# Subaru Legacy Automotive Repair Manual

**by Mike Stubblefield, Robert Maddox and John H Haynes**

Member of the Guild of Motoring Writers

**Models covered:**
All Legacy models
1990 through 1999
*Includes Legacy Outback and Legacy Brighton*

(89100 - 1S12)

ABCDE
FGHIJ
KLMNO

2

**Haynes Publishing Group**
Sparkford Nr Yeovil
Somerset BA22 7JJ England

**Haynes North America, Inc**
861 Lawrence Drive
Newbury Park
California 91320 USA

# About this manual

## Its purpose

The purpose of this manual is to help you get the best value from your vehicle. It can do so in several ways. It can help you decide what work must be done, even if you choose to have it done by a dealer service department or a repair shop; it provides information and procedures for routine maintenance and servicing; and it offers diagnostic and repair procedures to follow when trouble occurs.

We hope you use the manual to tackle the work yourself. For many simpler jobs, doing it yourself may be quicker than arranging an appointment to get the vehicle into a shop and making the trips to leave it and pick it up. More importantly, a lot of money can be saved by avoiding the expense the shop must pass on to you to cover its labor and overhead costs. An added benefit is the sense of satisfaction and accomplishment that you feel after doing the job yourself.

## Using the manual

The manual is divided into Chapters. Each Chapter is divided into numbered Sections, which are headed in bold type between horizontal lines. Each Section consists of consecutively numbered paragraphs.

At the beginning of each numbered Section you will be referred to any illustrations which apply to the procedures in that Section. The reference numbers used in illustration captions pinpoint the pertinent Section and the Step within that Section. That is, illustration 3.2 means the illustration refers to Section 3 and Step (or paragraph) 2 within that Section.

Procedures, once described in the text, are not normally repeated. When it's necessary to refer to another Chapter, the reference will be given as Chapter and Section number. Cross references given without use of the word "Chapter" apply to Sections and/or paragraphs in the same Chapter. For example, "see Section 8" means in the same Chapter.

References to the left or right side of the vehicle assume you are sitting in the driver's seat, facing forward.

Even though we have prepared this manual with extreme care, neither the publisher nor the author can accept responsibility for any errors in, or omissions from, the information given.

---

## NOTE

A **Note** provides information necessary to properly complete a procedure or information which will make the procedure easier to understand.

## CAUTION

A **Caution** provides a special procedure or special steps which must be taken while completing the procedure where the Caution is found. Not heeding a Caution can result in damage to the assembly being worked on.

## WARNING

A **Warning** provides a special procedure or special steps which must be taken while completing the procedure where the Warning is found. Not heeding a Warning can result in personal injury.

---

## Acknowledgements

We are grateful for the help and cooperation of Fuji Heavy Industries, Ltd., for their assistance with technical information and certain illustrations. Wiring diagrams were provided exclusively for Haynes North America, Inc. by Valley Forge Technical Communications.

---

© Haynes North America, Inc. 1998, 2006

With permission from J.H. Haynes & Co. Ltd.

---

**A book in the Haynes Automotive Repair Manual Series**

---

**Printed in the U.S.A.**

---

---

ISBN-13: 978-1-56392-646-4
ISBN-10: 1-56392-646-6

---

Library of Congress Control Number: 2006931626

---

---

# Contents

Haynes mechanic, author and photographer with 1998 Subaru Legacy Outback

# Introduction to the Subaru Legacy

These Subaru models are available as four-door sedan and wagon models. All models use a flat-four-cylinder engine mounted in the front. Both 2WD and 4WD models are available.

All models are equipped with a 2.2L SOHC engine or a 2.5L DOHC engine. Both engines use 16-valve cylinder heads and are equipped with multi-port fuel injection systems. Some earlier engines are turbocharged.

Power from the engine is transferred through a five-speed manual or four-speed automatic transaxle, then through a pair of driveaxles to the front wheels. On 4WD models, additional power is transferred through the driveshaft and a rear differential which drives the rear wheels through another pair of driveaxles.

Suspension is fully independent, utilizing MacPherson struts at all four wheels. The front suspension consists of steering knuckles bolted to the lower ends of the struts and to control arms. A stabilizer bar reduces vehicle roll. The rear suspension consists of a pair of rear knuckles, each of which is located by a trailing arm and a pair of control arms. A stabilizer bar reduces vehicle roll.

The steering gear is a power assisted rack-and-pinion type that is mounted to the bottom of the front crossmember with rubber insulators.

The brakes are disc at the front and disc or drums at the rear, with power assist standard. Some later models are equipped with an Anti-lock Brake System (ABS).

# Vehicle identification numbers

Modifications are a continuing and unpublicized process in vehicle manufacturing. Since spare parts lists and manuals are compiled on a numerical basis, the individual

**The VIN number is visible through the driver's side window**

vehicle numbers are necessary to correctly identify the component required.

## Vehicle Identification Number (VIN)

This very important identification number is stamped on a plate attached to the dashboard inside the windshield on the driver's side of the vehicle and on the engine compartment firewall **(see illustrations)**. The VIN also appears on the Vehicle Certificate of Title and Registration. It contains information such as where and when the vehicle was manufactured, the model year and the body style.

## VIN engine and model year codes

Two particularly important pieces of information found in the VIN are the engine code and the model year code. Counting from the left, the engine code letter designa-

tion is the 6th digit and the model year code letter designation is the 10th digit.

**On the models covered by this manual the engine codes are:**

| | |
|---|---|
| 6 | 1990 through 1994 2.2L |
| 3 | 1995 and later 2.2L (2WD) |
| 4 | 1995 and later 2.2L (4WD) |
| 6 | 1995 and later 2.5L (4WD) |

**On the models covered by this manual the model year codes are:**

| | |
|---|---|
| L | 1990 |
| M | 1991 |
| N | 1992 |
| P | 1993 |
| R | 1994 |
| S | 1995 |
| T | 1996 |
| V | 1997 |
| W | 1998 |
| X | 1999 |

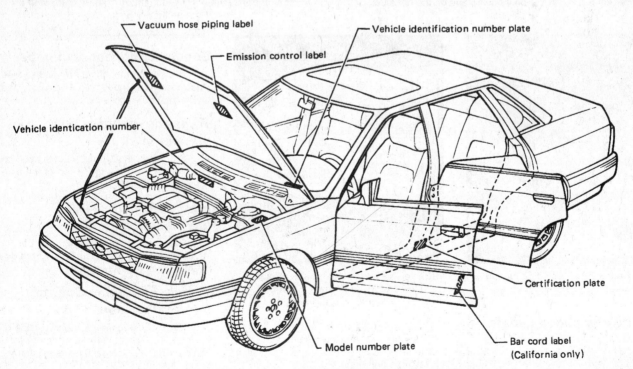

- Vacuum hose piping label
- Emission control label
- Vehicle identification number plate
- Vehicle identication number
- Certification plate
- Model number plate
- Bar cord label (California only)

**VIN number and other identification number locations**

The vehicle certification label is affixed the to the driver's side door pillar

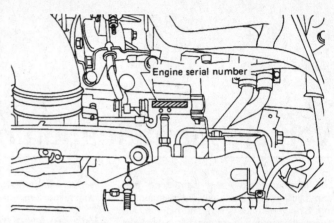

The engine identification number is located on top of the block, near the transaxle

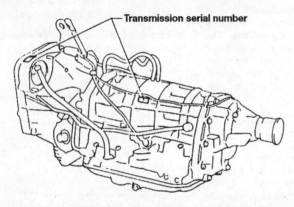

On automatic transaxles, the transaxle identification number is located on the top of the bellhousing and on the left side of the case

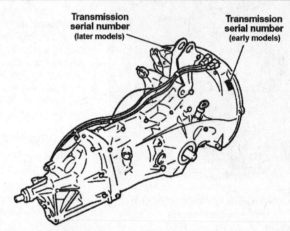

On manual transaxles, the identification number is located on the bellhousing

The rear differential identification tag is affixed to the differential cover

The vehicle emissions label is affixed to the underside of the hood in the engine compartment

## Vehicle Certification Label

The Vehicle Certification Label is attached to the driver's side door pillar (see illustration). Information on this label includes the name of the manufacturer, the month and year of production, and the Vehicle Identification Number.

## Engine identification number

The engine identification number (see illustration) is stamped onto a machined pad on the top of the engine block.

## Transaxle identification number(s)

The transaxle ID number is stamped on a tag which is riveted to the top of the bell-housing (see illustrations).

## Rear differential (4WD) identification number

The rear differential ID number is stamped on a tag which is affixed to the differential cover (see illustration).

## Vehicle Emissions Control Information label

This label is found on the underside of the hood in the engine compartment (see illustration). See Chapter 6 for more information on this label.

# Buying parts

Replacement parts are available from many sources, which generally fall into one of two categories - authorized dealer parts departments and independent retail auto parts stores. Our advice concerning these parts is as follows:

*Retail auto parts stores:* Good auto parts stores will stock frequently needed components which wear out relatively fast, such as clutch components, exhaust systems, brake parts, tune-up parts, etc. These stores often supply new or reconditioned parts on an exchange basis, which can save a considerable amount of money. Discount auto parts stores are often very good places to buy materials and parts needed for general vehicle maintenance such as oil, grease, filters, spark plugs, belts, touch-up paint, bulbs, etc. They also usually sell tools and general accessories, have convenient hours, charge lower prices and can often be found not far from home.

*Authorized dealer parts department:* This is the best source for parts which are unique to the vehicle and not generally available elsewhere (such as major engine parts, transmission parts, trim pieces, etc.).

*Warranty information:* If the vehicle is still covered under warranty, be sure that any replacement parts purchased - regardless of the source - do not invalidate the warranty!

To be sure of obtaining the correct parts, have engine and chassis numbers available and, if possible, take the old parts along for positive identification.

# Maintenance techniques, tools and working facilities

## Maintenance techniques

There are a number of techniques involved in maintenance and repair that will be referred to throughout this manual. Application of these techniques will enable the home mechanic to be more efficient, better organized and capable of performing the various tasks properly, which will ensure that the repair job is thorough and complete.

## Fasteners

Fasteners are nuts, bolts, studs and screws used to hold two or more parts together. There are a few things to keep in mind when working with fasteners. Almost all of them use a locking device of some type, either a lockwasher, locknut, locking tab or thread adhesive. All threaded fasteners should be clean and straight, with undamaged threads and undamaged corners on the hex head where the wrench fits. Develop the habit of replacing all damaged nuts and bolts with new ones. Special locknuts with nylon or fiber inserts can only be used once. If they are removed, they lose their locking ability and must be replaced with new ones.

Rusted nuts and bolts should be treated with a penetrating fluid to ease removal and prevent breakage. Some mechanics use turpentine in a spout-type oil can, which works quite well. After applying the rust penetrant, let it work for a few minutes before trying to loosen the nut or bolt. Badly rusted fasteners may have to be chiseled or sawed off or removed with a special nut breaker, available at tool stores.

If a bolt or stud breaks off in an assembly, it can be drilled and removed with a special tool commonly available for this purpose.

Most automotive machine shops can perform this task, as well as other repair procedures, such as the repair of threaded holes that have been stripped out.

Flat washers and lockwashers, when removed from an assembly, should always be replaced exactly as removed. Replace any damaged washers with new ones. Never use a lockwasher on any soft metal surface (such as aluminum), thin sheet metal or plastic.

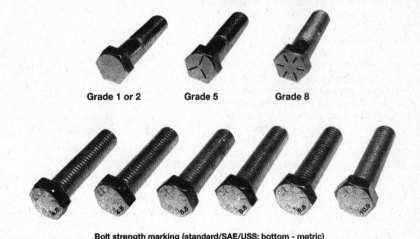

Grade 1 or 2    Grade 5    Grade 8

Bolt strength marking (standard/SAE/USS; bottom - metric)

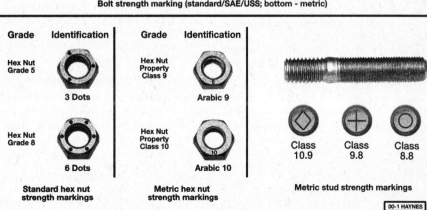

| Grade | Identification |
|---|---|
| Hex Nut Grade 5 | 3 Dots |
| Hex Nut Grade 8 | 6 Dots |

Standard hex nut strength markings

| Grade | Identification |
|---|---|
| Hex Nut Property Class 9 | Arabic 9 |
| Hex Nut Property Class 10 | Arabic 10 |

Metric hex nut strength markings

Class 10.9    Class 9.8    Class 8.8

Metric stud strength markings

00-1 HAYNES

## Fastener sizes

For a number of reasons, automobile manufacturers are making wider and wider use of metric fasteners. Therefore, it is important to be able to tell the difference between standard (sometimes called U.S. or SAE) and metric hardware, since they cannot be interchanged.

All bolts, whether standard or metric, are sized according to diameter, thread pitch and length. For example, a standard 1/2 - 13 x 1 bolt is 1/2 inch in diameter, has 13 threads per inch and is 1 inch long. An M12 - 1.75 x 25 metric bolt is 12 mm in diameter, has a thread pitch of 1.75 mm (the distance between threads) and is 25 mm long. The two bolts are nearly identical, and easily confused, but they are not interchangeable.

In addition to the differences in diameter, thread pitch and length, metric and standard bolts can also be distinguished by examining the bolt heads. To begin with, the distance across the flats on a standard bolt head is measured in inches, while the same dimension on a metric bolt is sized in millimeters (the same is true for nuts). As a result, a standard wrench should not be used on a metric bolt and a metric wrench should not be used on a standard bolt. Also, most standard bolts have slashes radiating out from the center of the head to denote the grade or strength of the bolt, which is an indication of the amount of torque that can be applied to it. The greater the number of slashes, the greater the strength of the bolt. Grades 0 through 5 are commonly used on automobiles. Metric bolts have a property class (grade) number, rather than a slash, molded into their heads to indicate bolt strength. In this case, the higher the number, the stronger the bolt. Property class numbers 8.8, 9.8 and 10.9 are commonly used on automobiles.

Strength markings can also be used to distinguish standard hex nuts from metric hex nuts. Many standard nuts have dots stamped into one side, while metric nuts are marked with a number. The greater the number of dots, or the higher the number, the greater the strength of the nut.

Metric studs are also marked on their ends according to property class (grade). Larger studs are numbered (the same as metric bolts), while smaller studs carry a geometric code to denote grade.

It should be noted that many fasteners, especially Grades 0 through 2, have no distinguishing marks on them. When such is the case, the only way to determine whether it is standard or metric is to measure the thread pitch or compare it to a known fastener of the same size.

Standard fasteners are often referred to as SAE, as opposed to metric. However, it should be noted that SAE technically refers to a non-metric fine thread fastener only. Coarse thread non-metric fasteners are referred to as USS sizes.

Since fasteners of the same size (both standard and metric) may have different

| Metric thread sizes | Ft-lbs | Nm |
|---|---|---|
| M-6 | 6 to 9 | 9 to 12 |
| M-8 | 14 to 21 | 19 to 28 |
| M-10 | 28 to 40 | 38 to 54 |
| M-12 | 50 to 71 | 68 to 96 |
| M-14 | 80 to 140 | 109 to 154 |

| Pipe thread sizes | | |
|---|---|---|
| 1/8 | 5 to 8 | 7 to 10 |
| 1/4 | 12 to 18 | 17 to 24 |
| 3/8 | 22 to 33 | 30 to 44 |
| 1/2 | 25 to 35 | 34 to 47 |

| U.S. thread sizes | | |
|---|---|---|
| 1/4 - 20 | 6 to 9 | 9 to 12 |
| 5/16 - 18 | 12 to 18 | 17 to 24 |
| 5/16 - 24 | 14 to 20 | 19 to 27 |
| 3/8 - 16 | 22 to 32 | 30 to 43 |
| 3/8 - 24 | 27 to 38 | 37 to 51 |
| 7/16 - 14 | 40 to 55 | 55 to 74 |
| 7/16 - 20 | 40 to 60 | 55 to 81 |
| 1/2 - 13 | 55 to 80 | 75 to 108 |

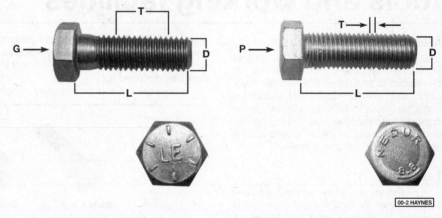

**Standard (SAE and USS) bolt dimensions/grade marks**

- G   Grade marks (bolt strength)
- L   Length (in inches)
- T   Thread pitch (number of threads per inch)
- D   Nominal diameter (in inches)

**Metric bolt dimensions/grade marks**

- P   Property class (bolt strength)
- L   Length (in millimeters)
- T   Thread pitch (distance between threads in millimeters)
- D   Diameter

strength ratings, be sure to reinstall any bolts, studs or nuts removed from your vehicle in their original locations. Also, when replacing a fastener with a new one, make sure that the new one has a strength rating equal to or greater than the original.

## Tightening sequences and procedures

Most threaded fasteners should be tightened to a specific torque value (torque is the twisting force applied to a threaded component such as a nut or bolt). Overtightening the fastener can weaken it and cause it to break, while undertightening can cause it to eventually come loose. Bolts, screws and studs, depending on the material they are

made of and their thread diameters, have specific torque values, many of which are noted in the Specifications at the beginning of each Chapter. Be sure to follow the torque recommendations closely. For fasteners not assigned a specific torque, a general torque value chart is presented here as a guide. These torque values are for dry (unlubricated) fasteners threaded into steel or cast iron (not aluminum). As was previously mentioned, the size and grade of a fastener determine the amount of torque that can safely be applied to it. The figures listed here are approximate for Grade 2 and Grade 3 fasteners. Higher grades can tolerate higher torque values.

Fasteners laid out in a pattern, such as cylinder head bolts, oil pan bolts, differential cover bolts, etc., must be loosened or tight-

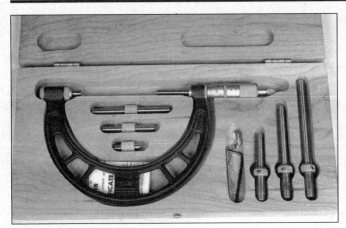

**Micrometer set**

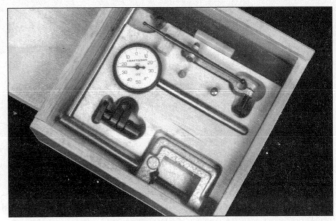

**Dial indicator set**

ened in sequence to avoid warping the component. This sequence will normally be shown in the appropriate Chapter. If a specific pattern is not given, the following procedures can be used to prevent warping.

Initially, the bolts or nuts should be assembled finger-tight only. Next, they should be tightened one full turn each, in a criss-cross or diagonal pattern. After each one has been tightened one full turn, return to the first one and tighten them all one-half turn, following the same pattern. Finally, tighten each of them one-quarter turn at a time until each fastener has been tightened to the proper torque. To loosen and remove the fasteners, the procedure would be reversed.

### Component disassembly

Component disassembly should be done with care and purpose to help ensure that the parts go back together properly. Always keep track of the sequence in which parts are removed. Make note of special characteristics or marks on parts that can be installed more than one way, such as a grooved thrust washer on a shaft. It is a good idea to lay the disassembled parts out on a clean surface in the order that they were removed. It may also be helpful to make sketches or take instant photos of components before removal.

When removing fasteners from a component, keep track of their locations. Sometimes threading a bolt back in a part, or putting the washers and nut back on a stud, can prevent mix-ups later. If nuts and bolts cannot be returned to their original locations, they should be kept in a compartmented box or a series of small boxes. A cupcake or muffin tin is ideal for this purpose, since each cavity can hold the bolts and nuts from a particular area (i.e. oil pan bolts, valve cover bolts, engine mount bolts, etc.). A pan of this type is especially helpful when working on assemblies with very small parts, such as the carburetor, alternator, valve train or interior dash and trim pieces. The cavities can be marked with paint or tape to identify the contents.

Whenever wiring looms, harnesses or connectors are separated, it is a good idea to identify the two halves with numbered pieces of masking tape so they can be easily reconnected.

### Gasket sealing surfaces

Throughout any vehicle, gaskets are used to seal the mating surfaces between two parts and keep lubricants, fluids, vacuum or pressure contained in an assembly.

Many times these gaskets are coated with a liquid or paste-type gasket sealing compound before assembly. Age, heat and pressure can sometimes cause the two parts to stick together so tightly that they are very difficult to separate. Often, the assembly can be loosened by striking it with a soft-face hammer near the mating surfaces. A regular hammer can be used if a block of wood is placed between the hammer and the part. Do not hammer on cast parts or parts that could be easily damaged. With any particularly stubborn part, always recheck to make sure that every fastener has been removed.

Avoid using a screwdriver or bar to pry apart an assembly, as they can easily mar the gasket sealing surfaces of the parts, which must remain smooth. If prying is absolutely necessary, use an old broom handle, but keep in mind that extra clean up will be necessary if the wood splinters.

After the parts are separated, the old gasket must be carefully scraped off and the gasket surfaces cleaned. Stubborn gasket material can be soaked with rust penetrant or treated with a special chemical to soften it so it can be easily scraped off. A scraper can be fashioned from a piece of copper tubing by flattening and sharpening one end. Copper is recommended because it is usually softer than the surfaces to be scraped, which reduces the chance of gouging the part. Some gaskets can be removed with a wire brush, but regardless of the method used, the mating surfaces must be left clean and smooth. If for some reason the gasket surface is gouged, then a gasket sealer thick enough to fill scratches will have to be used during reassembly of the components. For most applications, a non-drying (or semi-drying) gasket sealer should be used.

### Hose removal tips

**Warning:** *If the vehicle is equipped with air conditioning, do not disconnect any of the A/C hoses without first having the system depressurized by a dealer service department or a service station.*

Hose removal precautions closely parallel gasket removal precautions. Avoid scratching or gouging the surface that the hose mates against or the connection may leak. This is especially true for radiator hoses. Because of various chemical reactions, the rubber in hoses can bond itself to the metal spigot that the hose fits over. To remove a hose, first loosen the hose clamps that secure it to the spigot. Then, with slip-joint pliers, grab the hose at the clamp and rotate it around the spigot. Work it back and forth until it is completely free, then pull it off. Silicone or other lubricants will ease removal if they can be applied between the hose and the outside of the spigot. Apply the same lubricant to the inside of the hose and the outside of the spigot to simplify installation.

As a last resort (and if the hose is to be replaced with a new one anyway), the rubber can be slit with a knife and the hose peeled from the spigot. If this must be done, be careful that the metal connection is not damaged.

If a hose clamp is broken or damaged, do not reuse it. Wire-type clamps usually weaken with age, so it is a good idea to replace them with screw-type clamps whenever a hose is removed.

### Tools

A selection of good tools is a basic requirement for anyone who plans to maintain and repair his or her own vehicle. For the owner who has few tools, the initial investment might seem high, but when compared to the spiraling costs of professional auto maintenance and repair, it is a wise one.

To help the owner decide which tools are needed to perform the tasks detailed in this manual, the following tool lists are offered: *Maintenance and minor repair, Repair/overhaul* and *Special*.

The newcomer to practical mechanics

Dial caliper

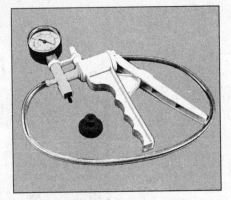

Hand-operated vacuum pump

Timing light

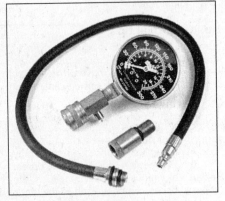

Compression gauge with spark plug
hole adapter

Damper/steering wheel puller

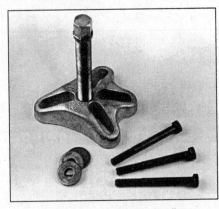

General purpose puller

Hydraulic lifter removal tool

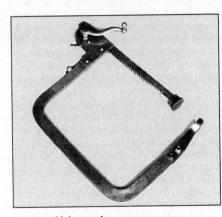

Valve spring compressor

Valve spring compressor

Ridge reamer

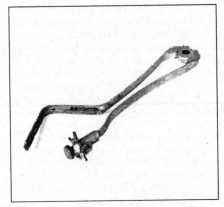

Piston ring groove cleaning tool

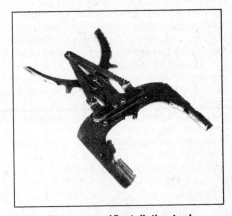

Ring removal/installation tool

**Ring compressor**

**Cylinder hone**

**Brake hold-down spring tool**

**Torque angle gauge**

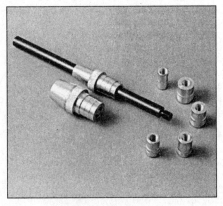

**Clutch plate alignment tool**

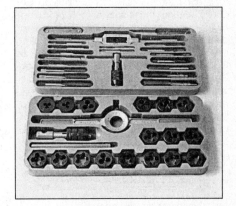

**Tap and die set**

should start off with the *maintenance and minor repair* tool kit, which is adequate for the simpler jobs performed on a vehicle. Then, as confidence and experience grow, the owner can tackle more difficult tasks, buying additional tools as they are needed. Eventually the basic kit will be expanded into the *repair and overhaul* tool set. Over a period of time, the experienced do-it-yourselfer will assemble a tool set complete enough for most repair and overhaul procedures and will add tools from the special category when it is felt that the expense is justified by the frequency of use.

## Maintenance and minor repair tool kit

The tools in this list should be considered the minimum required for performance of routine maintenance, servicing and minor repair work. We recommend the purchase of combination wrenches (box-end and open-end combined in one wrench). While more expensive than open end wrenches, they offer the advantages of both types of wrench.

*Combination wrench set (1/4-inch to 1 inch or 6 mm to 19 mm)*
*Adjustable wrench, 8 inch*
*Spark plug wrench with rubber insert*
*Spark plug gap adjusting tool*
*Feeler gauge set*
*Brake bleeder wrench*
*Standard screwdriver (5/16-inch x 6 inch)*

*Phillips screwdriver (No. 2 x 6 inch)*
*Combination pliers - 6 inch*
*Hacksaw and assortment of blades*
*Tire pressure gauge*
*Grease gun*
*Oil can*
*Fine emery cloth*
*Wire brush*
*Battery post and cable cleaning tool*
*Oil filter wrench*
*Funnel (medium size)*
*Safety goggles*
*Jackstands (2)*
*Drain pan*

**Note:** *If basic tune-ups are going to be part of routine maintenance, it will be necessary to purchase a good quality stroboscopic timing light and combination tachometer/dwell meter. Although they are included in the list of special tools, it is mentioned here because they are absolutely necessary for tuning most vehicles properly.*

## Repair and overhaul tool set

These tools are essential for anyone who plans to perform major repairs and are in addition to those in the maintenance and minor repair tool kit. Included is a comprehensive set of sockets which, though expensive, are invaluable because of their versatility, especially when various extensions and drives are available. We recommend the 1/2-inch drive over the 3/8-inch drive. Although the larger drive is bulky and more expensive,

it has the capacity of accepting a very wide range of large sockets. Ideally, however, the mechanic should have a 3/8-inch drive set and a 1/2-inch drive set.

*Socket set(s)*
*Reversible ratchet*
*Extension - 10 inch*
*Universal joint*
*Torque wrench (same size drive as sockets)*
*Ball peen hammer - 8 ounce*
*Soft-face hammer (plastic/rubber)*
*Standard screwdriver (1/4-inch x 6 inch)*
*Standard screwdriver (stubby - 5/16-inch)*
*Phillips screwdriver (No. 3 x 8 inch)*
*Phillips screwdriver (stubby - No. 2)*
*Pliers - vise grip*
*Pliers - lineman's*
*Pliers - needle nose*
*Pliers - snap-ring (internal and external)*
*Cold chisel - 1/2-inch*
*Scribe*
*Scraper (made from flattened copper tubing)*
*Centerpunch*
*Pin punches (1/16, 1/8, 3/16-inch)*
*Steel rule/straightedge - 12 inch*
*Allen wrench set (1/8 to 3/8-inch or 4 mm to 10 mm)*
*A selection of files*
*Wire brush (large)*
*Jackstands (second set)*
*Jack (scissor or hydraulic type)*

**Note:** *Another tool which is often useful is an electric drill with a chuck capacity of 3/8-inch and a set of good quality drill bits.*

## Special tools

The tools in this list include those which are not used regularly, are expensive to buy, or which need to be used in accordance with their manufacturer's instructions. Unless these tools will be used frequently, it is not very economical to purchase many of them. A consideration would be to split the cost and use between yourself and a friend or friends. In addition, most of these tools can be obtained from a tool rental shop on a temporary basis.

This list primarily contains only those tools and instruments widely available to the public, and not those special tools produced by the vehicle manufacturer for distribution to dealer service departments. Occasionally, references to the manufacturer's special tools are included in the text of this manual. Generally, an alternative method of doing the job without the special tool is offered. However, sometimes there is no alternative to their use. Where this is the case, and the tool cannot be purchased or borrowed, the work should be turned over to the dealer service department or an automotive repair shop.

*Valve spring compressor*
*Piston ring groove cleaning tool*
*Piston ring compressor*
*Piston ring installation tool*
*Cylinder compression gauge*
*Cylinder ridge reamer*
*Cylinder surfacing hone*
*Cylinder bore gauge*
*Micrometers and/or dial calipers*
*Hydraulic lifter removal tool*
*Balljoint separator*
*Universal-type puller*
*Impact screwdriver*
*Dial indicator set*
*Stroboscopic timing light (inductive pick-up)*
*Hand operated vacuum/pressure pump*
*Tachometer/dwell meter*
*Universal electrical multimeter*
*Cable hoist*
*Brake spring removal and installation tools*
*Floor jack*

## Buying tools

For the do-it-yourselfer who is just starting to get involved in vehicle maintenance and repair, there are a number of options available when purchasing tools. If maintenance and minor repair is the extent of the work to be done, the purchase of individual tools is satisfactory. If, on the other hand, extensive work is planned, it would be a good idea to purchase a modest tool set from one of the large retail chain stores. A set can usually be bought at a substantial savings over the individual tool prices, and they often come with a tool box. As additional tools are

needed, add-on sets, individual tools and a larger tool box can be purchased to expand the tool selection. Building a tool set gradually allows the cost of the tools to be spread over a longer period of time and gives the mechanic the freedom to choose only those tools that will actually be used.

Tool stores will often be the only source of some of the special tools that are needed, but regardless of where tools are bought, try to avoid cheap ones, especially when buying screwdrivers and sockets, because they won't last very long. The expense involved in replacing cheap tools will eventually be greater than the initial cost of quality tools.

## Care and maintenance of tools

Good tools are expensive, so it makes sense to treat them with respect. Keep them clean and in usable condition and store them properly when not in use. Always wipe off any dirt, grease or metal chips before putting them away. Never leave tools lying around in the work area. Upon completion of a job, always check closely under the hood for tools that may have been left there so they won't get lost during a test drive.

Some tools, such as screwdrivers, pliers, wrenches and sockets, can be hung on a panel mounted on the garage or workshop wall, while others should be kept in a tool box or tray. Measuring instruments, gauges, meters, etc. must be carefully stored where they cannot be damaged by weather or impact from other tools.

When tools are used with care and stored properly, they will last a very long time. Even with the best of care, though, tools will wear out if used frequently. When a tool is damaged or worn out, replace it. Subsequent jobs will be safer and more enjoyable if you do.

## How to repair damaged threads

Sometimes, the internal threads of a nut or bolt hole can become stripped, usually from overtightening. Stripping threads is an all-too-common occurrence, especially when working with aluminum parts, because aluminum is so soft that it easily strips out.

Usually, external or internal threads are only partially stripped. After they've been cleaned up with a tap or die, they'll still work. Sometimes, however, threads are badly damaged. When this happens, you've got three choices:

1) *Drill and tap the hole to the next suitable oversize and install a larger diameter bolt, screw or stud.*
2) *Drill and tap the hole to accept a threaded plug, then drill and tap the plug to the original screw size. You can also buy a plug already threaded to the original size. Then you simply drill a hole to the specified size, then run the threaded plug into the hole with a bolt and jam*

nut. *Once the plug is fully seated, remove the jam nut and bolt.*
3) *The third method uses a patented thread repair kit like Heli-Coil or Slimsert. These easy-to-use kits are designed to repair damaged threads in straight-through holes and blind holes. Both are available as kits which can handle a variety of sizes and thread patterns. Drill the hole, then tap it with the special included tap. Install the Heli-Coil and the hole is back to its original diameter and thread pitch.*

Regardless of which method you use, be sure to proceed calmly and carefully. A little impatience or carelessness during one of these relatively simple procedures can ruin your whole day's work and cost you a bundle if you wreck an expensive part.

## Working facilities

Not to be overlooked when discussing tools is the workshop. If anything more than routine maintenance is to be carried out, some sort of suitable work area is essential.

It is understood, and appreciated, that many home mechanics do not have a good workshop or garage available, and end up removing an engine or doing major repairs outside. It is recommended, however, that the overhaul or repair be completed under the cover of a roof.

A clean, flat workbench or table of comfortable working height is an absolute necessity. The workbench should be equipped with a vise that has a jaw opening of at least four inches.

As mentioned previously, some clean, dry storage space is also required for tools, as well as the lubricants, fluids, cleaning solvents, etc. which soon become necessary.

Sometimes waste oil and fluids, drained from the engine or cooling system during normal maintenance or repairs, present a disposal problem. To avoid pouring them on the ground or into a sewage system, pour the used fluids into large containers, seal them with caps and take them to an authorized disposal site or recycling center. Plastic jugs, such as old antifreeze containers, are ideal for this purpose.

Always keep a supply of old newspapers and clean rags available. Old towels are excellent for mopping up spills. Many mechanics use rolls of paper towels for most work because they are readily available and disposable. To help keep the area under the vehicle clean, a large cardboard box can be cut open and flattened to protect the garage or shop floor.

Whenever working over a painted surface, such as when leaning over a fender to service something under the hood, always cover it with an old blanket or bedspread to protect the finish. Vinyl covered pads, made especially for this purpose, are available at auto parts stores.

# Jacking and towing

## Jacking

**Warning:** *The jack supplied with the vehicle should only be used for changing a tire or placing jackstands under the frame. Never work under the vehicle or start the engine while this jack is being used as the only means of support.*

The vehicle should be on level ground. Place the shift lever in Park, if you have an automatic, or Reverse if you have a manual transaxle. Block the wheel diagonally opposite the wheel being changed. Set the parking brake.

Remove the spare tire and jack from stowage. Remove the wheel cover and trim ring (if so equipped) with the tapered end of the lug nut wrench by inserting and twisting the handle and then prying against the back of the wheel cover. Loosen the wheel lug nuts about 1/4-to-1/2 turn each.

Place the scissors-type jack under the side of the vehicle and adjust the jack height until it fits in the notch in the vertical rocker panel flange nearest the wheel to be changed. There is a front and rear jacking point on each side of the vehicle **(see illustration)**.

Turn the jack handle clockwise until the tire clears the ground. Remove the lug nuts and pull the wheel off. Replace it with the spare.

Install the lug nuts with the beveled edges facing in. Tighten them snugly. Don't attempt to tighten them completely until the vehicle is lowered or it could slip off the jack. Turn the jack handle counterclockwise to lower the vehicle. Remove the jack and tighten the lug nuts in a diagonal pattern.

Install the cover (and trim ring, if used) and be sure it's snapped into place all the way around.

Stow the tire, jack and wrench. Unblock the wheels.

## Towing

**Warning:** *Before towing models equipped with an automatic transaxle, the vehicle must be placed in front wheel drive mode. This is done by inserting a spare fuse into the FWD connector inside the engine compartment* **(see illustration)**. *If this isn't done, damage to the transfer clutch may occur.*

The vehicle can be towed with all four wheels on the ground, as long as speeds do not exceed 20 mph and the distance is not over six miles.

For distances exceeding six miles, towing equipment specifically designed for this purpose must be used and should be attached to the main structural members of the vehicle, not the bumper or brackets.

While towing, the parking brake should be fully released and the transaxle should be in Neutral. The steering must be unlocked (ignition switch in the Off position). Remember that power steering and power brakes will not work with engine off and never use the tie-down tabs to tow another vehicle.

Safety is a major consideration when towing and all applicable state and local laws must be obeyed. A safety chain system must be used at all times. Remember that power steering and power brakes will not work with the engine off.

Front jacking point - place the jack so it engages the notch in the rocker panel (the rear jacking point, which is located just in front of the rear wheels, has a similar notch)

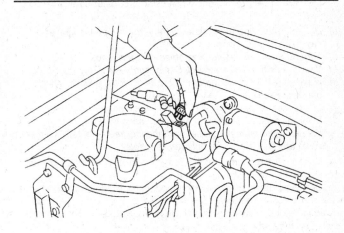

Before towing automatic models, insert a fuse into the FWD connector to disable the 4WD circuit

# Overriding the park lock system (automatic transaxle models)

To override the park lock system, pry off the trim piece surrounding the gear position indicator . . .

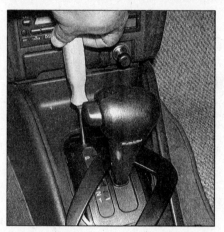

. . . then insert a screwdriver into the front left corner of the cavity around the gear position indicator and press down on the metal lever to release the park lock cable

If the park lock system malfunctions, it can be overridden. Simply pry off the gear position indicator trim piece, then insert a screwdriver into the front left corner of the cavity surrounding the gear position indicator and press down on the metal lever to release the park lock cable **(see illustrations)**.

# Booster battery (jump) starting

Observe these precautions when using a booster battery to start a vehicle:

a) *Before connecting the booster battery, make sure the ignition switch is in the Off position.*
b) *Turn off the lights, heater and other electrical loads.*
c) *Your eyes should be shielded. Safety goggles are a good idea.*
d) *Make sure the booster battery is the same voltage as the dead one in the vehicle.*
e) *The two vehicles MUST NOT TOUCH each other!*
f) *Make sure the transaxle is in Neutral (manual) or Park (automatic).*
g) *If the booster battery is not a maintenance-free type, remove the vent caps and lay a cloth over the vent holes.*

Connect the red jumper cable to the positive (+) terminals of each battery **(see illustration)**.

Connect one end of the black jumper cable to the negative (-) terminal of the booster battery. The other end of this cable should be connected to a good ground on the vehicle to be started, such as a bolt or bracket on the body.

Start the engine using the booster battery, then, with the engine running at idle speed, disconnect the jumper cables in the reverse order of connection.

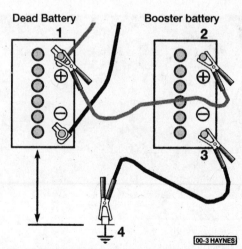

Make the booster battery cable connections in the numerical order shown (note that the negative cable of the booster battery is NOT attached to the negative terminal of the dead battery)

# Automotive chemicals and lubricants

A number of automotive chemicals and lubricants are available for use during vehicle maintenance and repair. They include a wide variety of products ranging from cleaning solvents and degreasers to lubricants and protective sprays for rubber, plastic and vinyl.

## Cleaners

**Carburetor cleaner and choke cleaner** is a strong solvent for gum, varnish and carbon. Most carburetor cleaners leave a dry-type lubricant film which will not harden or gum up. Because of this film it is not recommended for use on electrical components.

**Brake system cleaner** is used to remove brake dust, grease and brake fluid from the brake system, where clean surfaces are absolutely necessary. It leaves no residue and often eliminates brake squeal caused by contaminants.

**Electrical cleaner** removes oxidation, corrosion and carbon deposits from electrical contacts, restoring full current flow. It can also be used to clean spark plugs, carburetor jets, voltage regulators and other parts where an oil-free surface is desired.

**Demoisturants** remove water and moisture from electrical components such as alternators, voltage regulators, electrical connectors and fuse blocks. They are non-conductive and non-corrosive.

**Degreasers** are heavy-duty solvents used to remove grease from the outside of the engine and from chassis components. They can be sprayed or brushed on and, depending on the type, are rinsed off either with water or solvent.

## Lubricants

**Motor oil** is the lubricant formulated for use in engines. It normally contains a wide variety of additives to prevent corrosion and reduce foaming and wear. Motor oil comes in various weights (viscosity ratings) from 0 to 50. The recommended weight of the oil depends on the season, temperature and the demands on the engine. Light oil is used in cold climates and under light load conditions. Heavy oil is used in hot climates and where high loads are encountered. Multi-viscosity oils are designed to have characteristics of both light and heavy oils and are available in a number of weights from 5W-20 to 20W-50.

**Gear oil** is designed to be used in differentials, manual transmissions and other areas where high-temperature lubrication is required.

**Chassis and wheel bearing grease** is a heavy grease used where increased loads and friction are encountered, such as for wheel bearings, balljoints, tie-rod ends and universal joints.

**High-temperature wheel bearing grease** is designed to withstand the extreme temperatures encountered by wheel bearings in disc brake equipped vehicles. It usually contains molybdenum disulfide (moly), which is a dry-type lubricant.

**White grease** is a heavy grease for metal-to-metal applications where water is a problem. White grease stays soft under both low and high temperatures (usually from -100 to +190-degrees F), and will not wash off or dilute in the presence of water.

**Assembly lube** is a special extreme pressure lubricant, usually containing moly, used to lubricate high-load parts (such as main and rod bearings and cam lobes) for initial start-up of a new engine. The assembly lube lubricates the parts without being squeezed out or washed away until the engine oiling system begins to function.

**Silicone lubricants** are used to protect rubber, plastic, vinyl and nylon parts.

**Graphite lubricants** are used where oils cannot be used due to contamination problems, such as in locks. The dry graphite will lubricate metal parts while remaining uncontaminated by dirt, water, oil or acids. It is electrically conductive and will not foul electrical contacts in locks such as the ignition switch.

**Moly penetrants** loosen and lubricate frozen, rusted and corroded fasteners and prevent future rusting or freezing.

**Heat-sink grease** is a special electrically non-conductive grease that is used for mounting electronic ignition modules where it is essential that heat is transferred away from the module.

## Sealants

**RTV sealant** is one of the most widely used gasket compounds. Made from silicone, RTV is air curing, it seals, bonds, waterproofs, fills surface irregularities, remains flexible, doesn't shrink, is relatively easy to remove, and is used as a supplementary sealer with almost all low and medium temperature gaskets.

**Anaerobic sealant** is much like RTV in that it can be used either to seal gaskets or to form gaskets by itself. It remains flexible, is solvent resistant and fills surface imperfections. The difference between an anaerobic sealant and an RTV-type sealant is in the curing. RTV cures when exposed to air, while an anaerobic sealant cures only in the absence of air. This means that an anaerobic sealant cures only after the assembly of parts, sealing them together.

**Thread and pipe sealant** is used for sealing hydraulic and pneumatic fittings and vacuum lines. It is usually made from a Teflon compound, and comes in a spray, a paint-on liquid and as a wrap-around tape.

## Chemicals

**Anti-seize compound** prevents seizing, galling, cold welding, rust and corrosion in fasteners. High-temperature ant-seize, usually made with copper and graphite lubricants, is used for exhaust system and exhaust manifold bolts.

**Anaerobic locking compounds** are used to keep fasteners from vibrating or working loose and cure only after installation, in the absence of air. Medium strength locking compound is used for small nuts, bolts and screws that may be removed later. High-strength locking compound is for large nuts, bolts and studs which aren't removed on a regular basis.

**Oil additives** range from viscosity index improvers to chemical treatments that claim to reduce internal engine friction. It should be noted that most oil manufacturers caution against using additives with their oils.

**Gas additives** perform several functions, depending on their chemical makeup. They usually contain solvents that help dissolve gum and varnish that build up on carburetor, fuel injection and intake parts. They also serve to break down carbon deposits that form on the inside surfaces of the combustion chambers. Some additives contain upper cylinder lubricants for valves and piston rings, and others contain chemicals to remove condensation from the gas tank.

## Miscellaneous

**Brake fluid** is specially formulated hydraulic fluid that can withstand the heat and pressure encountered in brake systems. Care must be taken so this fluid does not come in contact with painted surfaces or plastics. An opened container should always be resealed to prevent contamination by water or dirt.

**Weatherstrip adhesive** is used to bond weatherstripping around doors, windows and trunk lids. It is sometimes used to attach trim pieces.

**Undercoating** is a petroleum-based, tar-like substance that is designed to protect metal surfaces on the underside of the vehicle from corrosion. It also acts as a sound-deadening agent by insulating the bottom of the vehicle.

**Waxes and polishes** are used to help protect painted and plated surfaces from the weather. Different types of paint may require the use of different types of wax and polish. Some polishes utilize a chemical or abrasive cleaner to help remove the top layer of oxidized (dull) paint on older vehicles. In recent years many non-wax polishes that contain a wide variety of chemicals such as polymers and silicones have been introduced. These non-wax polishes are usually easier to apply and last longer than conventional waxes and polishes.

# Conversion factors

### Length (distance)

| | | | | | |
|---|---|---|---|---|---|
| Inches (in) | X | 25.4 | = Millimetres (mm) | X 0.0394 | = Inches (in) |
| Feet (ft) | X | 0.305 | = Metres (m) | X 3.281 | = Feet (ft) |
| Miles | X | 1.609 | = Kilometres (km) | X 0.621 | = Miles |

### Volume (capacity)

| | | | | | |
|---|---|---|---|---|---|
| Cubic inches (cu in; in³) | X | 16.387 | = Cubic centimetres (cc; cm³) | X 0.061 | = Cubic inches (cu in; in³) |
| Imperial pints (Imp pt) | X | 0.568 | = Litres (l) | X 1.76 | = Imperial pints (Imp pt) |
| Imperial quarts (Imp qt) | X | 1.137 | = Litres (l) | X 0.88 | = Imperial quarts (Imp qt) |
| Imperial quarts (Imp qt) | X | 1.201 | = US quarts (US qt) | X 0.833 | = Imperial quarts (Imp qt) |
| US quarts (US qt) | X | 0.946 | = Litres (l) | X 1.057 | = US quarts (US qt) |
| Imperial gallons (Imp gal) | X | 4.546 | = Litres (l) | X 0.22 | = Imperial gallons (Imp gal) |
| Imperial gallons (Imp gal) | X | 1.201 | = US gallons (US gal) | X 0.833 | = Imperial gallons (Imp gal) |
| US gallons (US gal) | X | 3.785 | = Litres (l) | X 0.264 | = US gallons (US gal) |

### Mass (weight)

| | | | | | |
|---|---|---|---|---|---|
| Ounces (oz) | X | 28.35 | = Grams (g) | X 0.035 | = Ounces (oz) |
| Pounds (lb) | X | 0.454 | = Kilograms (kg) | X 2.205 | = Pounds (lb) |

### Force

| | | | | | |
|---|---|---|---|---|---|
| Ounces-force (ozf; oz) | X | 0.278 | = Newtons (N) | X 3.6 | = Ounces-force (ozf; oz) |
| Pounds-force (lbf; lb) | X | 4.448 | = Newtons (N) | X 0.225 | = Pounds-force (lbf; lb) |
| Newtons (N) | X | 0.1 | = Kilograms-force (kgf; kg) | X 9.81 | = Newtons (N) |

### Pressure

| | | | | | |
|---|---|---|---|---|---|
| Pounds-force per square inch (psi; lbf/in²; lb/in²) | X | 0.070 | = Kilograms-force per square centimetre (kgf/cm²; kg/cm²) | X 14.223 | = Pounds-force per square inch (psi; lbf/in²; lb/in²) |
| Pounds-force per square inch (psi; lbf/in²; lb/in²) | X | 0.068 | = Atmospheres (atm) | X 14.696 | = Pounds-force per square inch (psi; lbf/in²; lb/in²) |
| Pounds-force per square inch (psi; lbf/in²; lb/in²) | X | 0.069 | = Bars | X 14.5 | = Pounds-force per square inch (psi; lbf/in²; lb/in²) |
| Pounds-force per square inch (psi; lbf/in²; lb/in²) | X | 6.895 | = Kilopascals (kPa) | X 0.145 | = Pounds-force per square inch (psi; lbf/in²; lb/in²) |
| Kilopascals (kPa) | X | 0.01 | = Kilograms-force per square centimetre (kgf/cm²; kg/cm²) | X 98.1 | = Kilopascals (kPa) |

### Torque (moment of force)

| | | | | | |
|---|---|---|---|---|---|
| Pounds-force inches (lbf in; lb in) | X | 1.152 | = Kilograms-force centimetre (kgf cm; kg cm) | X 0.868 | = Pounds-force inches (lbf in; lb in) |
| Pounds-force inches (lbf in; lb in) | X | 0.113 | = Newton metres (Nm) | X 8.85 | = Pounds-force inches (lbf in; lb in) |
| Pounds-force inches (lbf in; lb in) | X | 0.083 | = Pounds-force feet (lbf ft; lb ft) | X 12 | = Pounds-force inches (lbf in; lb in) |
| Pounds-force feet (lbf ft; lb ft) | X | 0.138 | = Kilograms-force metres (kgf m; kg m) | X 7.233 | = Pounds-force feet (lbf ft; lb ft) |
| Pounds-force feet (lbf ft; lb ft) | X | 1.356 | = Newton metres (Nm) | X 0.738 | = Pounds-force feet (lbf ft; lb ft) |
| Newton metres (Nm) | X | 0.102 | = Kilograms-force metres (kgf m; kg m) | X 9.804 | = Newton metres (Nm) |

### Vacuum

| | | | | | |
|---|---|---|---|---|---|
| Inches mercury (in. Hg) | X | 3.377 | = Kilopascals (kPa) | X 0.2961 | = Inches mercury |
| Inches mercury (in. Hg) | X | 25.4 | = Millimeters mercury (mm Hg) | X 0.0394 | = Inches mercury |

### Power

| | | | | | |
|---|---|---|---|---|---|
| Horsepower (hp) | X | 745.7 | = Watts (W) | X 0.0013 | = Horsepower (hp) |

### Velocity (speed)

| | | | | | |
|---|---|---|---|---|---|
| Miles per hour (miles/hr; mph) | X | 1.609 | = Kilometres per hour (km/hr; kph) | X 0.621 | = Miles per hour (miles/hr; mph) |

### Fuel consumption*

| | | | | | |
|---|---|---|---|---|---|
| Miles per gallon, Imperial (mpg) | X | 0.354 | = Kilometres per litre (km/l) | X 2.825 | = Miles per gallon, Imperial (mpg) |
| Miles per gallon, US (mpg) | X | 0.425 | = Kilometres per litre (km/l) | X 2.352 | = Miles per gallon, US (mpg) |

### Temperature

Degrees Fahrenheit = (°C x 1.8) + 32

Degrees Celsius (Degrees Centigrade; °C) = (°F - 32) x 0.56

*It is common practice to convert from miles per gallon (mpg) to litres/100 kilometres (l/100km), where mpg (Imperial) x l/100 km = 282 and mpg (US) x l/100 km = 235

# Safety first!

Regardless of how enthusiastic you may be about getting on with the job at hand, take the time to ensure that your safety is not jeopardized. A moment's lack of attention can result in an accident, as can failure to observe certain simple safety precautions. The possibility of an accident will always exist, and the following points should not be considered a comprehensive list of all dangers. Rather, they are intended to make you aware of the risks and to encourage a safety conscious approach to all work you carry out on your vehicle.

## Essential DOs and DON'Ts

**DON'T** rely on a jack when working under the vehicle. Always use approved jackstands to support the weight of the vehicle and place them under the recommended lift or support points.

**DON'T** attempt to loosen extremely tight fasteners (i.e. wheel lug nuts) while the vehicle is on a jack - it may fall.

**DON'T** start the engine without first making sure that the transmission is in Neutral (or Park where applicable) and the parking brake is set.

**DON'T** remove the radiator cap from a hot cooling system - let it cool or cover it with a cloth and release the pressure gradually.

**DON'T** attempt to drain the engine oil until you are sure it has cooled to the point that it will not burn you.

**DON'T** touch any part of the engine or exhaust system until it has cooled sufficiently to avoid burns.

**DON'T** siphon toxic liquids such as gasoline, antifreeze and brake fluid by mouth, or allow them to remain on your skin.

**DON'T** inhale brake lining dust - it is potentially hazardous (see *Asbestos* below).

**DON'T** allow spilled oil or grease to remain on the floor - wipe it up before someone slips on it.

**DON'T** use loose fitting wrenches or other tools which may slip and cause injury.

**DON'T** push on wrenches when loosening or tightening nuts or bolts. Always try to pull the wrench toward you. If the situation calls for pushing the wrench away, push with an open hand to avoid scraped knuckles if the wrench should slip.

**DON'T** attempt to lift a heavy component alone - get someone to help you.

**DON'T** rush or take unsafe shortcuts to finish a job.

**DON'T** allow children or animals in or around the vehicle while you are working on it.

**DO** wear eye protection when using power tools such as a drill, sander, bench grinder, etc. and when working under a vehicle.

**DO** keep loose clothing and long hair well out of the way of moving parts.

**DO** make sure that any hoist used has a safe working load rating adequate for the job.

**DO** get someone to check on you periodically when working alone on a vehicle.

**DO** carry out work in a logical sequence and make sure that everything is correctly assembled and tightened.

**DO** keep chemicals and fluids tightly capped and out of the reach of children and pets.

**DO** remember that your vehicle's safety affects that of yourself and others. If in doubt on any point, get professional advice.

## Asbestos

Certain friction, insulating, sealing, and other products - such as brake linings, brake bands, clutch linings, torque converters, gaskets, etc. - may contain asbestos. Extreme care must be taken to avoid inhalation of dust from such products, since it is hazardous to health. If in doubt, assume that they do contain asbestos.

## Fire

Remember at all times that gasoline is highly flammable. Never smoke or have any kind of open flame around when working on a vehicle. But the risk does not end there. A spark caused by an electrical short circuit, by two metal surfaces contacting each other, or even by static electricity built up in your body under certain conditions, can ignite gasoline vapors, which in a confined space are highly explosive. Do not, under any circumstances, use gasoline for cleaning parts. Use an approved safety solvent.

Always disconnect the battery ground (-) cable at the battery before working on any part of the fuel system or electrical system. Never risk spilling fuel on a hot engine or exhaust component. It is strongly recommended that a fire extinguisher suitable for use on fuel and electrical fires be kept handy in the garage or workshop at all times. Never try to extinguish a fuel or electrical fire with water.

## Fumes

Certain fumes are highly toxic and can quickly cause unconsciousness and even death if inhaled to any extent. Gasoline vapor falls into this category, as do the vapors from some cleaning solvents. Any draining or pouring of such volatile fluids should be done in a well ventilated area.

When using cleaning fluids and solvents, read the instructions on the container carefully. Never use materials from unmarked containers.

Never run the engine in an enclosed space, such as a garage. Exhaust fumes contain carbon monoxide, which is extremely poisonous. If you need to run the engine, always do so in the open air, or at least have the rear of the vehicle outside the work area.

If you are fortunate enough to have the use of an inspection pit, never drain or pour gasoline and never run the engine while the vehicle is over the pit. The fumes, being heavier than air, will concentrate in the pit with possibly lethal results.

## The battery

Never create a spark or allow a bare light bulb near a battery. They normally give off a certain amount of hydrogen gas, which is highly explosive.

Always disconnect the battery ground (-) cable at the battery before working on the fuel or electrical systems.

If possible, loosen the filler caps or cover when charging the battery from an external source (this does not apply to sealed or maintenance-free batteries). Do not charge at an excessive rate or the battery may burst.

Take care when adding water to a non maintenance-free battery and when carrying a battery. The electrolyte, even when diluted, is very corrosive and should not be allowed to contact clothing or skin.

Always wear eye protection when cleaning the battery to prevent the caustic deposits from entering your eyes.

## Household current

When using an electric power tool, inspection light, etc., which operates on household current, always make sure that the tool is correctly connected to its plug and that, where necessary, it is properly grounded. Do not use such items in damp conditions and, again, do not create a spark or apply excessive heat in the vicinity of fuel or fuel vapor.

## Secondary ignition system voltage

A severe electric shock can result from touching certain parts of the ignition system (such as the spark plug wires) when the engine is running or being cranked, particularly if components are damp or the insulation is defective. In the case of an electronic ignition system, the secondary system voltage is much higher and could prove fatal.

# Troubleshooting

## Contents

## Engine

### 1 Engine will not rotate when attempting to start

1 Battery terminal connections loose or corroded (Chapter 1).
2 Battery discharged or faulty (Chapter 1).
3 Automatic transaxle not completely engaged in Park (Chapter 7) or clutch pedal not completely depressed (Chapter 8).
4 Broken, loose or disconnected wiring in the starting circuit (Chapters 5 and 12).
5 Starter motor pinion jammed in flywheel ring gear (Chapter 5).
6 Starter solenoid faulty (Chapter 5).
7 Starter motor faulty (Chapter 5).
8 Ignition switch faulty (Chapter 12).
9 Starter pinion or flywheel teeth worn or broken (Chapter 5).

### 2 Engine rotates but will not start

1 Fuel tank empty.
2 Battery discharged (engine rotates slowly) (Chapter 5).
3 Battery terminal connections loose or corroded (Chapter 1).
4 Leaking fuel injector(s), faulty fuel pump, pressure regulator, etc. (Chapter 4).
5 Broken or stripped timing belt (Chapter 2).
6 Ignition components damp or damaged (Chapter 5).
7 Worn, faulty or incorrectly gapped spark plugs (Chapter 1).
8 Broken, loose or disconnected wiring in the starting circuit (Chapter 5).
9 Broken, loose or disconnected wires at the ignition coil or faulty coil (Chapter 5).

### 3 Engine hard to start when cold

1 Battery discharged or low (Chapter 1).
2 Malfunctioning fuel system (Chapter 4).
3 Faulty coolant temperature sensor (Chapter 6).
4 Injector(s) leaking (Chapter 4B).
5 Faulty ignition system (Chapter 5).

### 4 Engine hard to start when hot

1 Air filter clogged (Chapter 1).
2 Fuel not reaching the fuel injection system (Chapter 4).
3 Corroded battery connections, especially ground (Chapter 1).
4 Faulty coolant temperature sensor (Chapter 6).

### 5 Starter motor noisy or excessively rough in engagement

1 Pinion or flywheel gear teeth worn or broken (Chapter 5).
2 Starter motor mounting bolts loose or missing (Chapter 5).

### 6 Engine starts but stops immediately

1 Loose or faulty electrical connections at coil or alternator (Chapter 5).
2 Insufficient fuel reaching the fuel injectors (Chapters 1 and 4).
3 Vacuum leak at the gasket between the intake manifold/plenum (Chapters 1 and 4).
4 Idle speed incorrect (Chapter 1).

### 7 Oil puddle under engine

1 Oil pan gasket and/or oil pan drain bolt washer leaking (Chapter 2).
2 Oil pressure sending unit leaking (Chapter 2).
3 Cylinder head covers leaking (Chapter 2).
4 Engine oil seals leaking (Chapter 2).
5 Oil pump housing leaking (Chapter 2).

### 8 Engine lopes while idling or idles erratically

1 Vacuum leakage (Chapters 2 and 4).
2 Leaking EGR valve (Chapter 6).
3 Air filter clogged (Chapter 1).
4 Fuel pump not delivering sufficient fuel to the fuel injection system (Chapter 4).
5 Leaking head gasket (Chapter 2).
6 Timing belt and/or pulleys worn (Chapter 2).
7 Camshaft lobes worn (Chapter 2).

### 9 Engine misses at idle speed

1 Spark plugs worn or not gapped properly (Chapter 1).
2 Faulty spark plug wires (Chapter 1).
3 Vacuum leaks (Chapter 1).
4 Incorrect ignition timing (Chapter 5).
5 Uneven or low compression (Chapter 2).
6 Problem with the fuel injection system (Chapter 4).

### 10 Engine misses throughout driving speed range

1 Fuel filter clogged and/or impurities in the fuel system (Chapter 1).
2 Low fuel output at the injectors (Chapter 4).
3 Faulty or incorrectly gapped spark plugs (Chapter 1).
4 Incorrect ignition timing (Chapter 5).
5 Cracked coil (Chapters 1 and 5).

6 Leaking spark plug wires (Chapters 1 or 5).
7 Faulty emission system components (Chapter 6).
8 Low or uneven cylinder compression pressures (Chapter 2).
9 Weak or faulty ignition system (Chapter 5).
10 Vacuum leak in fuel injection system, intake manifold or vacuum hoses (Chapter 4).

### 11 Engine stumbles on acceleration

1 Spark plugs fouled (Chapter 1).
2 Problem with fuel injection system (Chapter 4).
3 Fuel filter clogged (Chapters 1 and 4).
4 Incorrect ignition timing (Chapter 5).
5 Intake manifold air leak (Chapters 2 and 4).
6 Problem with the emissions control system (Chapter 6).

### 12 Engine surges while holding accelerator steady

1 Intake air leak (Chapter 4).
2 Fuel pump or fuel pressure regulator faulty (Chapter 4).
3 Problem with fuel injection system (Chapter 4).
4 Problem with the emissions control system (Chapter 6).

### 13 Engine stalls

1 Idle speed incorrect (Chapter 1).
2 Fuel filter clogged and/or water and impurities in the fuel system (Chapters 1 and 4).
3 Ignition components damp or damaged (Chapter 5).
4 Faulty emissions system components (Chapter 6).
5 Faulty or incorrectly gapped spark plugs (Chapter 1).
6 Faulty spark plug wires (Chapter 1).
7 Vacuum leak in the fuel injection system, intake manifold or vacuum hoses (Chapters 2 and 4).
8 Valve clearances incorrectly set (Chapter 1).

### 14 Engine lacks power

1 Incorrect ignition timing (Chapter 5).
2 Faulty spark plug wires or coil (Chapters 1 and 5).
3 Faulty or incorrectly gapped spark plugs (Chapter 1).
4 Problem with the fuel injection system (Chapter 4).

5    Plugged air filter (Chapter 1).
6    Brakes binding (Chapter 9).
7    Automatic transaxle fluid level incorrect (Chapter 1).
8    Clutch slipping (Chapter 8).
9    Fuel filter clogged and/or impurities in the fuel system (Chapters 1 and 4).
10   Emission control system not functioning properly (Chapter 6).
11   Low or uneven cylinder compression pressures (Chapter 2).
12   Obstructed exhaust system (Chapter 4).

### 15  Engine backfires

1    Emission control system not functioning properly (Chapter 6).
2    Ignition timing incorrect (Chapter 5).
3    Faulty secondary ignition system (cracked spark plug insulator, faulty plug wires) (Chapters 1 and 5).
4    Problem with the fuel injection system (Chapter 4).
5    Vacuum leak at fuel injector(s), intake manifold or vacuum hoses (Chapters 2 and 4).
6    Valve clearances incorrectly set and/or valves sticking (Chapter 1).

### 16  Pinging or knocking engine sounds during acceleration or uphill

1    Incorrect grade of fuel.
2    Ignition timing incorrect (Chapter 5).
3    Fuel injection system faulty (Chapter 4).
4    Improper or damaged spark plugs or wires (Chapter 1).
5    Worn or damaged ignition components (Chapter 5).
6    EGR valve not functioning (Chapter 6).
7    Vacuum leak (Chapters 2 and 4).

### 17  Engine runs with oil pressure light on

1    Low oil level (Chapter 1).
2    Idle rpm below specification (Chapter 1).
3    Short in wiring circuit (Chapter 12).
4    Faulty oil pressure sender (Chapter 2).
5    Worn engine bearings and/or oil pump (Chapter 2).

### 18  Engine diesels (continues to run) after switching off

1    Idle speed too high (Chapter 1).
2    Excessive engine operating temperature (Chapter 3).
3    Ignition timing incorrect (Chapter 5).

## Engine electrical system

### 19  Battery will not hold a charge

1    Alternator drivebelt defective or not adjusted properly (Chapter 1).
2    Battery electrolyte level low (Chapter 1).
3    Battery terminals loose or corroded (Chapter 1).
4    Alternator not charging properly (Chapter 5).
5    Loose, broken or faulty wiring in the charging circuit (Chapter 5).
6    Short in vehicle wiring (Chapter 12).
7    Internally defective battery (Chapters 1 and 5).

### 20  Alternator light fails to go out

1    Faulty alternator or charging circuit (Chapter 5).
2    Alternator drivebelt defective or out of adjustment (Chapter 1).
3    Alternator voltage regulator inoperative (Chapter 5).

### 21  Alternator light fails to come on when key is turned on

1    Warning light bulb defective (Chapter 12).
2    Fault in the printed circuit, dash wiring or bulb holder (Chapter 12).

## Fuel system

### 22  Excessive fuel consumption

1    Dirty or clogged air filter element (Chapter 1).
2    Incorrect ignition timing (Chapter 5).
3    Emissions system not functioning properly (Chapter 6).
4    Fuel injection system not functioning properly (Chapter 4).
5    Low tire pressure or incorrect tire size (Chapter 1).

### 23  Fuel leakage and/or fuel odor

1    Leaking fuel feed or return line (Chapters 1 and 4).
2    Tank overfilled.
3    Evaporative canister filter clogged (Chapters 1 and 6).
4    Problem with fuel injection system (Chapter 4).

## Cooling system

### 24  Overheating

1    Insufficient coolant in system (Chapter 1).
2    Water pump defective (Chapter 3).
3    Radiator core blocked or grille restricted (Chapter 3).
4    Thermostat faulty (Chapter 3).
5    Electric coolant fan inoperative or blades broken (Chapter 3).
6    Radiator cap not maintaining proper pressure (Chapter 3).
7    Ignition timing incorrect (Chapter 5).

### 25  Overcooling

1    Faulty thermostat (Chapter 3).
2    Inaccurate temperature gauge sending unit (Chapter 3).
3    Cooling fan runs continuously.

### 26  External coolant leakage

1    Deteriorated/damaged hoses; loose clamps (Chapters 1 and 3).
2    Water pump defective (Chapter 3).
3    Leakage from radiator core or coolant reservoir bottle (Chapter 3).
4    Engine drain or water jacket core plugs leaking (Chapter 2).

### 27  Internal coolant leakage

1    Leaking cylinder head gasket (Chapter 2).
2    Cracked cylinder bore or cylinder head (Chapter 2).

### 28  Coolant loss

1    Too much coolant in system (Chapter 1).
2    Coolant boiling away because of overheating (Chapter 3).
3    Internal or external leakage (Chapter 3).
4    Faulty radiator cap (Chapter 3).

### 29  Poor coolant circulation

1    Inoperative water pump (Chapter 3).
2    Restriction in cooling system (Chapters 1 and 3).
3    Water pump drivebelt defective/out of adjustment (Chapter 1).
4    Thermostat sticking (Chapter 3).

## Clutch

**Note:** *All clutch related service information is located in Chapter 8, unless otherwise noted.*

### 30 Fails to release (pedal pressed to the floor-shift lever does not move freely in and out of gear)

1   Freeplay incorrectly adjusted.
2   Clutch contaminated with oil. Remove clutch disc and inspect.
3   Clutch disc warped, distorted or otherwise damaged.
4   Diaphragm spring fatigued. Remove clutch cover/pressure plate assembly and inspect.
5   Leakage of fluid from clutch hydraulic system. Inspect master cylinder, operating cylinder and connecting lines.
6   Air in clutch hydraulic system. Bleed the system.
7   Insufficient pedal stroke. Check and adjust as necessary.
8   Piston seal in master or release cylinder deformed or damaged.
9   Lack of grease on pilot bearing.

### 31 Clutch slips (engine speed increase with no increase in vehicle speed)

1   Clutch cable in need of adjustment (Chapter 1).
2   Worn or oil-soaked clutch disc.
3   Clutch disc not broken in. It may take 30 or 40 starts for a new clutch to seat.
4   Diaphragm spring weak or damaged. Remove clutch cover/pressure plate assembly and inspect.
5   Debris in master cylinder preventing the piston from returning to its normal position.
6   Clutch hydraulic line damaged internally (not allowing fluid to return to the clutch master cylinder).
7   Binding in the release mechanism.

### 32 Grabbing (chattering) as clutch is engaged

1   Oil on clutch disc. Remove and inspect. Repair any leaks.
2   Worn or loose engine or transaxle mounts. These units may move slightly when clutch is released. Inspect mounts and bolts.
3   Worn splines on clutch disc. Remove clutch components and inspect.
4   Warped pressure plate or flywheel. Remove clutch components and inspect.
5   Diaphragm spring fatigued. Remove clutch cover/pressure plate assembly and inspect.
6   Clutch linings hardened or warped.
7   Clutch lining rivets loose.

### 33 Squeal or rumble with clutch fully engaged (pedal released)

1   Improper pedal adjustment. Adjust pedal freeplay.
2   Release bearing binding on transaxle input shaft. Remove clutch components and check bearing. Remove any burrs or nicks, clean and relubricate before reinstallation.
3   Pilot bearing worn or damaged.
4   Clutch rivets loose.
5   Clutch disc cracked.
6   Fatigued clutch disc torsion springs. Replace clutch disc.
7   Weak pedal return spring. Replace the spring.

### 34 Squeal or rumble with clutch fully disengaged (pedal depressed)

1   Worn, faulty or broken release bearing.
2   Worn or broken pressure plate diaphragm fingers.

### 35 Clutch pedal stays on floor when disengaged

1   Bind in cable or release bearing. Inspect cable or remove clutch components as necessary.
2   Clutch pressure plate weak or broken. Remove and inspect clutch pressure plate.

## Manual transaxle

**Note:** *All manual transaxle service information is located in Chapter 7A, unless otherwise noted.*

### 36 Noisy in Neutral with engine running

1   Mainshaft bearing worn.
2   Damaged pinion shaft bearing.
3   Insufficient transaxle lubricant.
4   Transaxle lubricant in poor condition. Drain and fill with proper grade (Chapter 1). Inspect old lubricant for water and debris.
5   Noise can be caused by variations in engine torque. Change the idle speed (Chapter 1) and see if noise disappears.

### 37 Noisy in all gears

1   Mainshaft bearing worn.
2   Damaged pinion shaft bearing.
3   Insufficient lubricant (see checking procedures in Chapter 1).

### 38 Noisy in one particular gear

1   Worn, damaged or chipped gear teeth for that particular gear.
2   Worn or damaged synchronizer for that particular gear.

### 39 Slips out of high gear

1   Transaxle mounting bolts loose.
2   Shift mechanism not working freely.
3   Damaged pilot bearing.
4   Dirt between transaxle housing and engine or misalignment of transaxle.
5   Worn or improperly adjusted linkage.

### 40 Difficulty in engaging gears

1   Clutch not releasing (Chapter 8).
2   Loose, damaged or misadjusted shift linkage. Make a thorough inspection, replacing parts as necessary. Adjust as described in Chapter 8.

### 41 Oil leakage

1   Excessive amount of lubricant in transaxle (see Chapter 1 for correct checking procedures). Drain lubricant as required.
2   Driveaxle oil seals defective.
3   Extension housing seal or speedometer driven-gear O-ring defective.

## Automatic transaxle

**Note:** *Due to the complexity of the automatic transaxle, it is difficult for the home mechanic to properly diagnose and service this component. For problems other than the following, the vehicle should be taken to a reputable mechanic.*

### 42 Fluid leakage

1   Automatic transaxle fluid is a deep red color and fluid leaks should not be confused with engine oil which can easily be blown by air flow to the transaxle.
2   To pinpoint a leak, first remove all built-up dirt and grime from around the transaxle. Degreasing agents and/or steam cleaning will achieve this. With the underside clean, drive the vehicle at low speeds so that air flow will not blow the leak far from its source. Raise the vehicle and determine where the leak is coming from. Common areas of leakage are:

a) *Fluid pan: tighten mounting bolts and/or replace pan gasket as necessary* (Chapter 1)

b) **Extension housing seal:** *replace seal as necessary (Chapter 7B)*
c) **Filler pipe:** *replace the rubber oil seal where pipe enters transaxle case*
d) **Transaxle fluid cooler lines:** *tighten connectors where lines enter transaxle case and/or replace lines*
e) **Vent pipe:** *transaxle over-filled and/or water in fluid (see checking procedures, Chapter 1)*
f) **Speedometer driven gear** *O-ring defective.*

## 43 General shift mechanism problems

Chapter 7 deals with checking and adjusting the shift linkage on automatic transaxles. Common problems which may be attributed to out-of-adjustment linkage are:

a) *Engine starts in gears other than P (Park) or N (Neutral)*
b) *Gear position indicator points to a gear other than the one the transaxle is actually in*
c) *Vehicle will not hold firm when in P (Park) position*

## 44 Transaxle will not downshift with the accelerator pedal pressed to the floor

Faulty electronics in transaxle control system. Take the vehicle to a dealer.

## 45 Engine will start in gears other than P (Park) or N (Neutral)

Check the Park/Neutral and back-up light switch.

## 46 Transaxle slips, shifts rough, is noisy or has no drive in forward or reverse gears

1    There are many probable causes for the above problems, but the home mechanic should concern himself only with one possibility: fluid level.
2    Before taking the vehicle to a repair shop, check the level of the fluid and condition of the fluid as described in Chapter 1. Correct fluid level as necessary or change the fluid and filter if needed. If problem persists, have a professional diagnose the probable cause.

## Driveshaft (4WD models)

## 47 Leakage of fluid at front of driveshaft

Defective extension housing seal (Chapter 7). Also, inspect the splined yoke for burrs or a rough condition which may be damaging the seal. If found, these can be dressed with crocus cloth or a fine whetstone.

## 48 Knock or clunk when the transaxle is under initial load (just after transaxle is put into gear)

1    Loose or disconnected rear suspension components. Check all mounting bolts and bushings (Chapters 1 and 10).
2    Loose driveshaft bolts. Inspect all bolts and nuts and tighten to the specified torque.
3    Worn or damaged universal joint bearings. Replace the driveshaft (Chapter 8).
4    Worn sleeve yoke and mainshaft splines (Chapter 8).

## 49 Metallic grating sound consistent with vehicle speed

Pronounced wear in the universal joint bearings. Replace the driveshaft (Chapter 8).

## 50 Vibration

**Note:** *Before it can be assumed that the driveshaft is at fault, make sure the tires are perfectly balanced and perform the following test.*
1    Install a tachometer inside the vehicle to monitor engine speed as it is driven. Drive the vehicle and note the engine speed at which the vibration (roughness) is most pronounced. Now shift the transaxle to a different gear and bring the engine speed to the same point.
2    If the vibration occurs at the same engine speed (rpm) regardless of which gear the transaxle is in, the driveshaft is NOT at fault since the driveshaft speed varies.
3    If the vibration decreases or is eliminated when the transaxle is in a different gear at the same engine speed, refer to the following probable causes.
4    Bent or dented driveshaft. Inspect and replace as necessary (Chapter 8).
5    Undercoating or built-up dirt, etc. on the driveshaft. Clean the shah thoroughly and test.
6    Worn universal joint bearings (Chapter 8).

## Front differential

## 51 Gear noise when driving

If noise increases as vehicle speed increases, it may be due to insufficient gear oil (Chapter 1), incorrect gear engagement or damaged gears. Remove the transaxle/differential unit and have it checked and repaired by a Subaru dealer service department.

## 52 Gear noise when coasting

Damaged gears caused by bearings and shims that are worn or out of adjustment.

## 53 Bearing noise

Usually caused by cracked, broken or otherwise damaged bearings (see Section 48).

## 54 Noise when turning

Damaged or worn differential side gear, pinion gear or pinion shaft (see Section 48).

## Rear differential (4WD models)

## 55 Oil leakage

1    Worn or incorrectly installed pinion seal or axleshaft oil seal.
2    Scored or excessively worn sliding surface of companion flange.
3    Clogged air vent.
4    Loose rear cover attaching bolts or damaged gasket.
5    Loose oil fill or drain plug.

## 56 Noise when starting or shifting gears

1    Excessive gear backlash.
2    Insufficient bearing preload.
3    Loose drive pinion nut.

## 57 Noise when turning

1    Damaged or worn side gears or bearings.
2    Broken or seized spider gear shaft.
3    Excessively worn side gear thrust washer.
4    Broken teeth on differential hypoid gears.

## Driveaxles

**Note:** *All driveaxle service procedures are in Chapter 8, unless otherwise noted.*

### 58 Clicking noise in turns

Worn or damaged outer CV joint. Check for cut or damaged boots. Repair as necessary.

### 59 Knock or clunk when accelerating after coasting

Worn or damaged inner CV joint. Check for cut or damaged boots. Repair as necessary.

### 60 Shudder or vibration during acceleration

1   Excessive joint angle. Check and correct as necessary.
2   Worn or damaged inner or outer CV joints. Repair or replace as necessary.
3   Sticking inner CV joint assembly. Correct or replace as necessary.

## Brakes

**Note:** *Before assuming that a brake problem exists, make sure that the tires are in good condition and inflated properly (see Chapter 1), the wheel alignment is correct (see Chapter 10) and that the vehicle is not loaded with weight in an unequal manner. All service procedures for the brakes are included in Chapter 9, unless otherwise noted.*

### 61 Vehicle pulls to one side during braking

1   Defective, damaged or oil-contaminated disc pad on one side. Inspect as described in Chapter 1. Replace as necessary.
2   Excessive wear of brake pad material or disc on one side. Inspect and correct as necessary.
3   Loose or disconnected front suspension components. Inspect and tighten all bolts to the torque listed in the Chapter 10 Specifications.
4   Defective caliper assembly. Remove caliper and inspect for stuck piston or damage.

### 62 Noise (high-pitched squeal without brake applied)

Front brake pads worn out. This noise comes from the wear sensor or pad backing plate rubbing against the disc. Replace pads with new ones immediately.

### 63 Excessive brake pedal travel

1   Partial brake system failure. Inspect entire system (Chapter 1) and correct as required.
2   Insufficient fluid in master cylinder. Check (Chapter 1), add fluid and bleed system if necessary.
3   Rear brakes not adjusting properly (models with rear drum brakes). Make a series of starts and stops while the vehicle is in Reverse. If this does not correct the situation, remove rear drums and inspect self-adjusters.

### 64 Brake pedal feels spongy when depressed

1   Air in hydraulic lines. Bleed the brake system.
2   Faulty flexible hoses. Inspect all system hoses and lines. Replace parts as necessary.
3   Master cylinder mount loose. Inspect master cylinder bolts (nuts) and tighten to the torque listed in the Chapter 9 Specifications.
4   Master cylinder faulty.

### 65 Excessive effort required to stop vehicle

1   Power brake booster not operating properly.
2   Excessively worn linings or pads. Inspect (Chapter 1) and replace if necessary.
3   One or more caliper pistons or wheel cylinders seized. Inspect and replace as required.
4   Brake linings or pads contaminated with oil or grease. Inspect and replace as required (Chapter 1).
5   New pads or linings installed and not yet seated. It will take a while for the new material to seat against the drum (or disc).

### 66 Pedal travels to floor with little resistance

Little or no fluid in the master cylinder reservoir (caused by leaking wheel cylinder(s), leaking caliper piston(s), loose, damaged or disconnected brake lines). Inspect entire system and correct as necessary.

### 67 Brake pedal pulsates during brake application

1   Wheel bearings not adjusted properly or in need of replacement (Chapter 1).
2   Caliper not sliding properly due to improper installation or obstructions.

Remove and inspect.
3   Disc not within specifications. Remove the disc and check for excessive lateral run-out and parallelism. Have the disc machined or replace it with a new one.
4   Out-of-round rear brake drums. Remove the drums and have them machined, or replace them.

### 68 Hill-holder fails to hold

1   Incline of hill may be too gentle to activate holder.
2   Pressure holder valve in need of adjustment.

## Suspension and steering

**Note:** *All service procedures related to suspension and steering are located in Chapter 10, unless otherwise noted.*

### 69 Excessive tire wear (not specific to one area)

1   Incorrect tire pressures (Chapter 1).
2   Tires out of balance. Have professionally balanced.
3   Wheel damaged. Inspect and replace as necessary.
4   Suspension or steering components excessively worn (Chapter 1).

### 70 Excessive tire wear on outside edge

1   Inflation pressures not correct (Chapter 1).
2   Excessive speed on turns.
3   Front end alignment incorrect (excessive toe-in). Have professionally aligned.
4   Suspension arm bent or twisted.

### 71 Excessive tire wear on inside edge

1   Inflation pressures incorrect (Chapter 1).
2   Front or rear toe incorrect. Have wheels aligned.
3   Loose or damaged steering components (Chapter 1).

### 72 Tire tread worn in one place

1   Tires out of balance. Balance tires professionally.
2   Damaged or buckled wheel. Inspect and replace if necessary.
3   Defective tire.

### 73  General vibration at highway speeds

1   Out-of-balance front wheels or tires. Have them professionally balanced.
2   Front or rear wheel bearings loose or worn. Check and replace as necessary.
3   Defective tire or wheel. Have them checked and replaced if necessary.

### 74  Noise whether coasting or in drive

1   Road noise. No corrective procedures available.
2   Tire noise. Inspect tires and tire pressures (Chapter 1).
3   Front wheel bearings loose, worn or damaged. Check (Chapter 1) and replace if necessary.
4   Damaged shock absorbers or mounts (Chapter 1).
5   Loose road wheel lug nuts. Check and tighten as necessary (Chapter 1).

### 75  Vehicle pulls to one side

1   Tire pressures uneven (Chapter 1).
2   Defective tire (Chapter 1).
3   Excessive wear in suspension or steering components (Chapter 1).
4   Front end in need of alignment.
5   Front brakes dragging. Inspect brakes as described in Chapter 1.

### 76  Shimmy, shake or vibration

1   Tire or wheel out of balance or out of round. Have professionally balanced.
2   Loose or worn wheel bearings. Replace as necessary.
3   Struts and/or suspension components worn or damaged.

### 77  Excessive pitching and/or rolling around corners or during braking

1   Defective struts. Replace as a set.
2   Broken or weak coil springs and/or suspension components. Inspect as described in Chapter 11.

### 78  Excessively stiff steering

1   Lack of fluid in power steering fluid reservoir (Chapter 1).
2   Incorrect tire pressures (Chapter 1).
3   Lack of lubrication at balljoints (Chapter 1).
4   Front end out of alignment.

### 79  Excessive play in steering

1   Loose wheel bearings (Chapter 1).
2   Excessive wear in suspension or steering components.

### 80  Lack of power assistance

1   Steering pump drivebelt faulty, broken or not adjusted properly (Chapter 1).
2   Fluid level low (Chapter 1).
3   Hoses or lines restricting the flow. Inspect and replace parts as necessary.
4   Air in power steering system. Bleed system.

# Chapter 1
# Tune-up and routine maintenance

## Contents

## Specifications

### Recommended lubricants and fluids

**Note:** *Listed here are manufacturer recommendations at the time this manual was written. Manufacturers occasionally upgrade their fluid and lubricant specifications, so check with your auto parts store for current recommendations.*

Engine oil
    Type .............................................................................. API "certified for gasoline engines"
    Viscosity ...................................................................... See accompanying chart

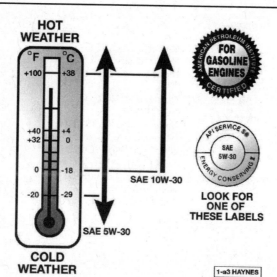

Engine oil viscosity chart - for best fuel economy and cold starting, select the lowest SAE viscosity grade for the expected temperature range

1-a3 HAYNES

## Recommended lubricants and fluids (continued)

| | |
|---|---|
| Coolant | Ethylene glycol based anti-freeze |
| Brake fluid | DOT 3 or DOT 4 |
| Clutch fluid | DOT 3 or DOT 4 |
| Power steering fluid | Dexron II or Dexron IIE ATF |
| Automatic transaxle fluid | Dexron II or Dexron IIE ATF |
| Manual transaxle lubricant | API GL-5 SAE 80W-90 gear oil |
| Differential lubricant | API GL-5 SAE 80W-90 gear oil |
| Chassis grease | NLGI no. 2 lithium base chassis grease |

## Capacities*

| | Quarts |
|---|---|
| Engine oil (with filter change) | |
|     2.2L engine | |
|         1990 through 1994 | 4.8 qts |
|         1995 on | 4.2 qts |
|     2.5L engine | 4.7 qts |
| Cooling system | |
|     2.2L engine | |
|         1990 through 1994 | |
|             2WD | 6.3 qts |
|             4WD | 7.4 qts |
|         1995 on | 6.1 qts |
|     2.5L engines | 6.3 qts |
| Automatic transaxle | |
|     Standard refill after fluid and filter change (approximate) | 4.0 qts |
|     Total capacity (refill after overhaul) | |
|         2.2L engines | |
|             1990 through 1993 | 8.8 qts |
|             1994 on | 8.4 qts |
|         2.5L engines | 10 qts |
| Manual transaxle | |
|     2.2L engines | |
|         2WD models | |
|             1990 through 1994 | 3.5 qts |
|             1995 on | 3.7 qts |
|         4WD models | |
|             1990 through 1994 | 4.2 qts |
|             1995 on | 3.7 qts |
|     2.5L engines | 3.7 qts |
| Differential | |
|     Front differential (vehicles equipped with automatic transaxle) | 1.5 qts |
|     Rear differential (4WD vehicles) | 0.8 qt |

*All capacities approximate. Add as necessary to bring to appropriate level.*

## Ignition system

| | |
|---|---|
| Spark plug type | |
|     2.2L engines (types are equivalents - use brand of preference) | |
|         1990 | |
|             Type I | Champion RC9YC-4 |
|             Type II | NGK BKR6E-11 |
|             Type III | Nippondenso K20PUR-11 |
|         1992 through 1994 | |
|             Type I | Champion RC7YC-4 |
|             Type II | NGK BKR6E-11 |
|             Type III | Nippondenso K20PUR-11 |
|         1995 on | |
|             Type I | Champion RC10YC-4 |
|             Type II | NGK BKR6E-11 |
|             Type III | Nippondenso K20PR-U11 |
|     2.5L engines | NGK PFR5B-11 |
| Spark plug gap | 0.039 to 0.043 inch |

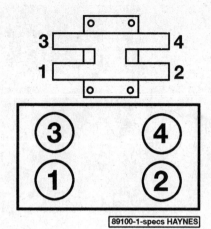

**Engine cylinder numbering and coil
pack terminal locations**

Idle speed

  No load on engine ........................................................................ 600 to 800 rpm in Neutral (man. trans) or Park (auto. trans)

  Load on engine (air conditioning on) .......................................... 800 to 900 rpm in Neutral (man. trans) or Park (auto. trans)

Firing order ................................................................................... 1-3-2-4

## Valve clearances (engine cold)

Intake ............................................................................................ 0.008 inch

Exhaust ......................................................................................... 0.010 inch

## Brakes

Disc brake pad lining thickness (minimum) .................................. 1/16 inch

Drum brake shoe lining thickness (minimum) .............................. 1/16 inch

Parking brake adjustment

  Drum brake

    1990 through 1994 .................................................................. 3 to 4 clicks

    1995 on ................................................................................... automatically adjusted

  Disc brake ................................................................................. 3 to 4 clicks

Brake pedal freeplay ..................................................................... 3/64 to 1/8 inch

## Clutch

Pedal freeplay

  Turbocharged models ................................................................ 1/8 to 19/32 inch

  Non-turbocharged models ......................................................... 3/8 to 13/16 inch

Fork lever freeplay ........................................................................ 1/8 to 5/32 inch

## Suspension and steering

Steering wheel freeplay limit ........................................................ 11/16 inch

Balljoint allowable movement ........................................................ 0.0 inch

Wheel bearing freeplay ................................................................. 0.002 inch

## Torque specifications

Ft-lbs

Automatic transaxle drain plug ..................................................... 18

Manual transaxle drain plug ......................................................... 30

Front differential drain plug (automatic transaxle) ....................... 30

Engine oil drain plug ..................................................................... 30

Spark plugs ................................................................................... 15

Wheel lug nuts .............................................................................. 72

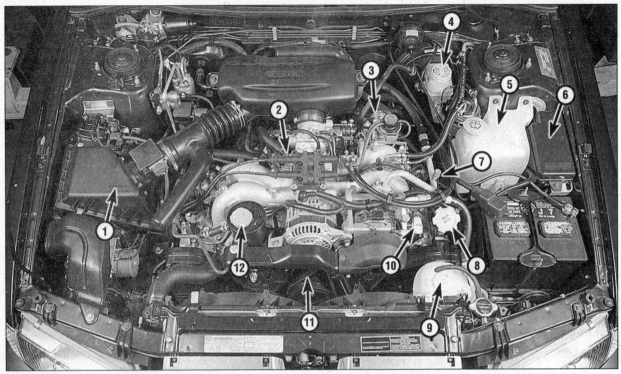

**Engine compartment component locations (typical)**

| | | | | | |
|---|---|---|---|---|---|
| 1 | Air filter housing | 6 | Fuse and relay center | 9 | Coolant reservoir |
| 2 | PCV valve and hose | 7 | Air conditioning refrigerant service | 10 | Engine oil dipstick |
| 3 | EGR valve | | fitting | 11 | Drivebelts |
| 4 | Brake fluid reservoir | 8 | Oil filler cap | 12 | Power steering fluid reservoir |
| 5 | Windshield washer fluid reservoir | | | | |

**Typical engine compartment underside component locations**

| | | | | | |
|---|---|---|---|---|---|
| 1 | Oil filter | 4 | Front brake disc | 7 | Exhaust pipe |
| 2 | Engine block coolant drain plugs | 5 | Driveaxle | 8 | Engine oil drain plug |
| 3 | Strut assembly | 6 | Automatic transaxle drain plug | | |

**Typical rear underside component locations**

| | | | |
|---|---|---|---|
| 1 | Muffler | 3 | Evaporative emissions canister |
| 2 | Rear differential | 4 | Rear driveaxle |

| | |
|---|---|
| 5 | Driveshaft |
| 6 | Rear differential drain plug |

# 1 Subaru Legacy Maintenance schedule

## Every 250 miles or weekly, whichever comes first

Check the engine oil level (Section 4)
Check the engine coolant level
(Section 4)
Check the windshield washer fluid level (Section 4)
Check the brake fluid level (Section 4)
Check the tires and tire pressures (Section 5)

## Every 3000 miles or 3 months, whichever comes first

*All items listed above, plus . . .*
Check the automatic transaxle fluid level (Section 6)
Check the power steering fluid level (Section 7)
Change the engine oil and filter (Section 8)

## Every 7500 miles or 6 months, whichever comes first

Check and service the battery (Section 9)
Check the cooling system (Section 10)
Inspect and replace, if necessary, all underhood hoses
(Section 11)
Inspect and replace, if necessary, the windshield wiper
blades (Section 12)
Rotate the tires (Section 13)
Inspect the suspension and steering components
(Section 14)
Inspect the exhaust system (Section 15)
Check the manual transaxle lubricant (Section 16)
Check the front differential lubricant (automatic transaxles)
(Section 16)
Check the rear differential lubricant level (Section 17)
Check the seat belts (Section 18)

## Every 15,000 miles or 12 months, whichever comes first

*All items listed above, plus . . .*
Check the brakes (Section 19)
Inspect the fuel system (Section 20)
Replace the fuel filter (Section 21)
Check the engine drivebelts (Section 22)
Check the clutch pedal height and hillholder adjustment
(Section 23)

## Every 30,000 miles or 24 months, whichever comes first

*All items listed above, plus . . .*
Replace the spark plugs (non-platinum plugs) (Section 24)
Inspect the spark plug wires (Section 25)
Check the idle speed adjustment (Section 26)
Replace the air filter and PCV filter (Section 27)*
Check the Positive Crankcase Ventilation (PCV) system
(Section 28)
Inspect the evaporative emissions control system
(Section 29)
Check the EGR valve (Section 30)
Service the cooling system (drain, flush and refill)
(Section 31)
Change the brake fluid (Section 32)
Change the automatic transaxle fluid (Section 33)**
Change the manual transaxle lubricant (Section 34)
Change the differential lubricant (Section 35)

## Every 60,000 miles or 48 months, whichever comes first

Replace the spark plugs on the 2.5L engine (Section 24)
Inspect the front and rear wheel bearings (Section 36)
Replace the timing belt on the 2.2L engine (Chapter 2A)

## Every 100,000 miles or 72 months, whichever comes first

Check the valve adjustment on 1997 and later models
(Section 37)
Replace the timing belt (on 2.5L engines replace platinum-
type plugs) (Chapter 2A)

*This item is affected by "severe" operating conditions, as
described below. If the vehicle is operated under severe
conditions, perform all maintenance indicated with an
asterisk (*) at 7500 mile/six-month intervals. Severe conditions exist if you mainly operate the vehicle . . .*
in dusty areas
towing a trailer
idling for extended periods and/or driving at low
speeds when outside temperatures remain below freezing
and most trips are less than four miles long

**If operated under one or more of the following conditions,
change the automatic transaxle fluid every 15,000 miles:*
in heavy city traffic where the outside temperature
regularly reaches 90-degrees F or higher
in hilly or mountainous terrain
frequent trailer pulling

## 2    Introduction

This Chapter is designed to help the home mechanic maintain the Subaru for peak performance, economy, safety and long life.

On the following pages is a master maintenance schedule, followed by Sections dealing specifically with each item on the schedule. Visual checks, adjustments, component replacement and other helpful items are included. Refer to the accompanying illustrations of the engine compartment and the underside of the vehicle for the location of various components.

Servicing your Subaru in accordance with the mileage/time maintenance schedule and the following Sections will provide it with a planned maintenance program that should result in a long and reliable service life. This is a comprehensive plan, so maintaining some items but not others at the specified service intervals will not produce the same results.

As you service your vehicle, you will discover that many of the procedures can, and should, be grouped together because of the nature of the particular procedure you're performing or because of the close proximity of two otherwise unrelated components to one another.

For example, if the vehicle is raised for any reason, you should inspect the exhaust, suspension, steering and fuel systems while you're under the vehicle. When you're rotating the tires, it makes good sense to check the brakes and wheel bearings since the wheels are already removed.

Finally, let's suppose you have to borrow or rent a torque wrench. Even if you only need to tighten the spark plugs, you might as well check the torque of as many critical fasteners as time allows.

The first step of this maintenance program is to prepare yourself before the actual work begins. Read through all Sections pertinent to the procedures you're planning to do, then make a list of and gather together all the parts and tools you will need to do the job. If it looks as if you might run into problems during a particular segment of some procedure, seek advice from your local parts man or dealer service department.

## 3    Tune-up general information

The term tune-up is used in this manual to represent a combination of individual operations rather than one specific procedure.

If, from the time the vehicle is new, the routine maintenance schedule is followed closely and frequent checks are made of fluid levels and high wear items, as suggested throughout this manual, the engine will be kept in relatively good running condition and the need for additional work will be minimized.

More likely than not, however, there will be times when the engine is running poorly due to lack of regular maintenance. This is even more likely if a used vehicle, which has not received regular and frequent maintenance checks, is purchased. In such cases, an engine tune-up will be needed outside of the regular routine maintenance intervals.

The first step in any tune-up or diagnostic procedure to help correct a poor running engine is a cylinder compression check. A compression check (see Chapter 2B) will help determine the condition of internal engine components and should be used as a guide for tune-up and repair procedures. If, for instance, the compression check indicates serious internal engine wear, a conventional tune-up won't improve the performance of the engine and would be a waste of time and money. Because of its importance, the compression check should be done by someone with the right equipment and the knowledge to use it properly.

The following procedures are those most often needed to bring a generally poor running engine back into a proper state of tune.

### *Minor tune-up*

    Check all engine related fluids (Section 4)
    Clean, inspect and test the battery (Section 9)
    Check the cooling system (Section 10)
    Check all underhood hoses (Section 11)
    Check and adjust the drivebelts (Section 22)
    Inspect the spark plug wires (Section 25)

    Replace the spark plugs (Section 24)
    Check and adjust the idle speed (Section 26)
    Check the air filter and the PCV filter (Section 27)
    Check the PCV valve (Section 28)

### *Major tune-up*

*All items listed under Minor tune-up, plus . . .*
    Check the fuel system (Section 20)
    Replace the fuel filter (Section 21)
    Check and adjust the valve clearances (Section 37)
    Check the EGR system (Section 30)
    Replace the spark plug wires (Section 25)
    Replace the air filter and the PCV filter (Section 27)
    Replace the PCV valve (Section 28)
    Check the ignition timing (Chapter 5)
    Check the charging system (Chapter 5)

## 4    Fluid level checks (every 250 miles or weekly)

**Note:** *The following are fluid level checks to be done on a 250 mile or weekly basis. Additional fluid level checks can be found in specific maintenance procedures which follow. Regardless of intervals, be alert to fluid leaks under the vehicle which would indicate a fault to be corrected immediately.*

1    Fluids are an essential part of the lubrication, cooling, brake and windshield washer systems. Because the fluids gradually become depleted and/or contaminated during normal operation of the vehicle, they must be periodically replenished. See *Recommended lubricants and fluids* at the beginning of this Chapter before adding fluid to any of the following components. **Note:** *The vehicle must be on level ground when fluid levels are checked.*

### *Engine oil*

*Refer to illustrations 4.2 and 4.4*

2    The engine oil level is checked with a dipstick that extends through a tube and into the oil pan at the bottom of the engine **(see illustration)**. The oil dipstick is located on the left side of the engine compartment near the battery.

3    The oil level should be checked before the vehicle has been driven, or about 5 minutes after the engine has been shut off. If the oil is checked immediately after driving the vehicle, some of the oil will remain in the upper engine components, resulting in an inaccurate reading on the dipstick.

4    Pull the dipstick out of the tube and wipe all the oil from the end with a clean rag or paper towel. Insert the clean dipstick all the way back into the tube, then pull it out again. Note the oil at the end of the dipstick. Add oil as necessary to keep the level between the ADD and FULL marks on the dipstick **(see illustration)**.

**Oil filler cap**

**Oil level dipstick**

**4.2  The engine oil dipstick is located on the left side of the engine near the oil filler cap**

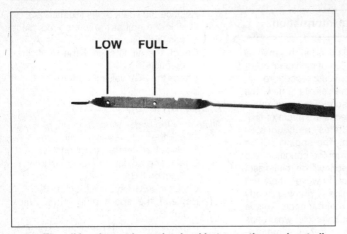

**4.4  The oil level must be maintained between the marks at all times - it takes one quart of oil to raise the level from the LOW mark to the FULL mark**

**4.8  Coolant can be added to the cooling system after removing the cap from the coolant reservoir (arrow)**

5    Do not overfill the engine by adding too much oil since this may result in oil-fouled spark plugs, oil leaks or oil seal failures.

6    Oil is added to the engine after removing the threaded cap from the oil filler tube **(see illustration 4.2)**. A funnel may help to reduce spills.

7    Checking the oil level is an important preventive maintenance step. A consistently low oil level indicates oil leakage through damaged seals, defective gaskets or past worn rings or valve guides. If the oil looks milky or has water droplets in it, the cylinder head gasket(s) may be blown or the head(s) or block may be cracked. The engine should be checked immediately. The condition of the oil should also be checked. Whenever you check the oil level, slide your thumb and index finger up the dipstick before wiping off the oil. If you see small dirt or metal particles clinging to the dipstick, the oil should be changed (see Section 8).

## Engine coolant

*Refer to illustration 4.8*

**Warning 1:** *Do not allow antifreeze to come in contact with your skin or painted surfaces of the vehicle. Flush contaminated areas immediately with plenty of water. Don't store new coolant or leave old coolant lying around where it's accessible to children or pets – they're attracted by its sweet smell. Ingestion of even a small amount of coolant can be fatal! Wipe up garage floor and drip pan spills immediately. Keep antifreeze containers covered and repair cooling system leaks as soon as they're noticed.*

**Warning 2:** *DO NOT remove the radiator cap or the coolant reservoir cap while the cooling system is hot, as escaping steam could cause serious injury.*

8    These models are equipped with a pressurized coolant recovery system. A white coolant reservoir, which is located by the radiator in the engine compartment, is connected by a hose to the base of the radiator cap **(see illustration)**. If the coolant gets too hot during engine operation, coolant can escape from the radiator through a pressurized filler cap, then through a connecting hose into the reservoir. As the engine cools, the coolant is automatically drawn back into the cooling system to maintain the correct level.

9    The coolant level should be checked regularly. The coolant level should be between the FULL and LOW lines on the reservoir tank. The level will vary with the temperature of the engine. When the engine is cold, the coolant level should be at or slightly above the LOW mark on the tank. Once the engine has warmed up, the level should be at or near the FULL mark. If it isn't, allow the fluid in the tank to cool, then remove the cap from the reservoir and add coolant to bring the level up to the FULL line.

10   Use only ethylene-glycol type coolant and water in the mixture ratio recommended by your owner's manual. Do not use supplemental inhibitor additives. If only a small amount of coolant is required to bring the system up to the proper level, water can be used. However, repeated additions of water will dilute the recommended antifreeze and water solution. In order to maintain the proper ratio of antifreeze and water, it is advisable to top up the coolant level with the correct mixture. Refer to your owners' manual for the recommended ratio.

11   If the coolant level drops within a short

**4.16a  The fluid level inside the brake reservoir can easily be checked by observing the level from the outside - fluid can be added to the reservoir after unscrewing the cap (later model shown)**

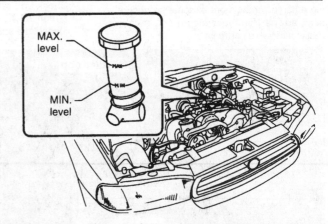

**4.16b  Location of the clutch master cylinder fluid reservoir on manual transmission models**

4.23 The windshield washer fluid reservoir is located at the left front of the engine compartment

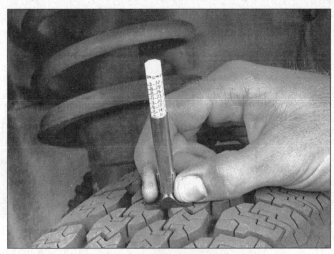

5.2 Use a tire tread depth gauge to monitor tire wear - they are available at auto parts stores and service stations and cost very little

time after replenishment, there may be a leak in the system. Inspect the radiator, hoses, engine coolant filler cap, drain plugs and water pump. If no leak is evident, have the radiator cap pressure tested by your dealer. **Warning:** *Never remove the radiator cap or the coolant recovery reservoir cap when the engine is running or has just been shut down, because the cooling system is hot. Escaping steam and scalding liquid could cause serious injury.*

12   If it is necessary to open the radiator cap, wait until the system has cooled completely, then wrap a thick cloth around the cap and turn it to the first stop. If any steam escapes, wait until the system has cooled further, then remove the cap.

13   When checking the coolant level, always note its condition. It should be relatively clear. If it is brown or rust colored, the system should be drained, flushed and refilled. Even if the coolant appears to be normal, the corrosion inhibitors wear out with use, so it must be replaced at the specified intervals.

14   Do not allow antifreeze to come in contact with your skin or painted surfaces of the vehicle. Flush contacted areas immediately with plenty of water.

### Brake and clutch fluid

*Refer to illustrations 4.16a and 4.16b*

15   The brake and clutch fluid level is checked by looking through the plastic reservoir mounted on the master cylinder. The brake master cylinder is mounted on the front of the power booster unit in the driver's side rear corner of the engine compartment and the clutch master cylinder is mounted near the firewall.

16   The fluid level should be between the MAX and MIN lines on the side of the reservoir **(see illustrations)**.

17   If the fluid level is low, wipe the top of the reservoir and the cap with a clean rag to prevent contamination of the system as the cap is unscrewed.

18   Add only the specified brake fluid to the reservoir (refer to *Recommended lubricants and fluids* at the front of this Chapter or your owner's manual). Mixing different types of brake fluid can damage the system. Fill the reservoir to the MAX line. **Warning:** *Brake fluid can harm your eyes and damage painted surfaces, so use extreme caution when handling or pouring it. Do not use brake fluid that has been standing open or is more than one year old. Brake fluid absorbs moisture from the air, which can cause a dangerous loss of braking effectiveness.*

19   While the reservoir cap is off, check the master cylinder reservoir for contamination. If rust deposits, dirt particles or water droplets are present, the system should be bled repeatedly until clean brake fluid emerges from the bleeder valves (see Section 32).

20   After filling the reservoir to the proper level, make sure the cap is seated to prevent fluid leakage and/or contamination.

21   The fluid level in the master cylinder will drop slightly as the brake shoes or pads at each wheel wear down during normal operation. If the brake fluid level drops consistently, check the entire system for leaks immediately. Examine all brake lines, hoses and connections, along with the calipers, wheel cylinders and master cylinder (see Section 19).

22   When checking the fluid level, if you discover one or both reservoirs empty or nearly empty, the brake system should be bled (see Chapter 9).

### Windshield washer fluid

*Refer to illustration 4.23*

23   Fluid for the windshield washer system is stored in a plastic reservoir located on the left side of the engine compartment **(see illustration)**.

24   In milder climates, plain water can be used in the reservoir, but it should be kept no more than 2/3 full to allow for expansion if the water freezes. In colder climates, use wind-

shield washer system antifreeze, available at any auto parts store, to lower the freezing point of the fluid. Mix the antifreeze with water in accordance with the manufacturer's directions on the container. **Caution:** *Do not use cooling system antifreeze - it will damage the vehicle's paint.*

### Battery electrolyte

25   Most vehicles covered by this manual are equipped with a battery which is permanently sealed (except for vent holes) and has no filler caps. Water does not have to be added to these batteries at any time; however, if a maintenance-type battery has been installed, remove all the cell caps on top of the battery. If the electrolyte level is low, add distilled water until the level is above the plates. There is usually a split-ring indicator in each cell to help you judge when enough water has been added. Add water until the electrolyte level is just up to the bottom of the split ring indicator. **Caution:** *Overfilling the cells may cause electrolyte to spill over during periods of heavy charging, causing corrosion or damage.*

### 5   Tire and tire pressure checks (every 250 miles or weekly)

*Refer to illustrations 5.2, 5.3, 5.4a, 5.4b and 5.8*

1   Periodic inspection of the tires may spare you the inconvenience of being stranded with a flat tire. It can also provide you with vital information regarding possible problems in the steering and suspension systems before major damage occurs.

2   The original tires on this vehicle are equipped with 1/2-inch wear bands that will appear when tread depth reaches 1/16-inch, at which time the tires can be considered worn out. Tread wear can be monitored with a simple, inexpensive device known as a tread depth indicator **(see illustration)**.

**UNDERINFLATION**

**CUPPING**

**Cupping may be caused by:**

● **Underinflation and/or mechanical irregularities such as out-of-balance condition of wheel and/or tire, and bent or damaged wheel.**
● **Loose or worn steering tie-rod or steering idler arm.**
● **Loose, damaged or worn front suspension parts.**

**OVERINFLATION**

**INCORRECT TOE-IN OR EXTREME CAMBER**

**FEATHERING DUE TO MISALIGNMENT**

5.3  This chart will help you determine the condition of the tires, the probable cause(s) of abnormal wear and the  corrective action necessary

3    Note any abnormal tread wear **(see illustration)**. Tread pattern irregularities such as cupping, flat spots and more wear on one side than the other are indications of front end alignment and/or balance problems. If any of these conditions are noted, take the vehicle to a tire shop or service station to correct the problem.

4    Look closely for cuts, punctures and embedded nails or tacks. Sometimes a tire will hold air pressure for a short time or leak down very slowly after a nail has embedded itself in the tread. If a slow leak persists, check the valve stem core to make sure it's tight **(see illustration)**. Examine the tread for an object that may have embedded itself in the tire or for a "plug" that may have begun to leak (radial tire punctures are repaired with a rubber plug that's installed in the hole). If a puncture is suspected, it can be easily verified by spraying a solution of soapy water onto the puncture area **(see illustration)**. The soapy solution will bubble if there's a leak. Unless the puncture is unusually large, a tire shop or service station can usually repair the tire.

5    Carefully inspect the inner sidewall of each tire for evidence of brake fluid leakage. If you see any, inspect the brakes immediately.

6    Correct air pressure adds miles to the

lifespan of the tires, improves mileage and enhances overall ride quality. Tire pressure cannot be accurately estimated by looking at a tire, especially if it's a radial. A tire pressure gauge is essential. Keep an accurate gauge in the vehicle. The pressure gauges attached to the nozzles of air hoses at gas stations are often inaccurate.

7    Always check tire pressure when the tires are cold. Cold, in this case, means the vehicle has not been driven over a mile in the three hours preceding a tire pressure check. A pressure rise of four to eight pounds is not uncommon once the tires are warm.

8    Unscrew the valve cap protruding from the wheel or hubcap and push the gauge

5.4a  If a tire loses air on a steady basis, check the valve core first to make sure it's snug (special inexpensive wrenches are commonly available at auto parts stores)

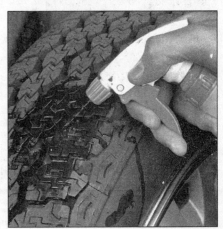

5.4b  If the valve core is tight, raise the corner of the vehicle with the low tire and spray a soapy water solution onto the tread as the tire is turned slowly - leaks will cause small bubbles to appear

**5.8  To extend the life of the tires, check the air pressure at least once a week with an accurate gauge (don't forget the spare)**

**6.4  The automatic transaxle fluid dipstick is located at the left rear of the engine compartment**

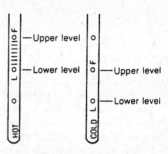

**6.6  The automatic transaxle fluid level must be maintained between the UPPER LEVEL mark and the LOWER LEVEL mark at the indicated operating temperature (Cold or Hot)**

firmly onto the valve stem **(see illustration)**. Note the reading on the gauge and compare the figure to the recommended tire pressure shown on the placard on the driver's side door pillar. Be sure to reinstall the valve cap to keep dirt and moisture out of the valve stem mechanism. Check all four tires and, if necessary, add enough air to bring them up to the recommended pressure.

9    Don't forget to keep the spare tire inflated to the specified pressure (consult your owner's manual). Note that the air pressure specified for the compact spare is significantly higher than the pressure of the regular tires.

## 6    Automatic transaxle fluid level check (every 3000 miles or 3 months)

*Refer to illustrations 6.4 and 6.6*

1    The level of the automatic transaxle fluid should be carefully maintained. Low fluid level can lead to slipping or loss of drive, while overfilling can cause foaming, loss of fluid and transaxle damage.

2    The transaxle fluid level should only be checked when the transaxle is hot (at its normal operating temperature). If the vehicle has just been driven over 10 miles (15 miles in a frigid climate), and the fluid temperature is 160 to 175-degrees F, the transaxle is hot. **Caution:** *If the vehicle has just been driven for a long time at high speed or in city traffic in hot weather, or if it has been pulling a trailer, an accurate fluid level reading cannot be obtained. Allow the fluid to cool down for about 30 minutes.*

3    If the vehicle has not been driven, park the vehicle on level ground, set the parking brake, then start the engine and bring it to operating temperature. While the engine is idling, depress the brake pedal and move the selector lever through all the gear ranges, beginning and ending in Park.

4    With the engine still idling, remove the dipstick from its tube **(see illustration)**.

Check the level of the fluid on the dipstick and note its condition.

5    Wipe the fluid from the dipstick with a clean rag and reinsert it back into the filler tube until the cap seats.

6    Pull the dipstick out again and note the fluid level. If the transaxle is cold, the level should be in the COLD or COOL range on the dipstick. If it is hot, the fluid level should be in the HOT range. If the level is at the low side of either range, add the specified automatic transaxle fluid through the dipstick tube with a funnel **(see illustration)**.

7    Add just enough of the recommended fluid to fill the transaxle to the proper level. It takes about one pint to raise the level from the low mark to the high mark when the fluid is hot, so add the fluid a little at a time and keep checking the level until it is correct.

8    The condition of the fluid should also be checked along with the level. If the fluid at the end of the dipstick is black or a dark reddish brown color, or if it emits a burned smell, the fluid should be changed (see Section 33). If you are in doubt about the condition of the fluid, purchase some new fluid and compare the two for color and smell.

## 7    Power steering fluid level check (every 3000 miles or 3 months)

*Refer to illustrations 7.2 and 7.6*

1    Unlike manual steering, the power steering system relies on fluid which may, over a period of time, require replenishing.

2    The fluid reservoir for the power steering pump is located on the pump body at the front of the engine **(see illustration)**.

3    For the check, the front wheels should be pointed straight ahead and the engine should be off.

4    Use a clean rag to wipe off the reservoir cap and the area around the cap. This will help prevent any foreign matter from entering the reservoir during the check.

5    Twist off the cap and determine the temperature of the fluid at the end of the dipstick with your finger.

6    Wipe off the fluid with a clean rag, reinsert the dipstick, then withdraw it and read the fluid level. The fluid should be at the proper level, depending on whether it was checked hot or cold **(see illustration)**. Never allow the fluid level to drop below the lower mark on the dipstick.

**7.2  The power steering fluid reservoir is located at the front of the engine compartment - turn the cap counterclockwise to remove it**

**7.6  The marks on the dipstick indicate the safe fluid range**

7    If additional fluid is required, pour the specified type directly into the reservoir, using a funnel to prevent spills.

8    If the reservoir requires frequent fluid additions, all power steering hoses, hose connections and the power steering pump should be carefully checked for leaks.

## 8    Engine oil and filter change (every 3000 miles or 3 months)

*Refer to illustrations 8.2, 8.7, 8.13 and 8.15*

1    Frequent oil changes are the best preventive maintenance the home mechanic can give the engine, because aging oil becomes diluted and contaminated, which leads to premature engine wear.

2    Make sure that you have all the necessary tools before you begin this procedure **(see illustration)**. You should also have plenty of rags or newspapers handy for mopping up any spills.

3    Access to the underside of the vehicle is greatly improved if the vehicle can be lifted on a hoist, driven onto ramps or supported by jackstands.

4    If this is your first oil change, get under the vehicle and familiarize yourself with the location of the oil drain plug. The engine and exhaust components will be warm during the actual work, so try to anticipate any potential problems before the engine and accessories are hot.

5    Park the vehicle on a level spot. Start the engine and allow it to reach its normal operating temperature (the needle on the temperature gauge should be at least above the bottom mark). Warm oil and contaminants will flow out more easily. Turn off the engine when it's warmed up. Remove the filler cap in the valve cover.

6    Raise the vehicle and support it on jackstands. **Warning:** *To avoid personal injury, never get beneath the vehicle when it is supported by only by a jack. The jack provided with your vehicle is designed solely for raising the vehicle to remove and install the wheels.*

*Always use jackstands to support the vehicle when it becomes necessary to place your body underneath the vehicle.*

7    Being careful not to touch the hot exhaust components, place the drain pan under the drain plug in the bottom of the pan and remove the plug **(see illustration)**. You may want to wear gloves while unscrewing the plug the final few turns if the engine is really hot.

8    Allow the old oil to drain into the pan. It may be necessary to move the pan farther under the engine as the oil flow slows to a trickle. Inspect the old oil for the presence of metal shavings and chips.

9    After all the oil has drained, wipe off the drain plug with a clean rag. Even minute metal particles clinging to the plug would immediately contaminate the new oil.

10    Clean the area around the drain plug opening, reinstall the plug and tighten it securely, but do not strip the threads.

11    Move the drain pan into position under the oil filter.

12    Remove all tools, rags, etc. from under the vehicle, being careful not to spill the oil in the drain pan, then lower the vehicle.

13    Loosen the oil filter **(see illustration)** by turning it counterclockwise with the filter wrench. Any standard filter wrench should work. Once the filter is loose, use your hands to unscrew it from the block. **Warning:** *The exhaust pipes may still be hot, so be careful.*

14    With a clean rag, wipe off the mounting surface on the block. If a residue of old oil is allowed to remain, it will smoke when the block is heated up. It will also prevent the new filter from seating properly. Also make sure that the none of the old gasket remains stuck to the mounting surface. It can be removed with a scraper if necessary.

15    Compare the old filter with the new one to make sure they are the same type. Smear some engine oil on the rubber gasket of the new filter and screw it into place **(see illustration)**. Because over-tightening the filter will damage the gasket, do not use a filter wrench to tighten the filter. Tighten it by hand

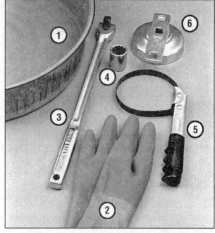

**8.2 These tools are required when changing the engine oil and filter**

1    ***Drain pan*** *- It should be fairly shallow in depth, but wide to prevent spills*

2    ***Rubber gloves*** *- When removing the drain plug and filter, you will get oil on your hands (the gloves will prevent burns)*

3    ***Breaker bar*** *- Sometimes the oil drain plug is tight, and a long breaker bar is needed to loosen it*

4    ***Socket*** *- To be used with the breaker bar or a ratchet (must be the correct size to fit the drain plug)*

5    ***Filter wrench*** *- This is a metal band-type wrench, which requires clearance around the filter to be effective*

6    ***Filter wrench*** *- This type fits on the bottom of the filter and can be turned with a ratchet or breaker bar (different size wrenches are available for different types of filters)*

until the gasket contacts the seating surface. Then seat the filter by giving it an additional 3/4-turn.

16    Add new oil to the engine through the oil filler cap in the valve cover. Use a spout or funnel to prevent oil from spilling onto the top

**8.7 The engine oil drain plug is located on the bottom of the oil pan - it is usually very tight, so use the proper size box end wrench or socket to avoid rounding it off**

**8.13 The oil filter is usually on very tight and will require a special wrench for removal - DO NOT use the wrench to tighten the new filter!**

**8.15 Lubricate the oil filter gasket with clean engine oil before installing the filter on the engine**

**9.1 Tools and materials required for battery maintenance**

**9.6a Battery terminal corrosion usually appears as light, fluffy powder**

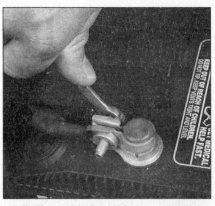

**9.6b Removing the cable from a battery post with a wrench - sometimes special battery pliers are required for this procedure if corrosion has caused deterioration of the nut hex (always remove the ground cable first and hook it up last!)**

of the engine. Pour three quarts of fresh oil into the engine. Wait a few minutes to allow the oil to drain into the pan, then check the level on the oil dipstick (see Section 4 if necessary). If the oil level is at or near the H mark, install the filler cap hand tight, start the engine and allow the new oil to circulate.

17   Allow the engine to run for about a minute. While the engine is running, look under the vehicle and check for leaks at the oil pan drain plug and around the oil filter. If either is leaking, stop the engine and tighten the plug or filter slightly.

18   Wait a few minutes to allow the oil to trickle down into the pan, then recheck the level on the dipstick and, if necessary, add enough oil to bring the level to the H mark.

19   During the first few trips after an oil change, make it a point to check frequently for leaks and proper oil level.

20   The old oil drained from the engine cannot be reused in its present state and should be discarded. Check with your local refuse disposal company, disposal facility or environmental agency to see if they will accept the oil for recycling. Don't pour used oil into drains or on the ground. After the oil has cooled, it can be drained into a suitable container (capped plastic jugs, topped bottles, milk cartons, etc.) for transport to one of these disposal sites.

## 9   Battery check, maintenance and charging (every 7500 miles or 6 months)

Refer to illustrations 9.1, 9.6a, 9.6b, 9.7a and 9.7b

**Warning:** *Certain precautions must be followed when checking and servicing the battery. Hydrogen gas, which is highly flammable, is always present in the battery cells, so keep lighted tobacco and all other open flames and sparks away from the battery. The electrolyte inside the battery is actually dilute sulfuric acid, which will cause injury if splashed on your skin or in your eyes. It will*

1   *Face shield/safety goggles - When removing corrosion with a brush, the acidic particles can easily fly up into your eyes*
2   *Baking soda - A solution of baking soda and water can be used to neutralize corrosion*
3   *Petroleum jelly - A layer of this on the battery posts will help prevent corrosion*
4   *Battery post/cable cleaner - This wire brush cleaning tool will remove all traces of corrosion from the battery posts and cable clamps*
5   *Treated felt washers - Placing one of these on each post, directly under the cable clamps, will help prevent corrosion*
6   *Puller - Sometimes the cable clamps are very difficult to pull off the posts, even after the nut/bolt has been completely loosened. This tool pulls the clamp straight up and off the post without damage*
7   *Battery post/cable cleaner - Here is another cleaning tool which is a slightly different version of Number 4 above, but it does the same thing*
8   *Rubber gloves - Another safety item to consider when servicing the battery; remember that's acid inside the battery!*

*also ruin clothes and painted surfaces. When removing the battery cables, always detach the negative cable first and hook it up last!*

### Maintenance

1   A routine preventive maintenance program for the battery in your vehicle is the only way to ensure quick and reliable starts. But before performing any battery maintenance, make sure that you have the proper equipment necessary to work safely around the battery **(see illustration)**.

2   There are also several precautions that should be taken whenever battery maintenance is performed. Before servicing the battery, always turn the engine and all accessories off and disconnect the cable from the negative terminal of the battery.

3   The battery produces hydrogen gas, which is both flammable and explosive. Never create a spark, smoke or light a match around the battery. Always charge the battery in a ventilated area.

4   Electrolyte contains poisonous and corrosive sulfuric acid. Do not allow it to get in your eyes, on your skin or on your clothes. Never ingest it. Wear protective safety glasses when working near the battery. Keep children away from the battery.

5   Note the external condition of the battery. If the positive terminal and cable clamp on your vehicle's battery is equipped with a rubber protector, make sure that it's not torn or damaged. It should completely cover the terminal. Look for any corroded or loose connections, cracks in the case or cover or loose hold-down clamps. Also check the entire length of each cable for cracks and frayed conductors.

6   If corrosion, which looks like white, fluffy deposits **(see illustration)** is evident, particularly around the terminals, the battery should be removed for cleaning. Loosen the cable

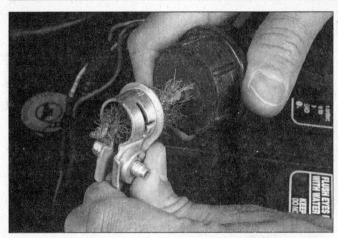

**9.7a  When cleaning the cable clamps, all corrosion must be removed (the inside of the clamp is tapered to match the taper on the post, so don't remove too much material)**

**9.7b  Regardless of the type of tool used on the battery posts, a clean, shiny surface should be the end result**

clamp bolts with a wrench, being careful to remove the ground cable first, and slide them off the terminals **(see illustration)**. Then disconnect the hold-down clamp bolt and nut, remove the clamp and lift the battery from the engine compartment.

7    Clean the cable clamps thoroughly with a battery brush or a terminal cleaner and a solution of warm water and baking soda **(see illustration)**. Wash the terminals and the top of the battery case with the same solution but make sure that the solution doesn't get into the battery. When cleaning the cables, terminals and battery top, wear safety goggles and rubber gloves to prevent any solution from coming in contact with your eyes or hands. Wear old clothes too - even diluted, sulfuric acid splashed onto clothes will burn holes in them. If the terminals have been extensively corroded, clean them up with a terminal cleaner **(see illustration)**. Thoroughly wash all cleaned areas with plain water.

8    Make sure that the battery tray is in good condition and the hold-down clamp bolts are tight. If the battery is removed from the tray, make sure no parts remain in the bottom of the tray when the battery is reinstalled. When reinstalling the hold-down clamp bolts, do not overtighten them.

9    Any metal parts of the vehicle damaged by corrosion should be covered with a zinc-based primer, then painted.

10    Information on removing and installing the battery can be found in Chapter 5. Information on jump starting can be found at the front of this manual. For more detailed battery checking procedures, refer to the *Haynes Automotive Electrical Manual*.

### Charging

**Warning:** *When batteries are being charged, hydrogen gas, which is very explosive and flammable, is produced. Do not smoke or allow open flames near a battery. Wear eye protection when near the battery during charging. Also, make sure the charger is unplugged before connecting or disconnect-*

*ing the battery from the charger.*
**Note:** *The manufacturer recommends the battery be removed from the vehicle for charging because the gas that escapes during this procedure can damage the paint. Fast charging with the battery cables connected can result in damage to the electrical system.*

11    Slow-rate charging is the best way to restore a battery that's discharged to the point where it will not start the engine. It's also a good way to maintain the battery charge in a vehicle that's only driven a few miles between starts. Maintaining the battery charge is particularly important in the winter when the battery must work harder to start the engine and electrical accessories that drain the battery are in greater use.

12    It's best to use a one or two-amp battery charger (sometimes called a "trickle" charger). They are the safest and put the least strain on the battery. They are also the least expensive. For a faster charge, you can use a higher amperage charger, but don't use one rated more than 1/10th the amp/hour rating of the battery. Rapid boost charges that claim to restore the power of the battery in one to two hours are hardest on the battery and can damage batteries not in good condition. This type of charging should only be used in emergency situations.

13    The average time necessary to charge a battery should be listed in the instructions that come with the charger. As a general rule, a trickle charger will charge a battery in 12 to 16 hours.

14    Remove all the cell caps (if equipped) and cover the holes with a clean cloth to prevent spattering electrolyte. Disconnect the negative battery cable and hook the battery charger cable clamps up to the battery posts (positive to positive, negative to negative), then plug in the charger. Make sure it is set at 12-volts if it has a selector switch.

15    If you're using a charger with a rate higher than two amps, check the battery regularly during charging to make sure it doesn't overheat. If you're using a trickle charger, you can safely let the battery charge overnight

after you've checked it regularly for the first couple of hours.

16    If the battery has removable cell caps, measure the specific gravity with a hydrometer every hour during the last few hours of the charging cycle. Hydrometers are available inexpensively from auto parts stores - follow the instructions that come with the hydrometer. Consider the battery charged when there's no change in the specific gravity reading for two hours and the electrolyte in the cells is gassing (bubbling) freely. The specific gravity reading from each cell should be very close to the others. If not, the battery probably has a bad cell(s).

17    Some batteries with sealed tops have built-in hydrometers on the top that indicate the state of charge by the color displayed in the hydrometer window. Normally, a bright-colored hydrometer indicates a full charge and a dark hydrometer indicates the battery still needs charging.

18    If the battery has a sealed top and no built-in hydrometer, you can hook up a voltmeter across the battery terminals to check the charge. A fully charged battery should read 12.6 volts or higher after the surface charge has been removed.

19    Further information on the battery and jump starting can be found in Chapter 5 and at the front of this manual.

### 10   Cooling system check (every 7500 miles or 6 months)

*Refer to illustration 10.4*

1    Many major engine failures can be attributed to a faulty cooling system. If the vehicle is equipped with an automatic transaxle, the cooling system also cools the transaxle fluid and thus plays an important role in prolonging transaxle life.

2    The cooling system should be checked with the engine cold. Do this before the vehicle is driven for the day or after it has been shut off for at least three hours.

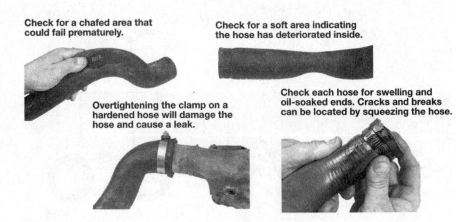

Check for a chafed area that could fail prematurely.

Check for a soft area indicating the hose has deteriorated inside.

Overtightening the clamp on a hardened hose will damage the hose and cause a leak.

Check each hose for swelling and oil-soaked ends. Cracks and breaks can be located by squeezing the hose.

**10.4 Hoses, like drivebelts, have a habit of failing at the worst possible time - to prevent the inconvenience of a blown radiator or heater hose, inspect them carefully as shown here**

3    Remove the radiator cap by turning it to the left until it reaches a stop. If you hear a hissing sound (indicating there is still pressure in the system), wait until this stops. Now press down on the cap with the palm of your hand and continue turning to the left until the cap can be removed. Thoroughly clean the cap, inside and out, with clean water. Also clean the filler neck on the radiator. All traces of corrosion should be removed. The coolant inside the radiator should be relatively transparent. If it is rust colored, the system should be drained and refilled (see Section 31). If the coolant level is not up to the top, add additional antifreeze/coolant mixture (see Section 4).

4    Carefully check the large upper and lower radiator hoses along with the smaller diameter heater hoses which run from the engine to the firewall. Inspect each hose along its entire length, replacing any hose which is cracked, swollen or shows signs of deterioration. Cracks may become more apparent if the hose is squeezed **(see illustration)**. Regardless of condition, it's a good idea to replace hoses with new ones every two years.

5    Make sure all hose connections are tight. A leak in the cooling system will usually show up as white or rust colored deposits on the areas adjoining the leak. If wire-type clamps are used at the ends of the hoses, it may be a good idea to replace them with more secure screw-type clamps.

6    Use compressed air or a soft brush to remove bugs, leaves, etc. from the front of the radiator or air conditioning condenser. Be careful not to damage the delicate cooling fins or cut yourself on them.

7    Every other inspection, or at the first indication of cooling system problems, have the cap and system pressure tested. If you don't have a pressure tester, most gas stations and repair shops will do this for a minimal charge.

## 11   Underhood hose check and replacement (every 7500 miles or 6 months)

### General

1    **Warning:** *The air conditioning system is under high pressure. Never remove air conditioning components or hoses until the system has been evacuated by a dealer service department or an air conditioning shop. Do not vent the refrigerant to the atmosphere.*

2    High temperatures in the engine compartment can cause the deterioration of the rubber and plastic hoses used for engine, accessory and emission systems operation. Periodic inspection should be made for cracks, loose clamps, material hardening and leaks. Information specific to the cooling system hoses can be found in Section 10.

3    Some, but not all, hoses are secured to the fittings with clamps. Where clamps are used, check to be sure they haven't lost their tension, allowing the hose to leak. If clamps aren't used, make sure the hose has not expanded and/or hardened where it slips over the fitting, allowing it to leak.

### Vacuum hoses

4    It's quite common for vacuum hoses, especially those in the emissions system, to be color coded or identified by colored stripes molded into them. Various systems require hoses with different wall thickness, collapse resistance and temperature resistance. When replacing hoses, be sure the new ones are made of the same material.

5    Often the only effective way to check a hose is to remove it completely from the vehicle. If more than one hose is removed, be sure to label the hoses and fittings to ensure correct installation.

6    When checking vacuum hoses, be sure to include any plastic T-fittings in the check. Inspect the fittings for cracks and the hose where it fits over the fitting for distortion, which could cause leakage.

7    A small piece of vacuum hose (1/4-inch inside diameter) can be used as a stethoscope to detect vacuum leaks. Hold one end of the hose to your ear and probe around vacuum hoses and fittings, listening for the "hissing" sound characteristic of a vacuum leak. **Warning:** *When probing with the vacuum hose stethoscope, be very careful not to come into contact with moving engine components such as the drivebelt, cooling fan, etc.*

### Fuel hose

**Warning:** *There are certain precautions which must be taken when inspecting or servicing fuel system components. Work in a well ventilated area and do not allow open flames (cigarettes, appliance pilot lights, etc.) or bare light bulbs near the work area. Mop up any spills immediately and do not store fuel soaked rags where they could ignite.*

8    Check all rubber fuel lines for deterioration and chafing. Check especially for cracks in areas where the hose bends and just before fittings, such as where a hose attaches to the fuel filter.

9    Only high quality fuel line should be used for fuel line replacement. Never, under any circumstances, use unreinforced vacuum line, clear plastic tubing or water hose for fuel lines.

10   Spring-type clamps are commonly used on fuel lines. These clamps often lose their tension over a period of time, and can be "sprung" during removal. Replace all spring-type clamps with screw clamps whenever a hose is replaced.

### Metal lines

*Refer to illustration 11.11*

11   Sections of metal line are often used in the fuel system. Check carefully to be sure the line has not been bent or crimped and that cracks have not started in the line **(see illustration)**.

12   If a section of metal fuel line must be replaced, only seamless steel tubing should be used, since copper and aluminum tubing don't have the strength necessary to withstand normal engine vibration.

**11.11 Check the condition of the metal fuel lines near the fuel tank (arrow)**

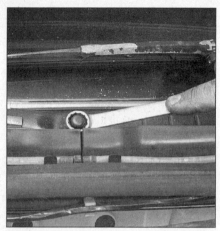

**12.3  Pry off the trim cap and check the tightness of the wiper arm retaining nut**

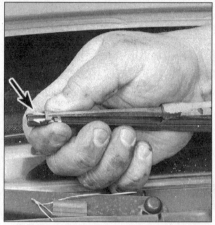

**12.5  Use needle-nose pliers to compress the wiper element retaining tabs (arrow) then slide the element out - slide the new element in and lock the retaining tabs of the wiper element onto the fingers of the wiper arm**

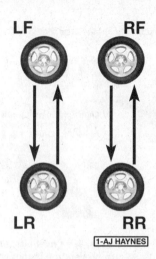

**13.2  Tire rotation diagram for radial tires**

13    Check the metal brake lines where they enter the master cylinder and brake proportioning unit (if used) for cracks in the lines or loose fittings. Any sign of brake fluid leakage calls for an immediate thorough inspection of the brake system.

## 12  Wiper blade inspection and replacement  (every 7500 miles or 6 months)

*Refer to illustrations 12.3 and 12.5*

1    The windshield wiper and blade assembly should be inspected periodically for damage, loose components and cracked or worn blade elements.
2    Road film can build up on the wiper blades and affect their efficiency, so they should be washed regularly with a mild detergent solution.
3    The action of the wiping mechanism can loosen bolts, nuts and fasteners, so they should be checked and tightened, as necessary **(see illustration)**, at the same time the wiper blades are checked.
4    If the wiper blade elements are cracked, worn or warped, or no longer clean adequately, they should be replaced with new ones.
5    Use needle-nose pliers to compress the blade element retaining tab, then slide the element out of the frame and discard it **(see illustration)**.
6    Installation is the reverse of removal.

## 13  Tire rotation (every 7500 miles or 6 months)

*Refer to illustration 13.2*

1    The tires should be rotated at the specified intervals and whenever uneven wear is noticed. Since the vehicle will be raised and the tires removed anyway, check the brakes (see Section 19) at this time.
2    Radial tires must be rotated in a specific pattern **(see illustration)**.
3    Refer to the information in *Jacking and*

*towing* at the front of this manual for the proper procedures to follow when raising the vehicle and changing a tire. If the brakes are to be checked, do not apply the parking brake as stated. Make sure the tires are blocked to prevent the vehicle from rolling.
4    Preferably, the entire vehicle should be raised at the same time. This can be done on a hoist or by jacking up each corner and then lowering the vehicle onto jackstands placed under the frame rails. Always use four jackstands and make sure the vehicle is firmly supported.
5    After rotation, check and adjust the tire pressures as necessary and be sure to check the lug nut tightness.
6    For further information on the wheels and tires, refer to Chapter 10.

## 14  Suspension and steering check (every 7500 miles or 6 months)

*Refer to illustrations 14.1, 14.6a, 14.6b and 14.9*
**Note:** *For detailed illustrations of the steering and suspension components, refer to Chapter 10.*

### With the wheels on the ground

1    With the vehicle stopped and the front wheels pointed straight ahead, rock the steering wheel gently back and forth. If freeplay **(see illustration)** is excessive, a front wheel bearing, main shaft yoke, intermediate shaft yoke, lower arm balljoint or steering system joint is worn or the steering gear is out of adjustment or broken. Refer to Chapter 10 for the appropriate repair procedure.
2    Other symptoms, such as excessive vehicle body movement over rough roads, swaying (leaning) around corners and binding as the steering wheel is turned, may indicate faulty steering and/or suspension components.

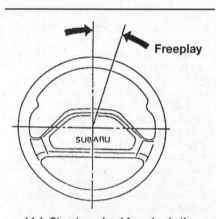

**14.1  Steering wheel freeplay is the amount of travel between an initial steering input and the point at which the front wheels begin to turn (indicated by a slight resistance)**

3    Check the shock absorbers by pushing down and releasing the vehicle several times at each corner. If the vehicle does not come back to a level position within one or two bounces, the shocks/struts are worn and must be replaced. When bouncing the vehicle up and down, listen for squeaks and noises from the suspension components.

### Under the vehicle

4    Raise the vehicle with a floor jack and support it securely on jackstands. See *jacking and towing* at the front of this book for proper jacking points.
5    Check the tires for irregular wear patterns and proper inflation. See Section 5 in this Chapter for information regarding tire wear.
6    Inspect the universal joint between the steering shaft and the steering gear housing. Check the steering gear housing for leakage. Make sure that the boots are not damaged and that the boot clamps are not loose **(see illustration)**. Check the steering linkage for looseness or damage. Check the tie-rod ends for excessive play. Look for loose bolts, bro-

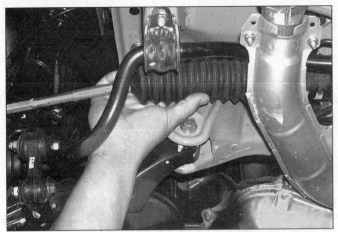

14.6a  Check the steering gear boots for cracks and leaking steering fluid

14.6b  Inspect the suspension for deteriorated rubber bushings and torn grease seals (arrow)

14.9  Check the driveaxle boot for cracks and/or leaking grease

15.2a  Check the exhaust pipes and connections for signs of leakage and corrosion

ken or disconnected parts and deteriorated rubber bushings on all suspension and steering components **(see illustration)**. While an assistant turns the steering wheel from side to side, check the steering components for free movement, chafing and binding. If the steering components do not seem to be reacting with the movement of the steering wheel, try to determine where the slack is located.

7    Check the balljoints by moving each lower arm up and down with a pry bar to ensure that its balljoint has no play. If any balljoint does have play, replace it. See Chapter 10 for the front balljoint replacement procedure.

8    Inspect the balljoint boots for damage and leaking grease. Replace the balljoints with new ones if they are damaged (see Chapter 10).

9    Inspect the front and rear driveaxle boots on 4WD models for tears and cracks as well as loose clamps **(see illustration)**. If there is any evidence of cracks or leaking lubricant, they must be replaced as described in Chapter 8. Oil and grease can cause the boot material to deteriorate prematurely, so it's a good idea to wash the boots

with soap and water.

10    Check the wheel bearings. Do this by spinning the front wheels. Listen for any abnormal noises and watch to make sure the wheel spins true (doesn't wobble). Grab the top and bottom of the tire and pull in-and-out on it. Notice any movement which would indicate a loose wheel bearing assembly. If the bearings are suspect, they should be checked (see Section 36).

11    Inspect the driveshaft on 4WD models for worn U-joints and for excessive play in the slip yoke and spline area (see Chapter 8).

12    Check the transaxle and differentials for evidence of fluid leakage.

## 15    Exhaust system check (every 7500 miles or 6 months)

*Refer to illustrations 15.2a and 15.2b*

1    With the engine cold (at least three hours after the vehicle has been driven), check the complete exhaust system from the cylinder head to the end of the tailpipe. Be careful around the catalytic converter (if equipped), which may be hot even after three

15.2b  Check the exhaust system rubber hangers for cracks and damage (arrows)

hours. The inspection should be done with the vehicle on a hoist to permit unrestricted access. If a hoist isn't available, raise the vehicle and support it securely on jackstands.

2    Check the exhaust pipes and connections for signs of leakage and/or corrosion indicating a potential failure. Make sure that all brackets and hangers are in good condition and tight **(see illustrations)**.

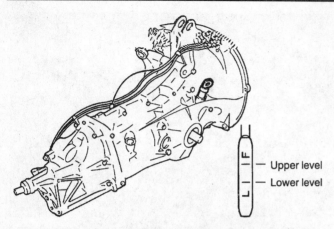

**16.1a The manual transaxle/front differential dipstick is located on the right side of the engine compartment**

**16.1b The automatic transaxle/front differential dipstick is located on the right side near the firewall**

3    Inspect the underside of the body for holes, corrosion, open seams, etc. which may allow exhaust gasses to enter the passenger compartment. Seal all body openings with silicone sealant or body putty.

4    Rattles and other noises can often be traced to the exhaust system, especially the hangers, mounts and heat shields. Try to move the pipes, mufflers and catalytic converter. If the components can come in contact with the body or suspension parts, secure the exhaust system with new brackets and hangers.

## 16    Manual transaxle/front differential lubricant level check (every 7500 miles or 6 months)

*Refer to illustrations 16.1a, 16.1b and 16.2*
**Note:** *Vehicles equipped with a manual transaxle have an integral front differential (meaning they share the same lubricant). Vehicles equipped with an automatic transaxle have a non-integral front differential (meaning they DO NOT share the same lubricant). The dipstick for the manual transaxle and the front differential on automatic transaxle equipped vehicles is approximately*

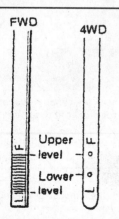

**16.2 The lubricant level must be maintained between the marks at all times**

*in the same position in the engine compartment and the lubricant level checking procedure is the same.*
1    The manual transaxle has a dipstick that extends through a tube and into the transaxle **(see illustrations)**.
2    Pull the dipstick out of the tube and wipe all the lubricant from the end with a clean rag or paper towel. Insert the clean dipstick all the way back into the tube, then pull it out again. Note the lubricant at the end of the dipstick. Add lubricant as necessary to keep the level between the ADD and FULL marks on the dipstick **(see illustration)**.
3    Lubricant is added to the transaxle through the dipstick tube. A funnel may help to reduce spills. Do not overfill the transaxle since this may result in lubricant leaks or lubricant seal failures.
4    Reinstall the dipstick and close the hood.

## 17    Differential lubricant level check (every 7500 miles or 6 months)

*Refer to illustration 17.2*
**Note:** *At the specified interval, the lubricant level in the front differential should be checked on vehicles equipped with automatic transaxles. Follow the procedures outlined in Section 16.*
1    The rear differential has a check/fill plug which must be removed to check the lubricant level. If the vehicle must be raised to gain access to the plug, be sure to support it safely on jackstands - DO NOT crawl under the vehicle when it's supported only by the jack.
2    Remove the check/fill plug from the back of the rear differential **(see illustration)**.
3    Use a finger to reach inside the housing to determine the lubricant level. The lubricant level should be at the bottom of the plug opening. If it isn't, use a hand pump (available at auto parts stores) to add the specified lubricant until it just starts to run out of the opening.
4    Install the plug and tighten it securely.

## 18    Seat belt check (every 7500 miles or 6 months)

1    Check the seat belts, buckles, latch plates and guide loops for any obvious damage or signs of wear.
2    Make sure the seat belt reminder light comes on when the key is turned on.
3    The seat belts are designed to lock up during a sudden stop or impact, yet allow free movement during normal driving. The retractors should hold the belt against your chest while driving and rewind the belt when the buckle is unlatched.
4    If any of the above checks reveal problems with the seat belt system, replace parts as necessary.

## 19    Brake system check (every 15,000 miles or 12 months)

**Warning:** *The dust created by the brake system may contain asbestos, which is harmful to your health. Never blow it out with compressed air and don't inhale any of it. An approved filtering mask should be worn when*

**17.2 The rear differential fill plug (A) and drain plug (B) are located on the differential cover - use your finger as a dipstick to check the lubricant level**

**19.5 With the wheels removed, the brake pad lining can be inspected through the caliper window (arrow) and at each end of the caliper**

**19.10 Check for any sign of brake fluid leakage at the line fittings and the brake hoses (arrow)**

**19.12 If the lining is bonded to the brake shoe, measure the lining thickness from the outer surface to the metal shoe, as shown here; if the lining is riveted to the shoe, measure from the lining outer surface to the rivet head**

working on the brakes. Do not, under any circumstances, use petroleum-based solvents to clean brake parts. Use brake system cleaner only! Try to use non-asbestos replacement parts whenever possible. **Note:** *For detailed photographs of the brake system, refer to Chapter 9.*

1    In addition to the specified intervals, the brakes should be inspected every time the wheels are removed or whenever a defect is suspected. Any of the following symptoms could indicate a potential brake system defect: The vehicle pulls to one side when the brake pedal is depressed; the brakes make squealing or dragging noises when applied; brake pedal travel is excessive; the pedal pulsates; brake fluid leaks, usually onto the inside of the tire or wheel.

2    Loosen the wheel lug nuts.

3    Raise the vehicle and place it securely on jackstands.

4    Remove the wheels (see *Jacking and towing* at the front of this book, or your owner's manual, if necessary).

## Disc brakes

*Refer to illustrations 19.5 and 19.10*

5    There are two pads (an outer and an inner) in each caliper. The pads are visible through inspection holes in each caliper **(see illustration).**

6    Check the pad thickness by looking at each end of the caliper and through the inspection hole in the caliper body. If the lining material is less than the thickness listed in this Chapter's Specifications, replace the pads. **Note:** *Keep in mind that the lining material is riveted or bonded to a metal backing plate and the metal portion is not included in this measurement.*

7    If it is difficult to determine the exact thickness of the remaining pad material by the above method, or if you are at all concerned about the condition of the pads, remove the caliper(s), then remove the pads from the calipers for further inspection (refer to Chapter 9).

8    Once the pads are removed from the calipers, clean them with brake cleaner and re-measure them with a ruler or a vernier caliper.

9    Measure the disc thickness with a micrometer to make sure that it still has service life remaining. If any disc is thinner than the specified minimum thickness, replace it (refer to Chapter 9). Even if the disc has service life remaining, check its condition. Look for scoring, gouging and burned spots. If these conditions exist, remove the disc and have it resurfaced (see Chapter 9).

10    Before installing the wheels, check all brake lines and hoses for damage, wear, deformation, cracks, corrosion, leakage, bends and twists, particularly in the vicinity of the rubber hoses at the calipers **(see illustration).** Check the clamps for tightness and the connections for leakage. Make sure that all hoses and lines are clear of sharp edges, moving parts and the exhaust system. If any of the above conditions are noted, repair, reroute or replace the lines and/or fittings as necessary (see Chapter 9).

## Drum brakes

*Refer to illustrations 19.12 and 19.14*

11    Refer to Chapter 9 and remove the rear brake drums.

12    Note the thickness of the lining material on the rear brake shoes **(see illustration)** and look for signs of contamination by brake fluid and grease. If the lining material is within 1/16-inch of the recessed rivets or metal shoes, replace the brake shoes with new ones. The shoes should also be replaced if they are cracked, glazed (shiny lining surfaces) or contaminated with brake fluid or grease. See Chapter 9 for the replacement procedure.

13    Check the shoe return and hold-down springs and the adjusting mechanism to make sure they're installed correctly and in good condition. Deteriorated or distorted springs, if not replaced, could allow the linings to drag and wear prematurely.

14    Check the wheel cylinders for leakage by carefully peeling back the rubber boots **(see illustration).** If brake fluid is noted

behind the boots, the wheel cylinders must be replaced (see Chapter 9).

15    Check the drums for cracks, score marks, deep scratches and hard spots, which will appear as small discolored areas. If imperfections cannot be removed with emery cloth, the drums must be resurfaced by an automotive machine shop (see Chapter 9 for more detailed information).

16    Refer to Chapter 9 and install the brake drums.

17    Install the wheels and snug the wheel lug nuts finger tight.

18    Remove the jackstands and lower the vehicle.

19    Tighten the wheel lug nuts to the torque listed in this Chapter's Specifications.

## Brake booster check

20    Sit in the driver's seat and perform the following sequence of tests.

21    With the engine stopped, depress the brake pedal several times to bleed off the vacuum in the booster.

22    With the brake pedal depressed, start

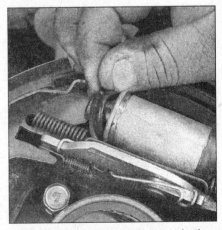

**19.14 Check for fluid leakage at both ends of the wheel cylinder dust covers**

**21.2  The fuel filter (arrow) is located in the left side of the engine compartment, near the brake master cylinder**

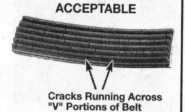

**ACCEPTABLE**

Cracks Running Across "V" Portions of Belt

1/2"

Missing Two or More Adjacent Ribs 1/2" or longer

**22.3  Small cracks in the underside of a V-ribbed belt are acceptable - lengthwise cracks, or missing pieces that cause the belt to make noise, are cause for replacement**

**UNACCEPTABLE**

Cracks Running Parallel to "V" Portions of Belt

the engine - the pedal should move down a little when the engine starts.

23   Depress the pedal, stop the engine and hold the pedal in for about 30 seconds - the pedal should neither sink nor rise.

24   Restart the engine, run it for about a minute and turn it off. Then firmly depress the pedal several times - the pedal travel should decrease with each application.

25   If your brakes do not operate as described above when the preceding tests are performed, the brake booster is in need of replacement. Refer to Chapter 9 for the removal procedure.

### Parking brake

**Note:** *Be sure to check the brake pedal freeplay and the hillholder adjustments as described in Section 23.*

26   Slowly pull up on the parking brake and count the number of clicks you hear until the handle is up as far as it will go. The adjustment should be within the specified number of clicks listed in this Chapter's Specifications. If you hear more or fewer clicks, it's time to adjust the parking brake (refer to Chapter 9).

27   An alternative method of checking the parking brake is to park the vehicle on a steep hill with the parking brake set and the transaxle in Neutral (be sure to stay in the vehicle during this check!). If the parking brake cannot prevent the vehicle from rolling, it is in need of adjustment (see Chapter 9).

## 20   Fuel system check (every 15,000 miles or 12 months)

**Warning:** *Gasoline is extremely flammable, so take extra precautions when you work on any part of the fuel system. Don't smoke or allow open flames or bare light bulbs near the work area, and don't work in a garage where a natural gas-type appliance (such as a water heater or clothes dryer) with a pilot light is present. Since gasoline is carcinogenic, wear latex gloves when there's a possibility of being exposed to fuel, and, if you spill any fuel on*

*your skin, rinse it off immediately with soap and water. Mop up any spills immediately and do not store fuel-soaked rags where they could ignite. The fuel system is under constant pressure, so, if any fuel lines are to be disconnected, the fuel pressure in the system must be relieved first (see Chapter 4 for more information). When you perform any kind of work on the fuel system, wear safety glasses and have a Class B type fire extinguisher on hand.*

1   The fuel system is most easily checked with the vehicle raised on a hoist so the components underneath the vehicle are readily visible and accessible.

2   If the smell of gasoline is noticed while driving or after the vehicle has been in the sun, the system should be thoroughly inspected immediately.

3   Remove the gas tank cap and check for damage, corrosion and an unbroken sealing imprint on the gasket. Replace the cap with a new one if necessary.

4   With the vehicle raised and safely supported, inspect the gas tank and filler neck for punctures, cracks and other damage. The connection between the filler neck and the tank is particularly critical. Sometimes a rubber filler neck will leak because of loose clamps or deteriorated rubber. These are problems a home mechanic can usually rectify. **Warning:** *Do not, under any circumstances, try to repair a fuel tank (except rubber components). A welding torch or any open flame can easily cause fuel vapors inside the tank to explode.*

5   Carefully check all rubber hoses and metal lines leading away from the fuel tank. Check for loose connections and deteriorated hoses, crimped lines and other damage. Follow the lines to the front of the vehicle, carefully inspecting them all the way to the fuel injection system. Repair or replace damaged sections as necessary.

6   If fuel odor is evident after the inspection, refer to Chapter 6 and check the EVAP system.

## 21   Fuel filter replacement (every 15,000 miles or 12 months)

*Refer to illustration 21.2*

**Warning:** *Gasoline is extremely flammable, so*

take extra precautions when you work on any part of the fuel system. Don't smoke or allow open flames or bare light bulbs near the work area, and don't work in a garage where a natural gas-type appliance (such as a water heater or clothes dryer) with a pilot light is present. Since gasoline is carcinogenic, wear latex gloves when there's a possibility of being exposed to fuel, and, if you spill any fuel on your skin, rinse it off immediately with soap and water. Mop up any spills immediately and do not store fuel-soaked rags where they could ignite. The fuel system is under constant pressure, so, if any fuel lines are to be disconnected, the fuel pressure in the system must be relieved first (see Chapter 4 for more information). When you perform any kind of work on the fuel system, wear safety glasses and have a Class B type fire extinguisher on hand.* **Warning 2:** *Refer to Chapter 4 and depressurize the fuel system before removing the filter!*

1   This job should be done with the engine cold (after sitting at least three hours). Place rags or newspapers under the filter to catch spilled fuel.

2   The fuel filter is located in the engine compartment on the left side **(see illustration)**.

3   To replace the filter, loosen the clamps and slide them down the hoses, past the fittings on the filter.

4   Carefully twist and pull on the hoses to separate them from the filter. If the hoses are in bad shape, now would be a good time to replace them with new ones.

5   Unclip the filter bracket, pull the filter out of the bracket and install the new one, then hook up the hoses and reposition the clamps. Make sure the hose from the fuel tank connects to the fitting marked IN. Start the engine and check carefully for leaks at the filter hose connections.

## 22   Drivebelt check, adjustment and replacement (every 15,000 miles or 12 months)

### Check

*Refer to illustrations 22.3 and 22.4*

1   The drivebelts are located at the front of the engine and play an important role in the

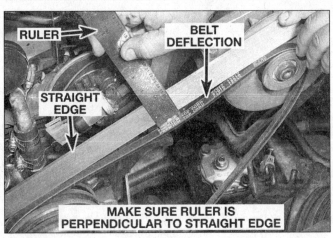

22.4 Measuring drivebelt deflection with a straightedge and ruler

22.6a Remove the drivebelt cover bolts (arrows)

overall operation of the vehicle and its components. Due to their function and material make-up, the belts are prone to failure after a period of time and should be inspected and adjusted periodically to prevent major engine damage.

2    The number of belts used on a particular vehicle depends on the accessories installed. Drivebelts are used to turn the alternator, power steering pump and air conditioning compressor.

3    With the engine off, open the hood and locate the belts at the front of the engine. Using your fingers (and a flashlight, if necessary), move along the belts checking for cracks and separation of the belt plies. Also check for fraying and glazing, which gives the belt a shiny appearance. Check the ribs on the underside of the belt. They should all be the same depth, with none of the surface uneven **(see illustration)**.

4    The tension of each belt is checked by pushing on the belt at a distance halfway between the pulleys. Push firmly with your thumb and see how much the belt moves (deflects) **(see illustration)**. As rule of thumb, the belt should deflect approximately 1/4-inch.

## Adjustment

*Refer to illustration 22.6a, 22.6b and 22.6c*

5    If it is necessary to adjust the belt tension, either to make the belt tighter or looser, it is done by either of two adjusting assemblies mounted on the front of the engine.

6    For each belt on the engine there will be one adjusting assembly with a slider bolt and a lock bolt. The lock bolts must be loosened slightly to enable you to move the assembly **(see illustrations)** while the slider bolt is rotated to loosen or tighten the belt tension.

7    After the lock bolt has been loosened, turn the slider bolt to loosen or tighten the drivebelt. Hold the accessory in position and check the belt tension. If it is correct, tighten the lock bolt until just snug, then recheck the tension. If the tension is all right, tighten the bolts.

8    Do not use a prybar to move the assembly while the belt is being adjusted. Be sure the drivebelt is correctly aligned within each pulley before applying complete tension to the drivebelt.

## Replacement

9    To replace a belt, follow the above pro-

cedures for drivebelt adjustment but slip the belt off the pulleys and remove it. Since belts tend to wear out more or less at the same time, it's a good idea to replace all of them at the same time. Mark each belt and the corresponding pulley grooves so the replacement belts can be installed properly.

10    Take the old belts with you when purchasing new ones in order to make a direct comparison for length, width and design.

11    Adjust the belts as described earlier in this Section.

## 23    Clutch pedal/brake pedal freeplay and hillholder - check and adjustment (every 15,000 miles or 12 months)

**Note:** *After checking the clutch pedal freeplay adjustments, refer to Chapter 9 for the hillholder adjustment procedure.*

## Brake pedal freeplay

*Refer to illustration 23.1*

1    The freeplay is the pedal slack, or the distance the pedal can be depressed before it

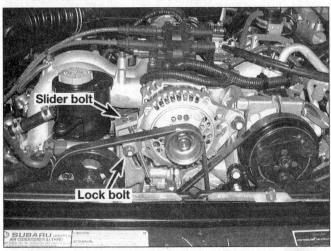

22.6b Alternator drivebelt adjustment details

22.6c Air conditioning drivebelt adjustment details

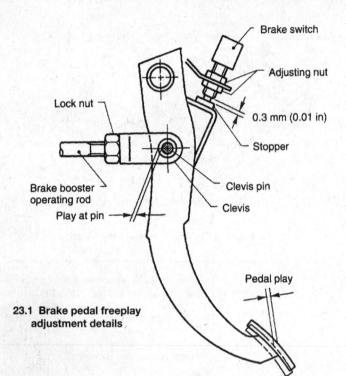

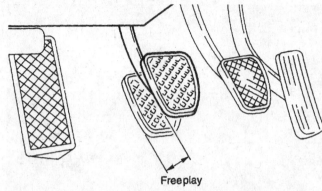

**23.3  Check the clutch pedal freeplay using two or three fingers on the clutch pedal by pushing carefully until resistance is felt**

**23.1  Brake pedal freeplay adjustment details**

**23.4  Adjust the freeplay by loosening the lock nut and turning the adjusting nut**

begins to have any effect on the brake system **(see illustration)**. If the pedal freeplay is not within the specified range, it must be adjusted.

2    To adjust the brake pedal freeplay, loosen the brake switch adjusting nut until the clearance between the stopper and the brake switch mechanism reaches the specified distance. Using your hand, depress the brake pedal several times and recheck the freeplay at the pedal. Make sure the engine is OFF and no vacuum is applied to the brake booster. This measurement is performed without the assistance of the power brake system.

### Clutch pedal freeplay

*Refer to illustrations 23.3 and 23.4*

3    The clutch pedal freeplay is the pedal slack, or the distance the pedal can be depressed before it begins to have any effect on the clutch system **(see illustration)**. If the pedal freeplay is not within the specified range, it must be adjusted.

4    To adjust the clutch pedal freeplay, loosen the lock nut at the end of the clutch cable at the release fork **(see illustration)**. Turn the adjusting nut until the specified amount of freeplay exists at the release fork.

### 24   Spark plug replacement (every 30,000 miles or 24 months)

*Refer to illustrations 24.1, 24.4a and 24.4b*
**Note:** *Replace non-platinum spark plugs at 30,000 mile intervals and platinum-type plugs at 60,000 mile intervals.*

1    Spark plug replacement requires a spark plug socket which fits onto a ratchet wrench. This socket is lined with a rubber grommet to protect the porcelain insulator of the spark plug and to hold the plug while you insert it into the spark plug hole. You will also need a wire-type feeler gauge to check and

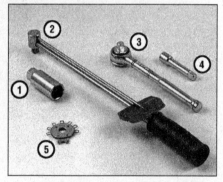

**24.1  Tools required for changing spark plugs**

1    *Spark plug socket - This will have special padding inside to protect the spark plug's porcelain insulator*
2    *Torque wrench - Although not mandatory, using this tool is the best way to ensure the plugs are tightened properly*
3    *Ratchet - Standard hand tool to fit the spark plug socket*
4    *Extension - Depending on model and accessories, you may need special extensions and universal joints to reach one or more of the plugs*
5    *Spark plug gap gauge - This gauge for checking the gap comes in a variety of styles. Make sure the gap for your engine is included*

adjust the spark plug gap and a torque wrench to tighten the new plugs to the specified torque **(see illustration)**.

2    If you are replacing the plugs, purchase the new plugs, adjust them to the proper gap and then replace each plug one at a time. **Note:** *When buying new spark plugs, it's essential that you obtain the correct plugs for your specific vehicle. This information can be found in the Specifications Section at the beginning of this Chapter or in the owner's manual.*

3    Inspect each of the new plugs for defects. If there are any signs of cracks in the porcelain insulator of a plug, don't use it.

4    Check the electrode gaps of the new plugs. Check the gap by inserting the wire gauge of the proper thickness between the electrodes at the tip of the plug **(see illustration)**. The gap between the electrodes should be identical to that listed in this Chapter's Specifications. If the gap is incorrect, use the notched adjuster on the feeler gauge body to bend the curved side electrode slightly **(see illustration)**.

5    If the side electrode is not exactly over the center electrode, use the notched adjuster to align them. **Caution:** *If the gap of a new plug must be adjusted, bend only the base of the ground electrode - do not touch the tip.*

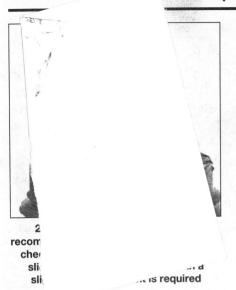

recom...
chec...
sli...
sli... ...is required

**24.4b To change the gap, bend the *side* electrode only, as indicated by the arrows, and be very careful not to crack or chip the porcelain insulator surrounding the center electrode**

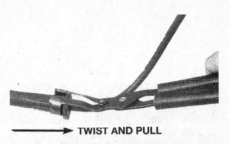

→ **TWIST AND PULL**

**24.6 Using a spark plug boot puller tool like this one will make the job of removing the spark plug boots much easier**

## Removal

*Refer to illustrations 24.6 and 24.8*

6    To prevent the possibility of mixing up spark plug wires, work on one spark plug at a time. Remove the wire and boot from one spark plug. Grasp the boot - not the cable - then give it a half twisting motion and pull straight up **(see illustration)**.

7    If compressed air is available, blow any dirt or foreign material away from the spark plug area before proceeding (a common bicycle pump will also work).

8    Remove the spark plug **(see illustration)**. **Note:** *On 2.5L engines, it will normally be necessary to remove the battery and coolant reservoir to access the spark plugs on the left side of the engine (see Chapters 3 and 5 for details, if necessary).*

9    Whether you are replacing the plugs at this time or intend to reuse the old plugs, compare each old spark plug with the chart shown on the inside back cover of this manual to determine the overall running condition of the engine.

## Installation

*Refer to illustrations 24.10a and 24.10b*

10    Prior to installation, apply a coat of anti-

seize compound to the plug threads **(see illustration)**. It's often difficult to insert spark plugs into their holes without cross-threading them. To avoid this possibility, fit a short piece of rubber hose over the end of the spark plug **(see illustration)**. The flexible hose acts as a universal joint to help align the plug with the plug hole. Should the plug begin to cross-thread, the hose will slip on the spark plug, preventing thread damage. Tighten the plug to the torque listed in this Chapter's Specifications.

11    Attach the plug wire to the new spark plug, again using a twisting motion on the boot until it is firmly seated on the end of the spark plug.

12    Follow the above procedure for the remaining spark plugs, replacing them one at a time to prevent mixing up the spark plug wires.

## 25   Spark plug wire check and replacement (every 30,000 miles or 24 months)

1    The spark plug wires should be checked whenever new spark plugs are installed.

2    Begin this procedure by making a visual check of the spark plug wires while the engine is running. In a darkened garage (make sure there is adequate ventilation) start the engine and observe each plug wire. Be careful not to come into contact with any moving engine parts. If there is a break in the wire, you will see arcing or a small spark at the damaged area. If arcing is noticed, make a note to obtain new wires, then allow the engine to cool.

3    The spark plug wires should be inspected one at a time to prevent mixing up the order, which is essential for proper engine operation. Each original plug wire should be numbered to help identify its location. If the number is illegible, a piece of tape can be marked with the correct number and wrapped around the plug wire.

4    Disconnect the plug wire from the spark plug. A removal tool can be used for this purpose or you can grasp the rubber boot, twist the boot half a turn and pull the boot free. Do not pull on the wire itself.

5    Check inside the boot for corrosion, which will look like a white crusty powder.

6    Push the wire and boot back onto the end of the spark plug. It should fit tightly onto the end of the plug. If it doesn't, remove the wire and use pliers to carefully crimp the metal connector inside the wire boot until the fit is snug.

**24.8 The spark plugs can be removed from under the vehicle on the right side of the engine compartment if necessary**

**24.10a Apply a thin coat of anti-seize compound to the spark plug threads**

**24.10b A length of rubber hose will save time and prevent damaged threads when installing the spark plugs**

**27.4  Lift the top cover and pull the filter element out of the housing**

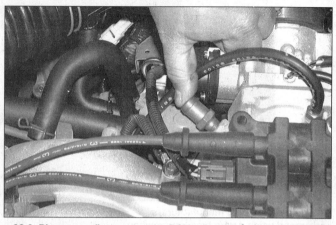

**28.3  Place your finger over the PCV valve to check for vacuum**

7    Using a clean rag, wipe the entire length of the wire to remove built-up dirt and grease. Once the wire is clean, check for burns, cracks and other damage. Do not bend the wire sharply, because the conductor might break.

8    Remove the rubber boot (if equipped) and disconnect the wire from the coil. Again, pull only on the rubber boot. Check for corrosion and a tight fit. Reconnect the wire to the coil.

9    Inspect the remaining spark plug wires, making sure that each one is securely fastened at the coil pack and spark plug when the check is complete.

10    If new spark plug wires are required, purchase a set for your specific engine model. Remove and replace the wires one at a time to avoid mix-ups in the firing order.

## 26  Idle speed check and adjustment (every 30,000 miles or 24 months)

**Note:** *Some common problems resulting in improper idle speed and rough idle include: 1) Sludge and deposits around the throttle plate in the throttle body. This can be cleaned with carburetor cleaner and a toothbrush. 2) A vacuum leak at the throttle body base, intake manifold or broken or disconnected vacuum hose. 3) A defective ISC valve (see Chapter 4).*

1    Engine idle speed is the speed at which the engine operates when no accelerator pedal pressure is applied. The idle speed is critical to the performance of the engine as well as many engine sub-systems.

2    Make sure the parking brake is firmly set and the wheels blocked to prevent the vehicle from rolling. An assistant inside the vehicle pressing on the brake pedal is the safest method.

3    A hand-held tachometer must be used when adjusting idle speed to get an accurate reading. The exact hook-up for these meters varies with the manufacturer, so follow the particular directions included with the instrument. **Note:** *These ignition systems are of the "waste spark" type. The companion cylinders*

*(1-2 and 3-4) will fire simultaneously. Some tachometers will register twice the actual idle speed because of the overlap in this Direct Ignition System. Be sure to read the instructions furnished with the tachometer. Refer to Chapter 5 for additional information on the ignition system.*

4    Warm the engine to normal operating temperature.

5    Check the idle speed with the engine unloaded. Turn off all headlights, A/C system, heater fan, rear defroster, radiator fan (wait until off), etc. Refer to the Specifications listed in this Chapter.

6    Since the idle speed is controlled by the computer, do not turn the stop screw on the throttle body to set an out-of-spec idle speed. Refer to the Idle Speed Control checks in Chapter 4 for diagnostics.

7    Most models have a tune-up decal or Vehicle Emission Control Information (VECI) label located in the engine compartment with instructions for setting idle speed. If no VECI label is found, refer to the Specifications Section at the beginning of this Chapter and to the diagnostic procedures specified in Chapter 4.

## 27  Air filter check and replacement (every 30,000 miles or 24 months)

*Refer to illustration 27.4*

1    At the specified intervals, the air filter should be replaced with a new one. A thorough preventive maintenance schedule would also require the filter to be inspected between filter changes.

2    The air filter housing is located on the right side of the engine compartment.

3    Remove the cover retaining clips. Then detach all hoses that would interfere with the removal of the air cleaner cover from the air cleaner housing. While the top cover is off, be careful not to drop anything down into the air cleaner assembly.

4    Lift the air filter element out of the housing **(see illustration)** and wipe out the inside of the air cleaner housing with a clean rag.

5    Inspect the outer surface of the filter element. If it is dirty, replace it. If it is only moderately dusty, it can be reused by blowing it clean from the back to the front surface with compressed air. Because it is a pleated paper type filter, it cannot be washed or oiled. If it cannot be cleaned satisfactorily with compressed air, discard and replace it. **Caution:** *Never drive the vehicle with the air cleaner removed. Excessive engine wear could result and backfiring could even cause a fire under the hood.*

6    Place the new filter in the air cleaner housing, making sure it seats properly.

7    Installation of the cover is the reverse of removal.

## 28  Positive Crankcase Ventilation (PCV) valve check and replacement (every 30,000 miles or 24 months)

*Refer to illustration 28.3*

**Note:** *This procedure requires an assistant.*

1    The PCV valve is located in the intake manifold.

2    With the engine off, pull the vent hose from the valve.

3    Start the engine and place your finger over the valve opening **(see illustration).** You should feel vacuum that should increase when an assistant depresses the accelerator slightly and releases it.

4    Remove your finger from the valve. You should hear a faint click as the valve operates.

5    If the valve does not operate as described, unscrew it from the intake manifold and replace it.

6    When purchasing a replacement PCV valve, make sure it's for your particular vehicle and engine size. Compare the old valve with the new one to make sure they're the same.

7    Push the hose onto the valve.

8    Inspect all rubber hoses and grommets for damage and hardening. Replace them, if necessary.

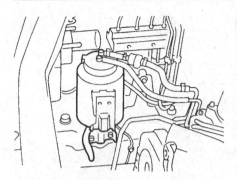

29.2a  On early models, the charcoal canister is located in the right front corner of the engine compartment

29.2b  On later models, the canister is located under the right rear corner of the vehicle (arrow)

30.2  The diaphragm in the EGR valve (which can be reached through the holes in the underside of the valve) should move easily with finger pressure

## 29  Evaporative emissions control system check (every 30,000 miles or 24 months)

*Refer to illustrations 29.2a and 29.2b*

1    The function of the evaporative emissions control system is to draw fuel vapors from the fuel tank and fuel system, store them in a charcoal canister and route them to the intake manifold during normal engine operation.

2    The most common symptom of a fault in the evaporative emissions system is a strong fuel odor in the engine compartment. If a fuel odor is detected, inspect the charcoal canister, located in the engine compartment or under the vehicle **(see illustrations)**. Check the canister and all hoses for damage and deterioration.

3    The evaporative emissions control system is explained in more detail in Chapter 6.

## 30  Exhaust Gas Recirculation (EGR) system check (every 30,000 miles or 24 months)

*Refer to illustration 30.2*

1    The EGR valve is usually located on the intake manifold. Most of the time when a

problem develops in this emissions system, it's due to a stuck or corroded EGR valve.

2    With the engine cold to prevent burns, push on the EGR valve diaphragm. Using moderate pressure, you should be able to push the diaphragm up into the housing **(see illustration)**.

3    If the diaphragm doesn't move or is hard to move, replace the EGR valve with a new one. If in doubt about the condition of the valve, compare the free movement of your EGR valve with a new valve.

4    Refer to Chapter 6 for more information on the EGR system.

## 31  Cooling system servicing (draining, flushing and refilling) (every 30,000 miles or 24 months)

*Refer to illustrations 31.3 and 31.4*
**Warning:** *Do not allow antifreeze to come in contact with your skin or painted surfaces of the vehicle. Rinse off spills immediately with plenty of water. Antifreeze is highly toxic if ingested. Never leave antifreeze lying around in an open container or in puddles on the floor; children and pets are attracted by it's*

sweet smell and may drink it. Check with local authorities about disposing of used antifreeze. Many communities have collection centers which will see that antifreeze is disposed of safely.

1    Periodically, the cooling system should be drained, flushed and refilled to replenish the antifreeze mixture and prevent formation of rust and corrosion, which can impair the performance of the cooling system and cause engine damage. When the cooling system is serviced, all hoses and the radiator cap should be checked and replaced if necessary.

2    Apply the parking brake and block the wheels. **Warning:** *If the vehicle has just been driven, wait several hours to allow the engine to cool down before beginning this procedure.*

3    Move a large container under the radiator drain to catch the coolant. The radiator drain plug is located at the lower right corner of the radiator **(see illustration)**. Attach a hose to the drain fitting (if possible) to direct the coolant into the container, then unscrew the drain fitting.

4    Remove the radiator cap and allow the radiator to drain, then, move the container

31.3  Radiator drain location (arrow)

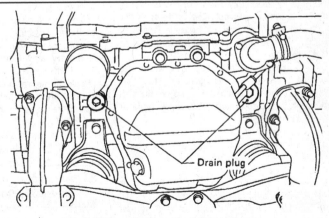

31.4  Engine block drain plug locations

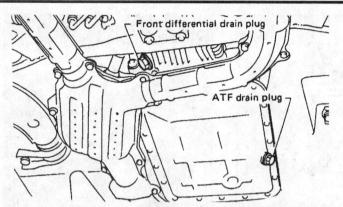

**33.7 The automatic transmission fluid drain plug is located on the bottom of the fluid pan, toward the rear; the drain plug for the differential is located on the right side, near the front of the transaxle**

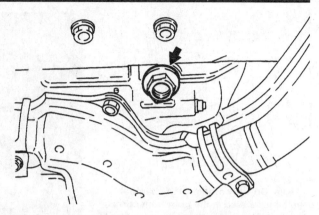

**34.3 On manual transaxles, the drain plug (arrow) is located on the bottom of the transaxle case**

under the engine block. Remove the engine block drain plugs and allow the coolant in the block to drain **(see illustration)**.

5    While the coolant is draining, check the condition of the radiator hoses, heater hoses and clamps (refer to Section 10 if necessary).

6    Replace any damaged clamps or hoses.

7    Once the system is completely drained, flush the radiator with fresh water from a garden hose until it runs clear at the drain. The flushing action of the water will remove sediments from the radiator but will not remove rust and scale from the engine and cooling tube surfaces.

8    These deposits can be removed with a chemical cleaner. Follow the procedure outlined in the manufacturer's instructions. If the radiator is severely corroded, damaged or leaking, it should be removed (see Chapter 3) and taken to a radiator repair shop.

9    Remove the cap and the overflow hose from the coolant reservoir and flush the reservoir with clean water, then reconnect the hose.

10    Close and tighten the radiator drain fitting. Install and tighten the block drain plugs.

11    Place the heater temperature control in the maximum heat position.

12    Slowly add new coolant (a 50/50 mixture of water and antifreeze) to the radiator until it's full. Add coolant to the reservoir up to the lower mark. **Note:** *On turbocharged models, remove the coolant hose from the reservoir, install a funnel and add the coolant to the radiator until it is full. Install the coolant hose back onto the reservoir and add coolant to the reservoir.*

13    Leave the radiator cap off and run the engine in a well-ventilated area until the thermostat opens (coolant will begin flowing through the radiator and the upper radiator hose will become hot).

14    Turn the engine off and let it cool. Add more coolant mixture to bring the level back up to the lip on the radiator filler neck.

15    Squeeze the upper radiator hose to expel air, then add more coolant mixture if necessary. Replace the radiator cap.

16    Start the engine, allow it to reach normal operating temperature and check for leaks.

## 32   Brake fluid change (every 30,000 miles or 24 months)

**Warning:** *Brake fluid can harm your eyes and damage painted surfaces, so use extreme caution when handling or pouring it. Do not use brake fluid that has been standing open or is more than one year old. Brake fluid absorbs moisture from the air. Excess moisture can cause a dangerous loss of braking effectiveness.*

1    At the specified intervals, the brake fluid should be drained and replaced. Since the brake fluid may drip or splash when pouring it, place plenty of rags around the master cylinder to protect any surrounding painted surfaces.

2    Before beginning work, purchase the specified brake fluid (see *Recommended lubricants and fluids* at the beginning of this Chapter).

3    Remove the cap from the master cylinder reservoir.

4    Using a hand suction pump or similar device, withdraw the fluid from the master cylinder reservoir.

5    Add new fluid to the master cylinder until it rises to the base of the filler neck.

6    Bleed the brake system as described in Chapter 9 at all four brakes until new and uncontaminated fluid expels from the bleeder screw. Be sure to maintain the fluid level in the master cylinder as you perform the bleeding process. If you allow the master cylinder to run dry, air will enter the system.

7    Refill the master cylinder with fluid and check the operation of the brakes. The pedal should feel solid when depressed, with no sponginess. **Warning:** *Do not operate the vehicle if you are in doubt about the effectiveness of the brake system.*

## 33   Automatic transaxle fluid change (every 30,000 miles or 24 months)

*Refer to illustration 33.7*

1    At the specified time intervals, the auto-

matic transaxle fluid should be drained and replaced.

2    Before beginning work, purchase the specified transmission fluid (see *Recommended fluids and lubricants,* and *Capacities* at the beginning of this Chapter).

3    Other tools necessary for this job include jackstands to support the vehicle in a raised position, a wrench, a drain pan capable of holding at least eight quarts, newspapers and clean rags.

4    The fluid should be drained after the vehicle has been driven and brought to operating temperature. Hot fluid is more effective than cold fluid at removing built up sediment. **Warning:** *Fluid temperature can exceed 350-degrees F in a hot transaxle. Wear protective gloves.*

5    Raise the vehicle and place it on jackstands.

6    Move the necessary equipment under the vehicle, being careful not to touch any of the hot exhaust components.

7    Place the drain pan under the drain plug in the transaxle housing or fluid pan and remove the drain plug **(see illustration)**. Be sure the drain pan is in position, as fluid will come out with some force. Once the fluid is drained, reinstall the drain plug securely.

8    Lower the vehicle.

9    With the engine off, add new fluid to the transaxle through the dipstick tube. Use a funnel to prevent spills. It is best to add a little fluid at a time, continually checking the level with the dipstick (see Section 6). Allow the fluid time to drain into the pan.

10    Start the engine and shift the selector into all positions from Park through Low then shift into Park and apply the parking brake.

11    With the engine idling, check the fluid level. Add fluid up to the lower level on the dipstick.

## 34   Manual transaxle lubricant change (every 30,000 miles or 24 months)

*Refer to illustration 34.3*

1    Drive the vehicle to warm the lubricant,

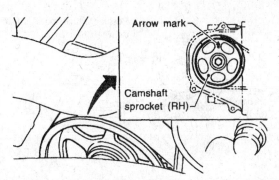

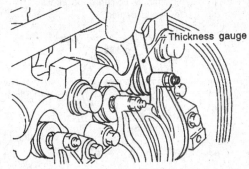

**37.2 With the no. 1 piston at TDC on the compression stroke, the arrow mark on the right side camshaft sprocket should point up**

**37.3 Check the clearance of the intake and exhaust valves on the no. 1 cylinder using a feeler (thickness) gauge**

then raise the vehicle and support it securely on jackstands.

2    Move a drain pan, rags, newspapers and wrenches under the transaxle.

3    Remove the transaxle drain plug at the bottom of the case and allow the lubricant to drain into the pan **(see illustration)**.

4    After the lubricant has drained completely, reinstall the plug and tighten it securely.

5    Fill the transaxle with the recommended lubricant as described in Section 16.

6    Lower the vehicle.

7    Drive the vehicle for a short distance, then check the drain plug for leakage.

---

### 35    Differential lubricant change (every 30,000 miles or 24 months)

**Note:** *The following procedure is used for the rear differential as well as the front differential on vehicles equipped with automatic transaxles.*

1    Drive the vehicle for several miles to warm up the differential oil, then raise the vehicle and support it securely on jackstands.

2    Move a drain pan, rags, newspapers and the proper tools under the vehicle.

3    With the drain pan under the differential, use a socket and ratchet to loosen the drain plug on the rear differential **(see illustration 17.2)**. On automatic transaxle models, also drain the front differential **(see illustration 33.7)**. Do not confuse the two drain plugs on automatic transaxle models! The differential fluid is dark, 80W gear oil while the transaxle fluid is reddish, thin Dexron II automatic transmission fluid.

4    Once the plug is loosened, carefully unscrew it with your fingers until you can remove it from the case.

5    Allow all of the oil to drain into the pan, then replace the drain plug and tighten it securely.

6    Feel with your hands along the bottom of the drain pan for any metal bits that may have come out with the oil. If there are any, it's a sign of excessive wear, indicating that the internal components should be carefully inspected in the near future.

7    Remove the rear differential check/fill

plug (see Section 17). Using a hand pump, syringe or funnel, fill the differential with the correct amount and grade of oil (see Specifications) until the level is just at the bottom of the plug hole.

8    Reinstall the plug and tighten it securely.

9    On vehicles equipped automatic transaxles, fill the front differential with the recommended lubricant as described in Section 16.

10    Lower the vehicle. Check for leaks at the drain plug after the first few miles of driving.

---

### 36    Wheel bearing check (every 60,000 miles or 48 months)

1    These models are equipped with sealed bearings in the front and rear hub assemblies. In most cases the wheel bearings will not need servicing. However, the bearings should be checked whenever the vehicle is raised for any reason. With the vehicle securely supported on jackstands, spin each wheel and check for noise, rolling resistance and freeplay.

2    Grasp the top of each tire with one hand and the bottom with the other. Move the wheel in and out on the spindle. If there's any noticeable movement, remove the front wheel and check the freeplay using a dial indicator. Refer to the Specifications listed in this Chapter.

3    Replace the bearing assembly if excess freeplay and bearing noise exists (refer to Chapter 10).

---

### 37    Valve clearance check and adjustment (1997 and later models) (every 100,000 miles or 6 years)

**Note:** *The valve clearances are checked with the engine cold.*

#### 2.2L engines

*Refer to illustrations 37.2, 37.3, 37.4 and 37.6*

1    Remove the air cleaner assembly and disconnect the Mass Airflow (MAF) sensor (see Chapter 4).

2    Refer to Chapter 2A and remove the valve covers, then use the timing marks to position the number one piston at TDC on the compression stroke **(see illustration)**. **Note:** *Verify TDC for the number one piston by observing that both valves are closed and the rocker arms are loose.*

3    With the number one piston at TDC, measure the clearance of the intake and exhaust valves on the number one cylinder **(see illustration)**. Insert a feeler gauge of the specified thickness (see this Chapter's Specifications) between the valve stem tip and the rocker arm. The feeler gauge should slip between the valve stem tip and rocker arm with a slight amount of drag.

4    If the clearance is incorrect (too loose or too tight), loosen the locknut and turn the adjusting screw slowly until you can feel a slight drag on the feeler gauge as you withdraw it from between the valve stem tip and the rocker arm **(see illustration)**.

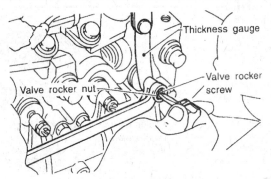

**37.4 Loosen the locknut and turn the adjusting screw until the feeler gauge slips between the valve stem tip and rocker arm with a slight amount of drag, then follow the firing order sequence to bring the remaining cylinders to their TDC position and adjust the valves for each of the remaining cylinders**

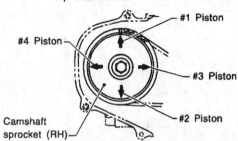

Position of compression stroke
top dead center

#1 Piston
#4 Piston
#3 Piston
#2 Piston
Camshaft
sprocket (RH)

**37.6  Rotate the crankshaft 180-degrees until the arrow on the camshaft sprocket indicates another valve clearance adjustment position**

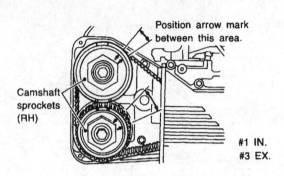

Position arrow mark
between this area.

Camshaft
sprockets
(RH)

#1 IN.
#3 EX.

**37.14  With the arrows in the 2:30 position, adjust the number 1 intake valve and the number 3 exhaust valve**

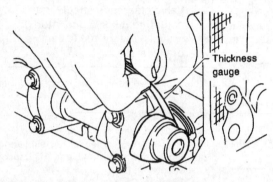

Thickness
gauge

**37.15  Use a feeler gauge between the camshaft and the shim to check the adjustment**

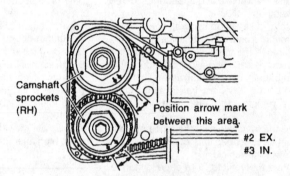

Camshaft
sprockets
(RH)

Position arrow mark
between this area.

#2 EX.
#3 IN.

**37.16  With the arrows in the 4:30 position, adjust the number 3 intake valve and the number 2 exhaust valve**

5    Once the clearance is adjusted, hold the adjusting screw with a screwdriver (to keep it from turning) and tighten the locknut lightly. Recheck the clearance to make sure it hasn't changed after tightening the locknut.

6    The valves in the remaining cylinders can now be checked. It is essential to adjust cylinder 3 next, followed by 2 and finally 4 (follow the firing order sequence). Before checking clearances, bring each cylinder (in order) to TDC by turning the crankshaft 180 degrees in a clockwise direction. Verify TDC by checking the position of the arrow on the camshaft sprocket **(see illustration)**. With the number 1 cylinder at TDC, the arrow should be pointing straight UP. Also, as the engine is rotated to adjust each individual cylinder, the valves should be closed and there should be slight clearance between the valve stem tip and the rocker arm when the cylinder is correctly positioned for adjustment.

7    If necessary, repeat the adjustment procedure described in Steps 3, 4 and 5 until all the valves are adjusted to specifications.

8    Install the valve covers (use new gaskets) and tighten the mounting bolts evenly and securely.

9    Install the spark plug wires and the various hoses and vacuum lines (if removed).

10    Start the engine and check for oil leakage between the valve covers and the cylinder heads.

## 2.5L engines

*Refer to illustrations 37.14, 37.15, 37.16, 37.17, 37.18, 37.19a, 37.19b, 37.19c, 37.19d, 37.19e, 37.19f, 37.19g and 37.21*

**Note 1:** *This procedure requires the use of special valve lifter tools, which are available at most aftermarket tool suppliers. It is impossible to perform this task without them.*

11    To check and adjust the valve clearances, the engine must be cold with the coolant temperature between 68 and 104 degrees F (20 and 40 degrees C).

12    Refer to Chapter 2A and remove the valve covers.

13    Remove the timing belt cover from the right side camshaft assemblies to expose the timing belt sprockets (see Chapter 2A).

14    Turn the crankshaft pulley clockwise

until the arrow mark on the camshaft sprocket is set approximately at the 2:30 clock position **(see illustration)**. Measure the number 1 intake valve and the number 3 exhaust valve clearances.

15    Measure the clearances of the number 1 and number 3 valves with feeler gauges **(see illustration)**. Record the measurements that are out of specification. They will be used later to determine the required replacement shims.

16    Turn the crankshaft until the timing marks on the sprocket are at approximately the 4:30 clock position **(see illustration)**. Measure the number 2 exhaust valve and the number 3 intake valve clearances.

17    Turn the crankshaft until the timing marks on the sprocket are at approximately

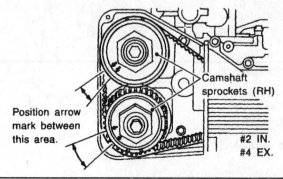

Position arrow
mark between
this area.

Camshaft
sprockets (RH)

#2 IN.
#4 EX.

**37.17  With the arrows in the 7:30 position, adjust the number 2 intake valve and the number 4 exhaust valve**

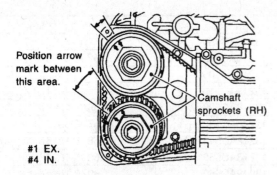

**37.18  With the arrows in the 10:30 position, adjust the number 4 intake valve and the number 1 exhaust valve**

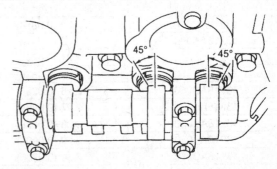

**37.19a  Rotate the notches in the lifters out to a 45-degree angle**

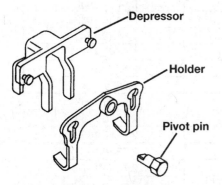

**37.19b  Valve adjusting tools for the 2.5L engine**

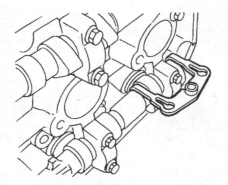

**37.19c  Install the holder to the camshaft first**

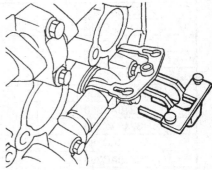

**37.19d  Next, attach the depressor to the bottom side of the holder**

the 7:30 clock position **(see illustration)**. Measure the number 2 intake valve and the number 4 exhaust valve clearances.

18   Turn the crankshaft until the timing marks on the sprocket are at approximately the 10:30 clock position **(see illustration)**. Measure the number 1 exhaust valve and the number 4 intake valve clearances.

19   After all the valve clearances are checked and recorded, replace the shim for any valve assembly that is out of specification. Rotate the notch in the valve lifter out by 45 degrees. Then depress the valve lifter with the special valve lifter tools **(see illustra-**

**tions)**. Follow the photo sequence. Place the special valve holder tool in position as shown, mounted to the intake camshaft. Install the depressor onto the holder and install the pivot pin to lock all three tools into place. Rotate the pivot pin to depress the valve lifter. Once the valve lifter is lowered (depressed), remove the adjusting shim with a small screwdriver or a pair of tweezers.

20   Measure the thickness of the shim with a micrometer. To calculate the correct thickness of a replacement shim that will place the valve clearance within the specified value, use the following formula:

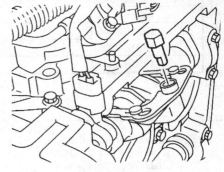

**37.19e  Install the pivot pin into both tools**

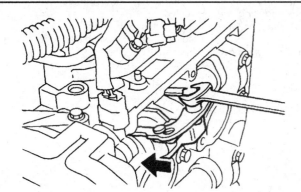

**37.19f  Rotate the pivot pin to force the depressor onto the bucket assembly**

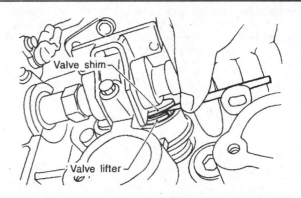

**37.19g  With the bucket depressed, remove the shim from the assembly**

| Part No. | Thickness mm (in) | Part No. | Thickness mm (in) |
|---|---|---|---|
| 13218AC230 | 2.22 (0.0874) | 13218AC480 | 2.52 (0.0992) |
| 13218AE000 | 2.23 (0.0878) | 13218AC490 | 2.53 (0.0996) |
| 13218AC240 | 2.24 (0.0882) | 13218AC500 | 2.54 (0.1000) |
| 13218AE010 | 2.25 (0.0886) | 13218AC510 | 2.55 (0.1004) |
| 13218AC250 | 2.26 (0.0890) | 13218AC520 | 2.56 (0.1008) |
| 13218AE020 | 2.27 (0.0894) | 13218AC530 | 2.57 (0.1012) |
| 13218AC260 | 2.28 (0.0898) | 13218AC540 | 2.58 (0.1016) |
| 13218AE030 | 2.29 (0.0902) | 13218AC550 | 2.59 (0.1020) |
| 13218AC270 | 2.30 (0.0906) | 13218AC560 | 2.60 (0.1024) |
| 13218AE040 | 2.31 (0.0909) | 13218AC570 | 2.61 (0.1028) |
| 13218AC280 | 2.32 (0.0913) | 13218AC580 | 2.62 (0.1031) |
| 13218AC290 | 2.33 (0.0917) | 13218AC590 | 2.63 (0.1035) |
| 13218AC300 | 2.34 (0.0921) | 13218AC600 | 2.64 (0.1039) |
| 13218AC310 | 2.35 (0.0925) | 13218AC610 | 2.65 (0.1043) |
| 13218AC320 | 2.36 (0.0929) | 13218AC620 | 2.66 (0.1047) |
| 13218AC330 | 2.37 (0.0933) | 13218AC630 | 2.67 (0.1051) |
| 13218AC340 | 2.38 (0.0937) | 13218AC640 | 2.68 (0.1055) |
| 13218AC350 | 2.39 (0.0941) | 13218AC650 | 2.69 (0.1059) |
| 13218AC360 | 2.40 (0.0945) | 13218AC660 | 2.70 (0.1063) |
| 13218AC370 | 2.41 (0.0949) | 13218AE050 | 2.71 (0.1067) |
| 13218AC380 | 2.42 (0.0953) | 13218AC670 | 2.72 (0.1071) |
| 13218AC390 | 2.43 (0.0957) | 13218AE060 | 2.73 (0.1075) |
| 13218AC400 | 2.44 (0.0961) | 13218AC680 | 2.74 (0.1079) |
| 13218AC410 | 2.45 (0.0965) | 13218AE070 | 2.75 (0.1083) |
| 13218AC420 | 2.46 (0.0969) | 13218AC690 | 2.76 (0.1087) |
| 13218AC430 | 2.47 (0.0972) | 13218AE080 | 2.77 (0.1091) |
| 13218AC440 | 2.48 (0.0976) | 13218AC700 | 2.78 (0.1094) |
| 13218AC450 | 2.49 (0.0980) | 13218AE090 | 2.79 (0.1098) |
| 13218AC460 | 2.50 (0.0984) | 13218AC710 | 2.80 (0.1102) |
| 13218AC470 | 2.51 (0.0988) | 13218AE100 | 2.81 (0.1106) |

**37.21  Shim sizes and part number chart**

Intake valve S = (V + T) - 0.008 inch
Exhaust valve S = (V + T) - 0.010 inch
T = *thickness of the old shim*
V = *valve clearance measured*
S = *thickness of the new shim*

21    Select a shim with a thickness as close as possible to the valve clearance calculated. Shims are available in sizes in increments of 0.0004 inch (0.01 mm). They range in size from 0.0874 inch (2.22 mm) to 0.1106 inch (2.81 mm) **(see illustration)**. **Note:** *Through careful analysis of the shim sizes needed to bring the out-of-specification valve clearance within specification, it is often possible to simply move a shim that has to come out anyway to another valve lifter requiring a shim of that particular size, thereby reducing the number of new shims that must be purchased.*

22    Place the special valve lifter tool in position and keep the lifter depressed while the shim is inserted. Measure the clearance with a feeler gauge to make sure that your calculations are correct.

23    Repeat this procedure until all the valves which are out of clearance have been corrected.

24    Installation of the spark plugs, valve cover, spark plug wires and boots, etc. is the reverse of removal.

# Chapter 2  Part A  Engines

## Contents

## Specifications

### General

| | |
|---|---|
| Firing order | 1-3-2-4 |
| Cylinder head gasket surface warpage limit | 0.002 inch |

### Camshaft

#### 2.2L engine

Lobe height

| | |
|---|---|
| 1990 and 1991 | 1.2752 to 1.2791 inches |
| 1992 through 1994 | |
| Non-turbocharged models | 1.2742 to 1.2781 inches |
| Turbocharged models | 1.2711 to 1.2750 inches |
| 1995 and 1996 | |
| Intake | 1.2596 to 1.2635 inches |
| Exhaust | 1.2844 to 1.2883 inches |
| 1997 and 1998 | |
| Intake | 1.2694 to 1.2734 inches |
| Exhaust | 1.2584 to 1.2624 inches |
| 1999 | |
| Intake | 1.3386 to 1.5268 |
| Exhaust | 1.3386 to 1.5475 |
| Wear limit (all) | 0.006 inch |

Journal diameter

| | |
|---|---|
| Rear | 1.2573 to 1.2579 inches |
| Center | 1.4738 to 1.4744 inches |
| Front | 1.4935 to 1.4941 inches |

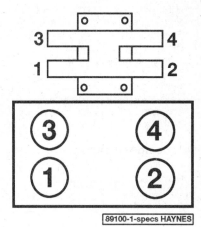

**Engine cylinder numbering and coil pack terminal locations**

## Camshaft (continued)

### 2.2L engine (continued)
Journal bores
    Rear .................................................................................... 1.2600 to 1.2608 inches
    Center ................................................................................ 1.4766 to 1.4774 inches
    Front .................................................................................. 1.4963 to 1.4970 inches
Journal oil clearance
    Standard ............................................................................ 0.0022 to 0.0035 inch
    Limit .................................................................................. 0.0039 inch
Thrust clearance (endplay) ...................................................... 0.0012 to 0.0102 inches

### 2.5L engine
Lobe height
    1996
        Intake ........................................................................... 1.6409 to 1.6449 inches
        Exhaust ......................................................................... 1.6528 to 1.6567 inches
    1997 on
        Intake ........................................................................... 1.6614 to 1.6654 inches
        Exhaust
            Front ......................................................................... 1.6732 to 1.6772 inches
            Rear .......................................................................... 1.6299 to 1.6339 inches
    Wear limit (all) .................................................................. 0.006 inch
Journal diameter
    Front .................................................................................. 1.2577 to 1.2584 inches
    Center ................................................................................ 1.1002 to 1.1009 inches
    Rear .................................................................................. 1.1002 to 1.1009 inches
Journal bore
    Front .................................................................................. 1.2598 to 1.2605 inches
    Center ................................................................................ 1.1024 to 1.1031 inches
    Rear .................................................................................. 1.1024 to 1.1031 inches
Journal oil clearance
    Standard ............................................................................ 0.0015 to 0.0028 inch
    Limit .................................................................................. 0.0039 inch
Thrust clearance (endplay) ...................................................... 0.0016 to 0.0031 inches

## Valve lifters (2.5L engine)
Outer diameter .......................................................................... 1.2976 to 1.2982 inch
Lifter bore diameter .................................................................. 1.2990 to 1.2998 inch
Lifter-to-bore clearance
    Standard ............................................................................ 0.0007 to 0.0022 inch
    Service limit ....................................................................... 0.0039 inch

## Oil pump
Inner and outer rotor tip clearance
    Standard ............................................................................ 0.0016 to 0.0055 inch
    Limit .................................................................................. 0.0071 inch
Outer rotor-to-pump housing clearance
    Standard ............................................................................ 0.0039 to 0.0069 inch
    Limit .................................................................................. 0.0079 inch
Rotor-to-cover clearance (endplay)
    Standard ............................................................................ 0.0008 to 0.0028 inch
    Limit .................................................................................. 0.0047 inch

## Torque specifications                                                     **Ft-lbs** (unless otherwise indicated)
Camshaft seal retainer/support (2.2L engine)
    Non-turbocharged models ................................................. 120 to 144 in-lbs
    Turbocharged models ........................................................ 72 to 84 in-lbs
Camshaft sprocket bolts
    2.2L ................................................................................... 47 to 54
    2.5L ................................................................................... 55 to 61
Crankshaft pulley bolt
    2.2L ................................................................................... 70 to 80
    2.5L ................................................................................... 90 to 100
Camshaft retainer caps (2.5L engine) ..................................... 70 to 90 in-lbs

## Torque specifications

Cylinder head bolts (refer to illustration 10.13)              **Ft-lbs** (unless otherwise indicated)

| | |
|---|---|
| Step 1 | 22 |
| Step 2 | 51 |
| Step 3 | Loosen all bolts 180-degrees |
| Step 4 | Loosen all bolts an additional 180-degrees |
| Step 5 (bolts 1 and 2 only) | |
|     Non-turbocharged models | 25 |
|     Turbocharged models | 27 |
| Step 6 (bolts 3, 4, 5 and 6) | |
|     Non-turbocharged models | 132 in-lbs |
|     Turbocharged models | 168 in-lbs |
| Step 7 | Tighten all bolts an additional 90-degrees |
| Step 8 | Tighten all bolts an additional 90-degrees |
| Flywheel/driveplate housing-to-engine bolts | 25 to 30 |
| Flywheel/driveplate-to-crankshaft bolts | 51 to 55 |
| Front exhaust pipe-to-engine | 18 to 22 |
| Intake manifold bolts | 168 to 192 in-lbs |
| Oil pan bolts | 36 to 48 in-lbs |
| Oil pressure sending unit | 14 to 18 |
| Oil pump mounting bolts | 48 to 60 in-lbs |
| Oil strainer mounting bolts | 72 to 84 in-lbs |
| Rocker arm assembly bolts (2.2L) | 96 to 108 in-lbs |
| Timing belt cover bolts | 36 to 48 in-lbs |
| Timing belt idler sprocket bolt | 26 to 32 |
| Timing belt tensioner mounting bolts | |
|     1997 and earlier | 17 to 20 |
|     1998 and 1999 | 26 to 32 |
| Valve cover bolts | 36 to 48 in-lbs |

## 1   General information

Both the 2.2L and 2.5L engines are a horizontally opposed, four cylinder configuration. The crankcase is made of aluminum and can be separated into right and left sections. The cylinder heads are also aluminum while the crankshaft is made of steel and supported by five main bearings. The aluminum pistons have two compression rings and one combination-type oil control ring. Each cylinder is equipped with two intake valves and two exhaust valves, for a total of 16 valves.

The 2.2L engine is a single overhead-cam (SOHC) design. Two camshafts (one mounted in each cylinder head) operate the valves with rocker arms and on 1996 and earlier models, hydraulic lash adjusters. The hydraulic lash adjusters are located in each rocker arm on the valve side. On 1997 and later models, the 2.2L engines are equipped with adjustable valves (see Chapter 1). On 2.2L engines, the camshafts can only be removed by first removing the cylinder heads from the engine.

The 2.5L engine, introduced in 1996, is available as an option in certain models. The 2.5L engine is a double overhead-cam (DOHC) design with four camshafts, two mounted on each cylinder head. The valves are operated directly by the camshafts and valve lifters. 1996 models are equipped with hydraulic valve lifters, while 1997 and later models are equipped with an adjustable valve train (see Chapter 1). On 2.5L engines, the camshafts can be removed without removing the cylinder head, if necessary.

The camshafts are driven by the crankshaft with a single timing belt. Timing belt tension is maintained by a tensioner mounted between the two camshafts. Belt tension is maintained by a compression spring that acts against a main spring and oil chamber to keep the tensioner balanced. The water pump is also driven directly by the timing belt. The timing belt is scheduled for replacement at prescribed service intervals (see Chapter 1).

The engine oil pump is driven by the crankshaft and it is mounted directly in the center of the engine behind the timing belt and covers.

## 2   Repair operations possible with the engine in the vehicle

Some major repair operations can be accomplished without removing the engine from the vehicle.

Clean the engine compartment and the exterior of the engine with some type of degreaser before any work is done. It will make the job easier and help keep dirt out of the internal areas of the engine.

Depending on the components involved, it may be helpful to remove the hood to improve access to the engine as repairs are performed (refer to Chapter 11 if necessary). Cover the fenders to prevent damage to the paint. Special pads are available, but an old bedspread or blanket will also work.

If vacuum, exhaust, oil or coolant leaks develop, indicating a need for gasket or seal replacement, the repairs can generally be made with the engine in the vehicle. The intake and exhaust gaskets, oil pan gasket, crankshaft oil seals and cylinder head gasket are all accessible with the engine in place. However, cylinder head gasket replacement is easier with the engine out of the chassis.

Exterior engine components, such as the intake and exhaust, the oil pan (and the oil pump), the water pump, the starter motor, the alternator, the ignition system and fuel system components can be removed for repair with the engine in place.

Since the cylinder heads can be removed without pulling the engine (although this is difficult), valve component servicing can also be accomplished with the engine in the vehicle. Replacement of the camshafts, rockers and lifters can be accomplished with the engine in the chassis.

**3.7  TDC mark on the pulley (arrow) aligned with zero mark on the timing scale**

**4.6  Remove the bolts from the valve cover (arrows)**

### 3    Top Dead Center (TDC) for number one piston - locating

*Refer to illustrations 3.7*

1    Top Dead Center (TDC) is the highest point in the cylinder that each piston reaches as it travels up the cylinder bore. Each piston reaches TDC on the compression stroke and again on the exhaust stroke, but TDC generally refers to piston position on the compression stroke.

2    Positioning the piston(s) at TDC is an essential part of many procedures such as valve timing, camshaft and timing belt/pulley removal.

3    Before beginning this procedure, be sure to place the transmission in Neutral and apply the parking brake or block the rear wheels. Also, disable the ignition system by disconnecting the harness connector from the coil pack (see Chapter 5). Remove the spark plugs (see Chapter 1).

4    In order to bring any piston to TDC, the crankshaft must be turned using one of the methods outlined below. When looking at the front of the engine, normal crankshaft rotation is clockwise.

 a) *The preferred method is to turn the crankshaft with a socket and ratchet attached to the bolt threaded into the front of the crankshaft. Turn the bolt in a clockwise direction only. Never turn the bolt counterclockwise.*

 b) *A remote starter switch, which may save some time, can also be used. Follow the instructions included with the switch. Once the piston is close to TDC, use a socket and ratchet as described in the previous paragraph.*

 c) *If an assistant is available to turn the ignition switch to the Start position in short bursts, you can get the piston close to TDC without a remote starter switch. Make sure your assistant is out of the vehicle, away from the ignition switch, then use a socket and ratchet as described in Paragraph (a) to complete the procedure.*

5    To find TDC on the compression stroke for the number one cylinder, install a compression gauge in the number one spark plug hole (refer to Chapter 2B).

6    Rotate the crankshaft using a socket and breaker bar on the crankshaft pulley while observing the compression gauge. When the compression stroke of number one cylinder is reached, compression pressure will begin to build and register on the gauge.

7    Continue rotating the crankshaft until the notch in the crankshaft pulley aligns with the "0" on the timing indicator **(see illustration)**. If you go past the marks, release the gauge pressure and rotate the crankshaft two revolutions. **Note:** *Because either cylinders 1 or 2 could be at the TDC position when the timing marks are aligned, it is important not to mistake the wrong cylinder at the TDC position; make sure compression is apparent at the number one cylinder as the crankshaft is rotated and the notch on the pulley is nearing the timing scale.*

### 4    Valve covers - removal and installation

*Refer to illustration 4.6*

1    Disconnect the cable from the negative battery terminal.

2    Remove the air intake ducts and the air cleaner assembly (see Chapter 4) to access the right side valve cover.

3    Disconnect the spark plug wires from each cylinder (see Chapter 1).

4    Remove the battery and the battery tray from the engine compartment to access the left side valve cover.

5    Remove the windshield washer reservoir from the engine compartment.

6    Remove the bolts from the valve cover **(see illustration)** and separate the cover from the cylinder head. Depending on the tools you are using, it may be easier to remove the lower bolts from under the vehicle. If this is the case, raise the vehicle and support it securely on the jackstands.

7    Installation is the reverse of removal. Be

sure to install a new valve cover gasket and tighten the bolts listed in this Chapter's Specifications.

### 5    Intake manifold - removal and installation

**Warning:** *Wait until the engine is completely cool before beginning this procedure.*

### *Removal*

*Refer to illustration 5.15a, 5.15b, and 5.18*

1    Relieve the fuel pressure (see Chapter 4).

2    Disconnect the cable from the negative battery terminal. Drain the cooling system (see Chapter 1).

3    Disconnect all of the hoses and wires from the air cleaner assembly and MAF sensor (see Chapters 4 and 6).

4    Remove the air cleaner assembly and air intake ducts.

5    Remove the alternator (see Chapter 5).

6    Remove the air conditioning compressor and its mount (see Chapter 3). Lay the compressor aside without disconnecting the refrigerant lines. **Warning:** *The air conditioning system is under high pressure. DO NOT loosen any fittings unless the system has been discharged. Air conditioning refrigerant should be properly discharged into an approved container at a dealer service department or an automotive air conditioning repair facility.*

7    Disconnect the fuel delivery and return hoses from the fuel rail (see Chapter 4).

8    Disconnect the vacuum hose, the vent hose and the purge hose from the evaporation pipe. Tag all of the hoses and wires with masking tape to help identify their location during reassembly.

9    Disconnect the brake booster vacuum hose from the intake manifold.

10    Disconnect the purge control solenoid harness connector.

11    Disconnect the spark plug wires from the plugs and the harness connector to the coil pack (see Chapter 5).

12    Disconnect the accelerator cable from

**5.15a Disconnect the EGR pipe fitting at the manifold (arrow)**

**5.15b Disconnect the EGR pipe fitting at the cylinder head (arrow)**

the throttle body (see Chapter 4).

13   Disconnect the coolant hose to the thermostat housing from the top of the radiator (see Chapter 3).

14   Disconnect the coolant hose from the intake manifold to the firewall. Place a rag under the connection to catch any coolant left in the hose.

15   Remove the EGR pipe (see illustrations).

16   Disconnect the hoses from the bypass air control solenoid valve (1990 through 1994 models) (see Chapter 4).

17   Disconnect the hose from the PCV valve.

18   Remove the intake manifold mounting bolts (see illustration) and carefully lift the manifold off of the engine with the throttle body and fuel injectors attached. There are more than one length of intake bolts, so mark them as to their location. Note: As you lift the manifold, check for any hoses or wires that may still be connected.

### Installation

19   Scrape away any traces of sealant or old gasket materials from the intake manifold mounting surfaces and clean the gasket surface with a rag and lacquer thinner. Note: When installing the manifold, always use new gaskets, and do not use sealant on the gaskets. Clean the threads of the bolts with a wire brush before installation.

20   Carefully place the intake manifold on the engine and bolt it into place with the

**5.18 Exploded view of the intake manifold and related components - 2.2L engine (2.5L similar)**

1   Intake manifold gasket
2   Intake manifold gasket
3   Fuel injector pipe insulator
4   Fuel injector pipe
5   O-ring
6   O-ring
7   Fuel injector
8   Insulator
9   Fuel injector cap
10   Plate
11   Seal
12   Gasket
13   Coolant hose
14   Air bypass hose
15   Idle air control solenoid valve
16   Coolant hose
17   Fitting
18   Plug
19   PCV valve
20   Purge control solenoid valve
21   Fitting
22   Back pressure transducer
23   Bracket
24   Hose
25   EGR vacuum hose
26   EGR vacuum hose
27   EGR valve
28   Gasket
29   EGR solenoid valve
30   EGR pipe
31   Pressure sensor
32   Pressure sensor switching valve
33   Vacuum hose
34   Vacuum hose
35   Vacuum hose
36   Bracket
37   Bracket
38   Intake manifold

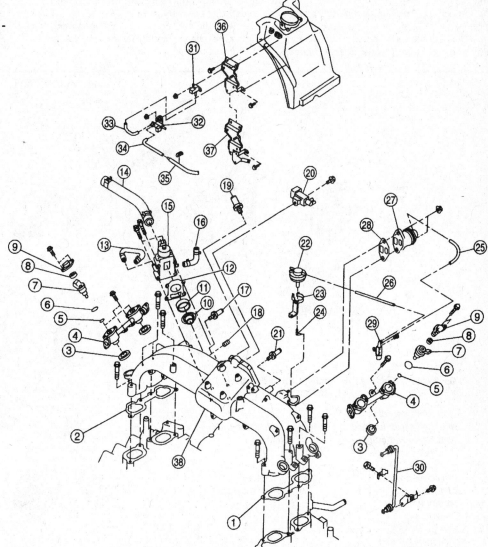

**6.7  Use a chain wrench to lock the crankshaft pulley in place while removing the crankshaft bolt with a breaker bar and socket**

**6.8  Remove the crankshaft pulley from the crankshaft**

mounting bolts, tightening them evenly to the torque listed this Chapter's Specifications.

21    Attach the hose to the PCV valve.

22    Install the oil fill tube and bracket on the engine.

23    Attach the EGR supply tube to the manifold.

24    Connect the wiring connectors and vacuum and fuel hoses. **Note:** *Check all hoses*

*for cracks and damage at this time. Replace them with new ones if necessary.*

25    Connect the coolant transfer hose and the radiator hose at the thermostat housing.

26    Connect the accelerator cable and adjust it, if necessary.

27    Refill the cooling system. When starting the engine, check carefully for coolant, fuel or vacuum leaks.

### 6    Timing belts and sprockets - removal, inspection and installation

#### *Removal*

> **\*\* CAUTION \*\***
>
> The timing system is complex. Severe engine damage will occur if you make any mistakes. Do not attempt this procedure unless you are highly experienced with this type of repair. If you are at all unsure of your abilities, consult an expert. Double-check all your work and be sure everything is correct before you attempt to start the engine.

*Refer to illustrations 6.7, 6.8, 6.9a, 6.9b, 6.10, 6.11a, 6.11b, 6.11c, 6.13a, 6.13b, 6.16, 6.17 and 6.18*

1    Disconnect the cable from the negative battery terminal.

2    Position the engine at TDC for cylinder number 1 (see Section 3).

3    Remove the drivebelts (see Chapter 1).

4    Remove the air cleaner assembly.

5    Remove the air conditioning compressor drivebelt tensioner.

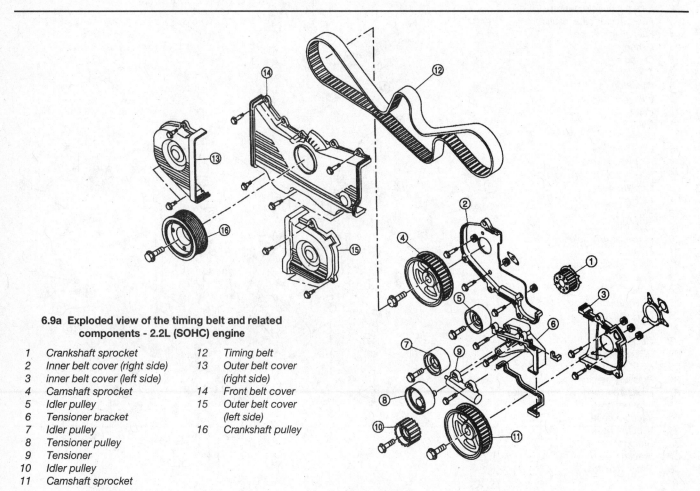

**6.9a  Exploded view of the timing belt and related components - 2.2L (SOHC) engine**

| | |
|---|---|
| 1    Crankshaft sprocket | 12    Timing belt |
| 2    Inner belt cover (right side) | 13    Outer belt cover |
| 3    inner belt cover (left side) | (right side) |
| 4    Camshaft sprocket | 14    Front belt cover |
| 5    Idler pulley | 15    Outer belt cover |
| 6    Tensioner bracket | (left side) |
| 7    Idler pulley | 16    Crankshaft pulley |
| 8    Tensioner pulley | |
| 9    Tensioner | |
| 10    Idler pulley | |
| 11    Camshaft sprocket | |

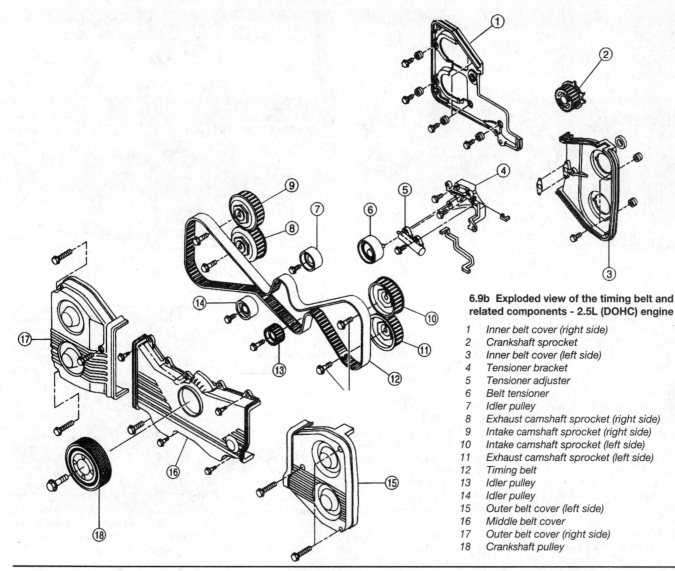

**6.9b Exploded view of the timing belt and related components - 2.5L (DOHC) engine**

1   Inner belt cover (right side)
2   Crankshaft sprocket
3   Inner belt cover (left side)
4   Tensioner bracket
5   Tensioner adjuster
6   Belt tensioner
7   Idler pulley
8   Exhaust camshaft sprocket (right side)
9   Intake camshaft sprocket (right side)
10  Intake camshaft sprocket (left side)
11  Exhaust camshaft sprocket (left side)
12  Timing belt
13  Idler pulley
14  Idler pulley
15  Outer belt cover (left side)
16  Middle belt cover
17  Outer belt cover (right side)
18  Crankshaft pulley

6    Remove the engine cooling fan(s) and shroud.
7    Use a breaker bar and socket to remove the bolt from the crankshaft pulley. Use a chain wrench to hold the pulley while loosening the bolt **(see illustration)**

8    The crankshaft pulley should come off by hand **(see illustration)**, if not, use a screwdriver on either side of it to lever it off evenly.
9    Remove the outer belt covers **(see illustrations)**. There are two side covers and one central cover.

10   Turn the crankshaft and align the marks on the crankshaft and left and right camshaft sprockets with the notches on the belt cover and the cylinder head **(see illustration)**.
11   Use white paint to clearly mark these alignment marks in relation to the engine

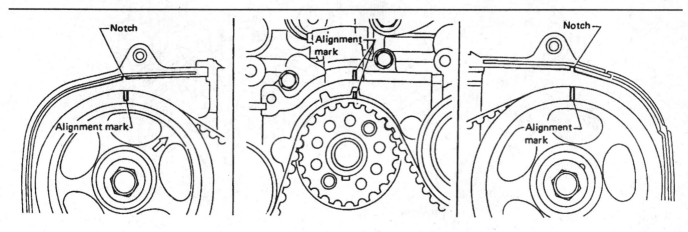

**6.10  Location of the timing marks - 2.2L engine**

6.11a  Location of the timing marks on the crankshaft sprocket (arrows) - 2.5L engine

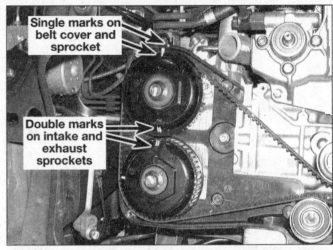

6.11b  Location of the timing marks on the right side intake and exhaust camshaft sprockets - 2.5L engine

block (center) and the inner belt covers (left and right) **(see illustrations)**.

12   Loosen the tensioner mounting bolts to relieve belt tension.

13   Remove the idler pulley **(see illustrations)**.

14   Remove the timing belt. **Caution:** *On DOHC models, do not rotate the camshaft sprockets with the timing belt removed or the valve heads may contact each other resulting in bent valves.*

15   If only the timing belt is to be replaced, proceed to the *Inspection* and *Installation* Steps. If the sprockets are to be replaced, continue with the following Steps.

16   Remove the crankshaft pulley sprocket from the crankshaft. If it doesn't slip off, use two screwdrivers behind it to evenly lever it off **(see illustration)**.

17   Remove the bolt(s) and the timing belt tensioner **(see illustration)**.

18   While keeping the camshaft sprocket timing mark aligned with the mark on the inner cover, remove the sprocket bolts, while holding the sprocket with a large pair of adjustable pliers or similar tool **(see illustration)**. Remove both camshaft sprockets and mark them left and right.

## Inspection

*Refer to illustrations 6.21, 6.22 and 6.23*

**Caution:** *Do not bend, twist or turn the timing belt inside out. Do not allow it to come in contact with oil, coolant or fuel. Do not use timing belt tension to keep the camshaft or crankshaft from turning when installing the sprocket bolt(s). Do not turn the crankshaft or camshaft more than a few degrees (necessary for tooth alignment) while the timing belt is removed.*

19   Rotate the tensioner pulley and idler pulley by hand and move it side-to-side to

6.11c  Location of the timing marks on the left side intake and exhaust camshaft sprockets - 2.5L engine

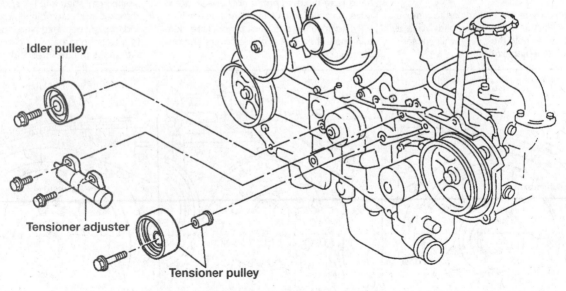

6.13a  Remove the idler pulley (2.2L engine)

6.13b  Remove the idler pulley (2.5L engine)

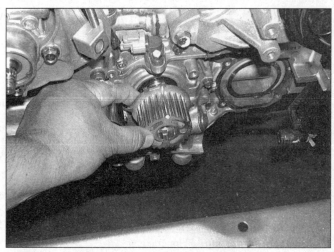

6.16  Remove the crankshaft sprocket

6.17  On 1998 models the tensioner assembly has been
redesigned and is retained by a single mounting bolt

6.18  Hold the camshaft sprocket with a suitable tool while
loosening the bolt

detect roughness and excessive play. Replace them if they don't turn smoothly or if play is noted.

20   If the timing belt was broken during engine operation, the belt may have been fouled by debris or may have been damaged by a defective component in the area of the timing belt; check for belt material in the teeth of the sprockets. Any defective parts or debris in the sprockets must be cleaned out of all the sprockets before installing the new belt or the belt will not mesh properly when installed. **Note:** *If one of the sprockets is damaged or worn, replace the sprockets as a set.*

21   If the belt teeth are cracked or pulled off **(see illustration)**, the oil pump or camshaft(s) may have seized.

22   If there is noticeable wear or cracks in the belt **(see illustration)**, check to see if there are nicks or burrs on the sprockets.

23   If there is wear or damage on only one side of the belt **(see illustration)**, check the belt guide and the alignment of all sprockets. Also check the oil seals at the front of the engine and replace them if they are leaking.

24   Replace the timing belt with a new one if obvious wear or damage is noted or if it is the least bit questionable. Correct any problems which contributed to belt failure prior to belt installation. **Note:** *We recommend replacing the belt whenever it is removed, since belt failure can lead to expensive engine damage.*

6.21  Check the timing belt for cracked
and missing teeth

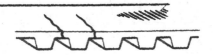

6.22  If the belt is cracked or worn, check
the sprockets for nicks and burrs

6.23  Wear on one side of the belt
indicates sprocket
misalignment problems

**6.26  Right side timing belt inner cover mounting bolts (arrows)**

## Installation

> ** ** CAUTION ** **
>
> Before starting the engine, carefully rotate the crankshaft by hand through at least two full revolutions (use a socket and breaker bar on the crankshaft pulley center bolt). If you feel any resistance, STOP! There is something wrong - most likely, valves are contacting the pistons. You must find the problem before proceeding. Check your work and see if any updated repair information is available.

Refer to illustrations 6.26, 6.30a, 6.30b, 6.30c, 6.31a, 6.31b, 6.34, 6.35a and 6.35b

**Note:** *If the inner timing belt covers were removed from the engine (only necessary if the cylinder heads had been removed or the engine was to be overhauled, continue as below. If the inner covers were not removed, proceed to Step 30.*

25   If removed as part of the camshaft sprocket removal procedure, attach the seals and belt cover mounts to the center inner belt cover, then install the assembly on the cylinder block.

26   Attach the seals and belt cover mounts to the left inner belt cover and the right inner belt cover **(see illustration)**, then install the assembly on the cylinder head and block.

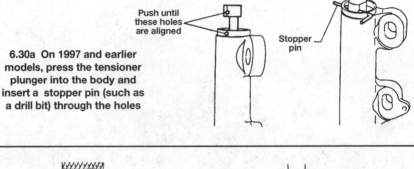

**6.30a  On 1997 and earlier models, press the tensioner plunger into the body and insert a stopper pin (such as a drill bit) through the holes**

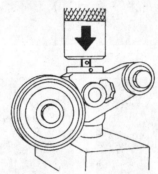

**6.30b  On 1998 models, place the tensioner assembly onto a vertical press and gradually press the plunger in until the holes align - press the plunger in very slowly, taking at least three minutes to complete the procedure**

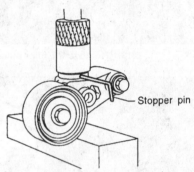

**6.30c  Insert a stopper pin through the holes - DO NOT force the adjuster rod past this point or damage to the tensioner assembly will occur**

27   Install the camshaft sprockets **(see illustrations 6.9a and 6.9b)**. Tighten the bolts to the torque listed in this Chapter's Specifications.

28   Install the crankshaft sprocket onto the crankshaft. Make sure the crankshaft and camshaft sprockets timing marks are still aligned **(see illustrations 6.10, 6.11a, 6.11b and 6.11c)**. If necessary rotate the sprockets slightly to align the timing marks. **Caution:** *If it's necessary to rotate the camshaft sprockets on a DOHC model, rotate the sprockets only slightly and independently of each other. Due to valve spring pressure the camshaft timing marks on the left bank may misalign when the belt is removed. Align these sprock-*ets *as the belt is installed, rotating the intake camshaft clockwise and the exhaust camshaft counterclockwise.*

29   If the tensioner idler pulley (1997 and earlier models) had been removed, reinstall it.

30   Reinstall the tensioner. First, depress the tensioner plunger in and lock it in place with a stopper pin **(see illustrations)**. Install the assembly onto the engine. On 1997 and earlier models, position the tensioner to the right (away from the belt) and temporarily tighten the bolts.

31   Install the timing belt onto the sprockets and pulleys noting the correct spacing between sprockets **(see illustration)**. On DOHC models install the belt around the sprockets in the numerical order shown.

32   Install the idler pulley(s).

33   On 1997 and earlier models, loosen the tensioner bolts and move the tensioner to the left (toward the belt) and tighten the mounting bolts.

34   Remove the stopper pin from the tensioner adjuster **(see illustration)**. Double-check all the timing marks for correct alignment.

35   Install the timing belt guide, if equipped, maintaining the proper clearance between the guide and timing belt **(see illustrations)**.

36   Install the timing belt covers and crankshaft pulley.

37   The remainder of installation is the reverse of the removal procedure.

**6.31a Install the timing belt making sure the timing belt alignment marks are aligned and verify the correct distance between the timing marks by counting the teeth on the timing belt (2.2L SOHC engine)**

$Z_1$     44 teeth
$Z_2$     40.5 teeth

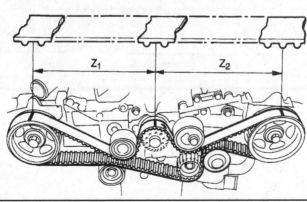

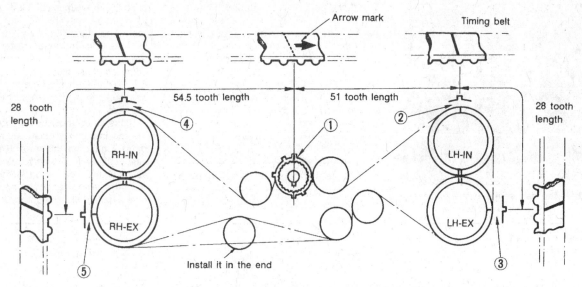

**6.31b Install the timing belt in the numerical order shown - make sure the timing belt alignment marks are aligned and verify the correct distance between the timing marks by counting the teeth on the timing belt (2.5L DOHC engine)**

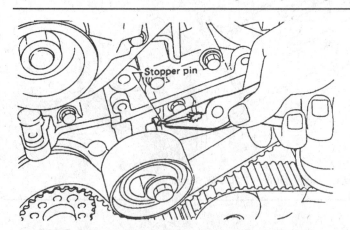

6.34 Pull the stopper pin out to apply tension to the belt

6.35a Install the timing belt guide bolts (arrows)

## 7 Crankshaft front oil seal - replacement

*Refer to illustrations 7.3 and 7.5*

1  Disconnect the negative battery cable.
2  Refer to Section 6 and remove the timing belt and crankshaft sprocket.
3  Carefully pry the seal out of the cover with a seal puller or a large screwdriver **(see illustration)**. **Caution:** *Be careful not to scratch, gouge or distort the area that the seal fits into or an oil leak will develop.* **Note:** *An alternative method if you don't have a seal puller is to drill two 1/8-inch holes in the seal, being careful not to hit the seal housing or crankshaft. Screw two self-tapping screws into the holes and pull on them, alternating side to side, with a slide-hammer or self-locking pliers on the screws.*

4  Clean the bore to remove any old seal material and corrosion. Position the new seal in the bore with the seal lip (usually the side with the spring) facing IN (toward the engine). A small amount of oil applied to the outer edge of the new seal will make installation easier - but don't overdo it!

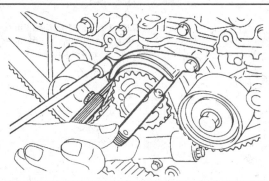

6.35b Check the clearance using a feeler gauge - it should be between 0.020 to 0.060 inch

7.3 Pull the seal from the oil pump housing taking care not to damage the crankshaft surface or the oil pump housing

**7.5 Drive the new seal in with a hammer and a deep socket**

5    Drive the seal into the bore with a large socket and hammer until it's completely seated **(see illustration)**. Select a socket that's the same outside diameter as the seal and make sure the new seal is pressed into place until it bottoms against the cover flange, to the same depth as the original seal.

6    Refer to Section 6 for installation of the sprockets and timing belts.

7    The remainder of installation is the reverse of the removal process.

## 8    Camshaft oil seals - replacement

1    Refer to Section 6 and remove the tim-

ing belts and camshaft sprockets.

2    Unbolt the camshaft seal retainer from the cylinder housing, if equipped **(see illustrations 9.9a and 9.9b)**. **Note:** *It is not necessary to remove the camshaft cover, camshaft housing or inner timing covers.*

3    Pull the retainer from the engine. Use a seal puller to pry the old seal from the cylinder head.

4    Install the new seal by gently tapping the seal into the cylinder head recess using a deep socket and hammer. **Note:** *Drive the seal in squarely and only to the same depth as the original seal was installed.*

5    The remainder of the procedure is the reverse of the disassembly process.

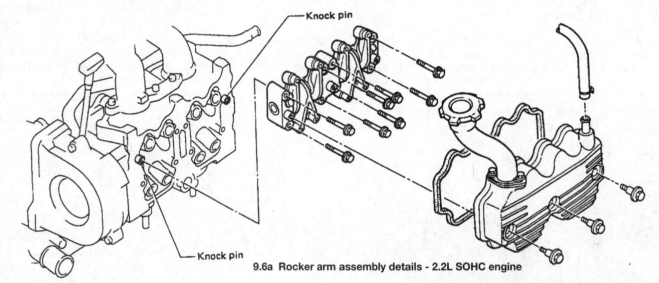

**9.6a  Rocker arm assembly details - 2.2L SOHC engine**

Knock pin

Knock pin

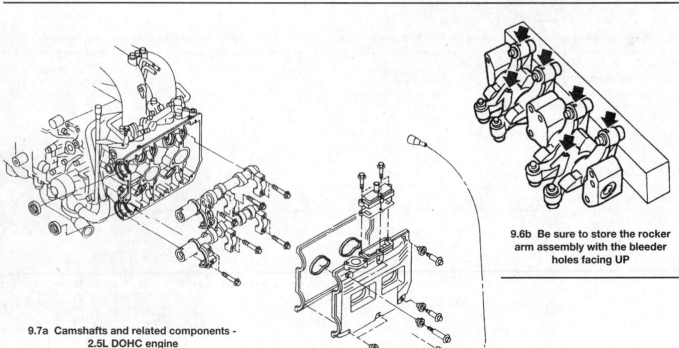

**9.7a  Camshafts and related components - 2.5L DOHC engine**

**9.6b  Be sure to store the rocker arm assembly with the bleeder holes facing UP**

## 9  Camshafts and valve actuating components - removal, inspection and installation

**Note:** *The cylinder heads must be removed for camshaft servicing on 2.2L engines.*

### Removal

*Refer to Illustrations 9.6a, 9.6b, 9.7a, 9.7b, 9.9a and 9.9b*

1  On 2.2L models, refer to Chapter 1 to drain the cooling system, then remove the engine block drain plugs to drain the engine coolant.

2  Refer to Section 6 and remove the timing belts and camshaft sprockets.

3  Remove the bolts and the inner timing belt covers **(see illustrations 6.9a and 6.9b)**.

4  Remove the valve covers (see Section 4). **Caution:** *Do not pry between the cover and the camshaft housing. Both are aluminum and the sealing surfaces could be damaged. If the cover is stuck, tap on the edge with a small block of wood and a hammer.*

5  Remove the camshaft sensor (see Chapter 6).

6  On 2.2L models, working from the center out, gradually loosen the rocker arm bolts and remove rocker arm assembly **(see illustration)**. Loosen the inner bolts first and work out in an even pattern and lift the rocker arm assembly horizontally from the plane of the cylinder head. Store the rocker arm assembly with the bleeder holes facing up **(see illustration)**.

7  On 2.5L engines, loosen the camshaft bearing caps in small increments, working from the ends to the center **(see illustration)**. Remove the bearing caps and camshaft from the cylinder head. On 1997 and later models, be very careful not to drop the adjusting shims when removing the camshafts, store all the components in an organized manner **(see illustration)**.

8  On 2.5L engines, withdraw the lifters from the cylinder head.

9  On 2.2L engines, remove the cylinder head (see Section 10). The camshaft can then be withdrawn from the cylinder head after

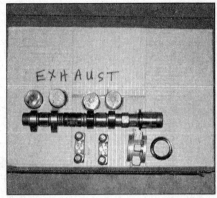

**9.7b Store the camshafts, bearing caps and lifters in an organized manner so the components can be returned to their original locations**

removing the seal retainer **(see illustrations)**. **Caution:** *Withdraw the camshaft carefully from the cylinder head, so that the lobes do not nick the journal bores.*

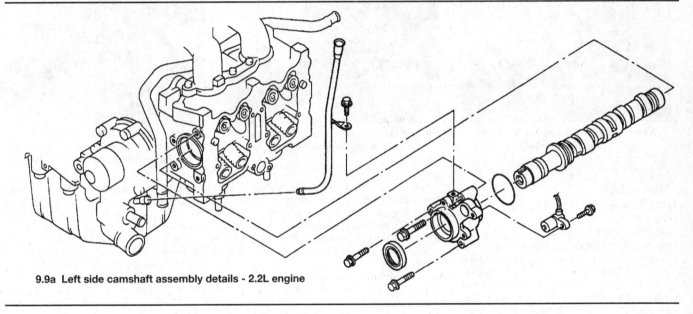

**9.9a  Left side camshaft assembly details - 2.2L engine**

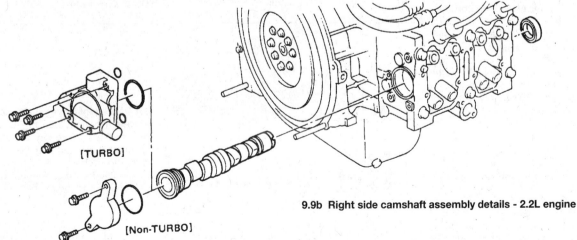

**9.9b  Right side camshaft assembly details - 2.2L engine**

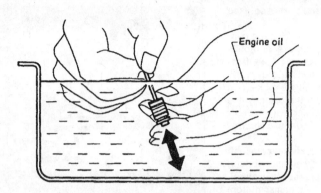

**9.10  After the lash adjuster is bled of all the air - leave it immersed in the oil until ready for installation**

**9.12  Check the lifter for scuffing, cracks or chips**

**9.14a  Measure the camshaft bearing journal diameter**

**9.14b  Measure the camshaft lobe at its greatest dimension . . .**

**9.14c  . . . and subtract the camshaft lobe diameter at its smallest dimension to obtain the lobe lift specification**

## Inspection

*Refer to illustrations 9.10, 9.12, 9.14a, 9.14b and 9.14c*

10   On 1990 through 1996 2.2L engines, remove the hydraulic lash adjusters from the rocker arms (if necessary). Keep the lash adjusters organized so they can be returned to their original locations. **Caution:** *Do not use pliers to remove the lash adjusters. If they are varnished and can't be removed easily, spray some carburetor cleaner around their bores and let it soak. The lash adjusters should come out by hand.* Check each lash adjuster for signs of wear. Place each adjuster in a pan of oil and push the plunger to "pump up" the hydraulic piston. Stand the lash adjuster on the bench after this treatment and depress the plunger by hand. If it depresses more than 0.5 mm, the adjuster should be replaced **(see illustration)**.

11   Check the pivot seat in each rocker arm and the pivot faces. Look for galling, stress cracks and unusual wear patterns. If the rocker arms are worn or damaged, replace them with new ones.

12   On 2.5L engines, inspect each lifter for scuffing and score marks **(see illustration)**.

13   Visually examine the camshaft lobes, journals, bearing caps, pivot points and metal-to-metal contact areas. Check for score marks, pitting and evidence of overheating (blue, discolored areas). If wear is excessive or damage is evident, the component will have to be replaced. Also check the front of the camshaft for wear where the seal rides.

14   Using a micrometer, measure camshaft journal diameter and lobe height **(see illustrations)**, and compare your measurements to this Chapter's Specifications. If the lobe height is less than the minimum allowable, the camshaft is worn and must be replaced.

15   On 2.2L engines, measure the inside diameter of each camshaft journal bore. If the oil clearance (bore diameter less the camshaft journal diameter) is greater than the Specifications, the cylinder head must be replaced. On 2.5L engines install the camshafts onto the cylinder head (with the lifters removed) and use Plastigage to determine the oil clearance.

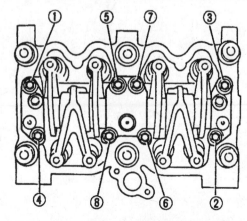

**9.17  When installing the rocker arm assembly on a 2.2L engine, first tighten bolts 1 through four until the assembly is seated on the cylinder head, next tighten bolts 5 through 8 to the specified torque, then tighten bolts 1 through 4 to the specified torque**

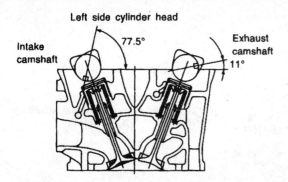

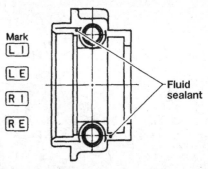

9.18b Apply a small amount of anaerobic sealant to the number one camshaft cap sealing surface - do not apply excessive sealant or it may flow into the oil seal area and oil leaks may develop

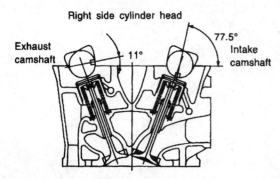

9.18a On 2.5L engines, it is important to install the camshaft at the correct angle to avoid damaging the valves during installation. The right side cylinder head camshafts do not have to be rotated after installation to align the timing marks. Only the left side intake camshaft will have to be rotated 80-degrees clockwise and the left side exhaust camshaft will have to be rotated 45-degrees counterclockwise after the camshafts have been installed

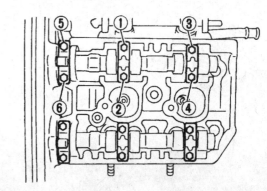

9.18c Camshaft bearing cap tightening sequence - 2.5L engine

## Installation

Refer to illustrations 9.17, 9.18a, 9.18b and 9.18c

16 Lubricate the camshaft journals and lobes with camshaft installation lubricant.

17 On 2.2L engines, install the camshafts carefully into the cylinder heads. Install the camshaft retainer with a new O-ring and tighten the bolts to the torque listed in this Chapter's Specifications. Install a new camshaft oil seal and install the cylinder heads onto the engine (see Section 10). Install the rocker arm assembly and tighten the bolts in the recommended sequence to the torque listed in this Chapter's Specifications (see illustration).

18 On 2.5L engines, lubricate the valve lifters with camshaft installation lubricant and install them in their original locations. Use camshaft installation lubricant to retain the shims (if equipped) and install them onto the valve lifters. Install the camshafts with the base circle of the camshaft lobes contacting the valve lifters (see illustration). Apply a small amount of anaerobic sealant to each number one cap sealing surface (see illustration). Lubricate the bearing surface of the camshaft caps with camshaft installation lubricant and install them in their original locations. Tighten the camshaft bearing cap bolts in the recommended sequence to the

torque listed in this Chapter's Specifications (see illustration). Install new camshaft oil seals.

19 Install the camshaft sprockets and timing belt (see Section 6). Check and adjust, if necessary, the valve clearance (see Chapter 1).

20 The remainder of the installation is the reverse of the disassembly process. Note: Be sure to use new gaskets on the valve covers.

21 Start the engine, listen for unusual valve train noses and check for oil leaks at the valve cover gaskets.

## 10 Cylinder heads - removal and installation

## Removal

Refer to Illustration 10.8

1 Relieve the fuel pressure (see Chapter 4), then disconnect the negative battery cable.

2 Drain the cooling system and remove the spark plugs (see Chapter 1).

3 Remove the timing belt, camshaft sprockets and inner timing belt covers (see Section 6). Remove the valve covers, rocker arm assembly (2.2L) or camshafts (2.5L) (see Section 9).

4 Disconnect the exhaust pipes from the cylinder heads. Note: Apply penetrating oil before beginning the procedure, and allow it

to soak-in on the exhaust bolts/nuts.

5 Refer to Section 5 and remove the intake manifold. Remove any hoses or brackets bolted to the cylinder heads, and on models equipped with air conditioning, remove the compressor bracket from the left cylinder head. Note: On some models, it may be necessary to remove the alternator and mount (see Chapter 5).

6 Remove the bottom stud/nuts of the front engine mounts (see Section 15), and raise the engine with a floor jack under the oil pan, using a block of wood to protect the oil pan.

7 On the left side, disconnect the EGR tube as described in Section 5, and unbolt the EGR bracket from the top-rear of the cylinder head.

8 Loosen the cylinder head bolts in the reverse of the tightening sequence (see the accompanying illustration and illustration 10.13).

9 Remove the cylinder heads and the old gaskets. Note: The block and cylinder heads are aluminum. Do not pry between the cylinder heads and the crankcase, as damage to the gasket sealing surfaces may result. Instead use a soft-faced hammer to tap the cylinder heads and break the gasket seal.

10 Cylinder head disassembly and inspection procedures are covered in detail in Chapter 2, Part B.

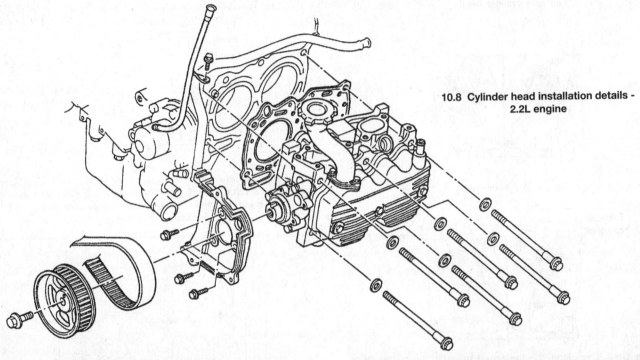

**10.8 Cylinder head installation details - 2.2L engine**

**10.11 Be careful not to gouge the aluminum surfaces of the cylinder head or block when removing the old gasket material**

**10.12 Place the new head gasket over the dowels (arrows) in the block - look for markings on the gaskets to indicate TOP or FRONT**

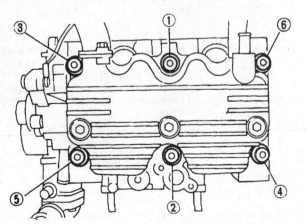

**10.13 Cylinder head bolt tightening sequence**

**11.4a Remove the oil pan bolts (arrows - not all bolts are visible in this view)**

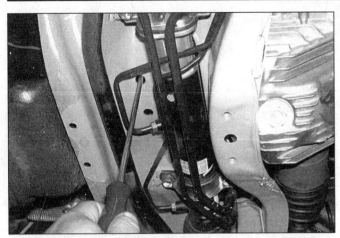

**11.4b Remove the rear oil pan bolts through the access holes in the crossmember**

**11.6 Remove the oil pump pickup tube bolts (arrows) and remove the pickup tube with the oil pan**

## Installation

*Refer to Illustrations 10.11, 10.12 and 10.13*

11   Clean the gasket mating surfaces of the cylinder heads and crankcase **(see illustration)** with lacquer thinner or acetone (they must be clean and oil-free).

12   Refer to the cylinder head gasket manufacturers instructions and if necessary, apply a thin, even coat of the recommended gasket sealant to both sides of the new head gasket then lay it in place **(see illustration)**.

13   Install the cylinder head(s). Lubricate the bolt threads and washers with engine oil, then install them hand-tight. Tighten the bolts in the recommended sequence to the torque listed in this Chapter's Specifications **(see illustration)**. **Caution:** *The cylinder head bolt tightening procedure must be followed exactly. Follow the steps as listed in this Chapter's Specifications. On the last two steps use a torque-angle meter (available at most automotive parts stores) or mark the bolt heads with white paint and tighten the bolts the required angle (90-degrees in each step) - DO NOT exceed a total of 180-degrees.*

14   The remainder of installation is the reverse of removal.

## 11   Oil pan - removal and installation

### Removal

*Refer to illustrations 11.4a, 11.4b and 11.6*

1   Disconnect the negative battery cable. Raise the vehicle and support it securely on jackstands (see Chapter 1).

2   Drain the engine oil and remove the oil filter (see Chapter 1).

3   Refer to Section 15 and remove the nuts from the engine mount studs at the chassis, then raise the engine two inches with an engine support fixture or hoist.

4   Remove the bolts securing the oil pan to the engine **(see illustrations)**.

5   Tap on the pan with a soft-faced hammer to break the gasket seal, then lower the oil pan from the engine. A thin putty knife can be inserted between the pan and the block to

break the gasket seal, but the block is aluminum, so do not use screwdriver or other sharp tool at the pan/block interface. **Caution:** *Before using force on the oil pan, be sure all the bolts have been removed.*

6   If the oil pump pickup tube interferes with oil pan removal, remove the pickup tube bolts and remove the oil pan and pickup tube from the vehicle **(see illustration)**.

### Installation

7   Using a gasket scraper, scrape off all traces of the old gasket from the engine block and the oil pan. Be especially careful not to nick or gouge the gasket sealing surfaces of the crankcases (they are made of aluminum and are quite soft).

8   Clean the oil pan with solvent and dry it thoroughly. Check the gasket sealing surfaces for distortion. If the oil pan is distorted at the bolt hole areas, straighten the flange by supporting it from below on a wood block and tapping the bolt holes with the rounded end of a ball-peen hammer. Wipe the gasket surfaces clean with a rag soaked in lacquer thinner or acetone.

9   Install a new O-ring on the pickup tube and place it in the oil pan.

10   Apply a thin coat of gasket sealant to the new oil pan gasket in place it carefully on the oil pan.

11   Raise the oil pan in position and install the pickup tube (be careful not to disturb the gasket). Install the oil pan to the engine block and tighten the bolts hand-tight. Working from the center of the pan out to the ends, tighten the bolts to the torque listed in this Chapter's Specifications. Do not overtighten the bolts or oil leaks may occur.

12   The remainder of installation is the reverse of the removal process. After refilling with fresh oil and installing a new filter, start the engine and check for oil leaks.

## 12   Oil pump - removal, inspection and installation

### Removal

*Refer to illustrations 12.1 and 12.5*

1   The oil pump is located in a housing mounted on the front of the engine and is driven directly by the crankshaft **(see illustration)**.

**12.1 Exploded view of the oil pump assembly**

1   *Inner rotor*
2   *Outer rotor*
3   *Oil seal*
4   *Oil pump housing*
5   *Oil pump cover*
6   *Plug*
7   *Washer*
8   *Relief valve spring*
9   *Relief valve*

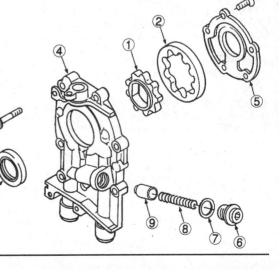

12.5  Remove the oil pump mounting bolts (arrows)

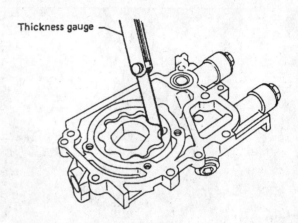

12.13a  Using a feeler gauge, measure the clearance between
the rotor tips

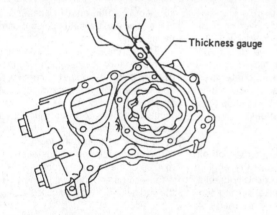

12.13b  Measure the clearance between the outer
rotor and the housing

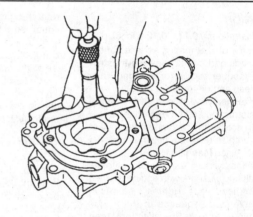

12.13c  Use a depth micrometer or a precision straightedge and
feeler gauge to measure the rotor-to-cover clearance (endplay)

2    Refer to Chapter 1 and drain the engine oil. Remove the oil filter.

3    Raise the front of the vehicle and place it on jackstands.

4    Refer to Section 6 and remove the timing belt and crankshaft sprocket.

5    Disconnect the electrical connector at the oil pressure sending unit. Remove the idler pulley(s). Remove the mounting bolts and the oil pump **(see illustration)**. Place a drain pan under the oil pump to catch the oil that will be spilled as the pump is removed.

### Inspection

*Refer to illustrations 12.13a, 12.13b and 12.13c*

6    Remove the pump cover from the back of the oil pump assembly.

7    Apply alignment marks to the inner and outer rotors so they can be installed in their original relationship to each other. Withdraw the rotors from the pump housing. Remove the relief valve plug, washer, spring and relief valve from the pump housing.

8    Clean the components with solvent, dry them thoroughly and inspect for any obvious damage.

9    Carefully check the interior surface of

the pump housing and the exterior surfaces of the rotors for score marks and damage.

10    Check the relief valve and spring for damage.

11    Check the pump housing for clogged oil passages, case cracks and damage.

12    If there is damage to any of the components, replace the oil pump assembly.

13    Install the rotors in the pump housing and measure the rotor tip clearance; the

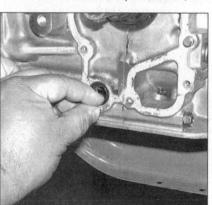

12.16  Be sure to install a new O-ring into
the oil pump housing or engine block

outer rotor-to-oil pump housing clearance; and the rotor-to-cover clearance (endplay) **(see illustrations)**. If any clearance exceeds the limit listed in this Chapter's Specifications, replace the oil pump assembly.

### Installation

*Refer to illustrations 12.16 and 12.17*

14    Lubricate the relief valve with clean

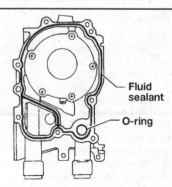

12.17  Apply a bead of anaerobic
sealant to the indicated area
on the oil pump housing

15.6a  Right side engine mount bolt (arrow)

15.5b  Left side engine mount bolt (arrow)

engine oil and install the relief valve, spring, washer and plug.

14   Lubricate the rotors with clean engine oil and install the rotors into the pump housing, aligning the matchmarks made previously. Install the rotor cover.

16   Be sure to replace the oil pump housing-to-engine block O-ring and install a new crankshaft oil seal **(see illustration)**.

17   Apply a bead of anaerobic sealant to the oil pump housing sealing surface **(see illustration)**. Install the oil pump onto the engine block and tighten the bolts to the torque listed in this Chapter's Specifications.

18   The remainder of installation is the reverse of the removal procedure. Refill the engine with fresh oil and install a new filter. Start the engine and check for proper oil pressure and oil leaks.

## 13   Flywheel/driveplate - removal and installation

### Removal

1   Remove the transaxle (see Chapter 7). If equipped with a manual transaxle, remove the clutch disc and pressure plate (see Chapter 8).

2   Remove the attaching bolts and separate the flywheel/driveplate from the crankshaft.

### Installation

3   Apply thread locking compound to the bolt threads. On automatic transmission models, align the small hole in the driveplate with the mark on the backplate. Hold the flywheel/driveplate in position and install the bolts. **Note:** *The flywheel/driveplate can only be installed in one position, since the bolt holes are not equally spaced. If the bolt holes do not align, rotate the flywheel/driveplate relative to the crankshaft until they all are in exact alignment.*

5   Hold the flywheel/driveplate so that it doesn't turn with an appropriate tool and

tighten the bolts (using a crisscross pattern) to the torque listed in this Chapter's Specifications.

6   Install the clutch disc and clutch cover assembly as described in Chapter 8, if equipped.

7   Install the transaxle (see Chapter 7).

## 14   Rear main oil seal - replacement

1   Refer to Chapters 7 and 8 for removal of the transaxle and clutch assembly.

2   Refer to Section 13 for removal of the flywheel or driveplate.

3   Pry the rear main oil seal from the back of the block with a screwdriver or a seal-removal tool. Be very careful not to nick the crankshaft seal surface with the tool.

4   Clean the seal bore and make sure the seal mounting surface is free of burrs.

5   Lubricate the new seal's inner lip with multi-purpose grease, and the outer diameter with clean engine oil.

6   Drive the new seal in place squarely with a seal driver, large socket, or section of pipe that's the same diameter as the outer diameter of the seal. Drive the seal to the original depth.

7   Install the flywheel/driveplate, clutch assembly (if equipped) and transaxle.

## 15   Engine mounts - check and replacement

### Check

1   Engine mounts seldom require attention, but broken or deteriorated mounts should be replaced immediately or the added strain placed on the driveline components may cause damage.

2   During the check, the engine must be raised slightly to remove the weight from the mounts. Disconnect the negative battery cable from the battery.

3   Raise the vehicle and support it securely on jackstands, then position the jack under the engine oil pan. Place a wood block between the jack head and the oil pan, then carefully raise the engine just enough to take the weight off the mounts.

4   Check the mounts to see if the rubber is cracked, hardened or separated from the metal plates. Sometimes the rubber will split right down the center. Rubber preservative may be applied to the mounts to slow deterioration.

5   Check for relative movement between the mount plates and the engine or frame (use a large screwdriver or pry bar to attempt to move the mounts). If movement is noted, lower the engine and tighten the mount fasteners.

### Replacement

*Refer to illustrations 15.6a and 15.6b*

6   Remove the engine mount locknut from the stud projecting through the crossmember **(see illustrations)**.

7   Raise the front of the engine high enough for the mount stud to clear the crossmember, but do not force the engine up too high. If anything interferes before the mounts are free, remove the component for clearance. Block the engine in this position with wood blocks.

8   Remove the two bolts securing the mount to the engine block and remove the mount.

9   Slip the new engine mount between the crossmember and the engine. Install the bolts into the engine block and tighten them securely.

10   Lower the engine slowly, making sure that both lower studs go through their respective holes in the crossmember. Remove the wood blocks and lower the engine to its original height and tighten the nuts securely. **Note:** *On vehicles equipped with self-locking nuts and bolts, replace the nuts with new ones whenever they are disassembled.*

# Notes

# Chapter 2  Part B
# General engine overhaul procedures

## Contents

## Specifications

### General

Bore and stroke
- 2.2L engine ... 3.82 x 2.95 inches
- 2.5L engine ... 3.92 x 3.11 inches

Displacement
- 2.2L engine ... 135 cubic inches
- 2.5L engine ... 149 cubic inches

Cylinder compression pressure
- 2.2L engine
  - Turbo ... 142 to 171 psi
  - Non turbo ... 156 to 185 psi
- 2.5L engine ... 137 to 176 psi

Oil pressure
- 2,000 rpm ... 14 to 26 psi
- 4,000 rpm ... 34 to 46 psi

### Cylinder head

Cylinder head gasket surface warpage limit ... 0.002 inch

## Valves

| | |
|---|---|
| Valve clearance | See Chapter 1 |
| Valve face angle | 45-degrees |

Margin width
  Standard
    2.2L

| | |
|---|---|
| Intake | 0.039 inch |
| Exhaust | 0.047 inch |

    2.5L

| | |
|---|---|
| Intake | 0.047 inch |
| Exhaust | 0.059 inch |

  Service limit

| | |
|---|---|
| Intake | 0.031 inch |
| Exhaust | 0.031 inch |

Stem diameter

| | |
|---|---|
| Intake | 0.2343 to 0.2348 inch |

  Exhaust

| | |
|---|---|
| 2.2L | 0.2341 to 0.2346 inch |
| 2.5L | 0.2343 to 0.2348 inch |
| Valve guide bore diameter | 0.2362 to 0.2367 inch |

Valve stem-to-guide clearance
  Standard

| | |
|---|---|
| Intake | 0.0014 to 0.0024 inch |
| Exhaust | 0.0016 to 0.0026 inch |
| Service limit | 0.006 inch |

## Valve springs

Free length
  2.2L

| | |
|---|---|
| 1990 through 1994 | 1.817 inches |
| 1995 through 1998 | 1.734 inches |
| 1999 | 2.1378 inches |
| 2.5L | 1.891 inches |

Out-of-square limit
  2.2L

| | |
|---|---|
| 1998 and earlier | 0.079 inch |
| 1999 | 0.094 inch |
| 2.5L | 0.083 inch |

## Valve lifters (2.5L engine only)

| | |
|---|---|
| Lifter diameter | 1.2976 to 1.2982 inch |
| Lifter bore diameter | 1.2990 to 1.2998 inch |

Lifter-to-bore clearance

| | |
|---|---|
| Standard | 0.0007 to 0.0022 inch |
| Service limit | 0.0039 inch |

## Cylinder bores

Diameter
  2.2L

| | |
|---|---|
| A | 3.8151 to 3.8155 inches |
| B | 3.8148 to 3.8151 inches |
| C | 3.8144 to 3.8148 inches |

  2.5L

| | |
|---|---|
| A | 3.9175 to 3.9179 inches |
| B | 3.9171 to 3.9175 inches |
| Taper limit | 0.0006 inch |
| Out-of-round limit | 0.0004 inch |
| Maximum increase in diameter (boring and honing) | 0.02 inch |
| Maximum difference in diameter between cylinders | 0.0012 inch |

## Pistons and rings

Piston diameter
  2.2L

| | |
|---|---|
| A | 3.8144 to 3.8148 inches |
| B | 3.8140 to 3.8144 inches |
| C | 3.8136 to 3.8140 inches |

  2.5L

| | |
|---|---|
| A | 3.9167 to 3.9171 inches |
| B | 3.9163 to 3.9167 inches |

Piston ring end gap
  Standard
    1990 through 1994
      Top ring
        Non-turbocharged engines ...................................... 0.0079 to 0.0138 inch
        Turbocharged engines ............................................. 0.0079 to 0.0098 inch
      Second ring .............................................................. 0.0146 to 0.0205 inch
      Oil ring ..................................................................... 0.0079 to 0.0276 inch
    1995 and later
      Top ring ................................................................... 0.0079 to 0.0138 inch
      Second ring
        1998 and earlier .................................................... 0.0079 to 0.0197 inch
        1999 ....................................................................... 0.0146 to 0.0205 inch
      Oil ring
        1998 and earlier .................................................... 0.0079 to 0.0276 inch
        1999 ....................................................................... 0.0079 to 0.0197 inch
  Service limit
    Top ring
      Non-turbocharged engines ...................................... 0.039 inch
      Turbocharged engines ............................................. 0.035 inch
    Second ring .............................................................. 0.039 inch
    Oil ring ..................................................................... 0.059 inch
Piston ring-to-groove clearance
  Top ring
    Standard .................................................................. 0.0016 to 0.0032 inch
    Service limit.............................................................. 0.006 inch
  Second ring
    Standard .................................................................. 0.0012 to 0.0026 inch
    Service limit.............................................................. 0.006 inch
Piston-to-cylinder bore clearance
  Standard...................................................................... 0.0004 to 0.0012 inch
  Service limit ................................................................. 0.002 inch
Piston pin-to-piston clearance
  Standard...................................................................... 0.0002 to 0.0006 inch
  Service limit ................................................................. 0.0008 inch

## Connecting rods

Side clearance
  Standard...................................................................... 0.0028 to 0.0130 inch
  Service limit ................................................................. 0.016 inch

## Crankshaft and bearings

Main bearing journal diameter
  1990 through 1994 ...................................................... 2.3616 to 2.3622 inches
  1995 through 1998 ...................................................... 2.3619 to 2.3625 inches
Connecting rod bearing journal diameter
  2.2L ............................................................................ 2.0466 to 2.0472 inches
  2.5L ............................................................................ 1.8891 to 1.8898 inches
Bearing journal taper limit................................................ 0.0027 inch
Bearing journal out-of-round limit
  2.2L ............................................................................ 0.0012 inch
  2.5L ............................................................................ 0.008 inch
Crankshaft runout limit ..................................................... 0.0014 inch
Crankshaft endplay
  Standard...................................................................... 0.0012 to 0.0045 inch
  Service limit ................................................................. 0.010 inch
Main bearing oil clearance
  Standard...................................................................... 0.0004 to 0.0012 inches
  Service limit ................................................................. 0.0016 inches
Connecting rod bearing oil clearance
  2.2L
    Non-turbocharged engine
      Standard .............................................................. 0.0006 to 0.0018 inch
      Service limit .......................................................... 0.0020 inch
    Turbocharged engine
      Standard .............................................................. 0.0010 to 0.0021 inch
      Service limit .......................................................... 0.0024 inch
  2.5L
    Standard .................................................................. 0.0004 to 0.0015 inch
    Service limit.............................................................. 0.0020 inch

## Crankcase

Mating surface warpage limit ................................................................... 0.002 inch
Surface grinding limit ............................................................................... 0.004 inch

## Torque specifications

**Ft-lbs** (unless otherwise indicated)

Engine-to-transaxle bolts ......................................................................... 34 to 40
Connecting rod nuts ................................................................................. 32 to 34
Crankcase bolts
  Short.......................................................................................................... 17 to 20
  Long ........................................................................................................... 35 to 37
Crankcase service hole plugs
  Plugs ......................................................................................................... 46 to 56
  Cover screws (left rear) ........................................................................... 48 to 60 in-lbs

## 1   General information

Included in this portion of Chapter 2 are the general overhaul procedures for the cylinder heads and internal engine components.

The information ranges from advice concerning preparation for an overhaul and the purchase of replacement parts to detailed, step-by-step procedures covering removal and installation of internal engine components and the inspection of parts.

The following Sections have been written based on the assumption that the engine has been removed from the vehicle. For information concerning in-vehicle engine repair, as well as removal and installation of the external components necessary for the overhaul, see Chapter 2A and Section 8 of this Chapter.

The Specifications included in this Part are only those necessary for the inspection and overhaul procedures which follow. Refer to Chapter 2, Part A for additional Specifications.

It's not always easy to determine when, or if, an engine should be completely overhauled, as a number of factors must be considered.

High mileage is not necessarily an indication that an overhaul is needed, while low mileage doesn't preclude the need for an overhaul. Frequency of servicing is probably the most important consideration. An engine that's had regular and frequent oil and filter changes, as well as other required maintenance, will most likely give many thousands of miles of reliable service. Conversely, a neglected engine may require an overhaul very early in its life.

Excessive oil consumption is an indication that piston rings, valve seals and/or valve guides are in need of attention. Make sure that oil leaks aren't responsible before deciding that the rings and/or guides are bad. Perform a cylinder compression check and an oil pressure check to determine the extent of the work required (see Sections 2 and 3). Also check the vacuum readings under various conditions (see Section 4).

Loss of power, rough running, knocking or metallic engine noises, excessive valve train noise and high fuel consumption rates may also point to the need for an overhaul,

especially if they're all present at the same time. If a complete tune-up doesn't remedy the situation, major mechanical work is the only solution.

An engine overhaul involves restoring the internal parts to the specifications of a new engine. During an overhaul, the piston rings are replaced and the cylinder walls are reconditioned (re-bored and/or honed). If a re-bore is done by an automotive machine shop, new oversize pistons will also be installed. The main bearings, connecting rod bearings and camshaft bearings are generally replaced with new ones and, if necessary, the crankshaft may be reground to restore the journals. Generally, the valves are serviced as well, since they're usually in less-than-perfect condition at this point. While the engine is being overhauled, other components, such as the distributor, starter and alternator, can be rebuilt as well. The end result should be a like new engine that will give many trouble free miles. **Note:** *Critical cooling system components such as the hoses, drivebelts, thermostat and water pump should be replaced with new parts when an engine is overhauled. The radiator should be checked carefully to ensure that it isn't clogged or leaking (see Chapter 3). If you purchase a rebuilt engine or short block, some rebuilders will not warranty their engines unless the radiator has been professionally flushed. Also, we don't recommend overhauling the oil pump - always install a new one when an engine is rebuilt.*

Before beginning the engine overhaul, read through the entire procedure to familiarize yourself with the scope and requirements of the job. Overhauling an engine isn't difficult, but it is time-consuming. Plan on the vehicle being tied up for a minimum of two weeks, especially if parts must be taken to an automotive machine shop for repair or reconditioning. Check on availability of parts and make sure that any necessary special tools and equipment are obtained in advance. Most work can be done with typical hand tools, although a number of precision measuring tools are required for inspecting parts to determine if they must be replaced. Often an automotive machine shop will handle the inspection of parts and offer advice concerning reconditioning and replacement. **Note:** *Always wait until the engine has been completely disassembled and all components,*

*especially the engine block, have been inspected before deciding what service and repair operations must be performed by an automotive machine shop. Since the block's condition will be the major factor to consider when determining whether to overhaul the original engine or buy a rebuilt one, never purchase parts or have machine work done on other components until the block has been thoroughly inspected. As a general rule, time is the primary cost of an overhaul, so it doesn't pay to install worn or substandard parts.*

As a final note, to ensure maximum life and minimum trouble from a rebuilt engine, everything must be assembled with care in a spotlessly-clean environment.

## 2   Oil pressure check

*Refer to illustrations 2.2 and 2.3*

1    Low engine oil pressure can be a sign of an engine in need of rebuilding. A "low oil pressure" indicator (often called an "idiot light") is not a test of the oiling system. Such indicators only come on when the oil pressure is dangerously low. Even a factory oil pressure gauge in the instrument panel is only a relative indication, although much better for driver information than a warning light. A better test is with a mechanical (not electrical) oil pressure gauge. When used in conjunction with an accurate tachometer, an engine's oil pressure can be compared to the Specifications at the beginning of this Chapter.

2    Locate the oil pressure indicator sending unit **(see illustration)**.

3    Remove the oil pressure sending unit and install a fitting which will allow you to directly connect your hand-held, mechanical oil pressure gauge **(see illustration)**. Use Teflon tape or sealant on the threads of the adapter and the fitting on the end of your gauge's hose.

4    Connect an accurate tachometer to the engine, according to the tachometer manufacturer's instructions.

5    Check the oil pressure with the engine running (full operating temperature) at the specified engine speed, and compare it to this Chapter's Specifications. If it's extremely low, the bearings and/or oil pump are probably worn out.

**2.2 The oil pressure sending unit (arrow) is located on top of the engine block near the alternator**

## 3 Cylinder compression check

*Refer to illustration 3.6*

1    A compression check will tell you what mechanical condition the upper end (pistons, rings, valves, head gaskets) of the engine is in. Specifically, it can tell you if the compression is down due to leakage caused by worn piston rings, defective valves and seats or a blown head gasket. **Note:** *The engine must be at normal operating temperature and the battery must be fully charged for this check.*

2    Begin by cleaning the area around the spark plugs before you remove them. Compressed air should be used, if available, otherwise a small brush or even a bicycle tire pump will work. The idea is to prevent dirt from getting into the cylinders as the compression check is being done.

3    Remove all of the spark plugs from the engine (see Chapter 1).

4    Block the throttle wide open.

5    Disable the ignition system by disconnecting the harness connector from the igni-

tion coil pack (see Chapter 5) and disable the fuel pump by disconnecting the fuel pump harness connector at the fuel pump (see Chapter 4).

6    Install the compression gauge in the number one spark plug hole **(see illustration)**.

7    Crank the engine over at least seven compression strokes and watch the gauge. The compression should build up quickly in a healthy engine. Low compression on the first stroke, followed by gradually increasing pressure on successive strokes, indicates worn piston rings. A low compression reading on the first stroke, which doesn't build up during successive strokes, indicates leaking valves or a blown head gasket (a cracked head could also be the cause). Deposits on the undersides of the valve heads can also cause low compression. Record the highest gauge reading obtained.

8    Repeat the procedure for the remaining cylinders, turning the engine over for the same length of time for each cylinder, and compare the results to this Chapter's Specifications.

9    If the readings are below normal, add some engine oil (about three squirts from a plunger-type oil can) to each cylinder, through the spark plug hole, and repeat the test.

10    If the compression increases after the oil is added, the piston rings are definitely worn. If the compression doesn't increase significantly, the leakage is occurring at the valves or head gasket. Leakage past the valves may be caused by burned valve seats and/or faces or warped, cracked or bent valves.

11    If two adjacent cylinders have equally low compression, there's a strong possibility the head gasket between them is blown. The appearance of coolant in the combustion chambers or the crankcase would verify this condition.

12    If one cylinder is about 20-percent lower than the others, and the engine has a slightly

rough idle, a worn exhaust lobe on the camshaft could be the cause.

13    If the compression is unusually high, the combustion chambers are probably coated with carbon deposits. If that's the case, the cylinder heads should be removed and decarbonized.

14    If compression is way down or varies greatly between cylinders, it would be a good idea to have a leak-down test performed by an automotive repair shop. This test will pinpoint exactly where the leakage is occurring and how severe it is.

15    Reconnect the coil and fuel pump and test drive the vehicle.

## 4 Vacuum gauge diagnostic checks

*Refer to illustrations 4.4 and 4.6*

1    A vacuum gauge provides valuable information about what is going on in the engine at a low cost. You can check for worn rings or cylinder walls, leaking head or intake manifold gaskets, incorrect throttle body adjustments, restricted exhaust, stuck or burned valves, weak valve springs, improper ignition or valve timing and ignition problems.

2    Unfortunately, vacuum gauge readings are easy to misinterpret, so they should be used in conjunction with other tests to confirm the diagnosis.

3    Both the gauge readings and the rate of needle movement are important for accurate interpretation. Most gauges measure vacuum in inches of mercury (in-Hg). The following references to vacuum assume the diagnosis is being performed at sea level. As elevation increases (or atmospheric pressure decreases), the reading will decrease. For every 1,000-foot increase in elevation above approximately 2,000 feet, the gauge readings will decrease about one inch of mercury.

4    Connect the vacuum gauge directly to

**2.3 Remove the alternator and the oil pressure sending unit and attach an oil pressure gauge - be sure the fittings you use have the same thread as the sending unit**

**3.6 A compression gauge with a threaded fitting for the spark plug hole is preferred over the type that requires hand pressure to maintain the seal - be sure to open the throttle valve as far as possible during the compression check**

**4.4 An inexpensive vacuum gauge can tell a lot about the tune and general condition of an engine - test it before beginning an overhaul**

intake manifold vacuum, not to ported (before throttle plate) vacuum **(see illustration)**. Be sure no hoses are left disconnected during the test or false readings will result.

5    Before you begin the test, allow the engine to warm up completely. Block the wheels and set the parking brake. With the transaxle in Park, start the engine and allow it to run at normal idle speed.

6    Read the vacuum gauge; an average, healthy engine should normally produce about 17 to 22 inches of vacuum with a fairly steady needle. Refer to the following vacuum gauge readings and what they indicate about the engine's condition **(see illustration)**:

7    A low, steady reading usually indicates a leaking gasket between the intake manifold and throttle body, a leaky vacuum hose, late ignition timing or incorrect camshaft timing. Eliminate all other possible causes, utilizing the tests provided in this Chapter before you remove the timing chain cover to check the timing marks.

8    If the reading is three to eight inches below normal and it fluctuates at that low reading, suspect an intake manifold gasket leak at an intake port.

9    If the needle has regular drops of about two to four inches at a steady rate, the valves are probably leaking. Perform a compression or leak-down test to confirm this.

10   An irregular drop or down-flick of the needle can be caused by a sticking valve or an ignition misfire. Perform a compression or leak-down test and read the spark plugs.

11   A rapid vibration of about four inches-Hg vibration at idle combined with exhaust smoke indicates worn valve guides. Perform a leak-down test to confirm this. If the rapid vibration occurs with an increase in engine speed, check for a leaking intake manifold gasket or head gasket, weak valve springs, burned valves or ignition misfire.

12   A slight fluctuation, say one inch up and down, may mean ignition problems. Check all the usual tune-up items and, if necessary, run the engine on an ignition analyzer.

13   If there is a large fluctuation, perform a compression or leak-down test to look for a weak or dead cylinder or a blown head gasket.

14   If the needle moves slowly through a wide range, check for a clogged PCV system, incorrect idle fuel mixture, throttle body or intake manifold gasket leaks.

15   Check for a slow return after revving the engine by quickly snapping the throttle open until the engine reaches about 2,500 rpm and let it shut. Normally the reading should drop to near zero, rise above normal idle reading (about 5 in-Hg over) and then return to the previous idle reading. If the vacuum returns slowly and doesn't peak when the throttle is snapped shut, the rings may be worn. If there is a long delay, look for a restricted exhaust system (often the muffler or catalytic converter). An easy way to check this is to temporarily disconnect the exhaust ahead of the suspected part and re-test.

## 5   Engine removal - methods and precautions

If you have decided that an engine must be removed for overhaul or major repair work, several preliminary steps should be taken.

Locating a suitable work area is extremely important. A shop is, of course, the most desirable place to work. Adequate work space, along with storage space for the vehicle, will be needed. If a shop or garage is not available, at the very least a flat, level, clean work surface made of concrete or asphalt is required.

Cleaning the engine compartment and engine before beginning the removal procedure will help keep tools clean and organized.

An engine hoist or A-frame will be needed. Make sure that the equipment is rated in excess of the combined weight of the engine and its accessories. Safety is of primary importance, considering the potential hazards involved in lifting the engine out of the vehicle.

If the engine is being removed by a novice, a helper should be available. Advice and aid from someone more experienced would also be helpful. There are many instances when one person cannot simultaneously perform all of the operations required when lifting the engine out of the vehicle.

Plan the operation ahead of time. Arrange for or obtain all of the tools and equipment you will need prior to beginning the job. Some of the equipment necessary to perform engine removal and installation safely and with relative ease are (in addition

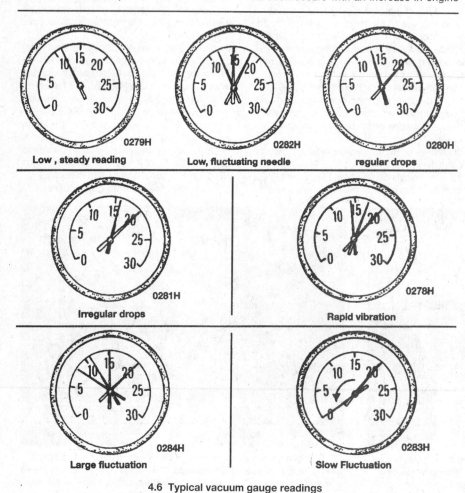

| Low , steady reading | Low, fluctuating needle | regular drops |
|---|---|---|
| 0279H | 0282H | 0280H |

| Irregular drops | Rapid vibration |
|---|---|
| 0281H | 0278H |

| Large fluctuation | Slow Fluctuation |
|---|---|
| 0284H | 0283H |

**4.6  Typical vacuum gauge readings**

**6.10 Remove the air conditioning compressor and set it to the side**

**6.17 Remove the power steering pump and set it to the side without disconnecting the lines**

to an engine hoist) a heavy duty floor jack, complete sets of wrenches and sockets as described in the front of this manual, wooden blocks and plenty of rags and cleaning solvent for mopping up spilled oil, coolant and gasoline. If the hoist is to be rented, make sure that you arrange for it in advance and perform beforehand all of the operations possible without it. This will save you money and time.

Plan for the vehicle to be out of use for a considerable amount of time. A machine shop will be required to perform some of the work which the do-it-yourselfer cannot accomplish due to a lack of special equipment. These shops often have a busy schedule, so it would be wise to consult them before removing the engine in order to accurately estimate the amount of time required to rebuild or repair components that may need work.

Always use extreme caution when removing and installing the engine. Serious injury can result from careless actions. Plan ahead, take your time and a job of this nature, although major, can be accomplished successfully.

## 6   Engine - removal

*Refer to illustrations 6.10, 6.17, 6.23a, 6.23b and 6.26*

**Warning 1:** *The air conditioning system is under high pressure. DO NOT loosen any fittings or remove any components until after the system has been discharged. Air conditioning refrigerant should be properly discharged into an EPA-approved container at a dealer service department or an automotive air conditioning repair facility. Always wear eye protection when disconnecting air conditioning system fittings.*

**Warning 2:** *Your vehicle is fuel injected and you must relieve the fuel system pressure before disconnecting any fuel lines. Gasoline is extremely flammable, so take extra precau-*

tions when you work on any part of the fuel system. Don't smoke or allow open flames or bare light bulbs near the work area. Don't work in a garage where a natural gas appliance (such as a water heater or clothes dryer) with a pilot light is present. Since gasoline is carcinogenic, wear latex gloves when there's a possibility of being exposed to fuel. If you spill any fuel on your skin, wash it off immediately with soap and water. Mop up any spills immediately; do not store fuel-soaked rags where they could ignite. The fuel system is under constant pressure, so if any fuel lines are to be disconnected, the fuel system pressure must be relieved first (see Chapter 4 for more information). When you do any kind of work on the fuel system, wear safety glasses and have a Class B fire extinguisher on hand.*

**Warning 3:** *Do not place any part of your body under the vehicle or the engine when the engine is supported only by a hoist. Keep your hands out of the engine compartment, away from areas between the engine and the body when raising or lowering the engine.*

**Note:** *The engine must be removed as a separate unit with the transaxle left in place in the vehicle. Do not attempt to remove the transaxle with the engine.*

1   Before starting this procedure, some method of lifting the engine must be devised. Ideally, a small crane mounted on wheels should be rented or borrowed. These are readily available and easy to use. An alternative would be to suspend a chain fall or cable hoist from the garage rafters or a framework fabricated from large timbers. ' Regardless of which type of hoist support is utilized, it must be strong enough to support the full weight of the engine. Do not take chances or cut corners here, as serious injury and damage to the engine and vehicle could result.

2   The following sequence of operations does not necessarily need to be performed in the order given. It is, rather, a checklist of everything that must be disconnected or removed before the engine can be lifted out of the vehicle. It is very important that all linkages, electrical wiring, hoses and cables be

removed or disconnected before attempting to lift the engine clear of the vehicle, so double-check everything thoroughly.

3   Scribe (or mark with paint) the location of the hood hinge brackets on the hood (to ensure proper alignment of the hood during reinstallation). Loosen and remove the bolts attaching the hood to the brackets and lift the hood carefully away from the vehicle (with the help of an assistant).

4   Remove the splash shields from the underside of the engine.

5   Relieve the fuel pressure (see Chapter 4).

6   Disconnect both cables from the battery (negative first, then positive).

7   Refer to Chapter 1 and drain the entire cooling system (including the engine), then remove the lower radiator hose.

8   Unplug the main cooling fan and the sub fan harness connectors (se Chapter 3).

9   Disconnect the hoses and wiring from the air cleaner and remove the air cleaner assembly. **Note:** *Plug the throttle body opening to keep dirt out.*

10   Refer to Chapter 3 and remove the engine cooling fans, radiator, radiator hoses, and the air conditioning compressor (if equipped) **(see illustration)**.

11   Refer to Chapter 5 and remove the alternator and mount, then the starter motor.

12   Remove the ground cable from the top-front of the left cylinder head.

13   Refer to Chapter 5 and remove the spark plug wires.

14   Refer to Part A of this Chapter and remove the intake manifold, tagging all of the vacuum, fuel and electrical connectors for ease of reassembly.

15   Disconnect the heater hoses at the bellhousing/transaxle parting line.

16   Remove the spark plug wire bracket from the top front of the engine.

17   If vehicle is equipped with power steering, refer to Chapter 10, disconnect the power steering pump mounts and place it carefully to the side of the engine compartment **(see illustration)**.

**6.23a Install the lifting chain on the eye bracket at the rear of the engine**

**6.23b Attach the chain to a solid mounting point on the front of engine block**

**6.26 Lift the engine from the vehicle using an engine hoist**

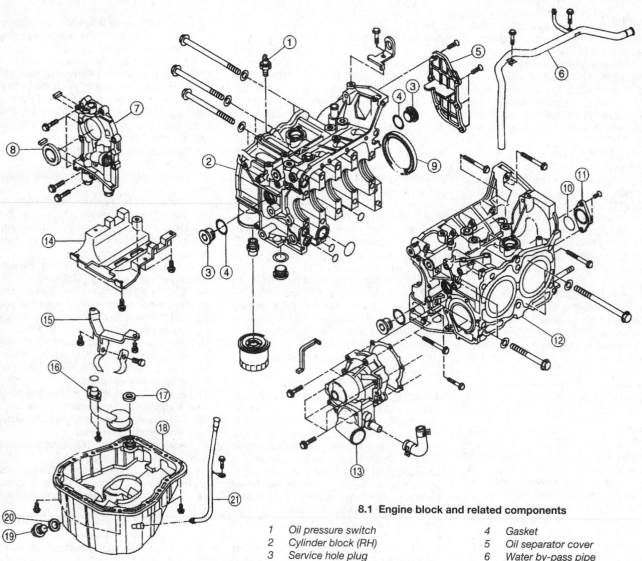

**8.1 Engine block and related components**

| | | | |
|---|---|---|---|
| 1 | Oil pressure switch | 4 | Gasket |
| 2 | Cylinder block (RH) | 5 | Oil separator cover |
| 3 | Service hole plug | 6 | Water by-pass pipe |

| | | | | | | | |
|---|---|---|---|---|---|---|---|
| 7 | Oil pump | 11 | Service hole cover | 15 | Oil strainer stay | 19 | Oil drain plug |
| 8 | Front oil seal | 12 | Cylinder block (LH) | 16 | Oil strainer | 20 | Gasket |
| 9 | Rear oil seal | 13 | Water pump | 17 | Gasket | 21 | Oil level gauge guide |
| 10 | O-ring | 14 | Baffle plate | 18 | Oil pan | | |

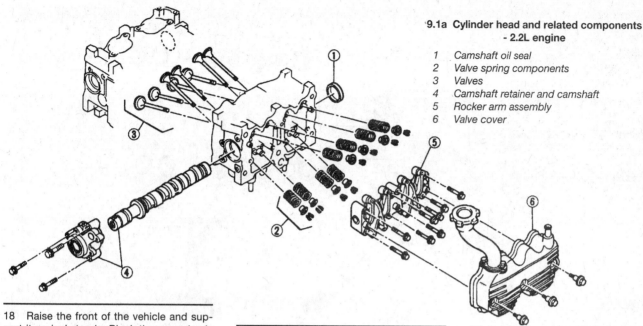

**9.1a Cylinder head and related components - 2.2L engine**

1   *Camshaft oil seal*
2   *Valve spring components*
3   *Valves*
4   *Camshaft retainer and camshaft*
5   *Rocker arm assembly*
6   *Valve cover*

18   Raise the front of the vehicle and support it on jackstands. Block the rear wheels to keep the vehicle from rolling.
19   Refer to Chapter 4 and disconnect the electrical lead from the oxygen sensor, then detach the front exhaust pipe from the head pipe flanges on each cylinder head.
20   If equipped with an automatic transaxle, refer to Chapter 7B for removing the torque converter-to-driveplate fasteners.
21   Remove the two upper engine-to-transaxle mounting bolts and loosen the two lower engine-to-transaxle mounting nuts. Remove the pitching stopper (brace) from the engine and body.
22   Refer to Part A of this Chapter and remove the front engine mount retaining nuts.
23   Attach the engine hoist chain or cables to the engine **(see illustrations)**, then support the transaxle with a hydraulic floor jack.
24   Take the slack out of the hoist chain or cables, then remove the two lower engine-to-transaxle mounting nuts.
25   Before proceeding, make sure that all wires, hoses, lines and brackets have been disconnected.
26   Very carefully lift the engine until the front engine mount studs clear the crossmember, then slowly move the engine forward and up **(see illustration)**. Be very careful not to allow the engine to strike or catch on the engine compartment components or the body as it is being removed.
27   With the engine clear of the vehicle, lower it to the shop floor and remove the flywheel/driveplate, then remove the flywheel housing.
28   Because of the unusual design of the Subaru engine, it may be more desirable to disassemble the engine on a large, suitably-strong workbench, rather than on a traditional engine stand. It is difficult to separate the crankcase halves on a stand, and when stripped of the exterior parts, the engine is light enough to maneuver around on the bench by hand.

## 7   Engine rebuilding alternatives

The do-it-yourselfer is faced with a number of options when performing an engine overhaul. The decision to replace the engine block, piston/connecting rod assemblies and crankshaft depends on a number of factors, with the number one consideration being the condition of the block. Other considerations are cost, access to machine shop facilities, parts availability, time required to complete the project and the extent of prior mechanical experience on the part of the do-it-yourselfer.

Some of the rebuilding alternatives include:

**Individual parts** - If the inspection procedures reveal that the engine block and most engine components are in reusable condition, purchasing individual parts may be the most economical alternative. The block, crankshaft and piston/connecting rod assemblies should all be inspected carefully. Even if the block shows little wear, the cylinder bores should be surface-honed.

**Crankshaft kit** - This rebuild package consists of a reground crankshaft and a matched set of pistons and connecting rods. Piston rings and the necessary bearings will be included in the kit. These kits are commonly available for standard cylinder bores, as well as for engine blocks which have been bored to a regular oversize.

**Short block** - A short block consists of an engine block with a crankshaft and piston/connecting rod assemblies already installed. All new bearings are incorporated and all clearances will be correct. The existing cylinder heads, camshafts, valve train components and external parts can be bolted to the short block with little or no machine shop work necessary.

**Long block** - A long block consists of a short block plus an oil pump, oil pan, cylinder heads, valve covers, camshaft and valve train

components, timing sprockets, and timing belts and covers on OHC models. All components are installed with new bearings, seals and gaskets incorporated throughout. The installation of manifolds and external parts is all that is necessary.

Give careful thought to which alternative is best for you and discuss the situation with local automotive machine shops, auto parts dealers or parts store countermen before ordering or purchasing replacement parts.

## 8   Engine overhaul - disassembly sequence

*Refer to illustrations 8.1*
To completely disassemble the engine, remove the following items in the order given **(see illustration)**:

*Engine external components*
*Flywheel/driveplate and housing*
*Timing belt and sprockets*
*Oil pan*
*Oil strainer/pick-up tube*
*Oil pump*
*Valve covers*
*Rocker arm assembly (2.2L)*
*Camshafts*
*Cylinder heads*
*Pistons*
*Separate the crankcase*
*Crankshaft and connecting rods*

## 9   Cylinder head - disassembly

*Refer to illustrations 9.1a, 9.1b, 9.2, 9.3a, 9.3b and 9.4*
**Note:** *Refer to Chapter 2A for the camshaft removal procedures.*

1   Cylinder head disassembly involves removal of the intake and exhaust valves and their related components **(see illustrations)**.

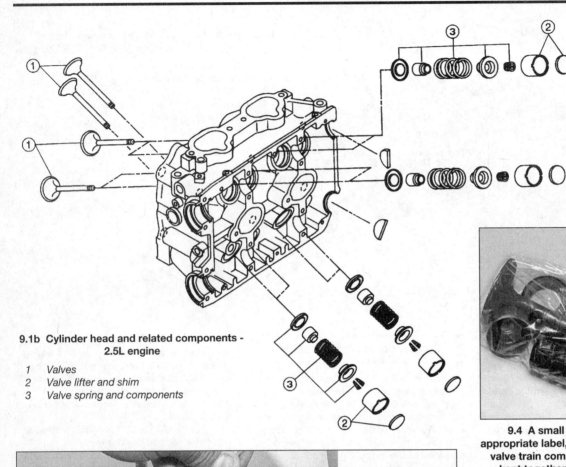

**9.1b Cylinder head and related components -
2.5L engine**

1　Valves
2　Valve lifter and shim
3　Valve spring and components

**9.4　A small plastic bag, with an
appropriate label, can be used to store the
valve train components so they can be
kept together and reinstalled in the
original position**

**9.3a　Use a spring
compressor with
the appropriate
adapter to
compress the
spring just enough
to remove the
keepers with
a magnet**

**9.3b　Typical valve
components**

1　Valve
2　Valve stem seal
3　Inner valve
    spring
4　Outer valve
    spring
5　Retainer

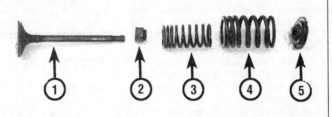

2　　Before the valves are removed, arrange
to label and store them, along with their
related components, so they can be kept
separate and reinstalled in the same valve
guides they were removed from. Use a separate plastic bag for the components for each
valve, including the valve lifter and shim (if
equipped), spring, retainer, seal, keepers and
valve **(see illustration)**.
3　　Compress the valve spring on the first
valve with a spring compressor, then remove
the keepers and the retainer from the valve
assembly **(see illustration)**. Carefully release
the valve spring compressor and remove the
springs, the seal, the spring seat and the
valve from the head **(see illustration)**. If the
valve binds in the guide (won't pull through),
push it back into the head and deburr the
area around the keeper groove with a fine file
or whetstone.
4　　Repeat the procedure for the remaining
valves. Remember to keep all the parts for
each valve in order so they can be reinstalled
in the same locations. Use a marked plastic
bag for each valve assembly **(see illustration)**.
5　　Once the valves have been removed
and safely stored, the head should be thoroughly cleaned and inspected. If a complete
engine overhaul is being done, finish the
engine disassembly procedures before
beginning the cylinder head cleaning and
inspection process.

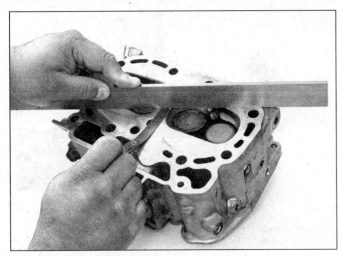

**10.12  Check the cylinder head gasket surface for warpage with a precision straightedge and feeler gauge**

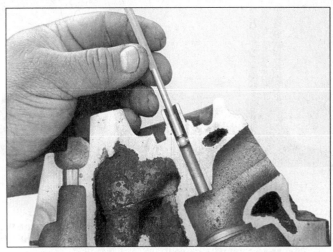

**10.14  Use a small-hole gauge inside the valve guide to check diameter at the top, middle and bottom of the guide**

## 10   Cylinder head - cleaning and inspection

1   Thorough cleaning of the cylinder head and related valve train components, followed by a detailed inspection, will enable you to decide how much valve service work must be done during the engine overhaul.

### Cleaning

**Note:** *Decarbonizing chemicals are available and may prove very useful when cleaning cylinder heads and valve train components. They are very caustic and should be used with caution. Be sure to follow the directions on the container.*

2   Scrape away any traces of old gasket material and sealing compound from the head gasket, the intake manifold and the exhaust pipe sealing surfaces. Work slowly and do not nick or gouge the soft aluminum of the head.

3   Carefully scrape all carbon deposits out of the combustion chamber areas. A hand-held wire brush or a piece of fine emery cloth can be used once the majority of deposits have been scraped away. Do not use a wire brush mounted in a drill motor, as the head material is soft and can be eroded away by the wire brush.

4   Remove any scale that may be built up around the coolant passages.

5   Run a stiff wire brush through the oil holes to remove any sludge deposits that may have formed in them.

6   It is a good idea to run an appropriate size tap into each of the threaded holes to remove any corrosion or thread sealant that may be present. Be very careful when cleaning aluminum threads; they can be damaged easily with a tap. If compressed air is available, use it to clear the holes of debris produced by this operation. **Warning:** *Always wear eye protection when using compressed air.*

7   Clean the exhaust pipe stud threads in a similar manner with an appropriate size die. Clean the rocker arm assembly bolt holes and the cylinder head stud holes with a wire brush.

8   Next, clean the cylinder head with solvent and dry it thoroughly. Compressed air will speed the drying process and ensure that all holes and recessed areas are clean.

9   Clean all the valve springs, keepers, retainers and spring seats with solvent and dry them thoroughly. Do the parts from one valve at a time, so that no mixing of parts between valves occurs.

10   Scrape off any heavy deposits that may have formed on the valves, then use a motorized wire brush to remove deposits from the valve heads and stems. Again, make sure the valves do not get mixed up.

### Inspection

#### Cylinder head

*Refer to illustrations 10.12 and 10.14*

11   Inspect the head very carefully for cracks, evidence of coolant leakage and other damage. If cracks are found, a new head is in order.

12   Using a straightedge and feeler gauge, check the head gasket mating surfaces for warpage **(see illustration)**. Lay the straightedge lengthwise, across the head and diagonally (corner-to-corner) and try to slip a feeler gauge under it at each location. See this Chapter's Specifications for the cylinder head warpage limit and use a feeler gauge of that thickness. If the feeler gauge can be inserted between the head and the straightedge, the head is warped. If the head is warped, it must be resurfaced at an automotive machine shop or replaced with a new one.

13   Examine the valve seats in each of the combustion chambers. If they are pitted, cracked or burned, the head will require valve service that is beyond the scope of the home mechanic.

14   Measure the inside diameters of the valve guides (at both ends and the center of

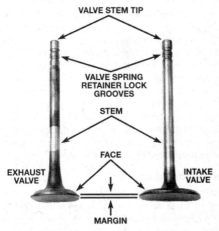

**10.15  Check for valve wear at the points shown here**

the guide) with a small hole gauge and micrometer **(see illustration)**. Record the measurements for future reference. These measurements, along with the valve stem diameter measurements, will enable you to compute the valve stem-to-guide clearance. This clearance, when compared to the Specifications, will be one factor that will determine the extent of the valve service work required. The guides are measured at the ends and at the center to determine if they are worn in a bell-mouth pattern (more wear at the ends). If they are, guide reconditioning or replacement is an absolute must.

#### Valves

*Refer to illustrations 10.15 and 10.16*

15   Carefully inspect each valve face for cracks, pits and burned spots **(see illustration)**. Check the valve stem and neck for cracks. Rotate the valve and check for any obvious indication that it is bent. Check the end of the stem for pits and excessive wear. The presence of any of the above conditions indicates a need for valve service by a professional.

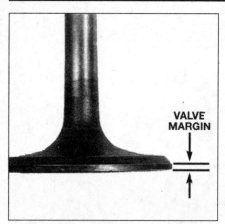

**10.16  The margin width on each valve must be as specified (if no margin exists, the valve cannot be reused)**

**10.18a  Measure the free length of each valve spring with a dial or vernier caliper**

**10.18b  Check each valve spring for squareness; replace the spring if bent**

16    Measure the width of the valve margin (on each valve) and compare it to the Specifications **(see illustration)**. Any valve with a margin narrower than specified will have to be replaced with a new one.

17    Measure the valve stem diameter. By subtracting the stem diameter from the valve guide diameter, the valve stem-to-guide clearance is obtained. Compare the results to the Specifications. If the stem-to-guide clearance is greater than specified, the guides will have to be reconditioned or replaced and new valves may have to be installed, depending on the condition of the old ones.

### Valve components

*Refer to illustrations 10.18a and 10.18b*

18    Check each valve spring for wear (on the ends) and pits. Measure the free length and compare it to the Specifications **(see illustrations)**. Any springs that are shorter than specified have sagged and should not be reused. Stand the spring on a flat surface and check it for squareness. Have the vehicle spring tension checked by an automotive machine shop.

19    Check the spring retainers and keepers for obvious wear and cracks. Any questionable parts should not be reused, as extensive damage will occur in the event of failure during engine operation.

### 11   Valves - servicing

1    Because of the complex nature of the job and the special tools and equipment required, servicing of the valves, the valve seats and the valve guides (commonly known as a "valve job") is best left to a professional.

2    The home mechanic can remove and disassemble the head, do the initial cleaning and inspection, then reassemble and deliver the head to a dealer service department or a reputable automotive machine shop for the actual valve servicing.

3    The dealer service department, or automotive machine shop, will remove the valves and springs, recondition or replace the valves

and valve seats, recondition or replace the valve guides, check and replace the valve springs, retainers and keepers (as necessary), replace the valve seals with new ones, reassemble the valve components and make sure the installed spring height is correct. The cylinder head gasket surface will also be resurfaced if it is warped.

4    After the valve job has been performed by a professional, the head will be in like-new condition. When the head is returned, be sure to clean it again, very thoroughly (before installation on the engine), to remove any metal particles and abrasive grit that may still be present from the valve service or head resurfacing operations. Use compressed air, if available, to blow out all the oil holes and passages. **Warning:** *Always wear eye protection when using compressed air.*

### 12   Cylinder head - reassembly

*Refer to illustrations 12.2a and 12.2b*

1    Regardless of whether or not the heads were sent to an automotive machine shop for valve servicing, make sure they are clean before beginning reassembly. If the heads were sent out for valve servicing, the valves

and related components will already be in place.

2    Install the valves in their original locations. Install new seals on the valve stem and guides. Lubricate the outside of the guides and press the seals over them, with an appropriate-size deep socket, until the tops of the seals are just seated fully **(see illustrations)**. Be careful not to cock or deform the seals as they are installed or they may not contact the valve stems properly.

3    Next, install the springs, the retainers and the keepers. **Note:** *The springs must be installed with the paint mark next to the retainer and the tightly wound coil end next to the head. Coat the valve stems with clean multi-purpose grease (or engine assembly lube) before slipping them into the guides. When compressing the springs with the valve spring compressor, do not let the retainers contact the valve guide seals.*

4    Repeat the procedure for the remaining head.

5    Support the heads (one at a time) on wood blocks so the valves cannot contact the workbench top and very gently tap each of the valve stem ends with a soft-faced hammer. This will help seat the keepers in their grooves.

**12.2a  Install the valve seal onto the valve stem**

**12.2b  Use a hammer and a deep socket to seat the seal on the valve guide**

**13.2 Remove the four access plugs (arrow indicates one) that allow piston pin removal**

## 13   Pistons - removal

*Refer to illustrations 13.2, 13.3, 13.4a, 13.4b*
**Note:** *Check for the presence of a wear ridge at the top of each cylinder. If a ridge has formed, it must be machined out before the pistons are removed. Special ridge reaming tools are available at tool and auto parts stores (follow the directions supplied with the tool).*

1    Temporarily install the crankshaft pulley bolt in the crankshaft front end so you can turn the crankshaft.

2    Remove the crankcase plugs from the four service holes with an Allen wrench for access to the piston pin circlips **(see illustration)**. **Note:** *These plugs may be difficult to remove. Soak them first with penetrating oil. If you have to hit the Allen wrench with a ham-*mer, make sure the wrench is fully into the plug to avoid rounding off the hexagonal opening.

3    To remove the piston pin circlips from a piston, position that piston at bottom dead center by turning the crankshaft, then insert needle-nose pliers through the service holes and remove the circlips **(see illustration)**. **Note:** *Use a small flashlight to see that the circlip is positioned directly at the access hole. You may have to make small movements of the crankshaft to align the piston just right.*

4    Remove the piston pins, using a special removal tool to pull the pins out through the service hole **(see illustrations)**.

5    Keep the pistons and pins together and mark the pistons so they can be reinstalled in their original locations.

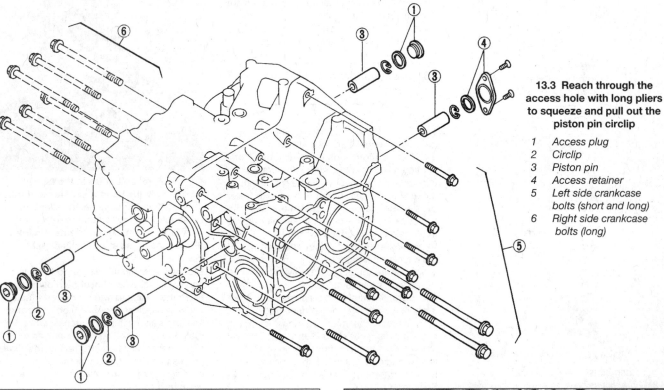

**13.3 Reach through the access hole with long pliers to squeeze and pull out the piston pin circlip**

1    *Access plug*
2    *Circlip*
3    *Piston pin*
4    *Access retainer*
5    *Left side crankcase bolts (short and long)*
6    *Right side crankcase bolts (long)*

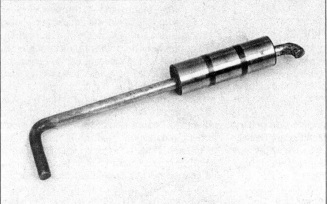

**13.4a  A special removal tool is needed to remove the piston pins - one can be fabricated from steel rod; bend the end to grab the rear edge and extract the pin**

**13.4b  If the pins are varnished from high mileage, you may have to use a slide hammer or hit the bent end of your homemade tool to force the pin out**

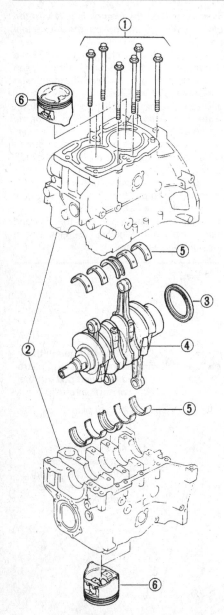

**14.3 Engine crankcase details**

1  *Long bolts*
2  *Crankcase halves*
3  *Rear main seal*
4  *Crankshaft and connecting rod*
   *assembly*
5  *Main crankshaft bearings*
6  *Piston*

6    The pistons can remain in the cylinder bores until the crankcase is separated and driven out with a wooden or plastic hammer handle, or they can be removed first.
7    If desired, remove the pistons before separating the crankcase as follows:

a) *Turn the crankshaft very slowly until the connecting rods push the pistons out slightly.*
b) *Insert the piston pins (clean and oil them first for easy installation) into the connecting rods (through the service holes),*

*then turn the crankshaft until the pin pushes the piston from the bore.*
c) *Pull the pistons out.*

## 14  Crankcase - separation

*Refer to illustrations 14.3*
1    In order to separate the crankcase halves, remove the bolts from the left side and loosen the right side bolts 1 to 2 turns.
2    Place the crankcase on a workbench with the right side (cylinder numbers 1 and 3) facing UP.
3    Remove the bolts from the right side of the crankcase **(see illustration)**.
4    Pull straight up on the right crankcase half to separate the two sections. You may have to tap the right crankcase section with a soft-faced hammer to break the gasket seal. Be careful when separating the halves, do not allow the connecting rods to fall and damage the crankcase. The crankshaft and connecting rod assembly will remain in the left half.

## 15  Crankshaft and connecting rods - removal

*Refer to illustration 15.2*
1    Separate the crankcase (Section 14) and remove the crankshaft rear oil seal.
2    Before lifting out the crankshaft/connecting rod assembly, check the crankshaft endplay. Gently pry or push the crankshaft all the way to the rear of the engine. Slip feeler gauges between the crankshaft and the thrust face of the center main bearing to determine the clearance (which is equivalent to crankshaft endplay) **(see illustration)**. If the endplay is greater than the specified limit, new main bearings *must* be installed when the engine is reassembled.
3    Carefully lift out the crankshaft and store it where it will not fall or get damaged.
4    Remove the main bearings from the case halves and store them in a clearly marked container so they can be reinstalled in their original locations (if they are reused).
5    Main bearing inspection is covered in Section 21.

## 16  Engine block - cleaning

*Refer to illustrations 16.6*
1    Using a gasket scraper, remove all traces of gasket material from the engine block. Be very careful not to nick or gouge the gasket sealing surfaces.
2    Remove all of the threaded oil gallery plugs from the block. The plugs are usually very tight - they may have to be drilled out and the holes re-tapped. Use new plugs when the engine is reassembled.
3    If the engine is extremely dirty it should be taken to an automotive machine shop to be steam cleaned or hot tanked.
4    After the block is returned, clean all oil holes and oil galleries one more time.

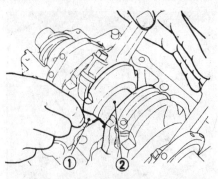

**15.2 Checking crankshaft end play**

1    *Feeler gauge*
2    *Crankshaft*

**16.6 All bolt holes in the block - particularly the head bolt holes and those that hold the case halves together - should be cleaned and restored with a tap (be sure to remove debris from the holes after this is done)**

Brushes specifically designed for this purpose are available at most auto parts stores. Flush the passages with warm water until the water runs clear, dry the block thoroughly and wipe all machined surfaces with a light, rust preventive oil. If you have access to compressed air, use it to speed the drying process and to blow out all the oil holes and galleries. **Warning:** *Wear eye protection when using compressed air.*
5    If the block isn't extremely dirty or sludged up, you can do an adequate cleaning job with hot soapy water and a stiff brush. Take plenty of time and do a thorough job. Regardless of the cleaning method used, be sure to clean all oil holes and galleries very thoroughly, dry the block completely and coat all machined surfaces with light oil.
6    The threaded holes in the block must be clean to ensure accurate torque readings during reassembly. Run the proper size tap into each of the holes to remove rust, corrosion, thread sealant or sludge and restore damaged threads **(see illustration)**. If possible, use compressed air to clear the holes of debris produced by this operation. Now is a good time to clean the threads on the head bolts and the main bearing cap bolts as well.
7    Apply non-hardening sealant (such as

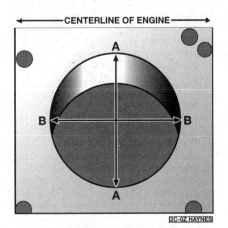

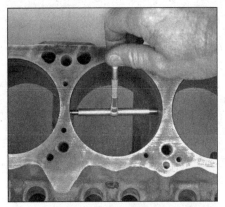

**17.4a  Measure the diameter of each cylinder at a right angle to the engine centerline (A), and parallel to engine centerline (B) - out-of-round is the difference between A and B; taper is the difference between A and B at the top of the cylinder and A and B at the bottom of the cylinder**

**17.4b  The ability to "feel" when the telescoping gauge is at the correct point will be developed over time, so work slowly and repeat the check until you're satisfied the bore measurement is accurate**

Permatex no. 2 or Teflon pipe sealant) to the new oil gallery plugs and thread them into the holes in the block. Make sure they're tightened securely.

8    If the engine isn't going to be reassembled right away, cover it with a large plastic trash bag to keep it clean.

## 17   Engine block - inspection

*Refer to illustrations 17.4a, 17.4b, 17.4c and 17.11*

1    Before the block is inspected, it should be cleaned as described in Section 16.
2    Visually check the block for cracks, rust and corrosion. Look for stripped threads in the threaded holes. It's also a good idea to

have the block checked for hidden cracks by an automotive machine shop that has the special equipment to do this type of work. If defects are found, have the block repaired, if possible, or replaced.

3    Check the cylinder bores for scuffing and scoring.

4    Check the cylinders for taper and out-of-round conditions as follows **(see illustrations)**:

5    Measure the diameter of each cylinder at the top (just under the ridge area), center and bottom of the cylinder bore, parallel to the crankshaft axis.

6    Next measure each cylinder's diameter at the same three locations perpendicular to the crankshaft axis.

7    The taper of the cylinder is the difference between the bore diameter at the top of the cylinder and the diameter at the bottom. The out-of-round specification of the cylinder bore is the difference between the parallel

and perpendicular readings. Compare your results to those listed in this Chapter's Specifications.

8    Repeat the procedure for the remaining pistons and cylinders.

9    If the cylinder walls are badly scuffed or scored, or if they're out-of-round or tapered beyond the limits given in this Chapter's Specifications, have the engine block rebored and honed at an automotive machine shop. If a rebore is done, oversize pistons and rings will be required.

10    If the cylinders are in reasonably good condition and not worn to the outside of the limits, and if the piston-to-bore clearance can be maintained properly, then they don't have to be rebored. Honing is all that's necessary (see Section 18).

11    A machined pad on the top front of the engine block is stamped with the crankshaft main journal size and the cylinder bore size grading marks **(see illustration)**. This information should be used when selecting main bearing inserts for the original crankshaft or standard sized pistons. If the original crankshaft was machined with an undersize journal, the undersize mark will be indicated; the standard bore size can be cross-referenced with the standard piston size grading listed in this Chapter's Specifications.

## 18   Cylinder honing

*Refer to illustrations 18.2a and 18.2b*

1    Prior to engine reassembly, the cylinder bores must be honed so the new piston rings will seat correctly and provide the best possible combustion chamber seal. **Note:** *If you don't have the tools or don't want to tackle the honing operation, most automotive machine shops will do it for a reasonable fee.*

2    Two types of cylinder hones are commonly available - the flex hone or "bottle

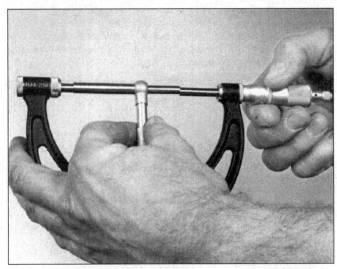

**17.4c  The gauge is then measured with a micrometer to determine the bore size**

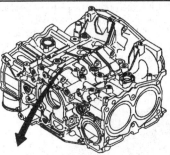

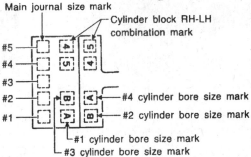

**17.11  The engine block is equipped with a stamped pad on the front top surface that indicates crankshaft main journal size and the cylinder bore size marks**

Main journal size mark

Cylinder block RH-LH combination mark

#5
#4
#3
#2 — #4 cylinder bore size mark
#1 — #2 cylinder bore size mark

#1 cylinder bore size mark
#3 cylinder bore size mark

brush" type and the more traditional surfacing hone with spring-loaded stones. Both will do the job, but for the less experienced mechanic the "bottle brush" hone will probably be easier to use and give better results. You'll also need some kerosene or honing oil, rags and an electric drill motor. Proceed as follows:

a) *Mount the hone in the drill motor, compress the stones and slip it into the first cylinder* **(see illustration)**. *Be sure to wear safety goggles or a face shield!*

b) *Lubricate the cylinder with plenty of honing oil, turn on the drill and move the hone up-and-down in the cylinder at a pace that will produce a fine crosshatch pattern on the cylinder walls. Ideally, the crosshatch lines should intersect at approximately a 60-degree angle* **(see illustration)**. *Be sure to use plenty of lubricant and don't take off any more material than is absolutely necessary to produce the desired finish.* **Note:** *Piston ring manufacturers may specify a smaller crosshatch angle than the traditional 60-degrees - read and follow any instructions included with the new rings.*

c) *Don't withdraw the hone from the cylinder while it's running. Instead, shut off the drill and continue moving the hone up-and-down in the cylinder until it comes to a complete stop, then compress the stones and withdraw the hone. If you're using a "bottle brush" type hone, stop the drill motor, then turn the chuck in the normal direction of rotation while withdrawing the hone from the cylinder.*

d) *Wipe the oil out of the cylinder and repeat the procedure for the remaining cylinders.*

3     After the honing job is complete, chamfer the top edges of the cylinder bores with a small file so the rings won't catch when the pistons are installed. Be very careful not to nick the cylinder walls with the end of the file.

4     The entire engine block must be washed again very thoroughly with warm, soapy water to remove all traces of the abrasive grit produced during the honing operation. **Note:** *The bores can be considered clean when a*

**18.2a  A "bottle brush" hone will produce better results if you've never honed cylinders before**

*lint-free white cloth - dampened with clean engine oil - used to wipe them out doesn't pick-up any more honing residue, which will show up as gray areas on the cloth. Be sure to run a brush through all oil holes and galleries and flush them with running water.*

5     After rinsing, dry the block and apply a coat of light rust preventive oil to all machined surfaces. Wrap the block in a plastic trash bag to keep it clean and set it aside until reassembly.

---

## 19  Connecting rods and bearings - removal

*Refer to illustration 19.1*

1     Before removing the connecting rods from the crankshaft, check the side clearance with a feeler gauge **(see illustration)**. If the side clearance is greater than specified, new connecting rods will be required for engine reassembly.

2     If the rods and caps are not numbered, use a center punch and hammer and carefully mark the connecting rods and caps so they can be reinstalled in the same position on the same crankshaft journal. Mark the connecting rod and cap at the front of the

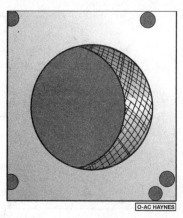

**18.2b  The cylinder hone should leave a smooth, crosshatch pattern with the lines intersecting at approximately a 60-degree angle**

crankshaft with one dot, the second connecting rod and cap with two dots and so on (both the rods and caps must be marked since they are going to be separated). Loosen the cap bolts on one connecting rod in three steps, carefully lift off the cap and bearing insert, then carefully remove the connecting rod and remaining bearing insert from the crankshaft journal. Temporarily reassemble the connecting rod, the bearing and the cap to prevent mixing up parts.

3     Repeat the procedure for the remaining connecting rods. Be very careful not to nick or scratch the crankshaft journals with the connecting rod bolts.

4     Without mixing them up, clean the parts with solvent and dry them thoroughly. Make sure the oil holes are clear.

5     Refer to Section 21 for the connecting rod bearing inspection procedures.

---

## 20  Crankshaft - inspection

*Refer to illustrations 20.1, 20.2, 20.5 and 20.7*

1     Remove all burrs from the crankshaft oil holes with a stone, file or scraper **(see illustration)**.

**19.1  Checking the connecting rod side clearance**

**20.1  The oil holes should be chamfered so sharp edges don't gouge or scratch the new bearings**

**20.2  Use a wire or stiff plastic bristle brush to clean the oil passages in the crankshaft**

**20.5 Measure the diameter of each crankshaft journal (mains and rods) at several points to detect taper and out-of-round conditions**

**20.7 If the seals have worn grooves in the crankshaft journals, or if the seal contact surfaces are nicked or scratched, the new seals will leak**

2    Clean the crankshaft with solvent and dry it with compressed air (if available). Be sure to clean the oil holes with a stiff brush **(see illustration)** and flush them with solvent.

3    Check the main and connecting rod bearing journals for uneven wear, scoring, pits and cracks.

4    Check the rest of the crankshaft for cracks and other damage. It should be magnafluxed to reveal hidden cracks - an automotive machine shop will handle the procedure.

5    Using a micrometer, measure the diameter of the main and connecting rod journals and compare the results to this Chapter's Specifications **(see illustration)**. By measuring the diameter at a number of points around each journal's circumference, you'll be able to determine whether or not the journal is out-of-round. Take the measurement at each end of the journal, near the crank throws, to determine if the journal is tapered.

6    If the crankshaft journals are damaged, tapered, out-of-round or worn beyond the limits given in the Specifications, have the crankshaft reground by an automotive machine shop. Be sure to use the correct size bearing inserts if the crankshaft is reconditioned. **Note:** *If the original crankshaft is to be installed, check the machined pad on the top front of the engine block for undersize markings and use this information to obtain the correct bearing inserts* **(see illustration 17.11)**.

7    Check the oil seal journals at each end of the crankshaft for wear and damage. If the seal has worn a groove in the journal, or if it's nicked or scratched **(see illustration)**, the new seal may leak when the engine is reassembled. In some cases, an automotive machine shop may be able to repair the journal by pressing on a thin sleeve. If repair isn't feasible, a new or different crankshaft should be installed.

8    Refer to Section 21 and examine the main and connecting rod bearing inserts.

## 21   Main and connecting rod bearings - inspection

*Refer to illustration 21.1*

1    Even though the main and connecting rod bearings should be replaced with new ones during the engine overhaul, the old bearings should be retained for close examination, as they may reveal valuable information about the condition of the engine **(see illustration)**.

2    Bearing failure occurs mainly because of lack of lubrication, the presence of dirt or other foreign particles, overloading the engine and/or corrosion. Regardless of the cause of bearing failure, it must be corrected before the engine is reassembled to prevent it from happening again.

3    When examining the bearings, remove them from the engine block, the connecting rods and caps and lay them out on a clean surface in the same general position as their location in the engine. This will enable you to match any noted bearing problems with the corresponding crankshaft journal.

4    Dirt and other foreign particles get into the engine in a variety of ways. It may be left in the engine during assembly, or it may pass through filters or breathers. It may get into the oil, and from there into the bearings. Metal chips from machining operations and normal engine wear are often present. Abrasives are sometimes left in engine components after reconditioning, especially when parts are not thoroughly cleaned using the proper cleaning methods. Whatever the source, these foreign objects often end up embedded in the soft bearing material and are easily recognized. Large particles will not embed in the bearing and will score or gouge the bearing and shaft. The best prevention for this cause of bearing failure is to clean all parts thoroughly and keep everything spotlessly-clean during engine assembly. Frequent and regular changes of engine oil, and oil filters, is also recommended.

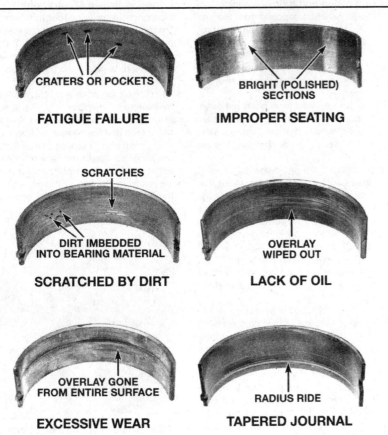

**21.1 Typical bearing failures**

5    Lack of lubrication (or lubrication breakdown) has a number of interrelated causes. Excessive heat (which thins the oil), overloading (which squeezes the oil from the bearing face) and oil leakage or throw-off (from excessive bearing clearances, worn oil pumps or high engine speeds) all contribute to lubrication breakdown. Blocked oil passages, which usually are the result of misaligned oil holes in a bearing shell, will also oil-starve a bearing and destroy it. When lack of lubrication is the cause of bearing failure, the bearing material is wiped or extruded from the steel backing of the bearing. Temperatures may increase to the point where the steel backing turns blue from overheating.

6    Driving habits can have a definite effect on bearing life. Too little throttle for the gear being used (or 'lugging' the engine) puts very high loads on bearings, which tends to squeeze out the oil film. These loads cause the bearings to flex, which produces fine cracks in the bearing face (fatigue failure). Eventually the bearing material will loosen in pieces and tear away from the steel backing. Short-trip driving leads to corrosion of bearings, as insufficient engine heat is produced to drive off the condensed water and corrosive gases produced. These products collect in the engine oil, forming acid and sludge. As the oil is carried to the engine bearings the acid attacks and corrodes the bearing material.

7    Incorrect bearing installation during engine assembly will lead to bearing failure as well. Tight-fitting bearings, which leave insufficient bearing oil clearance, result in oil starvation. Dirt or foreign particles trapped behind a bearing insert result in high spots on the bearing which lead to failure.

## 22   Engine overhaul - reassembly sequence

To assemble the engine, install the following items in the order given:

> Crankshaft and connecting rods
> Join the crankcase halves
> Pistons
> Cylinder heads
> Camshafts
> Rocker arm assembly (2.2L)
> Oil pump
> Timing belt and sprockets
> Valve covers
> Oil strainer/pick-up tube
> Oil pan
> Flywheel/driveplate and housing
> Engine external components

## 23   Pistons - inspection

*Refer to illustrations 23.4a, 23.4b, 23.10 and 23.11*

1    Before the inspection process can be carried out, the pistons must be cleaned and the old piston rings removed from the pistons.

**23.4a  The piston ring grooves can be cleaned with a special tool, as shown here . . .**

2    Using a piston ring installation tool, carefully remove the rings from the pistons. Do not nick or gouge the pistons in the process.

3    Scrape all traces of carbon from the top (or crown} of the piston. A hand-held wire brush or a piece of fine emery cloth can be used once the majority of the deposits have been scraped away. Do not, under any circumstances, use a wire brush mounted in a drill motor to remove deposits from the pistons. The piston material is soft and will be eroded away by the wire brush.

4    Use a piston-ring-groove cleaning tool to remove any carbon deposits from the ring grooves. If a tool is not available, a piece broken off the old ring will do the job (see illustrations). Be very careful to remove only the carbon deposits. Do not remove any metal and do not nick or scratch the sides of the ring grooves.

5    Once the deposits have been removed, clean the pistons with solvent and dry them thoroughly. Make sure that the oil return slots in the back sides of the oil ring grooves are clear.

6    If the pistons are not damaged or worn excessively, and if the cylinders are not rebored, new pistons will not be necessary. Normal piston wear appears as even vertical wear on the piston thrust surfaces and slight looseness of the top ring in its groove. New piston rings, on the other hand, should always be used when an engine is rebuilt.

7    Carefully inspect each piston for cracks around the skirt, at the pin bosses and at the ring lands.

8    Look for scoring and scuffing (on the thrust faces of the skirt), holes (in the piston crown) and burned areas (at the edge of the crown). If the skirts are scored or scuffed, the engine may have been suffering from overheating and/or abnormal combustion, which caused excessively high operating temperatures. The cooling and lubrication systems should be checked thoroughly. A hole in the piston crown, an extreme to be sure, is an indication that abnormal combustion (preignition) was occurring. Burned areas at the edge

**23.4b  . . . or a section of a broken ring**

of the piston crown are usually evidence of spark knock (detonation). If any of the above problems exist, the causes must be corrected or the damage will occur again.

9    Corrosion of the piston (evidenced by pitting) indicates that coolant is leaking into the combustion chambers and/or the crankcase. Again, the cause must be corrected or the problem may persist in the rebuilt engine.

10   Measure the piston ring-to-groove clearances by laying a new piston ring in each ring groove and slipping a feeler gauge in beside it (see illustration). Check the clearance at three or four locations around the groove. Be sure to use the correct ring for each groove; they are different. If the clearances are greater than specified, new pistons will have to be used and the cylinder rebored to accept them.

11   Check the piston-to-bore clearances by measuring the cylinder bores (see Section 17) and the piston diameter (see illustration). Make sure that the pistons and bores are correctly matched. Measure the pistons across the skirt, on the thrust faces (at 90-degree angle to the piston pin), about 1.5 to 2.0 inches from the top of the piston. Subtract the piston diameter from the corresponding

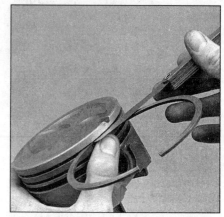

**23.10  Check the ring side clearance with a feeler gauge at several points around the groove**

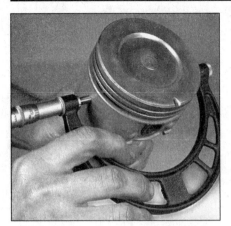

**23.11 Measure the piston diameter at a 90-degree angle to the piston pin and 1.5 to 2.0 inches from the top**

bore diameter to obtain the clearance. If *any* are greater than specified, the cylinders will have to be rebored and new pistons and rings installed. **Note:** *If standard size pistons can be used, check the machined pad on the top front of the engine block for cylinder bore size markings and use this information as a guide for selecting new pistons* **(see illustration 17.11)**.

12  Measure the piston pin outside diameter and the pin bore inside diameter. Subtract the two measurements to obtain the piston-to-piston pin clearance. If it is greater than specified, new pistons and possibly new pins must be installed.

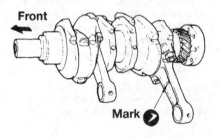

**24.3 The connecting rods must be installed with the mark facing the front of the crankshaft**

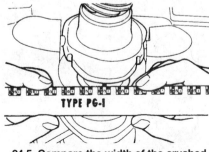

**24.5 Compare the width of the crushed Plastigage to the scale printed on the container to obtain the connecting rod bearing oil clearance**

## 24  Connecting rods and bearings - installation and oil clearance check

*Refer to illustrations 24.3 and 24.5*

1  Once the crankshaft and connecting rods have been cleaned and inspected and the decision has been made concerning bearing replacement, the connecting rods can be reinstalled on the crankshaft. **Note:** *If new bearings are being used, check the oil clearances before final installation of the connecting rods. If the clearances are within the specified limits, proceed with the installation. Never assume that the clearances are correct even though new bearings are involved.*

2  Make sure the bearing faces and backs are perfectly clean, then fit them to the connecting rod and cap. The tab on each bearing must be engaged in the recess in the cap or connecting rod.

3  Clean the number one connecting rod journal on the crankshaft, then slip the number one connecting rod into place. Make sure the mark on the connecting rod is facing the front of the crankshaft **(see illustration)**.

4  Apply a length of Plastigage to the crankshaft journal, just off center. Gently install the connecting rod cap in place, without turning the connecting rod on the journal. Make sure the mating mark on the cap is on the same side as the mark on the connecting rod. Tighten the connecting rod bolts to the torque listed in this Chapter's Specifications.

5  Remove the connecting rod bolts without allowing the connecting rod to turn on the journal, then remove the cap. Examine the Plastigage and compare its width to the scale on the Plastigage package **(see illustration)**. If the clearance is within Specifications, proceed with checking the other three connecting rods.

6  If the connecting rod clearances are all within Specifications, lubricate both halves of the bearings of connecting rod number 1 with moly-based assembly lube, and install the connecting rod bolts and tighten them to the specified torque, working up to it in three steps.

7  Repeat the procedure for the remaining

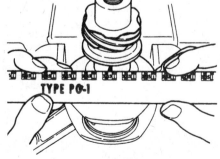

**25.9 Compare the width of the crushed Plastigage to the scale on the package to determine the main bearing oil clearance**

connecting rods: do not mix up the connecting rods and caps and do not install the connecting rods backwards.

8  After the connecting rods have been installed, rotate them by hand and check for any obvious binding.

9  As a final step, the connecting rod side clearance must be rechecked. Slide each connecting rod to one side of the journal and slip a feeler gauge between the side of each connecting rod and the crankshaft throw. Be sure to compare the measured clearance to the Specifications to make sure they are all correct.

## 25  Crankshaft and main bearings - installation and oil clearance check

*Refer to illustrations 25.9, 25.12 and 25.13*

1  Before installation of the crankshaft, the main bearing oil clearance must be checked.

2  Position the left crankcase section on a workbench with the bearing saddles facing up. Wipe the main bearing surfaces of the crankcase with a clean lint-free cloth. They must be kept spotlessly clean.

3  Clean the back sides of the main bearing inserts and lay one bearing half in each main bearing saddle in the crankcase on the workbench and the other bearing half from each set in the corresponding location in the remaining crankcase section. Make sure the tab on the bearing insert fits into the recess in the crankcase. Do not hammer the bearings into place and do not nick or gouge the bearing faces. No lubrication should be used at this time.

4  Clean the faces of the bearings in the crankcase and the crankshaft main bearing journals with a clean, lint-free cloth. Once you are certain that the crankshaft is clean, carefully lay it in position in the crankcase section on the workbench.

5  Trim three pieces of Plastigage so that they are slightly shorter than the width of the main bearings and place one piece on each crankshaft main bearing journal, parallel with the journal axis.

6  Clean the faces of the bearings in the right crankcase, then carefully lay it in position. Do not disturb the Plastigage.

7  Install the crankcase bolts. Start with the bolts on the 1-3 cylinder side (right crankcase half) and tighten them in three steps to the specified torque **(see illustration 14.3)**. Do not rotate the crankshaft at any time during this operation.

8  Remove the bolts and carefully lift off the right crankcase section. Do not disturb the Plastigage or rotate the crankshaft.

9  Compare the width of the crushed Plastigage on each journal to the scale printed on the Plastigage container to obtain the main bearing oil clearances **(see illustration)**. Check the Specifications to make sure they are correct.

**25.12 Apply engine assembly lube to the main bearing inserts before final assembly**

**25.13 Install the crankshaft/connecting rod assembly onto the bearings in the left crankcase**

**26.3a Apply a bead of anaerobic sealant to the face of the right crankcase**

10   If the clearance is not correct. double-check to make sure that you have the right size bearing inserts. Also, recheck the crankshaft main bearing journal diameters and make sure that no dirt or oil was between the bearing inserts and the main bearing caps or the block when the clearance was measured.
11   Be sure to remove all traces of the Plastigage from the bearing faces and/or journals. To prevent damage to the bearing surfaces, use a wood or plastic tool.
12   Carefully lift the crankshaft out of the crankcase. Clean the bearing faces, then apply a thin layer of engine assembly lube to each of the bearing faces in both crankcase sections **(see illustration)**. Be sure to coat the thrust bearing faces as well.
13   Carefully lay the crankshaft in the left crankcase section. Make sure the connecting rods are directed into the cylinder bores **(see illustration)**.
14   Refer to Section 26 and rejoin the two crankcase sections.

## 26   Crankcase - reassembly

*Refer to illustrations 26.3a and 26.3b*
1   Clean the block mating surfaces with lacquer thinner or acetone (they must be clean and oil-free).
2   Install the O-ring and backup ring **(see illustration 8.1)** in the left crankcase section.
3   Apply a thin layer of anaerobic sealant to the crankcase mating surfaces **(see illustrations)**.
4   Carefully lower the right crankcase section into position on the left crankcase and install the right-side bolts, tightening them to approximately 14 to 22 ft-lbs. Reposition the engine block horizontally and install the left-side bolts. First tighten the right-side bolts to the torque listed in this Chapter's Specifications in three steps starting with the center bolts and working outward in a circular pattern. Now tighten the left-side bolts to the torque listed in this Chapter's Specifications in three steps starting with the center bolts

and working outward in a circular pattern. Follow the tightening sequence carefully to allow the crankcase halves to mate evenly and uniformly.
5   Install a new rear main oil seal into the crankcase. Apply a thin bead of RTV sealer to the perimeter of the oil separator cover and install the cover.
6   Be sure to install a new front oil seal in the oil pump housing (see Chapter 2 Part A).

## 27   Piston rings - installation

*Refer to illustrations 27.3, 27.4, 27.11, 27.13 and 27.16*
1   Before installing the new piston rings, the ring end gaps and clearances must be checked.
2   Lay out the pistons and the new ring sets so the rings will be matched with the same piston and cylinder during the end gap measurement and engine assembly.
3   Insert one ring at a time into its groove on the piston, and measure its clearance to the groove with a feeler gauge **(see illustration)**. Compare your measurement to the value listed in this Chapter's Specifications.
4   Insert the top (number one) ring into the first cylinder and square it up with the cylinder walls by pushing it in with the top of the piston. The ring should be near the bottom of the cylinder at the lower limit of ring travel. To measure the end gap, slip a feeler gauge between the ends of the ring **(see illustration)**. Compare the measurement to the value listed in this Chapter's Specifications.
5   If the gap is larger or smaller than specified, double-check to make sure that you have the correct rings before proceeding.
6   If the gap is too small, it must be enlarged or the ring ends may come in contact with each other during engine operation, which can cause serious damage to the engine. The end gap can be increased by filing the ring ends very carefully with a fine file. Mount the file in a vise equipped with soft jaws, slip the ring over the file so that the

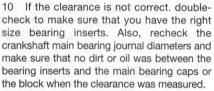

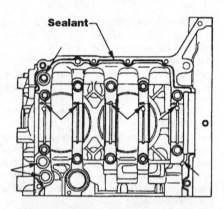

**26.3b Run the bead to the inside of the bolt holes to ensure proper sealing of the crankcase - DO NOT allow the sealant to flow into the O-ring grooves, oil passages or bearing grooves when the case is joined together!**

ends contact the file face and slowly move the ring to remove material from the ends. When performing this operation, file only from the outside in.
7   Use a fine file or whetstone to remove any burrs on the rings left from the filing procedure.

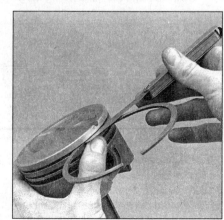

**27.3 Measuring piston ring-to-groove clearance with a feeler gauge**

**27.4  Checking piston ring end gap  with a feeler gauge**

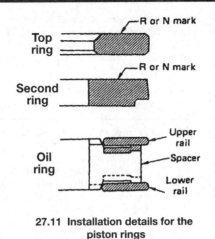

**27.11  Installation details for the piston rings**

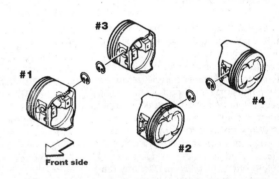

**27.13  The "R" or the "N" marks on the piston rings face the top of the piston**

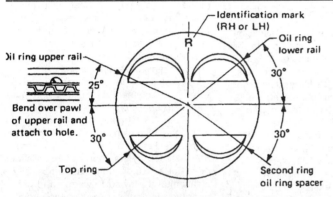

**27.16  Position the piston ring gaps exactly as shown before installing the pistons**

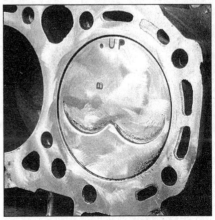

**28.2  Install a new piston pin circlip in the inner piston pin bore groove**

8    Repeat the procedure for each ring that will be installed in the first cylinder and for each ring in the remaining cylinders. Remember to keep rings, pistons and cylinders matched.

9    Once the ring end gaps have been checked/corrected, the rings can be installed on the pistons.

10    The oil control ring (lowest one on the piston) is installed first. It is composed of three separate components. Slip the oil ring spacer into the groove, then install the upper side rail. Do not use a piston ring installation tool on the oil ring side rails, as they may be damaged. Instead, place one end of the upper oil rail into the groove between the spacer and the ring land, hold it firmly in place and slide a finger around the piston while pushing the rail into the groove (above the spacer). Next, install the lower side rail in the same manner below the spacer.

11    After the three oil ring components have been installed, check to make sure that the upper and lower rails are positioned properly in relation to the spacer **(see illustration)**.

12    The number two (middle) ring is installed next. It can be readily distinguished from the top ring by its cross section shape, lack of chrome plating on the face and the fact that it is thicker than the top ring. Follow the instructions with the piston ring package for identification and proper orientation of the

new rings.

13    Use a piston ring installation tool and make sure that the identification mark is facing the top of the piston **(see illustration)**, then fit the ring into the middle groove on the piston. Do not expand the ring any more than is necessary to slide it over the piston.

14    Finally, install the number one (top) ring in the same manner. Make sure the identifying mark is facing up.

15    Repeat the procedure for the remaining pistons and rings. Be careful not to confuse the number one and number two rings.

16    When all rings on a piston are in place, make sure the gaps are staggered properly **(see illustration)**.

## 28    Pistons - installation

*Refer to illustrations 28.2, 28.5 and 28.6*

1    Position the engine on a workbench with crankshaft snout facing up.

2    Install <u>new</u> piston pin circlips in the inner piston pin bore groove of each piston **(see illustration)**. Make sure the piston is positioned correctly and the circlip is installed in the groove opposite the crankcase service hole when the piston is installed.

3    Make sure the ring end gaps are positioned correctly, then lubricate the skirt and rings with clean engine oil. Install a piston

ring compressor on the number one piston. Leave the skirt protruding about 1-inch to guide the piston into the cylinder. The rings must be compressed as far as possible.

4    Carefully rotate the crankshaft until the number one and two connecting rods are at bottom dead center. Align the connecting rods with the center of the cylinder.

5    Gently guide the number one piston into the cylinder. Make sure the word TOP or UP on the piston is facing the top of the engine as the piston is installed **(see illustration)**.

**28.5  The word UP or TOP must face the top of the engine as the piston is installed**

**28.6 Gently tap the piston into the bore while maintaining hand pressure to keep the ring compressor against the block - stop if resistance is felt**

Tap the exposed edge of the ring compressor so that it is contacting the crankcase around its entire circumference.

6    Carefully tap on the top of the piston with a soft-faced hammer **(see illustration)**. The piston rings may try to pop out of the ring compressor just before entering the cylinder bore, so keep some pressure on the ring compressor. Work slowly, and if any resistance is felt as the piston rings enter the cylinder, stop immediately. Find out what is hanging up and fix it before proceeding. Do not, for any reason, force the piston into the cylinder, as you will break a ring and/or the piston.

7    Push the piston in until the piston pin bore and the small end of the connecting rod are aligned in the service hole. **Note:** *Fabricate an alignment tool to insert into the service hole and align the connecting rod with the piston pin bore.*

8    Lubricate the piston pin with clean engine oil, then slip it through the service hole into the piston and connecting rod. If resistance is felt, do not force the pin. Instead, check to make sure the pin bore and connecting rod are aligned.

9    Install the outer circlip in the piston pin bore groove. **Caution:** *Make sure the circlip is seated properly in the groove or serious engine damage may result.*

10    Repeat the procedure for the number two piston. Apply gasket sealer the service hole plug gaskets and install the gaskets and plugs. Tighten the plugs to the torque listed in this Chapter's Specifications.

11    Turn the engine over (crankshaft snout facing down) and rotate the crankshaft until the number three and four connecting rods are at bottom dead center. Align the connecting rods with the center of the cylinder.

12    Repeat the piston and pin installation procedure for pistons three and four.

13    Apply gasket sealer to the service hole plug and cover gaskets and install the plug and cover. Tighten the plug and cover screws to the torque listed in this Chapter's Specifications.

## 29   Engine - installation

1    Apply grease to the splines of the transaxle mainshaft (manual transaxle equipped vehicles only).

2    Slowly and carefully raise the engine with the hoist and then lower it into the engine compartment while you tip the rear of the engine down towards the transaxle.

3    Align the engine crankshaft with the transaxle mainshaft. On manual transaxle models, turn the crankshaft pulley until the mainshaft is aligned with the clutch disc at the splines.

4    Attach the engine to the transaxle by installing the upper and then the lower engine-to-transaxle mounting bolts.

5    Make sure that the engine is properly aligned and seated with the transaxle. Do not use the bolts to force the components together. Tighten the bolts to the torque listed in this Chapter's Specifications.

6    Lower the jack supporting the transaxle and remove it from under the vehicle. Position the engine rubber mounts in place.

7    Lower the engine completely and remove the hoist from the area.

8    Raise the vehicle sufficiently to work underneath it and support it with jackstands.

9    Securely tighten all of the engine mounting nuts and bolts according to the torque listed in this Chapter's Specifications.

10    On automatic transaxle models, attach the torque converter to the driveplate as described in Chapter 7B, Section 9, Step 28.

11    Install the front exhaust pipe.

12    Now, lower the vehicle and install the engine pitching stopper as follows:

a)   *Attach the pitching stopper rod to the bracket on the engine, then tighten it at the body end.*

b)   *Tighten the rear nut on the pitching stopper so that 1/32 to 3/64 inch clearance is maintained between the rubber cushion and the washer.*

c)   *Attach a wrench to the rear nut on the engine side of the pitching stopper to prevent it from turning and tighten the front nut securely.*

13    Attach the clutch cable (manual transaxle) to the clutch release lever and adjust the cable (see Chapter 1).

14    The remainder of the installation is the reverse of the removal process.

15    Inspect the engine compartment and make sure that all hoses and wiring connec-tors are properly installed and connected.

16    Make sure that all mounting hardware is sufficiently tight.

17    Refer to Chapter 1 and adjust the engine drivebelts.

18    Refer to Chapter 1 and fill the engine and transaxle with the correct quantity and type of lubricants called for in the Specifications.

19    Make sure that the radiator is filled with new coolant.

## 30   Initial start-up and break-in after overhaul

1    Once the engine has been properly installed in the vehicle, double-check the engine oil and coolant levels. Disable the fuel pump by unplugging its electrical connector (see Chapter 4).

2    With the spark plugs out of the engine and the coil electrical connector (low voltage) unplugged, crank the engine over until oil pressure registers on the gauge.

3    Install the spark plugs, hook up the plug wires and reconnect the coil and fuel pump electrical connectors.

4    Start the engine. It may take a few moments, but the engine should start without a great deal of effort.

5    As soon as the engine starts, it should be set at a fast idle (to ensure proper oil circulation) and allowed to warm up to normal operating temperature. While the engine is warming up, make a thorough check for oil and coolant leaks.

6    After the engine reaches normal operating temperature, let it run for about 10 minutes then shut it off.

7    Recheck the engine oil and coolant levels. Also, check the ignition timing and the engine idle speed (refer to Chapter 1) and make any necessary adjustments.

8    Drive the vehicle to an area with no traffic, accelerate from 30 to 50 mph, then allow the vehicle to slow to 30 mph with the throttle closed. Repeat the procedure 10 or 12 times. This will load the piston rings and cause them to seat properly against the cylinder walls. Check again for oil and coolant leaks.

9    Drive the vehicle gently for the first 500 miles (no sustained high speeds) and keep a constant check on the oil level. It is not unusual for an engine to use oil during the break-in period.

10    At approximately 500 to 600 miles, change the oil and filter and recheck the valve clearances (if applicable).

11    For the next few hundred miles, drive the vehicle normally. Do not pamper it or abuse it.

12    After 2000 miles, change the oil and filter again and consider the engine fully broken in.

# Chapter 3
# Cooling, heating and air conditioning systems

## Contents

## Specifications

| | |
|---|---|
| Coolant type and capacity | See Chapter 1 |
| Thermostat | |
| Opening temperature | 169 to 176-degrees F |
| Fully open temperature | 196-degrees F |
| Radiator pressure cap | |
| Specified cap pressure | 11 to 14 psi |
| Test pressure | 10 psi |
| Refrigerant capacity | |
| R12 systems | 32.0 ounces |
| R134a systems | 24.0 ounces |

## Torque specifications

| | |
|---|---|
| Water pump-to-engine bolts | 84 to 120 in-lbs |
| Transmission oil line clamp-to-chassis | 72 to 120 in-lbs |
| Fan shroud-to-radiator | 48 to 72 in-lbs |
| Fan-to-electric motor nut | 24 to 48 in-lbs |
| Thermostat housing bolts | 48 to 60 in-lbs |
| Radiator mounting bolts | 72 to 120 in-lbs |
| Condenser mounting bolts | 60 to 108 in-lbs |
| Air conditioning lines-to-condenser | 72 to 132 in-lbs |
| Compressor mounting bolts | 18 to 24 ft-lbs |
| Air conditioning lines-to-compressor | 72 to 132 in-lbs |
| Air conditioning lines-to-evaporator | 14 to 20 ft-lbs |

## 1 General information

*Refer to illustration 1.1*

On all models, a cross-flow type radiator equipped with an electric-motor-driven fan is employed **(see illustration)**. With this system, cooling ability at idling speed, and warm-up characteristics, are improved. On models with air conditioning, a second fan is used in addition to the main cooling fan. This extra fan is called the radiator sub-fan. The radiator sub-fan is smaller than the main fan. The electric fan(s) are activated by the ECM in response to the temperature changes of the coolant in the engine block relayed by the coolant temperature sensor. The coolant temperature sensor also works in conjunction with the Electronic Fuel Injection system and Emission Control systems (refer to Chapters 4 and 6).

The radiator main cooling fan is mounted in a housing/shroud at the engine side of the radiator. It is designed to come on when the engine reaches a certain temperature, and shut off again when the engine cools down some, thereby keeping the engine in the desired operating temperature range.

The coolant temperature gauge on the dash is regulated by a coolant temperature switch located in the coolant pipe next to the ECT. The temperature gauge alerts the driver to the exact working temperature of the coolant inside the engine.

The system is sealed by a spring-loaded radiator cap, which, by maintaining pressure, increases the boiling point of the coolant. If the coolant temperature goes above this increased boiling point, the extra pressure in the system forces the radiator cap valve off its seat and exposes the overflow pipe or hose. The overflow pipe/hose leads to a coolant recovery system. This consists of a plastic reservoir, mounted to the left side of the radiator, into which the coolant that normally escapes due to expansion is retained. When the engine cools, the excess coolant is drawn back into the radiator by the vacuum created as the system cools, maintaining the system at full capacity. This is a continuous process and provided the level in the reservoir is correctly maintained, it is not necessary to add coolant to the radiator.

On models equipped with an automatic transaxle an oil cooler is built into the radiator to cool the automatic transmission fluid. Heated transmission fluid is circulated through the oil cooler and is cooled by the coolant, thus maintaining the fluid at an adequate temperature.

The heating system works by directing air through the heater core, which is like a small radiator mounted behind the dash. Hot engine coolant heats the core, over which air passes to the interior of the vehicle by a system of ducts. Temperature is controlled by mixing heated air with fresh air, using a system of flapper doors in the ducts, and a heater blower motor.

Air conditioning is an optional accessory, consisting of an evaporator core located under the dash, a condenser in front of the radiator, an accumulator/drier in the engine compartment and a belt-driven compressor mounted at the front of the engine.

## 2 Antifreeze - general information

*Refer to illustration 2.4*

**Warning:** *Do not allow antifreeze to come in contact with your skin or painted surfaces of the vehicle. Rinse off spills immediately with plenty of water. Antifreeze is highly toxic if ingested. Never leave antifreeze lying around in an open container or in puddles on the floor; children and pets are attracted by it's sweet smell and may drink it. Check with local authorities about disposing of used anti-*

**1.1 Typical cooling, heater and air conditioning systems underhood component locations**

| | | |
|---|---|---|
| 1 | Heater hoses | |
| 2 | Air conditioning refrigerant hose | |
| 3 | Air conditioning compressor | |
| 4 | Coolant reservoir | |
| 5 | Radiator cap | |
| 6 | Cooling fans | |
| 7 | Air conditioning condenser | |
| 8 | Upper radiator hose | |
| 9 | Receiver/drier | |

**2.4  An inexpensive hydrometer can be used to test the condition of your coolant**

freeze. *Many communities have collection centers which will see that antifreeze is disposed of safely. Never dump used antifreeze on the ground or pour it into drains.*

1    The cooling system should be filled with a water/ethylene glycol based antifreeze solution which will prevent freezing down to at least -20-degrees F (even lower in cold climates). It also provides protection against corrosion and increases the coolant boiling point. The engines in the vehicles covered by this manual have an aluminum block and heads. The manufacturer recommends that only coolant designated as safe for aluminum engine components be used.

2    The cooling system should be drained, flushed and refilled at least every other year (see Chapter 1). The use of antifreeze solutions for periods of longer than two years is likely to cause damage and encourage the formation of rust and scale in the system.

3    Before adding antifreeze to the system, check all hose connections. Antifreeze can leak through very minute openings.

4    The exact mixture of antifreeze to water which you should use depends on the relative weather conditions. The mixture should contain at least 50-percent antifreeze, but should

never contain more than 70-percent antifreeze. Consult the mixture ratio chart on the container before adding coolant. Hydrometers are available at most auto parts stores to test the coolant **(see illustration)**. Use antifreeze which meets specifications for engines with aluminum heads and blocks.

---

### 3    Thermostat - check and replacement

*Refer to illustrations 3.11 and 3.12*

1    The thermostat is located on the front of the engine block, directly below the water pump **(see illustrations 7.9a and 7.9b)**. The thermostat allows for quick warm-ups and governs the normal operating temperature of the engine.

### *Check*

2    If the thermostat is functioning properly, the temperature gauge should rise to the normal operating temperature quickly and then stay there, only rising above the normal position occasionally when the engine gets unusually hot. If the engine does not rise to normal operating temperature quickly, or if it overheats, the thermostat should be removed and checked or replaced.

3    Before condemning the thermostat, check the coolant level, cooling fans and temperature gauge (or light) operation.

4    If the engine takes a long time to warm up, the thermostat is probably stuck open. Replace the thermostat.

5    If the engine runs hot, check the temperature of the upper radiator hose. If the hose isn't hot, the thermostat is probably stuck shut. Replace the thermostat.

6    If the upper radiator hose is hot, it means the coolant is circulating and the thermostat is open. Refer to the *Troubleshooting* Section for the cause of overheating.

7    If an engine has been overheated, you may find damage such as leaking head gaskets, scuffed pistons and warped or cracked cylinder heads.

### *Replacement*

**Warning:** *Wait until the engine is completely cool before starting this procedure.*

8    Raise the front of the vehicle and support it securely on jackstands.

9    Drain the cooling system (see Chapter 1).

10    Place the drain pan under the thermostat housing. Loosen and slide back the hose clamp, then pull the radiator hose off the thermostat housing cover.

11    Remove the bolts and lift off the housing cover. You may have to tap the cover with a soft-faced hammer to break the gasket seal **(see illustration)**.

12    After the cover has been removed, note how the thermostat is installed and lift it out **(see illustration)**. If it is open when it is removed, it is defective and must be replaced with a new one.

13    To check the thermostat, submerge it in a container of water along with a thermometer. The thermostat should be suspended so it does not touch the container.

14    Gradually heat the water in the container with a hotplate or stove and check the temperature when the thermostat first starts to open.

15    Continue heating the water and check the temperature when the thermostat is fully open.

16    Lift the fully open thermostat out of the water and allow it to cool.

17    Compare the opening temperature and the fully open temperature to this Chapter's Specifications.

18    If these Specifications are not met, or if the thermostat does not open while the water is heated, replace it with a new one.

19    Clean the mating surfaces of the thermostat housing and cover. Do not nick or gouge the gasket sealing surfaces.

20    Install a new gasket on the thermostat, then place the thermostat into the housing with the proper end facing out **(see illustrations 7.9a and 7.9b)**. Make sure that the thermostat flange is properly seated in the recessed area of the housing.

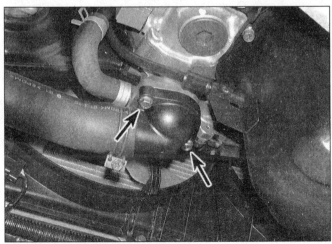

**3.11  Remove the two thermostat housing bolts (arrows) (2.5L engine shown)**

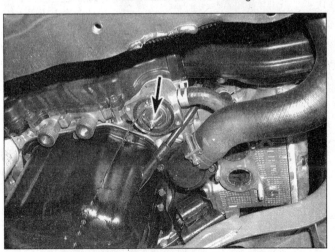

**3.12  Note the installed direction of the thermostat and remove it from the housing**

21　Carefully position the housing cover, install the bolts and tighten them to the torque listed in this Chapter's Specifications.

22　Slip the radiator hose onto the housing cover spigot, install the hose clamp and tighten it securely.

23　Refill the radiator with coolant (see Chapter 1). Start the engine and check for leaks around the thermostat housing and the upper radiator hose.

## 4　Cooling fan and relay - check, removal and installation

### *Check*

*Refer to illustrations 4.1, 4.2, 4.6a and 4.6b*

1　All models are equipped with an electric cooling fan and motor assembly **(see illustration)**. The cooling fans are actuated by a series of relays and the relays are controlled by the Electronic Control Module (ECM). The ECM receives information from the engine coolant temperature sensor (mounted on the engine block), and uses this information to determine when to operate the cooling fans. Models with air conditioning have an additional fan and motor assembly that is activated when the air conditioning is switched On. If the engine overheats because the cooling fans fail to operate, check the motor and relays as described in this Section. If further diagnosis is necessary, check the engine coolant temperature sensor as described in Chapter 6.

2　First check the fan fuse (see Chapter 12). If the fuse is good, check the fan motor for proper operation. Unplug the electrical connector and attach jumper wires to the two terminals in the connector half attached to the motor **(see illustration)**. **Caution:** *Make sure the jumper wires are not contacting each other.* **Note:** *Alternately attach the positive lead (+) to terminals 2 and 3 to activate the fan motor. One will be a low speed setting while the other is the high*

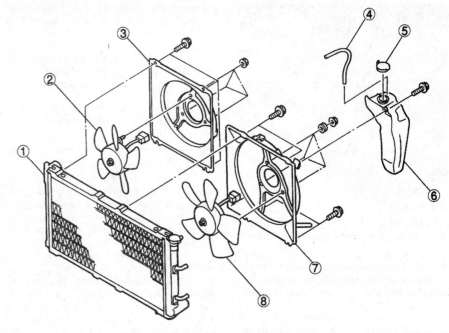

**4.1 Radiator cooling fan details**

| | | | |
|---|---|---|---|
| 1 | Radiator | 5 | Reservoir tank cap |
| 2 | Radiator sub-fan and motor | 6 | Coolant reservoir |
| 3 | Radiator sub-fan shroud | 7 | Radiator main fan shroud |
| 4 | Overflow hose | 8 | Radiator main fan and motor |

speed setting.

3　Connect the opposite ends of the jumper wires to the battery posts and see if the fan operates. **Caution:** *Keep your hands and the wires away from the cooling fan.*

4　Check the ground wire attached between the radiator and the chassis. If this wire is not well-grounded, the fan will not operate.

5　If the fan fails to operate when connected directly to battery power, replace the fan motor.

6　If the fan motor tested good in the previous steps but does not operate under normal

conditions, disconnect the connector and check for battery voltage at the connector with the engine hot. If battery voltage is not present at the connector check the fan relays mounted in the engine compartment fuse/relay box **(see illustrations)**. If the relay does not perform as described, replace it with a new part. **Note:** *1995 and later models are equipped with two main relays. Be sure to check both relays when diagnosing fan circuit problems. Refer to the relay designations stamped on the fuse/relay box for correct identification.*

7　If the relays tested good, check the

**4.2　Disconnect the harness connector (arrow) and apply battery voltage to the fan using a jumper wire from the battery**

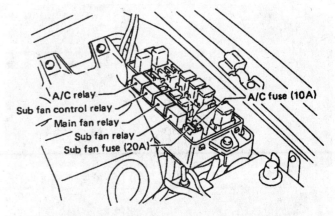

**4.6a　The cooling fan relays are located in the underhood fuse and relay box - refer to the inside of the fuse/relay box cover to locate the correct relays for the system**

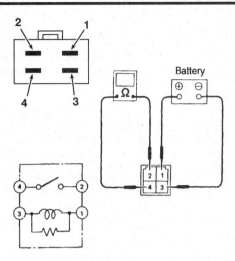

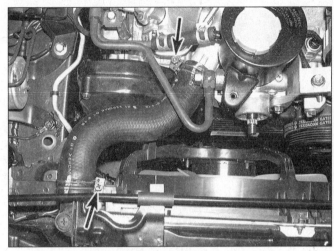

**4.6b  To test a relay, first check the resistance between terminals 1 and 3 - there should be approximately 100 ohms. Next, check the resistance between terminals 2 and 4 - there should be infinite resistance. Apply battery voltage to terminals 1 and 3 to activate the relay - continuity should now exist on terminals 2 and 4**

**5.3  Loosen the clamps and disconnect the upper radiator hose (arrows)**

engine coolant temperature sensor (see Chapter 6).

## *Removal and installation*

8    Disconnect the fan motor electrical connector(s).
9    Remove the fan motor shroud (with motor attached) from the radiator frame **(see illustration 5.7)**.
10   Remove the fan motor mounting bolts from the shroud and then remove the fan motor along with the fan.
11   If the fan motor is being replaced, remove the fan from the old motor and attach it to the new motor with the fan mounting nut.
12   Install the motor on the fan shroud and the shroud on the radiator frame.
13   Connect the electrical connector(s) to the motor and make sure that all of the mounting hardware is tight.

## 5    Radiator and coolant reservoir - removal and installation

**Warning:** *Wait until the engine is completely cool before starting this procedure.*

## *Radiator*

*Refer to illustrations 5.3, 5.6a, 5.6b and 5.7*
1    Drain the cooling system (see Chapter 1).
2    Disconnect the negative battery cable.
3    Disconnect the radiator hoses by loosening the hose clamps **(see illustration)**.
4    On automatic transaxle models, disconnect the hoses from the oil cooler in the radiator. **Note:** *Be prepared to catch any transmission fluid that may run out of these hoses when they are disconnected.*
5    Disconnect the fan motor wiring connector(s) and the radiator ground wire (see

Section 4).
6    Remove the radiator mounting bolts **(see illustrations)** and remove the radiator by lifting it up and out of the engine compartment. Radiator service and repair should be left to a reputable radiator shop.
7    Remove the cooling fan and shroud from the radiator **(see illustration)**. **Note:** *Models with air conditioning also have an additional fan assembly to remove.*
8    Installation is the reverse of removal. **Note:** *The bottom of the radiator sits in two rubber bushings on the body. Make sure the bushings are in place before tightening the upper radiator mounting bolts.*
9    Refill the cooling system (see Chapter 1). Run the engine until it is warm, while checking for leaks around each of the coolant hose attaching points. Allow the engine to cool completely before checking the coolant level again.

**5.6a  Remove the bolt from the left radiator mount (arrow) . . .**

**5.6b  . . . then remove the bolt (arrow) from the right radiator mount and pull the radiator up and out of the vehicle**

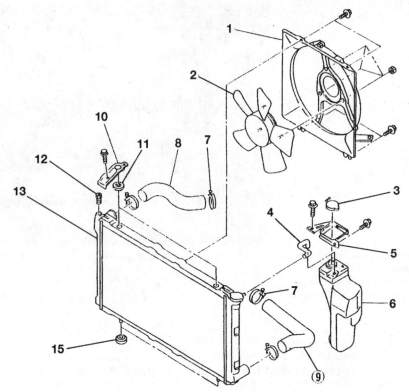

**5.7 Exploded view of a typical radiator and fan assembly**

1   Shroud
2   Fan and motor
3   Coolant reservoir cap
4   Overflow hose
5   Reservoir bracket
6   Coolant reservoir
7   Hose clamp
8   Radiator inlet hose
9   Radiator outlet hose
10   Radiator bracket
11   Upper cushion
12   Air vent plug
13   Radiator
15   Lower cushion
16   Radiator
17   Transmission fluid inlet hose
18   Transmission fluid outlet hose
19   Hose clamp
20   Transmission fluid pipe
21   Transmission fluid inlet hose
22   Transmission fluid outlet hose

— AT equipped model —

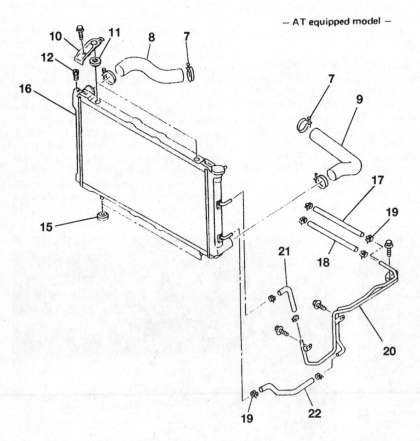

**5.11 On most models, the reservoir can be pulled straight up out of its bracket after removing the two mounting bolts (arrows)**

**6.3 If there's coolant leaking from the weep hole (arrow) the water pump must be replaced**

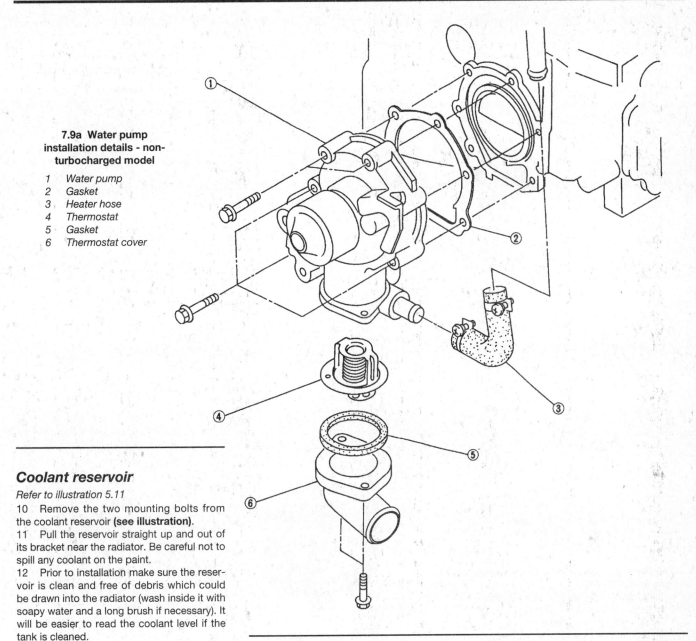

**7.9a  Water pump installation details - non-turbocharged model**

1   Water pump
2   Gasket
3   Heater hose
4   Thermostat
5   Gasket
6   Thermostat cover

## Coolant reservoir

*Refer to illustration 5.11*

10   Remove the two mounting bolts from the coolant reservoir **(see illustration)**.

11   Pull the reservoir straight up and out of its bracket near the radiator. Be careful not to spill any coolant on the paint.

12   Prior to installation make sure the reservoir is clean and free of debris which could be drawn into the radiator (wash inside it with soapy water and a long brush if necessary). It will be easier to read the coolant level if the tank is cleaned.

13   Installation is the reverse of removal.

## 6   Water pump - check

*Refer to illustration 6.3*

1   A failure in the water pump can cause serious engine damage due to overheating. If the pump is defective, it must be replaced with a new or rebuilt unit.

2   The two most common signs of water pump failure are coolant leakage and/or a howling or screeching sound. Don't mistake drivebelt slippage, which causes a squealing sound, for water pump bearing failure. If a squealing sound is heard, check the drivebelt tension and condition.

3   The water pump is driven by the timing belt and is located at the front of the engine. If you notice a puddle of coolant under the front of the vehicle, emanating from the timing belt cover, chances are that the water pump seal has failed. Water pumps are equipped with "weep" holes; if the seal fails, coolant will leak from the weep hole **(see illustration)**. To check this, the timing belt cover must be removed (see Chapter 2A).

4   If the water pump is making noise, the impeller shaft bearing has worn out. This can sometimes be confirmed by wiggling the water pump drive pulley (again, to check this the timing belt cover must be removed).

## 7   Water pump - replacement

*Refer to illustrations 7.9a, 7.9b and 7.11*
**Warning:** *Wait until the engine is completely cool before starting this procedure.*

1   Drain the cooling system (see Chapter 1).

2   Disconnect the radiator hose and the bypass hose(s) from the water pump.

3   Remove the fan assembly from the radiator (see Section 4).

4   Remove the drivebelt cover and remove the drivebelts (see Chapter 1).

5   Remove the timing belt (see Chapter 2A).

6   Remove the timing belt tensioner adjuster (see Chapter 2A) and the camshaft sensor (see Chapter 6).

7   Remove the sprocket(s) from the left side camshaft(s) (see Chapter 2A).

8   Remove the left side rear timing belt cover (see Chapter 2A).

9   Loosen the bolts to the water pump **(see illustrations)**, then separate the water pump and gasket from the engine. You may have to tap the pump gently with a soft-faced hammer to break the gasket seal.

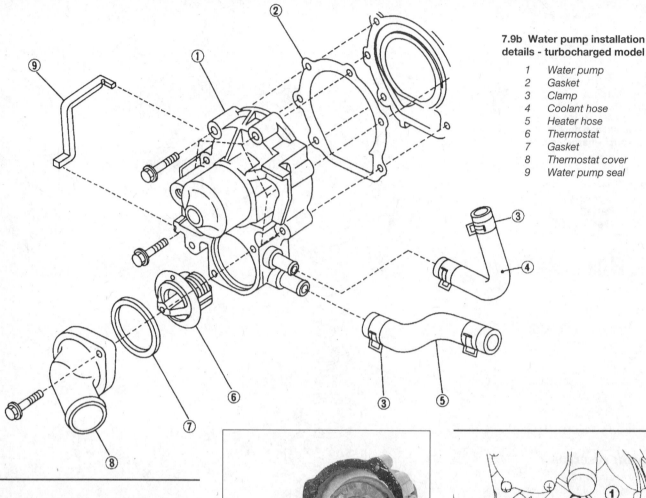

**7.9b  Water pump installation details - turbocharged model**

1   Water pump
2   Gasket
3   Clamp
4   Coolant hose
5   Heater hose
6   Thermostat
7   Gasket
8   Thermostat cover
9   Water pump seal

10   Scrape all traces of the old gasket and gasket sealer off of the engine. Do not nick or gouge the gasket sealing surfaces.

11   Coat both sides of a new gasket with gasket sealer **(see illustration)**, then install the new pump. Be sure to line up the bolt holes in the pump body and the gasket before placing the pump in position on the engine.

12   Install the pump mounting bolts and tighten them a little at a time to the torque listed in this Chapter's Specifications. Follow a criss-cross pattern when tightening the water pump bolts.

13   Attach the hoses to the pump and tighten the hose clamps securely.

14   Install the pump drivebelt and make the proper adjustments by referring to the appropriate Section in Chapter 1.

15   Refill the cooling system with coolant, start the engine and check for leaks and abnormal noises.

## 8   Coolant temperature sending unit - check and replacement

### *Check*

*Refer to illustration 8.1*

1   The coolant temperature indicator sys-

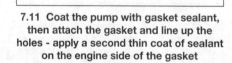

**7.11  Coat the pump with gasket sealant, then attach the gasket and line up the holes - apply a second thin coat of sealant on the engine side of the gasket**

tem is composed of a temperature gauge mounted in the dash and a coolant temperature sending unit mounted in the coolant pipe under the intake manifold **(see illustration)**.

2   If the temperature gauge indicates excessive temperature after running awhile, see the *Troubleshooting* section in the front of the manual. Check the coolant level, the wiring between the gauge and the sending unit and all the fuses that govern the circuit. Refer to the wiring diagrams at the end of Chapter 12.

3   If the temperature gauge indicates HOT as soon as the engine is started cold, disconnect the wire at the coolant temperature

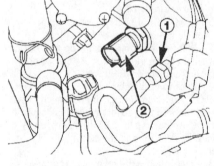

**8.1  The coolant temperature sensor (1) (used for the temperature gauge) and the engine coolant temperature sensor (2) (used by the computer) are located in the coolant pipe under the right-side intake manifold runner**

sending unit. If the gauge reading drops, replace the sending unit. If the reading remains high, the wire to the gauge may be shorted to ground or the gauge is faulty.

4   If the coolant temperature gauge fails to show any indication after the engine has been warmed up (approximately 10 minutes) and the fuses checked out OK, shut off the engine. Disconnect the wire at the sending unit and, using a jumper wire, connect the wire to a clean ground on the engine. Briefly turn on the ignition without starting the

engine. If the gauge now indicates Hot, replace the sending unit.

5    If the gauge fails to respond, the circuit may be open or the gauge may be faulty - see Chapter 12 for additional information.

### Replacement

**Warning:** *Wait until the engine is completely cool before beginning this procedure.*

6    Prepare the new sending unit by applying Teflon tape or thread sealant to the threads.

7    Disconnect the wiring connector from the sending unit.

8    Using a deep socket or a wrench, remove the sending unit.

9    Install the new unit as quickly as possible and tighten it securely. Be prepared for coolant spillage.

10    Reconnect the wiring connector, check the coolant level (see Chapter 1) and check for coolant leakage and proper gauge function.

---

### 9    Heater and air conditioning blower motor and circuit - check and replacement

**Warning:** *Some models covered by this manual are equipped with airbags. Always disconnect the negative battery cable and wait at least one minute before working in the vicinity of the impact sensors, steering column or instrument panel to avoid the possibility of accidental deployment of the airbag, which could cause personal injury (see Chapter 12).*

### Check

*Refer to illustration 9.6a, 9.6b and 9.8*

1    Current is supplied to the blower motor through the blower relay. The blower relay is controlled by the mode switch on the control assembly. The blower motor speed is controlled by the blower switch, which routes current through the various resistors contained in the blower resistor assembly. The blower resistor and blower switch are on the ground side of the blower motor circuit. Refer to the wiring diagrams at the end of Chapter 12 for additional information. Check the fuse and all connections in the circuit for looseness and corrosion. Make sure the battery is fully charged.

2    With the transmission in Park (automatic) or Neutral (manual) and the parking brake securely set, turn the ignition switch to ON (engine not running).

3    Switch the heater controls to FLOOR and the blower speed to HI. Listen at the ducts to hear if the blower is operating. If it is, then switch the blower speed to LO and listen again. Try all the speeds.

4    If the blower motor does not operate at any speed, disconnect the electrical connector at the blower motor, turn the ignition key ON (engine not running) and check for battery voltage. If battery voltage is not present, there is a problem in the blower motor relay

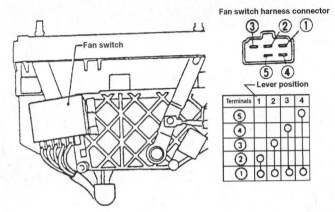

**9.6a  Check for continuity between the designated terminals - 1990 through 1994 models**

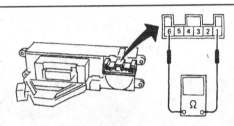

| Switch position | Terminals | | | | | |
|---|---|---|---|---|---|---|
| | 1 | 2 | 3 | 4 | 5 | 6 |
| 1 | ○ | ○ | | | | ○ |
| 2 | ○ | | ○ | | | ○ |
| 3 | ○ | | | | ○ | ○ |
| 4 | ○ | | | | ○ | ○ |
| | GND | | | | | IGN |

**9.6b  Blower switch terminal guide and continuity table - 1995 and later models**

or the ignition feed circuit. Refer to the wiring diagrams at the end of Chapter 12.

5    If battery voltage is present, reconnect the terminal to the blower motor. If the motor still does not operate, the motor or the ground circuit is faulty. With the harness connector in place, install a jumper wire into the back of the connector at the black/yellow wire and ground the other end to the chassis. Make sure your probe touches the metal terminal inside the connector. If battery power is present at the connector and the motor does not operate with the ground jumper in place, the motor is faulty.

6    If the motor is good, but doesn't operate at any speed, the blower switch on the heater/air conditioning control panel or the ground connection is probably faulty. Remove the control assembly (see Section 11) and check for continuity through the switch in each position **(see illustrations)**. Also check the black wire at the blower switch connector for continuity to ground.

7    If the blower motor operates at High speed, but not at one or more of the lower speeds, check the blower motor resistor, located under the instrument panel on the

passenger side next to the blower motor.

8    Disconnect the electrical connector from the blower motor resistor and withdraw the resistor from the housing. Using an ohmmeter, check for continuity between each of the blower resistor terminals **(see illustration)**.

9    The resistance indicated between the various terminals will vary, but if an open cir-

**9.8  Check for continuity between the terminals on the blower motor resistor**

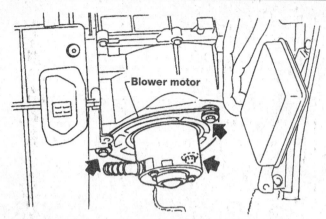

**9.13  Remove the blower mounting bolts (arrows)**

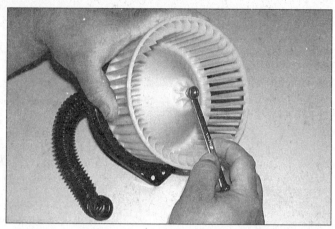

**9.14  Remove the nut that retains the blower fan to the motor**

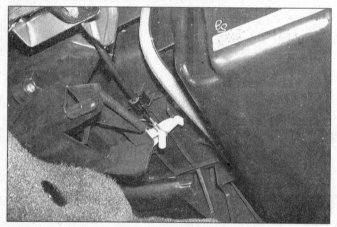

**10.4  Disconnect the temperature control cable
from the heater housing**

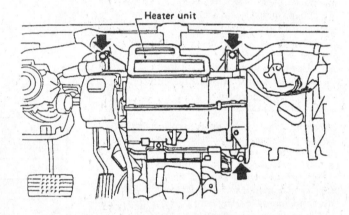

**10.8  Heater unit mounting bolts (arrows)**

cuit is indicated between any two terminals, replace the blower resistor.

### Replacement

*Refer to illustrations 9.13 and 9.14*

10   Disconnect the negative cable from the battery.

11   Refer to Chapter 11 and remove the glove box and the lower trim panel.

12   Disconnect the electrical connector from the blower motor.

13   Remove the three screws and washers and remove the blower assembly from the vehicle **(see illustration)**. Note: *On some models, disconnect the cooling hose before pulling the motor out, and on some early models, the fresh air duct may have to be removed first to access the blower motor.*

14   The motor may be replaced by removing the nut retaining the fan to the motor **(see illustration)**.

15   The installation is the reverse of the removal procedure.

---

### 10   Heater core - removal and installation

**Warning 1:** *Some models covered by this manual are equipped with airbags. Always*

disconnect the negative battery cable and wait at least one minute before working in the vicinity of the impact sensors, steering column or instrument panel to avoid the possibility of accidental deployment of the airbag, which could cause personal injury (see Chapter 12).

**Warning 2:** *The air conditioning system is under high pressure. DO NOT loosen any fittings or remove any components until after the system has been discharged. Air conditioning refrigerant should be properly discharged into an EPA-approved container at a dealer service department or an automotive air conditioning facility. Always wear eye protection when disconnecting air conditioning system fittings.*

### Removal

*Refer to illustrations 10.4, 10.8 and 10.9*

1   Disconnect the cable from the negative battery terminal.

2   Drain the cooling system (see Chapter 1).

3   Disconnect both the inlet and the outlet hoses from the heater pipes at the firewall.

4   Disconnect the temperature control cable from the heater unit **(see illustration)**.

5   Refer to Chapter 11 and remove the center console and the instrument panel from the vehicle. Also, remove the support beam from behind the instrument panel.

6   Detach the heater duct between the heater unit and the blower assembly.

7   Remove the evaporator unit if equipped with air conditioning (see Section 15).

8   Remove the bolts from the heater unit and lift the heater unit from the vehicle **(see illustration)**. Note: *Keep some shop towels on the vehicle's floor to protect the carpeting from spilled coolant. If the coolant spills on any painted surfaces, wash it off immediately with cold water.*

9   Remove the screws retaining the clamps over the heater core pipes on the heater core housing **(see illustration)**. Pull the heater core straight out of the housing. Note: *On some early models, the heater housing must be separated to remove the heater core. Pry the clips off the housing and separate the two halves to remove the heater core.*

### Installation

10   Slide the new heater core into the housing, making sure that the sealing foam is in place.

11   Install the heater unit in the vehicle.

12   Install the heater ducts.

13   Refer to Chapter 11 and reinstall the instrument panel and console. Connect the wires, cables and vacuum hoses discon-

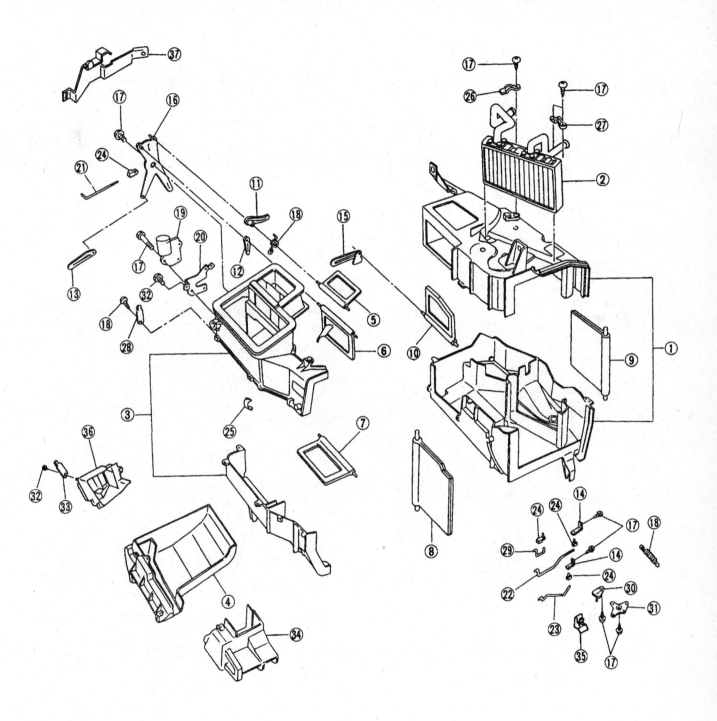

**10.9  An exploded view of the heater unit**

| | | | | | | | |
|---|---|---|---|---|---|---|---|
| 1 | Heater housing | 11 | Defrost lever | 21 | Actuator motor rod motor | 31 | Mix link |
| 2 | Heater core | 12 | Vent lever | 22 | Mix rod | 32 | Screw |
| 3 | Vent duct | 13 | Vent lever | 23 | Mix rod | 33 | Bracket |
| 4 | Heat duct | 14 | Mix lever | 24 | Rod holder | 34 | Foot duct |
| 5 | Defrost door | 15 | Lever heat | 25 | Clip | 35 | Cable clamp |
| 6 | Vent door | 16 | Main link | 26 | Pipe clamp | 36 | Foot duct |
| 7 | Vent door | 17 | Screw | 27 | Pipe clamp | 37 | Link cover |
| 8 | Mix door | 18 | Spring | 28 | Connector bracket | | |
| 9 | Mix door | 19 | Actuator motor | 29 | Mix rod | | |
| 10 | Heat door | 20 | Actuator motor bracket | 30 | Mix link | | |

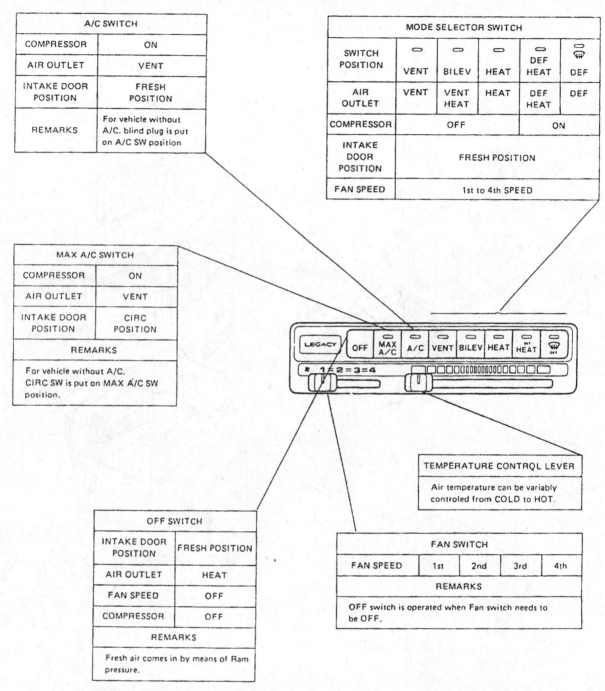

**A/C SWITCH**

| COMPRESSOR | ON |
| --- | --- |
| AIR OUTLET | VENT |
| INTAKE DOOR POSITION | FRESH POSITION |
| REMARKS | For vehicle without A/C, blind plug is put on A/C SW position |

**MODE SELECTOR SWITCH**

| SWITCH POSITION | VENT | BILEV | HEAT | DEF HEAT | DEF |
| --- | --- | --- | --- | --- | --- |
| AIR OUTLET | VENT | VENT HEAT | HEAT | DEF HEAT | DEF |
| COMPRESSOR | OFF | | | ON | |
| INTAKE DOOR POSITION | FRESH POSITION | | | | |
| FAN SPEED | 1st to 4th SPEED | | | | |

**MAX A/C SWITCH**

| COMPRESSOR | ON |
| --- | --- |
| AIR OUTLET | VENT |
| INTAKE DOOR POSITION | CIRC POSITION |
| REMARKS | |
| For vehicle without A/C. CIRC SW is put on MAX A/C SW position. | |

**TEMPERATURE CONTROL LEVER**

Air temperature can be variably controled from COLD to HOT.

**OFF SWITCH**

| INTAKE DOOR POSITION | FRESH POSITION |
| --- | --- |
| AIR OUTLET | HEAT |
| FAN SPEED | OFF |
| COMPRESSOR | OFF |
| REMARKS | |
| Fresh air comes in by means of Ram pressure. | |

**FAN SWITCH**

| FAN SPEED | 1st | 2nd | 3rd | 4th |
| --- | --- | --- | --- | --- |
| REMARKS | | | | |
| OFF switch is operated when Fan switch needs to be OFF. | | | | |

**11.1a  Manual heater and air conditioning control panel selection system - 1990 through 1994 models**

nected for removal.

14   Install the temperature control cable.

15   Connect both the inlet and the outlet hoses to the heater pipe. If either hose is hardened or split at the end, replace the heater hoses with new ones.

16   Fill the radiator with coolant (see Chapter 1) and connect the ground cable to the battery.

17   Start the vehicle and operate the heater controls. Check for any leakage around the hose connections.

## 11  Heater and air conditioning control assembly - check, removal and installation

**Warning:** *Some models covered by this manual are equipped with airbags. Always disconnect the negative battery cable and wait at least one minute before working in the vicinity of the impact sensors, steering column or instrument panel to avoid the possibility of accidental deployment of the airbag, which*

*could cause personal injury (see Chapter 12).*
**Note:** *Some models are equipped with an optional Automatic Climate Control system. The procedures in this section cover only the manual air conditioning system. Refer to Section 13 for information on the Automatic Climate Control system.*

### Check

*Refer to illustration 11.1a and 11.1b*

1   Start the engine and allow it to warm-up to operating temperature. Operate the fan

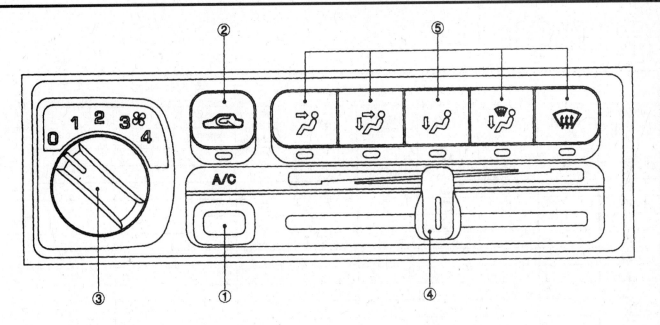

| | | Indicator | * ON | | OFF | |
|---|---|---|---|---|---|---|
| ① | A/C switch | Compressor | ON | | OFF | |
| | | *:  When fan switch is "ON", indicator light and compressor turn "ON". | | | | |
| ② | Recirc switch | Indicator | ON | | OFF | |
| | | Intake door position | Recirc | | Fresh | |
| ③ | Fan switch | Switch position | 1 | 2 | 3 | 4 |
| | | Fan speed | 1st (slow) | 2nd | 3rd | 4th (fast) |
| ④ | Temperature control lever | Outlet air temperature can be variably controlled from COLD to HOT. | | | | |
| ⑤ | Mode selector switch | Switch position | ⇗👤 | ⇗👤 | ↓👤 | 👤*1 🌊*2 |
| | | Air outlet | Vent | Vent Heat | Heat | DEF Heat    DEF |

*1:  When this switch is "ON", intake door position is FRESH.
*2:  When this switch is "ON", intake door position is FRESH and A/C switch is "ON".

**11.1b  Manual heater and air conditioning control panel selection system - 1995 and later models**

switch in each position, operate each mode switch, in turn, and slide the temperature control lever from cold to hot and back to cold. Compare the results of each test with the correct response shown in the accompanying illustrations **(see illustrations)**.

2    If the fan switch fails to respond, refer to Section 9 and check the blower motor and circuit.

3    If air does not come out of the proper duct when each mode switch is pressed, refer to the Steps below for control rod

adjustment and mode door operation. If necessary, remove the control panel and test the mode switches.

4    If the outlet air temperature does not respond to the temperature control lever operation, check the cable and air mix door for proper operation. Refer to Section 3 and check the thermostat for proper operation.

**Mode switch check**

*Refer to illustrations 11.5a and 11.5b*

5    Remove the control panel (see Step 16).

Using an ohmmeter, check for continuity on the indicated terminals with the indicated mode selector switch pressed **(see illustrations)**. If continuity is not indicated as shown, replace the control assembly.

**Control rod adjustments**

*Refer to illustrations 11.7 and 11.8*

6    First set the ventilation adjustment. Connect the mode door motor to the harness connector and turn the ignition switch to ACC. Set the mode button to VENT.

| Terminal | Mode selector switch | | | | | | RECIRC switch (MAX A/C switch) | | A/C switch | L.E.D. |
|---|---|---|---|---|---|---|---|---|---|---|
| | VENT | BILEV | HEAT | HEAT DEF | DEF | OFF (switch canceled) | ON RECIRC | OFF FRESH | ON | Mode selector switch* |
| ① | | | | | | | | | | |
| ② | | | | | | | | | | |
| ③ | | | | | | | | | | |
| ④ | | | | | | | | | | |
| ⑤ | | | | | | | | | | |
| ⑥ | | | | | | | | | | |
| ⑦ | | | | | | | | | | |
| ⑧ | | | | | | | | | | |
| ⑨ | | | | | | | | | | |
| ⑩ | | | | | | | | | | |
| ⑪ | | | | | | | | | | |
| ⑫ | | | | | | | | | | |
| ⑬ | | | | | | | | | | |
| ⑭ | | | | | | | | | | |
| ⑮ | | | | | | | | | | |

* Each switch is turned ON.

**11.5a Heater and air conditioning control assembly terminal guide and continuity table - 1990 through 1994 models**

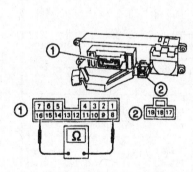

**11.5b Heater and air conditioning control assembly terminal guide and continuity table - 1995 and later models**

| Terminal No. | Mode selector switch | | | | | RECIRC switch | | A/C switch | Illumi. |
|---|---|---|---|---|---|---|---|---|---|
| | VENT | BI-LEV | HEAT | DEF/HEAT | DEF | RECIRC | FRESH | | |
| 1 | | | | | | | | | |
| 2 | | | | | | | | | |
| 3 | | | | | | | | | |
| 4 | | | | | | | | | |
| 5 | | | | | | | | | |
| 6 | | | | | | | | | |
| 7 | | | | | | | | | |
| 8 | | | | | | | | | |
| 9 | | | | | | | | | |
| 10 | | | | | | | | | |
| 11 | | | | | | | | | |
| 12 | | | | | | | | | |
| 13 | | | | | | | | | |
| 14 | | | | | | | | | |
| 15 | | | | | | | | | |
| 16 | | | | | | | | | |
| 17 | | | | | | | | | |
| 18 | | | | | | | | | |
| 19 | | | | | | | | | |

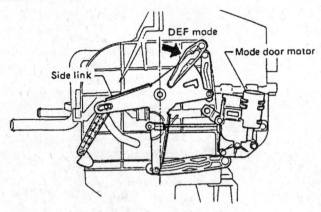

**11.7  VENT adjustment details**

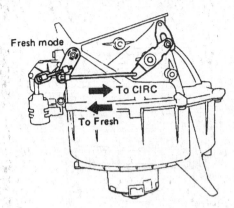

**11.8  FRESH mode selector adjustment details**

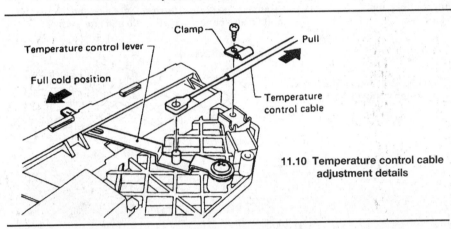

**11.10  Temperature control cable adjustment details**

## Temperature control lever adjustment

*Refer to illustration 11.10*

10   Connect the temperature control cable and set the temperature control lever to the FULL COLD position **(see illustration)**.

11   Install the clamp onto the temperature control cable and tighten until the cable seats firmly and the casing doesn't move when the lever is moved.

## Mode door motor check

*Refer to illustration 11.12*

12   Using jumper wires, apply battery voltage to the indicated terminals and observe the door motor rotation **(see illustration)**.

13   If the mode door motor fails to operate as indicated, replace the motor.

## Intake door motor check

*Refer to illustration 11.14*

14   On models with an electric INTAKE door motor, check the operation of the door as battery voltage is applied to the connector **(see illustration)**.

15   If the mode door motor fails to operate as indicated, replace the motor.

7   After connecting the mode door motor onto the heater unit, manually operate the side link to the vent mode position and secure the rod to the rod holder. Set the mode button to DEF and check that the side link moves over its full stroke range **(see illustration)**.

8   Next, set the fresh air adjustment. Remove the control rod from the FRESH AIR intake door motor. Connect the harness to the intake door motor. Turn the ignition switch to ACC, set RECIRC switch to ON and

check to see if the door moves into position **(see illustration)**.

9   Install the intake door onto the intake unit. Secure the rod holder to the link and install the link to the intake unit. Manually set the rod in the RECIRC mode and secure the rod holder. Observe that the door moves the complete range when the mode selector is set at RECIRC. **Note:** *The intake door will switch from RECIRC to FRESH when going from MAX A/C to A/C. Refer to the mode diagram at the beginning of this section.*

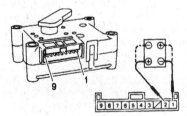

**11.12  To check the mode door motor, use jumper wires to apply battery voltage to the switch as indicated and check that the motor rotates in the proper direction**

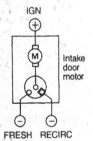

**11.14  To check the intake door motor, use jumper wires to apply battery voltage to the switch as indicated and see if the motor rotates in the proper direction**

| Terminal No. | | Mode door motor | |
| --- | --- | --- | --- |
| 2 | 1 | | |
| Polarity of power supply terminals | | Mode door motor operation | Direction of linkage rotation |
| – | + | VENT→DEF | Clockwise |
| + | – | DEF→VENT | Counterclockwise |

| Intake door motor position | Terminal | | Intake door motor operation |
| --- | --- | --- | --- |
| | ⊕ | ⊖ | |
| FRESH | 3 | 2 | Door motor moved to FRESH position. |
| RECIRC | | 1 | Door motor moved to RECIRC position. |

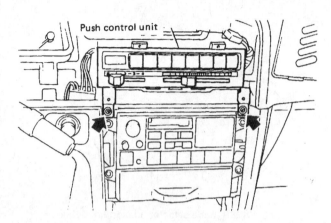

**11.18a  Location of the heater/air conditioning control panel mounting screws - 1990 through 1994 models**

**11.18b  Remove the screws (arrows) retaining the heating/air conditioning control panel - 1995 and later models**

## Removal

*Refer to illustrations 11.18a, 11.18b and 11.20*

16   Disconnect the negative cable from the battery.

17   Remove the center trim panel (see Chapter 11).

18   Remove the mounting screws and pull the control assembly out from the instrument panel **(see illustrations)**.

19   Disconnect the temperature control cable from the control assembly.

20   Disconnect the blower switch harness connector and remove the assembly **(see illustration)**.

## Installation

21   Installation is the reverse of removal. Adjust the temperature control cable (see Step 10).

## 12   Air conditioning and heating system - check and maintenance

*Refer to illustration 12.1*

**Warning:** *The air conditioning system is under high pressure. DO NOT loosen any fittings or remove any components until after the system has been discharged. Air conditioning refrigerant should be properly discharged into an approved container at a dealer service department or an automotive air conditioning repair facility. Always wear eye protection when disconnecting air conditioning system fittings.*

1   The following maintenance steps should be performed on a regular basis to ensure that the air conditioner continues to operate at peak efficiency **(see illustration)**.

a) *Check the tension of the drivebelt and adjust if necessary (see Chapter 1).*

b) *Check the condition of the hoses. Look for cracks, hardening and deterioration.* **Warning:** *Do not replace air conditioning hoses until the system has been discharged by a dealer or air conditioning shop.*

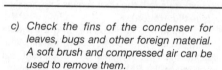

**11.20  Disconnect the blower switch connector as shown**

c) *Check the fins of the condenser for leaves, bugs and other foreign material. A soft brush and compressed air can be used to remove them.*

d) *Check the wire harness for correct routing, broken wires, damaged insulation, etc. Make sure the harness connections are clean and tight.*

e) *Maintain the correct refrigerant charge.*

2   The system should be run for about 10 minutes at least once a month. This is particularly important during the winter months because long-term non-use can cause hardening of the internal seals.

3   Because of the complexity of the air conditioning system and the special equipment required to effectively work on it, accurate troubleshooting of the system should be left to a professional technician. One probable cause for poor cooling that can be determined by the home mechanic is low refrigerant charge. Should the system lose its cooling ability, the following procedure will help you pinpoint the cause.

## Check

*Refer to illustrations 12.6 and 12.7*

4   Warm the engine up to normal operating temperature.

5   Place the air conditioning temperature selector at the coldest setting and put the blower at the highest setting. Open the doors

(to make sure the air conditioning system doesn't cycle off as soon as it cools the passenger compartment).

6   After the system reaches operating temperature, feel the two pipes connected to the evaporator at the firewall **(see illustration)**.

7   The pipe (thinner tubing) leading from the condenser outlet to the evaporator should be cold, and the evaporator outlet line (the thicker tubing that leads back to the compressor) should be slightly colder. If the evaporator outlet is considerably warmer than the inlet, the system needs a charge. Insert a thermometer in the center air distribution duct **(see illustration)** while operating the air conditioning system - the temperature of the output air should be 35 to 40 degrees F below the ambient air temperature (down to approximately 40 degrees F). If the ambient (outside) air temperature is very high, say 110 degrees F, the duct air temperature may be as high as 60 degrees F, but generally the air conditioning is 35 to 40 degrees F cooler than the ambient air. If the air isn't as cold as it used to be, the system probably needs a charge. Further inspection or testing of the system is beyond the scope of the home mechanic and should be left to a professional. **Note:** *Most R-12 systems have a sight glass on top of the receiver/drier. When the system is running, check the glass. A steady stream of bubbles or foam indicates the system is low on refrigerant.*

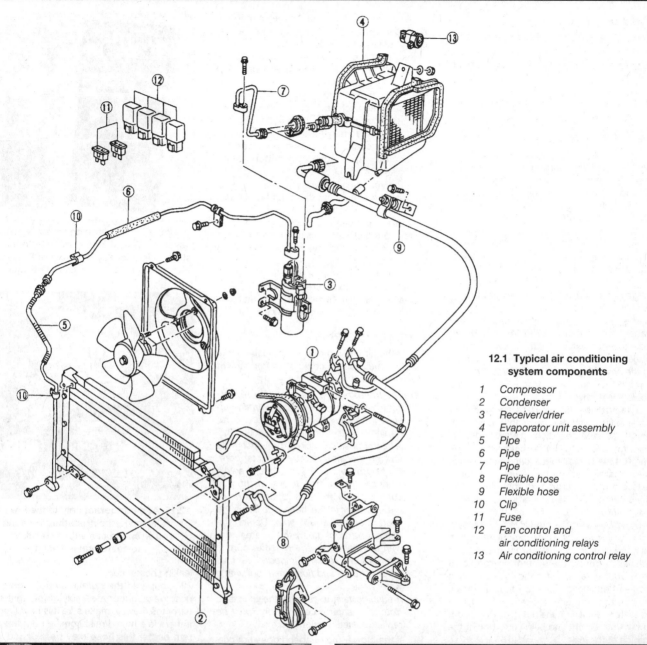

**12.1  Typical air conditioning system components**

1  Compressor
2  Condenser
3  Receiver/drier
4  Evaporator unit assembly
5  Pipe
6  Pipe
7  Pipe
8  Flexible hose
9  Flexible hose
10  Clip
11  Fuse
12  Fan control and
   air conditioning relays
13  Air conditioning control relay

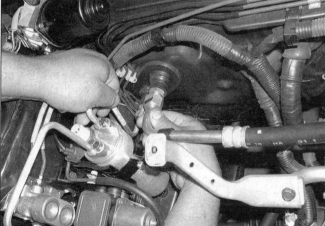

12.6  Feel the two refrigerant pipes at the firewall with the system operating

12.7  Insert a thermometer into one of the center dash air outlets to check the effectiveness of your air conditioning system

## Adding refrigerant

*Refer to illustrations 12.9 and 12.12*

8    Most models covered by this manual use refrigerant R-12, which was replaced by the environmentally friendly R-134a beginning with some 1994 models. When recharging or replacing air conditioning components, use only refrigerant, refrigerant oil and seals compatible with the system in your vehicle. The seals and compressor oil used with older, conventional R-12 refrigerant are not compatible with the components in the R-134a system. If in doubt about which refrigerant you have, look for labels on the air conditioning system. Only the R-134a systems have light-blue labels marked R-134a. **Note:** *Your Subaru dealer may have kits available for some 1990 to 1994 models that will convert the air conditioning system to accept R-134a refrigerant. If a kit is available for your specific vehicle, have your system's R-12 refrigerant discharged and recovered by an air conditioning shop, install the kit components according the to the manufacturer's instructions, then charge the system with R-134a refrigerant. Cooling performance after the conversion may not be as efficient as with the old refrigerant, but the new refrigerant is friendlier to the environment and much less expensive to replace should a leak develop.*

9    Refrigerant cans of R-12 are no longer available for home use. Have an R-12 system charged at an air conditioning shop or dealership, or convert it to R-134a if possible. However, R-134a is available in cans and you can buy a charging kit for home use at an auto parts store. A charging kit includes a 12-ounce can of R-134a refrigerant, a tap valve and a short section of hose that can be attached between the tap valve and the system low side service valve **(see illustration)**. Because one can of refrigerant may not be sufficient to bring the system charge up to the proper level, it's a good idea to buy a couple of additional cans. Try to find at least one can that contains red refrigerant dye. If the system is leaking, the red dye will leak out with the refrigerant and help you pinpoint the location of the leak.

10    Connect the charging kit by following the instructions furnished with the kit.

11    Back off the valve handle on the charging kit and screw the kit onto the refrigerant can, making sure first that the O-ring or rubber seal inside the threaded portion of the kit is in place. **Warning:** *Wear protective eye wear when dealing with pressurized refrigerant cans.*

12    Remove the dust cap from the low-side charging port and attach the quick-connect fitting on the kit hose **(see illustration)**. **Warning:** *DO NOT hook the charging kit hose to the system high side! The fittings on the charging kit are designed to fit* **only** *on the low side of the system.*

13    Warm the engine to normal operating temperature and turn on the air conditioning. Keep the charging kit hose away from the fan and other moving parts.

14    Turn the valve handle on the kit until the stem pierces the can, then back the handle out to release the refrigerant. You should be able to hear the rush of gas. Add refrigerant to the low side of the system until both the outlet and the evaporator inlet pipe feel about the same temperature. Allow stabilization time between each addition. **Warning:** *Never add more than two cans of refrigerant to the system.* The can may tend to frost up, slowing the procedure. Wet a shop towel with hot water and wrap it around the bottom of the can to keep it from frosting.

15    Put your thermometer back in the center register and check that the output air is getting colder.

16    When the can is empty, turn the valve handle to the closed position and release the connection from the low-side port. Replace the dust cap.

17    Remove the charging kit from the can and store the kit for future use with the piercing valve in the UP position, to prevent inadvertently piercing the can on the next use.

## Heating systems

18    If the air coming out of the heater vents isn't hot, the problem could stem from any of the following causes:

a) *The thermostat is stuck open, preventing the engine coolant from warming up enough to carry heat to the heater core. Replace the thermostat (see Section 3).*

b) *A heater hose is blocked, preventing the flow of coolant through the heater core. Feel both heater hoses at the firewall. They should be hot. If one of them is cold, there is an obstruction in one of the hoses or in the heater core, or the heater control valve is shut. Detach the hoses and back flush the heater core with a water hose. If the heater core is clear but circulation is impeded, remove the two hoses and flush them out with a water hose.*

c) *If flushing fails to remove the blockage from the heater core, the core must be replaced. (see Section 10).*

19    If the blower motor speed does not correspond to the setting selected on the blower switch, the problem could be a bad fuse, circuit, control panel or blower resistor (see Section 9).

20    If there isn't any air coming out of the vents:

a) *Turn the ignition ON and activate the fan control. Place your ear at the heating/air conditioning register (vent) and listen. Most motors are audible. Can you hear the motor running?*

b) *If you can't (and have already verified that the blower switch and the blower motor resistor are good), the blower motor itself is probably bad (see Section 9).*

21    If the carpet under the heater core is damp, or if antifreeze vapor or steam is coming through the vents, the heater core is leaking. Remove it (see Section 10) and install a new unit (most radiator shops will not repair a

**12.9 A basic charging kit for R-134a systems is available at most auto parts stores - it must say R-134a (not R-12) and so must the 12-ounce can of refrigerant**

**12.12 Add refrigerant only to the low-side port (arrow) - the procedure is easier if you wrap the can with a warm, wet towel to prevent icing**

leaking heater core).

22    Inspect the drain hose from the heater/evaporator assembly at the right-center of the firewall, make sure it is not clogged. If there is a humid mist coming from the system ducts, this hose may be plugged with leaves or road debris.

## Eliminating air conditioning odors

23    Unpleasant odors that often develop in air conditioning systems are caused by the growth of a bacteria and/or fungus, usually on the surface of the evaporator core. The warm, humid environment there is a perfect breeding ground for mildew to develop.

24    The evaporator core on most vehicles is difficult to access, and factory dealerships have a lengthy, expensive process for eliminating the fungus by opening up the evaporator housing and using a powerful disinfectant and rinse on the core until the fungus is gone. You can service your own system at home, but it takes something much stronger than basic household germ-killers or deodorizers.

25    Aerosol disinfectants for automotive air

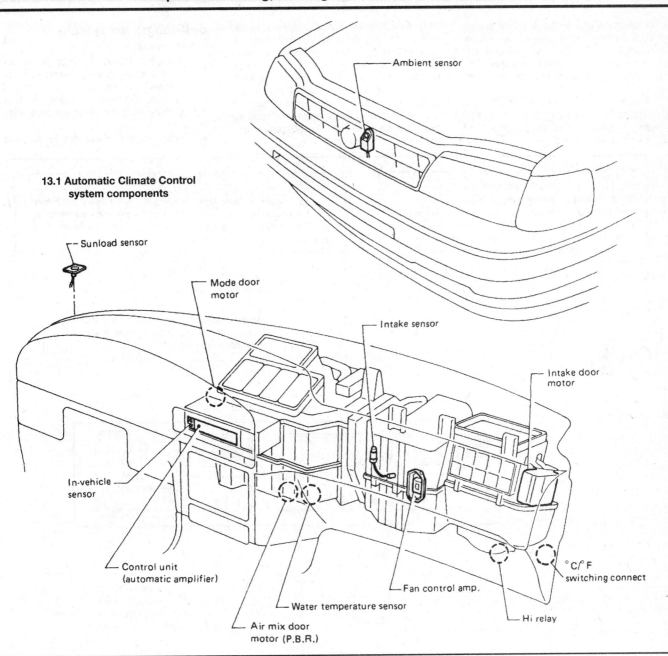

**13.1 Automatic Climate Control system components**

conditioning systems are available in most auto parts stores, but remember when shopping for them that the most effective treatments are also the most expensive. The basic procedure for using these sprays is to start by running the system in the RECIRC mode (MAX A/C) for ten minutes with the blower on its highest speed. Use the highest heat mode to dry out the system and keep the compressor from engaging by disconnecting the wiring connector at the compressor (see Section 14).
26   The disinfectant can usually comes with a long spray hose. Pry off the front clips on the evaporator housing, open the two halves enough to insert the nozzle and spray, according to the manufacturer's recommendations. Try to cover the whole surface of the evaporator core, by aiming the spray up, down and sideways. Follow the manufac-

turer's recommendations for the length of spray and waiting time between applications.
27   Once the evaporator has been cleaned, the best way to prevent the mildew from coming back again is to make sure your evaporator housing drain tube is clear, and to run your system with heat and RECIRC for a few minutes after a long continuous usage of the air conditioning on a hot, humid day.

**13   Automatic Climate Control system - general information and self-diagnosis system**

*General information*
*Refer to illustrations 13.1 and 13.2*
1   The Automatic Climate Control system

provides automatic regulation of the passenger compartment temperature based on the "set temperature" selected by the driver, regardless of the outside air temperature. A small microcomputer or automatic amplifier, receives input information from several sensors to allow the computer to automatically control the climate inside the vehicle. The water temperature sensor is located inside the heater unit, the intake air sensor is located external to the evaporator unit, the sunload sensor is located on the driver's side dash (left defroster grille), the ambient temperature sensor is located in the front grille and the computer is located behind the control panel **(see illustration)**.
2   There is also an in-vehicle sensor that is attached to the control unit on the dash **(see illustration)**. This sensor converts variations

in temperature of compartment air drawn from the aspirator into a resistance value for the computer. This sensor monitors the inside temperature constantly while The Automatic Climate Control system is operating.

3    The Automatic Climate Control system is equipped with a self-diagnosis system that gathers information from the computer and converts any system malfunctions into two-digit trouble codes. These codes are stored in the computer and when the self-diagnosis connector is accessed, the system will relay codes on the control panel display. This system is useful in diagnosing sensor malfunctions, door motor failures, defective blower motors and other system trouble areas. This section describes the method for extracting the Automatic Climate Control system trouble codes.

## Self-diagnosis system

*Refer to illustration 13.4*

4    Turn the ignition switch to ON (engine not running). Connect the self-diagnosis connector **(see illustration)** to ground by connecting the single terminal jumper wire to the designated slot in the air conditioning diagnostic connector.

5    There are four categories for self diag-

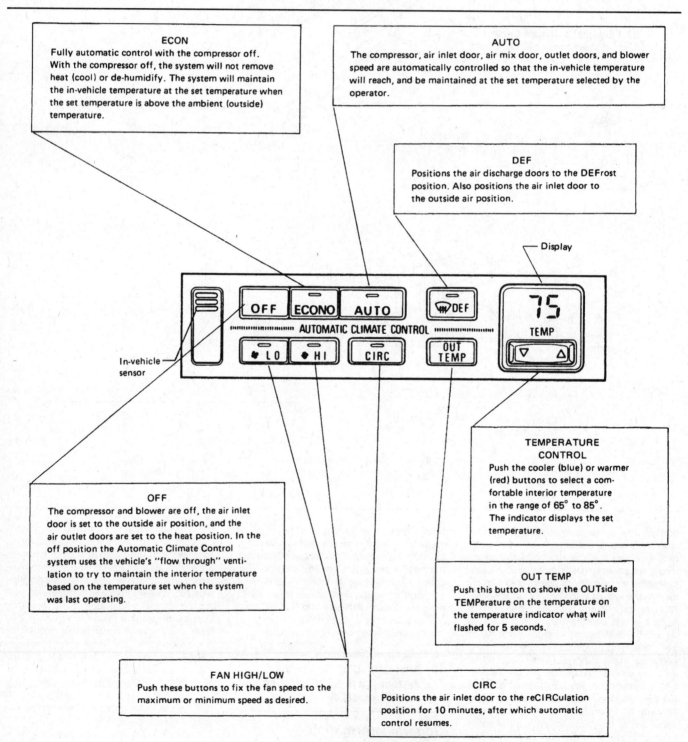

**ECON**
Fully automatic control with the compressor off. With the compressor off, the system will not remove heat (cool) or de-humidify. The system will maintain the in-vehicle temperature at the set temperature when the set temperature is above the ambient (outside) temperature.

**AUTO**
The compressor, air inlet door, air mix door, outlet doors, and blower speed are automatically controlled so that the in-vehicle temperature will reach, and be maintained at the set temperature selected by the operator.

**DEF**
Positions the air discharge doors to the DEFrost position. Also positions the air inlet door to the outside air position.

Display

In-vehicle sensor

**OFF**
The compressor and blower are off, the air inlet door is set to the outside air position, and the air outlet doors are set to the heat position. In the off position the Automatic Climate Control system uses the vehicle's "flow through" ventilation to try to maintain the interior temperature based on the temperature set when the system was last operating.

**TEMPERATURE CONTROL**
Push the cooler (blue) or warmer (red) buttons to select a comfortable interior temperature in the range of 65° to 85°. The indicator displays the set temperature.

**OUT TEMP**
Push this button to show the OUTside TEMPerature on the temperature on the temperature indicator what will flashed for 5 seconds.

**FAN HIGH/LOW**
Push these buttons to fix the fan speed to the maximum or minimum speed as desired.

**CIRC**
Positions the air inlet door to the reCIRCulation position for 10 minutes, after which automatic control resumes.

**13.2  Switch designations for the Automatic Climate Control system**

nosis available. Use the HOT or COLD switches on the temperature control button to select one of the four modes (categories);

Mode I - Displays all LED lights and segments for display problems
Mode II - Displays all the trouble codes
Mode III - Performs actuator checks and pattern displays
Mode IIII - Detects sensor temperatures for calibrating and diagnostics

6    Mode I is useful for checking the display features and the selection button lights that illuminate the dash. Carefully observe every segment of the temperature display to diagnose numeral misrepresentations that could give erroneous temperature readings. A segment that is defective will display a small dot along its path. Use a magnifying lens if necessary. **Note:** *When the HOT switch is pressed, Mode I will select Mode II. To jump back to Mode I, press the COLD button. So far the remaining selections, HOT will advance the mode selection while COLD returns the mode selection.*

7    Mode II will flash the trouble codes on the temperature display. Here is the list of trouble codes for the Automatic Climate Control system.

Code 20 - All sensors are normal
Code 21 - In-vehicle sensor circuit is open
Code -21 - In-vehicle sensor circuit is shorted
Code 22 - Ambient sensor circuit is open
Code -22 - Ambient sensor circuit is shorted
Code 23 - Intake sensor circuit is open
Code -23 - Intake sensor circuit is shorted
Code 24 - Water temperature sensor circuit is open
Code -24 - Water temperature sensor circuit is shorted
Code -25 - Sunload sensor circuit is shorted
Code 26 - PBR sensor circuit is open
Code -26 - PBR sensor circuit is shorted

8    In many cases the most common problem with the system will be a defective sen-

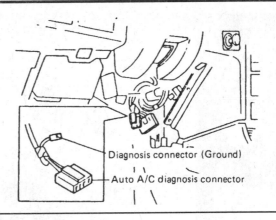

**13.4 Location of the Automatic Climate Control system diagnostic connector**

Diagnosis connector (Ground)

Auto A/C diagnosis connector

sor, a harness connector that is damaged or a poor ground connection causing incorrect information to be relayed to the computer.

## 14  Air conditioning receiver/drier-removal and installation

**Warning:** *The air conditioning system is under high pressure. DO NOT loosen any fittings or remove any components until after the system has been discharged. Air conditioning refrigerant should be properly discharged into an approved container at a dealer service department or an automotive air conditioning repair facility. Always wear eye protection when disconnecting air conditioning system fittings.*

### Removal

*Refer to illustrations 14.1 and 14.4*

1    The receiver/drier, which acts as a filter and reservoir for the refrigerant, is the canister-shaped object mounted on the passenger-side fender well in the engine compartment **(see illustration)**.

2    Before removing the receiver/drier, the system must be discharged by an air conditioning technician.

3    Disconnect the negative battery cable.

4    Disconnect the wiring from the pressure switch **(see illustration)**.

5    Remove both refrigerant lines from the receiver/drier.

6    Loosen the clamp and pull up on the receiver/drier to remove it from its mount.

### Installation

7    If installing a new receiver/drier, drain the refrigerant oil from the old receiver drier into a measured container. Pour that amount of new oil into the new receiver/drier.

8    Install the receiver/drier and tighten the clamp securely.

9    Install new O-rings on the refrigerant hose fittings and lubricate them with refrigerant oil. Install the fittings and tighten the bolts securely.

10   The remainder of installation is the reverse of removal.

## 15  Air conditioning compressor - removal and installation

**Warning:** *The air conditioning system is under high pressure. DO NOT loosen any fittings or remove any components until after the system has been discharged. Air conditioning refrigerant should be properly discharged into an approved container at a dealer service department or an automotive air conditioning repair facility. Always wear eye protection when disconnecting air conditioning system fittings.*

**14.1  Receiver/drier is located on the right side fenderwell (arrow)**

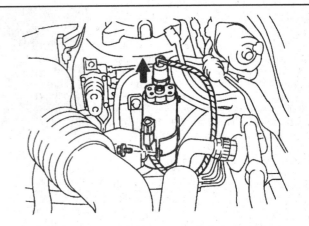

**14.4  Disconnect the electrical connector from the pressure switch on the receiver/drier (arrow)**

**15.4  The refrigerant line fittings are secured by bolts (arrow)**

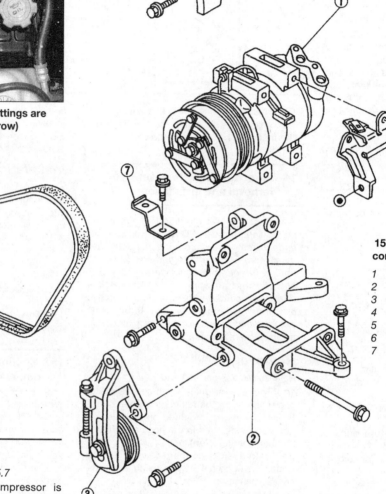

**15.7  Typical air conditioning compressor mounting details**

1   Compressor
2   Bracket
3   Tension pulley assembly
4   Drivebelt
5   Drivebelt cover
6   Bracket
7   Stay

## Removal

*Refer to illustrations 15.4 and 15.7*

1    The air conditioning compressor is mounted at the front of the engine on the left side and is driven by a belt from the crankshaft pulley.

2    Before removing the compressor, the system must be discharged by an air conditioning technician.

3    Loosen the drivebelt tensioner pulley and slip the drivebelt off the compressor clutch pulley (see Chapter 1). On later models, the alternator must be removed before removing the compressor (see Chapter 5).

4    Disconnect the refrigerant lines from the compressor **(see illustrations)**. **Note:** *Early models have the lines connected with large fittings, while on later models, the lines are bolted to the compressor with flanges.*

5    Disconnect the air conditioning compressor clutch electrical connectors.

6    Remove the compressor brace from the top of the assembly.

7    Remove the bolts attaching the compressor to the brackets and the compressor can be lifted out of the vehicle **(see illustration)**.

**16.4a  Remove the bolt (arrow) and detach the refrigerant line from the left side of the condenser . . .**

**16.4b  . . . and remove the bolt (arrow) and detach the refrigerant line from the right side of the condenser**

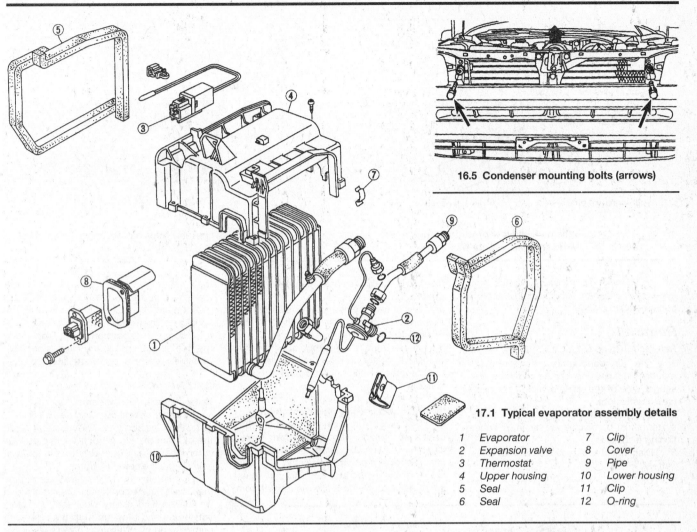

**16.5 Condenser mounting bolts (arrows)**

**17.1 Typical evaporator assembly details**

| | | | |
|---|---|---|---|
| 1 | Evaporator | 7 | Clip |
| 2 | Expansion valve | 8 | Cover |
| 3 | Thermostat | 9 | Pipe |
| 4 | Upper housing | 10 | Lower housing |
| 5 | Seal | 11 | Clip |
| 6 | Seal | 12 | O-ring |

## Installation

**Note:** *When a new compressor is installed, a new receiver/drier should also be installed.*

8    When installing a new compressor, drain the oil from the old compressor into a measured container. Drain the oil out of the new compressor and install only that amount of new oil recovered from the old unit.

9    Install the compressor on the mounting bracket and tighten the bolts to the torque listed in this Chapter's Specifications.

10    Install new O-rings on the refrigerant hose fittings and lubricate them with refrigerant oil. Carefully seat the hoses on the compressor fittings and install the bolts securely.

11    The remainder of installation is the reverse of removal. Install and adjust the drivebelt (see Chapter 1).

## 16  Air conditioning condenser - removal and installation

**Warning:** *The air conditioning system is under high pressure. DO NOT loosen any fittings or remove any components until after the system has been discharged. Air conditioning refrigerant should be properly discharged into an approved container at a*

dealer service department or an automotive air conditioning repair facility. Always wear eye protection when disconnecting air conditioning system fittings.

### Removal

*Refer to illustrations 16.4a, 16.4b and 16.5*

1    The air conditioning condenser is mounted in front of the radiator.

2    Before removing the condenser, the system must be discharged by an air conditioning technician.

3    Remove the grille (see Chapter 11) and the radiator mounting bolts (see Section 5).

4    Disconnect the refrigerant lines at the condenser **(see illustrations)**.

5    Remove the condenser mounting bolts **(see illustration)**. Lean the radiator back and carefully lift the condenser out of the vehicle; do not bend the cooling fins or coil.

### Installation

**Note:** *When a new condenser is installed, a new receiver/drier should also be installed.*

6    When installing a new condenser, drain the oil from the old condenser into a measured container. Install that amount of new oil into the new condenser.

7    Carefully lower the condenser in place

between the radiator and the radiator support. Make sure the lower guides are properly inserted in the holes in the radiator support.

8    When installing the refrigerant lines, lubricate the O-rings with refrigerant oil.

9    The remainder of installation is the reverse of removal.

## 17  Air conditioning evaporator and expansion valve - removal and installation

**Warning 1:** *Some models covered by this manual are equipped with airbags. Always disconnect the negative battery cable and wait at least one minute before working in the vicinity of the impact sensors, steering column or instrument panel to avoid the possibility of accidental deployment of the airbag, which could cause personal injury (see Chapter 12).*

**Warning 2:** *The air conditioning system is under high pressure. DO NOT loosen any fittings or remove any components until after the system has been discharged. Air conditioning refrigerant should be properly discharged into an approved container at a dealer service department or an automotive*

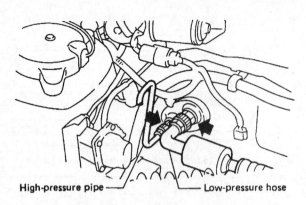

**17.5  Detach the high and low pressure refrigerant lines from the evaporator**

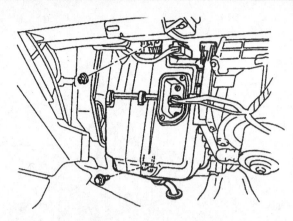

**17.7  Remove the evaporator housing mounting nut and bolt**

*air conditioning repair facility. Always wear eye protection when disconnecting air conditioning system fittings.*

## Removal

*Refer to illustrations 17.1, 17.5, 17.7 and 17.9*

1   The air conditioning evaporator is mounted in a housing located under the passenger side of the vehicle instrument panel **(see illustration)**.

2   Before removing the evaporator, the system must be discharged by an air conditioning technician.

3   Disconnect the negative terminal of the battery.

4   Remove the glove box and the glove box brace from the instrument panel (see Chapter 11).

5   Disconnect the refrigerant lines from the evaporator at the firewall **(see illustration)**. Remove the grommets from the pipes.

6   Remove the large clamps at either side of the evaporator housing that connect it to the heater core housing and blower motor housing.

7   Remove the mounting nut/bolt retaining the evaporator housing **(see illustration)**.

8   Disconnect the wiring harness and the drain hose from the evaporator housing. Carefully remove the housing from the vehicle.

9   Remove the clips retaining the two halves of the evaporator housing and separate the halves. Remove the thermostat from the upper housing, noting the location of the thermistor in the evaporator fins. The thermistor must be installed in exactly the same location on the new core. Remove the evaporator core and expansion valve. Disconnect the fittings and detach the expansion valve from the evaporator core **(see illustration)**.

## Installation

**Note:** *When a new evaporator is installed, a new receiver/drier should also be installed.*

10   When installing a new evaporator, drain the oil from the old evaporator into a measured container. Install only that amount of new oil into the new evaporator.

11   If installing the original evaporator core, make sure the evaporator fins are not clogged with debris. If necessary, clean the core with a soft brush and blow through the core with compressed air. **Warning:** *Always wear eye protection when using compressed air.* Never use water to clean the evaporator core.

12   When installing the expansion valve, wrap the capillary tube to the evaporator outlet pipe. Be sure to position the plastic ducts before slipping the evaporator into place. When installing the tubes, lubricate the inside surfaces and the outside of the fittings with refrigerant oil. The pipes must be positioned properly and tightened securely. Do not forget to install the drain pipe.

12   The remainder of installation is the reverse of removal.

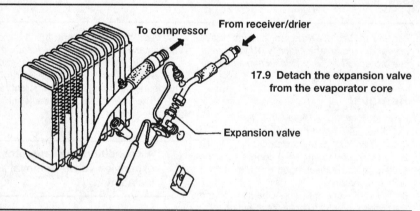

**17.9  Detach the expansion valve from the evaporator core**

# Chapter 4
# Fuel and exhaust systems

## Contents

## Specifications

### Fuel pressure

Non-turbocharged engines
    Fuel system pressure (at idle)
| | |
|---|---|
|       Vacuum hose attached to regulator | 26 to 32 psi |
|       Vacuum hose detached from regulator | 32 to 38 |

Turbocharged engines
    Fuel system pressure (at idle)
| | |
|---|---|
|       Vacuum hose attached to regulator | 34 to 40 psi |
|       Vacuum hose detached from regulator | 38 to 44 |
| Fuel pump hold pressure | 30 psi |

Injector resistance
| | |
|---|---|
|     1990 through 1994 | 11 to 12 ohms |
|     1995 through 1998 | 5 to 20 ohms |

### Torque specifications

**Ft-lbs** (unless otherwise indicated)

| | |
|---|---|
| Throttle body mounting bolts | 15 to 18 |
| Fuel rail mounting bolts | 84 to 108 in-lbs |
| Fuel injector pipe-to-manifold bolt | 13 to 15 |
| Fuel injector holder mounting bolts | 24 to 36 in-lbs |
| Turbocharger-to-exhaust manifold bolts | 18 to 24 |
| Cooling pipe-to-turbocharger bolt | 15 to 17 |
| Turbocharger oil inlet pipe bolt-to-engine block | 120 to 156 in-lbs |
| Oil inlet pipe bolt-to-turbocharger | 15 to 17 |
| Exhaust pipe-to-exhaust manifold bolts | 15 to 20 |
| EGR pipe | 23 to 26 |

**1.1a  Fuel injection system component locations**

| | | | | | |
|---|---|---|---|---|---|
| 1 | Fuel filter | 3 | Fuel pressure regulator | 5 | Air cleaner housing |
| 2 | Throttle body | 4 | Fuel injector | | |

## 1   General information

*Refer to illustrations 1.1a and 1.1b*

These models are equipped with an Electronic Fuel Injection (EFI) system. The fuel system consists of a fuel tank, an electric fuel pump (mounted in the fuel tank), a fuel pump relay, fuel injector(s), an air cleaner assembly and a throttle body unit **(see illustrations)**. 4WD models are also equipped with a fuel vapor separator to help filter fuel vapors for the EVAP system. The fuel vapor separator is located behind the trim panels in the trunk. Some early Legacy models (1990 through 1994) are equipped with a turbocharger. The fuel system for turbocharged engines is similar to the non-turbocharged models except for the higher fuel pressures delivered by the electric fuel pump to the injectors.

The fuel tank on 2WD models is equipped with a single fuel pump/fuel level sending unit. The rear seat can be removed to uncover the fuel pump access plate. The fuel pump and sending unit can be removed without dropping the fuel tank. 4WD models are equipped with a divided fuel tank to accommodate the rear differential, with two sending units to monitor the fuel levels in each compartment. The right side compartment is equipped with the fuel pump/sending unit assembly while the left side has the single sending unit. Both are accessible by removing the rear seat or trunk panel then lifting the access plate.

The fuel tank on 4WD models is equipped with a jet pump to circulate fuel from the left side to the right side to keep the weight of fuel distributed evenly. The jet pump utilizes the velocity of the fuel returning from the engine via the return line to produce negative pressure, which essentially creates a siphoning action.

### Multi Port Fuel Injection (MPFI) system

Multi Port Fuel Injection uses timed impulses to inject the fuel directly into the intake port of each cylinder. The injectors are controlled by the Electronic Control Module (ECM). The ECM monitors various engine parameters and delivers the exact amount of fuel required into the intake ports. The throttle body serves only to control the amount of air passing into the system. Because each cylinder is equipped with its own injector, much better control of the fuel/air mixture ratio is possible.

These models are equipped with gallery type (side feed) fuel injectors. The fuel circulates through the side to aid in cooling the injectors.

### Fuel pump and lines

Fuel is circulated from the fuel tank to the fuel injection system, and back to the fuel tank, through a pair of metal lines running along the underside of the vehicle. A vapor return system routes all vapors back to the fuel tank through a separate return line.

The fuel pump will operate as long as

the engine is cranking or running and the ECM is receiving ignition reference pulses from the electronic ignition system. If there are no reference pulses, the fuel pump will shut off after two or three seconds.

### Exhaust system

The exhaust system includes an exhaust pipe fitted with an oxygen sensor, a catalytic converter and a muffler.

The catalytic converter is an emission control device added to the exhaust system to reduce pollutants. A single-bed converter is used in combination with a three-way (reduction) catalyst. Refer to Chapter 6 for more information regarding the catalytic converter.

## 2   Fuel pressure relief

*Refer to illustration 2.2*

**Warning:** *Gasoline is extremely flammable, so take extra precautions when you work on any part of the fuel system. Don't smoke or allow open flames or bare light bulbs near the work area, and don't work in a garage where a natural gas-type appliance (such as a water heater or a clothes dryer) with a pilot light is present. Since gasoline is carcinogenic, wear latex gloves when there's a possibility of being exposed to fuel, and, if you spill any fuel on your skin, rinse it off immediately with soap and water. Mop up any spills immediately and do not store fuel-soaked rags where they could ignite. The fuel system is under*

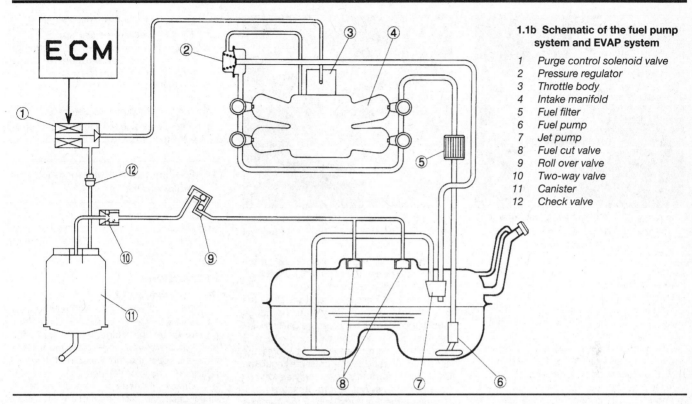

**1.1b Schematic of the fuel pump system and EVAP system**

1   Purge control solenoid valve
2   Pressure regulator
3   Throttle body
4   Intake manifold
5   Fuel filter
6   Fuel pump
7   Jet pump
8   Fuel cut valve
9   Roll over valve
10  Two-way valve
11  Canister
12  Check valve

constant pressure, so, if any fuel lines are to be disconnected, the fuel pressure in the system must be relieved first. When you perform any kind of work on the fuel system, wear safety glasses and have a Class B type fire extinguisher on hand.

**Note:** *After the fuel pressure has been relieved. it's a good idea to lay a shop towel over any fuel connection to be disassembled, to absorb the residual fuel that may leak out when servicing the fuel system.*

1   Remove the fuel filler cap to release any pressure that has built up in the tank.

2   Remove the rear seat (sedan) or trunk carpet liner (wagon) to access the fuel pump/sending unit access plate (see Section 5). Remove the cover then disconnect the electrical connector from the fuel pump **(see illustration)**. **Note:** *2WD models are*

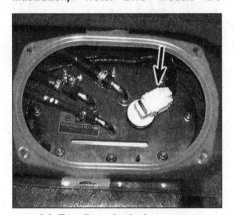

**2.2 To relieve the fuel pressure, disconnect the electrical connector at the fuel pump, then start the engine and allow it to die**

equipped with a single fuel pump/sending unit assembly while 4WD models are equipped with an extra fuel level sending unit mounted by itself on the left side of the fuel tank. The fuel pump is contained within the larger assembly (fuel pump/fuel level sending unit).

3   Start the engine and allow it to run until it stops. Disconnect the cable from the negative terminal of the battery before working on the fuel system.

4   The fuel system pressure is now relieved. When you're finished working on the fuel system, simply reconnect the fuel pump/sending unit harness connector and connect the negative cable to the battery.

---

**3   Fuel pump/fuel pressure check**

**Warning:** *Gasoline is extremely flammable, so take extra precautions when you work on any part of the fuel system. See the* **Warning** *in Section 2.*

### *Preliminary inspection*

*Refer to illustrations 3.2a and 3.2b*

1   Should the fuel system fail to deliver the proper amount of fuel, or any fuel at all, inspect it as follows. First, remove the fuel filler cap. Have an assistant turn the ignition key ON (engine not running) while you listen at the fuel filler opening. You should hear a whirring sound that lasts for a couple of seconds.

2   If you don't hear anything, check the fuel pump fuse. If the fuse is blown, replace it and see if it blows again. If it does, trace the fuel pump circuit for a short. If it isn't blown,

check the fuel pump relay (if so equipped) **(see illustrations)**. **Note:** *The fuel pump relay is located under the dash on the driver's side. The main relay and the fuel pump relay are*

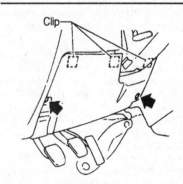

**3.2a Remove the driver's side lower trim panel**

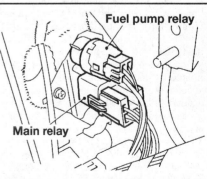

**3.2b To access the main and fuel pump relays, remove the fuse box mounting nuts and bracket and lower the fuse box to expose the relays**

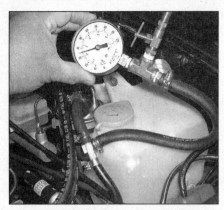

**3.6  Install a T-fitting between the fuel filter and fuel rail and check the fuel pressure at idle**

**3.8  The fuel pressure regulator (arrow) is located on the rear of the right-side fuel rail**

coupled together. *The main relay is square shaped (bottom location) while the fuel pump relay is round (top location).*

3    Remove the relay and check for battery voltage to the fuel pump relay connector. If there is battery voltage present, test the relay (see Chapter 12). Refer to the wiring diagrams at the end of Chapter 12 if necessary.

4    If battery voltage is present at the main relay and the fuel pump relay, unplug the fuel pump electrical connector at the fuel tank and check for battery voltage to the fuel pump with the ignition key ON (engine not running). **(see illustration 2.1)**. If there is no voltage, check the fuel pump circuit. If there is voltage present, make sure the fuel pump ground is good. If the circuit is properly grounded, replace the pump (see Section 4).

## *Operating pressure check*

*Refer to illustrations 3.6, 3.8 and 3.12*

5    Relieve the fuel system pressure (see Section 2). Detach the cable from the negative battery terminal.

6    Using a T-fitting, connect a fuel pressure gauge between the fuel filter and the fuel rail **(see illustration)**.

7    Attach the cable to the negative battery terminal. Start the engine and allow it to idle. Note the fuel pressure and compare it with the pressure listed in the Specifications.

8    Detach the vacuum hose from the fuel pressure regulator and watch the gauge **(see illustration)**. The fuel pressure should rise considerably when the vacuum hose is detached.

9    If the fuel pressure doesn't rise, connect a vacuum gauge to the pressure regulator vacuum hose. Start the engine and check for vacuum. If there isn't vacuum present, check for a clogged hose or vacuum port. If vacuum is present, replace the fuel pressure regulator.

10    Connect a hand-held vacuum pump to the port on the fuel pressure regulator. This test will simulate engine vacuum regulating working fuel pressure.

11    Read the fuel pressure gauge with vacuum applied to the pressure regulator and also with no vacuum applied. The fuel pressure should decrease as vacuum increases

(and increase as vacuum decreases). If the fuel pressure doesn't fluctuate as described, replace the fuel pressure regulator.

12    If the fuel pressure is too low, pinch the fuel return line shut and watch the gauge **(see illustration)**. If the pressure doesn't rise, the fuel pump is defective or there is a restriction in the fuel feed line. If the pressure rises sharply, replace the pressure regulator. **Caution:** *Perform this check only as long as necessary to verify that the pressure rises. Otherwise, the fuel pump and/or the fuel lines could be damaged.*

13    If the fuel pressure is still less than specified:

a)  *Inspect the system for a fuel leak. Repair any leaks and recheck the fuel pressure.*

b)  *If the fuel pressure is still low, replace the fuel filter (it may be clogged) and recheck the fuel pressure.*

14    If the fuel pressure is too high, turn the engine off. Disconnect the fuel return line from the pressure regulator and blow through it to check for a blockage. If there is no blockage, replace the fuel pressure regulator.

15    Turn the ignition switch to OFF, wait five minutes and recheck the pressure on the gauge. Compare the reading with the hold pressure listed in the Specifications. If the

**3.12  To determine if the cause of low fuel pressure is due to a faulty regulator, pinch the return line shut (it's the fuel line that is *not* connected to the filter); if the pressure rises, replace the regulator**

hold pressure is less than specified:

a)  *The fuel lines may be leaking.*

b)  *The fuel pressure regulator may be allowing the fuel pressure to bleed through to the return line*

c)  *A fuel injector (or injectors) may be leaking.*

d)  *The fuel pump may be defective.*

16    Before removing the fuel pressure gauge, relieve the fuel pressure (see Section 2).

## 4    Fuel lines and fittings - repair and replacement

**Warning:** *Gasoline is extremely flammable, so take extra precautions when you work on any part of the fuel system. See the* **Warning** *in Section 2.*

## *Inspection*

*Refer to illustration 4.2*

1    Once in a while, you will have to raise the vehicle to service or replace some component (an exhaust pipe hanger, for example). Whenever you work under the vehicle, always inspect the fuel lines and fittings for possible damage or deterioration.

2    Check all hoses and pipes for cracks, kinks, deformation or obstructions **(see illustration)**.

3    Make sure all hose and pipe clips attach their associated hoses or pipes securely to the underside of the vehicle.

4    Verify all hose clamps attaching rubber hoses to metal fuel lines or pipes are snug enough to assure a tight fit between the hoses and the metal pipes.

## *Replacement*

5    If you must replace any damaged sections, use hoses approved for use in fuel systems or tubing made from steel only (it's best to use an original-type pipe that's already flared and pre-bent). Do not install substitutes constructed from inferior or inappropriate material, as this could result in a fuel leak and a fire.

6    Always, before detaching or disassembling any part of the fuel system, note the routing of all hoses and pipes and the orientation of all clamps and clips to assure that replacement sections are installed in exactly the same manner.

7    Before detaching any part of the fuel system, be sure to relieve the fuel pressure (see Section 2).

8    Always use new hose clamps after loosening or removing them.

9    While you're under the vehicle, it's a good idea to check the following related components:

a)  *Check the condition of the fuel filter - make sure that it's not clogged or damaged* (see Chapter 1).

b)  *Inspect the evaporative emission control (EVAP) system. Verify that all hoses are attached and in good condition* (see Chapter 6).

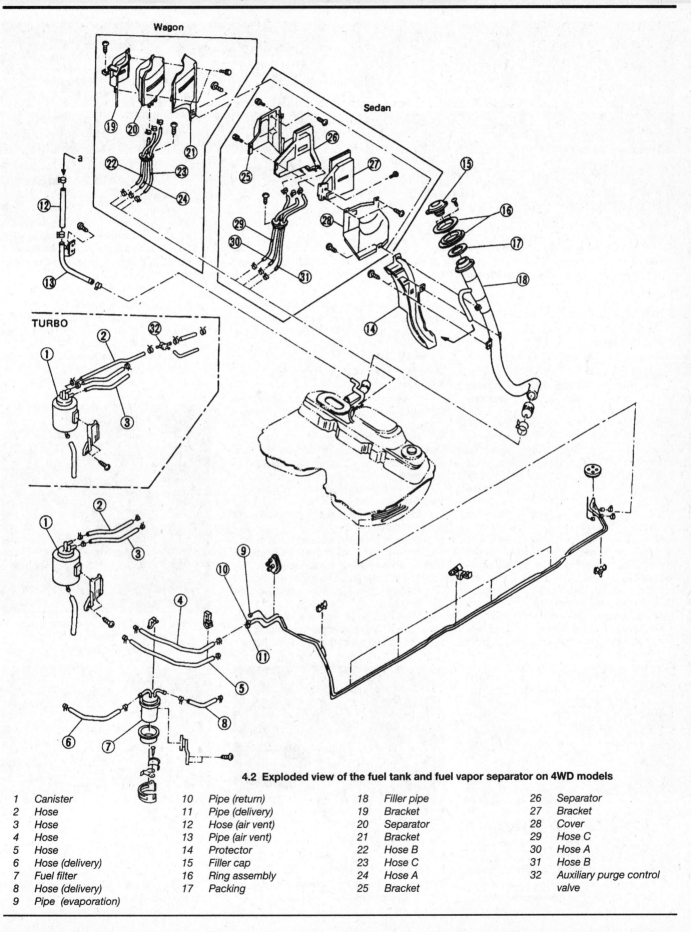

**4.2 Exploded view of the fuel tank and fuel vapor separator on 4WD models**

| | | | | | | | |
|---|---|---|---|---|---|---|---|
| 1 | Canister | 10 | Pipe (return) | 18 | Filler pipe | 26 | Separator |
| 2 | Hose | 11 | Pipe (delivery) | 19 | Bracket | 27 | Bracket |
| 3 | Hose | 12 | Hose (air vent) | 20 | Separator | 28 | Cover |
| 4 | Hose | 13 | Pipe (air vent) | 21 | Bracket | 29 | Hose C |
| 5 | Hose | 14 | Protector | 22 | Hose B | 30 | Hose A |
| 6 | Hose (delivery) | 15 | Filler cap | 23 | Hose C | 31 | Hose B |
| 7 | Fuel filter | 16 | Ring assembly | 24 | Hose A | 32 | Auxiliary purge control |
| 8 | Hose (delivery) | 17 | Packing | 25 | Bracket | | valve |
| 9 | Pipe (evaporation) | | | | | | |

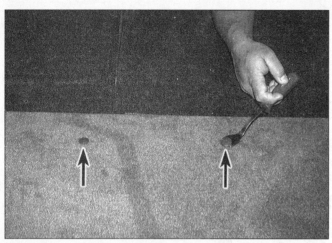

**5.2a Remove the two clips and pull up on the carpet to expose the fuel pump assembly and sending unit (Outback shown)**

**5.2b 4WD models are equipped with a fuel pump/sending unit assembly as well as an additional sending unit**

## 5 Fuel pump and fuel vapor separator - removal and installation

**Warning:** *Gasoline is extremely flammable, so take extra precautions when you work on any part of the fuel system. See the* **Warning** *in Section 2.*

**Note:** *Only 4WD models are equipped with the fuel vapor separator. The fuel vapor separator acts as a vapor filter for the evaporation system (EVAP). The vapor separator is located behind the trim panel in the trunk area, near the rear fender. Refer to illustration 4.2 for additional information.*

**Note:** *The fuel tank on 2WD systems are equipped with a single fuel pump/fuel level sending unit mounted in the fuel tank. The rear seat can be removed to uncover the fuel pump access plate. The fuel pump and sending unit can be removed without dropping the fuel tank. 4WD models are equipped with a divided fuel tank with two sending units to monitor the fuel level in each compartment. The right side compartment is equipped with the fuel pump/sending unit assembly while*

*the left side has the single sending unit. Both are accessible by removing the rear seat or trunk panel then lifting the access plate.*

### Fuel pump

*Refer to illustrations 5.2a, 5.2b, 5.5, 5.7, 5.8a, 5.8b and 5.8c*

1    Relieve the fuel system pressure (see Section 2). Disconnect the negative battery cable.

2    Remove the rear seat (sedan) or trunk liner (station wagon) to expose the fuel pump/sending unit access plate **(see illustrations)**.

3    Remove the access plate screws and lift the plate from the body.

4    Disconnect the fuel pump/sending unit electrical connector.

5    Loosen the fuel line clamps and detach the lines from the pump **(see illustration)**. Also, disconnect the return hose and, on 4WD models, the jet pump hose.

6    Remove the fuel pump/sending unit mounting bolts.

7    Lift the assembly from the fuel tank **(see illustration)**. Carefully angle the sending unit float and screen out of the tank without dam-

aging any of the components.

8    Disconnect the electrical connector, remove the fuel line clamp and detach the fuel pump **(see illustrations)**.

9    Installation is the reverse of removal. Run the engine and check for leaks.

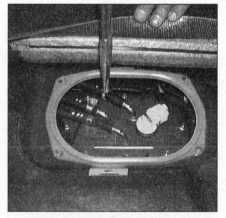

**5.5 Loosen the hose clamps and disconnect the fuel lines from the fuel pump**

**5.7 Carefully lift the fuel pump/sending unit assembly from the access hole**

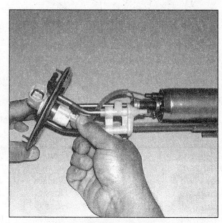

**5.8a Unplug the fuel pump electrical connector from the cover**

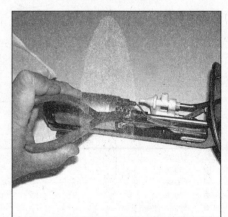

**5.8b Use needle-nose pliers to expand the fuel line hose clamp and slide the clamp up the hose**

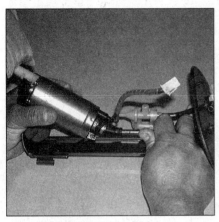

**5.8c  Separate the fuel pump from the cover**

## Fuel vapor separator (4WD models)

*Refer to illustration 5.13a and 5.13b*

10   The vapor separator is located behind the trim panel in the trunk **(see illustration 4.2)**.

11   Remove the right trim panel from the trunk or rear seat area (see Chapter 11).

12   Disconnect the breather hoses from the fuel separator assembly. Be sure to use paint or tape to mark each hose before disassembly.

13   Disconnect the fuel separator evaporation hose and remove the separator as an assembly **(see illustrations)**.

14   Place the fuel vapor separator on the bench and remove the remaining hoses.

15   Installation is the reverse of removal.

---

## 6   Fuel level sending unit - check and replacement

**Warning:** *Gasoline is extremely flammable, so take extra precautions when you work on any part of the fuel system. See the* **Warning** *in Section 2.*

### Check

*Refer to illustrations 6.2 and 6.3*

1   Relieve the fuel system pressure (see Section 2). Disconnect the negative battery cable.

2   Remove the fuel pump/fuel level sending unit from the fuel tank (see Section 5).

**Note:** *4WD models are equipped with a fuel pump/sending unit assembly in the fuel tank right side chamber and a fuel level sending unit in the left side chamber. Be sure to check both sending units* **(see illustration)**.

3   Using an ohmmeter, check the resistance of the sending unit with the float arm completely down (tank empty) and with the arm up (tank full) **(see illustration)**. The resistance should change steadily from empty to full.

4   When the tank is nearly empty (arm down), the resistance of the sending unit should be approximately 50 ohms.

5   With the fuel tank completely full (arm up), the resistance should be approximately 1 ohm.

6   If the readings are incorrect, replace the sending unit.

### Replacement

*Refer to illustrations 6.11a, 6.11b and 6.11c*

7   Lift up the carpet from the trunk area to expose the sending unit access plate **(see illustration 5.2a)**. Remove the access plate.

8   Remove the nuts and remove the unit from the fuel tank **(see illustration 6.2)**.

9   Lift the sending unit from the tank. Carefully angle the sending unit out of the opening without damaging the fuel level float located at the bottom of the assembly.

10   If the sealing gasket is damaged while lifting the sending unit from the fuel tank, replace it with a new one.

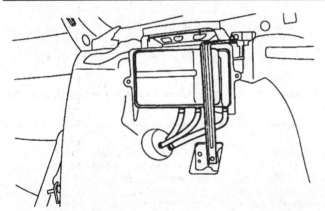

**5.13a  Location of the fuel vapor separator on a station wagon**

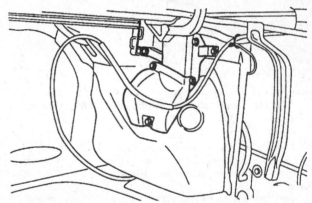

**5.13b  Location of the fuel vapor separator on a sedan**

**6.2  Remove the sending unit mounting nuts**

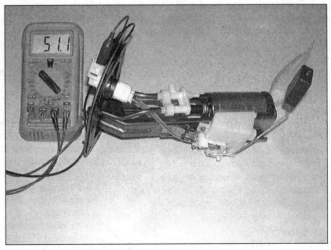

**6.3  Checking the fuel level sending unit resistance**

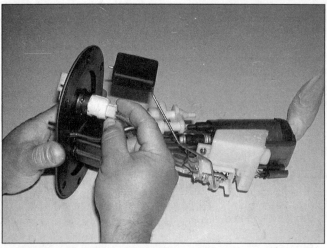

**6.11a  To change the sending unit, first disconnect the electrical connector from the cover . . .**

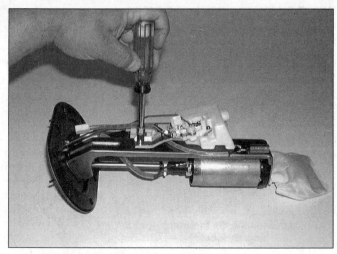

**6.11b  . . . then remove the mounting bolt . . .**

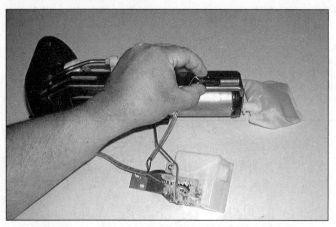

**6.11c  . . . and slide the sending unit off the bracket**

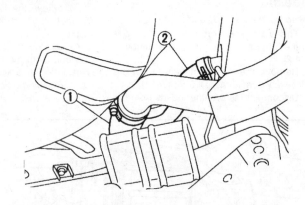

**7.8  Remove the filler pipe (1) and the fuel vapor pipe (2) from the fuel tank**

11   Disconnect the electrical connector, remove the mounting bolt and separate the sending unit from the bracket **(see illustrations).**
12   Installation is the reverse of removal.

## 7   Fuel tank - removal and installation

*Refer to illustrations 7.8 and 7.9*
**Warning:** *Gasoline is extremely flammable, so take extra precautions when you work on any part of the fuel system. See the* **Warning** *in Section 2.*
**Note:** *The following procedure is much easier to perform if the fuel tank is empty. Some tanks have a drain plug for this purpose. If the tank does not have a drain plug, drain the fuel into an approved fuel container using a commercially available siphoning kit (NEVER start a siphoning action by mouth) or wait until the fuel tank is nearly empty, if possible.*
1   Remove the fuel tank filler cap to relieve fuel tank pressure.
2   Detach the cable from the negative terminal of the battery.

3   Raise the vehicle and place it securely on jackstands.
4   If there is fuel remaining in the tank, siphon it out from the fuel inlet and allow the fuel to drain in an approved gasoline container. Remember - NEVER start the siphoning action by mouth! Use a siphoning kit, which can be purchased at most auto parts stores.
5   Remove the rear exhaust pipe and muffler (see Section 17).
6   On 4WD models, remove the rear differential (see Chapter 8).
7   On 4WD models, detach the lower control arms from the rear crossmember (see Chapter 10), remove the bolts retaining the rear crossmember to the body and remove the rear crossmember.
8   Disconnect the fuel filler tube from the pipe on the vehicle **(see illustration)**.
9   Disconnect the fuel lines and the vapor return line **(see illustration)**. **Note:** *The fuel feed and return lines and the vapor return line are three different diameters, so reattachment is simplified. If you have any doubts, however, clearly label the three lines and the fittings. Be sure to plug the hoses to prevent leakage and contamination of the fuel system.*

10   Support the fuel tank with a floor jack. Position a piece of wood between the jack head and the fuel tank to protect the tank.
11   Remove the fuel tank shields, then remove the bolts that retain the fuel tank straps to the chassis.
12   Remove the tank from the vehicle.
13   Installation is the reverse of removal.

## 8   Fuel tank cleaning and repair - general information

1   All repairs to the fuel tank or filler neck should be carried out by a professional who has experience in this critical and potentially dangerous work. Even after cleaning and flushing of the fuel system, explosive fumes can remain and ignite during repair of the tank.
2   If the fuel tank is removed from the vehicle, it should not be placed in an area where sparks or open flames could ignite the fumes coming out of the tank. Be especially careful inside garages where a natural gas-type appliance is located, because the pilot light could cause an explosion.

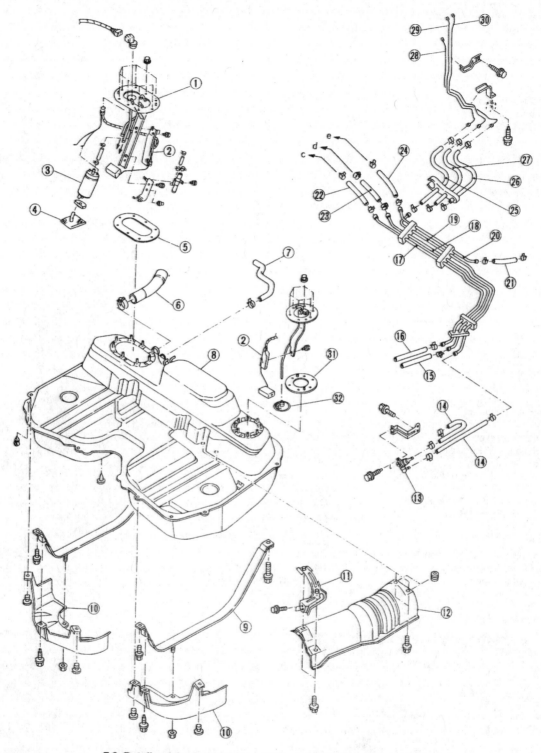

**7.9 Details of the fuel tank on a 4WD model (2WD models similar)**

| | | | | | | | | |
|---|---|---|---|---|---|---|---|---|
| 1 | Fuel pump assembly | 9 | Band | 17 | Pipe (return) | 25 | Hose (evaporation) |
| 2 | Fuel level sending unit | 10 | Protector | 18 | Pipe (delivery) | 26 | Hose (air breather) |
| 3 | Fuel pump | 11 | Bracket | 19 | Pipe (evaporation) | 27 | Hose (air breather) |
| 4 | Fuel filter | 12 | Cover | 20 | Pipe (sub delivery) | 28 | Pipe (evaporation) |
| 5 | Gasket | 13 | Roll over valve | 21 | Hose (sub delivery) | 29 | Pipe (air breather) |
| 6 | Filler hose | 14 | Hose (evaporation) | 22 | Hose (return) | 30 | Pipe (air breather) |
| 7 | Air vent hose | 15 | Hose (delivery) | 23 | Hose (delivery) | 31 | Gasket |
| 8 | Tank | 16 | Hose (return) | 24 | Hose (sub delivery) | 32 | Filter |

## 9   Air cleaner housing - removal and installation

*Refer to illustrations 9.4a and 9.4b*

1   Detach the cable from the negative terminal of the battery.

2   Remove the air filter from the air cleaner housing (see Chapter 1).

3   Loosen the clamp on the air intake duct and separate the duct from the housing.

4   Unclip the upper half of the air cleaner housing and remove it **(see illustrations)**. Leave the airflow meter and air intake duct attached to the upper cover.

5   Remove the mounting bolts from the air cleaner housing.

6   Remove the housing from the engine compartment.

7   Installation is the reverse of removal.

## 10   Accelerator cable - removal, installation and adjustment

### Removal

*Refer to illustrations 10.2 and 10.4*

1   Remove the air filter assembly (see Section 2).

2   Detach the accelerator cable from the throttle lever **(see illustration)**.

3   If equipped, remove the cruise control cable from the cable bracket.

4   Separate the accelerator cable from the cable bracket **(see illustration)**.

5   Detach the nylon collar from the upper end of the accelerator pedal arm.

6   Remove the cable through the firewall from the engine compartment side.

### Installation

7   Installation is the reverse of removal. Be sure the cable is routed correctly.

8   If necessary, at the engine compartment side of the firewall, apply sealant around the accelerator cable to prevent water from entering the passenger compartment.

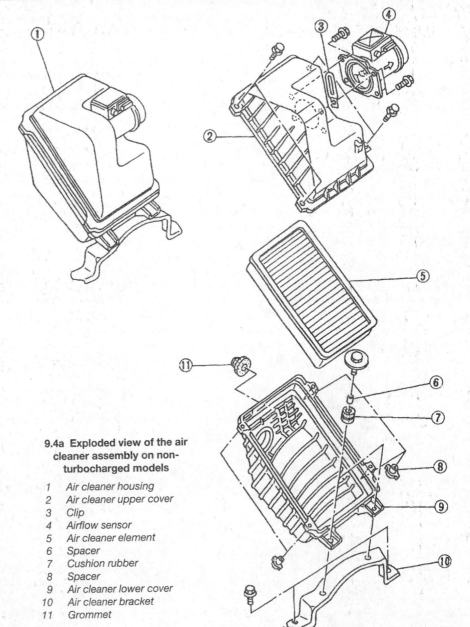

**9.4a Exploded view of the air cleaner assembly on non-turbocharged models**

1   *Air cleaner housing*
2   *Air cleaner upper cover*
3   *Clip*
4   *Airflow sensor*
5   *Air cleaner element*
6   *Spacer*
7   *Cushion rubber*
8   *Spacer*
9   *Air cleaner lower cover*
10   *Air cleaner bracket*
11   *Grommet*

**10.2 Rotate the throttle cable end until the cable aligns with the slot in the throttle lever**

**10.4 Unscrew the locknut (on the left), then pass the cable casing through the slot in the bracket**

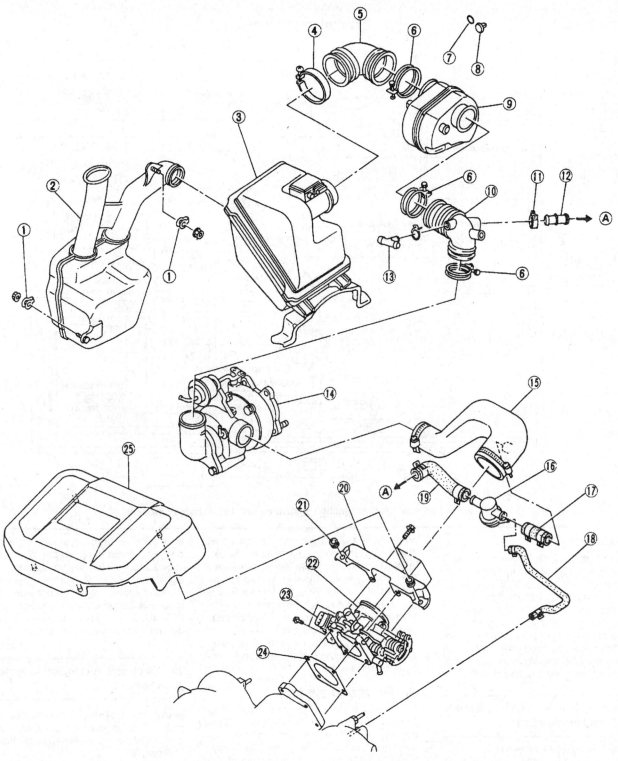

**9.4b  Exploded view of the air cleaner assembly on turbocharged models**

| | | | | | | |
|---|---|---|---|---|---|---|
| 1 | Cushion | 9 | Resonator chamber | 15 | Air outlet duct | 20 | Cushion |
| 2 | Resonator | 10 | Air inlet duct | 16 | Air by-pass valve | 21 | Collector cover bracket |
| 3 | Air cleaner assembly | 11 | Hose clamp | 17 | Connector hose A (to | 22 | Throttle body |
| 4 | Hose clamp | 12 | Connector hose (By-pass | | intake duct) | 23 | Throttle sensor |
| 5 | Air intake duct | | valve) | 18 | By-pass valve vacuum | 24 | Gasket |
| 6 | Hose clamp | 13 | Connector hose (PCV | | hose | 25 | Collector cover |
| 7 | O-ring | | valve) | 19 | Connector hose B | | |
| 8 | Clip | 14 | Turbocharger | | | | |

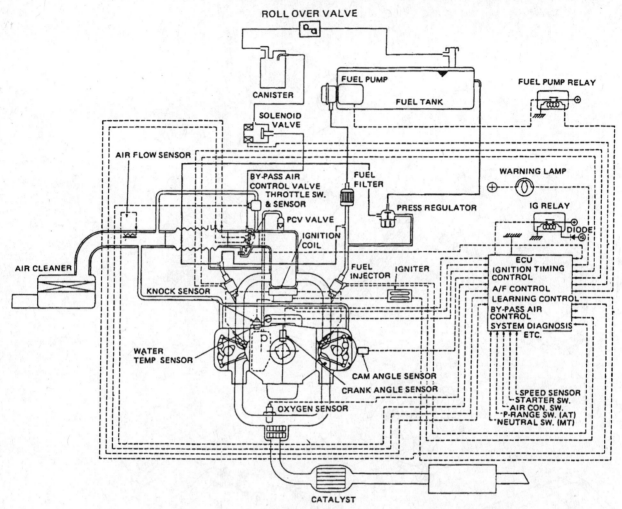

**11.1a  Schematic of the fuel injection system on non-turbocharged models**

## Adjustment

9    To adjust the cable. move the adjusting nut and lock nut as necessary to produce a cable deflection of 3/8 to 1/2-inch.

10   After you have adjusted the throttle cable, have an assistant help you verify that the throttle valve opens all the way when you depress the accelerator pedal to the floor and that it returns to the idle position when you release the accelerator. Verify the cable operates smoothly. It must not bind or stick.

## 11   Electronic fuel injection system - general information

*Refer to illustrations 11.1a and 11.1b*

1    These models are equipped with a multi-point Electronic Fuel Injection (EFI) system. The EFI system is composed of three basic subsystems: fuel system, air induction system and electronic control system **(see illustrations)**.

## Fuel system

2    An electric fuel pump located inside the fuel tank supplies fuel under constant pres-

sure to the fuel rail, which distributes fuel evenly to all injectors. From the fuel rail, fuel is injected into the intake ports, just above the intake valves, by fuel injectors. The amount of fuel supplied by the injectors is precisely controlled by an Electronic Control Module (ECM). A pressure regulator controls system pressure in relation to intake manifold vacuum. A fuel filter between the fuel pump and the fuel rail filters fuel to protect the components of the system.

## Air induction system

3    The air induction system consists of an air cleaner housing, the throttle body and the ducting. An airflow sensor monitors the amount of incoming air. This information helps the ECM determine the amount of fuel to be injected by the injectors.

## Electronic control system

4    The computer control system controls the fuel injection and other systems by means of an Electronic Control Module (ECM), which employs a microcomputer. The ECM receives signals from a number of information sensors which monitor such variables

as intake air temperature, throttle angle, coolant temperature, engine rpm, vehicle speed and exhaust oxygen content. These signals help the ECM determine the injection duration necessary for the optimum air/fuel ratio. For further information regarding the ECM and its relationship to the engine electrical and ignition system, see Chapter 6.

## 12   Electronic fuel injection system - check

**Warning:** *Gasoline is extremely flammable, so take extra precautions when you work on any part of the fuel system. See the* **Warning** *in Section 2.*
**Note:** *The following procedure is based on the assumption that the fuel pump is working and the fuel pressure is adequate.*

## Preliminary checks

1    Check all electrical connectors that are related to the system. Loose electrical connectors and poor grounds can cause many problems that resemble more serious malfunctions.

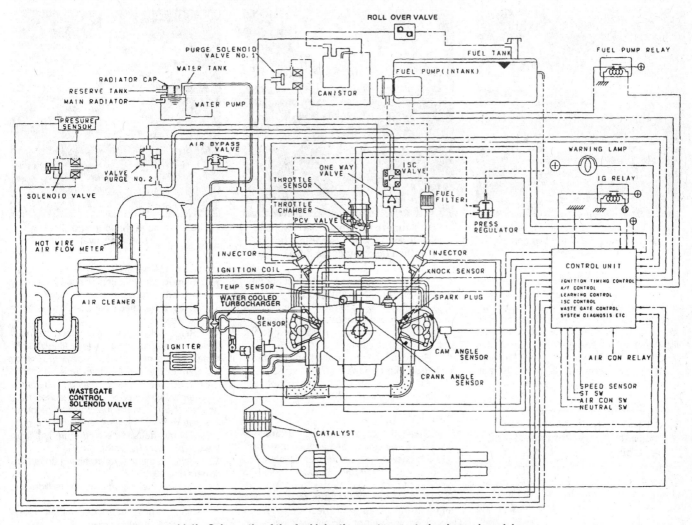

**11.1b Schematic of the fuel injection system on turbocharged models**

2    Check to see that the battery is fully charged, as the control unit and sensors depend on an accurate supply voltage in order to properly meter the fuel.

3    Check the air filter element - a dirty or partially blocked filter will severely impede performance and economy (see Chapter 1).

4    Check the gas cap - a damaged cap or clogged cap vents can cause vapor lock. Clean the vents or replace the cap.

5    If a blown fuse is found, replace it and see if it blows again. If it does, search for a grounded wire in the harness to the fuel pump (see Chapter 12).

### System checks

*Refer to illustration 12.8, 12.9 and 12.10*

6    Check the condition of the vacuum hoses connected to the intake manifold.

7    Remove the air intake duct from the throttle body and check for dirt, carbon or other residue build-up in the throttle body, particularly around the throttle plate. If it's dirty, clean it with aerosol carburetor cleaner, a rag and a toothbrush, if necessary.

8    With the engine running, place an automotive stethoscope against each injector, one at a time, and listen for a clicking sound, indicating operation **(see illustration)**. If you don't have a stethoscope, you can place the tip of a long screwdriver against the injector and listen through the handle.

9    If an injector isn't functioning (not click-ing), purchase a special injector test light (sometimes called a noid light) and install it into the injector electrical connector. Start the engine and check to see if the noid light flashes **(see illustration)**. If it does, the injector is receiving proper voltage. If it doesn't

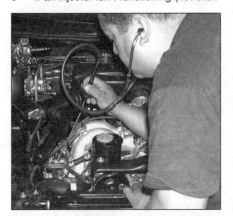

**12.8  Use a stethoscope or screwdriver to determine if the injectors are working properly - they should make a steady clicking sound that rises and falls with engine speed changes**

**12.9  Install the "noid" light into the fuel injector electrical connector and check to see that it blinks with the engine running**

**12.10 Using an ohmmeter, measure the resistance across the terminals of the injector**

**13.4 Squeeze the clamps (arrows) and slide them back on the coolant hoses, then disconnect the hoses**

**13.5 Remove the four throttle body bolts (arrows)**

flash, further diagnosis should be performed.
10   With the engine OFF and the fuel injector electrical connectors disconnected, measure the resistance of each injector **(see illustration)**. Compare your measurements with the injector resistance listed in this Chapter's Specifications. If any injector is shorted, open or has an abnormally high resistance, replace it with a new one.

## 13   Electronic Fuel Injection (EFI) system - component check and replacement

**Warning:** *Gasoline is extremely flammable, so take extra precautions when you work on any part of the fuel system. See the* **Warning** *in Section 2.*

### *Throttle body*

#### Removal

*Refer to illustration 13.4 and 13.5*
**Warning:** *Wait until the engine is completely cool before beginning this procedure.*
1   Detach the cable from the negative terminal of the battery.
2   Detach the electrical connector from the throttle position sensor.

3   Disconnect the accelerator cable (see Section 10) from the throttle body.
4   Carefully mark and remove the vacuum hoses and coolant hoses **(see illustration)** from the throttle body. Plug the coolant hoses to prevent leakage.
5   Remove the four throttle body mounting bolts **(see illustration)**.
6   Remove and discard the gasket between the throttle body and intake manifold.

#### Installation

7   Clean the gasket mating surfaces. If scraping is necessary, be careful not to damage the gasket surfaces or allow material to drop into the manifold. Installation is the reverse of removal. Be sure to tighten the throttle body mounting bolts to the torque listed in this Chapter's Specifications. If a significant amount of coolant was lost when the hoses were disconnected, check the coolant level and add some, if necessary (see Chapter 1).

### *Fuel rail*

*Refer to illustration 13.11*

#### Removal

8   Relieve the fuel pressure (see Section 2). Detach the cable from the negative

terminal of the battery.
9   Remove any ducting or hoses that may interfere with removal of the fuel rail(s).
10   Unplug the electrical connectors from the fuel injectors.
11   Remove the screws and detach the metal fuel line(s) from the fuel rail **(see illustration)**. **Note:** *The fuel rail on the left side of the engine has a metal fuel line attached to each end of the fuel rail. The fuel rail on the right side of the engine has only one metal line attached to it; on the other end is the fuel pressure regulator and return line. If you're removing the right side fuel rail, detach the fuel return line from the fuel pressure regulator.*
12   Remove the fuel rail retaining bolts **(see illustration 13.11)**.
13   Pull the fuel rail and injectors from the intake manifold.
14   Plug the holes in the manifold with rags to prevent the entry of debris.

#### Installation

15   Inspect the rubber seals for cracks and deterioration. It's a good idea to replace them whenever the fuel rail is removed.
16   Install the fuel rail and injector assembly onto the engine. Tighten the mounting bolts to the torque listed in this Chapter's Specifications.
17   Connect the fuel line(s) to the fuel rail, using new O-rings. Tighten the screws securely. If you removed the right-side fuel rail, connect the fuel return line to the fuel pressure regulator.
18   Reconnect the electrical connectors to the fuel injectors. Install any components that were removed for access to the fuel rail.

### *Fuel pressure regulator*

*Refer to illustration 13.26*

#### Check

19   Refer to Section 3 for fuel pressure regulator diagnosis.
20   Start the engine and check for leakage around the fuel rail, fuel lines and the fuel pressure regulator.
21   If the fuel pressure regulator is faulty or leaking, replace it.

**13.11 Fuel rail mounting details**

A   *Fuel line attaching screws*
B   *Fuel rail mounting bolts*
C   *Fuel return line*

**13.26  Remove the screws and detach the fuel pressure regulator from the fuel rail, then separate the regulator from the fuel return line**

**13.32  Remove the screws from the injector cap (arrows) . . .**

**13.33  . . . then twist and pull the fuel injector out of the fuel rail**

## Replacement

22   Relieve the fuel pressure from the system (see Section 2).
23   Disconnect the cable from the negative terminal of the battery.
24   Remove the air intake duct.
25   Clean any dirt from around the fuel pressure regulator. Disconnect the vacuum hose from the regulator.
26   Loosen the hose clamp and remove the fuel pressure regulator mounting screws. Separate the regulator from the fuel rail, then detach the regulator from the fuel return line **(see illustration)**.
27   Install new O-rings on the pressure regulator and lubricate them with a light coat of oil.
28   Installation is the reverse of removal. Tighten the pressure regulator mounting screws and the hose clamp securely.

## Fuel injectors

*Refer to illustrations 13.32, 13.33 and 13.34*

### Check

29   Refer to Section 12 for the fuel injector checking procedure.

### Removal

30   Relieve the system fuel pressure (see Section 2).
31   Unplug the electrical connector from the fuel injector.
32   Remove the screws from the injector cap **(see illustration)**.
33   Grasping the injector body, pull up while gently twisting the injector **(see illustration)**.
34   Inspect the injector O-rings and insulator for signs of deterioration **(see illustration)**. **Note:** *It's a good idea to replace the O-rings and insulator whenever an injector is removed.*

### Installation

35   Lubricate the new O-rings with light grade oil and install them on the injector. **Caution:** *Do not use silicone grease. It will clog the injectors.*
36   Using a light twisting motion, install the injector.
37   The remainder of installation is the reverse of removal.

## Idle Air Control (IAC) solenoid valve

**Note:** *In the event the idle speed is incorrect, there may be many different sources of trou-*

ble. The most common is an intake manifold leak, a vacuum hose broken or missing or a defective IAC valve that is not regulating air properly. Also check the throttle body and clean it, if necessary, as described in Section 12.

### General information

38   The IAC solenoid valve is controlled by the ECM and allows air to bypass the throttle plate to regulate the idle speed.

### Check

*Refer to illustrations 13.39 and 13.41*

39   With the engine completely cold, turn the ignition key On and check for the presence of battery voltage on the IAC solenoid valve electrical connector **(see illustration)**. Battery voltage should be present.
40   Allow the engine to warm up to normal operating temperature, turn the ignition key OFF and remove the IAC valve. Check to make sure the shutter has been activated and is completely closed (no air flow). If the shutter is open, replace the IAC solenoid valve.
41   Check the IAC solenoid valve resistance **(see illustration)**. If the resistance indicates a short or open, replace the IAC solenoid valve.

**13.34  Check the condition of the fuel injector O-rings and the insulator on the underside of the cap**

**13.39  Check for battery voltage on the middle terminal with the ignition key ON (engine not running)**

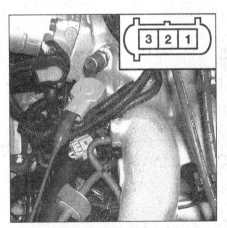

**13.41  First check the IAC resistance between terminals 1 and 2. Next, check the resistance between terminals 2 and 3. Both readings should be 9 ohms**

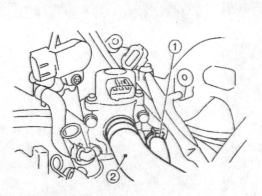

**13.43 Disconnect the air hose (2) and the coolant line (1) from the IAC solenoid valve**

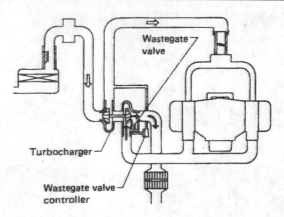

**14.1 Schematic of the turbocharger system**

## Replacement

*Refer to illustration 13.43*

42   Detach the IAC solenoid valve electrical connector and disconnect the two hoses.
43   Remove the mounting bolts **(see illustration)**.
44   Lift the assembly from the intake manifold.
45   Installation is the reverse of removal. Be sure to use a new gasket and tighten the mounting bolts securely.

## 14  Turbocharger - general information

*Refer to illustration 14.1*

The turbocharger increases power by using an exhaust gas-driven turbine to pressurize the air entering the combustion chambers **(see illustration)**. The amount of boost (intake manifold pressure) is controlled by the wastegate (exhaust bypass valve). The wastegate is operated by a spring-loaded actuator assembly which controls the maximum boost level by allowing some of the exhaust gas to bypass the turbine. While the

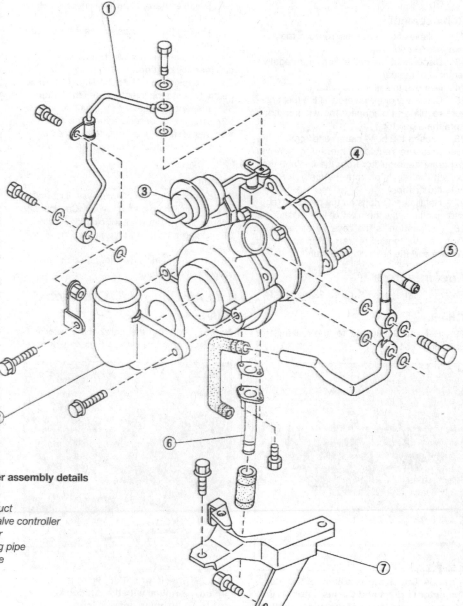

**15.8 Turbocharger assembly details**

1   *Oil inlet pipe*
2   *Turbo inlet duct*
3   *Wastegate valve controller*
4   *Turbocharger*
5   *Turbo cooling pipe*
6   *Oil outlet pipe*
7   *Bracket*

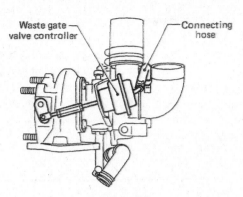

**15.11 Check the wastegate solenoid for proper operation**

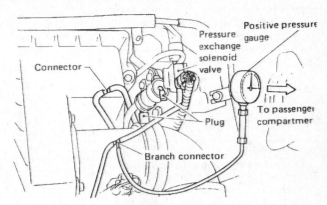

**15.14 Connect an air pressure gauge as shown to check turbocharger boost pressure**

supercharging pressure is lower than the pre-determined level, the wastegate is closed allowing all the exhaust gas through to the turbine inside the turbocharger. When exhaust pressure exceeds the specified level, it is diverted to the exhaust pipe by way of the wastegate valve.

These turbocharger systems are equipped with a pressure sensor and a pressure exchange solenoid valve. The pressure sensor relays the correct pressure readings according to altitude to the computer while the pressure exchange solenoid is an output actuator that indirectly controls the activation of the wastegate valve.

## 15 Turbocharger - check

### Turbocharger check

*Refer to illustration 15.8*

1    While it is a relatively simple device, the turbocharger is also a precision component which can be severely damaged by an interrupted oil or coolant supply or loose or damaged ducts.

2    Due to the special techniques and equipment required, checking and diagnosis of suspected problems dealing with the turbocharger should be left to a dealer service department or other qualified repair shop. The home mechanic can, however, check the connections and linkages for security, damage and other obvious problems. Also, the home mechanic can check components that govern the turbocharger such as the wastegate solenoid and wastegate actuator. Refer to the checks later in this Section.

3    Because each turbocharger has its own distinctive sound, a change in the noise level can be a sign of potential problems.

4    A high-pitched or whistling sound is a symptom of an inlet air or exhaust gas leak.

5    If an unusual sound comes from the vicinity of the turbine, the turbocharger can be removed and the turbine wheel inspected. **Caution:** *All checks must be made with the engine off and cool to the touch and the turbocharger stopped or personal injury could*

*result. Operating the engine without all the turbocharger ducts and filters installed is also dangerous and can result in damage to the turbine wheel blades.*

6    With the engine OFF, reach inside the housing and turn the turbine wheel to make sure it spins freely. If it doesn't, it's possible the oil has sludged or coked from overheating. Push in on the turbine wheel and check for binding. The turbine should rotate freely with no binding or rubbing on the housing. If it does the turbine bearing is worn out.

7    Check the exhaust manifold for cracks and loose connections.

8    Because the turbine wheel rotates at speeds up to 140,000 rpm, severe damage can result from the interruption of coolant or contamination of the oil supply to the turbine bearings. Check for leaks in the coolant and oil inlet lines **(see illustration)** and obstructions in the oil drain-back line, as this can cause severe oil loss through the turbocharger seals. Burned oil on the turbine housing is a sign of this. **Caution:** *Whenever a major engine bearing such as a main, connecting rod or camshaft bearing is replaced, the turbocharger should be flushed with clean oil.*

### Wastegate actuator check

*Refer to illustration 15.11 and 15.14*

9    The turbocharger wastegate provides additional low speed boost without overboost at high speeds. This increases low speed torque and improves driveability. It is important that the wastegate is properly adjusted. The wastegate actuator (solenoid) is controlled by the pressure signal produced by the release of warm, compressed air from the turbocharger.

10    Remove the pressure hose from the wastegate valve (solenoid).

11    Connect a hand-held pressure pump to the hose and apply approximately 9 to 10 psi pressure to the actuator **(see illustration)** and make sure the actuator rod moves. **Caution:** *Do not apply more than the specified pressure to avoid damaging the actuator.*

12    The control rod should move slightly and hold its position. Make sure the wastegate lever and wastegate are not binding.

13    If the test results are incorrect, replace the wastegate valve (solenoid).

14    Check the boost pressure. If the boost is too high, the engine may knock and air will be released through the air relief valve. Overboost is usually caused by the wastegate actuator being faulty or stuck closed. Too little boost causes a lack of engine power, poor acceleration or increased fuel consumption. Too little boost is often caused by leaks in the turbo system hoses. With the engine at operating temperatures, connect a T-fitting to the intake pipe pressure hose and install a pressure gauge **(see illustration)**.

15    With the clutch pedal pressed down (manual transmission), raise the engine rpm to 4,600 rpm and check the boost pressure. It should be 6 to 7 psi. If the pressure is less, check the intake and exhaust system for leaks. Also, check the air relief valve (if equipped) for hissing sounds. Replace if necessary. If there are no leaks, replace the turbocharger.

16    If the boost pressure is more than specified, check for a possible damaged wastegate valve.

### General checks

*Refer to illustration 15.17*

17    If oil leakage is detected inside the intake system, check for a loose or damaged turbine shaft. Although slight amounts of oil does not necessarily indicate problems with the turbocharger, it is best to examine the unit carefully. Install a dial indicator and confirm that the axial play does not exceed 0.0035 inch **(see illustration)**. Replace the turbocharger if the axial play is excessive.

18    If the system checks out correctly but the TURBO light on the dash remains on or illuminates at the incorrect rpm range, check the pressure switch and other sensors directly involved with the fuel and emissions system. Refer to Chapter 6 for the testing and replacement procedures.

19    Also, check the knock control system. This system detects excessive engine knocking and retards the ignition timing to prevent excessive detonation. Refer to Chapter 6 for checking procedures.

## 16  Turbocharger - removal and installation

**Caution:** *The turbocharger is a high-speed component, assembled and balanced to very fine tolerances. Do not disassemble it or try to repair it.*

### Removal

1    Disconnect the negative battery cable from the battery.
2    Drain the engine coolant from the radiator and engine block (see Chapter 1).
3    Remove the collector cover and disconnect the PCV from the intake system (see Chapter 6).

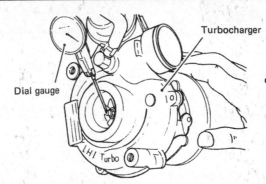

**15.17  Use a dial indicator to check the turbine shaft axial play**

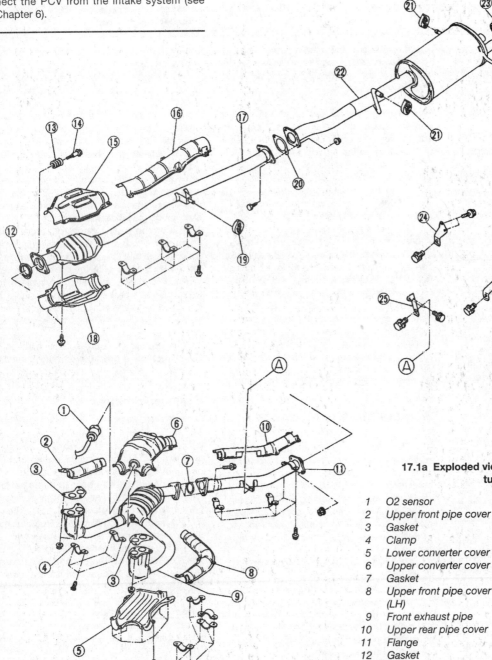

**17.1a  Exploded view of the exhaust system on a non-turbocharged model**

| | | | |
|---|---|---|---|
| 1 | O2 sensor | 15 | Upper cover |
| 2 | Upper front pipe cover | 16 | Upper cover |
| 3 | Gasket | 17 | Rear exhaust pipe |
| 4 | Clamp | 18 | Lower cover |
| 5 | Lower converter cover | 19 | Rubber hanger |
| 6 | Upper converter cover | 20 | Gasket |
| 7 | Gasket | 21 | Rubber hanger |
| 8 | Upper front pipe cover (LH) | 22 | Muffler |
| 9 | Front exhaust pipe | 23 | Tailpipe tips |
| 10 | Upper rear pipe cover | 24 | Bracket (automatic transaxle models) |
| 11 | Flange | 25 | Bracket (manual transaxle, 2WD) |
| 12 | Gasket | | |
| 13 | Spring | 26 | Bracket (manual transaxle, 4WD) |
| 14 | Bolt | | |

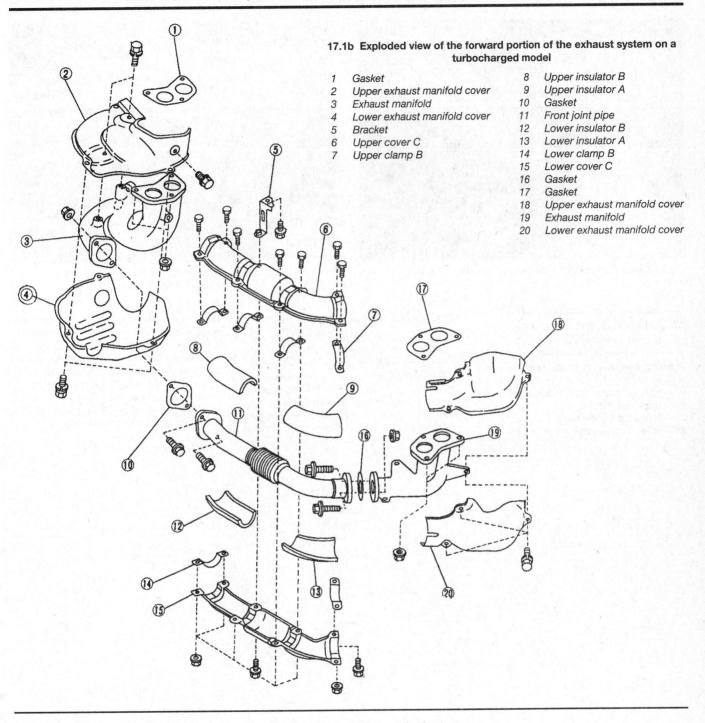

**17.1b Exploded view of the forward portion of the exhaust system on a turbocharged model**

| | | | |
|---|---|---|---|
| 1 | Gasket | 8 | Upper insulator B |
| 2 | Upper exhaust manifold cover | 9 | Upper insulator A |
| 3 | Exhaust manifold | 10 | Gasket |
| 4 | Lower exhaust manifold cover | 11 | Front joint pipe |
| 5 | Bracket | 12 | Lower insulator B |
| 6 | Upper cover C | 13 | Lower insulator A |
| 7 | Upper clamp B | 14 | Lower clamp B |
| | | 15 | Lower cover C |
| | | 16 | Gasket |
| | | 17 | Gasket |
| | | 18 | Upper exhaust manifold cover |
| | | 19 | Exhaust manifold |
| | | 20 | Lower exhaust manifold cover |

4    Disconnect the air inlet ducts, the air cleaner assembly and the resonator and remove the assembly from the top of the engine **(see illustration 9.4b)**.

5    Disconnect the hose from the turbo coolant pipe **(see illustration 15.8)**.

6    Remove the turbocharger mounting bracket.

7    Remove the turbocharger inlet duct.

8    Remove the bolts that retain the oil supply line and the oil return line **(see illustration 15.8)**. The oil return line is bolted to the bottom of the turbocharger. Be ready with a rag to catch any oil from the lines as they are disconnected.

9    Remove the nuts that retain the turbocharger to the exhaust manifold, being careful not to damage the wastegate actuator rod, line or bracket. **Note:** *The wastegate valve is precisely adjusted. Be careful when laying the complete turbocharger unit on the bench, so as not to disturb wastegate actuator alignment.*

## Installation

10    Use a die to clean the studs in the turbocharger mounting portion of the exhaust manifold and coat them with anti-seize compound. Bolt the turbocharger onto the exhaust manifold, using a new gasket. Tighten the bolts to the torque listed in this Chapter's Specifications.

11    Reinstall the oil drain line fitting and line with a new gasket.

12    Prime the center bearing of the turbocharger with oil by squirting some clean engine oil into the oil supply hole on top, while turning the compressor wheel, then install the supply line. **Warning:** *The turbine or compressor wheels have very sharp blades; do not turn the blades with your fingers. Use a plastic pen.*

13    The remainder of installation is the reverse of removal.

**17.1c Spray the exhaust nuts with penetrating oil before removal**

**17.1d Check the condition of the rubber hangers for the muffler (arrows)**

## 17 Exhaust system servicing - general information

**Warning:** *The vehicle's exhaust system generates very high temperatures and must be allowed to cool down completely before any of the components are touched. Be especially careful around the catalytic converter, where the highest temperatures are generated.*

### General Information

*Refer to illustrations 17.1a, 17.1b, 17.1c and 17.1d*

1   Replacement of exhaust system components is basically a matter of removing the heat shields, disconnecting the component and installing a new one **(see illustrations)**. The heat shields and exhaust system hangers must be reinstalled in the original locations or damage could result. Due to the high temperatures and exposed locations of the exhaust system components, rust and corrosion can seize parts together. Penetrating oils are available to help loosen frozen fasteners. However, in some cases it may be necessary to cut the pieces apart with a hacksaw or cutting torch. The latter method should be employed only by persons experienced in this work.

# Chapter 5
# Engine electrical systems

## Contents

## Specifications

### Battery voltage
| | |
|---|---|
| Engine off | 12 volts |
| Engine running | 14 to 15 volts |

### Spark plug wire resistance (approximate)
| | |
|---|---|
| Number 1 | 4,950 to 11,560 ohms |
| Number 2 | 4,860 to 11,330 ohms |
| Number 3 | 4,950 to 11,560 ohms |
| Number 4 | 5,240 to 12,230 ohms |

### Ignition coil resistance (approximate)
Hitachi
| | |
|---|---|
| Primary resistance | 0.63 to 0.77 ohms |
| Secondary resistance | 10.4 to 15.6 k-ohms |

Diamond
| | |
|---|---|
| Primary resistance | 0.40 to 1.00 ohms |
| Secondary resistance | 17.9 to 24.5 k-ohms |

### Ignition timing and idle speed*
1990 through 1994
Manual transaxle
| | |
|---|---|
| Non-turbo | 18 to 22 degrees BTDC @ 700 rpm |
| Turbo | 7 to 23 degrees BTDC @ 700 rpm |

Automatic transaxle
| | |
|---|---|
| Non-turbo | 12 to 28 degrees BTDC @ 700 rpm |
| Turbo | 7 to 23 degrees BTDC @ 700 rpm |

1995 and later
Sedan models
| | |
|---|---|
| Manual transaxle | 14 degrees BTDC @ 700 rpm |
| Automatic transaxle | 20 degrees BTDC @ 700 rpm |
| Station wagon and Outback models | 15 degrees BTDC @ 700 rpm |

* Use the information printed on the Vehicle Emissions Control Information label, if different than the Specifications listed here.

### Alternator brush length
| | |
|---|---|
| New | 45/64-inch |
| Minimum | 1/4-inch |

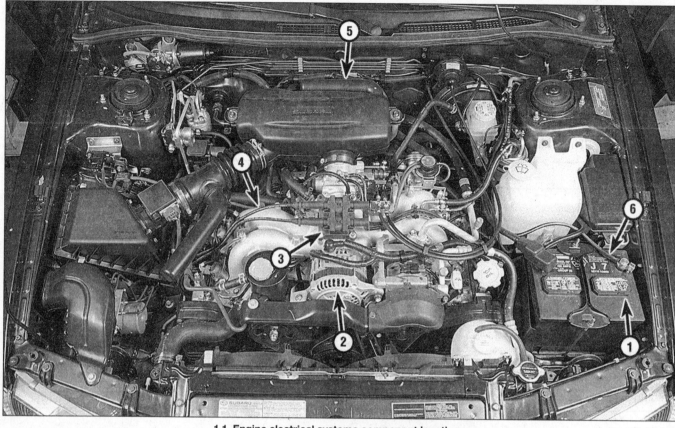

**1.1 Engine electrical systems component locations**

| | | | | | |
|---|---|---|---|---|---|
| 1 | Battery | 3 | Ignition coil | 5 | Igniter |
| 2 | Alternator | 4 | Spark plug wire | 6 | Battery cable |

## 1   General information

*Refer to illustration 1.1*

The engine electrical systems include all ignition, charging and starting components **(see illustration)**. Because of their engine-related functions, these components are considered separately from chassis electrical devices like the lights, instruments, etc.

Be very careful when working on the engine electrical components. They are easily damaged if checked, connected or handled improperly. The alternator is driven by an engine drivebelt which could cause serious injury if your hands, hair or clothes become entangled in it with the engine running. Both the starter and alternator are connected directly to the battery and could arc or even cause a fire if mishandled, overloaded or shorted out.

Never leave the ignition switch on for long periods of time with the engine off. Do not disconnect the battery cables while the engine is running. Correct polarity must be maintained when connecting battery cables from another source, such as another vehicle, during jump starting. Always disconnect the negative cable first and hook it up last or the battery may be shorted by the tool being used to loosen the cable clamps.

Additional safety related information on the engine electrical systems can be found in *Safety first* near the front of this manual. It should be referred to before beginning any operation included in this Chapter.

## 2   Battery - emergency jump starting

Refer to the *Booster battery (jump) starting* procedure at the front of this manual.

**3.2  Remove the nuts (arrows) that retain the battery strap to the hold-down bolts**

## 3   Battery - removal and installation

*Refer to illustrations 3.2 and 3.4*

1    Disconnect both cables from the battery terminals. **Caution:** *Always disconnect the negative cable first and hook it up last or the battery may be shorted by the tool being used to loosen the cable clamps.*

2    Locate the battery hold-down clamp straddling the top of the battery. Remove the nuts and the hold-down clamp **(see illustration)**.

**3.4  Lift the battery tray from the engine compartment**

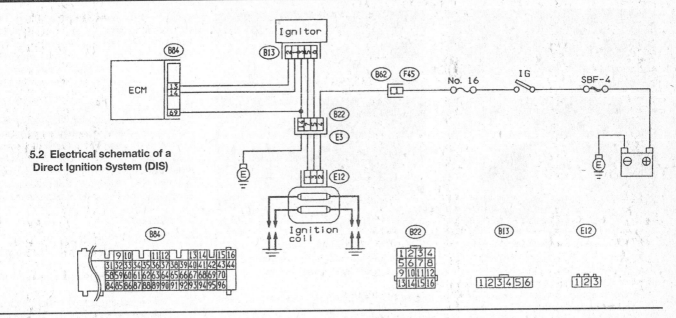

5.2 Electrical schematic of a Direct Ignition System (DIS)

3    Lift out the battery. Use the special straps that attach to the battery posts - lifting and moving the battery is much easier if you use one.
4    Remove the battery tray and inspect the area beneath it for corrosion deposits or fluid leakage from the battery **(see illustration)**.
5    Installation is the reverse of removal.

## 4    Battery cables - check and replacement

1    Periodically inspect the entire length of each battery cable for damage, cracked or burned insulation and corrosion. Poor battery cable connections can cause starting problems and decreased engine performance.
2    Check the cable-to-terminal connections at the ends of the cables for cracks, loose wire strands and corrosion. The presence of white, fluffy deposits under the insulation at the cable terminal connection is a sign that the cable is corroded and should be replaced. Check the terminals for distortion, missing mounting bolts and corrosion.
3    When replacing the cables, always disconnect the negative cable first and hook it up last or the battery may be shorted by the tool used to loosen the cable clamps. Even if only the positive cable is being replaced, be sure to disconnect the negative cable from the battery first.
4    Disconnect and remove the cable. Make sure the replacement cable is the same length and diameter.
5    Clean the threads of the starter solenoid or ground connection with a wire brush to remove rust and corrosion. Apply a light coat of petroleum jelly to the threads to prevent future corrosion.
6    Attach the cable to the relay or ground connection and tighten the mounting nut/bolt securely.
7    Before connecting the new cable to the

battery, make sure that it reaches the battery post without having to be stretched. Clean the battery posts thoroughly (see Chapter 1) and apply a light coat of petroleum jelly to prevent corrosion.
8    Connect the positive cable first, followed by the negative cable.

## 5    Ignition system - general information

*Refer to illustration 5.2*
1    The ignition system is designed to ignite the fuel/air charge entering each cylinder at just the right moment. It does this by producing a high-voltage spark between the electrodes of each spark plug.
2    These models are equipped with the Direct Ignition System (DIS) **(see illustration)**. These systems are also referred to as a distributorless ignition system because they are not equipped with a conventional distributor. The DIS system includes an ignition coil assembly, an igniter, the Electronic Control Module (ECM) and the ignition wires to each of the spark plugs from the coil pack. The ECM generates cylinder identification signals which allow the igniter to trigger the coil in the correct sequence. The ECM determines the correct ignition timing based on the input signals from the information sensors that are incorporated into the EFI and ignition system (refer to Chapter 6 for additional information on the sensors). The igniter distributes the signal to the proper coil driver circuit and determines dwell period based on coil primary current flow.
3    The DIS system uses a waste spark method for distribution. The coil pack is actually comprised of two separate coils. Two cylinders are fired simultaneously by each coil while one cylinder is on its compression stroke and the other is on its exhaust stroke.

Only the cylinder set to fire (compression) will use the majority of the voltage supplied to the two spark plugs due to the load demand on the cylinder. The companion cylinder will fire minimally only to disperse any remaining air/fuel molecules for combustion and emission efficiency. The engine is paired 1-2 and 3-4. Refer to Chapter 1 for cylinder locations.
4    When working on the ignition system, take the following precautions:
a)    *Do not keep the ignition switch on for more than 10 seconds if the engine will not start.*
b)    *Always connect a tachometer in accordance with the manufacturer's instructions. Some tachometers may be incompatible with this ignition system. Consult the tool manufacturers representative before buying a tachometer for use with this vehicle.*
c)    *Never allow the ignition coil terminals to touch ground. Grounding the coil could result in damage to the igniter and/or the ignition coil.*
d)    *Do not disconnect the battery when the engine is running.*
e)    *Make sure that the igniter is properly grounded.*

## 6    Ignition system - check

*Refer to illustrations 6.1, 6.4 and 6.6*
**Warning:** *Because of the high voltage generated by the ignition system, extreme care should be taken whenever an operation is performed involving ignition components. This not only includes the igniter, coil and spark plug wires, but related components such as plug connectors, tachometer and other test equipment also.*
1    If the engine turns over but won't start, disconnect the coil pack from any spark plug and attach it to a calibrated ignition tester

**6.1  To use a calibrated ignition tester, simply disconnect a spark plug wire and connect it to the tester, clip the tester to a convenient ground and operate the starter - if there is enough power to fire the plug, sparks will be visible between the electrode tip and the tester body**

(available at most auto parts stores) **(see illustration)**. Make sure the tester is designed for direct ignition systems (DIS) if a universal tester isn't available.

2    Connect the clip on the tester to a bolt or metal bracket on the engine, crank the engine and watch the end of the tester to see if bright blue, well-defined sparks occur.

3    If sparks occur, sufficient voltage is reaching the spark plug to fire it (repeat the check at the remaining spark plugs to verify that all the ignition coils are functioning). However, the plugs themselves may be fouled, so remove and check them as described in Chapter 1 or install new ones.

4    If no sparks or intermittent sparks occur, check for battery voltage to the ignition coil **(see illustration)**. Check the coils (see Section 7). Check the camshaft and crankshaft position sensors (see Chapter 6).

5    Also check for an igniter voltage signal to the coil packs. Remove the electrical connector from the coil pack. Connect a 12 volt test light to the battery positive terminal. Make sure it is an LED (Light Emitting Diode)

**6.4  Check for battery voltage on the middle terminal with the ignition key ON (engine not running)**

type test light. Touch the test light probe to each of the outside terminals of the coil pack connector in turn as an assistant cranks the engine over with the starter. See if the test light blinks as the igniter provides the trigger signal to the coil pack. If the test light does not blink, there is a problem with the igniter, crankshaft sensor, ECM or related wiring.

6    If the ignition system is experiencing an intermittent driveability problem, check the engine grounds **(see illustration)**. The terminal end should be free of corrosion and secure to the engine. Repair the harness if necessary.

7    If there is no response from the ignition system, check the ignition relay. Refer to Chapter 12 and the wiring diagrams at the end of Chapter 12 for additional information and relay testing procedures.

## 7    Ignition coil - check and replacement

### Check

*Refer to illustrations 7.1 and 7.2*

1    Check the primary resistance. With the ignition off, disconnect the three-terminal

connector from the coil. Connect an ohmmeter across terminals 1 and 2 **(see illustration)**. This will test the 1-2 coil pack. Next, connect the ohmmeter across terminals 2 and 3. This will test the 3-4 coil pack. The resistance should be as listed in this Chapter's Specifications for the primary resistance. If not, replace the coil.

2    Check the secondary resistance. Connect an ohmmeter between the companion cylinder coil towers. First test cylinder numbers 1 and 2, then cylinders 3 and 4 **(see illustration)**. The resistance should be as listed in this Chapter's Specifications for the secondary resistance. If not, replace the coil.

### Replacement

*Refer to illustration 7.6*

3    Detach the cable from the negative terminal of the battery.

4    Detach the three-wire connector from the ignition coil.

5    Disconnect the coil secondary leads.

6    Remove the mounting bolts **(see illustration)** and detach the coil assembly.

7    Installation is the reverse of removal.

## 8    Ignition timing - check

*Refer to illustrations 8.2 and 8.9*

**Note:** *Ignition timing is controlled by the Electronic Control Module (ECM) and is not adjustable on the models covered by this manual. The following procedure is only a check of the function of the ignition timing control system.*

1    Locate the Tune-up or VECI label under the hood and read through and perform all preliminary instructions concerning ignition timing. If no VECI label is found refer to the Specifications Section at the beginning of this Chapter.

2    Before attempting to check the timing, some special tools will be needed for this procedure **(see illustration)**.

3    Check that the idle speed is as specified (see Chapter 1).

4    Connect a timing light in accordance

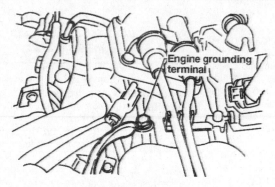

**6.6  Check the condition of the ground wires located near the coil pack**

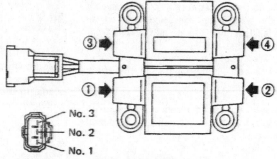

**7.1  To check the ignition coil primary resistance, measure the resistance across terminals 1 and 2, then 2 and 3 of the ignition coil electrical connector**

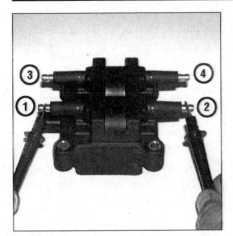

7.2 Check the coil secondary resistance across the paired coil towers of each coil

7.6 Coil pack mounting bolts (arrows)

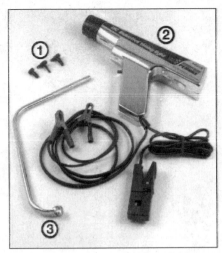

8.2 Tools needed to check and adjust the ignition timing

1   *Vacuum plugs* - Vacuum hoses will, in most cases, have to be disconnected and plugged. Molded plugs in various shapes and sizes are available for this

2   *Inductive pick-up timing light* - Flashes a bright, concentrated beam of light when the number one spark plug fires. Connect the leads according to the instructions supplied with the light

3   *Distributor wrench* - Not used on the models covered by this manual

with the tool manufacturer's instructions. Generally, the light will be connected to power and ground sources and to the number one spark plug wire (refer to the cylinder location diagram in Chapter 1 Specifications).

5   Locate the timing marks on the engine. Clean them off with solvent if necessary so you can see the numbers or marks and small grooves.

6   Use chalk or paint to mark the groove in the crankshaft pulley.

7   Mark the timing tab in accordance with the number of degrees called for on the VECI label or the tune-up label in the engine compartment.

8   Make sure timing light is clear of all moving engine components, then start the engine and warm it up to normal operating temperature.

9   Aim the flashing timing light at the timing mark by the crankshaft pulley (see illustration), again being careful not to come in contact with moving parts. The marks should appear to be stationary. If the marks are in alignment, the timing is correct. Raise the engine speed and observe the timing marks advance on the scale.

10   If the notch on the crankshaft pulley is not aligned with the correct mark on the

timing tab, then the ignition timing control system is malfunctioning. The problem could be a malfunctioning crankshaft or camshaft sensor, igniter or ECM.

11   Turn off the engine and disconnect the timing light. Reconnect any other components which were disconnected.

## 9   Igniter - replacement

*Refer to illustration 9.3*

1   Detach the cable from the negative terminal of the battery.

2   Disconnect the electrical connector from the igniter.

3   Remove the screws that retain the igniter to the body (see illustration).

4   Installation is the reverse of removal.

## 10   Charging system - general information and precautions

The charging system includes the alternator, an internal voltage regulator, a charge indicator or warning light, the battery, a fusible link and the wiring between all the

components. The charging system supplies electrical power for the ignition system, the lights, the radio, etc. The alternator is driven by a drivebelt at the front of the engine.

The purpose of the voltage regulator is to limit the alternator's voltage to a preset value. This prevents power surges, circuit overloads, etc., during peak voltage output.

One type of fusible link is a short length of insulated wire. The link is several wire gauges smaller in diameter than the circuit it protects. Other fusible links resemble large fuses. Refer to Chapter 12 for additional information on fusible links.

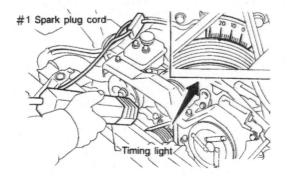

8.9 Point the timing light at the timing scale in the flywheel bellhousing and confirm that the timing marks advance with rpm increase

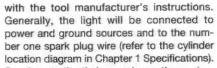

9.3 Igniter mounting screw locations (arrows)

11.2  **Connect the leads of a voltmeter to the battery terminals**

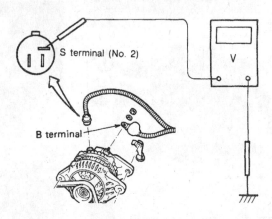

11.10  **Check for battery voltage on the S terminal and on the B terminal**

The charging system doesn't ordinarily require periodic maintenance. However, the drivebelt, battery and wires and connections should be inspected at the intervals outlined in Chapter 1.

Be very careful when making electrical circuit connections to a vehicle equipped with an alternator and note the following:

a) *When reconnecting wires to the alternator from the battery, be sure to note the polarity.*

b) *Before using arc welding equipment to repair any part of the vehicle, disconnect the wires from the alternator and the battery terminals.*

c) *Never start the engine with a battery charger connected.*

d) *Always disconnect both battery cables before using a battery charger (negative cable first, positive cable last).*

## 11   Charging system - check

*Refer to illustrations 11.2, 11.10, 11.11 and 11.12*

1    If a malfunction occurs in the charging circuit, do not immediately assume that the alternator is causing the problem. First check the following items:

a) *The battery cables where they connect to the battery. Make sure the connections are clean and tight.*

b) *The battery electrolyte specific gravity. If it is low, charge the battery.*

c) *Check the external alternator wiring and connections.*

d) *Check the drivebelt condition and tension (see Chapter 1).*

e) *Check the alternator mounting bolts for tightness.*

f) *Run the engine and check the alternator for abnormal noise.*

2    Using a voltmeter, check the battery voltage with the engine off. It should be approximately 12-volts **(see illustration)**.

3    Start the engine and check the battery voltage again. It should now be approximately 14 to 15-volts.

4    If the indicated voltage reading is less or more than the specified charging voltage, the problem may be within the alternator.

5    Due to the special equipment necessary to test or service the alternator, it is recommended that if a fault is suspected the vehicle be taken to a repair shop with the proper equipment. But if the home mechanic feels confident in the use of an ohmmeter, and in

some cases a soldering iron, the component check and replacement procedures for the most common alternator type are included in Section 13.

6    Some models are equipped with an ammeter on the instrument panel that indicates charge or discharge - current passing in or out of the battery. With all electrical equipment switched ON, and the engine idling, the gauge needle may show a discharge condition. At fast idle or normal driving speeds the needle should stay on the charge side of the gauge, with the charged state of the battery determining just how far over (the lower the battery state of charge, the farther the needle should swing toward the charge side).

7    Some models are equipped with a voltmeter on the instrument panel that indicates battery voltage with the key ON (engine not running), and alternator output when the engine is running.

8    The charge light on the instrument panel illuminates with the key ON and the engine not running, and should go out when the engine runs.

9    If the gauge does not show a charge when it should or the alternator light (if equipped) remains on, there is a fault in the system. Before inspecting the brushes or

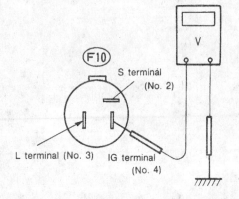

11.11  **Check for battery voltage on the IG terminal**

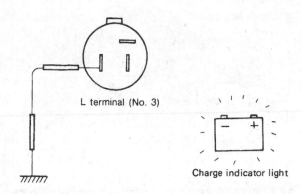

11.12  **The dash light should illuminate when the L terminal is grounded**

**12.4 Remove the tensioner assembly and the pivot bolt from the alternator (arrows)**

**13.2 Make a mark across the front cover, stator and rear cover to aid in reassembly**

replacing the alternator, the battery condition, alternator belt tension and electrical cable connections should be checked.

10 Check the alternator harness between the alternator and the battery for damage, broken terminals or defective bulbs (charging light). Disconnect the alternator harness connectors and check for battery voltage to the S terminal **(see illustration)** and the B terminal (single connector). Battery voltage should be available.

11 Check for battery voltage to the IG terminal **(see illustration)**. Battery voltage should be available with the ignition key ON (engine not running).

12 Ground the L terminal and observe that the charge indicator light is illuminated **(see illustration)**. Replace the bulb if necessary.

## 12 Alternator - removal and installation

*Refer to illustration 12.4*
1 Detach the cable from the negative terminal of the battery.
2 Disconnect the electrical connectors from the alternator.

3 Remove the drivebelt cover and detach the drivebelt (see Chapter 1).
4 Remove the adjustment and pivot bolts and separate the alternator from the engine **(see illustration)**.
5 Installation is the reverse of removal.
6 After the alternator is installed, adjust the drivebelt tension (see Chapter 1).

## 13 Alternator components - check and replacement

### *Disassembly*

*Refer to illustrations 13.2, 13.3, 13.4a, 13.4b, 13.4c, 13.5a, 13.5b, 13.6a, 13.6b, 13.6c and 13.7*
1 Remove the alternator from the vehicle (Section 12).
2 Scribe or paint marks on the front and rear end-frame housings of the alternator to facilitate reassembly **(see illustration)**.
3 Remove the nut retaining the fan pulley to the rotor shaft and remove the pulley **(see illustration)**. This can be done with a pneumatic impact wrench or with a socket and breaker bar. If the latter method is used, the

**13.3 The use of an air tool (impact wrench) is the easiest way to remove the pulley nut**

pulley will have to be immobilized with a strap wrench (in some cases this may have to be done even if an impact wrench is used).
4 Remove the four through-bolts holding the front and rear covers together, then remove the front cover. Remove the rotor **(see illustrations)**.

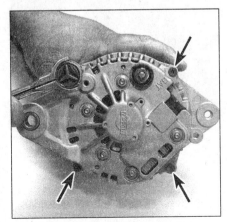

**13.4a Remove the four bolts from the rear cover (arrows)**

**13.4b Separate the front cover from the alternator body**

**13.4c Remove the rotor from the alternator assembly**

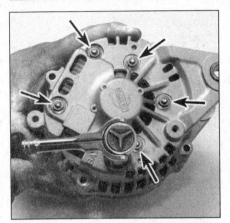

13.5a  Remove the mounting nuts (arrows)

13.5b  Separate the rear cover from the
stator and diode assembly

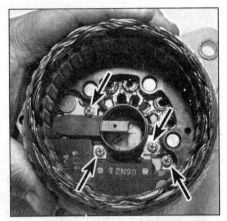

13.6a  Remove the diode assembly
mounting screws (arrows)

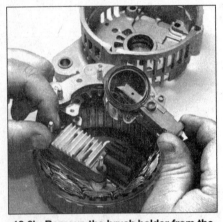

13.6b  Remove the brush holder from the
diode assembly

13.6c Remove the voltage regulator

13.7  Remove the four set screws and lift
the diode from the pick-up coil

5    Remove the nuts, then detach the rear
cover **(see illustrations)**. **Note:** *On some
Hitachi alternators it will necessary to remove
the diode assembly and the voltage regulator
as a complete unit. First, disconnect the stator coil leads with a soldering iron and be sure
to attach a heat sink to avoid damaging the
diodes. Then, disconnect the diode assembly
from the voltage regulator by melting the L-*

*connection with a soldering iron. Here again,
use a heat sink to avoid damaging the diodes.*
6    Remove the screws attaching the brush
holder and regulator to the diode and remove
the brush holder **(see illustrations)**.
7    Remove the diode from the pick-up coil
**(see illustration)**. On some types of alternators it will be necessary to use a soldering
iron and heat sink to melt the solder joints

that connect the pick-up coil leads to the
diode.

## Component checks

*Refer to illustrations 13.8a, 13.8b, 13.9
and 13.10*
8    Check the rotor for an open between the
two slip rings **(see illustration)**. There should

13.8a  Continuity should exist between
the rotor slip rings

13.8b  No continuity should exist between
the slip ring(s) and rotor shaft

13.9  Check for continuity on each stator
lead. There should be no breaks in the
windings; therefore, continuity should
exist between each terminal

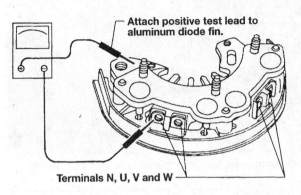

**13.10  Check each diode to make sure continuity exists only in ONE direction (typical diode assembly shown)**

Attach positive test lead to aluminum diode fin.

Terminals N, U, V and W

| | Ohmmeter probes | | Continuity |
|---|---|---|---|
| | Positive ⊕ | Negative ⊖ | |
| **Diodes check (Positive side)** | Positive diode plate | Diode terminals | Yes |
| | Diode terminals | Positive diode plate | No |
| **Diodes check (Negative side)** | Negative diode plate | Diode terminals | No |
| | Diode terminals | Negative diode plate | Yes |

be continuity between the slip rings. Check for grounds between each slip ring and the rotor shaft **(see illustration)**. There should be no continuity (infinite resistance) between the rotor shaft and either slip ring. If the rotor fails either test, or if the slip rings are excessively worn, the rotor is defective.

9     Check for opens between the center terminal and each end terminal of the stator windings **(see illustration)**. If either reading is high (infinite resistance), the stator is defective. Check for a grounded stator winding between each stator terminal and the frame. If there's continuity between any stator winding and the frame, the stator is defective.

10    Start the checks on the diode by touching one probe (positive +) of the ohmmeter on the diode plate and the other probe on one of the other designated diode terminals (negative -) **(see illustration)**. Then reverse the probes and check again. Follow the chart carefully. The diode should have continuity with the ohmmeter one way and no continuity when the probes are reversed. Check each of the terminals in this manner. If any of the diodes fail the test, the diode is defective.

**13.14  Insert a paper clip into the backside of the alternator to hold the brushes in place - after the alternator has been assembled, pull the paper clip out**

**Note:** *Because there are different Hitachi alternators installed on these models, many of the diode assemblies are slightly different in construction but not in operation. Follow the same terminal checks for each type of diode assembly.*

11    To check the sub-diodes, connect the probes of the ohmmeter to the sub-diode terminals and check for continuity in the same way as the previous diode checks. Be sure to probe only the sub-diode terminals. If any sub-diode fails the test, the diode assembly is defective.

12    Measure the length of the brushes and replace them if they are at or near the minimum brush length found in this Chapter's Specifications. **Note:** *On some models the brush leads are soldered onto the voltage regulator assembly.*

### Reassembly

*Refer to illustration 13.14*

13    Install the components in the reverse order of removal, noting the following:

14    Before installing the brush holder, push the brushes into the holder and slip a straightened paper clip or other suitable pin through the hole in the brush holder to hold the brushes in a retracted position. After the front and rear end frames have been bolted together, remove the paper clip **(see illustration)**.

## 14  Starting system - general information and precautions

1     The function of the starting system is to crank the engine quickly enough to start it. The system is composed of the starter motor, starter solenoid, battery, ignition switch, clutch start switch (manual transaxle models), neutral start switch (automatic transaxle models), diode box and connecting wires.

2     Turning the ignition key to the START position actuates the starter relay through the starter control circuit. The starter solenoid then connects battery voltage to the starter.

3     All models are equipped with a starter/solenoid assembly that is mounted to the transaxle bellhousing.

4     All vehicles are equipped with a clutch start switch or a neutral start switch in the starter control circuit, which prevents operation of the starter unless the shift lever is in Neutral or Park (automatic) or the clutch pedal is depressed (manual).

5     Never operate the starter motor for more than 15 seconds at a time without pausing to allow it to cool for at least two minutes. Excessive cranking can cause overheating, which can seriously damage the starter.

6     These models are equipped with a gear reduction type starter. Although similar in design, these Nippondenso starters are constructed differently for the automatic and manual transaxles and they cannot be interchanged. Gear reduction type starter assemblies incorporate the gear assembly and the solenoid as a combined unit. Although the solenoids can be replaced, it is advised that the starter be replaced as a complete unit in the event of solenoid trouble.

## 15  Starter motor and circuit - in-vehicle check

**Note:** *Before diagnosing starter problems, make sure the battery is fully charged.*

### General check

1     If the starter motor doesn't turn at all when the switch is operated, make sure the shift lever is in Neutral or Park (automatic) or the clutch is fully depressed (manual).

2     Make sure the battery is charged and that all cables at the battery and starter solenoid terminals are secure.

3     If the starter motor spins but the engine doesn't turn over, then the drive assembly in the starter motor is slipping and the starter motor must be replaced (see Section 16).

**16.4a  Location of the upper starter mounting bolt (arrow)**

**16.4b  Location of the lower starter mounting bolt (arrow)**

4    If, when the switch is actuated, the starter motor doesn't operate at all but the starter solenoid operates (clicks), then the problem lies with either the battery, the starter solenoid contacts or the starter motor connections.

5    If the starter solenoid doesn't click when the ignition switch is actuated, either the starter solenoid circuit is open, the starter relay is defective (manual transaxle models) or the solenoid itself is defective. Check the starter circuit (see the wiring diagrams at the end of Chapter 12) or replace the solenoid (see Section 17).

6    To check the starter solenoid circuit, remove the push-on connector from the solenoid wire. Make sure that the connection is clean and secure and the relay bracket is grounded. If the connections are good, check the operation of the solenoid with a jumper wire. To do this, place the transaxle in Park or Neutral and apply the parking brake. Remove the push-on connector from the solenoid. Connect a jumper wire between the battery positive terminal and the exposed terminal on the solenoid. If the starter motor now operates, the starter solenoid is okay. The problem is in the ignition switch, Neutral start switch or in the starting circuit wiring (look for open or loose connections).

7    If the starter motor still doesn't operate, replace the starter solenoid (see Section 17).

8    If the starter motor cranks the engine at an abnormally slow speed, first make sure the battery is fully charged and all terminal connections are clean and tight. Also check the connections at the starter solenoid and battery ground. Eyelet terminals should not be easily rotated by hand. Also check for a short to ground. If the engine is partially seized, or has the wrong viscosity oil in it, it will crank slowly.

### Starter cranking circuit test

9    Disconnect the electrical connector from the ignition coil to disable the ignition system.

10    Connect a remote control starter switch from the battery terminal of the starter solenoid to the S terminal of the solenoid.

11    Connect a voltmeter positive lead to the starter motor terminal of the starter solenoid, then connect the negative lead to ground.

12    Actuate the ignition switch and take the voltmeter readings as soon as a steady figure is indicated. Do not allow the starter motor to turn for more than 15 seconds at a time. A reading of 9-volts or more, with the starter motor turning at normal cranking speed, is normal. If the reading is 9-volts or more but the cranking speed is slow, the motor is faulty. If the reading is less than 9-volts and the cranking speed is slow, the solenoid contacts are probably burned.

### 16  Starter motor - removal and installation

*Refer to illustration 16.4a and 16.4b*

1    Detach the cable from the negative terminal of the battery.

2    Raise the vehicle and support it securely on jackstands.

3    Disconnect the wire and the large cable from the terminals on the starter solenoid.

4    Remove the starter motor mounting bolts **(see illustrations)** and detach the starter from the engine.

5    If necessary, turn the wheels to one side to provide removal access.

6    Installation is the reverse of removal.

### 17  Starter solenoid - replacement

*Refer to illustrations 17.1, 17.2 and 17.3*

1    Remove the nut and disconnect the lead wire from the solenoid electrical terminal **(see illustration)**.

2    Remove the two bolts from the solenoid and separate the solenoid from the end frame **(see illustration)**.

3    Separate the solenoid from the yoke **(see illustration)**.

4    Installation is the reverse of removal.

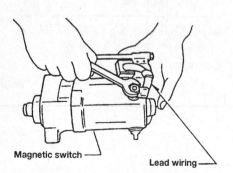

**17.1  Disconnect the lead wire from the solenoid electrical connector terminal**

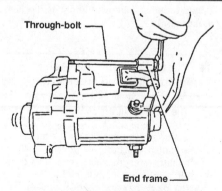

**17.2  Remove the two through-bolts from the starter assembly**

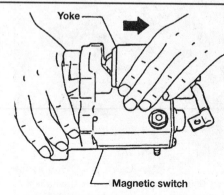

**17.3  Slip the solenoid off the yoke while sliding the unit out (arrow)**

# Chapter 6
# Emissions and engine control systems

## Contents

## Specifications

| | |
|---|---|
| Oxygen sensor heater resistance | 30 ohms |
| Crankshaft position sensor resistance | 1,000 to 4,000 ohms |
| Camshaft position sensor resistance | 1,000 to 4,000 ohms |

## 1  General information

*Refer to illustrations 1.1 and 1.7*

To prevent pollution of the atmosphere from incompletely burned and evaporating gases, and to maintain good driveability and fuel economy, a number of emission control systems are incorporated **(see illustration)**. They include the:

*Exhaust Gas Recirculation (EGR) system*
*Evaporative Emission Control (EVAP) system*
*Multi Port Fuel Injection (MPFI) system*
*Positive Crankcase Ventilation (PCV) system*
*Catalytic converter*

All of these systems are linked, directly or indirectly, to the emission control system.

The Sections in this Chapter include general descriptions, checking procedures within the scope of the home mechanic and component replacement procedures (when possible) for each of the systems listed above.

Before assuming that an emissions control system is malfunctioning, check the fuel and ignition systems carefully. The diagnosis of some emission control devices requires specialized tools, equipment and training. If checking and servicing become too difficult or if a procedure is beyond your ability, consult a dealer service department or other qualified repair facility. Remember, the most frequent cause of emissions problems is simply a loose or broken vacuum hose or wire, so always check the hose and wiring connections first.

This doesn't mean, however, that emission control systems are particularly difficult to maintain and repair. You can quickly and easily perform many checks and do most of the regular maintenance at home with com-

**1.1 Typical emissions and engine control systems underhood component locations**

1  Knock sensor (under intake manifold)
2  EGR valve
3  Camshaft position sensor (behind left inner timing belt cover)
4  Crankshaft sensor (above crankshaft pulley)
5  PCV valve
6  Pressure sensor
7  Airflow sensor
8  Throttle position sensor
9  Engine coolant temperature sensor (on coolant pipe under intake manifold runner)

**1.7  The Vehicle Emission Control Information (VECI) label on some models is located in the engine compartment under the hood and contains information on the emission devices on your vehicle, vacuum line routing, etc.**

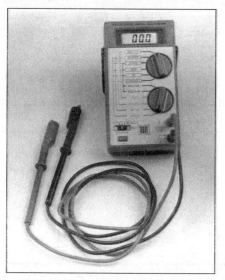

**2.1  Digital multimeters can be used for testing all types of circuits; because of their high impedance, they are much more accurate than analog meters for measuring millivolts in low-voltage computer circuits**

**2.2  Scanners like these from Actron and AutoXray are powerful diagnostic aids - they can tell you just about anything you want to know about your engine management system**

mon tune-up and hand tools. **Note:** *Because of a Federally mandated extended warranty which covers the emission control system components, check with your dealer about warranty coverage before working on any emissions-related systems. Once the warranty has expired, you may wish to perform some of the component checks and/or replacement procedures in this Chapter to save money.*

Pay close attention to any special precautions outlined in this Chapter. It should be noted that the illustrations of the various systems may not exactly match the system installed on the vehicle you're working on because of changes made by the manufacturer during production or from year-to-year.

A Vehicle Emissions Control Information (VECI) label is located in the engine compartment. This label contains important emissions specifications and adjustment information. A vacuum hose schematic with emissions components identified should also be present **(see illustration)**. When servicing the engine or emissions systems, the VECI label in your particular vehicle should always be checked for up-to-date information.

---

**2    On Board Diagnostic (OBD) system and trouble codes**

**Note:** *1990 through 1994 models are equipped with OBD I self diagnosis system, while 1995 through 1998 models are equipped with OBD II self diagnosis system. OBD I systems can be accessed by disconnecting or connecting the test terminals located under the dash (depending on what state they are in when you find them), but OBD II systems require the use of a Scan tool to access trouble codes. However, many of the information sensor checks and replacement procedures do apply to both systems.*

The OBD II five-digit codes indicated in the text are designed and mandated by the EPA for all 1995 and later OBD II vehicles produced by automobile manufacturers. These generic trouble codes do not include the manufacturer's specific trouble codes. Refer to the troubleshooting tips in the beginning of this manual to gain some insight to the most likely causes of a problem.

### Diagnostic tool information

*Refer to illustrations 2.1 and 2.2*

1    A digital multimeter is a necessary tool for checking fuel injection and emission related components **(see illustration)**. A digital volt-ohmmeter is preferred over the older style analog multimeter for several reasons. The analog multimeter cannot display the volts-ohms or amps measurement in hundredths and thousandths increments. When working with electronic circuits which are often very low voltage, this accurate reading is most important. Another good reason for the digital multimeter is the high impedance circuit. The digital multimeter is equipped with a high resistance internal circuitry (10 million ohms). Because a voltmeter is hooked up in parallel with the circuit when testing, it is vital that none of the voltage being measured be allowed to travel the parallel path set up by the meter itself. This dilemma does not show itself when measuring larger amounts of voltage (9 to 12 volt circuits) but if you are measuring a low voltage circuit such as the oxygen sensor signal voltage, a fraction of a volt may be a significant amount when diagnosing a problem.

2    Hand-held scanners are the most powerful and versatile tools for analyzing engine management systems used on later model vehicles **(see illustration)**. Early model scan-

ners handle codes and some diagnostics for many OBD I systems. Each brand scan tool must be examined carefully to match the year, make and model of the vehicle you are working on. Often interchangeable cartridges are available to access the particular manufacturer.

3    With the arrival of the federally mandated emission control system (OBD II), a scan tool specifically designed for OBD II systems must be used to access the trouble codes.

### General description

4    The electronically controlled fuel and emissions system is linked with many other related engine management systems. It consists mainly of sensors, output actuators and an Electronic Control Module (ECM). Completing the system are various other components which respond to commands from the ECM.

5    In many ways, this system can be compared to the central nervous system in the human body. The sensors (nerve endings) constantly gather information and send this data to the ECM (brain), which processes the data and, if necessary, commands the actuators (limbs).

6    Here's a specific example of how one portion of this system operates: An oxygen sensor, mounted in the exhaust manifold and protruding into the exhaust gas stream, constantly monitors the oxygen content of the exhaust gas as it travels through the exhaust pipe. If the percentage of oxygen in the exhaust gas is incorrect, an electrical signal is sent to the ECM. The ECM takes this information, processes it and then sends a command to the fuel injectors, telling it to change the fuel/air mixture. To be effective, all this happens in a fraction of a second, and it goes on continuously while the engine is running. The end result is a fuel/air mixture which is constantly kept at a predetermined ratio, regardless of driving conditions.

Test mode connector

**2.9 To access the self diagnosis system, locate the test mode connectors under the dash and disconnect them from each other if they're connected (if they're disconnected, plug the connector halves together)**

## Obtaining OBD I trouble codes (1990 through 1994 models)

### Self diagnosis

*Refer to illustration 2.9*

7    The self diagnosis mode is useful to diagnose malfunctions in major sensors and actuators of the Electronic Fuel Injection system. There are four different modes available for diagnosing driveability problems. Only the first mode, U-check Mode, is used by home mechanics. The other Modes are used by professional mechanics for self diagnosis. It is important to know that these other modes are used to detect driveability problems that store trouble codes because of random faults that may not be easily detected. The U-check Mode covers malfunctions that are constant or easily detected. Sometimes it will be necessary to double-check the symptoms before proceeding with the actual self diagnostics.

8    There are four modes in the self diagnosis system. The computer will illuminate the CHECK ENGINE light when it detects a problem in U-check Mode but not in D-check Mode. Therefore, it is also important to remember that there may be a problem in the system despite the fact that the CHECK ENGINE light is OFF. The D-CHECK mode level of diagnostics is difficult and is best handled by a professional.

   **U-check Mode** - user friendly self-diagnosis mode easily accessed by the home mechanic.

   **Read Memory Mode** - dealer service department mode for checking stored fault codes that detect past problems.

   **D-check Mode** - dealer service department mode for checking faulty parts.

   **Clear memory Mode** - selected mode for canceling stored trouble codes from the computer (ECM).

9    Find the TEST MODE connector under the dash **(see illustration)**. If it is disconnected, connect it; if it is connected, disconnect it. **Note:** *It will be necessary to partially remove the driver's (right side of column) side trim panels under the dash (see Chapter 11) to expose the diagnostic connectors.*

10   Turn the ignition key ON (engine not running) and make sure the CHECK ENGINE inspection light on the instrument panel is on.

If the light is off, replace the bulb.

11   Observe the CHECK ENGINE light on the dash. It will flash the trouble codes that have been stored within the computer. If there are no trouble codes stored, the CHECK ENGINE inspection light on the dash will not flash. If the CHECK ENGINE inspection light on the dash flickers, connect or disconnect the Test Mode connectors (depending on which state they are in) to enter the U-check Mode.

12   Observe the CHECK ENGINE light on the dash. It will flash the trouble codes in a clear and distinct manner. The first long flash will represent the first digit of the code designation. Next, the computer will flash the second digit of the code using short flashes. For example, four long flashes will represent the first digit, 4, followed by two short flashes is code 42. Record all the trouble codes onto a notepad and observe the computer codes once again to double-check the accuracy as the ECM repeats the list of trouble codes after all the codes have been displayed one time.

### Clearing codes

13   The easiest method for clearing trouble codes is simply disconnecting the negative battery terminal and waiting 30 seconds. Be sure to write the radio presets for easy reprogramming. Use a special battery pack that plugs into the cigarette lighter to keep the radio short term memory alive while the battery is disconnected. This tool can be purchased at most auto parts stores.

## OBD I trouble code chart

| Trouble codes | Circuit or system | Probable cause |
| --- | --- | --- |
| **Code 11** (1 long flash, 1 short flash) | Crank angle sensor/circuit | No reference pulse (see Chapter 5) |
| **Code 12** (1 long flash, 2 short flashes) | Starter switch | Starter switch remains in ON or OFF position (see Chapter 12) |
| **Code 13** (1 long flash, 3 short flashes) | Cam angle sensor | No position pulse (see Chapter 5) |
| **Code 14** (1 long flash, 4 short flashes) | Fuel injector #1 | Abnormal injector output (see Chapter 4) |
| **Code 15** (1 long flash, 5 short flashes) | Fuel injector #2 | Abnormal injector output (see Chapter 4) |
| **Code 16** (1 long flash, 6 short flashes) | Fuel injector #3 | Abnormal injector output (see Chapter 4) |
| **Code 17** (1 long flash, 7 short flashes) | Fuel injector #4 | Abnormal injector output (see Chapter 4) |
| **Code 21** (2 long flashes, 1 short flash) | Coolant temperature sensor | Sensor circuit or sensor malfunctioning (see Section 4) |
| **Code 22** (2 long flashes, 2 short flashes) | Knock sensor | Open or shorted knock sensor circuit (see Section 4) |
| **Code 23** (2 long flashes, 3 short flashes) | Airflow sensor | Open or shorted airflow sensor circuit (see Section 4) |
| **Code 24** (2 long flashes, 4 short flashes) | Air control valve | Open or shorted air control valve circuit (see Section 4) |
| **Code 31** (3 long flashes, 1 short flash) | Throttle position sensor | TPS sensor circuit is open or shorted (see Section 4). |
| **Code 32** (3 long flashes, 2 short flashes) | Oxygen sensor | The oxygen sensor circuit is open (see Section 4). |
| **Code 33** (3 long flashes, 3 short flashes) | Vehicle speed sensor | No speed sensor signal during operation (see Section 4). |
| **Code 35** (3 long flashes, 5 short flashes) | Purge control solenoid valve | Purge control solenoid remains in the ON or OFF position during operation (see Section 6) |
| **Code 41** (4 long flashes, 1 short flash) | Fuel mixture LEAN | Computer detects LEAN air/fuel ratio (see Chapter 4) |
| **Code 42** (4 long flashes, 2 short flashes) | Idle switch | Idle switch signal incorrect (see Chapter 4) |
| **Code 44** (4 long flashes, 4 short flashes) | Wastegate control solenoid | Wastegate solenoid valve (see Chapter 4) |
| **Code 45** (4 long flashes, 5 short flashes) | Atmospheric sensor | Faulty atmospheric pressure sensor or pressure exchange solenoid (see Chapter 4) |

## OBD I trouble code chart (continued)

| Trouble codes | Circuit or system | Probable cause |
|---|---|---|
| **Code 49** (4 long flashes, 9 short flashes) | Airflow sensor | Use of incorrect airflow sensor (see Section 4) |
| **Code 51** (5 long flashes, 1 short flash) | Neutral switch | Neutral switch remains in the ON position during operation (manual transaxle) (see Chapter 7) |
| **Code 51** (5 long flashes, 1 short flash) | Inhibitor switch | Inhibitor switch remains in the ON position during operation (automatic transaxle) (see Chapter 7) |
| **Code 52** (5 long flashes, 2 short flashes) | Parking switch | Parking switch remains in the ON position during operation |

### Obtaining OBD II trouble codes (1995 and later models)

*Refer to illustration 2.15*

14   1995 and later models are equipped with OBD II self diagnosis system. This updated diagnostic system indicates a problem by turning on a "CHECK ENGINE" light on the instrument panel when a fault has been detected. More importantly, the ECM will recognize this fault, in a particular system monitored by one of the various information sensors, and store it in its memory in the form of a trouble code. Although the trouble code cannot reveal the exact cause of the malfunction, it greatly facilitates diagnosis as you or a dealer mechanic can "tap into" the ECM's memory and be directed to the problem area. The SCAN tool can then be used to monitor "real time" values of sensors and output actuators for comparison with specified working parameters of the various components of the fuel and emissions control system. OBD II systems use a series of five-digit trouble codes designed to be compatible with all OBD II systems.

15   To retrieve this information from the ECM on all OBD II systems, a SCAN tool must be connected to the 16-pin Diagnostic Test Connector **(see illustration)**. The SCAN tool is a hand-held digital computer scanner that interfaces with the on-board computer. The SCAN tool is a very powerful tool; it not only reads the trouble codes but also displays the actual operating conditions of the sensors and actuators. SCAN tools are expensive, but they are necessary to accurately diagnose a modern computerized fuel-injected engine. SCAN tools are available from automotive parts stores and specialty tool companies.

16   The self-diagnosis feature built into this system does not detect all possible faults. Furthermore, when diagnosing an engine performance, fuel economy or exhaust emissions problem (which is not accompanied by a CHECK ENGINE light) do not automatically assume the fault lies in this system. Perform all standard troubleshooting procedures, as indicated at the beginning of this manual, before turning to the On Board Diagnostic (OBD) system.

17   Finally, since this is an electronic system, you should have a basic knowledge of automotive electronics before attempting any diagnosis. Damage to the ECM or related components can easily occur if care is not exercised.

### Clearing trouble codes

18   To clear codes from the ECM memory on OBD II systems, install the SCAN tool, consult the tools menu for the function that describes "clearing codes" and follow the prescribed method for that particular SCAN tool. On OBD I vehicles, momentarily remove the EFI fuse from the fuse box for 30 seconds. Clearing codes may also be accomplished by removing the fusible link (main power fuse) located near the battery positive terminal (see Chapter 12) or by disconnecting the cable from the positive terminal (+) of the battery (always disconnect the negative cable before disconnecting the positive cable). **Caution:** *To prevent damage to the ECM, the ignition switch must be OFF when disconnecting or connecting power to the ECM.*

### Trouble Code Identification

19   Following is a list of the typical Trouble Codes which may be encountered while diagnosing the On Board Diagnostic (OBD II) system. Also included are simplified troubleshooting procedures. If the problem persists after these checks have been made, the vehicle must be diagnosed by a professional mechanic who can use specialized diagnostic tools and advanced troubleshooting methods to check the system. Component replacements may not cure the problem in all cases. For this reason, you may want to seek professional advice before purchasing replacement parts.

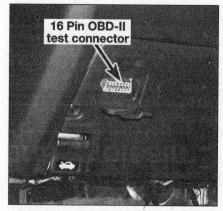

**2.15  16-pin Diagnostic Test Connector**

## OBD II Trouble Codes*

| Code | Code Definition |
|---|---|
| P0100 | Mass Air Flow (MAF) sensor or circuit malfunction |
| P0101 | Mass Air Flow (MAF) sensor range error |
| P0102 | Mass Air Flow (MAF) sensor circuit low input |
| P0103 | Mass Air Flow (MAF) sensor circuit high input |
| P0105 | Pressure sensor or circuit malfunction |
| P0106 | Pressure sensor range error |
| P0107 | Pressure sensor circuit low input |
| P0108 | Pressure sensor circuit high input |
| P0115 | Electronic Coolant Temperature (ECT) sensor or circuit malfunction |
| P0116 | Electronic Coolant Temperature (ECT) sensor circuit low input |
| P0117 | Electronic Coolant Temperature (ECT) sensor circuit high input |
| P0120 | Throttle Position Sensor (TPS) or circuit malfunction |
| P0121 | Throttle Position Sensor (TPS) range error |
| P0122 | Throttle Position Sensor (TPS) circuit low input |

| Code | Code Definition |
|------|-----------------|
| P0123 | Throttle Position Sensor (TPS) high input |
| P0125 | Insufficient coolant temperature for closed loop |
| P0130 | Upstream $O_2$ sensor or circuit malfunction |
| P0133 | Upstream $O_2$ sensor slow  response |
| P0135 | Upstream $O_2$ sensor heater circuit malfunction |
| P0136 | Downstream $O_2$ sensor circuit malfunction |
| P0139 | Downstream $O_2$ sensor circuit slow response |
| P0141 | Downstream $O_2$ sensor heater circuit malfunction |
| P0170 | Fuel trim malfunction (too lean or rich) |
| P0181 | Fuel temperature sensor range error |
| P0182 | Fuel temperature sensor circuit low input |
| P0183 | Fuel temperature sensor circuit high input |
| P0201 | Fuel injector number 1 malfunction |
| P0202 | Fuel injector number 2 malfunction |
| P0203 | Fuel injector number 3 malfunction |
| P0204 | Fuel injector number 4 malfunction |
| P0261 | Fuel injector number 1 circuit low input |
| P0262 | Fuel injector number 1 circuit high input |
| P0264 | Fuel injector number 2 circuit low input |
| P0265 | Fuel injector number 2 circuit high input |
| P0267 | Fuel injector number 3 circuit low input |
| P0268 | Fuel injector number 3 circuit high input |
| P0270 | Fuel injector number 4 circuit low input |
| P0271 | Fuel injector number 4 circuit high input |
| P0301 | Cylinder number 1 misfire detected |
| P0302 | Cylinder number 2 misfire detected |
| P0303 | Cylinder number 3 misfire detected |
| P0304 | Cylinder number 4 misfire detected |
| P0325 | Knock sensor circuit malfunction |
| P0335 | Crankshaft Position Sensor circuit malfunction |
| P0336 | Crankshaft Position Sensor circuit range error |
| P0340 | Camshaft Position sensor circuit malfunction |
| P0341 | Camshaft Position sensor circuit range error |
| P0400 | EGR flow malfunction |
| P0403 | EGR circuit malfunction |
| P0420 | Catalyst system efficiency below threshold |
| P0440 | EVAP system malfunction |
| P0441 | EVAP system incorrect purge flow |
| P0443 | EVAP system purge control valve or circuit malfunction |
| P0446 | EVAP vent control malfunction |
| P0451 | EVAP fuel tank pressure sensor range error |
| P0452 | EVAP fuel tank pressure sensor circuit low input |
| P0453 | EVAP fuel tank pressure sensor circuit high input |
| P0461 | Fuel level  sensor range error |
| P0462 | Fuel level sensor circuit low input |
| P0463 | Fuel level sensor circuit high input |
| P0500 | VSS  or circuit malfunction |
| P0505 | IAC system malfunction |
| P0506 | IAC system rpm low |
| P0507 | IAC system rpm high |
| P0600 | Serial communications link malfunction |
| P0601 | Internal control module memory error |
| P0703 | Brake switch malfunction |
| P0705 | Transmission range sensor or circuit malfunction |
| P0710 | Transmission fluid temperature sensor or circuit malfunction |
| P0720 | VSS circuit malfunction |
| P0725 | Engine speed circuit malfunction |
| P0731 thru P0734 | Incorrect gear ratio |
| P0740 and P0743 | Torque converter clutch system malfunction |
| P0748 thru P0763 | Shift solenoid circuit malfunction |

*Not all codes apply to all models*

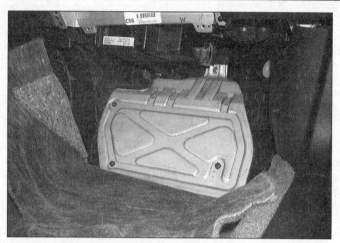

**3.6  Pull back the carpet on the right side of the passenger compartment to expose the ECM access cover**

**3.7  Disconnect the ECM lock by turning the handle (arrow) counterclockwise**

## 3    Electronic Control Module (ECM) - check and replacement

**Warning:** *Some models covered by this manual are equipped with airbags. Always disconnect the negative battery cable and wait at least one minute before working in the vicinity of the impact sensors, steering column or instrument panel to avoid the possibility of accidental deployment of the airbag, which could cause personal injury (see Chapter 12).*

### Check

1    The ECM on all models is located in the right front corner of the passenger compartment behind the glovebox. Remove the glovebox (see Chapter 11) for access to the ECM.

2    Using the tips of your fingers, tap vigorously on the side of the computer while the engine is running. If the computer is not functioning properly, the engine may stumble or stall and display glitches on the engine data stream obtained using a SCAN tool or other diagnostic equipment.

3    If the ECM fails this test, check the electrical connectors. Each connector is color coded to fit the respective slot in the computer body.

### Replacement

*Refer to illustration 3.6, 3.7 and 3.9*

**Caution:** *To prevent damage to the ECM, the ignition switch must be turned Off when disconnecting or connecting the ECM connectors.*

4    The ECM on all models is located in the right side of the passenger compartment under the carpet behind the glovebox **(see illustrations)**. Refer to Chapter 11 and remove the glovebox assembly.

5    Disconnect the cable from the negative battery terminal.

6    Pull back the carpet to expose the ECM access cover. Remove the mounting screws **(see illustration). Caution:** *Be sure to use a*

special computer anti-static device to eliminate the chance of ECM damage when handling the ECM.

7    Disconnect the ECM harness connectors by turning the LOCK handle counterclockwise **(see illustration)**.

8    Remove the ECM mounting bolts.

9    Disconnect the ECM harness electrical connectors. Each connector is color coded to fit its respective receptacle in the ECM **(see illustration)**.

10    Carefully lift the ECM from the passenger compartment without damaging the electrical connectors and wiring harness to the computer.

11    Installation is the reverse of removal.

## 4    Information sensors - general information and testing

**Caution:** *When performing the following tests, use only a high-impedance (10 mega ohms) digital multi-meter to prevent damage to the ECM or sensors.*

**Note:** *Refer to Chapter 5 for additional information concerning the ignition system testing and replacement procedures.*

### Engine coolant temperature sensor

*Refer to illustrations 4.1a and 4.1b*

1    The engine coolant temperature sensor is a thermistor type sensor (a variable resistor that sense temperature level changes). As the sensor temperature DECREASES, the resistance will INCREASE. As the sensor temperature INCREASES, the resistance will DECREASE. to check a thermistor type sensor, disconnect the harness connector at the sensor and connect an ohmmeter to the sensor terminals **(see illustration)**. The resistance reading should be high when the sensor is cold, and low when the sensor is hot **(see illustration)**. Be sure the tips of the probe make clean contact with the terminals inside the sensor to insure an accurate

**3.9  Separate the harness connectors from the ECM**

reading.

2    After the resistance of the sensor has been checked, test the system for the proper reference voltage from the computer. Disconnect the harness connector at the sensor, select the voltage range on the multi-meter and probe the terminals on the harness for the voltage signal. Reference voltage should be approximately 5.0 volts. The ignition switch must be in the ON position (engine not running). If there is no reference voltage available to the sensor, then the sensor circuit and the computer must be checked. Refer to the wiring diagrams at the end of Chapter 12 for wire designations.

### Throttle position sensor

*Refer to illustrations 4.3, 4.4, 4.5 and 4.6*

3    The throttle position sensor is a variable resistor that varies resistance according to throttle angle. The signal the throttle position sensor generates is used by the computer to determine position of the throttle. There are two different diagnostic methods that can be used on this sensor. The first method checks the resistance changes of the throttle position sensor as it is moved through its operating range (closed to wide open throttle). The other method checks the voltage signal

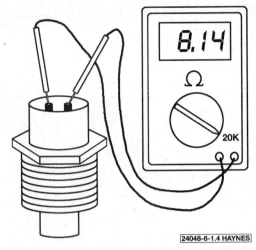

**4.1a  Check the resistance of the coolant temperature sensor with the engine completely cold and then again with the engine at operating temperature - or remove the sensor and check it in a heated pan of water**

| Temperature (degrees-F) | Resistance (ohms) |
|---|---|
| 212 | 176 |
| 194 | 240 |
| 176 | 332 |
| 158 | 458 |
| 140 | 668 |
| 122 | 972 |
| 112 | 1182 |
| 104 | 1458 |
| 95 | 1800 |
| 86 | 2238 |
| 76 | 2795 |
| 68 | 3520 |
| 58 | 4450 |
| 50 | 5670 |
| 40 | 7280 |
| 32 | 9420 |

**4.1b  Coolant temperature sensor approximate temperature vs. resistance relationships**

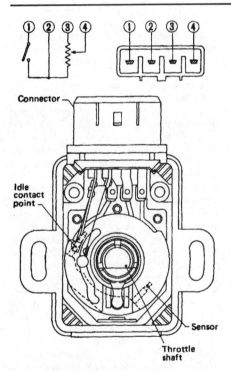

**4.3  4-terminal throttle position switch/sensor - 1994 and earlier models**

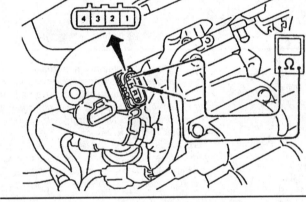

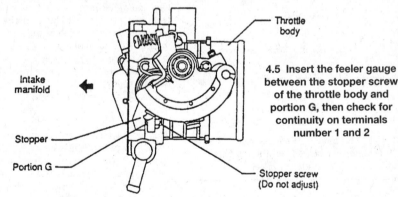

**4.4  Check the operation of the throttle switch on terminals number 1 and 2 - there should be zero resistance with the throttle closed and infinite resistance with the throttle open**

**4.5  Insert the feeler gauge between the stopper screw of the throttle body and portion G, then check for continuity on terminals number 1 and 2**

changes during operation. The first method is used to check 4-terminal sensors equipped on 1994 and earlier models. Later style sensors use 3-terminal harness connectors. This testing method is preferred because the older style sensors are equipped with an idle switch that detects an ON/OFF signal when the accelerator is first opened in addition to the normal throttle detection capabilities **(see illustration)**. This circuit is designated by terminals 1 and 2 on the four terminal connector on the accompanying illustration.

4    On 1994 and earlier models, disconnect the electrical connector from the throttle

position sensor and install the probes of the ohmmeter onto terminal number 1 and 2 **(see illustration)**. With the throttle lever completely closed, the meter should indicate continuity (zero ohms). With the throttle lever completely open, the meter should indicate an open circuit (infinite ohms). If the throttle position sensor does not operate as described, the throttle switch within the sensor is defective.

5    Disconnect the electrical connector from the throttle position sensor (TPS). Insert a feeler gauge of the specified thickness

between the throttle stop screw and the throttle stopper. Using an ohmmeter, measure the resistance between terminals number 1 and 2 **(see illustrations)**. With a 0.028 inch feeler gauge, there should be continuity. With a 0.035 gauge, there should be no continuity. This procedure serves as an adjustment and a check. Loosen the TPS mounting screws and slowly rotate the sensor until the ohmmeter needle (or readout) just deflects, then stop. Tighten the mounting screws, and using the proper feeler gauge, recheck the continuity between the specified terminals.

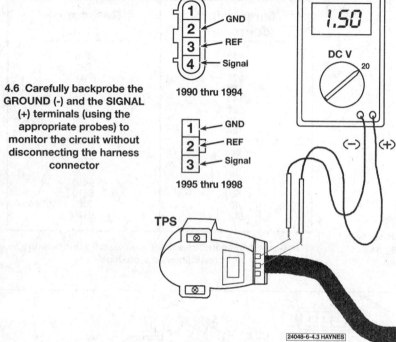

**4.6 Carefully backprobe the GROUND (-) and the SIGNAL (+) terminals (using the appropriate probes) to monitor the circuit without disconnecting the harness connector**

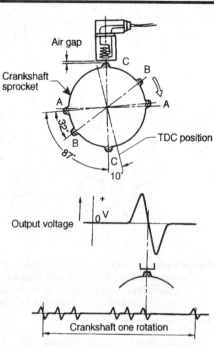

**4.8a The crankshaft sensor reads the number of pulses from the protrusions on the perimeter of the crankshaft sprocket**

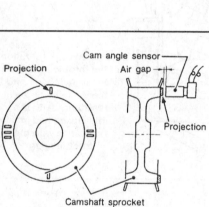

● Cylinder descrimination signal

**4.8b The camshaft sensor reads the number of pulses from the left side camshaft sprocket**

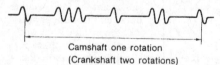

Camshaft one rotation
(Crankshaft two rotations)

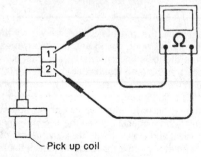

**4.8c Testing the crankshaft sensor resistance**

6    The second method monitors the voltage changes through the operating range of the sensor with voltage applied. This method requires the throttle position sensor harness to be backprobed with long pins to link the voltmeter probes to the circuit. This method can be used on older and newer style (3 and 4 terminal) sensors. Select the DC volts function on the multi-meter, carefully backprobe the harness connector using straight pins inserted into the correct terminals and connect the meter probes to the pins **(see illustration)**. Connect the negative probe (-) to the ground terminal and the positive probe (+) to the SIGNAL terminal. Turn the ignition On (engine not running) and observe the meter as the throttle is moved through its complete range. The voltage should vary from 0.5 to 1.0 volt at closed throttle to 4.5 to 5.0 volts wide-open-throttle.

7    After the SIGNAL voltage has been checked, test the system for the proper reference voltage from the computer. Simply disconnect the harness connector at the sensor, select the voltage range on the volt/ohmmeter and probe the correct terminals on the harness for the voltage signal. Reference voltage should be approximately 5.0 volts. The ignition switch must be in the ON position (engine not running). If there is no reference voltage available to the sensor, then the circuit and the computer must be checked.

## Crankshaft, camshaft and vehicle speed sensors

*Refer to illustration 4.8a, 4.8b, 4.8c and 4.9*

8    Crankshaft, camshaft and vehicle speed sensors are magnetic reluctance type sensors. Magnetic reluctance type sensors consist of a permanent magnet with a coil wire wound around the assembly. A steel disk mounted on a gear (crankshaft, input shaft, etc.) has tabs that pass between the pole pieces of the magnet causing a break in the magnetic field when passed near the sensor **(see illustrations)**. This break in the field causes a magnetic flux producing reluctance (resistance) thereby changing the voltage signal. This voltage signal is used to determine crankshaft position, vehicle speed, etc. There are two methods for testing these types of sensors. The first test checks the resistance across the sensor leads **(see illustration)**. This test checks the circuit within the sensor. If the sensor indicates the incorrect resistance, replace it with a new part.

9    The second test checks the operating condition of the sensor. Because magnetic energy is a free-standing source of energy and does not require battery power to produce voltage, this type of sensor must be checked by observing voltage fluctuations with an AC voltmeter. Simply switch the voltmeter to the AC scale and connect the probes to the sensor. On vehicle speed sensors it will be necessary to place the transaxle in neutral, then with the help of an assistant, hold one tire still while spinning the other tire (approximately 2 MPH or faster) and, observe the voltage fluctuations. This test can also be performed with the sensor removed from the vehicle, by turning the sensor's drive gear **(see illustration)**. **Note:** *Some vehicle speed sensors don't have a drive gear - this type of sensor will have to be checked in place.* On crankshaft position sensors it will be necessary to turn the engine over slowly using a breaker bar and socket on the pulley while you observe the voltage fluctuations. The meter should register slight

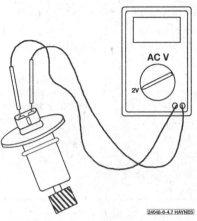

**4.9 Connect the probes of the voltmeter directly to the vehicle speed sensor and observe AC voltage fluctuations as the drive gear is slowly rotated**

voltage fluctuations that are constant and relatively the same range. These small voltage fluctuations indicate that the magnetic portion of the sensor is producing a magnetic field and "sensing" engine parameters for the computer.

## Oxygen sensor

*Refer to illustration 4.11*

10   The oxygen sensor(s) monitors the oxygen content of the exhaust gas stream. The oxygen content in the exhaust reacts with the oxygen sensor to produce a voltage output which varies from 0.1-volt (high oxygen, lean mixture) to 0.9-volts (low oxygen, rich mixture). The ECM constantly monitors this variable voltage output to determine the ratio of oxygen to fuel in the mixture. The ECM alters the air/fuel mixture ratio by controlling the pulse width (open time) of the fuel injectors. The ECM and the oxygen sensor(s) attempt to maintain a mixture ratio of 14.7 parts air to 1 part ratio of fuel at all times. The oxygen sensor produces no voltage when it is below its normal operating temperature of about 600-degrees F. During this initial period before warm-up, the ECM operates in OPEN

LOOP mode. When checking the oxygen sensor system, it will be necessary to test all oxygen sensors. **Note:** *Because the oxygen sensor(s) are difficult to access, probing the harness electrical connectors for testing purposes will require patience. The exhaust manifolds and pipes are extremely hot and will melt stray electrical probes and leads that touch the surface during testing. If possible, use a SCAN tool that plugs into the Diagnostic Test Connector **(see illustration 2.15)**. This tool will access the ECM data stream and indicates the millivolt changes for each individual oxygen sensor.*

11   Check the oxygen sensor millivolt signal. Locate the oxygen sensor electrical connector **(see illustration)** and carefully backprobe it using a long pin(s) into the appropriate wire terminals. In most models, connect the positive probe (+) of a voltmeter onto the SIGNAL wire and the negative probe (-) to the ground wire. Consult the wiring diagrams at the end of Chapter 12 for additional information on the oxygen sensor electrical connector wire color designations. Monitor the SIGNAL voltage (millivolts) as the engine goes from cold to warm.

12   The oxygen sensor will produce a steady voltage signal of approximately 0.1 to 0.2 volts (100 to 200 millivolts) with the engine cold (open loop). After a period of approximately two minutes, the engine will reach operating temperature and the oxygen sensor will start to fluctuate between 0.1 to 0.9 volts (100 to 900 millivolts) (closed loop). If the oxygen sensor fails to reach the closed loop mode or there is a very long period of time until it does switch into closed loop mode, replace the oxygen sensor with a new part. **Note:** *Downstream oxygen sensors will not change voltage values as quickly as upstream oxygen sensors. Because the downstream oxygen sensors detect oxygen content after the exhaust has been catalyzed, voltage values should fluctuate much slower and deliberate.*

13   Also inspect the oxygen sensor heater. Disconnect the oxygen sensor electrical connector and working on the oxygen sensor side, connect an ohmmeter between the ter-

minal numbers 1 and 2. Refer to the Specifications listed in this Chapter for the correct resistance measurements. Next, check for proper supply voltage to the heater. Disconnect the oxygen sensor electrical connector and working on the engine side of the harness, measure the voltage at terminal number 2. There should be battery voltage with the ignition key ON (engine not running). If there is no voltage, check the circuit between the main relay (see Chapter 4), the fuse and the sensor. **Note:** *It is important to remember that supply voltage will only reach the $O_2$ sensor with the ignition key ON (engine not running). If the oxygen sensor fails any of these tests, replace it with a new part.* **Note:** *Refer to the wiring diagrams at the end of Chapter 12 for additional information concerning the wire color codes and designations.*

## Air flow sensor

*Refer to illustrations 4.15*

14   The airflow sensor measures the amount of air passing through the sensor body and ultimately entering the engine through the throttle body. The ECM uses this information to control fuel delivery - the more air entering the engine (acceleration), the more fuel needed. These models use the vortex-type air flow sensor, which uses a hotwire to measure air mass (volume and weight). This information is relayed to the computer to inject the correct amount of fuel into the combustion chamber for the volume of air (load) that is demanded. This type of airflow sensor is referred to as a Mass Air Flow (MAF) sensor.

15   To test the airflow sensor, disconnect the airflow harness connector and, working on the harness side, check for battery voltage to the MAF sensor with the ignition key ON (engine not running) **(see illustration)**. Battery voltage should be present. If battery voltage is not present, have the ignition circuit and/or the ECM checked by a dealer service department. If battery voltage is available, check the MAF sensor using a SCAN tool.

16   A SCAN tool is recommended to check the output of the MAF sensor. The SCAN tool displays the sensor output in grams per second. With the engine idling at normal operating temperature, the display should read 4 to 7 grams per second. When the engine is accelerated the values should raise and remain steady at any given RPM. A failure in the MAF sensor or circuit will also set a diagnostic trouble code.

## Knock sensor

*Refer to illustration 4.18*

17   Knock sensors detect abnormal vibration in the engine. The knock control system is designed to reduce spark knock during periods of heavy detonation. This allows the engine to use maximum spark advance to improve driveability. Knock sensors produce AC output voltage which increases with the severity of the knock. The signal is fed into the ECM and the timing is retarded to compensate for the severe detonation.

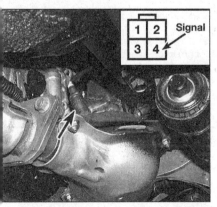

**4.11 Insert a pin into the backside of the oxygen sensor connector (arrow) on the correct terminal and check for a millivolt output signal generated by the sensor**

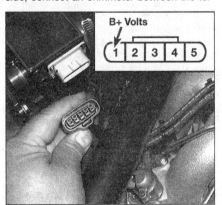

**4.15 Check for battery voltage on terminal number 1 with the ignition key ON (engine not running)**

18   To check a knock sensor, disconnect the electrical connector and check for continuity between the sensor terminal and ground (engine block). Continuity should not exist, if it does, replace the sensor **(see illustration)**.

### Neutral Start switch

19   The Neutral Start switch, located on the rear upper part of the automatic transaxle, indicates to the ECM when the transaxle is in Park or Neutral. This information is used for Exhaust Gas Recirculation (EGR) and Idle Air Control (IAC) valve operation. **Caution:** *The vehicle should not be driven with the Neutral Start switch disconnected because idle quality will be adversely affected.*

20   For more information regarding the Neutral Start switch, which is part of the Neutral start and back-up light switch assembly, see Chapter 7.

### Air conditioning control

21   During air conditioning operation, the ECM controls the application of the air conditioning compressor clutch. The ECM controls the air conditioning clutch control relay to delay clutch engagement after the air conditioning is turned ON to allow the IAC valve to adjust the idle speed of the engine to compensate for the additional load. The ECM also controls the relay to disengage the clutch on WOT (wide open throttle) to prevent excessively high rpm on the compressor. Be sure to check the air conditioning system as detailed in Chapter 3 before attempting to diagnose the air conditioning clutch or electrical system.

### Power steering pressure sensor

22   Turning the steering wheel increases power steering fluid pressure and engine load. The pressure switch will close before the load can cause an idle problem. A pressure switch that will not open or an open circuit from the ECM will cause timing to retard at idle and this will affect idle quality. A pressure switch that will not close or an open circuit may cause the engine to die when the power steering system is used heavily.

### Pressure sensor

*Refer to illustration 4.23a, 4.23b, 4.24 and 4.25*

23   The pressure sensor monitors the intake manifold pressure changes resulting from changes in engine load and speed and converts the information into a voltage output. The pressure sensor is used on turbocharged and 1995 and later automatic transaxle models only and it is mounted in the front, right side of the engine compartment **(see illustration)**. These models are equipped with a pressure exchange solenoid which switches pressure between inlets (engine intake and fresh air) to detect both atmospheric pressure and intake manifold pressure. The PCM uses the sensor to control fuel delivery and ignition timing. Select the volts function on

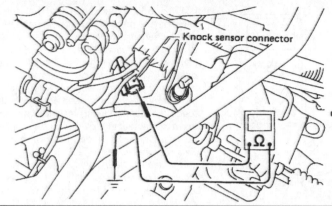

**4.18 Check to make sure that continuity does not exist between the sensor terminal and ground**

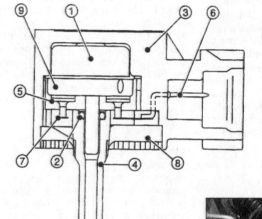

**4.23a  Pressure sensor details**

1   *Sensor unit*
2   *O-ring*
3   *Case*
4   *Pipe*
5   *Capacitor*
6   *Terminal*
7   *Inner lead*
8   *Resin*
9   *Cover*

the voltmeter. Test the system for the proper reference voltage from the computer. Reference voltage is a constant 5.0 volt signal to the sensor while the engine is operating. Simply disconnect the harness connector at the sensor and probe the correct terminals on the harness for the voltage signal. Reference voltage should be approximately 5 volts **(see illustration)**. The ignition switch must be in the ON position (engine not running). If there is no reference voltage available to the sensor, then the circuit and the computer must be checked.

24   After the reference voltage has been checked, check the SIGNAL voltage. The sensor SIGNAL voltage to the PCM varies from below 3 volts at idle (high vacuum) to 2 volts with wide open throttle (WOT) (low vacuum). These values correspond with the altitude and pressure changes the vehicle experiences while driving. Use long pins and carefully backprobe the harness connector terminals and position the voltmeter probes onto the pins. Connect the negative probe to the ground connection and the positive probe to the SIGNAL terminal. Observe the meter as the engine idles and then slowly raise the engine rpm to wide open throttle. The voltage should decrease from approximately 3 volts (high vacuum) to 2 volts (low vacuum). If the engine stalls or runs roughly, it is possible to simulate conditions by attaching a hand-held vacuum pump to the pressure/vacuum sen-

**4.23b  Check for a 5-volt reference voltage to pressure sensor**

sor to simulate running conditions **(see illustration)**.

25   Check the pressure exchange solenoid for correct operation. Disconnect the harness connector and measure the resistance across the two terminals **(see illustration)**. It should be 37 to 48 ohms. If not, replace the solenoid.

---

### 5   Information sensors - replacement

### Engine coolant temperature sensor

*Refer to illustrations 5.1 and 5.3*

**Warning:** *Wait until the engine is completely cool before beginning this procedure.*

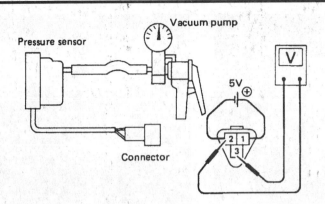

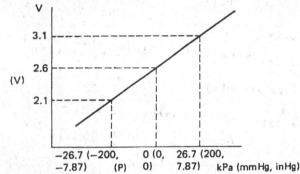

**4.24  Attach a hand-held vacuum pump to the pressure sensor and check the SIGNAL voltage - voltage should increase as vacuum is applied**

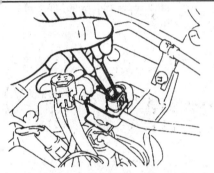

**4.25  Checking the resistance on the pressure exchange solenoid on a turbocharged model**

1    The coolant temperature sensor is located on the engine coolant pipe under the intake manifold **(see illustration)**.
2    To remove the sensor, release the locking tab, unplug the electrical connector, then carefully unscrew the sensor. Be sure to drain two to three quarts of the coolant from the radiator to prevent leakage when the ECT sensor is removed (see Chapter 1). **Caution:** *Handle the coolant sensor with care. Damage to this sensor will affect the operation of the entire fuel injection system.*
3    Before installing the new sensor, wrap

the threads with Teflon sealing tape to prevent leakage and thread corrosion **(see illustration)**.
4    Installation is the reverse of removal. Check the coolant level and add some, if necessary (see Chapter 1).

### Airflow sensor

*Refer to illustrations 5.5*
5    The Mass Airflow Sensor (MAF) is located in the air intake duct **(see illustration)**.
6    Disconnect the electrical connector from the MAF sensor.
7    Remove the air cleaner assembly from the air intake duct (see Chapter 4).
8    Remove the nuts and lift the MAF sensor assembly from the air cleaner.
9    Installation is the reverse of removal.

### Oxygen sensor(s)

*Refer to illustrations 5.10*
**Note:** *Because it is installed in the exhaust manifold or pipe, which contracts when cool, the oxygen sensor may be very difficult to loosen when the engine is cold. Rather than risk damage to the sensor (assuming you are planning to reuse it in another manifold or pipe) or the threads which it screws into, start and run the engine for a minute or two, then shut it off. Be careful not to burn yourself dur-*

**5.1  The coolant temperature sensor (arrow) is located on the coolant pipe under the intake manifold runner**

*ing the following procedure.*
10    1990 through 1994 models are equipped with a single heated oxygen sensor located upstream of the catalytic converter while 1995 through 1998 models are equipped with an upstream O2 sensor (before the catalytic converter) and a downstream O2 sensor (after the catalytic converter) **(see illustration)**.
11    The following is a list of special precautions which must be taken whenever the sen-

**5.3  To prevent coolant leakage, be sure to wap the temperature sensor threads with Teflon tape before installation**

**5.5  The MAF sensor (arrow) is located in the air intake duct near the air cleaner assembly**

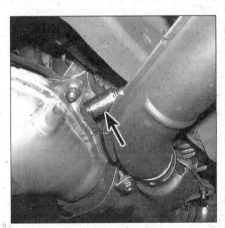

**5.10  Location of the upstream oxygen sensor (arrow)**

sor is serviced.

a) *The oxygen sensor has a permanently attached pigtail and electrical connector which should not be removed from the sensor. Damage or removal of the pigtail or electrical connector can adversely affect operation of the sensor.*

b) *Grease, dirt and other contaminants should be kept away from the electrical connector and the louvered end of the sensor.*

c) *Do not use cleaning solvents of any kind on the oxygen sensor.*

d) *Do not drop or roughly handle the sensor.*

e) *The silicone boot must be installed in the correct position to prevent the boot from being melted and to allow the sensor to operate properly.*

f) *The sensor is designed to allow air circulation to the internal portion of the sensor. Whenever the sensor is removed and installed or replaced, make sure the air passages are not restricted.*

12    Disconnect the cable from the negative terminal of the battery.
13    Raise the vehicle and place it securely on jackstands.
14    Remove any exhaust heat shields which would interfere with the removal of the oxygen sensor(s), then disconnect the electrical connector from the sensor.
15    Carefully remove the oxygen sensor from the exhaust pipe.
16    Anti-seize compound must be used on the threads of the sensor to facilitate future removal. The threads of new sensors will already be coated with this compound, but if an old sensor is removed and reinstalled, recoat the threads.
17    Install the sensor and tighten it securely.
18    Reconnect the electrical connector of the pigtail lead to the main engine wiring harness.
19    Lower the vehicle.

### Throttle position sensor

*Refer to illustrations 5.20*
20    The throttle position sensor is located on the throttle body **(see illustration)**.
21    Disconnect the electrical connector from the sensor. **Note:** *It may be necessary to remove the air inlet tube (air duct) to access the sensor connector.*
22    Remove the mounting screws from the throttle position sensor and remove the sensor from the throttle body.
23    When installing the throttle position sensor, be sure to align the socket locating tangs on the sensor with the throttle shaft in the throttle body.
24    Installation is the reverse of removal.
**Note:** *Refer to Section 4 for the adjustment procedure on 1994 and earlier models.*

### Crankshaft position sensor

*Refer to illustration 5.25*
25    The crankshaft sensor is mounted on the oil pump housing near the crankshaft pulley **(see illustration)**. Remove the mounting

**5.20  The throttle position sensor is located on the side of the throttle body (arrow)**

bolt. Remove the sensor slowly to avoid damaging the component.
26    Installation is the reverse of removal.

### Camshaft position sensor

*Refer to illustration 5.27*
27    The camshaft sensor is behind the left camshaft timing belt cover **(see illustration)**.
28    Disconnect the negative terminal from the battery.
29    Disconnect the electrical connector from the camshaft sensor.
30    Remove the bolt from the camshaft sensor and remove the sensor.
31    Installation is the reverse of removal.

### Knock sensor

**Warning:** *Wait for the engine to cool completely before performing this procedure.*
32    The knock sensor is located under the intake manifold runner on the left rear of the engine. Refer to Chapter 2A and remove the intake manifold to access the knock sensor.
33    The knock sensor is threaded into the engine block, when it is removed, the coolant will drain from the engine block. Drain the cooling system (see Chapter 1). Place a drain pan under the sensor, disconnect the electrical connector and remove the knock sensor. A new sensor is pre-coated with thread sealant, do not apply any additional sealant or the operation of the sensor may be effected. Install the knock sensor and tighten it securely (approximately 14 ft-lbs). Don't overtighten the sensor or damage may occur. The remainder of installation is the reverse of removal.

### Vehicle speed sensor

*Refer to illustrations 5.34*
34    The vehicle speed sensor is located in various places depending upon engine and drivetrain. On 2WD models, it is located on the transaxle near the axle spline. On 4WD models, speed sensor number 1 is located on the backside of the transfer case **(see illustration)**. Also on 4WD models, speed sensor

**5.25  The crankshaft sensor is located above the crankshaft pulley (arrow)**

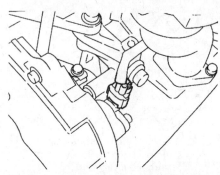

**5.27  The camshaft sensor is located behind the left camshaft timing belt cover**

number 2 is located on the top of the transaxle. Most of these models are equipped with a speed sensor buffer located in the instrument cluster. This sensor transfers the voltage signal from the drivetrain mounted sensor(s) to the ECM for processing.
35    To replace the vehicle speed sensor, detach the sensor retaining bolt(s) and or bracket, unplug the sensor and remove it from the transaxle.
36    Installation is the reverse of removal.

**5.34  Location of the vehicle speed sensor number 1 on the transfer case (4WD model)**

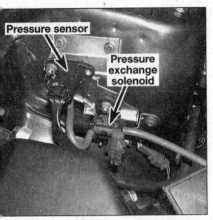

**5.37 The pressure sensor is mounted on the inner fender**

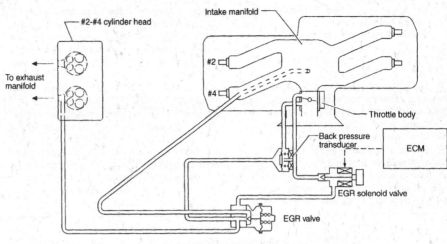

**6.2 Typical EGR system**

## Pressure sensor (turbocharged and automatic transaxle models)

*Refer to illustration 5.37*

37   The pressure sensor is mounted on the inner fender in the engine compartment **(see illustration)**.

38   Disconnect the harness connector for the pressure sensor and remove the sensor from the engine compartment. Installation is the reverse of removal.

## 6  Exhaust Gas Recirculation (EGR) system

### General description

*Refer to illustrations 6.2*

1   The EGR system is used to lower NOx (oxides of nitrogen) emission levels caused by high combustion temperatures. The EGR recirculates a small amount of exhaust gases into the intake manifold. The additional mixture lowers the temperature of combustion thereby reducing the formation of NOx compounds.

2   This system is equipped with an EGR valve, an EGR solenoid valve, a backpressure transducer (BPT), the Electronic Control Module (ECM) and the vacuum lines connecting the various components **(see illustration)**. The BPT controls the vacuum pressure to control the amount of EGR according to the engine load. The EGR valve is opened in response to the vacuum signal from the EGR control solenoid which is controlled by the ECM. The ECM detects engine driving conditions from the various sensors (MAF, ECT, TPS, etc) and translates the information into the correct On/Off EGR time.

### Check

*Refer to illustration 6.5*

3   Check all hoses for cracks, kinks, broken sections and proper connection. Inspect all system connections for damage, cracks and leaks.

4   To check the EGR system operation, bring the engine up to operating temperature and, with the transaxle in Neutral (parking brake set and tires blocked to prevent movement), allow it to idle for 1 to 2 minutes. Open the throttle abruptly so the engine speed is between 2,000 and 3,000 rpm and then allow it to close. The EGR valve stem should move if the control system is working properly. The test should be repeated several times. Movement of the stem indicates the control system is functioning correctly.

5   If the EGR valve stem does not move, check all of the hose connections to make sure they are not leaking or clogged. Disconnect the vacuum hose and apply ten inches of vacuum with a hand-held pump **(see illustration)**. If the stem still does not move, replace the EGR valve with a new one. If the valve does open, measure the valve travel to make sure it is approximately 1/8-inch. Also, the engine should run roughly or even stall when the valve is open. If it doesn't, the passages are probably clogged.

6   Apply vacuum with the pump and then clamp the hose shut. The valve should stay open for 30 seconds or longer. If it does not, the diaphragm is leaking and the valve should be replaced with a new one.

7   If the engine idles roughly and it is suspected the EGR valve is not closing, remove the EGR valve and inspect the poppet and seat area for deposits.

8   If the deposits are more than a thin film of carbon, the valve should be cleaned. To clean the valve, apply solvent and allow it to penetrate and soften the deposits, making sure that none gets on the valve diaphragm, as it could be damaged.

9   Use a vacuum pump to hold the valve open and carefully scrape the deposits from the seat and poppet area with a tool. Inspect the poppet and stem for wear and replace the valve with a new one if wear is found.

10   If the EGR valve is functioning properly, check the EGR control solenoid for correct operation. First, check for a vacuum signal from the throttle body to the EGR control solenoid. Disconnect the vacuum line from

the EGR solenoid and install a vacuum gauge onto the vacuum line. With the engine idling, the vacuum gauge should indicate manifold vacuum. Now increase the throttle opening (acceleration) and observe that manifold vacuum decreases with the change in engine speed. If the vacuum readings are incorrect, check for a damaged vacuum line or plugged vacuum port(s).

11   Check the EGR control solenoid. Using an ohmmeter, measure the resistance of the EGR control solenoid. It should be between 10 and 100 ohms.

12   Measure the power supply to the EGR control solenoid. With the ignition key ON (engine not running), measure the voltage to the EGR control solenoid. Battery voltage should be present. If battery voltage is present but the solenoid is out of range with high or low resistance, replace the EGR control solenoid.

### Component replacement

#### EGR valve

*Refer to illustration 6.18*

13   When replacing an EGR valve, make sure that you obtain the correct part. Use the stamped code located on the top of the EGR valve.

**6.5 Use a hand-held vacuum pump to apply vacuum to the EGR valve**

14 Detach the cable from the negative terminal of the battery.

15 Remove the air cleaner housing assembly (see Chapter 4).

16 Detach the vacuum line from the EGR valve.

17 Raise the vehicle and support it securely on jackstands. Remove the EGR pipe from the exhaust manifold. Lower the vehicle.

18 Remove the EGR valve mounting bolts **(see illustration)**.

19 Remove the EGR valve and gasket from the manifold. Discard the gasket.

20 Remove all exhaust deposits from the EGR valve mounting surface on the manifold and, if you plan to use the same valve, the mounting surface of the valve itself. Look for exhaust deposits in the valve outlet. Remove deposit build-up with a scraper or screwdriver. **Caution:** *Never wash the valve in solvents or degreaser - both agents will permanently damage the diaphragm. Sandblasting is also not recommended because it will affect the operation of the valve.*

21 If the EGR passage contains an excessive build-up of deposits, clean it out with a wire wheel. Make sure that all loose particles are completely removed to prevent them from clogging the EGR valve or from being ingested into the engine.

22 Installation is the reverse of removal.

**6.18 Location of the EGR valve and backpressure transducer**

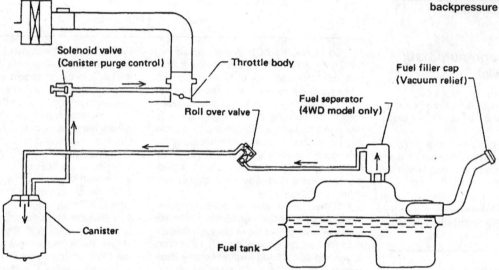

**Non-Turbocharged Models**

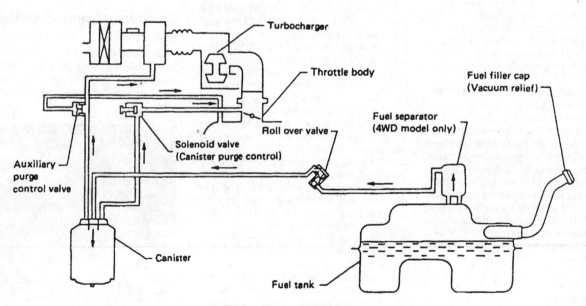

**Turbocharged Models**

**7.2 Typical EVAP system on non-turbocharged and turbocharged models**

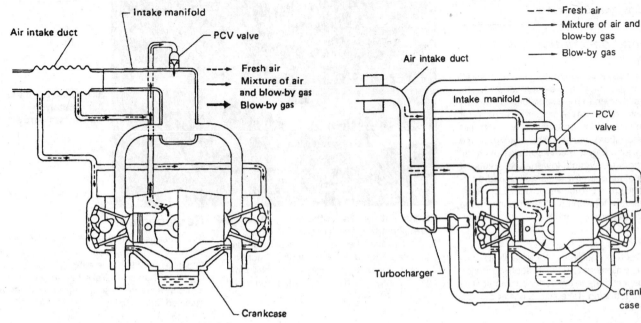

**8.1a  Diagram of a typical PCV system on non-turbocharged models**

**8.1b  Diagram of a typical PCV system on turbocharged models**

### EGR vacuum control solenoid

23   Detach the cable from the negative terminal of the battery.

24   Remove the air intake duct from the air cleaner assembly (see Chapter 4).

25   Unplug the electrical connector from the solenoid.

26   Clearly label and detach both vacuum hoses.

27   Remove the solenoid mounting screw and remove the solenoid.

28   Installation is the reverse of removal.

### 7   Evaporative Emissions Control System (EVAP)

#### General description

*Refer to illustration 7.2*

1   This system is designed to trap and store fuel vapors that evaporate from the fuel tank, throttle body and intake manifold.

2   The Evaporative Emission Control System (EVAP) consists of a charcoal-filled canister and the lines connecting the canister to the fuel tank, ported vacuum line to the purge control solenoid valve, a rollover valve and a two way valve (later models) mounted near the charcoal canister **(see illustration)**.

3   Fuel vapors are transferred from the fuel tank, throttle body and intake manifold to a canister where they are stored when the engine is not operating. When the engine is running, the fuel vapors are purged from the canister by a purge control solenoid and consumed in the normal combustion process.

#### Check

4   Poor idle, stalling and poor driveability can be caused by an inoperative purge control solenoid, a damaged canister, split or cracked hoses or hoses connected to the wrong tubes.

5   Evidence of fuel loss or fuel odor can be caused by fuel leaking from fuel lines or the throttle body, a cracked or damaged canister, an inoperative bowl vent valve, an inoperative purge valve, disconnected, misrouted, kinked, deteriorated or damaged vapor or control hoses or an improperly seated air cleaner or air cleaner gasket.

6   Inspect each hose attached to the canister for kinks, leaks and breaks along its entire length. Repair or replace as necessary.

7   Inspect the canister. If it is cracked or damaged, replace it.

8   Look for fuel leaking from the bottom of the canister. If fuel is leaking, replace the canister and check the hoses and hose routing.

9   Check the purge control solenoid for correct operation. First, check for a vacuum signal from the throttle body to the purge control solenoid. Disconnect the vacuum line from the purge control solenoid and install a vacuum gauge onto the vacuum line. Raise the engine rpm and observe the vacuum increase (ported vacuum signal). If the vacuum readings are incorrect, check for a damaged vacuum line or plugged vacuum port(s).

10   Check the purge control solenoid. Using an ohmmeter, measure the resistance of the purge control solenoid. It should be between 10 and 100 ohms.

11   Measure the power supply to the purge control solenoid. With the ignition key ON (engine not running), measure the voltage to the purge control solenoid. Battery voltage should be present. If battery voltage is present but the solenoid is out of range with high or low resistance, replace the purge control solenoid.

#### Component replacement

12   Raise the vehicle and support it securely on jackstands.

13   Clearly label, then detach, all vacuum lines from the canister.

14   Loosen the canister mounting clamp bolt(s) and pull the canister out **(see Chapter 1)**.

15   Installation is the reverse of removal.

### 8   Positive Crankcase Ventilation (PCV) system

*Refer to illustration 8.1a and 8.1b*

1   The Positive Crankcase Ventilation (PCV) system reduces hydrocarbon emissions by scavenging crankcase vapors. It does this by circulating fresh air from the air cleaner through the crankcase, where it mixes with blow-by gases and is then rerouted through a PCV valve to the intake manifold **(see illustrations)**.

2   The main components of the PCV system are the PCV valve, a fresh air filtered inlet and the vacuum hoses connecting these two components with the engine.

3   To maintain idle quality, the PCV valve restricts the flow when the intake manifold vacuum is high. If abnormal operating conditions arise, the system is designed to allow excessive amounts of blow-by gases to flow back through the crankcase vent tube into the air cleaner to be consumed by normal combustion.

4   Checking and replacement of the PCV valve and filter is covered in Chapter 1.

## 9    Catalytic Converter

### *General description*

*Refer to illustration 9.1*

1    The catalytic converter **(see illustration)** is an emission control device added to the exhaust system to reduce pollutants from the exhaust gas stream. A single-bed converter design is used in combination with a three-way (reduction) catalyst. The coating on the three-way catalyst media contains platinum and rhodium, which lowers the levels of oxides of nitrogen (NOx) as well as hydrocarbons (HC) and carbon monoxide (CO). Refer to Chapter 4 for additional information on the exhaust system.

### *Check*

2    The test equipment for a catalytic converter is expensive and highly sophisticated. If you suspect that the converter on your vehicle is malfunctioning, take it to a dealer service

**9.1 Location of the catalytic converters (arrows)**

department or an authorized emissions inspection facility for diagnosis and repair.

3    Whenever the vehicle is raised for servicing of underbody components, check the converter for leaks, corrosion and other damage. If damage is discovered, the converter should be replaced.

### *Replacement*

4    Because the converter is part of the exhaust system, converter replacement requires removal of the exhaust pipe assembly (see Chapter 4). Take the vehicle, or the exhaust system, to a muffler shop or other qualified repair facility.

# Chapter 7 Part A
# Manual transaxle

## Contents

## Specifications

### Torque specifications

| | Ft-lbs |
|---|---|
| Back-up light switch/neutral switch | 16 to 19 |
| Transaxle-to-engine fasteners | |
|     Lower nuts | 34 to 39 |
|     Upper right bolt | 34 to 39 |

## 1   General information

The manual transaxle is a fully-synchronized five-speed unit. The "transaxle" is actually several components bolted together into a single assembly: the clutch housing; the main case, which houses the differential and transaxle; and the rear case. On 4WD models the rear case consists of a transfer case/transfer control system and an extension housing where the driveshaft connects to the output shaft. However, the transaxle is removed and installed as a single assembly; do not try to separate any of these components from the transaxle. If the transaxle must be replaced, obtain a complete new, rebuilt or used assembly.

## 2   Shift lever - removal and installation

Refer to illustrations 2.1, 2.5a, 2.5b and 2.6
1   Unscrew the shift lever knob from the shift lever (see illustration).
2   Remove the center console and the shift lever boot (see Chapter 11).

**2.5a  To disconnect the stay rod, remove these two bolts (arrows) . . .**

**2.5b  . . . then remove the spring (4WD model shown)**

**2.6  To disconnect the shift rod, remove this nut and bolt (4WD model shown)**

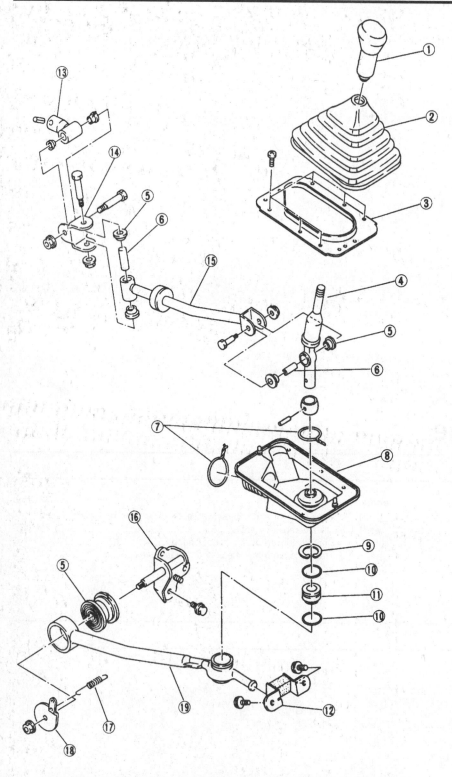

**2.1  An exploded view of a typical shift lever assembly (4WD model shown, 2WD models similar)**

| 1 | Shift lever knob | 8 | Boot | 14 | Joint |
|---|---|---|---|---|---|
| 2 | Shift lever boot | 9 | Snap-ring | 15 | Shift rod |
| 3 | Boot plate | 10 | O-rings | 16 | Bracket |
| 4 | Shift lever | 11 | Bushing | 17 | Spring |
| 5 | Bushing | 12 | Cushion rubber | 18 | Dynamic damper |
| 6 | Spacer | 13 | Boss | 19 | Stay rod |
| 7 | Retaining wires | | | | |

3    Remove the shift lever boot plate screws and detach the plate from the floor.
4    Raise the vehicle and place it securely on jackstands.
5    Disconnect the front end of the stay rod from the transaxle and remove the spring **(see illustrations)**.
6    Disconnect the front end of the shift rod from the transaxle **(see illustration)**.
7    Installation is the reverse of removal. Make sure that all fasteners are tight.
8    Remove the jackstands and lower the vehicle.

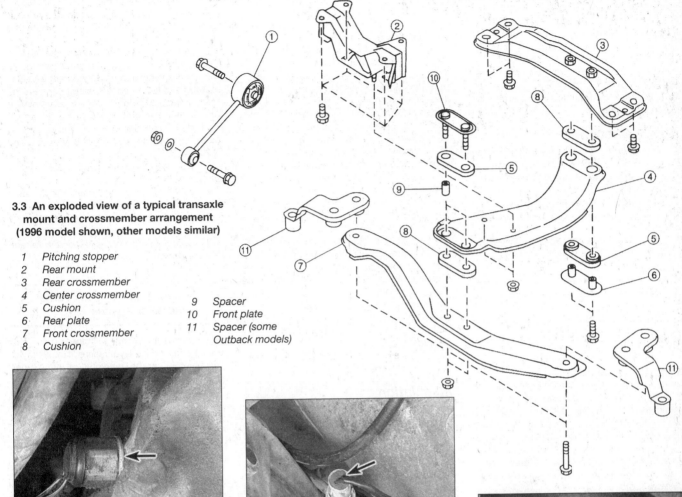

**3.3 An exploded view of a typical transaxle mount and crossmember arrangement (1996 model shown, other models similar)**

1  Pitching stopper
2  Rear mount
3  Rear crossmember
4  Center crossmember
5  Cushion
6  Rear plate
7  Front crossmember
8  Cushion
9  Spacer
10  Front plate
11  Spacer (some Outback models)

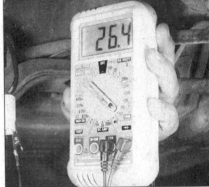

**4.2 The back-up light switch (arrow) is located on the left side of the rear case (2WD models) or the transfer case (4WD models); the neutral start switch (not visible in this photo) is also located here, right behind the back-up light switch**

**4.3 To check either switch, trace the electrical lead back to its connector (arrow), unplug the connector and hook up an ohmmeter to the connector terminals**

**4.4 The back-up light switch should have continuity only in Reverse; the neutral start switch should have continuity only in Neutral**

## 3  Transaxle mounts - check and replacement

*Refer to illustration 3.3*

1    Raise the vehicle and place it securely on jackstands.

2    Insert a large screwdriver or prybar into the space between the transaxle and the crossmember and try to pry the transaxle up slightly. The transaxle should move very little. If it moves a lot, inspect the rubber portions of the two mounts. If either mount is damaged, replace it.

3    To replace a mount, remove the bolts attaching the mount to the crossmember and to the transaxle **(see illustration)**.

4    Raise the transaxle slightly with a jack and remove the mount.

5    Installation is the reverse of the removal procedure. Be sure to tighten the bolts securely.

6    Remove the jackstands and lower the vehicle.

## 4  Back-up light and neutral switches - check and replacement

### Check

*Refer to illustrations 4.2, 4.3 and 4.4*

1    Raise the vehicle and place it securely on jackstands.

2    The back-up light switch and the neutral

switch **(see illustration)** are located on the left side of the rear case (2WD models) or the transfer case (4WD models).

3    To check either switch, trace the electrical lead back to its connector **(see illustration)** and hook up an ohmmeter.

4    To check the back-up light switch, put the transaxle into reverse and verify that there's continuity (zero or low resistance) **(see illustration)**. Then put the transaxle in

any other gear and verify that there's no continuity (high or infinite resistance).

5    To check the neutral switch, put the transaxle in Neutral and verify that there's continuity (zero or low resistance). Then put the transaxle in any other gear and verify that there's no continuity (high or infinite resistance).

6    If either switch fails to operate as described, replace it.

### Replacement

7    Simply unscrew the old switch, install the new switch (make sure the washer is installed) and tighten it to the torque listed in this Chapter's Specifications.

8    Verify that the new switch works properly (see above), then plug in the electrical connector.

9    Remove the jackstands and lower the vehicle.

---

## 5    Manual transaxle - removal and installation

### Removal

1    Open the hood and hold it securely in place with the hood stay.

2    Disconnect the negative battery cable.

3    If the vehicle is equipped with a cable-actuated clutch release system, disconnect the clutch cable; if it's equipped with a hydraulic release system, detach the release cylinder from the transaxle and support it out of the way (see Chapter 8). **Caution:** *Don't depress the clutch pedal after the release cylinder has been removed.*

4    Remove the pitching stopper **(see illustration 3.3)**. In place of the pitching stopper, Subaru recommends installing a special tool to adjust the angle of the engine to facilitate transaxle removal. If you are unable to obtain the special Subaru tool, you'll need an extra jack or engine hoist to slightly raise the front of the engine. Removing and installing the transaxle without either of these tools is very difficult.

5    Clearly label, then unplug, any electrical connectors accessible from above. (Some connectors can be unplugged from above, others are more accessible from underneath.)

6    Remove the starter motor (see Chapter 5).

7    Remove the upper right transaxle-to-engine bolt.

8    Raise the vehicle and place it securely on jackstands. Drain the lubricant from the transaxle (see Chapter 1).

9    Remove any parts of the exhaust system which are in the way (see Chapter 4).

10    Unplug the electrical connectors for the back-up light switch and the neutral start switch **(see illustration 4.2)** and the oxygen sensor (see Chapter 6). Disconnect any ground wires too. On 4WD models, unplug the connector for the 4WD indicator light switch.

11    Disconnect the speedometer cable from the right side of the transaxle.

12    On 4WD vehicles, remove the driveshaft (see Chapter 8).

13    Disconnect the stay rod, spring and shift rod **(see illustrations 2.5a, 2.5b and 2.6)**.

14    Disconnect the driveaxle assemblies from the transaxle (see Chapter 8).

15    Place a transaxle jack or a floor jack under the transaxle. As a safety measure, secure the transaxle to the jack head with a tie-down or a length of chain.

16    Remove the front, center and rear crossmembers **(see illustration 3.3)**.

17    Remove the two lower transaxle-to-engine nuts.

18    Using the special Subaru tool installed in place of the pitching stopper, or using a jack or an engine hoist, raise the front of the engine slightly so that the rear of the engine is angled down. Slide the transaxle to the rear slightly to disengage the transaxle input shaft from the clutch hub, then slowly lower the transaxle assembly.

19    While the transaxle is separated from the engine, inspect the clutch assembly and replace any worn or damaged parts (see Chapter 8).

20    While the transaxle is removed, inspect the transaxle mount (see Section 3).

### Installation

21    Support the transaxle on the floor jack then raise it into alignment with the engine. Apply a little multi-purpose grease to the input shaft splines.

22    Slowly and carefully slide the transaxle forward and insert the input shaft into the clutch hub. If the input shaft hangs up, rotate the crankshaft or the transaxle output shaft until the input shaft splines are aligned with the clutch hub splines. Guide the transaxle forward until the transaxle and engine are fully engaged, then install the lower transaxle-to-engine fasteners and tighten them to the torque listed in this Chapter's Specifications.

23    Install the rear, center and front crossmembers. Tighten all crossmember and mount nuts and bolts securely.

24    Remove the jack supporting the transaxle.

25    Reattach the driveaxles (see Chapter 8).

26    Install the shift linkage and tighten all fasteners securely (see Section 2).

27    On 4WD vehicles, install the driveshaft (see Chapter 8).

28    Install the exhaust pipe assembly (see Chapter 4).

29    Plug in the oxygen sensor connector and the connectors for the back-up light switch and the neutral start switch.

30    Connect the speedometer cable to the transaxle.

31    Remove the jackstands and lower the vehicle.

32    Install the upper right transaxle-to-engine bolt and tighten it to the torque listed in this Chapter's Specifications.

33    Install the starter motor (see Chapter 5).

34    Remove the special Subaru tool, if used, and install the stopper. Tighten the nuts and bolts securely.

35    Plug in any remaining unplugged electrical connectors. Reattach all ground wires.

36    If the vehicle is equipped with a cable-actuated clutch release system, connect the clutch cable and adjust the cable freeplay; if the clutch release system is hydraulic, attach the release cylinder to the transaxle, making sure the pushrod is positioned correctly (see Chapter 8).

37    Connect the battery ground cable to the battery.

38    Add lubricant to the transaxle by referring to the appropriate Section in Chapter 1.

39    Start the engine and check the exhaust system for any leaks or noise.

40    Check the clutch cable and shift linkage for smooth operation.

---

## 6    Manual transmission overhaul - general information

Overhauling a manual transaxle is a difficult job for the do-it-yourselfer. It involves the disassembly and reassembly of many small parts. Numerous clearances must be precisely measured and, if necessary, changed with select fit spacers and snap-rings. If transaxle problems arise, you can remove and install the transaxle yourself, but overhaul should be left to a transaxle repair shop. Rebuilt transaxles may be available - check with your dealer parts department and auto parts stores. At any rate, the time and money involved in an overhaul are almost sure to exceed the cost of a rebuilt unit.

Nevertheless, it's not impossible for an inexperienced mechanic to rebuild a transaxle if the special tools are available and the job is done in a deliberate step-by-step manner so nothing is overlooked.

The tools necessary for an overhaul include internal and external snap-ring pliers, a bearing puller, a slide hammer, a set of pin punches, a dial indicator and possibly a hydraulic press. In addition, a large, sturdy workbench and a vise or transaxle stand will be required.

During disassembly of the transaxle, make careful notes of how each piece comes off, where it fits in relation to other pieces and what holds it in place. Be sure to note how the parts are installed as you remove them; this will make it much easier to get the transaxle back together.

Before taking the transaxle apart for repair, it will help if you have some idea what area of the transaxle is malfunctioning. Certain problems can be closely tied to specific areas in the transaxle, which can make component examination and replacement easier. Refer to the *Troubleshooting* section at the front of this manual for information regarding possible sources of trouble.

# Chapter 7 Part B
# Automatic transaxle

## Contents

## Specifications

### Torque specifications

Ft-lbs (unless otherwise indicated)

Band adjusting screw
Screw
Step 1 .......... 78 in-lbs
Step 2 .......... Back off three turns
Locknut .......... 18 to 21
Shift cable adjustment nut .......... 48 to 81 in-lbs
Torque converter mounting bolts .......... 17 to 19
Transaxle-to-engine nuts/bolts
Lower transaxle-to-engine nuts .......... 34 to 40
Upper right bolt .......... 34 to 40

## 1  General information

All vehicles covered in this manual are equipped with either a five-speed manual transaxle or a four-speed automatic transaxle. All information on the automatic transaxle is included in this Part of Chapter 7. Information for the manual transaxle can be found in Part A.

Special tools and equipment are needed to service automatic transaxles because of their complexity. This Chapter is restricted to routine maintenance, general diagnosis and transaxle removal and installation.

If the transaxle requires major repair work, it should be left to a dealer service department or an automotive transaxle repair shop. You can, however, save money by removing and installing the transaxle yourself.

## 2  Diagnosis - general

**Note:** *Automatic transaxle malfunctions may be caused by five general conditions: poor engine performance, improper adjustments, hydraulic malfunctions, mechanical malfunctions or computer malfunctions. Diagnosis of these problems should always begin with a check of the easily repaired items: fluid level and condition (see Chapter 1), and shift linkage adjustment. Next, perform a road test to determine if the problem has been corrected or if more diagnosis is necessary. If the problem persists after the preliminary tests and corrections are completed, additional diagnosis should be done by a dealer service department or transaxle repair shop. Refer to the Troubleshooting section at the front of this manual for information on symptoms of transaxle problems.*

### Preliminary checks

1    Drive the vehicle to warm the transaxle to normal operating temperature.

2    Check the fluid level as described in Chapter 1:

a) *If the fluid level is unusually low, add enough fluid to bring the level within the designated area of the dipstick, then check for external leaks (see below).*

b) *If the fluid level is abnormally high, drain off the excess, then check the drained fluid for contamination by coolant. The presence of engine coolant in the automatic transaxle fluid indicates that a failure has occurred in the internal radiator walls that separate the coolant from the transaxle fluid (see Chapter 3).*

c) *If the fluid is foaming, drain it and refill the transaxle, then check for coolant in the fluid or a high fluid level.*

**3.4 To detach the shift cable from the manual lever, remove this snap-pin; to unbolt the cable clamp from the transaxle, remove these two bolts (arrows)**

3   Check the engine idle speed. **Note:** *If the engine is malfunctioning, do not proceed with the preliminary checks until it has been repaired and runs normally.*

4   Inspect the shift linkage (see Section 4). Make sure that it's properly adjusted and that the linkage operates smoothly.

## Fluid leak diagnosis

5   Most fluid leaks are easy to locate visually. Repair usually consists of replacing a seal or gasket. If a leak is difficult to find, the following procedure may help.

6   Identify the fluid. Make sure it's transaxle fluid and not engine oil or brake fluid (automatic transaxle fluid is a deep red color).

7   Try to pinpoint the source of the leak. Drive the vehicle several miles, then park it over a large sheet of cardboard. After a minute or two, you should be able to locate the leak by determining the source of the fluid dripping onto the cardboard.

8   Make a careful visual inspection of the suspected component and the area immediately around it. Pay particular attention to gasket mating surfaces. A mirror is often helpful for finding leaks in areas that are hard to see.

9   If the leak still cannot be found, clean the suspected area thoroughly with a degreaser or solvent, then dry it.

10   Drive the vehicle for several miles at normal operating temperature and varying speeds. After driving the vehicle, visually inspect the suspected component again.

11   Once the leak has been located, the cause must be determined before it can be properly repaired. If a gasket is replaced but the sealing flange is bent, the new gasket will not stop the leak. The bent flange must be straightened.

12   Before attempting to repair a leak, check to make sure that the following conditions are corrected or they may cause another leak. **Note:** *Some of the following conditions cannot be fixed without highly specialized tools and expertise. Such problems must be referred to a transaxle repair shop or a dealer service department.*

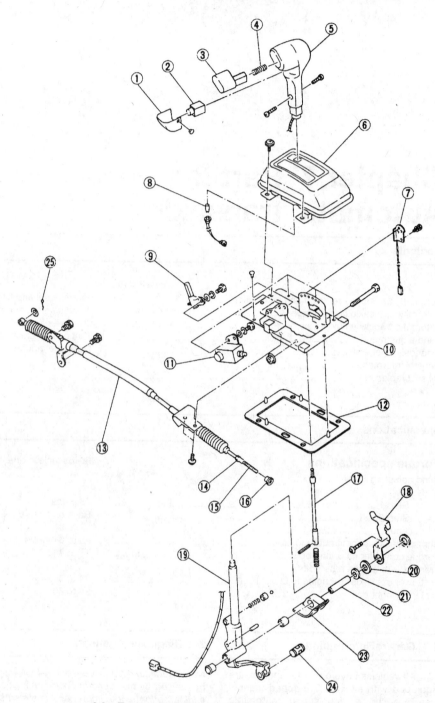

**3.6a Typical 1990 through 1994 shift lever assembly**

| 1 | Cover | 14 | Nut |
|---|---|---|---|
| 2 | Hold switch | 15 | Inner cable |
| 3 | Grip button | 16 | Nut |
| 4 | Spring | 17 | Rod |
| 5 | Grip | 18 | Lock plate |
| 6 | Gear position indicator panel | 19 | Shift lever |
| 7 | Park position switch | 20 | Washer |
| 8 | Indicator light bulb | 21 | Spacer |
| 9 | Shift-lock release button | 22 | Spacer |
| 10 | Shift lever base | 23 | Boot |
| 11 | Solenoid | 24 | Pin |
| 12 | Gasket | 25 | Snap-pin |
| 13 | Outer cable | | |

**3.6b  Typical 1995 and later shift lever assembly**

| | | | |
|---|---|---|---|
| 1 | Grip button | 14 | Clip |
| 2 | Spring | 15 | Rod |
| 3 | Grip | 16 | Shift lever |
| 4 | Gear position indicator panel | 17 | Lock plate |
| 5 | Park position switch | 18 | Detention spring |
| 6 | Indicator light bulb | 19 | Pin |
| 7 | Shift lock solenoid | 20 | Spacer |
| 8 | Shift lever base | 21 | Washer |
| 9 | Gasket | 22 | Boot |
| 10 | Outer cable | 23 | Spacer |
| 11 | Nut | 24 | Snap-pin |
| 12 | Nut | | |
| 13 | Inner cable | | |

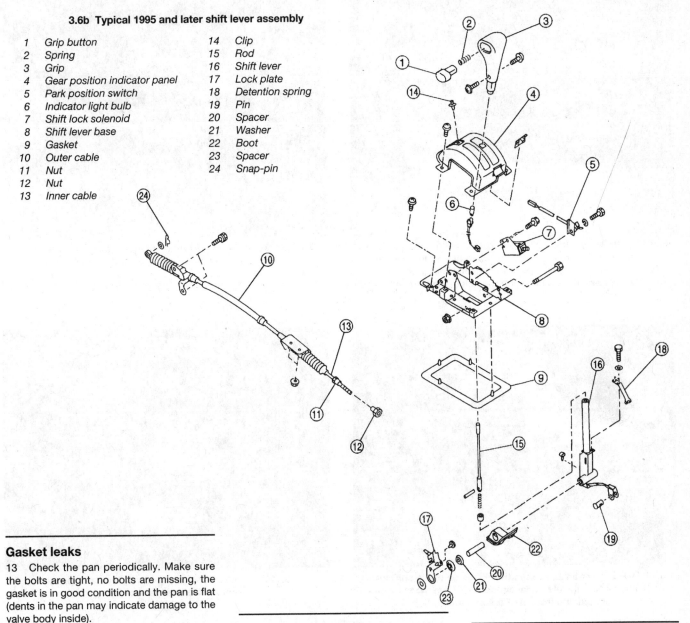

## Gasket leaks

13   Check the pan periodically. Make sure the bolts are tight, no bolts are missing, the gasket is in good condition and the pan is flat (dents in the pan may indicate damage to the valve body inside).

14   If the pan gasket is leaking, the fluid level or the fluid pressure may be too high, the vent may be plugged, the pan bolts may be too tight, the pan sealing flange may be warped, the sealing surface of the transaxle housing may be damaged, the gasket may be damaged or the transaxle casting may be cracked or porous. If sealant instead of gasket material has been used to form a seal between the pan and the transaxle housing, it may be the wrong sealant.

## Seal leaks

15   If a transaxle seal is leaking, the fluid level or pressure may be too high, the vent may be plugged, the seal bore may be damaged, the seal itself may be damaged or improperly installed, the surface of the shaft protruding through the seal may be damaged or a loose bearing may be causing excessive shaft movement.

16   Make sure the dipstick tube seal is in good condition and the tube is properly seated. Periodically check the area around the speedometer gear or sensor for leakage. If transaxle fluid is evident, check the O-ring for damage.

## Case leaks

17   If the case itself appears to be leaking, the casting is porous and will have to be repaired or replaced.

18   Make sure the oil cooler hose fittings are tight and in good condition.

## Fluid comes out vent pipe or fill tube

19   If this condition occurs, the transaxle is overfilled, there is coolant in the fluid, the case is porous, the dipstick is incorrect, the vent is plugged or the drain back holes are plugged.

## 3   Shift lever and cable - removal and installation

*Refer to illustrations 3.4, 3.6a, 3.6b, 3.6c, 3.9, 3.10, 3.11a, 3.11b and 3.12*

1   Place the shift lever in Neutral.

2   Raise the vehicle and place it securely on jackstands.

3   Remove the front exhaust pipe (see Chapter 4).

4   Disconnect the shift cable from the manual lever on the transaxle (see illustration).

5   Detach the cable clamp from the transaxle case.

6   Disconnect the shift cable from the shift lever (see illustrations).

7   Detach the cable casing from the bracket (see illustration 3.6c).

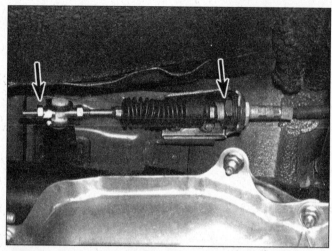

3.6c To disconnect the shift cable from the shift lever, unscrew the nut on the inner cable (left arrow); to disengage the cable from the cable bracket, loosen the adjuster nut (right arrow) and pass the cable through the slot in the bracket

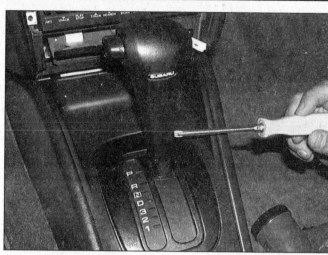

3.9 To release the grip from the shift lever, remove these two screws (one on each side) and lift off the grip

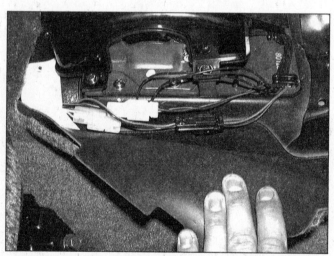

3.10 Peel back the carpet from the right side of the shift lever base and unplug the electrical connectors from the shift-lock solenoid and from the Park position switch

3.11a To detach the gear position indicator panel, remove these screws (arrows)

8    Remove the center console (see Chapter 11).
9    Remove the shift lever grip (see illustration).
10   Unplug the electrical connectors for the shift-lock solenoid and the Park position switch (see illustration).
11   Remove the gear position indicator retaining screws, lift up the panel and unplug the electrical connector for the gear position indicator illumination bulb (see illustrations).
12   Remove the shift lever base mounting screws (see illustration) and remove the shift lever assembly.
13   Installation is the reverse of removal. Adjust the shift cable as described in Section 4.

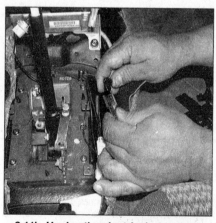

3.11b Unplug the electrical connector from the gear position indicator panel

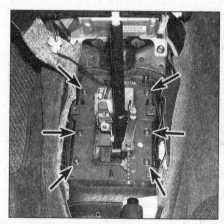

3.12 To detach the shift lever assembly from the floorpan, remove these mounting screws (arrows)

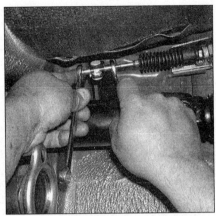

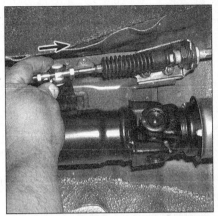

**4.9 Locate the cable connection at the lower end of the shift lever and loosen the rear nut; back it off far enough to allow the manual lever to move through its entire range of motion without moving the cable**

**4.10 To put the manual lever in Neutral, move it all the way forward, then move it back two clicks (the manual lever is attached to the selector shaft, which "clicks" as it rotates into each detent position; you'll feel it click as you move the manual lever)**

**4.11 Push the spacer between the two adjustment nuts forward until it touches the front nut, then tighten the rear nut to the torque listed in this Chapter's Specifications**

## 4  Shift cable - check and adjustment

### Check

1    As you move the shift lever (inside the vehicle) from the Park to the 1st gear position, you should hear an audible "click" in each gear as the manual valve (in the transaxle) is brought into each detent position. Verify that the shift lever position corresponds to the indicated gear on the gear position indicator, and that it's properly aligned with the corresponding notch in the guide plate, in each gear.
2    Verify that the shift lever cannot be moved from Neutral to Reverse unless the release button in the grip is pushed.
3    Verify that the engine cannot be started in any gear other than Neutral or Park.
4    Verify that the back-up light comes on only in the Reverse position.
5    Verify that the vehicle remains stationary on a slope when the shift lever is in the Park position.
6    If the shift linkage fails any part of this check, adjust it.

### Adjustment

*Refer to illustrations 4.9, 4.10 and 4.11*

7    Put the shift lever in the Neutral position.
8    Raise the vehicle and place it securely on jackstands.
9    At the lower end of the shift lever, loosen the *rear* cable adjustment nut **(see illustration)**; back it off far enough so that the manual lever (on the transaxle) is free to move through its range of motion without moving the shift cable.
10    Put the manual lever in the Neutral position by moving it all the way forward, then moving it two clicks to the rear **(see illustration)**.
11    Push the spacer between the two adjustment nuts forward until it touches the front nut **(see illustration)**, then tighten the rear nut to the torque listed in this Chapter's Specifications.
12    Verify that the shift lever operates smoothly.
13    Lower the vehicle.

## 5  Park/Neutral and back-up light switch - check, adjustment and replacement

### Check

1    Verify that the engine can only be started in the Park or Neutral position, and that the back-up lights work only when the shift lever is in the Reverse position.
2    If the Park/Neutral and back-up light switch doesn't operate as described, adjust it.

### Adjustment

*Refer to illustrations 5.4, 5.5, 5.6a, 5.6b and 5.6c*

3    Raise the vehicle and support it securely on jackstands.
4    Unplug the switch electrical connector **(see illustration)**.
5    Loosen the switch retaining bolts **(see illustration)**.

**5.4 Unplug the electrical connector from the Park/Neutral and back-up light switch**

**5.5 Locations of the Park/Neutral and back-up light switch retaining bolts (arrows)**

6    Hook up an ohmmeter to the indicated switch connector terminals **(see illustrations)** and move the switch until it produces continuity in Park and Reverse, then tighten the switch retaining bolts and verify that the switch produces no continuity at the indicated terminals in any other gear position except Reverse.

7    If the switch operates as described, tighten the switch bolts securely, plug in the electrical connector and lower the vehicle. If the switch still doesn't operate properly, even after adjustment, replace it.

### Replacement

*Refer to illustration 5.11*

8    Raise the vehicle and support it securely on jackstands.

9    Unplug the switch electrical connector **(see illustration 5.4)**.

10    Disconnect the shift cable from the manual lever **(see illustration 3.4)**.

11    Remove the nut that secures the manual lever to the selector shaft **(see illustration)**

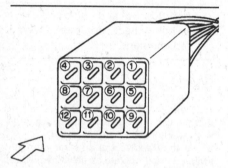

**5.6a Terminal guide for earlier models**

| 1 | 2 | 3 | 4 | 5 | 6 |
|---|---|---|---|---|---|
| 7 | 8 | 9 | 10 | 11 | 12 |

**5.6b Terminal guide for later models**

and remove the manual lever from the shaft.

12    Remove the switch retaining bolts **(see illustration 5.5)**.

13    Remove the switch.

14    Installation is the reverse of removal. Be sure to adjust the switch before tightening the bolts.

---

## 6    Oil seal replacement

---

1    Oil leaks frequently occur as a result of a worn extension housing oil seal, or a worn seal at the speedometer driven gear, back-up light switch or neutral start switch. Replacement of these seals is relatively easy, since the repairs can be performed without removing the transaxle from the vehicle. If you see puddles of lubricant under the transaxle, raise the vehicle and place it securely on jackstands. First, try to determine where the leak is coming from.

### Extension housing seal (4WD models only)

*Refer to illustrations 6.4 and 6.6*

2    The extension housing oil seal is located at the extreme rear end of the transaxle, where the driveshaft is attached. If the extension housing seal is leaking, there will be a buildup of lubricant on the front end of the driveshaft, and lubricant may even be dripping from the rear of the transaxle.

3    Disconnect the driveshaft from the transaxle (see Chapter 8).

4    Using a seal removal tool or screwdriver **(see illustration)**, carefully pry the oil seal out of the rear of the transaxle. Do not damage the splines on the output shaft.

5    If the oil seal cannot be removed with a screwdriver or prybar, a special oil seal removal tool (available at auto parts stores) will be required.

6    Using a large section of pipe or a large deep socket as a drift, install the new oil seal **(see illustration)**. Drive it into the bore

squarely and make sure it's completely seated.

7    Lubricate the splines of the output shaft and the outside of the driveshaft sleeve yoke with lightweight grease, then install the driveshaft. Be careful not to damage the lip of the new seal.

8    Remove the jackstands and lower the vehicle.

### Speedometer/speed sensor O-ring

*Refer to illustrations 6.10 and 6.11*

9    The speedometer cable is attached to the right side of the transaxle. The speedometer cable is driven by the speedometer shaft inside the transaxle case. A seal prevents lubricant from leaking past the shaft. If you see transaxle lubricant around the cable housing, this seal is probably leaking.

10    On earlier models, disconnect the speedometer cable from the transaxle. On later models, unplug the electrical connector from the speed sensor. Remove the speedometer driven gear/speed sensor hold-down bolt **(see illustration)** and remove the driven gear or sensor.

11    Remove the old O-ring **(see illustration)** and install a new one. Wipe a little oil on the O-ring before installing the speedometer driven gear/speed sensor.

12    Installation is the reverse of removal.

13    Remove the jackstands and lower the vehicle.

---

## 7    Transaxle mount - check and replacement

---

*Refer to illustrations 7.2 and 7.3*

1    Raise the vehicle and place it securely on jackstands.

2    Insert a large screwdriver or prybar into the space between the transaxle and the crossmember and try to pry the transaxle up slightly **(see illustration)**. The transaxle

| PIN NO. | 4 | 3 | 2 | 1 | 8 | 7 | 6 | 5 | 12 | 11 | 10 | 9 |
|---|---|---|---|---|---|---|---|---|---|---|---|---|
| CODE POSITION | B | Y | Br | YG | W | BY | R | GW | BY | BW | BW | RW |
| P | ○—| —○ | | | | | | | ○— | —○ | | |
| R | ○— | | —○ | | | | | | | | ○— | —○ |
| N | ○— | | | —○ | | | | | ○— | —○ | | |
| D | ○— | | | | —○ | | | | | | | |
| 3 | ○— | | | | | —○ | | | | | | |
| 2 | ○— | | | | | | —○ | | | | | |
| 1 | ○— | | | | | | | —○ | | | | |

**5.6c Continuity table for the Park/Neutral and back-up light switch**

5.11 To detach the manual lever from the selector shaft, remove this nut

6.4 Remove the extension housing seal with a seal removal tool (shown), or a large screwdriver; make sure you don't damage the splines on the output shaft

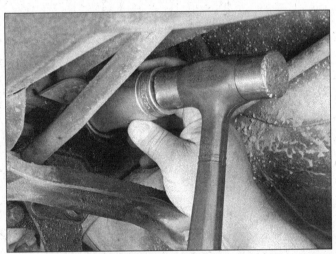

6.6 Make sure the seal is square to the bore, then use a hammer and large socket to tap the new extension housing seal into place; make sure the outside diameter of the socket is slightly smaller than the outside diameter of the new seal

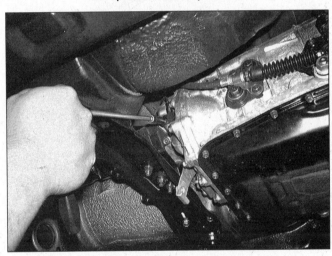

6.10 Remove the speedometer driven gear or speed sensor hold-down bolt

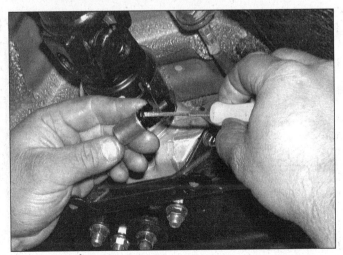

6.11 Remove the old O-ring and install a new one; put a little clean oil on the O-ring before installing the driven gear/speed sensor

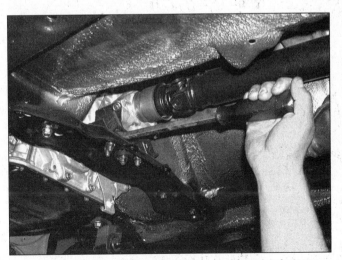

7.2 To check a transaxle mount, insert a large prybar between the rubber portion of the mount and the crossmember, then try to lever the transaxle up slightly; if it moves easily and excessively, replace the mount

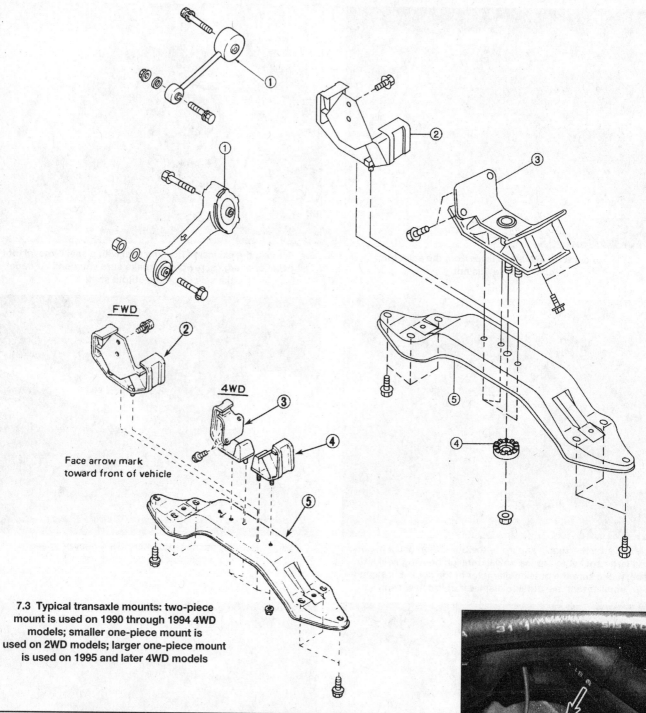

**7.3 Typical transaxle mounts: two-piece mount is used on 1990 through 1994 4WD models; smaller one-piece mount is used on 2WD models; larger one-piece mount is used on 1995 and later 4WD models**

should move very little. If it moves a lot, inspect the rubber portions of the two mounts. If either mount is damaged, replace it.

3    To replace a mount, remove the bolts attaching the mount to the crossmember and to the transaxle **(see illustration)**.

4    Raise the transaxle slightly with a jack and remove the mount.

5    Installation is the reverse of the removal procedure. Be sure to tighten the bolts securely.

6    Remove the jackstands and lower the vehicle.

## 8    Band adjustment

*Refer to illustration 8.3*

1    Road test the vehicle and note the following:

a) *If the transaxle upshifts directly from 1st to 3rd, the band clearance is too big. Tighten the band adjusting screw (see Steps 3 and 5).*

b) *If engine rpm increases abruptly when the transaxle shifts up from 1st to 2nd or from 3rd to 4th gear, or if there's more*

**8.3 The band adjustment screw (arrow) is located on the left side of the transaxle; to loosen the locknut, hold the screw with a wrench and break the nut loose with an offset-head wrench**

**9.6 Remove the pitching stopper nuts and bolts (arrows)**

**9.7a To gain access to the four driveplate-to-torque converter bolts from above, remove the timing hole plug (arrow)**

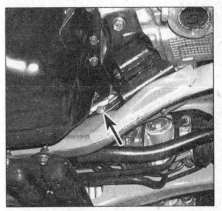

**9.7b The driveplate-to-torque converter bolts (arrow) can also be accessed from below**

than a one-second delay when the transaxle is downshifted from 3rd to 2nd, the band clearance is slightly too big. Tighten the band adjusting screw slightly (see Steps 3 and 4).

c) If you notice a "braking" effect when the transaxle upshifts from 2nd to 3rd, the band clearance is slightly too small. Loosen the adjusting screw slightly (see Steps 3 and 4).

d) If the transaxle repeatedly upshifts from 2nd to 4th and downshifts from 4th to 2nd, the band clearance is too small. Loosen the band adjusting screw (see Steps 3 and 5).

2    Raise the vehicle and support it securely on jackstands.

3    To adjust the band, locate the band adjusting screw on the left side of the transaxle, hold the end of the screw with a wrench and loosen the locknut with another wrench **(see illustration)**. Proceed to Step 4 or 5 as indicated.

4    If one of the problems described in Step 1b or Step 1c occurred, tighten or loosen the adjusting screw as indicated, in slight increments, retesting after each adjustment. Do NOT exceed 3/4-turn total. **Caution:** *Do NOT loosen the adjusting screw excessively, or the band strut on the servo piston will fall off.*

5    If one of the problems described in Step

1a or Step 1d occurred, tighten the adjusting screw to the torque listed in this Chapter's Specifications, then back it off three turns. Hold the adjusting screw with a wrench and tighten the locknut to the torque listed in this Chapter's Specifications.

6    Remove the jackstands and lower the vehicle. Road test the vehicle to verify that the transaxle is operating correctly.

## 9    Automatic transaxle - removal and installation

### Removal

*Refer to illustrations 9.6, 9.7a, 9.7b, 9.7c, 9.9, 9.15a, 9.15b, 9.15c, 9.20 and 9.22*

1    Open the hood and prop it in place with the stay.

2    Disconnect the cable from the negative terminal of the battery.

3    Remove the air intake duct (see Chapter 4).

4    Clearly label, then unplug, the electrical connectors for the front oxygen sensor, the transaxle harness, the transaxle ground, the Park/Neutral and back-up light switch and the vehicle speed sensor. Remove the bracket for the transaxle harness connector.

5    Remove the starter motor (see Chapter 5).

6    Remove the pitching stopper **(see illustration)**. In place of the pitching stopper, Subaru recommends installing a special tool to adjust the angle of the engine to facilitate transaxle removal. If you are unable to obtain the special tool, you'll need an extra jack or engine hoist to slightly raise the front of the engine. Removing and installing the transaxle without either of these tools is very difficult.

7    There are two ways to access the torque converter-to-driveplate bolts. There's a timing hole plug up top **(see illustration)**, and the driveplate is exposed underneath **(see illustration)**. Mark the relationship of the torque converter to the driveplate and remove the four bolts which attach the torque converter to the driveplate **(see illustration)**.

8    Remove the dipstick.

9    Remove the upper right transaxle-to-engine bolt **(see illustration)**.

10    Raise the vehicle and support it securely on jackstands.

11    Clearly label, then unplug, the electrical connector for the rear oxygen sensor.

12    Remove the exhaust system (see Chapter 4). On 4WD models, remove the rear exhaust pipe heat shield.

13    On 4WD models, remove the hanger bracket from the right side of the transaxle.

**9.7c Mark the relationship of the torque converter to the driveplate, then remove the four driveplate-to-torque converter bolts**

**9.9 Remove the upper right transaxle-to-engine bolt (arrow)**

**9.15a  Disconnect the oil cooler hoses from the metal lines (arrows)**

**9.15b  To detach the dipstick tube, remove this upper bracket bolt . . .**

**9.15c  . . . and this hold-down bolt**

14   Drain the fluid from the transaxle (see Chapter 1).
15   Disconnect the fluid cooler hoses from the metal lines on the transaxle side and the dipstick tube **(see illustrations)**.
16   On 4WD models, remove the driveshaft (see Chapter 8).
17   Disconnect the shift cable from the manual lever and detach the cable bracket from the transaxle **(see illustration 3.4)**.
18   Detach the stabilizer bar bushing clamps from the crossmember (see Chapter 10).
19   Remove the front driveaxles (see Chapter 10).
20   Remove the lower transaxle-to-engine nuts **(see illustration)**.
21   Place a transaxle jack or a floor jack under the transaxle. As a safety measure, secure the transaxle to the jack head with a tie-down, or a piece of chain or rope.
22   Remove the rear crossmember **(see illustration)**.
23   If you don't have the special pitching stopper replacement device recommended by Subaru, install an engine support, either a hoist, an engine support fixture or a floor jack positioned under the engine and slightly raise the front of the engine to facilitate transaxle removal.
24   Move the transaxle jack to the rear slightly to disengage the torque converter from the engine, then slowly lower the transaxle and

torque converter assembly. Keep a hand on the torque converter, which can fall out once the transaxle is detached from the engine.

## Installation

25   Support the transaxle on the floor jack then raise it into alignment with the engine.
26   Install the rear crossmember. Tighten the crossmember bolts and nuts securely.
27   Slowly and carefully slide the transaxle forward until the engine and transaxle are fully engaged, then install the lower transaxle-to-engine mounting nuts and tighten them to the torque listed in this Chapter's Specifications. In the engine compartment, install the upper right transaxle-to-engine bolt and tighten it to the torque listed in this Chapter's Specifications.
28   Line up the marks you made on the torque converter and driveplate, install the torque converter-to-driveplate bolts and tighten them to the torque listed in this Chapter's Specifications. Install the timing plug in the service hole if it was removed.
29   Remove the jack supporting the transaxle.
30   Install the driveaxles (see Chapter 8).
31   Reattach the stabilizer bar bushing clamps (see Chapter 10).
32   Attach the shift cable to the manual lever and the cable bracket to the transaxle

(see illustration 3.4); make sure the cable is correctly adjusted (see Section 4).
33   On 4WD models, install the driveshaft (see Chapter 8).
34   Reattach the cooler hoses and install the dipstick tube.
35   On 4WD models, install the hanger bracket on the right side of the transaxle.
36   On 4WD models, install the rear exhaust pipe heat shield.
37   Install the exhaust system (see Chapter 4).
38   Plug in the electrical connector for the rear oxygen sensor.
39   Remove the jackstands and lower the vehicle.
40   Install the pitching stopper and tighten the bolts and nuts securely.
41   Install the starter motor (see Chapter 5).
42   Plug in the connectors for the front oxygen sensor, transaxle harness, transaxle ground, Park/Neutral and back-up light switch, and vehicle speed sensor.
43   Add the recommended automatic transmission fluid to the transaxle by referring to the appropriate Section in Chapter 1. Install the dipstick.
44   Connect the negative battery cable.
45   Start the engine and check the exhaust system for any leaks or noise.
46   Check the shift cable for smooth operation.

**9.20  Remove the two lower transaxle-to-engine nuts (arrows)**

**9.22  To detach the rear crossmember, remove these nuts and bolts (arrows)**

# Chapter 8
# Clutch and driveline

## Contents

## Specifications

### Clutch

| Clutch cable adjustment | |
|---|---|
| Clutch pedal freeplay | 3/8 to 13/16 inch |
| Release lever freeplay | 1/8 to 3/16 inch |
| Release lever full stroke | 1 inch |

### Torque specifications
**Ft-lbs** (unless otherwise indicated)

| | |
|---|---|
| Center bearing retaining bolts | 35 to 41 |
| Center bearing flange nut | 180 to 220 |
| Clutch pressure plate bolts | 132 to 144 in-lbs |
| Driveshaft-to-pinion flange nuts/bolts | 18 to 28 |
| Driveaxle nut (front and rear) | 123 to 151 |
| Rear differential pinion flange nut | 123 to 144 |

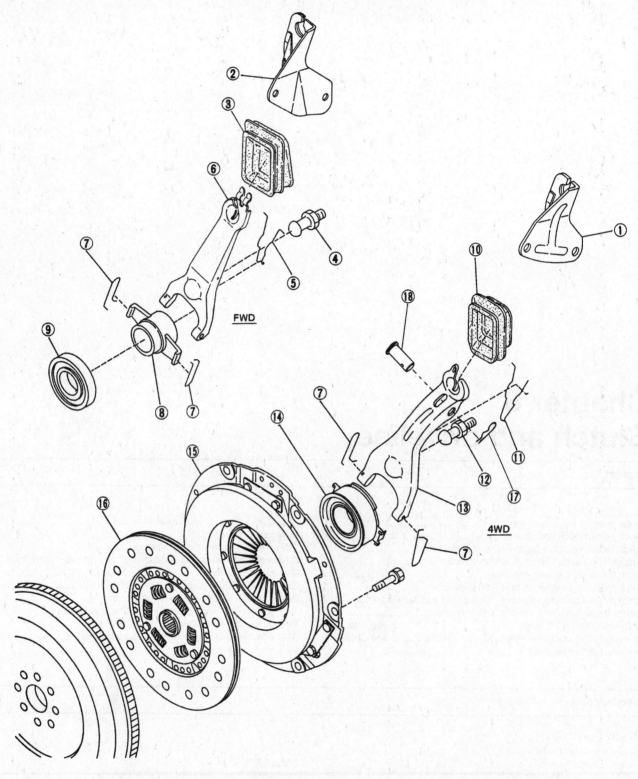

**2.2a  An exploded view of a typical clutch assembly with a cable-operated release system**

| | | | | | | | |
|---|---|---|---|---|---|---|---|
| 1 | Clutch cable bracket | 8 | Release bearing holder | 14 | Clutch release bearing assembly (no |
| 2 | Clutch cable bracket | 9 | Release bearing | | separate bearing holder on this type) |
| 3 | Clutch release lever dust boot | 10 | Release lever dust boot | 15 | Clutch pressure plate |
| 4 | Ballstud (lever fulcrum) | 11 | Retainer spring | 16 | Clutch disc |
| 5 | Retainer spring | 12 | Ballstud (lever fulcrum) | 17 | Cotter pin |
| 6 | Clutch release lever | 13 | Clutch release lever | 18 | Clevis pin |
| 7 | Clip | | | | |

## General information

The Sections in this Chapter deal with the components from the rear of the engine to the rear wheels (except for the transaxle, which is covered in Chapter 7) and, on four-wheel drive (4WD) models, to the front wheels. In this Chapter, the components are grouped into three categories: clutch, drive-shaft and driveaxles. Separate Sections in this Chapter cover checks and repair proce-dures for components in each group.

Since nearly all these procedures involve working under the vehicle, make sure it's safely supported on sturdy jackstands or a hoist where the vehicle can be safely raised and lowered.

## 2   Clutch - description and check

*Refer to illustrations 2.2a and 2.2b*

1   Vehicles with a manual transaxle use a single dry-plate diaphragm spring type clutch. The clutch disc has a splined hub which allows it to slide along the splines of the transaxle input shaft. The clutch and pressure plate are held in contact by spring pressure exerted by the diaphragm in the pressure plate.

2   The clutch release system is cable-operated or hydraulic, depending on the model **(see illustrations)**. The cable type release system consists of the clutch pedal, the clutch cable, a release lever and a release bearing which rides on the transaxle input shaft. On hydraulically actuated models, the system uses a master cylinder, a release cylinder and the hydraulic line between them, instead of a clutch cable; on hydraulic mod-els, the release lever is also different: instead of a ballstud (lever fulcrum), it pivots on a shaft.

3   When pressure is applied to the clutch pedal on a cable-operated system, the clutch cable pulls the outer end of the release lever. When the lever pivots at its fulcrum point on a ballstud, the inner end of the lever pushes against the release bearing, which slides for-ward on the transaxle input shaft against the diaphragm fingers, releasing the pressure plate from the clutch disc. When pressure is applied to the pedal on a hydraulically actu-ated system, the piston inside the clutch master cylinder pushes against the hydraulic fluid, which pushes against the piston inside the release cylinder at the other end of the line. The release cylinder piston moves a pushrod which pushes against the outer end of the release lever. The rest of the hydrauli-cally actuated system works just like a cable-operated system.

4   Terminology can be a problem when discussing the clutch components because common names are in some cases different from those used by the manufacturer. For example, the driven plate is also called the clutch plate or disc, the clutch release bear-ing is sometimes called a throw-out bearing, and so on.

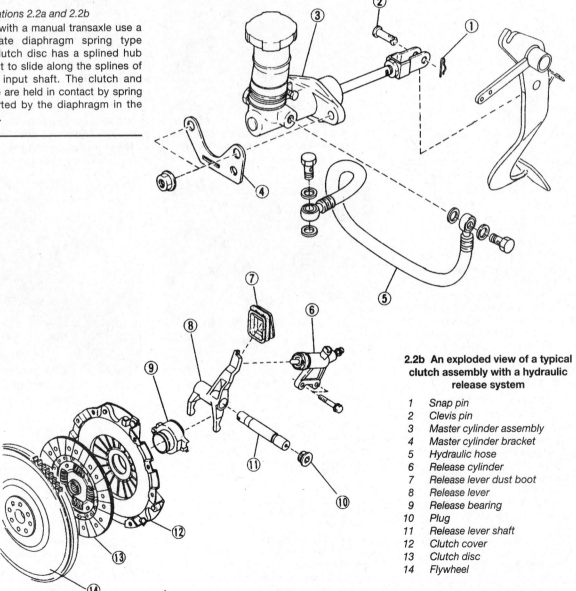

**2.2b   An exploded view of a typical clutch assembly with a hydraulic release system**

1    Snap pin
2    Clevis pin
3    Master cylinder assembly
4    Master cylinder bracket
5    Hydraulic hose
6    Release cylinder
7    Release lever dust boot
8    Release lever
9    Release bearing
10   Plug
11   Release lever shaft
12   Clutch cover
13   Clutch disc
14   Flywheel

5   Unless you're replacing parts with obvious damage, you can use the following preliminary checks to determine the condition of the clutch components:

  a) *On cable-operated models, always check the clutch cable adjustment (see Section 3).*

  b) *On hydraulically operated models, always check the clutch fluid level and make sure that the release system has no leaks.*

  c) *Check clutch "spin-down time": Run the engine at normal idle speed with the transaxle in Neutral (pedal released, clutch engaged). Disengage the clutch (depress the pedal), wait several seconds and shift the transaxle into Reverse. You should not hear any grinding noises. Assuming the transaxle is in good condition, the most likely cause of a grinding noise is a defective pressure plate or clutch disc.*

  d) *Verify that the clutch is releasing completely: With the parking brake applied to prevent the vehicle from moving, run the engine and hold the clutch pedal about 1/2-inch from the floor. Shift the transaxle between 1st gear and Reverse several times. If the shift is rough, the clutch assembly is defective.*

  e) *Visually inspect the pivot bushing at the top of the clutch pedal to make sure there is no binding or excessive play.*

## 3   Clutch cable - check, adjustment and replacement

### Check

*Refer to illustration 3.1*

1   To check the adjustment of the clutch cable, check clutch pedal freeplay. Measure the distance that the pedal travels, from its fully released position (all the way up), to the point at which you feel resistance **(see illustration)**. Compare this measurement to the pedal freeplay listed in this Chapter's Specifications. If the freeplay isn't with the allowable range, adjust the clutch cable.

### Adjustment

*Refer to illustrations 3.2a and 3.2b*

2   Disengage the release lever return spring from the release lever. There are two nuts on the end of the clutch cable at the release lever **(see illustration)**. Back off the locknut (the smaller nut), then turn the adjusting nut (the nut closer to the release lever) to bring release lever freeplay and full stroke **(see illustration)** within the dimensions listed in this Chapter's Specifications.

3   Tighten the locknut securely.

4   Install the release lever return spring.

### Replacement

*Refer to illustrations 3.7, 3.8 and 3.10*

5   Remove the release lever return spring.

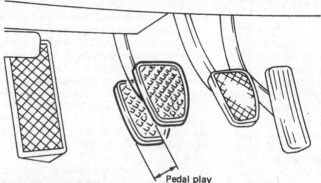

**3.1 To check clutch cable adjustment, measure clutch pedal freeplay, which is the distance the pedal travels from its fully released (up) position to the point at which you first feel resistance**

*Pedal play*

**3.2a There are two nuts on the forward end of the clutch cable; the front (smaller) nut is the locknut and the rear (larger) nut is the adjusting nut**

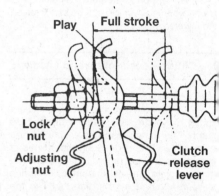

**3.2b To adjust clutch release lever freeplay and stroke, back off the locknut, then turn the adjusting nut to adjust the lever freeplay and full stroke**

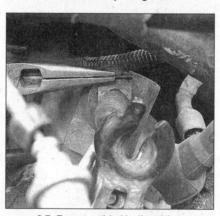

**3.7 Remove this U-clip with a pair of pliers, . . .**

**3.8 . . . then detach the clutch cable from its bracket**

6   Remove both the locknut and the adjusting nut from the end of the clutch cable.

7   Remove the U-clip which attaches the cable to the bracket **(see illustration)**.

8   Detach the cable from the bracket **(see illustration)**.

9   Working inside the vehicle, locate the other end of the clutch cable at the top of the clutch pedal.

10   Remove the cotter pin from the clevis pin which attaches the cable to the clutch pedal **(see illustration)**, then remove the clevis pin and detach the cable from the pedal.

11   Pull the cable through the firewall and into the engine compartment.

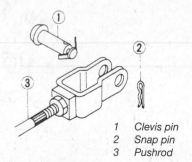

    *1   Clevis pin*
    *2   Snap pin*
    *3   Pushrod*

**3.10 Clevis pin details**

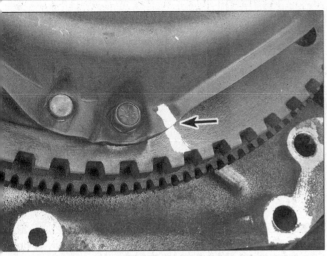

**6.4  If you're planning to re-use the same pressure plate, mark its relationship to the flywheel (arrow)**

**6.5a  Jam a large screwdriver between the flywheel ring gear and the flywheel housing to lock the flywheel while you loosen the clutch pressure plate bolts (arrows)**

12  Install the new cable by inserting the correct end through the firewall and into the passenger compartment. Be sure to route the cable correctly, so that there are no sharp bends or kinks. Make sure the grommet seats in the firewall completely

13  Lightly grease the clevis pin, then attach the cable to the clutch pedal with the clevis pin and secure it with the snap pin (use a new snap pin if the old one is deformed or weak).

14  Lightly grease the cable "pocket" on the end of the release lever, then attach the cable to the release lever with the adjusting nut, adjust the lever freeplay (see Step 2), then tighten the locknut securely.

15  Install the release lever return spring.

## 4  Clutch master cylinder - removal and installation

### Removal

**Caution:** *Do not allow brake fluid to contact any painted surfaces of the vehicle, as damage to the finish may result.*

1  Disconnect the cable from negative terminal of the battery.

2  Disconnect the master cylinder pushrod from the clutch pedal **(see illustration 2.2b)**. Remove the banjo bolt, disconnect the hydraulic line from the master cylinder and drain the fluid into a suitable container. Discard the sealing washers - new ones should be used when reinstalling the cylinder.

3  Remove the master cylinder flange mounting nuts **(see illustration 2.2b)** and withdraw the unit from the engine compartment.

### Installation

4  Installation is the reverse of removal, but be sure to bleed the hydraulic system (see Section 9) and check the pedal height and freeplay as described in Chapter 1.

## 5  Clutch release cylinder - removal and installation

### Removal

1  Disconnect the cable from negative terminal of the battery.

2  Raise the vehicle and support it securely on jackstands.

3  Remove the banjo bolt and disconnect the hydraulic line at the release cylinder **(see illustration 2.2b)**. Discard the sealing washers - new ones should be used upon installation. Have a small can and rags handy, as some fluid will be spilled as the line is removed.

4  Remove the release cylinder mounting bolts **(see illustration 2.2b)**.

5  Remove the release cylinder.

### Installation

6  Install the release cylinder on the clutch housing. Make sure the pushrod is seated in the release lever pocket.

7  Connect the hydraulic line to the release cylinder, using new sealing washers. Tighten the connection.

8  Fill the clutch master cylinder with brake fluid (conforming to DOT 3 specifications).

9  Bleed the system (see Section 9).

10  Lower the vehicle and connect the cable to the negative terminal of the battery.

## 6  Clutch components - removal and installation

**Warning:** *Dust produced by clutch wear and deposited on clutch components may contain asbestos, which is hazardous to your health. DO NOT blow it out with compressed air and DO NOT inhale it. DO NOT use gasoline or petroleum-based solvents to remove the dust. Brake system cleaner should be used to flush the dust into a drain pan. After*

*the clutch components are wiped clean with a rag, dispose of the contaminated rags and cleaner in a covered, marked container.*

### Removal

*Refer to illustrations 6.4, 6.5a and 6.5b*

1  Access to the clutch components is normally accomplished by removing the transaxle, leaving the engine in the vehicle. However, if the engine is being removed for major overhaul, then check the clutch for wear and replace worn components as necessary. The relatively low cost of the clutch components compared to the time and trouble spent gaining access to them warrants their replacement anytime the engine or transaxle is removed, unless they are new or in near-perfect condition. The following procedures are based on the assumption that the engine will stay in place.

2  On cable-actuated release systems, disconnect the clutch cable from the release lever (see Section 3). On hydraulic systems, remove the release cylinder (see Section 5).

3  Remove the transaxle (see Chapter 7A). Support the engine while the transaxle is out. An engine hoist should be used to support it from above. If you use a jack underneath the engine instead, make sure a piece of wood is positioned between the jack and oil pan to spread the load. **Caution:** *The pick-up for the oil pump is very close to the bottom of the oil pan. If the pan is bent or distorted in any way, engine oil starvation could occur.*

4  Carefully inspect the flywheel and pressure plate for indexing marks. The marks are usually an X, an O or a white letter. If they cannot be found, paint a mark so the pressure plate and the flywheel will be in the same alignment during installation **(see illustration)**.

5  Using a screwdriver jammed between the ring gear and the clutch housing **(see illustration)**, loosen the pressure plate-to-flywheel bolts in 1/4-turn increments until they can be removed by hand. Work in a crisscross pattern until all spring pressure is

**6.5b You can use a clutch alignment tool to support the pressure plate so it doesn't fall off when the bolts are removed; you'll also need this tool to center the clutch disc during installation**

**6.7 Inspect the surface of the flywheel for cracks, dark-colored areas (signs of overheating) and other obvious defects; resurfacing will correct minor defects (the surface of this flywheel is in good condition, but resurfacing is always a good idea)**

relieved, then hold the pressure plate securely and completely remove the bolts, followed by the pressure plate and clutch disc. If you don't have someone to hold the clutch pressure plate and disc while you're loosening the bolts, use an alignment tool to support them **(see illustration)**.

### Inspection

*Refer to illustrations 6.7, 6.9, 6.11a and 6.11b*
6    Ordinarily, when a clutch problem occurs, it's caused by clutch disc wear. Nevertheless, it's a good idea to inspect all clutch components at this time. If the clutch components are contaminated with oil, there will be shiny, black glazed spots on the clutch disc lining, which will cause the clutch to slip. Replacing clutch components won't completely solve the problem - be sure to check the crankshaft rear oil seal and the transaxle input shaft seal for leaks. If it looks like a seal is leaking, be sure to install a new one to avoid the same problem with the new clutch.
7    Check the flywheel for cracks, heat checking, grooves and other obvious defects **(see illustration)**. If the imperfections are slight, a machine shop can machine the surface flat and smooth, which is highly recommended regardless of the surface appearance. Refer to Chapter 2, Part A, for the flywheel removal and installation procedure.

8    Inspect the pilot bearing (see Section 8).
9    Check the lining on the clutch disc. There should be at least 1/16-inch of lining above the rivet heads. Check for loose rivets, distortion, cracks, broken springs and other obvious damage **(see illustration)**. As mentioned above, ordinarily the clutch disc is routinely replaced, so if you're in doubt about its condition, replace it.
10    The release bearing should also be replaced along with the clutch disc (see Section 7).
11    Check the machined surface and the diaphragm spring fingers of the pressure plate **(see illustrations)**. If the surface is grooved or otherwise damaged, replace the pressure plate. Also check for obvious damage, distortion, cracks, etc. Light glazing can be removed with sandpaper or emery cloth. If a new pressure plate is required, new and factory-rebuilt units are available.

### Installation

*Refer to illustration 6.15*
12    Before installation, clean the machined surfaces of the flywheel and pressure plate with lacquer thinner, acetone or brake system cleaner. It's vital that these surfaces and the clutch disc lining be free of all grease and oil. Be sure to wash your hands before handling these parts.

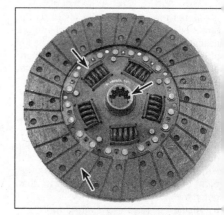

**6.9 Inspect the clutch disc lining, springs, and splines (arrows) for wear**

13    Position the clutch disc and pressure plate against the flywheel with the clutch held in place with an alignment tool **(see illustration 6.5b)**. Make sure the clutch disc is correctly installed (most replacement clutch plates will be marked "flywheel side" or something similar.
14    Tighten the pressure plate-to-flywheel bolts only finger-tight, working around the pressure plate.
15    Center the clutch disc by ensuring the alignment tool extends through the splined

**NORMAL FINGER WEAR**

EXCESSIVE WEAR

**EXCESSIVE FINGER WEAR**

**BROKEN OR BENT FINGERS**

**6.11a Replace the pressure plate if excessive wear is noted**

**6.11b  Examine the pressure plate friction surface for score marks, cracks and evidence of overheating**

**6.15  Tighten the clutch pressure plate bolts in a criss-cross pattern as shown, gradually and evenly tightening them to the torque listed in this Chapter's Specifications**

**7.2a  Disengage the retaining clips from the release bearing . . .**

**7.2b  . . . and slide the release bearing off the input shaft; note which end of the bearing faces toward the clutch pressure plate diaphragm fingers - this is the bearing surface, and the bearing must be installed this way**

hub and into the pilot bearing in the crankshaft. Wiggle the tool up, down or from side-to-side as needed to bottom the tool in the pilot bearing. Working in a criss-cross pattern **(see illustration)**, tighten the pres-

sure plate-to-flywheel bolts a little at a time, to prevent distorting the cover. After all the bolts are snug, tighten them to the torque listed in this Chapter's Specifications. Remove the alignment tool.

16  Lubricate the friction surfaces and contact points of the release lever and release bearing and install them, if removed (see Section 7).
17  Install the transaxle (see Chapter 7A).

**7    Clutch release bearing - removal, inspection and installation**

*Removal*

*Refer to illustrations 7.2a, 7.2b, 7.3a and 7.3b*
1    Remove the transaxle (see Chapter 7A).
2    Remove the release bearing retaining clips (or springs) from the bearing and remove the bearing from the input shaft **(see illustrations)**.
3    If the release lever pivots on a ballstud, pry off the release lever from the ballstud and remove the lever and the rubber sealing boot from the transaxle **(see illustrations)**. If it is necessary to remove the lever of the type that pivots on a cross shaft, remove the plug **(see illustration 2.2b)** and knock out the release lever shaft.

**7.3a  The release lever is secured to the ballstud by a wire retainer spring on the backside of the lever; to disengage the lever from the ballstud, insert a screwdriver behind the lever and carefully but firmly pry it off . . .**

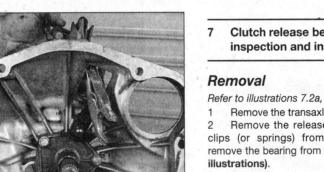

**7.3b  . . . then pull the release lever and the old rubber dust boot out through the hole in the bellhousing**

**7.4  To check the release bearing, turn it while pushing on it at the same time; the bearing should rotate smoothly and quietly; if it's rough or noisy, replace it**

**7.6a  Lubricate the sleeve of the input shaft bearing retainer (arrow) and the end of the ballstud (arrow) with high-temperature grease**

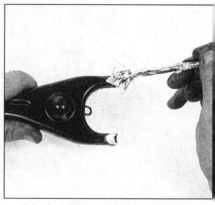

**7.6b  Lubricate the lever-to-bearing contact points of the two release lever fingers . . .**

## Inspection

*Refer to illustration 7.4*

4    Hold the bearing and rotate the outer portion while applying pressure **(see illustration)**. If the bearing doesn't turn smoothly or if it's noisy, replace it. Wipe the bearing with a clean shop rag and inspect it for cracks, wear and other damage. Do NOT immerse the bearing in solvent; it's a sealed unit, so putting it into solvent will ruin it.

## Installation

*Refer to illustrations 7.6a, 7.6b and 7.6c*

5    Replace the release bearing retaining clips, or the release bearing/ballstud retainer spring, if they're deformed or weak

6    Apply a light coat of grease to the sleeve of the input shaft bearing retainer and the input shaft splines **(see illustration)**, and to the contact surfaces of the release lever **(see illustrations)**.

7    Installation is essentially the reverse of removal. Make sure the release lever is properly positioned on the ballstud, then push it firmly until the ballstud pops into place between the two sides of the retainer spring.

8    Install the release bearing and secure it with the retaining clips.

9    Install the transaxle (see Chapter 7A).

## 8    Pilot bearing - inspection and replacement

*Refer to illustrations 8.5 and 8.6*

1    The clutch pilot bearing is a needle roller type bearing which is pressed into the rear of the crankshaft. It's greased at the factory and does not require additional lubrication. Its primary purpose is to support the front of the transaxle input shaft. The pilot bearing should be inspected whenever the clutch components are removed from the engine, and replaced, if you have any doubt about its condition. **Note:** *If the engine has been removed from the vehicle, disregard the following steps which don't apply.*

2    Remove the transaxle (see Chapter 7A).

3    Remove the clutch components (see Section 6).

4    Using a flashlight, inspect the bearing for excessive wear, scoring, dryness, roughness and any other obvious damage. If any of these conditions are noted, replace the bearing.

5    Removal can be accomplished with a special puller available at most auto parts stores **(see illustration)**, or with a slide hammer and an internal puller attachment.

6    To install the new bearing, lightly lubri-

cate the outside surface with grease, then drive it into the recess with a soft-face hammer **(see illustration)**. Some bearings have an O-ring seal, which must face out.

7    Install the clutch components, transaxle and all other components removed previously. Tighten all fasteners to the recommended torque values.

## 9    Clutch hydraulic system - bleeding

1    The hydraulic system should be bled of all air whenever any part of the system has been removed or if the fluid level has been allowed to fall so low that air has been drawn into the master cylinder. The procedure is very similar to bleeding a brake system.

2    Fill the clutch master cylinder with new brake fluid conforming to DOT 3 specifications. **Caution:** *Do not re-use any of the fluid coming from the system during the bleeding operation or use fluid which has been inside an open container for an extended period of time.*

3    Raise the vehicle and place it securely on jackstands to gain access to the release cylinder, which is located on the left side of the clutch housing.

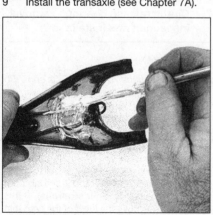

**7.6c  . . . then turn over the lever and lubricate the pocket for the ballstud and the retainer spring**

**8.5  Removing the pilot bearing with a special puller designed for the job**

**8.6  Tap the bearing into place with a bushing driver or a socket slightly smaller than the outside diameter of the bearing**

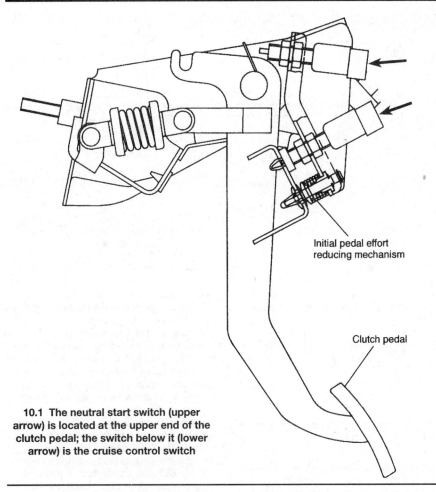

**10.1 The neutral start switch (upper arrow) is located at the upper end of the clutch pedal; the switch below it (lower arrow) is the cruise control switch**

master cylinder reservoir; if the level drops too low, air will be sucked back into the system and the process will have to be started all over again.

7    Install the dust cap and lower the vehicle. Check carefully for proper operation before placing the vehicle in normal service.

## 10    Clutch start switch - check and replacement

### *Check*

*Refer to illustration 10.1*

1    The clutch start switch **(see illustration)** is located under the dash, at the top of the clutch pedal (you'll need a flashlight to locate it). Remove the lower trim panel from the dash to provide more room to work (see Chapter 11).

2    To check the clutch start switch, unplug the electrical connector, hook up an ohmmeter to the switch connector terminals, depress the clutch pedal and verify that there is continuity, then release the pedal and verify that there's no continuity. (If the vehicle is equipped with cruise control, you will see two identical switches. The lower switch is the cruise control switch which turns off the cruise control system when the clutch pedal is depressed.)

3    If the switch doesn't operate as described, replace it.

### *Replacement*

4    Unplug the electrical connector from the switch.

5    Remove the adjustment nut on the underside of the pedal bracket (the nut that's NOT next to the switch) and pull the switch out of the clutch pedal bracket. Note the position of the upper adjustment nut (the one next to the switch) on the old switch, turn the upper nut to the same position on the threaded barrel of the new switch, insert the switch barrel through the pedal bracket, install the lower adjustment nut and adjust the switch with an ohmmeter by verifying that it's open when the pedal is released and closed when the pedal is depressed. When the switch is satisfactorily adjusted, tighten the lower nut securely.

6    Plug in the electrical connector.

7    Install the lower trim panel.

4    Remove the dust cap which fits over the bleeder valve and push a length of plastic hose over the valve. Place the other end of the hose into a clear container partially filled with clean brake fluid. The hose end must be submerged in the fluid.

5    Have an assistant depress the clutch pedal and hold it. Open the bleeder valve on the release cylinder, allowing fluid to flow through the hose. Close the bleeder valve when fluid stops flowing from the hose. Once closed, have your assistant release the pedal.

6    Continue this process until all air is evacuated from the system, indicated by a full, solid stream of fluid being ejected from the bleeder valve each time and no air bubbles in the hose or container. Keep a close watch on the fluid level inside the clutch

## 11    Driveshafts, universal joints and driveaxles - general information

### *Driveshafts and universal joints*

*Refer to illustration 11.1*

1    The driveshaft **(see illustration)** transmits power between the transaxle and the rear differential. Universal joints are located at either end of the driveshaft; a third U-joint is installed right behind the center bearing.

**11.1 An exploded view of a typical driveshaft assembly**

*1    Front driveshaft assembly*
*2    Center bearing assembly*
*3    Rear driveshaft assembly*
*4    Companion flange*
*5    Washer*

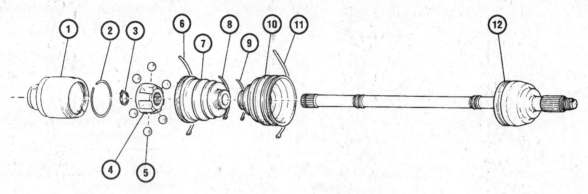

**11.8  An exploded view of a typical driveaxle assembly**

| | | | |
|---|---|---|---|
| 1 | Inner CV joint housing/outer race | 5 | Ball bearings |
| 2 | Wire retainer ring | 6 | Boot clamp |
| 3 | Snap-ring | 7 | Inner CV joint boot |
| 4 | Inner race | 8 | Boot clamp |

| | |
|---|---|
| 9 | Boot clamp |
| 10 | Outer CV joint boot |
| 11 | Boot clamp |
| 12 | Axleshaft/outer CV joint assembly |

2     The driveshaft employs a splined sleeve yoke at the front end, which slips into the extension housing. This arrangement allows the driveshaft to slide back-and-forth within the extension housing during vehicle operation. An oil seal prevents fluid from leaking out of the extension housing and keeps dirt from entering the transaxle. If leakage is evident at the front of the driveshaft, replace the oil seal (see Chapter 7A).

3     The rear end of the driveshaft is bolted to the differential pinion flange.

4     A center bearing supports the connection between the front and rear tubes of the driveshaft. The center bearing is a ball-type bearing mounted in a rubber cushion attached to the vehicle floorpan. The bearing is pre-lubricated and sealed at the factory.

5     The driveshaft assembly requires very little service. The universal joints are lubricated for life, and cannot be rebuilt; if a U-joint on one of these models is worn or damaged, replace the driveshaft.

6     Since the driveshaft is a balanced unit, it's important that no undercoating, mud, etc. be allowed to stay on it. When the vehicle is raised for service it's a good idea to clean the driveshaft and inspect it for any obvious damage. Also, make sure the small weights used to originally balance the driveshaft are in place and securely attached. Whenever the driveshaft is removed it must be reinstalled in the same relative position to preserve the balance.

7     Problems with the driveshaft are usually indicated by a noise or vibration while driving the vehicle. A road test should verify if the problem is the driveshaft or another vehicle component. Refer to the *Troubleshooting* section at the front of this manual. If you suspect trouble, inspect the driveline (see the next Section).

## Driveaxles

*Refer to illustration 11.8*

8     All models are equipped with a pair of front driveaxles; 4WD models also have two rear driveaxles. The front and rear driveaxle assemblies **(see illustration)** are identical in

design. Some driveaxles consist of an inner and outer ball-and-cage type CV joint connected by an axleshaft; others have a "tripot" inner joint and a ball-and-cage outer joint. The inner CV joint can be disassembled; the axleshaft and outer CV joint are a single assembly and cannot be disassembled; they can, however, be cleaned and inspected, and the boots can be replaced.

## 12  Driveline inspection

1     If the vehicle is equipped with air suspension, make sure that the vehicle is in the normal (low) position, the height control switch is turned off, and the battery ground cable is disconnected.

2     Raise the rear of the vehicle and support it securely on jackstands. Block the front wheels to keep the vehicle from rolling off the stands.

3     Crawl under the vehicle and visually inspect the driveshaft. Look for any dents or cracks in the tubing. If any are found, the driveshaft must be replaced.

4     Check for oil leakage at the front and rear of the driveshaft. Leakage where the driveshaft enters the transaxle indicates a defective transaxle/transfer case seal (see Chapter 7A). Leakage where the driveshaft joins the differential indicates a defective pinion seal (see Section 13).

5     While under the vehicle, have an assistant rotate a rear wheel so the driveshaft will rotate. As it does, make sure the universal joints are operating properly without binding, noise or looseness. Listen for any noise from the center bearing (if equipped), indicating it's worn or damaged. Also check the rubber portion of the center bearing for cracking or separation, which will necessitate replacement.

6     The universal joint can also be checked with the driveshaft motionless, by gripping your hands on either side of the joint and attempting to twist the joint. Any movement at all in the joint is a sign of considerable wear. Lifting up on the shaft will also indicate

movement in the universal joints.

7     Check all driveshaft U-joint mounting bolts; make sure they're tight.

8     Finally, check for looseness in the CV joints of the front and rear driveaxles. Also check for grease or oil leakage from around the driveaxles by inspecting the rubber boots and both ends of each axle. Leakage at the wheel end of a driveaxle indicates a torn or damaged rubber boot (see Section 18). (If the tear is serious, the surface of the wheel housing will be splattered with grease.) Oil leakage at the differential end of a driveaxle could also indicate a damaged boot (again, look for signs of oil being thrown onto the surrounding components), or it could indicate a defective side gear oil seal.

## 13  Driveshaft - removal and installation

### Removal

*Refer to illustrations 13.3 and 13.4*

1     If the vehicle is equipped with air suspension, make sure that the vehicle is in the normal (low) position, the height control switch is turned off, and the battery ground cable is disconnected. Raise the vehicle and place it securely on jackstands.

2     Place match marks on the rear U-joint yoke and the differential pinion flange.

3     Remove the bolts and nuts which attach the yoke to the pinion flange **(see illustration)**.

4     Remove the center bearing retaining bolts **(see illustration)**.

5     Pull the sleeve yoke out of the extension housing and remove the driveshaft. Plug the extension housing to prevent transaxle lubricant from leaking out.

6     If you're replacing the center bearing, refer to Section 14.

### Installation

7     Lubricate the sleeve yoke splines, then remove the extension housing plug and carefully insert the sleeve yoke into the extension

**13.3  Remove the four yoke-to-flange nuts and bolts - notice the match marks applied across the U-joint and differential pinion flange**

**13.4  Remove the center bearing retaining bolts (arrows)**

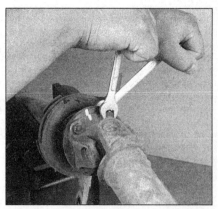

**14.3  Mark the relationship of the center U-joint to the front driveshaft flange, then remove the nuts and bolts that attach the U-joint to the flange**

**14.4  Mark the relationship of the flange to the front driveshaft, then unstake the nut and remove it**

**14.5  Remove the flange with a puller (if you don't have a suitable puller, have it pressed off at an automotive machine shop)**

housing. Make sure you don't damage the extension housing seal or the splines of the transaxle output shaft.

8    Raise the center bearing into place, install the center bearing retaining bolts and tighten them to the torque listed in this Chapter's Specifications.

9    Align the match marks you made on the rear U-joint yoke and the pinion flange, connect the yoke to the flange with the nuts and bolts and tighten them to the torque listed in this Chapter's Specifications.

10   Remove the jackstands and lower the vehicle.

**14   Center bearing - replacement**

*Refer to illustrations 14.3, 14.4, 14.5, 14.6 and 14.7*

1    Remove the driveshaft assembly (see Section 13).

2    Put the driveshaft assembly in a bench vise.

3    Mark the relationship of the center U-joint to the front driveshaft flange, then unbolt the U-joint from the flange **(see illustration)** and remove the rear driveshaft.

4    Mark the relationship of the flange to the front driveshaft, then unstake the nut **(see illustration)** and remove it.

5    Remove the flange with a puller **(see illustration)**, or have it pressed off at an automotive machine shop.

6    To separate the front driveshaft from the center bearing, lightly tap the threaded nose with a brass hammer **(see illustration)**. Remove the flange and the washer.

7    Inspect the center bearing. Make sure it rotates smoothly and quietly **(see illustration)**. If you detect any sign of roughness, noise or excessive play, replace the center bearing.

**14.6  Carefully tap the driveshaft through the center bearing with a brass hammer (be sure to hold the driveshaft with one hand while striking it so that it doesn't fall on the floor when it breaks free)**

**14.7  Make sure the center bearing rotates smoothly and quietly; if it doesn't, replace it**

**15.3 Using an inch-pound torque wrench, measure the turning torque of the pinion flange, jot down this number and save it for reassembly**

**15.4 Holding the flange with a suitable tool (such as this pin spanner braced by an exhaust hanger bracket), remove the retaining nut (if you don't have a pin spanner, try a pair of large water pump pliers or a plumber's wrench)**

8    Install the center bearing on the front driveshaft. If you have trouble getting the center bearing onto the front driveshaft, take the front driveshaft and center bearing to an automotive machine shop and have the center bearing installed.

9    Coat both sides of the large washer and the driveshaft splines with grease, then install the washer and the flange. Make sure the marks you made on the flange and the front driveshaft are aligned. Tighten the flange nut to the torque listed in this Chapter's Specifications, then stake it with a hammer and punch. Again, if the flange is difficult to install, take the front driveshaft and flange to an automotive machine shop and have the flange installed.

10    Make sure the marks you made on the flange and the U-joint are aligned, then attach the rear driveshaft. Tighten the U-joint-to-flange bolts and nuts to the torque listed in this Chapter's Specifications.

11    Install the driveshaft assembly (see Section 13).

## 15    Rear differential pinion seal - replacement

*Refer to illustrations 15.3, 15.4, 15.5, 15.6 and 15.7*

1    If the vehicle is equipped with air suspension, make sure that the vehicle is in the normal (low) position, the height control switch is turned off, and the battery ground cable is disconnected. Raise the vehicle and place it securely on jackstands.

2    Remove the driveshaft (see Section 13).

3    Using an inch-pound torque wrench, measure the turning torque of the pinion flange **(see illustration)**. Jot down this figure and save it for reassembly.

4    Holding the flange with a suitable tool, remove the retaining nut **(see illustration)**.

5    Remove the pinion flange; use a puller if necessary **(see illustration)**.

6    Remove the old seal **(see illustration)**.

7    Install a new seal **(see illustration)**.

8    Installation is the reverse of removal. Gradually tighten the pinion flange retaining nut to the minimum torque listed in this Chapter's Specifications; as you're tightening the nut, use the figure you recorded prior to disassembly to periodically check the pinion flange turning torque. By the time the retaining nut's minimum specified torque is reached, the turning torque of the pinion

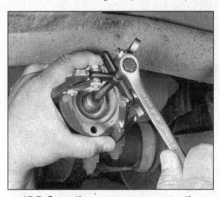

**15.5 Sometimes you can remove the pinion flange by simply pulling it off; if not, use a small puller**

**15.6 Remove the old seal with a seal removal tool (shown) or with a large screwdriver**

**15.7 Install the new seal with a large socket; make sure the seal is square to the bore, then carefully tap it into place until it's fully seated**

flange should be the same as it was before disassembly. When this figure is attained, tighten the nut to increase the turning torque by five inch-pounds.

9    Install the driveshaft (see Section 13).
10   Lower the vehicle.

## 16   Driveaxles - removal and installation

1    If the vehicle is equipped with air suspension, make sure that the vehicle is in the normal (low) position, the height control switch is turned off, and the battery ground cable is disconnected.

### *Front driveaxle*

*Refer to illustrations 16.2a, 16.2b, 16.6a, 16.6b, 16.7 and 16.8*

2    Remove the wheel cover. Unstake, then loosen, the driveaxle nut **(see illustrations)**. **Caution:** Just break the nut loose at this time. If it is loosened very much or removed with the wheel on the ground (supporting the weight of the vehicle) the front hub bearings can be damaged.
3    Loosen the wheel lug nuts, raise the vehicle and place it securely on jackstands.
4    Remove the wheel.

**16.2a  Before you can remove the driveaxle nut, "unstake" it: Using a small punch, restore the inner edge of the nut where it's been peened over to lock the nut onto the driveaxle**

**16.2b  With the vehicle on the ground, have an assistant put the transaxle in gear and apply the brakes while you break the driveaxle nut loose with a breaker bar**

5    Disconnect the control arm from the steering knuckle (see Chapter 10).
6    Remove the driveaxle nut, then pull the driveaxle assembly out of the steering knuckle **(see illustration)**. Make sure you don't damage the lip of the inner steering knuckle seal. If the outer CV joint splines are stuck in the hub, knock the driveaxle loose with a hammer and punch **(see illustration)**. If that doesn't break

the splines loose, remove the brake disc (see Chapter 9) and push the driveaxle from the hub using a two-jaw puller.
7    Locate the spring pin that locks the inner end of the driveaxle assembly to the differential side gear shaft. Knock out the spring pin **(see illustration)**.
8    Disengage the inner end of the driveaxle from the transaxle **(see illustration)**.
9    If you're planning to replace a CV joint

**16.6a  Disengage the driveaxle from the steering knuckle**

**16.6b  If the splines on the stub shaft hang up on the splines in the hub, knock them loose with a hammer and punch**

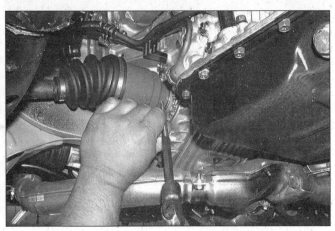

**16.7  To disconnect the front driveaxle from the differential, knock out the spring pin with a hammer and punch**

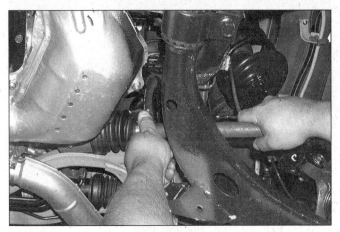

**16.8  Disengage the front driveaxle from the front differential**

**16.16  Detach the rear driveaxle from the rear knuckle**

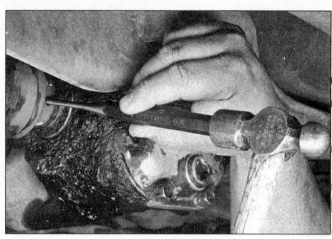

**16.17a  On earlier models, to unlock the rear driveaxle assembly from the differential, knock out this spring pin . . .**

boot or overhaul an inner CV joint, proceed to the next section. This is also a good time to inspect the inner and outer bearings in the knuckle and decide whether to reuse them or install new ones (see Chapter 10).

10    Installation is the reverse of removal. If you damaged the lip of the inner steering knuckle seal, be sure to replace the seal before installing the driveaxle assembly (see Chapter 10). Be sure to use a new spring pin to lock the inner CV joint to the differential stub shaft. Make sure you install the spring pin *from the chamfered side of the hole*. Tighten the driveaxle nut as securely as you can with the vehicle raised, then install the wheel and lug nuts and lower the vehicle to the ground. Tighten the driveaxle nut to the torque listed in this Chapter's Specifications, and the wheel lug nuts to the torque listed in the Chapter 1 Specifications.

### Rear driveaxle (4WD models)

*Refer to illustrations 16.16, 16.17a, 16.17b and 16.18*

11    Unstake, then loosen, the driveaxle nut

(see illustrations 16.2a and 16.2b).

12    Loosen the rear wheel lug nuts, raise the vehicle and place it securely on jackstands. Remove the rear wheel.

13    Remove the ABS sensor lead clamps and the parking brake cable bracket from the trailing arm.

14    Remove the bolts which secure the control arms to the rear knuckle (see Chapter 10).

15    On sedan models, remove the lower crossmember reinforcement, if equipped, from the crossmember.

16    Remove the driveaxle nut, then pull the driveaxle assembly out of the rear knuckle **(see illustration)**. Make sure you don't damage the lip of the inner rear knuckle seal. If the splines on the outer CV joint spindle hang up on the splines in the hub, knock them loose with a hammer and punch **(see illustration 16.6b)**.

17    On earlier models, which use a spring pin to lock the driveaxle to the rear differential, remove the spring pin, then pry the inner CV joint from the differential side gear shaft **(see illustrations)**.

18    On later models, which do not use a spring pin to lock the driveaxle to the rear differential, pry the inner CV joint from the differential **(see illustration)**. Use a bearing retainer bolt as a fulcrum for the lever; do NOT use force directly against the bearing retainer.

19    If you're planning to replace a CV joint boot, proceed to the next section. This is also a good time to inspect the inner and outer bearings in the rear knuckle and decide whether to reuse them or install new ones (see Chapter 10).

20    Installation is the reverse of removal. Be sure to use a new spring pin (if equipped) to lock the inner CV joint to the differential stub shaft. On these models, make sure you install the spring pin *from the chamfered side of the hole*. Tighten the driveaxle nut as securely as you can with the vehicle raised, then install the wheel and lug nuts and lower the vehicle to the ground. Tighten the driveaxle nut to the torque listed in this Chapter's Specifications, and the wheel lug nuts to the torque listed in the Chapter 1 Specifications.

**16.17b  . . . then pry the inner CV joint from the rear differential side gear shaft**

**16.18  On models that do not use a spring pin to secure the driveaxle to the differential, pry the inner CV joint out of the differential; use one of the bearing retainer bolts as a fulcrum for the lever - do NOT use the bearing retainer itself or you may crack it**

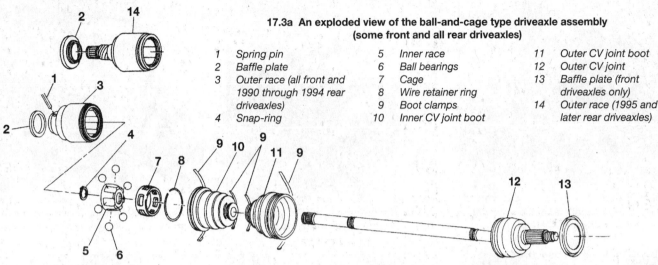

**17.3a  An exploded view of the ball-and-cage type driveaxle assembly (some front and all rear driveaxles)**

| | | | | | |
|---|---|---|---|---|---|
| 1 | Spring pin | 5 | Inner race | 11 | Outer CV joint boot |
| 2 | Baffle plate | 6 | Ball bearings | 12 | Outer CV joint |
| 3 | Outer race (all front and 1990 through 1994 rear driveaxles) | 7 | Cage | 13 | Baffle plate (front driveaxles only) |
| 4 | Snap-ring | 8 | Wire retainer ring | 14 | Outer race (1995 and later rear driveaxles) |
| | | 9 | Boot clamps | | |
| | | 10 | Inner CV joint boot | | |

**17.3b  To remove the boot clamps, pry open the locking tabs**

**17.4  Pry the wire retainer ring from the CV joint housing with a small screwdriver**

**17.5  With the retainer removed, the outer race can be pulled off the bearing assembly**

## 17  Driveaxle boot replacement

**Note:** *If the CV joints exhibit signs of wear indicating need for an overhaul (usually due to torn boots), explore all options before beginning the job. Complete rebuilt driveaxles are available on an exchange basis, which eliminates much time and work. Whichever route you choose to take, check on the cost and availability of parts before disassembling the vehicle.*

1    Remove the driveaxle (see Section 16).
2    Mount the driveaxle in a vise. The jaws of the vise should be lined with wood or rags to prevent damage to the axleshaft.

### Inner CV joint

#### Ball-and-cage type

##### Disassembly

*Refer to illustrations 17.3a, 17.3b, 17.4, 17.5, 17.7, 17.9, 17.10 and 17.11*

3    Pry open the locking tabs on the boot clamps, remove the clamps from the boot and discard them **(see illustrations)**.
4    Slide the boot back on the axleshaft and pry the wire ring ball retainer from the outer

race **(see illustration)**.
5    Pull the outer race off the inner bearing assembly **(see illustration)**.
6    Wipe as much grease as possible off the inner bearing.
7    Remove the snap-ring from the end of

the axleshaft **(see illustration)**.
8    Slide the inner bearing assembly off the axleshaft.
9    Mark the inner race and cage to ensure that they are reassembled with the correct sides facing out **(see illustration)**.

**17.7  Remove the snap-ring from the end of the axleshaft**

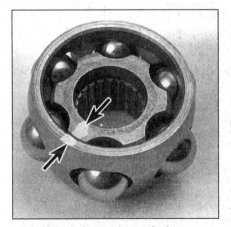

**17.9  Make index marks on the inner race and cage so they'll both be facing the same direction when reassembled**

**17.10  Pry the balls from the cage with a screwdriver (be careful not to nick or scratch them)**

**17.11  Tilt the inner race 90-degrees and rotate it out of the cage**

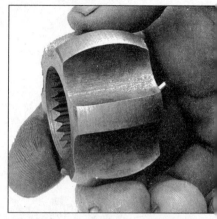

**17.12a  Inspect the inner race lands and grooves for pitting and score marks**

**17.12b  Inspect the cage for cracks, pitting and score marks (shiny spots are normal and don't affect operation)**

**17.14  Press the balls into the cage through the windows**

**17.15  Wrap the splined area of the axle with tape to prevent damage to the boot**

10   Using a screwdriver or piece of wood, pry the balls from the cage (see illustration). Be careful not to scratch the inner race, the balls or the cage.

11   Rotate the inner race 90-degrees, align the inner race lands with the cage windows and rotate the race out of the cage (see illustration).

### Inspection

*Refer to illustrations 17.12a and 17.12b*

12   Clean the components with solvent to remove all traces of grease. Inspect the cage and races for pitting, score marks, cracks and other signs of wear and damage. Shiny, polished spots are normal and will not adversely affect CV joint performance (see illustrations). If the outer CV joint boot is torn or damaged, now is the time to set aside the inner CV joint parts, remove the outer boot, and clean and inspect the outer CV joint.

### Reassembly

*Refer to illustrations 17.14, 17.15, 17.17, 17.20, 17.23, 17.24a, 17.24b, 17.24c and 17.24d*

13   Insert the inner race into the cage. Verify that the matchmarks are on the same side. However, it's not necessary for them to be in direct alignment with each other.

14   Press the balls into the cage windows with your thumbs (see illustration).

15   Wrap the axleshaft splines with tape to avoid damaging the boot (see illustration).

16   Slide the small boot clamp and boot onto the axleshaft, then remove the tape.

17   Install the inner race and cage assembly on the axleshaft with the larger diameter side or "bulge" of the cage facing the axleshaft

end (see illustration).

18   Install the snap-ring (see illustration 17.7).

19   Fill the boot with CV joint grease (normally included with the new boot kit).

20   Pack the inner race and cage assembly with grease, by hand, until grease is worked completely into the assembly (see illustration).

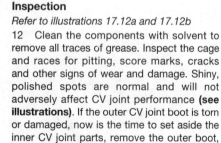

**17.17  Install the inner race and cage assembly with the large diameter end toward the splined end of the axleshaft**

**17.20  Pack grease into the bearing until it's completely full**

**17.23 Equalize the pressure inside the boot by inserting a small screwdriver between the boot and the outer race**

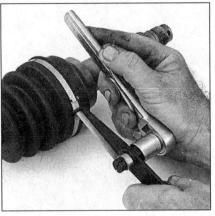

**17.24a Secure the boot clamps with a special banding tool such as the one shown here (available at most auto parts stores): install the clamp, thread it onto the tool, pull the clamp tight . . .**

**17.24b . . . peen over the locking tabs . . .**

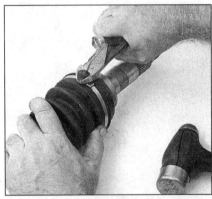

**17.24c . . . and cut off the excess**

21   Slide the outer race down onto the inner race and install the wire ring retainer.

22   Wipe any excess grease from the axle boot groove on the outer race. Seat the small diameter of the boot in the recessed area on the axleshaft and install the clamp. Push the other end of the boot onto the outer CV joint housing and seat it into the recessed area on the housing.

23   Position the CV joint mid-way through its travel, then equalize the pressure in the boot by inserting a dull screwdriver between the boot and the outer race **(see illustration)**. Don't damage the boot with the tool.

24   Install the boot clamps **(see illustrations)**. A special clamp installation tool is needed. The tool is available at most auto parts stores.

25   Install the driveaxle assembly (see Section 16).

### Tri-pot type

#### Disassembly

*Refer to illustrations 17.27a, 17.27b, 17.28 and 17.29*

26   Pry open the locking tabs on the boot clamps **(see illustration 17.3b)**, remove the boot clamps from the boot and discard them **(see illustrations)**.

27   Remove the wire retainer ring **(see illustration 17.4)**, then slide the outer race off the tri-pot bearing assembly **(see illustration)**. Before removing the race, wipe the grease off the tri-pot bearing assembly and scribe or paint alignment marks on the outer race and the tri-pot bearing assembly **(see illustration)** so they can be returned to their original position.

**17.24d Install the rubber protector over the big boot clamp (if equipped) when you're done**

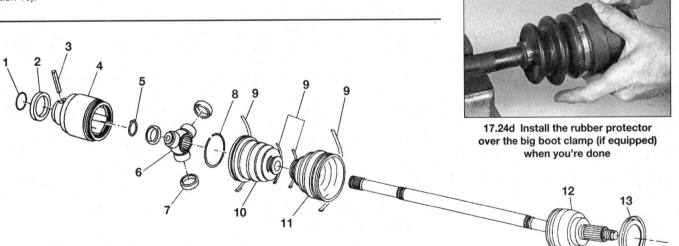

**17.27a An exploded view of the tri-pot type front driveaxle assembly used on some 1994 and later models**

| | | | |
|---|---|---|---|
| 1  O-ring | 5  Snap-ring | 8  Wire retainer ring | 11  Outer CV joint boot |
| 2  Baffle plate | 6  Tri-pot assembly (or | 9  Boot clamps | 12  Outer CV joint |
| 3  Spring pin |    "spider") | 10  Inner CV joint boot | 13  Baffle plate |
| 4  Outer race | 7  Bearings | | |

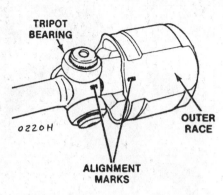

**17.27b  Scribe or paint alignment marks on the tri-pot assembly and the outer race, then slide the outer race off**

**17.28  Remove the snap-ring from the end of the axleshaft, then mark the relationship of the tri-pot bearing assembly to the axleshaft**

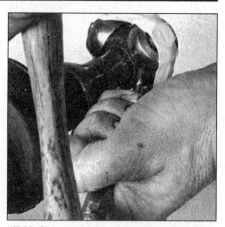

**17.29  Secure the bearing rollers with tape and drive the tri-pot off the shaft with a hammer and brass drift**

**17.35  Install the tri-pot assembly on the axleshaft, making sure the punch marks are lined up, then install the snap-ring**

**17.36  Use plenty of CV joint grease to hold the needle bearings in place when you install the roller assemblies on the tri-pot, and make sure you put each roller in its original position**

**17.37  Pack the outer race with grease and slide it over the tri-pot assembly - make sure the match marks on the outer race and tri-pot line up**

28    Remove the snap-ring from the end of the axleshaft, then mark the relationship of the tri-pot bearing assembly to the axleshaft **(see illustration)**.

29    Secure the bearing rollers with tape, then remove the tri-pot bearing assembly from the axleshaft with a brass drift and a hammer **(see illustration)**. Remove the tape, but don't let the rollers fall off and get mixed up.

30    Remove the old boot and discard it.

### Inspection

31    Clean the old grease from the outer race and the tri-pot bearing assembly. Carefully disassemble each section of the tri-pot assembly, one at a time so as not to mix up the parts, and clean the needle bearings with solvent.

32    Inspect the rollers, tri-pot, bearings and outer race for scoring, pitting or other signs of abnormal wear, which will warrant the replacement of the inner CV joint.

### Reassembly

*Refer to illustrations 17.35, 17.36 and 17.37*

33    Wrap the splines of the axleshaft with tape to avoid damaging the new boot, then slide the boot onto the axleshaft **(see illustration 17.15)**. Remove the tape.

34    Align the match marks you made before disassembly and tap the tri-pot assembly onto the axleshaft with a hammer and brass drift.

35    Install the outer snap-ring **(see illustration)**.

36    Apply a coat of CV joint grease to the inner bearing surfaces to hold the needle bearings in place when reassembling the tri-pot assembly **(see illustration)**. Make sure each roller is installed on the same post as before.

37    Pack the outer race with half of the grease furnished with the new boot and place the remainder in the boot. Install the outer race **(see illustration)**. Make sure the marks you made on the tri-pot assembly and the outer race are aligned.

38    Seat the inner ridges in the ends of the boot in their respective grooves in the outer race and in the axleshaft.

39    Position the CV joint mid-way through its travel, then equalize the pressure in the boot by inserting a dull screwdriver between the boot and the outer race **(see illustration 17.23)**. Don't damage the boot with the tool.

40    Install and tighten the new boot clamps

**(see illustrations 17.24a through 17.24d)**.

41    Install the driveaxle assembly (see Section 16).

## Outer CV joint and boot

*Refer to illustration 17.44*

**Note:** *The outer CV joint is a non-serviceable item and is permanently retained to the driveaxle. If any damage or excessive wear occurs to the axle or the outer CV joint, the entire driveaxle assembly must be replaced (excluding the inner CV joint). Service to the outer CV joints is limited to boot replacement and grease repacking only.*

42    Remove inner CV joint and boot (see Steps 4 through 11).

43    Cut the boot clamps from both inner and outer boots and discard them **(see illustrations 17.3a and 17.3b)**.

44    Remove the outer CV joint boot. Wash the outer CV joint assembly in solvent and inspect it **(see illustration)** as described in Step 12. If any outer CV joint components are excessively worn, replace the axleshaft and outer CV joint assembly.

45    Install the new, outer boot and clamp

**17.44 After the old grease has been rinsed away and the cleaning solvent has been blown out with compressed air, rotate the outer joint housing through its full range of motion and inspect the bearing surfaces for wear or damage - if any of the balls, the race or cage look damaged, replace the driveaxle and outer joint**

onto the axleshaft **(see illustration 17.15)**.

46  Repack the outer CV joint with CV joint grease and spread grease inside the new boot as well.

47  Position the outer boot on the CV joint and install new boot clamps **(see illustrations 17.24a through 17.24d)**. Make sure the boot is not twisted or kinked.

48  Reassemble the inner CV joint and boot (see Steps 13 through 24 or Steps 33 through 40).

49  Install the driveaxle (see Section 16).

## 18  Rear differential side gear seals - replacement

### *All models*

*Refer to illustration 18.1*

1  The rear differential side gear seals can become worn and leak gear lubricant onto

**18.1 If your rear differential looks like this, it's time to change the side gear seals!**

the differential housing and inner CV joint **(see illustration)**. If your differential is covered with gear lube, replace the seals.

2  If the vehicle is equipped with air suspension, make sure that the vehicle is in the normal (low) position, the height control switch is turned off, and the battery negative cable is disconnected. Loosen the rear wheel lug nuts, block the front wheels, raise the rear of the vehicle and support it securely on jackstands. Remove the rear wheel(s).

3  Drain the gear lubricant from the differential (see Chapter 1).

4  Remove the rear driveaxle(s) (see Section 16).

### *1990 through 1994 models*

*Refer to illustrations 18.5, 18.6, 18.7, 18.8 and 18.10*

**Note:** *The side gear oil seals can be replaced with the differential in the vehicle, even though this procedure shows it being done with the differential removed.*

5  Remove the side gear bearing retainer bolts **(see illustration)**, then remove the side gear bearing retainer and bearing spacer (washer). Note the position of the notch in the retainer; the retainer must be installed with

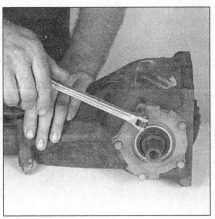

**18.5 Remove the bearing retainer bolts and the retainer; don't lose the big washer on the stub shaft - it's a critical spacer that must be installed before installing the driveaxle (1990 through 1994 models)**

the notch in the same position. **Caution:** *When you remove the retainer from the differential, be careful not to move any of the internal parts, or you might change the bearing preload.*

6  With the retainer removed, remove the retainer O-ring **(see illustration)**. Also remove the metal shims.

7  To remove the oil seal from the retainer, place the retainer on two blocks of wood as shown, then, using a socket with the same outside diameter as the outside diameter of the seal, drive the seal out of the retainer **(see illustration)**.

8  To install a new seal, use the same socket and one block of wood and carefully drive the new seal into position **(see illustration)**. Make sure that the seal is installed *flush* with the surface of the retainer.

9  Install the metal shims. If using new shims, they must be the same thicknesses as the ones that were removed. Install a new O-ring on the retainer.

10  Install the bearing retainer onto the differential, making sure that the notch is in the

**18.6 Remove and discard the retainer O-ring; a new O-ring must be installed before installing the retainer (1990 through 1994 models)**

**18.7 Use a socket to drive the old oil seal out of the retainer (1990 through 1994 models)**

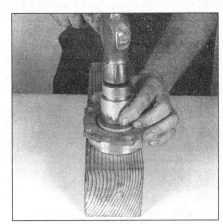

**18.8 Carefully install the new seal flush with the retainer (1990 through 1994 models)**

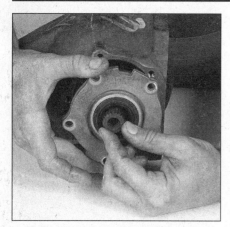

**18.10 Install the side bearing retainer with the notch in the upper position (1990 through 1994 models)**

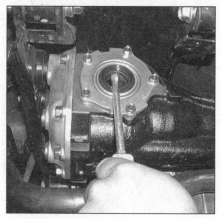

**18.12 To remove an old rear differential seal on 1995 and later models, simply pry it out of the bearing retainer with a seal removal tool or a big screwdriver**

**18.13 To install a new rear differential seal on 1995 and later models, tap it into place with a seal installer tool or with a big socket**

same place as when it was removed **(see illustration)**.

11    Install the bearing retainer bolts and tighten them to the torque listed in this Chapter's Specifications. Install the side bearing spacer washer.

### 1995 and later models

*Refer to illustrations 18.12 and 18.13*
**Note:** *The side gear seals on these models can be replaced without removing the bearing retainer, but differential lubricant could also be leaking out from between the bearing retainer and the differential housing. If you suspect this might be the case, follow the procedure described for 1990 through 1994 models to replace the seal **and** the O-ring.*

12    Pry out the old seal with a seal removal tool or a screwdriver **(see illustration)**.
13    Install the new seal with a seal installer or with a large socket **(see illustration)**.

### All models

14    Install the rear driveaxle(s) (see Section 16).
15    Fill the rear differential with the type and quantity of lubricant specified in Chapter 1.
16    Install the wheel and lug nuts, then lower the vehicle. Tighten the lug nuts to the torque listed in the Chapter 1 Specifications.

17    Drive the vehicle, then inspect for leaks around the seal and retainer.

### 19    Rear differential - removal and installation

*Refer to illustrations 19.6 and 19.7*

## Removal

1    If the vehicle is equipped with air suspension, make sure that the vehicle is in the normal (low) position, the height control switch is turned off, and the battery ground cable is disconnected. Loosen the rear wheel lug nuts, block the front wheels and raise the rear of the vehicle. Support it securely on jackstands. Remove the rear wheels.
2    Drain the lubricant from the differential (see Chapter 1).
3    Disconnect the driveshaft from the rear differential (see Section 13).
4    Disconnect the driveaxles from the rear differential (see Section 16).
5    Support the rear of the differential with a floor jack.
6    Remove the mounting nuts that attach the differential to the rear crossmember **(see**

illustration)**.
7    Remove the four front mounting nuts **(see illustration)**.
8    Carefully lower the differential and remove it from under the vehicle.
9    With the differential removed from the vehicle, now would be a good time to check or replace the rubber mounts for the differential mounting brackets and/or the rear crossmember.

## Installation

10    Place the differential on the jack head and position it directly underneath the mounting bracket and crossmember.
11    Raise the differential into position and install the rear mounting nuts loosely. Then install the front mounting nuts. Tighten all mounting fasteners securely.
12    Install the driveaxles (see Section 16) and the driveshaft (see Section 14).
13    If it was drained, fill the differential with the type and amount of lubricant specified in Chapter 1.
14    Install the wheels, remove the jack and lower the vehicle to the ground. Tighten the wheel lug nuts to the torque listed in the Chapter 1 Specifications.

**19.6 To detach the differential from the rear crossmember, remove these two nuts (arrows)**

**19.7 To detach the front end of the differential, remove these four nuts (arrows)**

# Chapter 9   Brakes

## Contents

## Specifications

### General

| | |
|---|---|
| Brake fluid type | See Chapter 1 |
| Brake light switch plunger stroke | 1/16 to 5/64 inch |
| Brake pedal adjustments | |
| Pedal freeplay | 3/64 to 1/8 inch |
| Pedal height | |
| 1990 through 1994 | 6-7/32 inches |
| 1995 on | 5-53/64 inches |
| Power brake booster pushrod length (1995 on) | 5-23/32 inches |

### Disc brakes (front and rear)

| | |
|---|---|
| Minimum brake pad thickness | See Chapter 1 |
| Disc minimum thickness | Refer to the dimension marked on the disc |
| Disc runout limit | |
| 1990 through 1994 | 0.0039 inch |
| 1995 on | 0.0030 inch |

### Rear drum brake

| | |
|---|---|
| Minimum brake shoe lining thickness | See Chapter 1 |
| Brake drum maximum diameter | Refer to the dimension marked on the drum |

### Torque specifications

| | Ft-lbs (unless otherwise indicated) |
|---|---|
| Brake hose-to-caliper banjo bolt | 132 to 180 in-lbs |
| Caliper support bracket bolts | |
| Front support bracket | 51 to 65 |
| Rear support bracket | 16 to 23 |
| Front caliper lock pin | 25 to 33 |
| Master cylinder mounting nut | 96 to 156 in-lbs |
| Proportioning valve mounting bolts | 15 to 21 |
| Rear caliper lock pin | 144 to 204 in-lbs |
| Wheel cylinder mounting nuts | 72 to 96 in-lbs |

**2.4 Wash the brake assembly with brake system cleaner; do NOT use compressed air to blow off the brake dust**

**2.5a Depress the piston(s) into the caliper with a C-clamp to make room for the new brake pads**

## 1    General information

The vehicles covered by this manual are equipped with hydraulically operated front and rear brake systems. The front brakes are disc-type **(see illustration)**. The rear brakes are either drum or disc type.

These models are equipped with a dual-circuit hydraulic system. One circuit serves the right front and the left rear brakes; the other circuit serves the left front and the right rear brakes. Thus, if one circuit should fail, the other circuit will still enable the vehicle to stop.

The brake hydraulic system also employs a proportioning valve which limits pressure to the rear brakes under heavy braking to prevent rear wheel lock-up.

All models are equipped with a power brake booster which uses engine vacuum to amplify braking force.

The parking brake system consists of a parking brake lever and cables used to apply either the rear brake shoes (rear drum brake models) or special parking brake shoes (rear disc brake models).

Later models with a manual transaxle feature a "hill-holder" system. This device, which is connected to the clutch release lever, is activated when the clutch pedal is depressed. The hill-holder activates the brakes on a steep incline so the clutch does not wear out as rapidly and also makes it easier to start the vehicle in motion when on a hill. The hill-holder is deactivated when the clutch pedal is released.

There are some notes and cautions involving the brake system on this vehicle:

a) *Use only DOT 3 brake fluid in this system.*
b) *The brake pads and linings may contain asbestos fibers which are hazardous to your health if inhaled. Whenever you work on the brake system components, carefully clean all parts with brake system cleaner. Do not allow the fine asbestos dust to become airborne.*

c) *Safety should be paramount whenever any servicing of the brake components is performed. Do not use parts or fasteners which are not in perfect condition, and be sure that all clearances and torque specifications are adhered to. If you are at all unsure about a certain procedure, seek professional advice. Upon completion of any brake system work, test the brakes carefully in a controlled area before putting the vehicle into normal service. If a problem is suspected in the brake system, do not drive the vehicle until the fault is corrected.*
d) *Tires, load and front end alignment are factors which also affect braking performance.*

## 2    Disc brake pads - replacement

*Refer to illustrations 2.4 and 2.5a through 2.5s*

**Warning:** *Disc brake pads must be replaced on both wheels at the same time - never replace the pads on only one wheel. Also, brake system dust may contain asbestos, which is hazardous to your health. DO NOT blow it out with compressed air and DO NOT inhale it. An approved filtering mask should be worn when working on the brakes. DO NOT use gasoline or petroleum-based solvents to remove the dust. Use brake system cleaner only!*

1    If the vehicle is equipped with air suspension, make sure that the vehicle is in the normal (low) position, the height control switch is turned off, and the battery ground cable is disconnected.

2    Block the wheels opposite the end to be worked on, loosen the wheel lugs nuts, raise the vehicle and place it securely on jackstands. Remove the wheels. Release the parking brake lever if you're working on the rear brakes.

3    Remove about two-thirds of the fluid from the master cylinder reservoir and discard it; when the pistons are depressed to

allow the caliper to fit over the disc with the new pads installed, fluid will be forced back into the reservoir. Position a drain pan under the brake assembly.

4    Before beginning, wash down the entire brake assembly with brake system cleaner **(see illustration)**.

5    To replace the front brake pads, follow the accompanying photos, beginning with **illustration 2.5a**. Be sure to stay in order and read the caption under each illustration. Work on one brake assembly at a time so that you'll have something to refer to if you get in trouble. To replace the rear brake pads, follow the same photos (the rear brake pad and caliper are slightly smaller than the front setup but are otherwise virtually identical; refer to **illustration 2.5s** if necessary.

6    While the pads are removed, inspect the caliper for brake fluid leaks and ruptures in the piston boot. Replace the caliper if necessary (see Section 3). Also inspect the brake disc carefully (see Section 4). If machining is necessary, follow the information in that Section to remove the disc. If you're replacing the rear pads, this would be a good time to remove the caliper and disc and inspect the parking brake shoes (see Section 13).

7    Before installing the caliper guide and lock pins, make sure you clean them and inspect them for corrosion, scoring and other damage. If they're damaged or worn, replace them. Be sure to tighten the caliper lock pins to the torque listed in this Chapter's Specifications.

8    Install the brake pads on the opposite wheel, then install the wheels and lower the vehicle. Tighten the wheel lug nuts to the torque listed in the Chapter 1 Specifications.

9    Add brake fluid to the reservoir until it's full (see Chapter 1). Pump the brakes several times to seat the pads against the discs, then check the fluid level again.

10    Check the operation of the brakes before driving the vehicle in traffic. Try to avoid heavy brake applications until the brakes have been applied lightly several times to seat the pads.

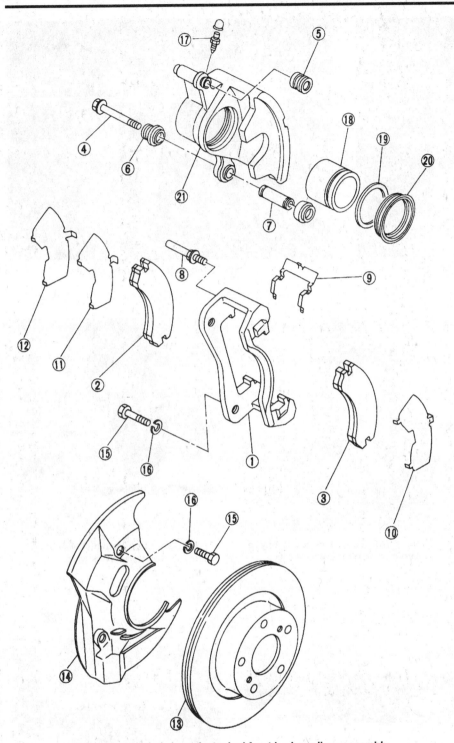

**2.5c** Remove the caliper lock pin (the lower pin), swing the caliper up for access to the brake pads (it's not necessary to disconnect the brake hose from the caliper)

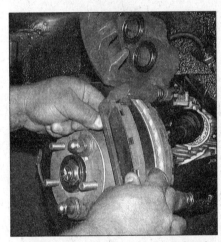

**2.5d** Remove the outer brake pad and shims, then remove the shim(s) from the pad (if a shim is damaged, replace it)

**2.5e** Remove the inner brake pad and shims, then remove the shims from the pad

**2.5b  An exploded view of a typical front brake caliper assembly**

| | |
|---|---|
| 1 | Caliper support bracket |
| 2 | Inner brake pad |
| 3 | Outer brake pad |
| 4 | Caliper lock pin |
| 5 | Guide pin dust boot |
| 6 | Lock pin dust boot |
| 7 | Lock pin sleeve (bushing) |
| 8 | Caliper guide pin |
| 9 | Anti-rattle clip (upper clip shown, lower clip identical) |
| 10 | Shim |
| 11 | Shim |
| 12 | Shim |
| 13 | Front brake disc |
| 14 | Brake disc splash shield |
| 15 | Bolt |
| 16 | Washer |
| 17 | Bleeder screw |
| 18 | Piston |
| 19 | Piston seal |
| 20 | Piston dust boot |
| 21 | Caliper body |

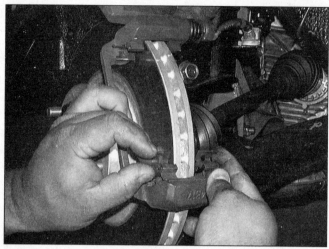

2.5f  Remove the lower anti-rattle clip, clean and inspect it, then set it aside for re-use; if it is damaged, replace it

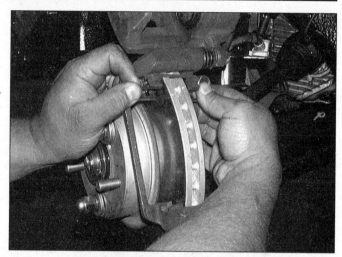

2.5g  Remove the upper anti-rattle clip also

2.5h  If the caliper doesn't slide well on the guide and lock pins, remove the caliper from the caliper support, then clean and inspect both pins; if either pin is damaged or worn, replace it (caliper support bracket removed for clarity)

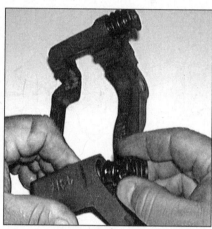

2.5i  Inspect the pin dust boots; if they're torn or cracked, replace them

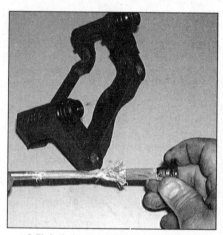

2.5j  Lubricate the pin(s) with high-temperature grease

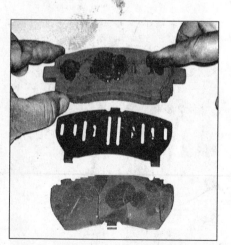

2.5k  The brake pads may have either one or two shims; apply anti-squeal compound to the backing plates of the new pads . . .

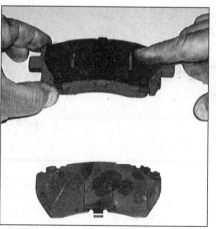

2.5l  . . . install the inner shim on the pad . . .

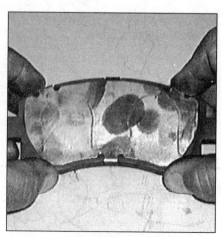

2.5m  . . . followed by the outer shim (if applicable)

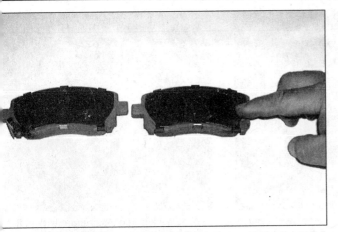

2.5n  Assemble the other pad and shim(s), then apply anti-squeal compound to the outer shims of both pads

2.5o  Install the lower anti-rattle clip on the caliper support bracket . . .

2.5p  . . . and the upper anti-rattle clip

2.5q  Install the inner and outer brake pads and shims; make sure the pads are correctly seated in the caliper support

2.5r  Slide the caliper back onto the guide pin, if removed, then pivot it down over the new pads, install the caliper lock pin and tighten it to the torque listed in this Chapter's Specifications

2.5s  An exploded view of a typical rear brake caliper assembly

1   Shims
2   Inner brake pad
3   Caliper support bracket
4   Outer brake pad
5   Caliper guide pin
6   Caliper lock pin
7   Lock pin boot
8   Lock pin sleeve (bushing)
9   Caliper body
10  Piston
11  Piston dust boot
12  Bleeder screw
13  Pad anti-rattle clip

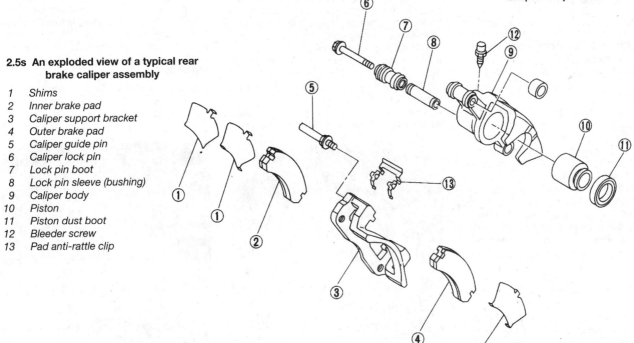

### 3   Brake caliper - removal and installation

#### *Removal*

*Refer to illustration 3.2*

1   If the vehicle is equipped with air suspension, make sure that the vehicle is in the normal (low) position, the height control switch is turned off, and the battery negative cable is disconnected. Block the wheels opposite the end being worked on. Release the parking brake lever if you're working on the rear brakes. Raise the vehicle and place it securely on jackstands. Initially follow the instructions in the previous Section and remove the disc brake pads.

2   Place a container under the caliper and have some rags handy to catch any spilled brake fluid. Remove the brake hose-to-caliper banjo bolt **(see illustration)**. Plug the hose to prevent contaminants from entering the brake hydraulic system and to prevent fluid from leaking out the hose.

3   Unbolt and remove the caliper from the caliper support bracket (see Section 2).

#### *Installation*

4   Install the brake pads, if removed (see Section 2).

5   Before installing the caliper assembly on the caliper support, apply high-temperature grease to the caliper lock pin and guide pin.

6   Install the caliper assembly and reconnect the brake line to the caliper. Use new sealing washers and tighten the banjo bolt to the torque listed in this Chapter's Specifications.

7   Bleed the brake system (see Section 10).

### 4   Brake disc - inspection, removal and installation

#### *Inspection*

*Refer to illustrations 4.4a, 4.4b, 4.5a and 4.5b*

1   If the vehicle is equipped with air suspension, make sure that the vehicle is in the normal (low) position, the height control switch is turned off, and the battery negative cable is disconnected. Loosen the wheel lug nuts, raise the vehicle and support it securely on jackstands. Remove the wheel.

2   Unbolt the brake caliper **(see illustration 2.5c)**. It's not necessary to disconnect the brake hose. After removing the caliper lock pin, suspend the caliper out of the way with a piece of wire. Don't let the caliper hang by the hose and don't stretch or twist the hose.

3   Visually check the disc surface for score marks and other damage. Light scratches and shallow grooves are normal after use and may not always be detrimental to brake operation, but deep score marks - over 0.015-inch (0.38 mm) - require disc removal and refinishing by an automotive machine shop.

**3.2 If you're replacing the caliper, remove the banjo bolt that attaches the brake hose to the caliper; discard the old sealing washers and install new ones when you reattach the brake hose to the caliper**

Be sure to check both sides of the disc. If pulsating has been noticed during application of the brakes, suspect excessive disc runout.

4   To check disc runout, place a dial indicator at a point about 1/2-inch from the outer edge of the disc **(see illustration)**. Set the indicator to zero and turn the disc. The indicator reading should not exceed the specified allowable runout limit. If it does, the disc should be refinished by an automotive machine shop. Measure runout on both the outside and inside faces of the disc. **Note:** *Professionals recommend resurfacing of brake discs regardless of the dial indicator reading (to produce a smooth, flat surface, that will eliminate brake pedal pulsations and other undesirable symptoms related to questionable discs). At the very least, if you elect not to have the discs resurfaced, deglaze the brake pad surface with sandpaper or emery cloth (use a swirling motion to ensure a non-directional finish)* **(see illustration)**.

5   The disc must not be machined to a thickness less than the specified minimum refinish thickness. The minimum wear thickness is cast into the inside of the disc **(see illustration)**. Disc thickness can be checked with a micrometer **(see illustration)**. Also

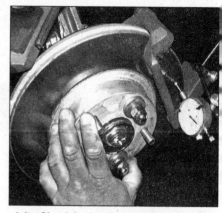

**4.4a   Check brake disc runout with a dial indicator; check both sides of the disc**

**4.4b   Using a swirling motion, remove the glaze from the disc with sandpaper or emery cloth**

measure the thickness at several different points around the disc to check for variation in thickness (parallelism) and compare your findings with the value listed in this Chapter's Specifications. If the disc has worn down below the minimum thickness, replace it.

#### *Removal*

*Refer to illustrations 4.6a and 4.6b*

6   Remove the caliper support bracket bolts **(see illustrations)** and remove the support bracket.

**4.5a   The minimum thickness of the disc is cast into the hub area**

**4.5b   Measure the thickness of the disc with a micrometer and compare it to the specified minimum thickness**

**4.6a  To remove the front caliper support bracket, remove these bolts (arrows)**

**4.6b  To remove the rear caliper support bracket, remove these bolts (arrows)**

7   Slide the disc off the hub.
8   If you're removing a rear disc, inspect the parking brake shoes (see Section 13).

## Installation

8   Thoroughly clean all parts. Install the disc.
9   Install the caliper support bracket and tighten the bracket bolts to the torque listed in this Chapter's Specifications.
10   Install the brake pads and caliper (see Sections 2 and 3) and tighten the caliper pin to the torque listed in this Chapter's Specifications.
11   Install the wheels, then lower the vehicle to the ground. Depress the brake pedal a few times to bring the brake pads into contact with the disc. Bleeding of the system will not be necessary unless the brake hose was disconnected from the caliper. Check the operation of the brakes carefully before placing the vehicle into normal service.

## 5   Drum brake shoes - replacement

*Refer to illustrations 5.3a, 5.3b and 5.13*
**Warning:** *Brake shoes must be replaced on both wheels at the same time - never replace the shoes on only one wheel. Also, brake system dust may contain asbestos, which is hazardous to your health. DO NOT blow it out*

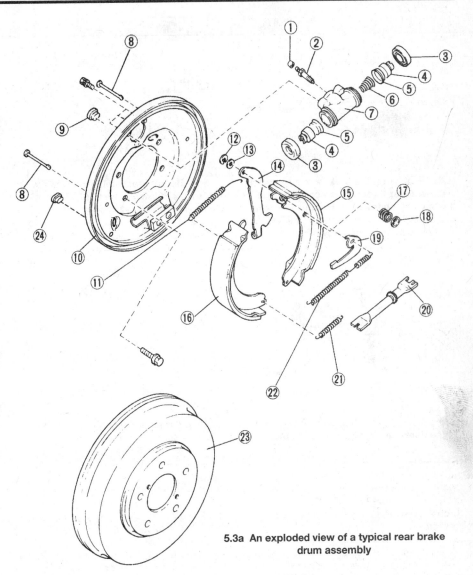

**5.3a  An exploded view of a typical rear brake drum assembly**

| | | | |
|---|---|---|---|
| 1 | Bleeder cap | 13 | Washer |
| 2 | Bleeder screw | 14 | Parking brake lever |
| 3 | Dust boot | 15 | Trailing brake shoe |
| 4 | Piston | 16 | Leading brake shoe |
| 5 | Cup | 17 | Hold-down spring |
| 6 | Spring | 18 | Cup |
| 7 | Wheel cylinder body | 19 | Adjusting lever |
| 8 | Hold-down pin | 20 | Adjuster |
| 9 | Adjuster access plug | 21 | Lower brake shoe return spring |
| 10 | Backing plate | 22 | Adjuster spring |
| 11 | Upper brake shoe return spring | 23 | Brake drum |
| 12 | Retaining clip | 24 | Plug |

*with compressed air and DO NOT inhale it. An approved filtering mask should be worn when working on the brakes. DO NOT use gasoline or petroleum-based solvent to remove the dust. Use brake system cleaner only.*
1   If the vehicle is equipped with air suspension, make sure that the vehicle is in the normal (low) position, the height control switch is turned off, and the battery negative cable is disconnected.
2   Loosen the wheel lug nuts, raise the rear of the vehicle and support it securely on jack-

stands. Block the front wheels to keep the vehicle from rolling off the stands. Remove the rear wheels. Release the parking brake.
3   Pull off the brake drums **(see illustration)**. The brake drums may be difficult or impossible to remove if the shoes have worn the drums excessively. If you can't pull off the drums, remove the access hole plug for the adjuster from the backing plate and, using a brake adjuster tool and a narrow screwdriver (or two screwdrivers), push the adjuster lever off the star wheel and turn the star wheel to retract the shoes **(see illustration)**.

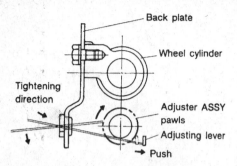

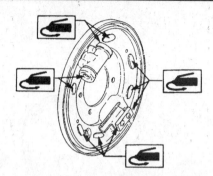

**5.3b  To back off the brake shoes, insert a screwdriver through the access hole in the backing plate, push the adjusting lever off the adjuster wheel and turn the wheel with another screwdriver**

**5.13  Before reassembling the brake assembly, lubricate the raised pads, the slots in the wheel cylinder pistons and the ends of the lower shoe retaining plate (arrows) with high-temperature grease**

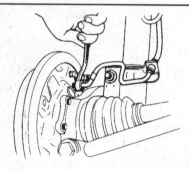

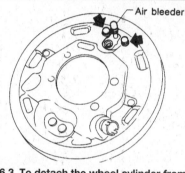

**6.2  Disconnect the brake line fitting with a flare-nut wrench (to protect the corners of the nut)**

**6.3  To detach the wheel cylinder from the backing plate, remove these two retaining bolts**

4    Wash the brake assembly with brake system cleaner before beginning work. Do NOT use compressed air to blow off the brake assembly, which may contain asbestos, a known carcinogen.

5    Clean the brake drums and check them for score marks, deep grooves, hard spots (which will appear as small discolored areas) and cracks. If the drums are worn, scored or out-of-round, they can be resurfaced by an automotive machine shop. **Note:** *Professionals recommend resurfacing the drums whenever a brake job is done. Resurfacing will eliminate the possibility of out-of-round drums. If the drums are worn so much they can't be resurfaced without exceeding the maximum allowable diameter (stamped into the drum), new ones will be required. At the very least, if you elect not to have the drums resurfaced, remove the glazing from the surface with sandpaper or emery cloth using a swirling motion.*

6    Work on only one drum brake assembly at a time. Do not begin disassembling the other brake until you have reassembled the first one. That way, you can use the other one as a reference, if necessary.

7    Using a hold-down spring tool, push down and give each hold-down cup a 90-degree twist, disconnect the hold-down cups and remove the hold-down springs.

8    Disconnect the lower shoe return spring from the brake shoes.

9    Remove the leading and trailing shoes and the adjuster mechanism from the back-ing plate.

10    Disconnect the parking brake cable from the parking brake lever.

11    Place the leading and trailing brake shoe and adjuster assembly on a bench and remove the rest of the parts.

12    Inspect and, if necessary, replace the wheel cylinder (see Section 6).

13    Clean off the backing plate and apply brake grease or high-temperature grease to the brake shoe contact areas on the backing plate **(see illustration)**.

14    Apply brake grease to the threaded portion of the adjuster and to the tips of the adjuster, where it engages the brake shoes. Engage the slots in the brake shoes with the ends of the adjuster. Attach the upper return spring to both shoes to hold them in place.

15    Position the shoes and adjuster on the brake backing plate and engage the upper ends of the shoes, one at a time, with the slots on the ends of the wheel cylinder pistons.

16    Attach the lower return spring to the leading and trailing shoes.

17    Install the hold-down pins, springs and cups.

18    Repeat this procedure for the other rear brake assembly.

19    Install the brake drums. To adjust the brake shoes, turn the adjuster **(see illustration 5.3b)** until the wheel stops turning, then back off the adjuster slightly. The wheel should now turn freely and you shouldn't be able to hear the shoes dragging on the drum;

if it doesn't turn freely and you can hear the shoes drag, back off the adjuster a little more.

20    Install the wheels and lug nuts, lower the vehicle and tighten the lug nuts to the torque listed in the Chapter 1 Specifications. Test the brakes for proper operation before driving the vehicle in traffic.

## 6    Wheel cylinder - removal and installation

*Refer to illustrations 6.2 and 6.3*

### *Removal*

1    Remove the brake drum and brake shoes (see Section 5).

2    Unscrew the brake line fitting from the rear of the wheel cylinder **(see illustration)**. If available, use a flare-nut wrench to avoid rounding off the corners on the fitting. Don't pull the metal line out of the wheel cylinder - it could bend, making installation difficult.

3    Remove the two nuts securing the wheel cylinder to the brake backing plate **(see illustration)**.

4    Remove the wheel cylinder.

5    Plug the end of the brake line to prevent the loss of brake fluid and the entry of dirt.

### *Installation*

6    Place the wheel cylinder in position and, while it's still loose, connect the brake line to it, being careful not to cross thread the fitting. Don't tighten the fitting yet.

7    Install the bolts and tighten them to the torque listed in this Chapter's Specifications. Tighten the line fitting securely.

8    Bleed the brakes (see Section 10). Don't drive the vehicle in traffic until the operation of the brakes has been thoroughly tested.

## 7    Master cylinder - removal and installation

*Refer to illustrations 7.2, 7.3 and 7.4*
**Caution:** *Brake fluid will damage paint. Cover all body parts and be careful not to spill fluid during this procedure.*
**Note:** *New and rebuilt master cylinders are readily available at auto parts stores. Rebuilding of the master cylinder is not recommended.*

### *Removal*

1    Place some shop rags underneath the master cylinder to catch spilled brake fluid, then remove the brake fluid from the reservoir using a suction gun or a poultry baster. **Warning:** *If a poultry baster is used, never again use it for the preparation of food.*

2    Unplug the electrical connector for the brake fluid level indicator **(see illustration)**.

3    Place some rags or newspapers under the brake line fittings. Using a flare-nut wrench, unscrew the brake line tube nuts **(see illustration)** and allow any residual fluid to drain onto the rags.

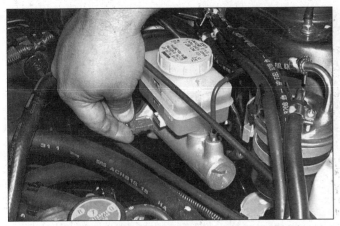

7.2 Unplug the electrical connector for the brake fluid level indicator

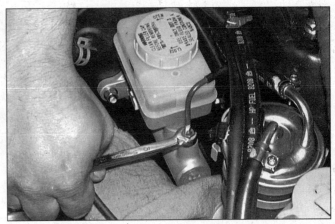

7.3 To disconnect the brake lines from the master cylinder, unscrew the tube nuts with a flare-nut wrench

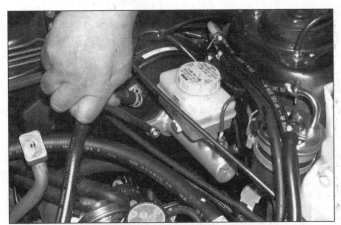

7.4 To detach the master cylinder from the power brake booster, remove the mounting nuts

8.3 To protect brake line tube nuts, use a flare-nut wrench so the corners of the nut don't become rounded off

4    Remove the nuts that attach the master cylinder to the power brake booster (see illustration).
5    Remove the master cylinder from the engine compartment, being careful not to spill any fluid.

## Installation

Note: Whenever the master cylinder is removed, the complete hydraulic system must be bled (see Section 10). The time required to bleed the system can be reduced if the master cylinder is filled with fluid and bench bled (refer to Steps 6 through 9) before it's installed on the vehicle.

6    Insert threaded plugs of the correct size into the brake line outlet holes and fill the reservoirs with brake fluid. The master cylinder should be supported so brake fluid won't spill during the bench bleeding procedure.
7    Loosen one plug at a time and push the piston assembly into the bore to force air from the master cylinder. To prevent air from being drawn back in, the appropriate plug must be replaced before allowing the piston to return to its original position.
8    Stroke the piston three or four times for each outlet to ensure that all air has been expelled.

9    Since high pressure isn't involved in the bench bleeding procedure, there is an alternative to the removal and replacement of the plugs with each stroke of the piston assembly. Before pushing in on the piston assembly, remove one of the plugs completely. Before releasing the piston, however, instead of replacing the plug, simply put your finger tightly over the hole to keep air from being drawn back into the master cylinder. Wait several seconds for the brake fluid to be drawn from the reservoir into the piston bore, then repeat the procedure. When you push down on the piston it'll force your finger off the hole, allowing the air inside to be expelled. When only brake fluid is being ejected from the hole, replace the plug and go on to the other port.
10    Installation is the reverse of removal. Tighten the mounting nuts to the torque listed in this Chapter's Specifications. Tighten the fittings securely.
11    If brake fluid spilled onto the paint in the engine compartment, rinse it off with water.
12    Fill the master cylinder reservoir with the recommended fluid (see Chapter 1). Bleed the brake system (see Section 10) and test the operation of the brakes before driving the vehicle in traffic.

## 8    Brake hoses and lines - check and replacement

1    About every six months, inspect the flexible hoses which connect the steel brake lines with the front and rear brake assemblies for cracks, chafing of the outer cover, leaks, blisters and other damage. These are important and vulnerable parts of the brake system and your inspection should be thorough. You'll need a light and mirror. If a hose exhibits any of the above defects, replace it with a new one.
2    If the vehicle is equipped with air suspension, make sure that the vehicle is in the normal (low) position, the height control switch is turned off, and the battery negative cable is disconnected. Raise the vehicle and place it securely on jackstands.

## Flexible hoses

Refer to illustrations 8.3, 8.4a and 8.4b

3    Clean all dirt away from the ends of the hose. Using a flare-nut wrench, disconnect the brake line from the hose fitting (see illustration). Be careful not to bend the bracket or kink the metal line. If necessary, soak the connections with penetrating oil.

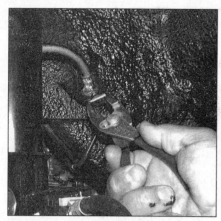

**8.4a  Remove the U-clip from the bracket on the inner fender panel . . .**

**8.4b  . . . and from the bracket on the strut**

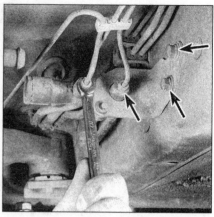

**9.2  To replace the proportioning valve, loosen all four tube nuts (rear two shown), then remove the two mounting bracket bolts**

4    Remove the U-clips from the brackets on the strut and inner fender panel **(see illustrations)**.

5    Unscrew the banjo bolt, disconnect the hose from the caliper and pass it through the bracket on the strut. Discard the sealing washers on either side of the banjo fitting (new ones should be used on installation).

6    Attach the hose to the caliper with the banjo bolt. Be sure to use new sealing washers and tighten the fitting bolt to the torque listed in this Chapter's Specifications.

7    Route the hose so that it doesn't touch any suspension components. Make sure there are no kinks or twists, then attach the hose to the metal line at the bracket by loosely tightening the tube nut.

8    Install the U-clip.

9    Tighten the brake line tube nut securely. Make sure that the hose doesn't turn, and the metal line doesn't kink, as you tighten the tube nut.

10    Make sure no suspension or steering components contact the hose. Have an assistant push down on the vehicle and also turn the steering wheel lock-to-lock during inspection.

11    Bleed the brake system (see Section 10).

## Metal brake lines

12    When replacing metal brake lines, be sure to use the correct parts. Don't use copper tubing for any brake system components. Purchase genuine steel brake lines from a dealer parts department or auto parts store.

13    Prefabricated brake line, with the tube ends already flared and fittings installed, is available at auto parts stores and dealer parts departments. If pre-bent lines are not available, remove the defective line and purchase a straight section of brake line (with the ends already flared and the fittings attached) that measures as close as possible to the length of the original line (including the bends). Using the proper tubing bending tools, bend the new line to resemble the original.

14    When installing the new line make sure it's well supported by all clips and brackets, and has plenty of clearance between moving or hot components.

15    After installation, check the master cylinder fluid level and add fluid as necessary. Bleed the brake system as outlined in the next Section and test the brakes carefully before placing the vehicle into normal service.

## 9    Proportioning valve - replacement

*Refer to illustration 9.2*

1    If the vehicle is equipped with air suspension, make sure that the vehicle is in the normal (low) position, the height control switch is turned off, and the battery negative cable is disconnected. Raise the vehicle and support it securely on jackstands.

2    Unscrew all four brake line tube nuts with a flare nut wrench **(see illustration)**.

3    Unbolt the proportioning valve.

4    Installation is the reverse of removal. Be sure to bleed the brake system (see Section 10) when you're done.

## 10    Brake hydraulic system - bleeding

*Refer to illustrations 10.1 and 10.8*

**Warning:** *Wear eye protection when bleeding the brake system. If the fluid comes in contact with your eyes, immediately rinse them with water and seek medical attention.*

**Note:** *Bleeding the brake system is necessary to remove any air that's trapped in the system when it's opened during removal and installation of a hose, line, caliper, wheel cylinder or master cylinder.*

1    It will probably be necessary to bleed the system at all four brakes if air has entered the system due to low fluid level, or if the brake lines have been disconnected at the master cylinder. **Note:** *If the master cylinder has run dry (due to a leak in the system) or has been rebuilt or replaced, begin by bleeding the master cylinder* **(see illustration)**.

2    If a brake line was disconnected only at a wheel, then only that caliper or wheel cylinder must be bled.

3    If a brake line is disconnected at a fitting

**10.1  Have an assistant depress the brake pedal and hold it down, then loosen the fitting nut, allowing the air and fluid to escape. Repeat this procedure on both fittings until the fluid is clear of air bubbles**

located between the master cylinder and any of the brakes, that part of the system served by the disconnected line must be bled.

4    Remove any residual vacuum from the power brake booster by applying the brake several times with the engine off.

5    Remove the master cylinder reservoir cap and fill the reservoir with brake fluid. Reinstall the cap. **Note:** *Check the fluid level often during the bleeding operation and add fluid as necessary to prevent the fluid level from falling low enough to allow air bubbles into the master cylinder.*

6    Have an assistant on hand, as well as a supply of new brake fluid, a clear container partially filled with clean brake fluid, a length of plastic, rubber or vinyl tubing to fit over the bleeder valve and a wrench to open and close the bleeder valve.

7    Beginning at the right front wheel, loosen the bleeder screw slightly, then tighten it to a point where it's snug but can still be loosened quickly and easily.

8    Place one end of the tubing over the

**10.8  When bleeding the brakes, a hose is connected to the bleeder screw at the caliper or wheel cylinder and then submerged in brake fluid - air will be seen as bubbles in the tube and container (all air must be expelled before moving to the next wheel)**

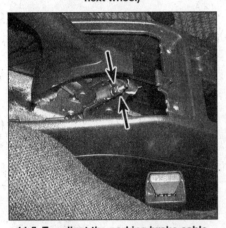

**11.5  To adjust the parking brake cable, loosen this locknut (upper arrow) and tighten or loosen the adjuster nut (lower arrow) so that the parking brake is fully applied when the lever "clicks" seven to eight times**

bleeder screw fitting and submerge the other end in brake fluid in the container **(see illustration)**.

9    Have the assistant push down on the brake pedal and hold the pedal firmly depressed.

10    While the pedal is held depressed, open the bleeder screw just enough to allow a flow of fluid to leave the valve. Watch for air bubbles to exit the submerged end of the tube. When the fluid flow slows after a couple of seconds, tighten the screw and have your assistant release the pedal.

11    Repeat Steps 9 and 10 until no more air is seen leaving the tube, then tighten the bleeder screw and proceed to the left rear wheel, the left front wheel and the right rear wheel, in that order, and perform the same procedure. Be sure to check the fluid in the master cylinder reservoir frequently.

12    Never use old brake fluid. It contains moisture which can boil, rendering the brakes useless.

13    Refill the master cylinder with fluid at the end of the operation.

14    Check the operation of the brakes. The pedal should feel solid when depressed, with no sponginess. If necessary, repeat the entire process. **Warning:** *Do not operate the vehicle if you are in doubt about the effectiveness of the brake system.*

## 11  Parking brake - adjustment

*Refer to illustration 11.5*

1    Before adjusting the parking brake, make sure that the brake hydraulic system is free of all air (see Section 10) and that the rear brakes have been adjusted properly (rear

drum brake models, see Section 5; rear disc brake models, see Section 13).

2    Firmly apply the parking brake lever three to five times.

3    Count how many clicks the brake lever travels before it becomes fully engaged. The correct number is seven to eight clicks. If the parking brake lever needs more than this number of clicks before it's fully applied, the cable is stretched. If it applies the brakes in less than this number, the cable is too tight. Adjust the parking brake as follows.

4    Remove the center console (see Chapter 11).

5    Back off the locknut **(see illustration)**, then turn the adjuster nut clockwise to tighten the cable or counterclockwise to loosen it.

6    Pull up on the parking brake lever again and count how many clicks it takes to fully apply the parking brake. Repeat the adjustment procedure if necessary.

7    After the adjustment is made, tighten the locknut against the adjuster nut.

8    If it is impossible to achieve the correct adjustment, the cables are stretched beyond adjustment. Replace them (see Section 12).

9    Install the center console (see Chapter 11).

## 12  Parking brake cables - replacement

*Refer to illustrations 12.4a, 12.4b, 12.4c, 12.5, 12.7a and 12.7b*

1    Remove the center console (see Chapter 11).

2    Loosen the cable locknut and adjuster nut **(see illustration 11.5)**.

3    If the vehicle is equipped with air suspension, make sure that the vehicle is in the normal (low) position, the height control switch is turned off, and the battery negative cable is disconnected. Loosen the rear wheel lug nuts, raise the rear of the vehicle and place it securely on jackstands. Remove the rear wheels.

4    Trace the routing of the rear cable you intend to replace and remove all clamps and/or clips attaching the cable to the vehicle body **(see illustrations)**.

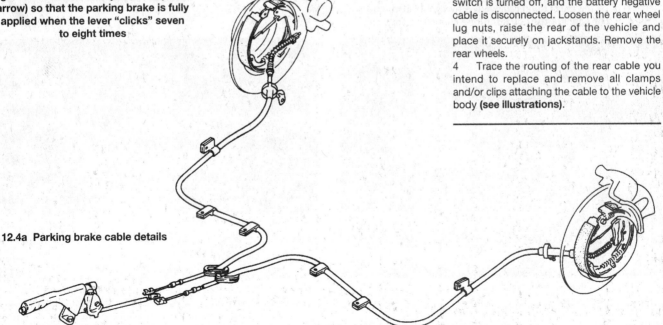

**12.4a  Parking brake cable details**

12.4b  To detach either parking brake cable from the floorpan, remove these clamps (arrows) and disengage the cable from the forward clip (arrow)

12.4c  To detach either parking brake cable from the trailing arm bracket, remove this bolt (arrow)

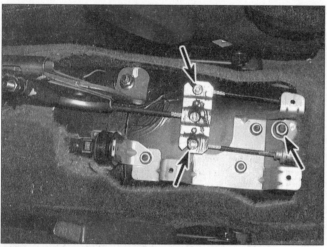

12.5  Loosen the cable locknut and adjuster nut, disengage the parking brake cable you're replacing (arrows) from the equalizer, peel back the carpet and remove the two cable clamp nuts (arrow) right behind the equalizer (one clamp nut not visible)

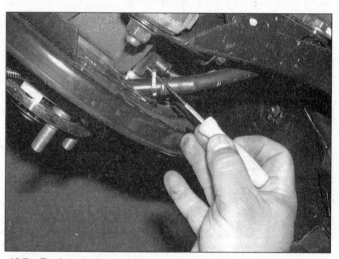

12.7a  To detach the parking brake cable from the brake backing plate, remove this retainer clip . . .

12.7b  . . . then pull the cable through the backing plate

13.3  If a rear disc proves difficult or impossible to remove, pull out the adjuster hole access plug from the backing plate and back off the parking brake shoes by turning the star wheel on the adjuster with an adjuster tool or a screwdriver

5    Disengage the cable from the equalizer, peel back the carpet and remove the two cable clamp nuts right behind the equalizer **(see illustration)**.

6    Disengage the cable from the rear brake assembly (rear drum brake models, see Section 5; rear disc brake models, see Section 13).

7    Detach the cable from the brake backing plate **(see illustrations)**.

8    Installation is the reverse of removal. Make sure that the cables are routed so that they're not kinked and so that nothing interferes with them.

9    Adjust the new cables (see Section 11).

10   Install the center console (see Chapter 11).

## 13  Parking brake shoes (rear disc brakes only) - inspection and replacement

*Refer to illustrations 13.3, 13.4, 13.5 and 13.6a through 13.6o*

**Warning:** *Parking brake shoes must be replaced on both wheels at the same time - never replace the shoes on only one wheel. Also, brake system dust may contain asbestos, which is hazardous to your health. DO NOT blow it out with compressed air and DO NOT inhale it. An approved filtering mask should be worn when working on the parking brakes. DO NOT use gasoline or petroleum-based solvent to remove the dust. Use brake system cleaner only.*

1    If the vehicle is equipped with air suspension, make sure that the vehicle is in the normal (low) position, the height control switch is turned off, and the battery negative cable is disconnected.

2    Loosen the wheel lug nuts, raise the rear of the vehicle and support it securely on jackstands. Block the front wheels to keep the vehicle from rolling off the stands. Remove the rear wheels. Release the parking brake.

3    Remove the brake discs (see Section 4). It's not necessary to disconnect the brake hoses from the brake calipers. Make sure you support the calipers with coat hangers or pieces of wire. It may be difficult or impossible to remove the discs if the parking brake shoes have worn them excessively. If you can't pull off the discs, remove the access hole plug for the parking brake shoe adjuster from the backing plate and, using a brake adjuster tool or a narrow screwdriver, back off the brake shoes by turning the star wheel on the adjuster **(see illustration)**.

4    Wash the parking brake assemblies with brake system cleaner before beginning work **(see illustration)**. Do not use compressed air to blow off the brake assembly.

5    Wash the disc brakes and check the parking brake drums for score marks, deep grooves, hard spots (which will appear as small discolored areas) and cracks. If the parking brake drums are worn, scored or out-of-round, they can be resurfaced by an automotive machine shop. **Note:** *Professionals recommend resurfacing drums whenever a brake job is done. Resurfacing will eliminate the possibility of out-of-round drums. If the drums are worn so much they can't be resurfaced without exceeding the maximum allowable diameter - which is stamped into the drum portion of the disc* **(see illustration)** *- new ones will be required. At the very least, if you elect not to have the drums resurfaced, remove the glazing from the surface with sandpaper or emery cloth using a swirling motion. This is also a good time to inspect the discs themselves for wear (see Section 4).*

6    To replace the parking brake shoes, follow the accompanying photos, beginning with **illustration 13.6a**. Be sure to stay in order and read the caption under each illustration. Work on only one parking brake

**13.4  Wash the parking brake assembly with brake system cleaner before disassembling anything**

**13.5  Don't be confused by the two specifications cast into the drum area of the disc: the spec on the left is the minimum thickness for the brake disc; the spec on the right is the maximum diameter for the drum**

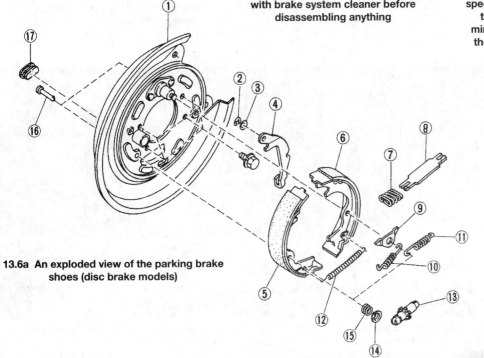

**13.6a  An exploded view of the parking brake shoes (disc brake models)**

| | |
|---|---|
| 1 | Backing plate |
| 2 | C-clip |
| 3 | Spring washer |
| 4 | Parking brake lever |
| 5 | Primary parking brake shoe |
| 6 | Secondary parking brake shoe |
| 7 | Strut spring |
| 8 | Strut |
| 9 | Shoe guide plate |
| 10 | Primary shoe return spring |
| 11 | Secondary shoe return spring |
| 12 | Adjusting spring |
| 13 | Adjuster |
| 14 | Shoe hold-down cup |
| 15 | Shoe hold-down spring |
| 16 | Shoe hold-down pin |
| 17 | Adjusting hole plug |

**13.6b Using a hold-down spring tool, push down and give the hold-down cup a 90-degree twist, disconnect the hold-down cup and remove the hold-down spring**

**13.6c Remove the secondary (rear) shoe hold-down spring the same way**

**13.6d Unhook the secondary shoe return spring from the anchor pin with a brake spring tool, then unhook the spring from the secondary shoe**

assembly at a time. Do not begin disassembling the second parking brake assembly until you have reassembled the first. That way, you will have one assembled parking brake to use as a reference, if necessary.

7  Repeat this procedure for the other parking brake assembly.

8  Install the brake discs (see Section 4). To adjust the parking brake shoes, turn the adjuster **(see illustration 13.3)** until the shoes rub on the drum, then back off the adjuster until they don't.

9  Install the caliper support brackets, the brake pads and the calipers (see Sections 2 and 3).

10  Install the rear wheels and lug nuts, lower the vehicle and tighten the lug nuts to the torque listed in the Chapter 1 Specifications. Adjust the parking brake (see Section 11). Test the brakes for proper operation before driving the vehicle in traffic.

**13.6e Remove the strut and strut spring**

**13.6f Unhook the primary shoe return spring from the anchor pin with a brake spring tool then unhook the spring from the shoe**

**13.6g Remove the brake shoes, lower return spring and adjuster as a single unit, remove the adjuster and spring, then detach the parking brake cable from the lever**

**13.6h Clean off the backing plate, then lubricate the brake shoe contact areas with high-temperature grease**

13.6i  Transfer the parking brake lever to the new secondary shoe, then connect the cable to the lever and position the shoe on the backing plate

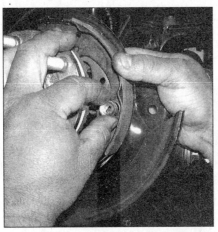

13.6j  Install the hold-down pin, spring and cup, then lock down the spring by pushing in on the cup and turning it 90-degrees

13.6k  Install the strut and strut spring; make sure that the slot in the rear end of the strut is correctly engaged with the slot in the secondary shoe

13.6l  Hook the lower return spring to the bottom of each shoe and install the adjuster between them

13.6m  Place the primary shoe and shoe guide plate in position . . .

13.6n  . . . then install the hold-down pin, spring and retainer

13.6o  Hook the upper return springs to each shoe and, using a brake spring tool, hook them over the anchor pin

## 14  Hill-holder system - adjustment and component replacement

### *Adjustment*

*Refer to illustrations 14.3a and 14.3b*

1    Check the clutch cable adjustment (see Chapter 8). If necessary, adjust it. The clutch and hill-holder valve work hand in hand - when one is engaged, the other isn't, and vice versa.
2    Find a hill with at least three degrees of incline (the valve doesn't engage on a hill with less than three degrees of slope).
3    Start the vehicle up the hill, stop, then depress the clutch pedal. If the vehicle starts to roll backward, the cable is too loose. Locate the adjusting nut and tighten it **(see illustrations)**.
4    Repeat the test: start up the hill, stop, depress the clutch pedal, and note whether the vehicle remains in place or rolls backward. If it still rolls, tighten the adjusting nut a little more.
5    Follow this procedure until the hill-holder operates properly. Do not tighten the cable any more than necessary.
6    It's the brakes that actually hold the vehicle in place when the valve is actuated (the hill-holder valve is connected directly to the master cylinder).
7    If the brakes are still applied, preventing the vehicle from rolling freely, the hill-holder cable is probably adjusted too tightly. Take the vehicle to a three-degree or steeper hill and loosen the cable adjuster nut until the vehicle rolls freely under power.
8    If the brakes will not release your vehicle at all, check the hill-holder return spring. If it is broken, replace the hill-holder mechanism immediately. You can get the vehicle home by removing the hill-holder cable adjusting nuts, disconnecting the cable from the clutch release lever and manually retracting the hill-holder valve lever until the brakes are released.

### *Component replacement*

9    Raise the vehicle and support it securely on jackstands.

#### Hill-holder cable

10    Loosen and remove the locknut from the end of the hill-holder cable.
11    Loosen the adjuster nut for the hill-holder cable enough to release it from the clutch release lever.
12    Pull the end of the cable out of the clutch release lever, then remove the clip which secures the cable in place on the engine bracket.
13    Remove the clip holding the cable to the lever assembly on the hill-holder valve.
14    Remove the cable end from the hill-holder valve.
15    Remove any clamps holding the cable in place along its length, then remove the cable.
16    Installation is the reverse of removal. Make sure that the cable is installed correctly at both ends. Do not tighten the adjusting nut

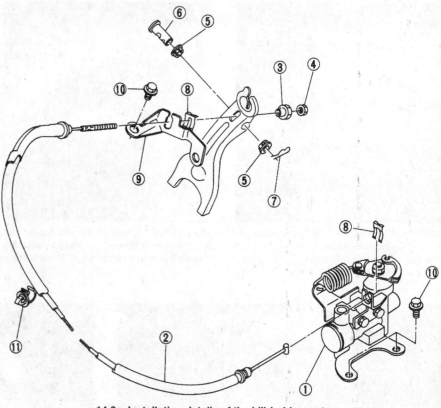

**14.3a  Installation details of the hill-holder system**

| | | | |
|---|---|---|---|
| 1 | Hill-holder valve | 7 | Retainer pin |
| 2 | Hill-holder cable | 8 | U-clips |
| 3 | Cable adjusting nut | 9 | Cable bracket |
| 4 | Cable locknut | 10 | Hill-holder valve retaining bolts |
| 5 | Clevis bushings | 11 | Cable clip |
| 6 | Cable clevis pin | | |

at the clutch release lever until the cable has been adjusted.
17    Adjust the hill-holder cable (see above).

#### Hill-holder valve

18    Place shop rags underneath the master cylinder and the hill-holder valve to catch any brake fluid which leaks out. Drain the fluid from the reservoir on the primary side of the master cylinder. Open the valve, with a piece of tubing attached to it, and let it drain into a container by gravity.
19    Disconnect the hill-holder cable at the clutch release lever end and the hill-holder valve end.
20    Disconnect the brake line fittings (top, bottom and rear) from the valve.
21    Detach the electrical connector from the valve bracket. Remove the hill-holder valve mounting bolts and remove the valve.
22    Inspect the return spring. If it's worn or damaged, replace it.
23    To inspect the valve, rotate it back and forth in your hands. If the sound of a rolling ball is heard, then the valve is probably still good.
24    Apply a lithium-based grease to all of the moving parts of the valve mechanism. Work the lever a few times to make sure it is working correctly and to loosen it up.

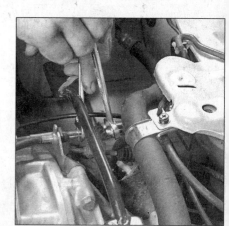

**14.3b  Turn this adjusting nut to tighten or loosen the hill-holder cable**

25    Install the valve to the frame of your vehicle and attach the three-way electrical connector to the valve bracket. Tighten all of the mounting hardware securely.
26    Attach the three brake lines and make sure the tube nut fittings are tight.
27    Install both cable ends but do not tighten the locknut on the clutch release lever until the cable has been adjusted (see above).
28    Bleed the brakes (see Section 10).

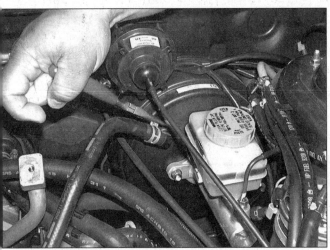

15.7  Detach the vacuum hose from the power brake booster

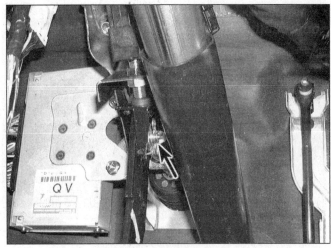

15.9  To disconnect the power brake booster pushrod from the brake pedal, remove the retaining clip and pull out the clevis pin (arrow)

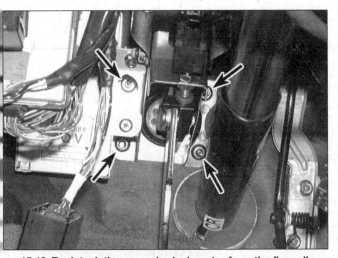

15.10  To detach the power brake booster from the firewall, remove these four nuts (arrows)

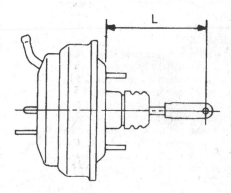

15.12  On 1995 and later models, measure the length (L) of the booster pushrod and compare your measurement to the length listed in this Chapter's Specifications; if the pushrod is out of specification, loosen the locknut and screw the pushrod in or out

## 15  Power brake booster - check, removal and installation

Refer to illustrations 15.7, 15.9, 15.10 and 15.12

1  The power brake booster unit requires no special maintenance apart from periodic inspection of the vacuum hose and the case.

### Operating check

2  Depress the brake pedal several times with the engine off and make sure there is no change in the pedal reserve distance (the minimum distance to the floor).
3  Depress the pedal and start the engine. If the pedal goes down slightly, operation is normal.

### Airtightness check

4  Start the engine and turn it off after one or two minutes. Depress the pedal several times slowly. If the pedal goes down farther the first time but gradually rises after the second or third depression, the booster is airtight.
5  Depress the brake pedal while the engine is running, then stop the engine with the brake pedal depressed. If there is no change in the pedal reserve travel after holding the pedal for 30 seconds, the booster is airtight.

### Removal

6  If the booster is defective, replace it with a new or rebuilt unit. The booster cannot be overhauled.
7  Disconnect the vacuum hose from the booster unit **(see illustration)**.
8  Remove the master cylinder (see Section 7).
9  Working on the inside of the vehicle, remove the pedal return spring, the cotter pin and the pushrod clevis pin, and disconnect the booster pushrod clevis from the brake pedal **(see illustration)**.
10  Remove the four booster-to-firewall nuts **(see illustration)**, then remove the booster from the vehicle. Discard the old seals.

### Installation

11  Installation is the reverse of removal. Tighten the booster-to-firewall nuts to the torque listed in this Chapter's Specifications.
12  If you're installing a new power brake booster, adjust the pushrod length as follows: On 1990 through 1994 models, verify that there's a little freeplay between the pushrod clevis and the brake pedal (you should be able to depress the brake pedal slightly before it begins to move the pushrod). If there isn't, loosen the locknut and turn the pushrod until there is. On 1995 and later models, verify that the pushrod is the length listed in this Chapter's Specifications **(see illustration)**. If it isn't, loosen the locknut and turn the pushrod until it's the specified length.
13  Bleed the brake system (see Section 10).

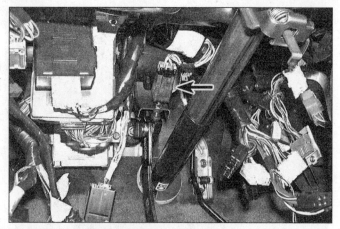

**16.1 The brake light switch (arrow), is located near the top of the brake pedal**

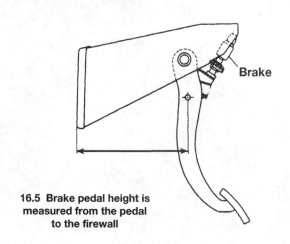

**16.5 Brake pedal height is measured from the pedal to the firewall**

## 16   Brake light switch - check, adjustment and replacement

### Check

*Refer to illustration 16.1*

1   The brake light switch **(see illustration)** is located at the top of the brake pedal. You'll need a flashlight to locate it. If the vehicle is equipped with cruise control, the switch performs two functions: the brake light portion of the switch is normally open, and is closed when the brake pedal is depressed; the cruise control portion of the switch is normally closed, and is opened when the brake pedal is depressed.

2   To check the switch, trace the switch lead to the electrical connector, unplug the connector and hook up an ohmmeter to the terminals on the switch side of the connector.

3   With the brake pedal released, the switch should have no continuity; when the pedal is depressed, there should be continuity. If the switch doesn't operate as described, adjust it and retest. (If the switch operates exactly opposite to this, you're checking the cruise control portion of the switch.)

### Adjustment

*Refer to illustrations 16.5, 16.7 and 16.9*

4   First, make sure that the brake pedal height and freeplay are adjusted correctly.

5   To adjust brake pedal height, unplug the electrical connector for the brake light switch. Loosen the switch locknut and turn the brake light switch until the pedal height **(see illustration)** listed in this Chapter's Specifications is obtained.

6   Tighten the locknut, plug in the electrical connector and check the brake lights for proper operation. They should come on when the brake pedal is depressed, and go out when it is released.

7   To adjust pedal freeplay (the distance the pedal travels before it begins to move the power brake pushrod), loosen the locknut on the power brake pushrod (at the clevis that

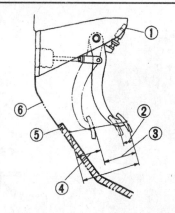

**16.7 Brake pedal freeplay and reserve clearance (the distance between the pedal and the floor mat) are measured between the indicated points**

1   *Brake light switch*
2   *Brake pedal freeplay*
3   *Brake pedal stroke*
4   *Reserve clearance*
5   *Floor mat*
6   *Firewall*

attaches the pushrod to the brake pedal) and turn the pushrod (pliers may be necessary) until the proper amount of freeplay **(see illustration)** is obtained. Tighten the locknut securely.

8   Depress the pedal as far as possible and make sure that the pedal height (pedal-to-floor clearance) is as specified. If the pedal has an excessively long stroke, check the brake shoe lining-to-drum clearance (see Chapter 1).

9   Adjust the switch by loosening the locknut and turning the threaded switch barrel up or down until the stroke of the switch plunger is within the range **(see illustration)** listed in this Chapter's Specifications. Apply the brake pedal and verify that the brake lights come on; release the pedal and verify that the brake lights go off. If the lights come on and go off as described, the switch is correctly adjusted.

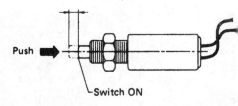

**16.9 Adjust the brake light switch so that the plunger stroke is within the dimension listed in this Chapter's Specifications**

### Replacement

10   Unplug the switch electrical connector.

11   Remove the switch locknut and remove the switch from its bracket.

12   Installation is the reverse of removal. Be sure to adjust the switch, then check it to verify that it operates properly.

## 17   Anti-lock Brake System (ABS) - general information

### Description

*Refer to illustration 17.1*

The Anti-lock Brake System (ABS) **(see illustration)** is designed to maintain vehicle maneuverability, directional stability and optimum deceleration under severe braking conditions on most road surfaces. It does so by monitoring the rotational speed of the wheels and controlling the brake line pressure during braking. This prevents the wheels from locking up prematurely.

### Electronic control unit (ECU)

*Refer to illustration 17.2*

The ABS control module for the anti-lock brake system is mounted in the dash on 1990 through 1996 models, and is an integral part of the hydraulic control unit, in the engine compartment, on 1997 and 1998 models **(see illustration)**.

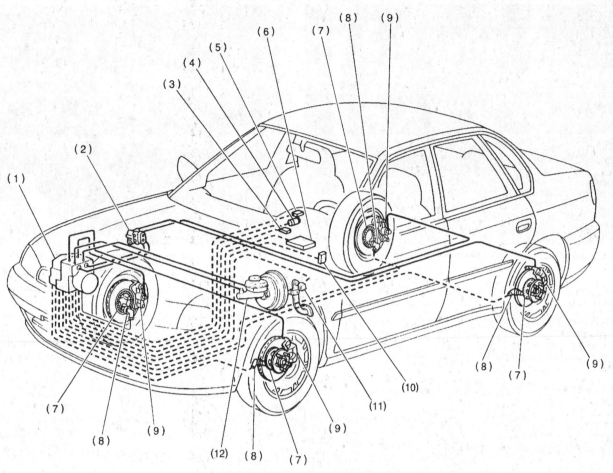

**17.1  Anti-lock Brake System (ABS) (1997 and later model shown, earlier models similar)**

| | | | | | |
|---|---|---|---|---|---|
| 1 | ABS control module and hydraulic control unit (on pre-1997 models, module is located in the dash) | 5 | Data link connector (for Subaru select monitor) | 9 | Brake caliper |
| 2 | Proportioning valve | 6 | Transaxle control module (automatics only) | 10 | G sensor (4WD models only) |
| 3 | Diagnosis connector | 7 | Tone wheel | 11 | Brake light switch |
| 4 | ABS warning light | 8 | ABS sensor | 12 | Master cylinder |

The module monitors the rotation of each wheel with four wheel speed sensors, processes this information and avoids wheel lockup by controlling the hydraulic line pressure accordingly. Here's how it works: When the brakes are applied too firmly during a "panic stop," hydraulic line pressure inside the brake lines builds to such a high level that it "locks up" the wheels, causing the vehicle to skid out of control. On a vehicle equipped with ABS, the module prevents the hydraulic pressure from reaching this dangerously high level by monitoring the rotational speed of the wheels. When a wheel begins to slow down more rapidly in relation to the other wheels, the module energizes the solenoid (inside the hydraulic control unit) controlling the hydraulic brake fluid circuit to that wheel. The energized solenoid opens the circuit, allowing some of the brake fluid into a reservoir, thereby lowering the pressure and preventing the wheel from locking up. As soon as the rotation speed of the wheel equals that of the other wheels, the solenoid closes and

pressure begins to build again. This cycle of opening and closing the circuit occurs many times a second. The module can regulate the pressure to a single wheel, or to two, three or all four wheels, simultaneously.

The module also monitors the ABS system for malfunctions while the engine is running. If the module detects a problem, the ABS warning light on the instrument cluster lights up and a diagnostic code is stored which, when retrieved by a service technician, will indicate the problem area or component. When the engine is started, the ABS warning light glows for about three seconds (indicating that the module is monitoring the system for faults), then goes out; if the ABS light remains on, there's a problem in the ABS system. Take the vehicle to a dealer service department or other qualified service facility.

### Hydraulic control unit

The hydraulic control unit, which is mounted inside the engine compartment on

**17.2  The ABS control module and hydraulic control unit are integrated into one unit on 1997 and later models**

all models, houses the solenoids which regulate brake fluid pressure in response to signals from the ABS control modules. On 1997 and 1998 models, the module is an integral part of the hydraulic control unit.

**17.6a  The front wheel speed sensor (arrow) is installed in the steering knuckle**

**17.6b  The rear wheel speed sensor (arrow) is installed in the rear knuckle**

## Speed sensors

*Refer to illustrations 17.6a and 17.6b*

Each wheel has its own speed sensor **(see illustrations)**. The speed sensor is small variable reluctance sensor (pick-up coil) which sends a variable voltage signal (actually, an alternating current sine wave output) to the ABS control module. The module converts this analog signal into a digital code which it compares to its "map" (program), then either ignores it (if the wheel is rotating at the same speed as the other wheels) or executes a command to open a solenoid for the circuit to that wheel (if the wheel is starting to slow down in relation to the other wheels).

## Brake light switch

The brake light switch signals the control unit when the driver steps on the brake pedal. Without this signal the anti-lock system won't activate.

## Diagnosis and repair

If the ABS warning light on the instrument cluster comes on and stays on, make sure the parking brake is released and there's no problem with the brake hydraulic system. If neither of these is the cause, the anti-lock system is probably malfunctioning. Although special test procedures are necessary to properly diagnose the system, the home mechanic can perform a few simple checks.

a) *Make sure the brake linings, calipers and wheel cylinders are in good condition.*
b) *Inspect the electrical connectors at the ABS control module. Make sure they're clean and tight.*
c) *Check the fuses.*
d) *Follow the wiring harness to the speed sensor(s) and brake light switch and make sure all connections are clean and tight and the wiring isn't damaged.*

If the above preliminary checks don't rectify the problem, the vehicle should be diagnosed by a dealer service department or other qualified repair shop.

# Chapter 10
# Suspension and steering systems

## Contents

## Specifications

### Torque specifications

**Ft-lbs** (unless otherwise indicated)

#### Front suspension

| | |
|---|---|
| Balljoint-to-control arm nut | 29 |
| Control arms | |
| Front pivot bolt/nut | 61 to 83 |
| Rear pivot stud nut | 130 to 144 |
| Rear bushing bolts | 145 to 217 |
| Stabilizer bar | |
| Stabilizer bar bushing clamp bolts | 16 to 21 |
| Stabilizer-to-link bolts/nuts | 28 to 37 |
| Link-to-control arm bolts/nuts | 16 to 22 |
| Steering knuckle-to-balljoint pinch bolt | 28 to 37 |
| Strut/coil spring assembly | |
| Damper rod-to-mount nut | 37 to 50 |
| Strut-to-steering knuckle bolts/nuts | 98 to 119 |
| Strut upper mounting nuts | 120 to 192 in-lbs |

## Torque specifications (continued)

**Ft-lbs** (unless otherwise indicated)

### Rear suspension

Control arms
| | |
|---|---|
| Control arm-to-crossmember bolt/nut | 87 to 116 |
| Control arm-to-rear knuckle bolt/nut | 87 to 116 |
| Rear hub and bearing retaining nut (2WD) | 123 to 151 |

Stabilizer bar
| | |
|---|---|
| Stabilizer bar bushing clamp bolts | 16 to 21 |

Stabilizer-to-link bolts/nuts
| | |
|---|---|
| 1990 through 1994 | 120 to 228 in-lbs |
| 1995 on | 29 to 36 |

Link-to-control arm nut
| | |
|---|---|
| 1990 through 1994 | 132 to 240 in-lbs |
| 1995 on | 29 to 36 |

Strut assembly
| | |
|---|---|
| Damper rod-to-mount nut | 37 to 50 |
| Strut-to-knuckle bolts/nuts | 98 to 119 |
| Strut upper mounting nuts | 120 to 228 in-lbs |

Trailing arms
| | |
|---|---|
| Trailing arm-to-body bolt/nut | 72 to 94 |
| Trailing arm-to-rear knuckle bolt/nut | 72 to 94 |

### Steering

Power steering pump pulley nut
| | |
|---|---|
| 1990 through 1994 | 31 to 46 |
| 1995 on | 40 to 49 |
| Tie-rod end-to-steering knuckle nut | 19 to 21 |
| Steering gear mounting bolts | 35 to 52 |
| Steering shaft U-joint pinch bolt | 15 to 19 |
| Steering wheel nut | 22 to 29 |

**1.1  Typical front suspension components**

| | | | |
|---|---|---|---|
| 1 | Stabilizer bar | 5 | Steering knuckle | 9 | Steering gear boot |
| 2 | Stabilizer bar bushing clamp | 6 | Balljoint | 10 | Steering gear clamp bolt |
| 3 | Tie-rod | 7 | Control arm | | |
| 4 | Tie-rod end | 8 | Control arm bushing clamp | | |

**1.2 Typical rear suspension components (4WD model)**

| | | | | | |
|---|---|---|---|---|---|
| 1 | Stabilizer bar | 4 | Rear control arm | 6 | Trailing arm |
| 2 | Stabilizer bar bushing clamp | 5 | Front control arm | 7 | Rear knuckle |
| 3 | Stabilizer bar link | | | | |

## 1  General information

### Suspension

*Refer to illustrations 1.1 and 1.2*

The front suspension **(see illustration)** is fully independent. It consists of strut/coil spring assemblies, control arms, steering knuckles and a stabilizer bar. The upper end of each strut is attached to the body and the lower end is bolted to the steering knuckle. The lower end of the knuckle is attached to the control arm by a balljoint. The inner end of the control arm is bolted to a crossmember. The stabilizer bar is attached to the crossmember by a pair of clamps and is connected to the control arms by links.

The rear suspension **(see illustration)** is also fully independent. It consists of strut/coil spring assemblies, trailing arms, control arms, knuckles and a stabilizer bar. The upper end of each strut is attached to the body and the lower end is bolted to the knuckle. The knuckle is positioned by the control arms and the trailing arms. The inner ends of the control arms are bolted to the crossmember; the outer ends of the control arms are bolted to the knuckle. The front ends of the trailing arms are bolted to the body; the rear ends of the trailing arms are

bolted to the knuckles. The stabilizer bar is attached to the crossmember by a pair of clamps and is connected to the control arms by links.

### Steering

All models use a rack-and-pinion type steering gear. Some units are manual, but most are power-assisted. The steering gear is connected to the steering knuckles by a pair of tie-rods.

## 2  Strut/coil spring assembly (front) - removal and installation

### Removal

*Refer to illustrations 2.5a, 2.5b and 2.6*

1    If the vehicle is equipped with air suspension, make sure that the vehicle is in the normal (low) position, the height control switch is turned off, and the battery negative cable is disconnected.

2    Loosen the front wheel lug nuts, block the rear wheels, raise the front of the vehicle and place it securely on jackstands. Remove the front wheels.

3    Detach the brake hose from the caliper and its bracket on the strut (see Chapter 9). Plug the hose to prevent excessive fluid loss

and contamination.

4    On ABS models, unbolt the ABS sensor from the steering knuckle **(see illustration 7.4)**. It's not absolutely necessary to remove the sensor from the knuckle, but the sensor lead could be damaged if the knuckle drops down too far when the strut is detached.

5    Detach the ABS sensor lead from the strut, mark the relationship of the upper camber adjustment bolt to the strut flange, then remove the strut-to-knuckle nuts and bolts

**2.5a  Mark the relationship of the upper strut-to-knuckle bolt**

**2.5b On models with ABS, remove the sensor lead bracket bolt (left arrow) from the strut; on all models, remove the strut-to-knuckle nuts and bolts (right arrows)**

**2.6 To detach the upper end of the strut/coil spring assembly from the body, remove these nuts (arrows)**

**(see illustrations). Note:** *If a new strut is being installed, it is still important to mark the bolt position; there is an indexing mark on the strut flange, and the proper alignment mark on the bolt must line up with it when installed to preserve the camber setting.*

6    In the engine compartment, remove the mounting nuts that attach the top of the strut to the strut tower **(see illustration)**. Support the strut with one hand (or have an assistant hold it) while doing this.

7    Remove the strut assembly. If you're planning to replace either the strut or the coil spring, refer to Section 3.

## Installation

8    Place the strut assembly in position and install, but don't tighten, the upper mounting nuts.

9    Insert the steering knuckle into the strut flange, install the strut-to-knuckle bolts and align the mark you made on the upper bolt with the mark on the strut flange. Tighten the bolts and nuts to the torque listed in this Chapter's Specifications.

10    Install the ABS sensor, if equipped.

11    Reattach the brake hose bracket to the

strut and to the brake caliper (using new sealing washers). Tighten the brake hose-to-caliper banjo bolt to the torque listed in the Chapter 9 Specifications.

12    Bleed the brakes (see Chapter 9).

13    Install the wheels and lug nuts.

14    Lower the vehicle and tighten the lug nuts to the torque listed in the Chapter 1 Specifications. Tighten the upper strut mounting nuts to the torque listed in this

Chapter's Specifications.

15    Have the front end alignment checked and, if necessary, adjusted.

## 3    Strut/coil spring - replacement

1    If the struts or coil springs exhibit the telltale signs of wear (leaking fluid, loss of damping capability, chipped, sagging or

**3.3 Install the spring compressor in accordance with the tool manufacturer's instructions and compress the spring until all pressure is relieved from the upper spring seat**

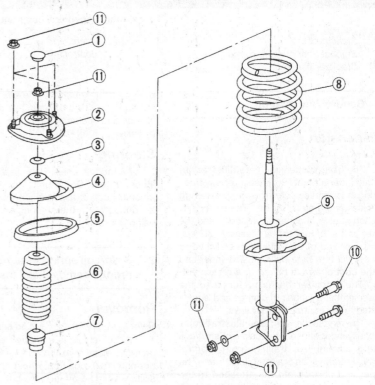

**3.4a An exploded view of the front strut/coil spring assembly**

| | | | |
|---|---|---|---|
| 1 | Dust cover | 7 | Rubber bumper |
| 2 | Strut mount | 8 | Coil spring |
| 3 | Spacer | 9 | Strut |
| 4 | Upper spring seat | 10 | Camber adjusting bolt |
| 5 | Rubber seat | 11 | Self-locking nuts |
| 6 | Dust boot | | |

**3.4b Remove the damper shaft nut**

**3.5 Remove the upper mount from the damper shaft**

**3.6 Remove the upper spring seat from the damper shaft**

cracked coil springs) explore all options before beginning any work. The strut/shock absorber assemblies are not serviceable and must be replaced if a problem develops. However, strut assemblies complete with springs may be available on an exchange basis, which eliminates much time and work. Whichever route you choose to take, check on the cost and availability of parts before disassembling your vehicle. **Warning:** *Disassembling a strut is potentially dangerous and utmost attention must be directed to the job, or serious injury may result. Use only a high quality spring compressor and carefully follow the manufacturer's instructions furnished with the tool. After removing the coil spring from the strut assembly, set it aside in a safe, isolated area.*

## Disassembly

*Refer to illustrations 3.3, 3.4a, 3.4b, 3.5, 3.6 and 3.7*

2    Remove the strut and spring assembly (see Section 2).
3    Mount the strut assembly in a vise. Line the vise jaws with wood or rags to prevent damage to the unit and don't tighten the vise excessively. Following the tool manufacturer's instructions, install the spring compressor (which can be obtained at most auto parts stores or equipment yards on a daily rental basis) on the spring and compress it sufficiently to relieve all pressure from the upper spring seat **(see illustration)**. This can be verified by wiggling the spring.
4    Loosen the damper shaft nut with a socket wrench **(see illustrations)**.
5    Remove the nut and lift off the upper strut mount **(see illustration)**. Remove the spacer. Inspect the bearing in the strut mount for smooth operation. If it doesn't turn smoothly, replace the strut mount. Check the rubber portion of the strut mount for cracking and general deterioration. If there is any separation of the rubber, replace it.
6    Remove the upper spring seat **(see illustration)**, the rubber seat and the dust cover. Inspect the upper seat, the rubber seat and the dust cover for cracking and hardness. Replace all damaged parts.
7    Carefully lift the compressed spring

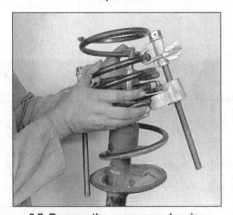

**3.7 Remove the compressed spring assembly; keep the ends of the spring pointed away from your body**

from the assembly **(see illustration)** and set it in a safe place. **Warning:** *Never place your head near the end of the spring!*
8    Slide the rubber bumper off the damper shaft. Inspect it for cracking and hardness. If it's worn or damaged, replace it.

## Reassembly

*Refer to illustration 3.10*

9    Extend the damper rod to its full length and install the rubber bumper.
10    Carefully place the coil spring onto the lower insulator, with the end of the spring resting in the lowest part of the insulator **(see illustration)**.
11    Install the dust cover, the rubber seat and the upper spring seat.
12    Install the spacer and the upper strut mount. Install a new self-locking nut and tighten it to the torque listed in this Chapter's Specifications.
13    Install the strut/coil spring assembly (see Section 2).

## 4    Stabilizer bar (front) - removal and installation

*Refer to illustrations 4.3 and 4.4*

1    If the vehicle is equipped with air suspension, make sure that the vehicle is in the

**3.10 When installing the spring, make sure the end fits into the recessed portion of the lower seat (arrow)**

normal (low) position, the height control switch is turned off, and the battery negative cable is disconnected.
2    Loosen the wheel lug nuts. Block the rear wheels, raise the front of the vehicle and place it securely on jackstands. Remove the front wheels.
3    Unbolt the stabilizer bar from the links that connect it to the control arms **(see illustration)**.

**4.3 To detach the stabilizer bar from the links, remove the upper nut and bolt (arrow); to detach the links from the control arms, remove the lower nut and bolt (arrow)**

**4.4  To detach the bushing clamps from the crossmember, remove these bolts (arrows) (right clamp shown, left clamp identical)**

**5.4a  Remove the balljoint pinch bolt (arrow) from the steering knuckle . . .**

**5.4b  . . . insert a large prybar between the control arm and the steering knuckle and lever the balljoint out of the knuckle**

**5.5a  To detach the inner end of the control arm from the crossmember, remove the pivot bolt and nut from the front . . .**

4    Remove the stabilizer bar bushing clamps **(see illustration)**.
5    Remove the stabilizer bar.
6    Remove the bushings from the stabilizer and inspect them for cracks or deterioration. Inspect the stabilizer bar for cracks in the curved portions and deformation. Replace any parts, as necessary.
7    Installation is the reverse of removal. Tighten the fasteners to the torque listed in this Chapter's Specifications.
8    Install the wheels and lug nuts and lower the vehicle.
9    Tighten the lug nuts to the torque listed in the Chapter 1 Specifications.

## 5    Control arm (front) - removal and installation

*Refer to illustrations 5.4a, 5.4b, 5.5a and 5.5b*
1    If the vehicle is equipped with air suspension, make sure that the vehicle is in the normal (low) position, the height control switch is turned off, and the battery negative cable is disconnected.
2    Loosen the wheel lug nuts, block the rear wheels, raise the front of the vehicle and place it securely on jackstands. Remove the front wheel.
3    Disconnect the stabilizer bar from the control arm (see Section 4).
4    Remove the balljoint pinch bolt from the steering knuckle, then separate the balljoint from the steering knuckle **(see illustrations)**.
5    Remove the front pivot bolt and nut and the rear bushing clamp bolts **(see illustrations)** and remove the control arm.
6    Inspect the control arm bushings for cracks or deterioration. Inspect the control arm for cracks and deformations. Replace any damaged parts. To separate the balljoint from the control arm, refer to Section 6.
7    Installation is the reverse of removal. Tighten the balljoint pinch bolt to the torque listed in this Chapter's Specifications. Before tightening the control arm pivot bolt and bracket bolts, raise the outer end of the control arm with a floor jack to simulate normal ride height, then tighten the fasteners to the

torque listed in this Chapter's Specifications.
8    Install the wheel and lug nuts, then lower the vehicle.
9    Tighten the wheel lug nuts to the torque listed in the Chapter 1 Specifications.

**5.5b  . . . and remove the bushing bracket bolts (arrows) from the rear**

6.7  Remove the cotter pin and loosen the nut . . .

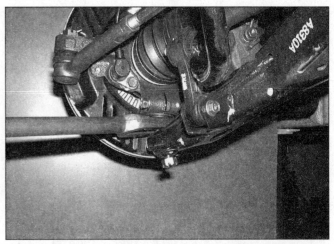

6.8  . . . then separate the balljoint from the control arm with a pickiefork-type balljoint separator

# 6   Balljoints - check and replacement

## *Check*

1    Inspect the control arm balljoints for looseness anytime either of them is separated from the control arm. See if you can turn the ballstud in its socket with your fingers. If the balljoint is loose, or if the ballstud can be turned, replace the balljoint. You can also check the balljoints with the suspension assembled as follows.

2    If the vehicle is equipped with air suspension, make sure that the vehicle is in the normal (low) position, the height control switch is turned off, and the battery negative cable is disconnected. Raise the front of the vehicle and support it securely on jackstands.

3    Wipe each balljoint clean and inspect the seal for cuts and tears. If the seal is damaged it can be replaced, but it's a good idea to go ahead and replace the balljoint.

4    Place a large prybar under the balljoint and resting on the wheel, then try to pry the balljoint up while feeling for movement between the balljoint and steering knuckle. Now, pry between the control arm and the steering knuckle and try to lever the down while feeling for movement between the balljoint and steering knuckle. If any movement is evident in either check, the balljoint is worn and should be replaced.

5    Have an assistant grasp the tire at the top and bottom and move the top of the tire in-and-out. Touch the balljoint stud castellated nut. If any looseness is felt, suspect a worn balljoint stud or a widened hole in the control arm. If the latter problem exists, the control arm should be replaced as well as the balljoint.

## *Replacement*

*Refer to illustrations 6.7, 6.8, 6.9 and 6.10*

6    If the vehicle is equipped with air suspension, make sure that the vehicle is in the normal (low) position, the height control switch is turned off, and the battery negative

6.9  Use a screwdriver to pry open the slot in the steering knuckle to facilitate removal of the balljoint from the knuckle

cable is disconnected. Loosen the wheel lug nuts. Block the rear wheels, raise the front of the vehicle and place it on jackstands. Remove the front wheel.

7    Remove the cotter pin and loosen, but don't remove, the castle nut on the ballstud **(see illustration)**.

8    Separate the control arm from the balljoint with a two-jaw puller or a picklefork-type balljoint separator **(see illustration)**. **Note:** *The use of a picklefork tool will most likely damage the balljoint boot, but it doesn't matter since the balljoint is being replaced. For all other operations requiring the control arm to be separated from the steering knuckle, the balljoint can easily be detached from the steering knuckle (see Section 5).*

9    Remove the balljoint pinch bolt from the steering knuckle **(see illustration 5.4a)** Use a large screwdriver to pry open the slot in the steering knuckle, then install the castle nut onto the end of the ballstud and use it as a handle to pull the balljoint out of the knuckle **(see illustration)**.

10    Remove the boot ring from the balljoint **(see illustration)** and remove the rubber boot.

6.10  Pry the boot ring from the balljoint with a small screwdriver

11    Inspect the boot for cracks or deterioration. Check the balljoint for rust, pitting and abnormal wear. Replace any parts, if necessary, with new ones.

12    Apply chassis grease to the balljoint and pack the inside of the rubber boot. Also apply a thin coat of grease to the part of the balljoint that fits into the steering knuckle.

13    Install the balljoint into the knuckle and tighten the pinch bolt to the torque listed in this Chapter's Specifications.

14    Reattach the control arm to the steering knuckle and tighten the castle nut to the torque listed in this Chapter's Specifications. Install a new cotter pin.

# 7   Steering knuckle/hub assembly - removal and installation

*Refer to illustration 7.4*

1    If the vehicle is equipped with air suspension, make sure that the vehicle is in the normal (low) position, the height control switch is turned off, and the battery negative cable is disconnected.

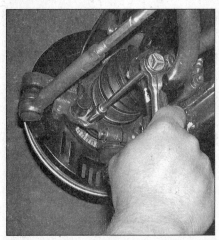

**7.4 On models with ABS, remove the ABS sensor retaining bolt and detach the sensor from the steering knuckle**

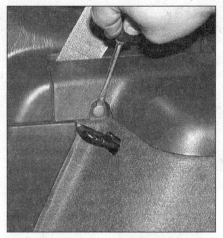

**10.2 To gain access to the upper mount of either rear strut/coil spring assembly on Wagon models, pry out this plastic retainer, then remove the trim piece (on Sedan models, you'll have to remove the seat back to get to the upper ends of the struts)**

**10.6 To detach the strut from the rear knuckle, remove these nuts and bolts (arrows)**

2    Unstake and loosen the driveaxle nut (see Chapter 8).
3    Loosen the wheel lug nuts, block the rear wheels, raise the front of the vehicle and place it securely on jackstands. Remove the front wheel.
4    Remove the brake caliper, the brake pads, the caliper support bracket and the disc (see Chapter 9). On models with ABS, remove the front wheel sensor retaining bolt, detach the sensor and set it aside **(see illustration)**.
5    Disconnect the tie-rod end from the steering knuckle (see Section 19).
6    Loosen the strut-to-steering knuckle nuts **(see illustrations 2.5a and 2.5b)**. **Note:** *Be sure to mark the relationship of the upper bolt to the strut flange to preserve the camber angle on reassembly.*
7    Remove the balljoint pinch bolt and pry the balljoint out of the steering knuckle **(see illustrations 5.4a and 5.4b)**. Now remove the strut-to-knuckle nuts and bolts.
8    Remove the driveaxle nut and pull the steering knuckle off the outer CV joint. If the hub sticks to the CV joint splines, push the stub shaft out of the hub with a two-jaw puller (see Chapter 8). **Caution:** *Be careful not to overextend the inner CV joint.*
9    While the steering knuckle is removed, have an automotive machine remove the hub and check and, if necessary, replace the front wheel bearings (they're pressed into the steering knuckle). If either CV joint boot is damaged, now is the time to replace it (see Chapter 8).
10    While the suspension is disassembled, inspect and, if necessary, replace the control arm balljoint (see Section 6).
11    Installation is the reverse of removal. Be sure to align the mark on the upper strut-to-knuckle bolt with the mark on the strut flange, and tighten all fasteners to the torque listed in this Chapter's Specifications.
12    Install the wheel and lug nuts, then lower the vehicle.
13    Tighten the lug nuts to the torque listed

in the Chapter 1 Specifications.
14    Have the front end alignment checked and, if necessary, adjusted.

## 8    Hub (front) - replacement

1    Remove the steering knuckle/hub assembly (see Section 7).
2    The front hub is pressed into the bearings, which in turn are pressed into the steering knuckle. It cannot be removed or installed at home without a hydraulic press and the right adapters.
3    Take the steering knuckle/hub assembly to an automotive machine shop and have the hub pressed out of the knuckle and a new hub pressed in.
4    Make sure that the shop inspects the seals and bearings while the hub is removed (the outer seal can only be replaced with the hub removed).
5    Install the steering knuckle/hub assembly (see Section 7).
6    Have the front end alignment checked and, if necessary, adjusted by an alignment shop.

## 9    Wheel bearings (front) - replacement

1    Remove the steering knuckle/hub (see Section 7).
2    The bearings are pressed into the steering knuckle. They cannot be removed and installed at home without a hydraulic press and the right adapters.
3    Take the steering knuckle/hub assembly to an automotive machine shop and have the hub separated from the steering knuckle, then have it inspect and, if necessary, replace

the front wheel bearings. Make sure new inner and outer seals are installed (the outer seal can only be replaced with the hub removed).
4    Install the steering knuckle/hub assembly (see Section 7).
5    Have the front alignment checked and, if necessary, adjusted by an alignment shop.

## 10    Strut/coil spring assembly (rear) - removal and installation

*Refer to illustrations 10.2, 10.6 and 10.7*
1    If the vehicle is equipped with air suspension, make sure that the vehicle is in the normal (low) position, the height control switch is turned off, and the battery negative cable is disconnected.
2    On Sedan models, remove the rear seat back (see Chapter 11). On Wagon models, remove the trim piece covering the strut upper mounting nuts **(see illustration)**.
3    Loosen the rear wheel lug nuts, block the front wheels, raise the rear of the vehicle and support it securely on jackstands. Remove the rear wheels.
4    On models with rear drum brakes, unscrew the metal brake line from the flexible brake hose at the bracket on the strut, remove the U-clip and detach the hose and line from the bracket (see Chapter 9). On models with rear disc brakes, remove the brake hose banjo bolt from the caliper and detach the hose from the bracket on the strut (see Chapter 9).
5    Place a floor jack under the rear knuckle and raise it to a point just before the jack head contacts the knuckle.
6    Remove the strut-to-knuckle nuts and bolts **(see illustration)**. If the bolts are difficult to remove, raise the jack slightly until the bolts come out easily.
7    Have an assistant support the strut, then remove the strut upper mounting nuts **(see illustration)**.

**10.7 To detach the strut from the body, remove these nuts (arrows)**

**11.2 To disconnect the rear stabilizer bar from each link, remove the upper nut and bolt; to disconnect the link from the rear control arm, remove the lower nut and bolt**

8   Installation is the reverse of removal. Use the jack to raise or lower the knuckle to align the holes in the strut bracket with the holes in the knuckle. Make sure that all fasteners are tightened to the torque listed in this Chapter's Specifications.

9   If you need to disassemble the strut/coil spring assembly in order to replace either the strut or the coil spring, refer to Section 3.

10   Repeat this procedure for the other strut/coil spring assembly.

11   Install the wheels and lug nuts, then lower the vehicle.

12   Tighten the wheel lug nuts to the torque listed in the Chapter 1 Specifications.

## 11   Stabilizer bar (rear) - removal and installation

*Refer to illustrations 11.2 and 11.3*

1   If the vehicle is equipped with air suspension, make sure that the vehicle is in the normal (low) position, the height control switch is turned off, and the battery negative cable is disconnected. Raise the rear of the vehicle and support it securely on jackstands. Block the front wheels to prevent the vehicle from rolling.

2   Remove the nuts and bolts that attach the stabilizer bar to the links **(see illustration)**.

3   Remove the stabilizer bar bushing clamp bolts **(see illustration)**.

4   Remove the stabilizer bar.

5   Inspect the rubber bushings for cracks and deterioration and replace as necessary.

6   Installation is the reverse of removal. Be sure to tighten the fasteners to the torque values listed in this Chapter's Specifications.

## 12   Trailing arm - removal and installation

*Refer to illustrations 12.4 and 12.5*

1   If the vehicle is equipped with air sus-

pension, make sure that the vehicle is in the normal (low) position, turn off the height control switch, and disconnect the battery negative cable.

2   Loosen the rear wheel lug nuts, block the front wheels, raise the rear of the vehicle and place it on jackstands. Remove the rear wheel.

3   Detach the parking brake cable from the trailing arm (see Chapter 9).

4   Remove the nut and pivot bolt that attach the forward end of the trailing arm to the trailing arm bracket **(see illustration)**.

5   Remove the nut and bolt that attaches the trailing arm to the rear knuckle **(see illustration)**.

6   Remove the trailing arm.

7   Inspect the trailing arm bushings. If they're cracked, hardened or otherwise worn, have them pressed out and new ones pressed in at an automotive machine shop.

8   Installation is the reverse of removal. After the bolts and nuts have been installed, raise the rear knuckle with a floor jack to sim-

**11.3 To detach the rear stabilizer bar from the underside of the vehicle, remove these bushing clamp bolts (arrows)**

**12.4 To detach the forward end of a trailing arm from its bracket, remove this nut and bolt (arrows)**

**12.5 To detach the rear end of the trailing arm from the rear knuckle, remove this nut and bolt (arrow)**

**13.5  To ensure that the correct toe-in is maintained, scribe or paint alignment marks on the adjuster bolt and crossmember before removing the bolt**

**13.7  To detach the rear control arms from the rear knuckle, remove this nut and bolt**

ulate normal ride height, then tighten the trailing arm bolts to the torque listed in this Chapter's Specifications.

### 13  Control arms (rear) - removal and installation

*Refer to illustrations 13.5, 13.7 and 13.8*

1    If the vehicle is equipped with air suspension, make sure that the vehicle is in the normal (low) position, turn off the height control switch, and disconnect the battery negative cable.

2    Loosen the rear wheel lug nuts, block the front wheels, raise the rear of the vehicle and place it on jackstands. Remove the rear wheel.

3    On some 2WD models, it may be necessary to remove the rear part of the exhaust system for clearance (see Chapter 4).

4    On models with ABS, detach the ABS sensor lead from the trailing arm.

5    Scribe or paint alignment marks on the rear control arm adjusting bolt and the rear crossmember **(see illustration)**.

6    Disconnect the rear stabilizer link from the rear control arm (see Section 11).

7    Remove the nut and bolt that attach the control arms to the rear knuckle **(see illustration)**.

8    Remove the nut(s) and bolt(s) which attach the inner ends of the control arms to the rear crossmember **(see illustration)**. 2WD models have one long through-bolt and a nut; 4WD models have a pair of nuts and short bolts, to allow for driveaxle clearance.

9    Inspect the control arm bushings. If they're cracked or dried out or otherwise worn, have them pressed out and new ones pressed in at an automotive machine shop.

10    Installation is the reverse of removal. Be sure to align the matchmarks on the inner pivot bolt and the crossmember. After all the

bolts and nuts have been installed, raise the rear knuckle with a floor jack to simulate normal ride height, then tighten the control arm bolts to the torque listed in this Chapter's Specifications.

11    Have the rear wheel alignment checked and, if necessary, adjusted.

### 14  Hub (rear) - removal and installation

1    If the vehicle is equipped with air suspension, make sure that the vehicle is in the normal (low) position, turn off the height control switch, and disconnect the battery negative cable.

2    On 4WD models, loosen the rear driveaxle nut (see Chapter 8).

3    Loosen the rear wheel lug nuts, block the front wheels, raise the rear of the vehicle and place it on jackstands. Remove the rear wheel.

4    On models with rear drum brakes, remove the brake drum (see Chapter 9).

5    On models with rear disc brakes, remove the caliper and hang it out of the way with a piece of wire, remove the caliper support bracket and the brake disc (see Chapter 9).

#### *2WD models*

*Refer to illustration 14.6*

6    Remove the grease cap **(see illustration)**.

7    Unstake the hub retaining nut and remove the nut and washer. Discard the nut and obtain a new nut for reassembly.

8    Remove the hub and bearing assembly.

9    Wipe off and inspect the spindle bearing surface for scoring or other damage. If it's worn or damaged, replace the rear knuckle.

10    Installation is the reverse of removal. Be sure to lubricate the spindle with wheel bear-

ing grease before installing the hub and bearing assembly. Tighten the hub and bearing retaining nut to the torque listed in this Chapter's Specifications and stake the nut.

#### *4WD models*

11    Remove the rear knuckle (see Section 15).

12    The rear hub is pressed into the bearings, which in turn are pressed into the rear knuckle. It cannot be removed or installed at home without a hydraulic press and the right adapters.

13    Take the rear knuckle to an automotive machine shop and have the hub pressed out of the knuckle and a new hub pressed in.

14    Make sure that the shop inspects the seals and bearings while the hub is removed (the outer seal can only be replaced with the hub removed).

15    Install the rear knuckle (see Section 15).

**13.8 To detach the rear control arms from the crossmember, remove these two pairs of nuts and bolts (4WD model shown; 2WD models have one long bolt instead of two short ones)**

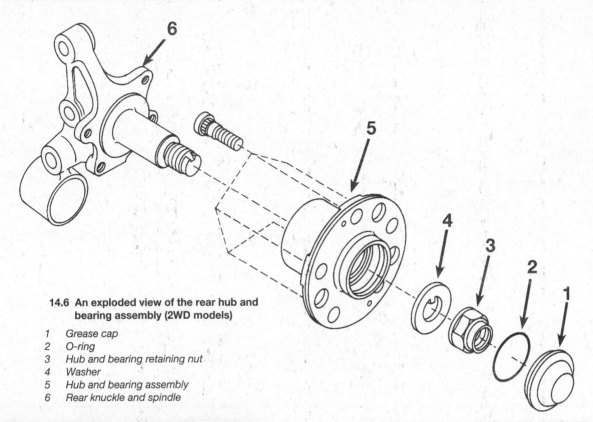

**14.6  An exploded view of the rear hub and bearing assembly (2WD models)**

1   Grease cap
2   O-ring
3   Hub and bearing retaining nut
4   Washer
5   Hub and bearing assembly
6   Rear knuckle and spindle

**15.6  If the vehicle is equipped with ABS, be sure to remove the retaining bolt for the rear wheel speed sensor, detach the sensor from the backing plate and set it aside**

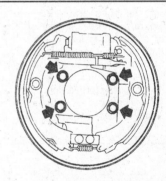

**15.8  To detach the brake backing plate from the rear knuckle, remove these four bolts (arrows) (backing plate for rear drum brake model shown; bolt pattern identical for rear disc brake models)**

## 15  Rear knuckle/hub assembly - removal and installation

*Refer to illustrations 15.6 and 15.8*

1   If the vehicle is equipped with air suspension, make sure that the vehicle is in the normal (low) position, turn off the height control switch, and disconnect the battery negative cable.
2   On 4WD models, loosen the rear driveaxle nut (see Chapter 8).
3   Loosen the rear wheel lug nuts, block the front wheels, raise the rear of the vehicle and place it on jackstands. Remove the rear wheel.
4   On models with rear drum brakes, remove the brake drum and the brake shoe assembly, disconnect the brake line from the

wheel cylinder and remove the wheel cylinder (see Chapter 9).
5   On models with rear disc brakes, remove the caliper and hang it out of the way with a piece of wire, remove the caliper support bracket, the brake disc and the parking brake assembly (see Chapter 9).
6   Detach the parking brake cable from the backing plate (see Chapter 9). On models with ABS, detach the rear wheel speed sensor from the backing plate **(see illustration)**.
7   On 2WD models, pry off the grease cap, loosen and remove the rear hub nut, remove the washer and remove the rear hub (see Section 14).
8   Remove the four brake backing plate bolts **(see illustration)** and remove the backing plate.
9   Disconnect the trailing arm from the rear

knuckle **(see illustration 12.5)**.
10   Disconnect the control arms from the rear knuckle **(see illustration 13.7)**.
11   Disconnect the rear knuckle from the rear strut/coil spring assembly **(see illustration 10.6)**.
12   Remove the rear knuckle. On 4WD models, remove the rear driveaxle nut and pull the rear knuckle and hub off the splined spindle of the outer CV joint; if the spindle is "frozen" in the splines of the hub, apply penetrating oil, wait a while, then use a puller to force the hub off the spindle.
13   If you need to remove the hub from the rear knuckle on a 4WD model, refer to Section 14. If the bearings are in need of replacement, refer to Section 16.

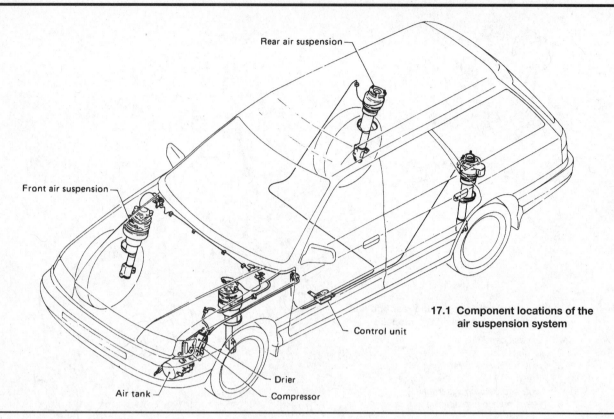

**17.1 Component locations of the air suspension system**

15   Installation is the reverse of removal. After all the bolts and nuts have been installed, raise the rear knuckle with a floor jack to simulate normal ride height, then tighten the control arm bolts and trailing arm bolts to the torque values listed in this Chapter's Specifications. Tighten the rear driveaxle nut to the torque listed in the Chapter 8 Specifications. On models with rear drum brakes, bleed the brakes (see Chapter 9).

### 16  Wheel bearings (rear) - replacement

**Note:** *This procedure applies to 4WD models only. On 2WD models, the wheel bearings are inside the hub; rear hub removal for 2WD models is in Section 14.*

1   Remove the rear knuckle (see Section 14).
2   The bearings are pressed into the rear knuckle. They cannot be removed and installed without a hydraulic press and the right adapters.
3   Take the rear knuckle/hub assembly to an automotive machine shop to have the hub separated from the rear knuckle and the wheel bearings replaced. Make sure new seals are installed (the outer seal can only be replaced with the hub removed).
4   Install the rear knuckle/hub assembly (see Section 15).

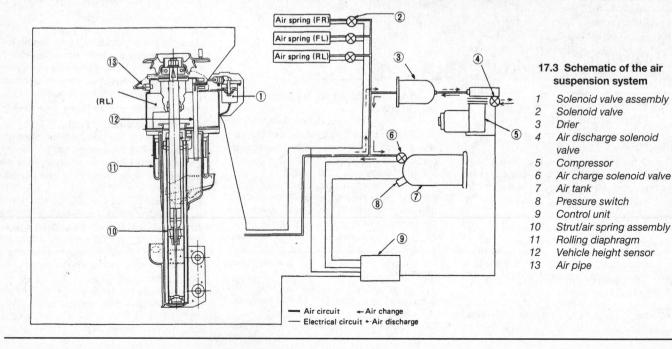

**17.3 Schematic of the air suspension system**

1   Solenoid valve assembly
2   Solenoid valve
3   Drier
4   Air discharge solenoid valve
5   Compressor
6   Air charge solenoid valve
7   Air tank
8   Pressure switch
9   Control unit
10   Strut/air spring assembly
11   Rolling diaphragm
12   Vehicle height sensor
13   Air pipe

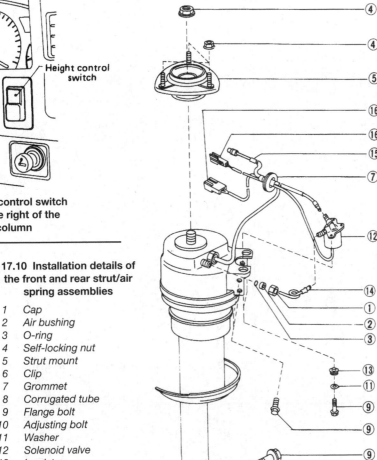

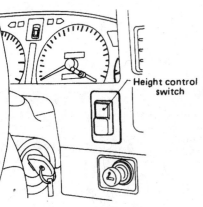

**17.5  The height control switch is located to the right of the steering column**

**17.10  Installation details of the front and rear strut/air spring assemblies**

1.  Cap
2.  Air bushing
3.  O-ring
4.  Self-locking nut
5.  Strut mount
6.  Clip
7.  Grommet
8.  Corrugated tube
9.  Flange bolt
10. Adjusting bolt
11. Washer
12. Solenoid valve
13. Insulator
14. Air pipe for solenoid valve
15. Air pipe
16. Connector

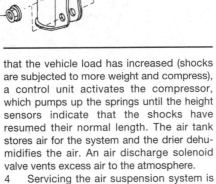

## 17  Air suspension system - general information and component replacement

### General information

*Refer to illustrations 17.1, 17.3 and 17.5*

1   Some models are equipped with an air suspension system **(see illustration)** which controls vehicle ground clearance. A height control switch allows selection of either of two levels of ground clearance - Normal or High. The difference in height between high and normal is 1.57 inches.

2   The system also maintains a constant ground clearance by altering the clearance in response to vehicle load. This is accomplished by altering the air volume in each air spring in response to a signal from a vehicle height sensor installed in each spring.

3   The system **(see illustration)** consists of four strut/air spring assemblies, an air compressor, an air tank, a drier and the air lines connecting these components. When the height sensors inside each shock indicate

that the vehicle load has increased (shocks are subjected to more weight and compress), a control unit activates the compressor, which pumps up the springs until the height sensors indicate that the shocks have resumed their normal length. The air tank stores air for the system and the drier dehumidifies the air. An air discharge solenoid valve vents excess air to the atmosphere.

4   Servicing the air suspension system is generally beyond the scope of the home mechanic. However, there are a few procedures that can be done at home, such as replacing the front struts, rear shocks, or the compressor or drier.

5   When working on any part of the suspension system, make sure that the vehicle is in the normal (low) position, the height control switch on the dash **(see illustration)** is turned off, and the battery negative cable is disconnected.

6   When installing components, do not reuse old O-rings. Apply grease to all O-rings and make sure you don't damage the grooves for the O-rings.

7   Do not apply an undercoating to the shock/spring assemblies or to the air compressor. When the shock oil temperature increases, it generates heat, which melts the undercoating, which may trap dust, dirt and sand between the rolling diaphragm and the surface of the shock body on which it rolls up and down as it's inflated and deflated, resulting in a damaged diaphragm. Undercoating on the air inlet of the compressor can block the vent.

### Component replacement
#### Front strut/air spring assembly

*Refer to illustration 17.10*

8   Make sure that the vehicle is in the normal (low) position, the height control switch is turned off, and the battery negative cable is disconnected.

9   Block the rear wheels. Loosen the front wheel lug nuts, raise the front of the vehicle and support it securely on jackstands. Remove the front wheels.

10  Disconnect the air pipes **(see illustration)**.

11  Unplug the electrical connector for the vehicle height sensor harness.

12  The rest of the procedure is similar to removing a conventional strut assembly (see Section 2).

13  Installation is the reverse of removal.

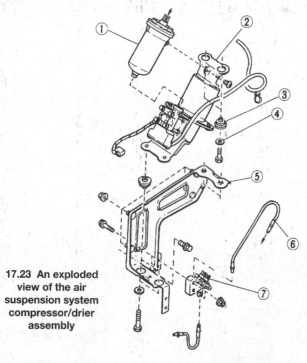

**17.23 An exploded view of the air suspension system compressor/drier assembly**

| | | | |
|---|---|---|---|
| 1 | Drier | 5 | Compressor bracket |
| 2 | Compressor | 6 | Compressor pipe |
| 3 | Insulator | 7 | Manifold assembly |
| 4 | Washer | | |

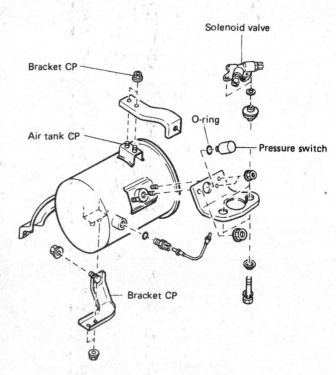

**17.28 Mounting details of the air suspension system air tank**

## Rear strut/air spring assembly

14   Make sure that the vehicle is in the normal (low) position, the height control switch is turned off, and the battery negative cable is disconnected.

15   Put the transaxle in gear and block the front wheels. Loosen the rear wheel lug nuts, raise the rear of the vehicle and support it securely on jackstands. Remove the rear wheels.

16   Remove the solenoid valve from the rear air suspension assembly **(see illustration 17.10)**. If you're going to replace the solenoid valve, disconnect the air pipe from the solenoid valve.

17   Pull out the vehicle height sensor harness from the access hole in the shock body and unplug the harness electrical connector.

18   The rest of the procedure is similar to removing a conventional strut/coil spring assembly (see Section 10).

19   Installation is the reverse of removal.

## Compressor and drier assembly

*Refer to illustration 17.23*

20   Make sure that the vehicle is in the normal (low) position, the height control switch is turned off, and the battery negative cable is disconnected.

21   Apply the parking brake. Loosen the left front wheel lug nuts. Raise the front of the vehicle and support it securely on jackstands. Remove the left front wheel.

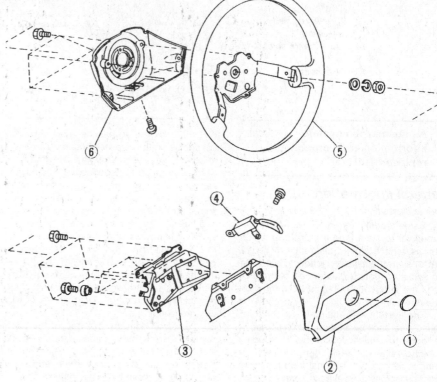

**18.2a Typical steering wheel details (earlier model without an airbag)**

| | | | |
|---|---|---|---|
| 1 | Ornament | 4 | Cruise control sub-switch |
| 2 | Horn pad | 5 | Steering wheel |
| 3 | Sub-switch contact sheet | 6 | Lower cover |

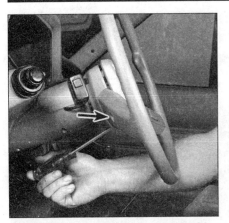

**18.2b  On models without a driver's side airbag module, remove the horn pad retaining screws . . .**

**18.2c  . . . grasp the horn pad and pull it off**

**18.3a  On airbag-equipped models, remove the airbag module Torx retaining bolts from the holes in the sides of the steering wheel . . .**

22  Remove the front half of the mud guard (see Section 13 in Chapter 11).
23  Disconnect the air pipes from the drier **(see illustration)**.
24  Remove the couplers.
25  Remove the compressor and drier mounting bolts and nuts and remove the compressor and drier.
26  Installation is the reverse of removal.

**18.3b  . . . lift off the airbag module . . .**

### Air tank assembly

*Refer to illustration 17.28*
27  Make sure that the vehicle is in the normal (low) position, the height control switch is turned off, and the battery negative cable is disconnected.
28  Detach the air pipe from the solenoid valve, then remove the solenoid valve coupler **(see illustration)**.
29  Remove the mounting nuts and bolts and detach the air tank assembly.
30  Installation is the reverse of removal.

## 18  Steering wheel - removal and installation

*Refer to illustrations 18.2a, 18.2b, 18.2c, 18.3a, 18.3b, 18.3c, 18.4, 18.5, 18.6a and 18.6b*
**Warning:** *Some models covered by this manual are equipped with Supplemental Restraint Systems (SRS), more commonly known as airbags. Always disconnect the negative battery cable and wait for at least one minute before working in the vicinity of the impact sensors, steering column or instrument panel to avoid the possibility of accidental deployment of the airbag, which could cause injury.*

*Do not use electrical test equipment on any of the airbag system wiring or tamper with them in any way. The steering shaft must not be rotated while the steering wheel is removed; to do so could damage the airbag roll connector assembly. See Chapter 12 for more information on the airbag system.*
1  Turn the steering wheel so the front wheels are pointing straight ahead, turn the ignition switch to Off, disconnect the cable from the negative terminal of the battery and, on models equipped with an airbag, wait for at least one minute before proceeding (the system has a back-up capacitor which must fully discharge).
2  On models without a driver's side airbag, remove the horn pad retaining screws, then pull off the horn pad **(see illustrations)**.
3  On models with a driver's side airbag, remove the bolts attaching the airbag module to the steering wheel, lift off the airbag module and unplug the electrical connectors for the airbag and horn **(see illustrations)**.
**Warning:** *When carrying the airbag module, keep the trim side of it away from your body, and when you place it on the bench, have the trim side facing up.*
4  Remove the steering wheel-to-steering shaft nut **(see illustration)**.

**18.3c  . . . and unplug the electrical connectors for the airbag module and for the horn**

**18.4  Remove the steering wheel retaining nut**

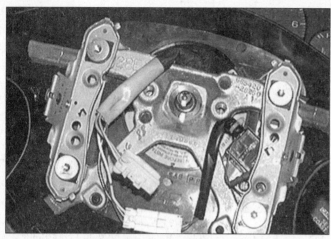

**18.5  Mark the relationship of the steering wheel to the steering shaft**

**18.6a  If the vehicle is equipped with cruise control, unplug the electrical connectors for the cruise control system**

**18.6b  If the steering wheel doesn't come right off the shaft, install a steering wheel puller to separate the wheel from the shaft**

**19.3a  Loosen and back off the jam nut from the tie-rod end . . .**

5     Mark the relationship of the steering wheel to the steering shaft **(see illustration)**.
6     Unplug the electrical connectors for the cruise control system, if equipped **(see illustration)**, then remove the steering wheel from the steering shaft. If the steering wheel is difficult to remove, install a steering wheel puller to separate the wheel from the shaft **(see**

**19.3b  . . . and mark the position of the tie-rod end on the tie-rod**

**illustration)**. **Warning:** *Once the steering wheel has been removed on an airbag-equipped vehicle, make sure that the steering shaft is not turned. If it is, the roll connector must be re-centered before installing the steering wheel, or the airbag system may be damaged and be rendered inoperative. If the steering shaft is turned, refer to Section 26 in Chapter 12 for the roll connector re-centering procedure.*

7     Installation is the reverse of removal. Be sure to align the mark on the steering wheel hub with the mark on the steering shaft, and tighten the steering wheel nut to the torque listed in this Chapter's Specifications.

## 19  Tie-rod ends - removal and installation

*Refer to illustrations 19.3a, 19.3b, 19.4, 19.5 and 19.7*

1     If the vehicle is equipped with air suspension, make sure that the vehicle is in the normal (low) position, the height control switch is turned off, and the battery negative cable is disconnected.

2     Loosen the wheel lug nuts. Block the rear wheels. Raise the front of the vehicle and support it securely. Remove the front wheel.
3     Loosen the jam nut enough to mark the position of the tie-rod end in relation to the threads **(see illustrations)**.
4     Remove the cotter pin and loosen - but don't remove - the nut on the tie-rod end stud **(see illustration)**.
5     Disconnect the tie-rod end from the steering knuckle with a puller **(see illustration)**. Remove the nut and separate the tie-rod end from the steering knuckle.
6     Unscrew the tie-rod end from the tie-rod.
7     If you're planning to install the old tie-rod end, you should inspect the tie-rod end boot for cracks or tears. If it's damaged, simply remove the boot ring **(see illustration)**, slide off the old boot, wipe off the balljoint with a clean rag, lubricate it with chassis grease, slide on a new boot and install the boot ring.
8     Thread the tie-rod end on to the marked position and insert the tie-rod end stud into the steering knuckle. Tighten the jam nut securely.

**19.4  Remove the cotter pin from the castellated nut and loosen - but don't remove - the nut**

**19.5  Install a suitable small puller or tie-rod removal tool such as the one shown to force the tie-rod end ballstud out of the steering knuckle**

**19.7  To replace the old boot on the tie-rod end, remove the boot retaining ring**

9    Install the nut on the stud and tighten it to the torque listed in this Chapter's Specifications. Install a new cotter pin.
10   Install the wheel and lug nuts. Lower the vehicle and tighten the wheel lug nuts to the torque listed in the Chapter 1 Specifications.
11   Have the alignment checked and, if necessary, adjusted.

## 20   Steering gear boots - replacement

*Refer to illustrations 20.4a and 20.4b*
1    If the vehicle is equipped with air suspension, make sure that the vehicle is in the normal (low) position, the height control switch is turned off, and the battery negative cable is disconnected.
2    Loosen the front wheel lug nuts, raise the vehicle and support it securely on jackstands. Remove the wheel.
3    Remove the tie-rod end (see Section 19).
4    Remove the steering gear boot clamps **(see illustrations)** and slide off the boot.
5    Before installing the new boot, wrap the threads and serrations on the end of the tie-rod with a layer of tape so the small end of the new boot isn't damaged.
6    Slide the new boot into position on the steering gear until it seats in the groove in the steering gear and install new clamps.
7    Remove the tape from the tie-rod and install the tie-rod end (see Section 19).
8    Install the wheel and lug nuts. Lower the

vehicle and tighten the lug nuts to the torque listed in the Chapter 1 Specifications.
9    Have the alignment checked and, if necessary, adjusted.

## 21   Steering gear - removal and installation

*Refer to illustrations 21.5, 21.7 and 21.8*
**Warning 1:** *Some models covered by this manual are equipped with airbags. Always disconnect the negative battery cable and wait at least one minute before working in the vicinity of the impact sensors, steering column or instrument panel to avoid the possibility of accidental deployment of the airbag, which could cause personal injury (see Chapter 12)*
**Warning 2:** *On models equipped with airbags, DO NOT allow the steering column shaft to rotate with the steering gear removed or damage to the airbag roll connector may occur. To prevent the steering column from turning, place the ignition switch in the Lock position and remove the key.*

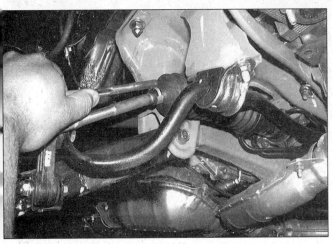

**20.4a  To detach a boot from the steering gear, remove the outer boot retaining clamp . . .**

**20.4b  . . . and the inner retaining wire**

21.5  To remove the jacking plate, remove these bolts (center arrows); to detach the steering gear, remove the four clamp bolts (outer arrows)

21.7  Disconnect the power steering lines (arrows) from the steering gear lines at the right (passenger's) side of the steering gear. Note: *Access may be easier from the engine compartment*

21.8  Mark the relationship of the steering shaft U-joint to the steering gear input shaft, then remove the pinch bolt (arrow)

22.2  To remove the cover bracket for the power steering pump pulley belt, remove these two bolts and the nut (arrows)

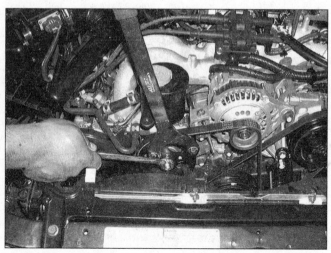

22.3  To loosen the power steering pump pulley retaining nut, you'll need to immobilize the pulley with a pin spanner tool

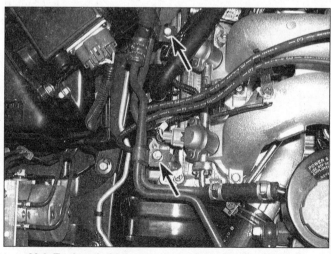

22.6  To detach the two power steering fluid line clamps, remove these bolts (arrows)

**22.7 Disconnect the power steering fluid lines from the power steering pump and from the reservoir**

**22.8 To detach the power steering pump from its mounting bracket, remove these three bolts (arrows)**

1    If the vehicle is equipped with air suspension, make sure that the vehicle is in the normal (low) position, the height control switch is turned off, and the battery negative cable is disconnected.

2    Loosen the wheel lug nuts. Block the rear wheels, raise the front of the vehicle and place it securely on jackstands. Remove the front wheels.

3    Disconnect the tie-rod ends from the steering knuckles (see Section 19).

4    Remove the front exhaust pipes, if necessary (see Chapter 4).

5    Remove the jacking plate **(see illustration)**.

6    Remove the stabilizer bar (see Section 4).

7    Disconnect the power steering fluid lines from the steering gear **(see illustration)**.

8    Mark the relationship of the U-joint, if equipped, that connects the steering shaft to the steering gear input shaft **(see illustration)**.

9    Remove the steering shaft U-joint pinch bolt **(see illustration 21.8)**.

10    Remove the steering gear mounting bolts **(see illustration 21.5)** and remove the steering gear from the passenger's side of the vehicle. **Warning:** *On models equipped with airbags, DO NOT allow the steering column shaft to rotate with the steering gear removed.*

11    Installation is the reverse of removal. Be sure to align the mark on the U-joint with the mark on the shaft, and tighten the steering gear mounting bolts, the U-joint pinch bolt, and the tie-rod end-to-steering knuckle nuts to the torque values listed in this Chapter's Specifications.

11    Install the wheels and lug nuts. Lower the vehicle and tighten the lug nuts to the torque listed in this Chapter's Specifications.

12    Fill the steering system with the recommended fluid and then check for leaks (see Chapter 1). Bleed the system (see Section 25).

13    Have the wheel alignment checked and, if necessary, adjusted.

## 22  Power steering pump - removal and installation

*Refer to illustrations 22.2, 22.3, 22.6, 22.7, 22.8 and 22.10*

1    Using a syringe, remove the power steering fluid from the power steering pump reservoir.

2    Remove the cover bracket for the power steering pump pulley **(see illustration)**.

3    Loosen the power steering pump pulley retaining nut **(see illustration)**.

4    Remove the alternator/power steering pump drivebelt (see Chapter 1).

5    Remove the power steering pump pulley nut.

6    Detach the power steering fluid line clamps **(see illustration)**.

7    Disconnect the power steering fluid lines from the power steering pump and from the fluid reservoir **(see illustration)**.

8    Remove the three bolts from the front of the power steering pump **(see illustration)** and remove the pump.

9    The power steering pump bracket doesn't need to be removed, but if you wish to do so, it's bolted to the engine by three bolts.

10    If you haven't yet removed the reservoir from the power steering pump, do so now. Put the pump in a bench vise and remove the two bolts that secure the reservoir to the pump **(see illustration)**. Protect the pump by placing wood or plastic jaw liners between the vise and the pump. Don't over tighten the vise! The pump can be easily distorted.

11    Installation is the reverse of removal. Be sure to tighten all fasteners securely. Refer to Chapter 1 to adjust the drivebelt tension.

12    Install new power steering fluid and check for any leaks in the system (see Chapter 1). Tighten the fittings if necessary. Bleed the power steering system (see Section 23).

## 23  Power steering system - bleeding

1    Check the fluid level and add fluid as necessary (see Chapter 1).

2    If the vehicle is equipped with air suspension, make sure that the vehicle is in the normal (low) position, the height control switch is turned off, and the battery negative cable is disconnected.

3    Raise and support the front of the vehicle with jackstands.

4    Slowly turn the steering wheel from lock-to-lock two or three times and recheck the fluid level.

5    Lower the vehicle and reconnect the negative battery cable. Start the engine and let it idle. Slowly turn the steering wheel from lock-to-lock again (two or three times) and recheck the fluid level one more time. **Caution:** *Don't hold the steering wheel against the stops.*

6    Recheck the fluid level. Position the wheels in the straight-ahead position.

7    Bleeding is complete if no groaning noise is heard when the engine is running or the steering wheel is turned, and if no foaming is observed after the engine is stopped.

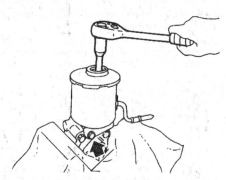

**22.10 To detach the reservoir from the power steering pump, remove the bolt at the base of the reservoir (arrow) and the other one inside the reservoir**

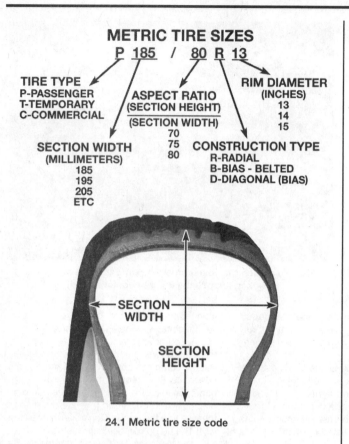

**24.1 Metric tire size code**

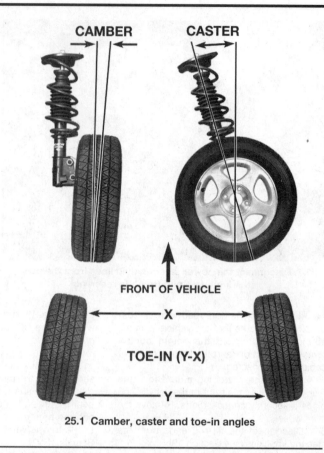

**25.1 Camber, caster and toe-in angles**

## 24   Wheels and tires - general information

*Refer to illustration 24.1*

All models covered by this manual are equipped with metric-sized radial tires **(see illustration)**. Use of other size or type of tires may affect the ride and handling of the vehicle. Don't mix different types of tires, such as radials and bias belted, on the same vehicle as handling may be seriously affected. It's recommended that tires be replaced in pairs on the same axle, but if only one tire is being replaced, be sure it's the same size, structure and tread design as the other.

Because tire pressure has a substantial effect on handling and wear, the pressure on all tires should be checked at least once a month or before any extended trips (see Chapter 1).

Wheels must be replaced if they are bent, dented, leak air, have elongated bolt holes, are heavily rusted, out of vertical symmetry or if the lug nuts won't stay tight. Wheel repairs that use welding or peening are not recommended.

Tire and wheel balance is important to the overall handling, braking and performance of the vehicle. Unbalanced wheels can adversely affect handling and ride characteristics as well as tire life. Whenever a tire is installed on a wheel, the tire and wheel should be balanced by a shop with the proper equipment.

## 25   Wheel alignment - general information

*Refer to illustration 25.1*

A wheel alignment refers to the adjustments made to the wheels so they are in proper angular relationship to the suspension and the ground. Wheels that are out of proper alignment not only affect vehicle control, but also increase tire wear. The alignment angles normally measured are camber, caster and toe-in **(see illustration)**. Toe-in and camber on the front, and toe-in on the rear are the only adjustable angles on these vehicles. The other angles should be measured to check for bent or worn suspension parts.

Wheel alignment is a very exacting process, one in which complicated and expensive machines are necessary to perform the job properly. You should have a technician with the proper equipment perform these tasks. We will, however, use this space to give you a basic idea of what is involved with a wheel alignment so you can better understand the process and deal intelligently with the shop that does the work.

Toe-in is the turning in of the wheels. The purpose of a toe specification is to ensure parallel rolling of the wheels. In a vehicle with zero toe-in, the distance between the front edges of the wheels will be the same as the distance between the rear edges of the wheels. The actual amount of toe-in is normally only a fraction of an inch. On the front end, toe-in is controlled by the tie-rod end position on the tie-rod. On the rear end, it's controlled by a cam bolt on the inner end of the rearmost control arm. Incorrect toe-in will cause the tires to wear improperly by making them scrub against the road surface.

Camber is the tilting of the wheels from vertical when viewed from one end of the vehicle. When the wheels tilt out at the top, the camber is said to be positive (+). When the wheels tilt in at the top the camber is negative (-). The amount of tilt is measured in degrees from vertical and this measurement is called the camber angle. This angle affects the amount of tire tread which contacts the road and compensates for changes in the suspension geometry when the vehicle is cornering or traveling over an undulating surface. On the front end, camber is adjusted by a cam bolt ( the upper strut-to-knuckle bolt). Rear camber is not adjustable.

Caster is the tilting of the front steering axis from the vertical. A tilt toward the rear is positive caster and a tilt toward the front is negative caster.

# Chapter 11   Body

## Contents

## 1   General information

These models feature a "unibody" construction, using a floor pan with front and rear frame side rails which support the body components, front and rear suspension systems and other mechanical components. Certain components are particularly vulnerable to accident damage and can be unbolted and repaired or replaced. Among these parts are the body moldings, front fenders, bumpers, hood, doors, trunk lid and all glass.

Only general body maintenance practices and body panel repair procedures within the scope of the do-it-yourselfer are included in this Chapter.

## 2   Body - maintenance

1   The condition of your vehicle's body is very important, because the resale value depends a great deal on it. It's much more difficult to repair a neglected or damaged body than it is to repair mechanical components. The hidden areas of the body, such as the wheel wells, the frame and the engine compartment, are equally important, although they don't require as frequent attention as the rest of the body.
2   Once a year, or every 12,000 miles, it's a good idea to have the underside of the body steam cleaned. All traces of dirt and oil will be removed and the area can then be inspected

carefully for rust, damaged brake lines, frayed electrical wires, damaged cables and other problems. The front suspension components should be greased after completion of this job.
3   At the same time, clean the engine and the engine compartment with a steam cleaner or water-soluble degreaser.
4   The wheel wells should be given close attention, since undercoating can peel away and stones and dirt thrown up by the tires can cause the paint to chip and flake, allowing rust to set in. If rust is found, clean down to the bare metal and apply an anti-rust paint.
5   The body should be washed about once a week. Wet the vehicle thoroughly to soften the dirt, then wash it down with a soft sponge

and plenty of clean soapy water. If the surplus dirt is not washed off very carefully, it can wear down the paint.

6    Spots of tar or asphalt thrown up from the road should be removed with a cloth soaked in solvent.

7    Once every six months, wax the body and chrome trim. If a chrome cleaner is used to remove rust from any of the vehicle's plated parts, remember that the cleaner also removes part of the chrome, so use it sparingly.

## 3    Vinyl trim - maintenance

Don't clean vinyl trim with detergents, caustic soap or petroleum-based cleaners. Plain soap and water works just fine, with a soft brush to clean dirt that may be ingrained. Wash the vinyl as frequently as the rest of the vehicle. After cleaning, application of a high-quality rubber and vinyl protectant will help prevent oxidation and cracks. The protectant can also be applied to weatherstripping, vacuum lines and rubber hoses, which often fail as a result of chemical degradation, and to the tires.

## 4    Upholstery and carpets - maintenance

1    Every three months remove the floor mats and clean the interior of the vehicle (more frequently if necessary). Use a stiff whisk broom to brush the carpeting and loosen dirt and dust, then vacuum the upholstery and carpets thoroughly, especially along seams and crevices.

2    Dirt and stains can be removed from carpeting with basic household or automotive carpet shampoos available in spray cans. Follow the directions and vacuum again, then use a stiff brush to bring back the "nap" of the carpet.

3    Most interiors have cloth or vinyl upholstery, either of which can be cleaned and maintained with a number of material-specific cleaners or shampoos available in auto supply stores. Follow the directions on the product for usage, and always spot-test any upholstery cleaner on an inconspicuous area (bottom edge of a back seat cushion) to ensure that it doesn't cause a color shift in the material.

4    After cleaning, vinyl upholstery should be treated with a protectant. **Note:** *Make sure the protectant container indicates the product can be used on seats - some products may make a seat too slippery.* **Caution:** *Do not use protectant on vinyl-covered steering wheels.*

5    Leather upholstery requires special care. It should be cleaned regularly with saddlesoap or leather cleaner. Never use alcohol, gasoline, nail polish remover or thinner to clean leather upholstery.

6    After cleaning, regularly treat leather upholstery with a leather conditioner, rubbed in with a soft cotton cloth. Never use car wax on leather upholstery.

7    In areas where the interior of the vehicle is subject to bright sunlight, cover leather seating areas of the seats with a sheet if the vehicle is to be left out for any length of time.

## 5    Body repair - minor damage

### *Repair of scratches*

1    If the scratch is superficial and does not penetrate to the metal of the body, repair is very simple. Lightly rub the scratched area with a fine rubbing compound to remove loose paint and built-up wax. Rinse the area with clean water.

2    Apply touch-up paint to the scratch, using a small brush. Continue to apply thin layers of paint until the surface of the paint in the scratch is level with the surrounding paint. Allow the new paint at least two weeks to harden, then blend it into the surrounding paint by rubbing with a very fine rubbing compound. Finally, apply a coat of wax to the scratch area.

3    If the scratch has penetrated the paint and exposed the metal of the body, causing the metal to rust, a different repair technique is required. Remove all loose rust from the bottom of the scratch with a pocket knife, then apply rust inhibiting paint to prevent the formation of rust in the future. Using a rubber or nylon applicator, coat the scratched area with glaze-type filler. If required, the filler can be mixed with thinner to provide a very thin paste, which is ideal for filling narrow scratches. Before the glaze filler in the scratch hardens, wrap a piece of smooth cotton cloth around the tip of a finger. Dip the cloth in thinner and then quickly wipe it along the surface of the scratch. This will ensure that the surface of the filler is slightly hollow. The scratch can now be painted over as described earlier in this Section.

### *Repair of dents*

*See photo sequence*

4    When repairing dents, the first job is to pull the dent out until the affected area is as close as possible to its original shape. There is no point in trying to restore the original shape completely as the metal in the damaged area will have stretched on impact and cannot be restored to its original contours. It is better to bring the level of the dent up to a point which is about 1/8-inch below the level of the surrounding metal. In cases where the dent is very shallow, it is not worth trying to pull it out at all.

5    If the back side of the dent is accessible, it can be hammered out gently from behind using a soft-face hammer. While doing this, hold a block of wood firmly against the opposite side of the metal to absorb the hammer blows and prevent the metal from being stretched.

6    If the dent is in a section of the body which has double layers, or some other factor makes it inaccessible from behind, a different technique is required. Drill several small holes

through the metal inside the damaged area, particularly in the deeper sections. Screw long, self tapping screws into the holes just enough for them to get a good grip in the metal. Now the dent can be pulled out by pulling on the protruding heads of the screws with locking pliers.

7    The next stage of repair is the removal of paint from the damaged area and from an inch or so of the surrounding metal. This is easily done with a wire brush or sanding disk in a drill motor, although it can be done just as effectively by hand with sandpaper. To complete the preparation for filling, score the surface of the bare metal with a screwdriver or the tang of a file or drill small holes in the affected area. This will provide a good grip for the filler material. To complete the repair, see the Section on *filling and painting*.

### *Repair of rust holes or gashes*

8    Remove all paint from the affected area and from an inch or so of the surrounding metal using a sanding disk or wire brush mounted in a drill motor. If these are not available, a few sheets of sandpaper will do the job just as effectively.

9    With the paint removed, you will be able to determine the severity of the corrosion and decide whether to replace the whole panel, if possible, or repair the affected area. New body panels are not as expensive as most people think and it is often quicker to install a new panel than to repair large areas of rust.

10   Remove all trim pieces from the affected area except those which will act as a guide to the original shape of the damaged body, such as headlight shells, etc. Using metal snips or a hacksaw blade, remove all loose metal and any other metal that is badly affected by rust. Hammer the edges of the hole on the inside to create a slight depression for the filler material.

11   Wire brush the affected area to remove the powdery rust from the surface of the metal. If the back of the rusted area is accessible, treat it with rust inhibiting paint.

12   Before filling is done, block the hole in some way. This can be done with sheet metal riveted or screwed into place, or by stuffing the hole with wire mesh.

13   Once the hole is blocked off, the affected area can be filled and painted. See the following subsection on *filling and painting*.

### *Filling and painting*

14   Many types of body fillers are available, but generally speaking, body repair kits which contain filler paste and a tube of resin hardener are best for this type of repair work. A wide, flexible plastic or nylon applicator will be necessary for imparting a smooth and contoured finish to the surface of the filler material. Mix up a small amount of filler on a clean piece of wood or cardboard (use the hardener sparingly). Follow the manufacturer's instructions on the package, otherwise the filler will set incorrectly.

15   Using the applicator, apply the filler paste to the prepared area. Draw the applicator across the surface of the filler to achieve

the desired contour and to level the filler surface. As soon as a contour that approximates the original one is achieved, stop working the paste. If you continue, the paste will begin to stick to the applicator. Continue to add thin layers of paste at 20-minute intervals until the level of the filler is just above the surrounding metal.

16    Once the filler has hardened, the excess can be removed with a body file. From then on, progressively finer grades of sandpaper should be used, starting with a 180-grit paper and finishing with 600-grit wet-or-dry paper. Always wrap the sandpaper around a flat rubber or wooden block, otherwise the surface of the filler will not be completely flat. During the sanding of the filler surface, the wet-or-dry paper should be periodically rinsed in water. This will ensure that a very smooth finish is produced in the final stage.

17    At this point, the repair area should be surrounded by a ring of bare metal, which in turn should be encircled by the finely feathered edge of good paint. Rinse the repair area with clean water until all of the dust produced by the sanding operation is gone.

18    Spray the entire area with a light coat of primer. This will reveal any imperfections in the surface of the filler. Repair the imperfections with fresh filler paste or glaze filler and once more smooth the surface with sandpaper. Repeat this spray-and-repair procedure until you are satisfied that the surface of the filler and the feathered edge of the paint are perfect. Rinse the area with clean water and allow it to dry completely.

19    The repair area is now ready for painting. Spray painting must be carried out in a warm, dry, windless and dust free atmosphere. These conditions can be created if you have access to a large indoor work area, but if you are forced to work in the open, you will have to pick the day very carefully. If you are working indoors, dousing the floor in the work area with water will help settle the dust which would otherwise be in the air. If the repair area is confined to one body panel, mask off the surrounding panels. This will help minimize the effects of a slight mismatch in paint color. Trim pieces such as chrome strips, door handles, etc., will also need to be masked off or removed. Use masking tape and several thickness of newspaper for the masking operations.

20    Before spraying, shake the paint can thoroughly, then spray a test area until the spray painting technique is mastered. Cover the repair area with a thick coat of primer. The thickness should be built up using several thin layers of primer rather than one thick one. Using 600-grit wet-or-dry sandpaper, rub down the surface of the primer until it is very smooth. While doing this, the work area should be thoroughly rinsed with water and the wet-or-dry sandpaper periodically rinsed as well. Allow the primer to dry before spraying additional coats.

21    Spray on the top coat, again building up the thickness by using several thin layers of paint. Begin spraying in the center of the repair area and then, using a circular motion, work out until the whole repair area and about two inches of the surrounding original paint is covered. Remove all masking material 10 to 15 minutes after spraying on the final coat of paint. Allow the new paint at least two weeks to harden, then use a very fine rubbing compound to blend the edges of the new paint into the existing paint. Finally, apply a coat of wax.

## 6    Body repair - major damage

1    Major damage must be repaired by an auto body shop specifically equipped to perform body and frame repairs. These shops have the specialized equipment required to do the job properly.

2    If the damage is extensive, the body must be checked for proper alignment or the vehicle's handling characteristics may be adversely affected and other components may wear at an accelerated rate.

3    Due to the fact that all of the major body components (hood, fenders, etc.) are separate and replaceable units, any seriously damaged components should be replaced rather than repaired. Sometimes the components can be found in a wrecking yard that specializes in used vehicle components, often at considerable savings over the cost of new parts.

## 7    Hinges and locks - maintenance

Once every 3000 miles, or every three months, the hinges and latch assemblies on the doors, hood and trunk should be given a few drops of light oil or lock lubricant. The door latch strikers should also be lubricated with a thin coat of grease to reduce wear and ensure free movement. Lubricate the door and trunk locks with spray-on graphite lubricant.

## 8    Windshield and fixed glass - replacement

Replacement of the windshield and fixed glass requires the use of special fast-setting adhesive/caulk materials and some specialized tools and techniques. These operations should be left to a dealer service department or a shop specializing in glass work.

## 9    Hood - removal, installation and adjustment

**Note:** *The hood is heavy and somewhat awkward to remove and install - at least two people should perform this procedure.*

### Removal and installation

*Refer to illustration 9.2*

1    Use blankets or pads to cover the cowl area of the body and fenders. This will protect the body and paint as the hood is lifted off.

2    Make marks or scribe a line around the

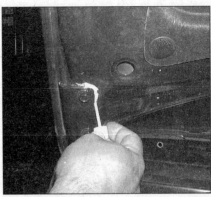

**9.2  Before removing the hood, draw a line around the hinge plate**

hood hinge to ensure proper alignment during installation **(see illustration)**.

3    Disconnect any wires that will interfere with removal.

4    With an assistant helping you support the hood, remove the hinge-to-hood bolts.

5    Lift off the hood.

6    Installation is the reverse of removal.

### Adjustment

*Refer to illustrations 9.10 and 9.11*

7    Fore-and-aft and side-to-side adjustment of the hood is done by moving the hinge plate slot after loosening the bolts or nuts.

8    Scribe a line around the entire hinge plate so you can determine the amount of movement **(see illustration 9.2)**.

9    Loosen the bolts or nuts and move the hood into correct alignment. Move it only a little at a time. Tighten the hinge bolts and carefully lower the hood to check the position.

10    After installing the hood, adjust the striker, if necessary. The striker can be adjusted fore-and-aft as well as from side-to-side so that the hood closes securely and flush with the fenders. To make the adjustment, scribe a line or mark around the striker mounting flange to provide a reference point, then loosen the striker bolts and reposition the striker as necessary **(see illustration)**. Be sure to tighten the striker mounting bolts securely.

**9.10  To adjust the position of the hood, mark the relationship of the striker to the hood, then loosen the striker bolts and slide the striker fore-and-aft or side-to-side as necessary**

These photos illustrate a method of repairing simple dents. They are intended to supplement *Body repair - minor damage* in this Chapter and should not be used as the sole instructions for body repair on these vehicles.

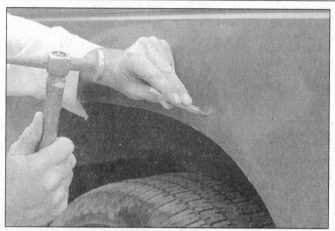

1   If you can't access the backside of the body panel to hammer out the dent, pull it out with a slide-hammer-type dent puller. In the deepest portion of the dent or along the crease line, drill or punch hole(s) at least one inch apart . . .

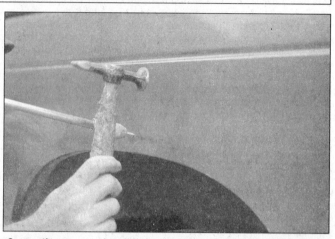

2   . . . then screw the slide-hammer into the hole and operate it. Tap with a hammer near the edge of the dent to help 'pop' the metal back to its original shape. When you're finished, the dent area should be close to its original contour and about 1/8-inch below the surface of the surrounding metal

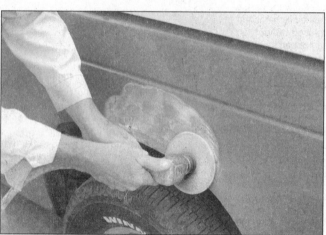

3   Using coarse-grit sandpaper, remove the paint down to the bare metal. Hand sanding works fine, but the disc sander shown here makes the job faster. Use finer (about 320-grit) sandpaper to feather-edge the paint at least one inch around the dent area

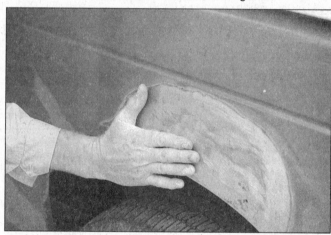

4   When the paint is removed, touch will probably be more helpful than sight for telling if the metal is straight. Hammer down the high spots or raise the low spots as necessary. Clean the repair area with wax/silicone remover

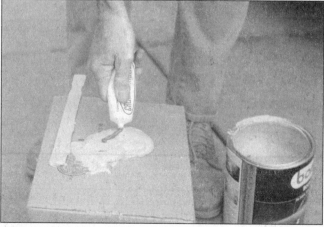

5   Following label instructions, mix up a batch of plastic filler and hardener. The ratio of filler to hardener is critical, and, if you mix it incorrectly, it will either not cure properly or cure too quickly (you won't have time to file and sand it into shape)

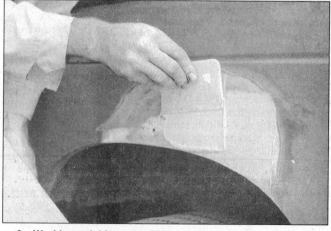

6   Working quickly so the filler doesn't harden, use a plastic applicator to press the body filler firmly into the metal, assuring it bonds completely. Work the filler until it matches the original contour and is slightly above the surrounding metal

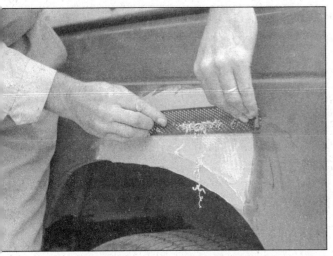

7   Let the filler harden until you can just dent it with your fingernail. Use a body file or Surform tool  (shown here) to rough-shape  the filler

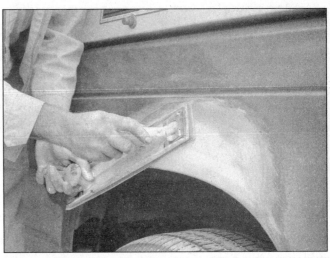

8   Use coarse-grit sandpaper and a sanding board or block to work the filler down until it's smooth and even. Work down to finer grits of sandpaper - always using a board or block - ending up with 360 or 400 grit

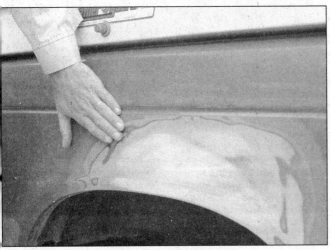

9   You shouldn't be able to feel any ridge at the transition from the filler to the bare metal or from the bare metal to the old paint. As soon as the repair is flat and uniform, remove the dust and mask off the adjacent panels or trim pieces

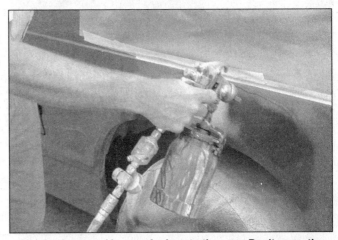

10   Apply several layers of primer to the area. Don't spray the primer on too heavy, so it sags or runs, and make sure each coat is dry before you spray on the next one. A professional-type spray gun is being used here, but aerosol spray primer is available inexpensively from auto parts stores

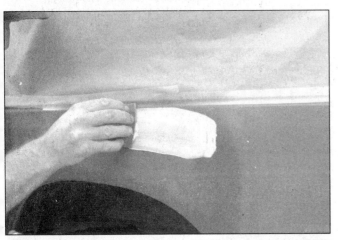

11   The primer will help reveal imperfections or scratches. Fill these with glazing compound. Follow the label instructions and sand it with 360 or 400-grit sandpaper until it's smooth. Repeat the glazing, sanding and respraying until the primer reveals a perfectly smooth surface

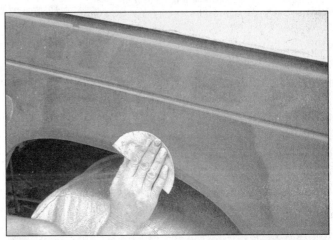

12   Finish sand the primer with very fine sandpaper (400 or 600-grit) to remove the primer overspray. Clean the area with water and allow it to dry. Use a tack rag to remove any dust, then apply the finish coat. Don't attempt to rub out or wax the repair area until the paint has dried completely (at least two weeks)

9.11 Screw the hood bumpers in or out to adjust the hood flush with the fenders

10.2 To detach the hood latch, remove these three retaining bolts (arrows)

10.3 Flip the hood latch over and disengage the hood release cable from the latch mechanism (make sure to remember how the cable is routed before you disconnect it)

10.6 As you trace the routing of the hood release cable back toward the firewall, you'll find several cable clips, such as these two above the headlight (arrows); be sure to disconnect all clips before removing the old cable

11  Also, if necessary, adjust the hood bumpers **(see illustration)** so that the hood is flush with the fenders when it's closed.
12  The hood latch assembly, as well as the hinges, should be periodically lubricated with lithium-base grease to prevent binding and wear.

## 10  Hood release latch and cable - removal and installation

### *Latch*

*Refer to illustrations 10.2 and 10.3*
1  Remove the radiator grille (see Section 11).

2  Scribe a line around the latch to aid alignment when installing, then detach the latch retaining bolts from the radiator support **(see illustration)** and remove the latch.
3  Disengage the hood release cable from the latch assembly **(see illustration)**.
4  Installation is the reverse of the removal procedure.

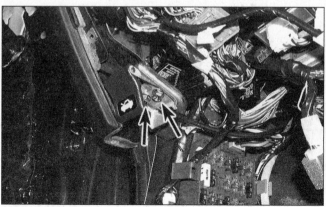

10.8 After removing the driver's side panel lower cover, detach the hood release lever retaining screws (arrows) and pull the cable rearward into the passenger compartment

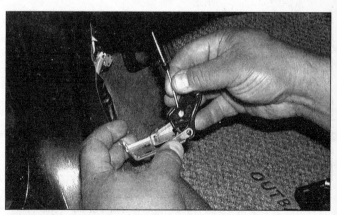

10.9 Disengage the cable from the hood release lever mechanism

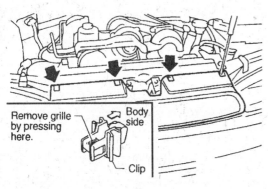

**11.1 The grille is secured by four clips across the top of the upper radiator crossmember (and by a pair of clips on the headlights, not visible in this illustration)**

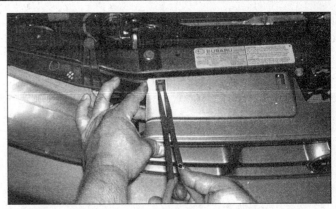

**11.2 To detach the top of the grille from the upper radiator crossmember, squeeze the clips with a pair of needle-nose pliers**

## Cable

*Refer to illustrations 10.6, 10.8 and 10.9*

5   Disconnect the hood release cable from the latch assembly as described above.

6   Attach a piece of stiff wire to the end of the cable, trace the cable back to the firewall and detach all cable retaining clips **(see illustration)**.

7   Working in the passenger compartment, remove the driver's side panel lower cover (see Section 27).

8   Detach the screws securing the hood release lever **(see illustration)**.

9   Disengage the cable from the hood release lever **(see illustration)**.

10   Pull the old cable into the passenger compartment until you can see the stiff wire that you attached to the cable. A grommet insulates the cable hole in the firewall from the elements. The new cable should have a new grommet, so you can remove and discard the old cable grommet. Make sure the new grommet is already on the new cable (if not, slip the old grommet onto the new cable), then detach the old cable from the wire and attach the new cable to the wire.

11   Working from the engine compartment side of the firewall, pull the wire through the cable hole in the firewall.

12   Installation is otherwise the reverse of the removal. Working from the passenger compartment side, push the grommet into place with your fingers. Make sure it's fully seated in the hole in the firewall.

## 11   Radiator grille - removal and installation

*Refer to illustrations 11.1, 11.2 and 11.3*

1   The radiator grille is held in place by four clips across the top of the radiator upper crossmember **(see illustration)** and by a pair of clips near the headlights.

2   To release the upper edge of the grille from the four upper clips, squeeze the locking tangs on the side of each clip with a pair of needle-nose pliers **(see illustration)**.

3   Once the four upper clips are released, pull the upper part of the grille forward **(see illustration)** and disengage it from the lower clips.

4   Installation is the reverse of removal.

## 12   Bumpers - removal and installation

**Warning:** *Some models covered by this manual are equipped with airbags. Always disconnect the negative battery cable and wait at least one minute before working in the vicinity of the impact sensors, steering column or instrument panel to avoid the possibility of accidental deployment of the airbag, which could cause personal injury (see Chapter 12).*

### Front

*Refer to illustrations 12.2, 12.3a, 12.3b, 12.3c, 12.3d, 12.3e, 12.4a, and 12.4b*

1   Loosen the front wheel lug nuts. Raise the vehicle and support it securely on jackstands. Remove the wheels.

2   Working behind and below the bumper assembly, remove the front part of the wheel housing mud guard and the small splash shield ahead of it **(see illustration)**.

3   Remove the bumper cover retaining screws and bolts **(see illustrations)**.

4   Remove the bumper retaining bolts **(see illustrations)** and remove it from the vehicle.

5   Installation is the reverse of removal.

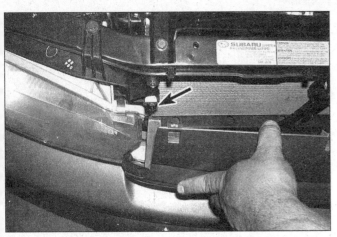

**11.3 To disengage the grille from the lower clip (arrow) next to each headlight, pull the upper edge of the grille forward and lift up**

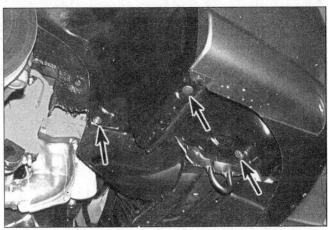

**12.2 To gain access to the fasteners that attach the ends of the bumper cover, detach the front part of the mud guard and the small splash shield in front of it by prying up the plastic pop-up type fasteners (arrows) (Outback model shown, other models similar)**

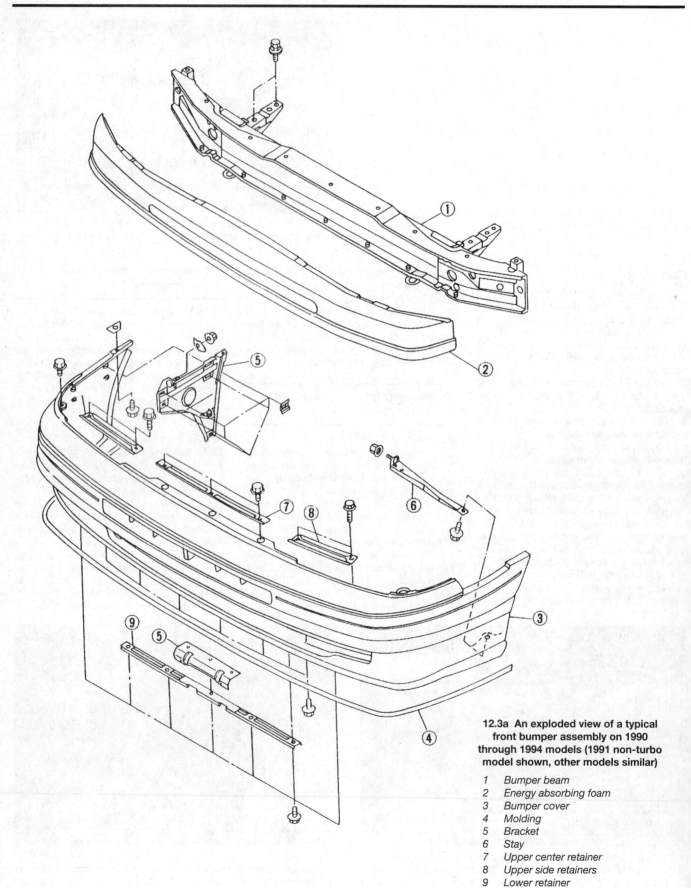

12.3a  An exploded view of a typical
front bumper assembly on 1990
through 1994 models (1991 non-turbo
model shown, other models similar)

1    Bumper beam
2    Energy absorbing foam
3    Bumper cover
4    Molding
5    Bracket
6    Stay
7    Upper center retainer
8    Upper side retainers
9    Lower retainer

**12.3b An exploded view of a typical front bumper assembly on 1995 and later models (1996 Outback model shown, other models similar)**

1   Bumper cover
2   Bumper beam
3   Bracket
4   Stay
5   Back beam
6   Energy absorbing foam
7   Retainer
8   Back beam brackets

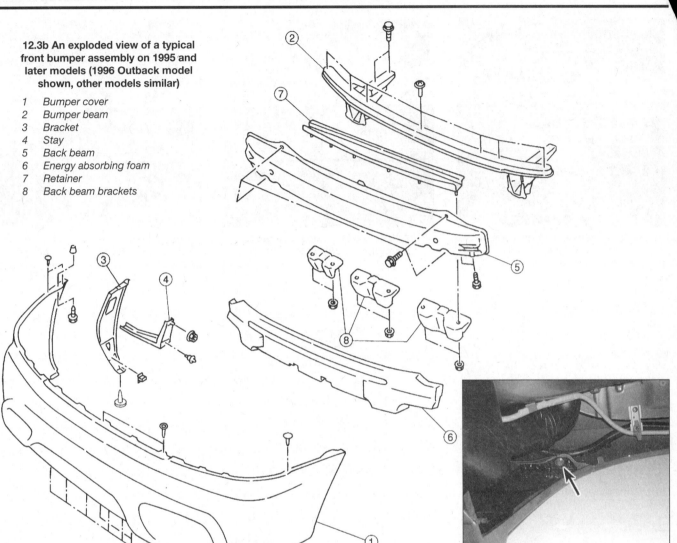

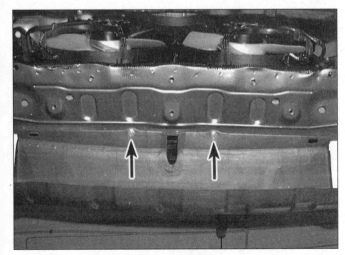

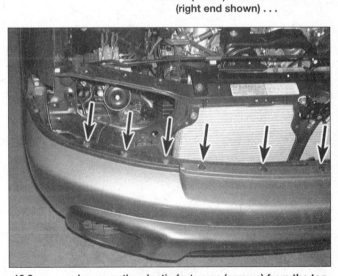

12.3c  Remove the bumper cover retaining screws (arrow) from each end (right end shown) . . .

12.3d  . . . remove the plastic Philips screws (arrows) from the underside of the cover . . .

12.3e  . . . and remove the plastic fasteners (arrows) from the top of the cover; besides the six fasteners shown here, there are five more, not visible in this photo, on the left end of the cover

12.4a  To detach the front bumper assembly, remove the upper left bolts (arrows) . . .

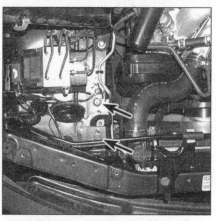

12.4b  . . . and the upper right bolts (arrows), then pull off the bumper

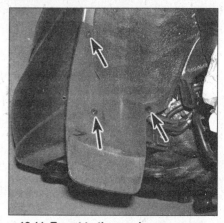

12.11  To get to the rear bumper cover bolts inside the rear wheel housings, remove the mud guard fasteners (arrows) and detach the mud guards

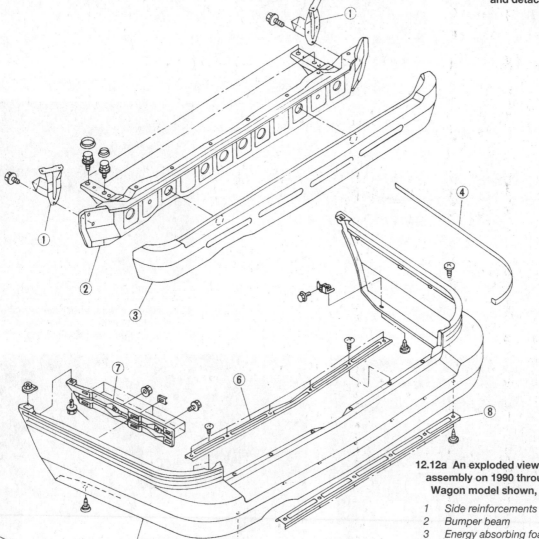

12.12a  An exploded view of a typical rear bumper assembly on 1990 through 1994 models (1990 Wagon model shown, other models similar)

1  Side reinforcements
2  Bumper beam
3  Energy absorbing foam
4  Molding
5  Bumper cover
6  Upper retainer
7  Bracket
8  Lower center retainer
9  Lower side retainers

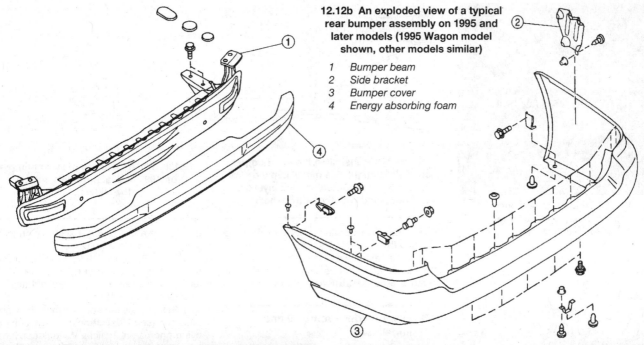

**12.12b  An exploded view of a typical rear bumper assembly on 1995 and later models (1995 Wagon model shown, other models similar)**

1  Bumper beam
2  Side bracket
3  Bumper cover
4  Energy absorbing foam

**12.12c  To detach the forward ends of the rear bumper, remove the single bolt (arrow) inside each wheel housing (right side shown, left side identical)**

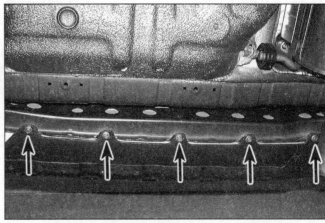

**12.12d  To detach the rear bumper cover, remove these bolts (arrows)**

**12.13a  Remove any rear quarter panel trim pieces from the trunk or cargo area to gain access to the rear bumper bolts; on wagon and Outback models, this cargo hook bolt (arrow) and the cargo hook must be removed to remove the trim panel**

**12.13b  Once the trunk/cargo area trim panels are removed, you'll find a pair of plastic plugs (arrows) in each corner; remove all four plugs**

### Rear

*Refer to illustrations 12.11, 12.12a, 12.12b, 12.12c, 12.12d, 12.13a, 12.13b, 12.13c, 12.15a, 12.15b, 12.15c and 12.15d*

10   Loosen the rear wheel lug nuts, raise the vehicle and support it securely on jackstands. Remove the rear wheels.

11   Remove the mud guard from the wheel housing **(see illustration)**.

12   Remove the bumper cover bolts inside both wheel housings and remove the lower bumper cover bolts **(see illustrations)**.

13   Working in the trunk (sedan models) or the cargo area (wagon models), remove the rear quarter trim panel **(see illustration)**. Pry out the bumper bolt covers, then remove all four bumper bolts (two per side) from the trunk or cargo area **(see illustrations)**. Have an assistant support the bumper as the bolts are removed.

14   Pull the bumper out slightly and unplug or detach the electrical connectors and/or

**12.13c  To detach the rear bumper, remove these bolts (arrows) from each corner**

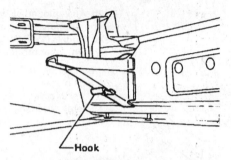

**12.15a  When installing the rear bumper on 1990 through 1994 models, make sure these hooks (located on the stays) are engaged with the body panels**

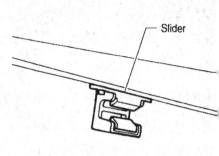

**12.15b  When installing the rear bumper on 1995 and later models, attach the sliders . . .**

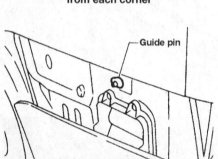

**12.15c  . . . to the guide pins . . .**

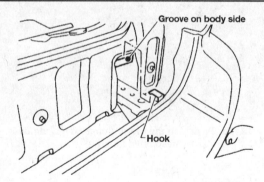

**12.15d  . . . and insert the bumper hooks into the body grooves**

wiring harnesses for any lights in or near the bumper (license plate light, etc.) that interfere with bumper removal.

15    Installation is basically the reverse of removal **(see illustrations)**.

## 13   Front fender - removal and installation

*Refer to illustrations 13.3a, 13.3b, 13.3c, 13.3d, 13.5a, 13.5b, 13.5c, 13.5d, 13.5e and 13.5f*

1    Loosen the front wheel lug nuts, raise the vehicle and support it securely on jack stands. Remove the wheel.

2    On 1990 through 1994 models, remove the turn signal light assemblies; on 1995 and later models, remove the headlight assemblies (see Chapter 12).

3    Remove the mud guards from the wheel housings **(see illustrations)**. The accompanying photos are typical. Various combinations of bolts, screws and rivets are used to secure the mud guards on various models. If rivets are used, drill them out; on these models, use small bolts and nuts or sheet metal screws when reattaching the mud guards.

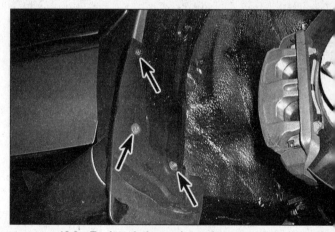

**13.3a  To detach the mud guard, remove these three fasteners (arrows)**

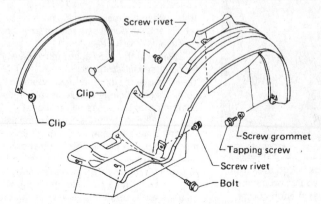

**13.3b  Front fender inner splash shield mounting details (1990 through 1994 models)**

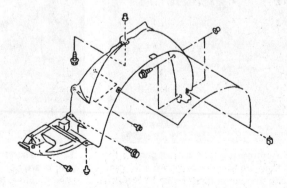

**13.3c  Front fender inner splash shield mounting details (1995 and later models)**

13.3d To remove the front fender inner splash shield, remove these fasteners and clips (arrows)

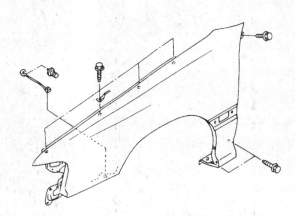

13.5a Front fender mounting details (1990 through 1994 models)

13.5b To detach the front of the fender, remove these bolts (arrows) (1995 and later models)

13.5c To detach the top of the fender, remove these bolts (arrows) (1995 and later models)

4    Remove the front bumper cover (see Section 12).
5    Remove the fender mounting bolts and nuts **(see illustrations)**. The accompanying photos, of a 1998 Outback model, are typical. However, note that 1990 through 1994 models have four upper fender bolts while 1995 and later models have five.
6    Detach the fender. It's a good idea to have an assistant support the fender while it's being moved away from the vehicle to prevent damage to the surrounding body panels.
7    Installation is the reverse of removal. Be sure to tighten all fasteners securely. Install sheet metal screws or small nuts and bolts where rivets were used to attach the mud guards.

13.5d To detach the upper rear corner of the fender, open the door and remove this bolt (arrow) (1995 and later models)

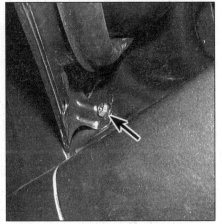

13.5e To detach the lower rear corner of the fender, open the door and remove this bolt (arrow) . . .

13.5f . . . and remove these two bolts (arrows) from the rocker panel area below the door (1995 and later models)

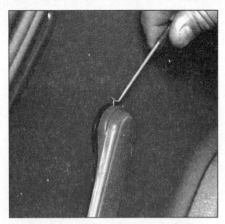

**14.2 On models with manual window regulators, use a hooked tool like this to remove the window crank retaining clip**

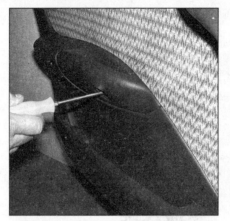

**14.3 Use a small screwdriver to pry out the trim caps, then remove the armrest retaining screw**

**14.4a Pry off this trim cap . . .**

## 14 Door trim panel - removal and installation

*Refer to illustrations 14.2, 14.3, 14.4a, 14.4b, 14.4c, 14.5a, 14.5b, 14.6 and 14.7*

1    Disconnect the negative cable from the battery.

2    On manual window equipped models, remove the window crank, using a hooked tool to remove the retainer clip **(see illustration)**. A special tool is available for this purpose, but it's not essential. With the clip removed, pull off the handle.

3    Detach the armrest **(see illustrations)**.

4    Remove the door trim panel retaining screws **(see illustrations)**.

5    Insert a putty knife, screwdriver or a special trim panel removal tool between the trim panel and the head of each retaining clip **(see illustration)** to detach the door trim panel from the door. The trim panel retaining clips **(see illustration)** are about five to six inches apart. Pry only at the clip locations.

**14.4b . . . remove the retaining screw . . .**

Prying on the trim panel in the areas between the clips will distort or damage the panel.

6    Once all of the clips are disengaged, carefully detach the trim panel from the door, unplug any electrical connectors **(see illustration)** and remove the trim panel.

7    For access to the handle, latch, lock and

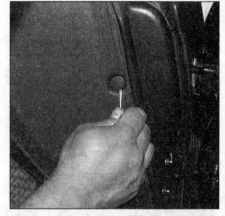

**14.4c . . . then remove this trim cap and the retaining screw behind it**

window regulator mechanisms, carefully peel back the plastic watershield **(see illustration)**.

8    Before installing the door trim panel, inspect the condition of all clips and reinstall any clips which may have fallen out.

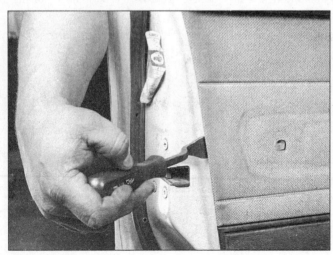

**14.5a Insert a putty knife or trim removal tool between the door and the door trim panel, then carefully pry out the trim panel retaining clips**

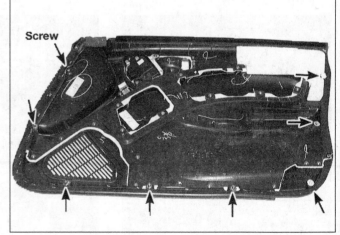

**14.5b Door trim panel retaining clip locations (arrows)**

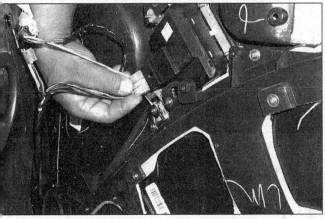

**14.6  Pull the door trim panel off the door and unplug the electrical connector(s) for the power windows, door locks, etc.**

**14.7  To get to the door handles, relay rods, latch, etc., carefully peel back the watershield**

Installation is the reverse of the removal procedure. **Note:** *When installing door trim panel retaining clips, make sure the clips are lined up with their mating holes first, then gently tap the clips in with the palm of your hand.*

## 15  Door handles, key lock cylinder and latch - removal and installation

Raise the window, then remove the door trim panel and peel away the watershield (see Section 14).

### Inside handle

*Refer to illustrations 15.2a, 15.2b, 15.2c, 15.2d, 15.2e, 15.3 and 15.5*

2  Detach the actuating rods between the inside door handle and the latch assembly **(see illustrations)**.

3  Unclip the actuating rod guides, then remove the door handle retaining screws **(see illustration)**.

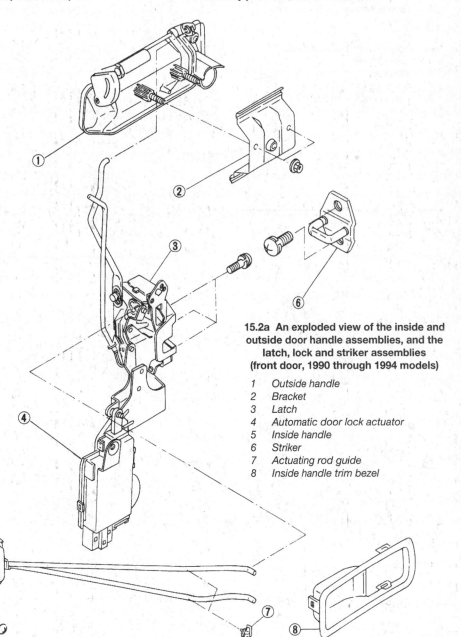

**15.2a  An exploded view of the inside and outside door handle assemblies, and the latch, lock and striker assemblies (front door, 1990 through 1994 models)**

1  *Outside handle*
2  *Bracket*
3  *Latch*
4  *Automatic door lock actuator*
5  *Inside handle*
6  *Striker*
7  *Actuating rod guide*
8  *Inside handle trim bezel*

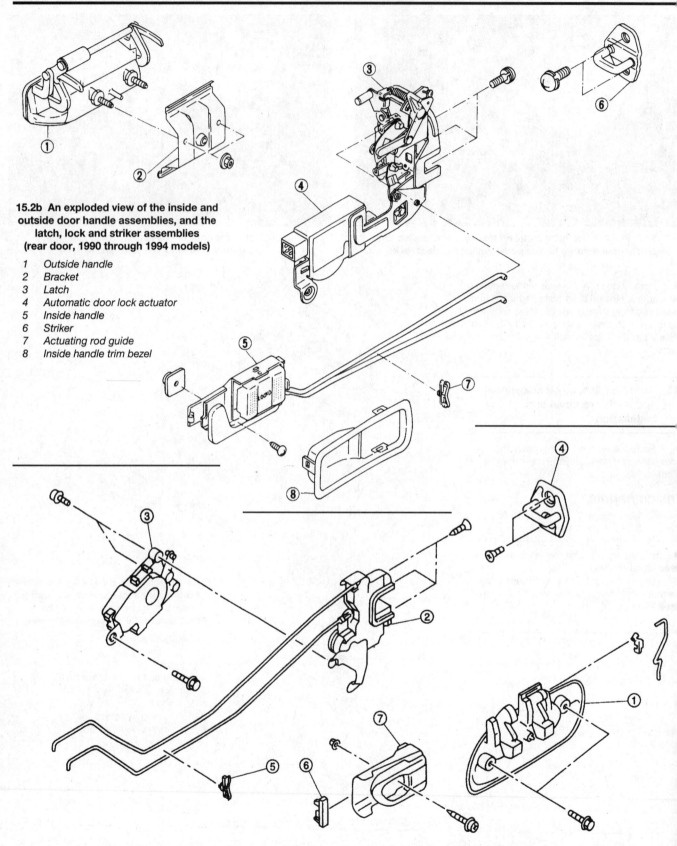

**15.2b  An exploded view of the inside and outside door handle assemblies, and the latch, lock and striker assemblies (rear door, 1990 through 1994 models)**

1　Outside handle
2　Bracket
3　Latch
4　Automatic door lock actuator
5　Inside handle
6　Striker
7　Actuating rod guide
8　Inside handle trim bezel

**15.2c  An exploded view of the inside and outside door handle assemblies, and the latch, lock and striker assemblies (rear door, 1995 and later models)**

| 1 | Outside handle | 3 | Automatic door lock | 4 | Striker | 6 | Inside handle retainer |
| 2 | Latch | | actuator | 5 | Actuating rod guide | 7 | Inside handle |

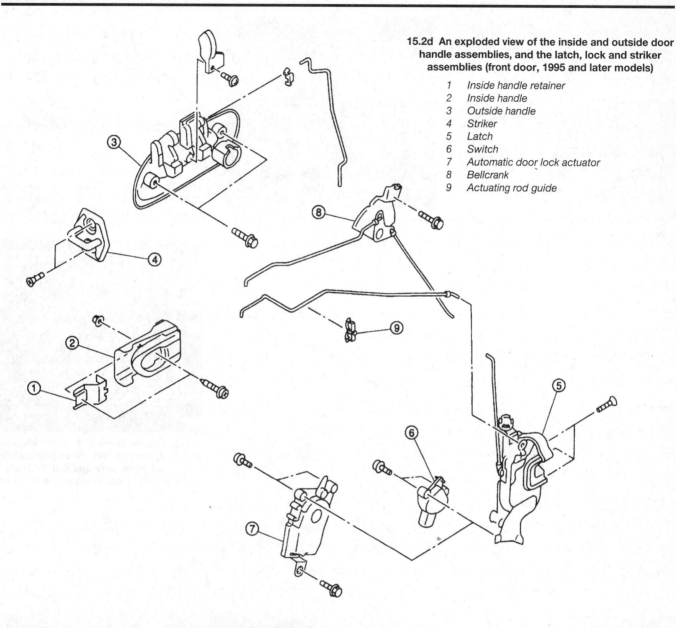

**15.2d  An exploded view of the inside and outside door
handle assemblies, and the latch, lock and striker
assemblies (front door, 1995 and later models)**

1  Inside handle retainer
2  Inside handle
3  Outside handle
4  Striker
5  Latch
6  Switch
7  Automatic door lock actuator
8  Bellcrank
9  Actuating rod guide

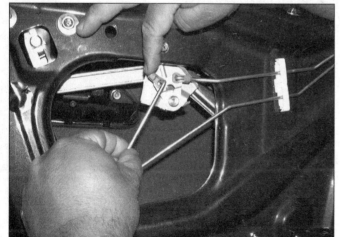

15.2e  To disengage the actuating rods, flip up each locking
device as shown and pull the rods out

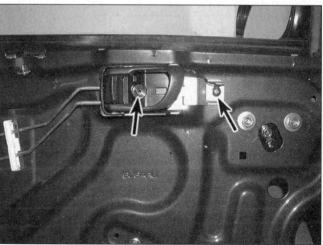

15.3  Disengage the actuating rod guide, then remove the
inside handle retaining screws (arrows) and
detach the handle from the door

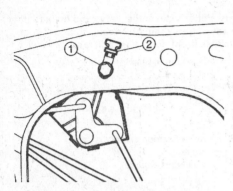

15.5 If you're installing the inside door handle on the front door of a 1995 or later model, lock the door, loosen the bellcrank bolt (1), push down on the tab (2) to lower the bellcrank, then tighten the bolt

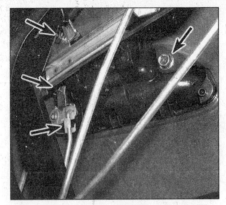

15.6 To remove the outside door handle, disengage the actuating rod from the handle, then remove the handle mounting nuts (arrows)

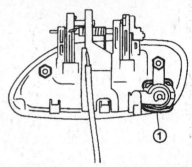

15.8 To remove the key lock cylinder from the outside handle, loosen the spring clip (1) securing the cylinder to the handle, then pull the cylinder out of the handle

**16.5a An exploded view of a typical front door window and regulator assembly (1990 model shown, other models similar)**

1   Drip guide
2   Nut
3   Spacer
4   Window glass
5   Washers
6   Rear window retainer
7   Center window retainer
8   Front window retainer
9   Outer weatherstrip
10   Stabilizer
11   Rear sash
12   Front sash
13   Window regulator assembly
14   Regulator handle

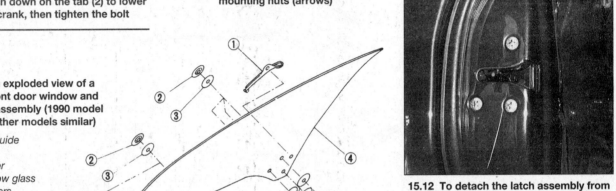

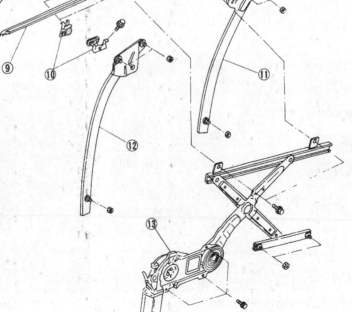

15.12 To detach the latch assembly from the door, remove these three screws from the end of the door and pull the latch assembly through the access hole

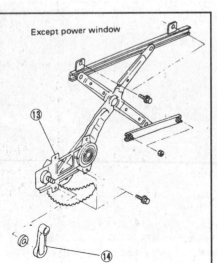

Except power window

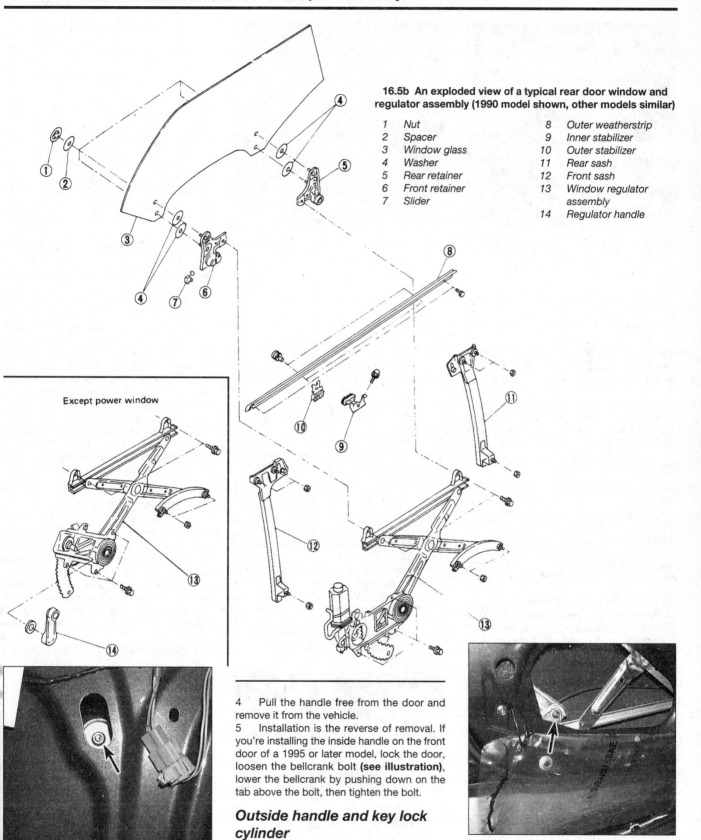

**16.5b  An exploded view of a typical rear door window and regulator assembly (1990 model shown, other models similar)**

1   Nut
2   Spacer
3   Window glass
4   Washer
5   Rear retainer
6   Front retainer
7   Slider
8   Outer weatherstrip
9   Inner stabilizer
10  Outer stabilizer
11  Rear sash
12  Front sash
13  Window regulator assembly
14  Regulator handle

Except power window

**16.5c  On 1995 and later models, you can access the stabilizer (arrow) through this small hole in the middle of the door near the lower edge**

4    Pull the handle free from the door and remove it from the vehicle.
5    Installation is the reverse of removal. If you're installing the inside handle on the front door of a 1995 or later model, lock the door, loosen the bellcrank bolt **(see illustration)**, lower the bellcrank by pushing down on the tab above the bolt, then tighten the bolt.

### Outside handle and key lock cylinder

*Refer to illustrations 15.6 and 15.8*

6    Working through the access hole, disengage the actuating rods from the outside door handle and from the key lock cylinder **(see illustration)**.

**16.6  To detach the window from the regulator, remove the bolt (arrow) from each lower corner of the glass (rear bolt shown, forward bolt can be reached through large access hole at lower front corner of door)**

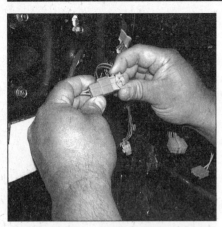

**17.3 On 1995 and later models with power mirrors, unplug the electrical connector for the power mirror motor**

**17.4 To detach the window regulator, remove these four mounting bolts (arrows)**

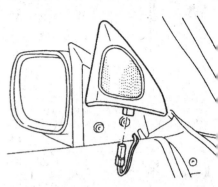

**18.1 Carefully pry off the mirror trim cover**

7  Detach the outside handle retaining nuts, then remove the handle and lock cylinder assembly from the door.

8  To separate the key lock cylinder from the outside handle, loosen the spring **(see illustration)** securing the cylinder to the handle and remove the cylinder from the handle.

9  Installation is the reverse of removal. If you removed the key lock cylinder from the outside handle, make sure that the key slot in the lock cylinder comes to the center of the hole in the outside handle.

### *Door latch*

*Refer to illustration 15.12*

10  Detach the inside door handle assembly from the door and disengage the handle-to-latch actuating rods from the latch (see Steps 2 through 4).

11  Working through the access hole, disengage the outside handle-to-latch rods and the lock cylinder-to-latch rod from the outside assembly.

12  Remove the three screws securing the latch to the door **(see illustration)**, then remove the latch assembly from the door. If the vehicle is equipped with automatic door locks, remove the actuator retaining bolt, which is located either below the three latch bolts in the end of the door, or on the inside surface of the door, near the rear edge of the door.

13  Installation is the reverse of removal. When installing the inside handle assembly on 1995 and later front doors, refer to Step 5.

## 16 Door window glass - removal and installation

*Refer to illustrations 16.5a, 16.5b, 16.5c and 16.6*

1  Remove the door trim panel and the plastic watershield (see Section 14).

2  Lower the window glass all the way down into the door.

3  On 1995 and later models, unplug the

electrical connector for the power mirror and remove the triangular mirror trim panel from the door (see Section 18).

4  Remove the inside door handle and rods (see Section 15).

5  Remove the window glass stabilizer bolt **(see illustrations)** and remove the stabilizer.

6  Remove the window glass retainer bolts **(see illustration)**.

7  Remove the glass by carefully pulling it up and out.

8  Installation is the reverse of removal. If it is necessary to adjust the glass, loosen the adjustment bolts on the stabilizers, sashes and up-stops, carefully raise the window and position the glass in the window opening so it is level and contacting the weatherstrip evenly all the way around. Have an assistant press in slightly on the window to give it a bit of preload on the weatherstrip, then tighten the adjustment bolts. To fine-tune the adjustment, loosen the necessary adjustment bolts and move the up-stops, sashes or stabilizers as required, then tighten them securely. Verify that the window goes up and down smoothly, and that the door opens and closes easily. If the door "pops" when you open it or is hard to close, there is too much preload on the glass

### 17 Door window glass regulator - removal and installation

*Refer to illustrations 17.3 and 17.4*

1  Remove the door trim panel and the plastic watershield (see Section 14).

2  Remove the door window glass assembly (see Section 16).

3  On power operated windows, unplug the electrical connector from the window regulator motor **(see illustration)**.

4  Remove the regulator mounting bolts **(see illustration)**.

5  Pull the regulator assembly through the service hole in the door frame to remove it.

6  Installation is the reverse of removal. Adjust the window glass as described in the previous Section.

### 18 Outside mirrors - removal and installation

*Refer to illustrations 18.1, 18.3 and 18.4*

1  Pry off the mirror trim cover **(see illustration)**.

2  If the vehicle has power mirrors, remove the door trim panel (see Section 14).

3  If the vehicle has power mirrors, unplug the mirror electrical connector **(see illustration)**.

4  Remove the mirror retaining screws **(see**

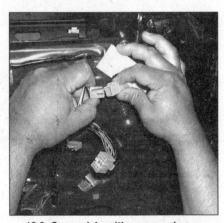

**18.3 On models with power mirrors, remove the door trim panel and unplug the mirror electrical connector**

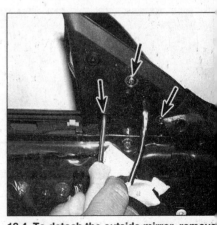

**18.4 To detach the outside mirror, remove these retaining screws (arrows)**

**19.6 Before loosening the door retaining bolts (arrows), draw a line around the hinge plate for a reinstallation reference**

**19.11 Scribe or paint alignment marks around the striker to establish a baseline, then adjust the striker by loosening the mounting screws and gently tapping the striker in the desired direction (arrows)**

**20.3 Scribe a mark around the hinge plate (arrow) for realignment of the trunk lid on installation**

illustration) and detach the mirror from the vehicle.

5    Installation is the reverse of removal.

## 19   Door - removal, installation and adjustment

**Note:** *The door is heavy and somewhat awkward to remove and install - at least two people should perform this procedure.*

### Removal and installation

*Refer to illustration 19.6*

1    Raise the window completely in the door and then disconnect the negative cable from the battery.
2    Open the door all the way and support it on jacks or blocks covered with rags to prevent damaging the paint.
3    Remove the door trim panel and watershield (see Section 14).
4    Disconnect all electrical connections, ground wires and harness retaining clips from the door. **Note:** *It is a good idea to label all connections to simplify reassembly.*
5    From the door side, detach the rubber conduit between the body and the door. Then pull the wiring harness through the conduit hole and remove it from the door.
6    Mark around the door hinges with a pen or a scribe to facilitate realignment during reassembly **(see illustration)**.
7    With an assistant holding the door, remove the hinge to door bolts and lift off the door.
8    Installation is the reverse of removal.

### Adjustment

*Refer to illustration 19.11*

9    Having proper door to body alignment is a critical part of a well functioning door assembly. First check the door hinge pins for excessive play. Fully open the door and lift up and down on the door without lifting the body. If a door has 1/16-inch or more excessive play, the hinges should be replaced.

10   Door-to-body alignment adjustments are made by loosening the hinge-to-body bolts or hinge-to-door bolts and moving the door. Proper body alignment is achieved when the top of the doors are parallel with the roof section, the front door is flush with the fender, the rear door is flush with the rear quarter panel and the bottom of the doors are aligned with the lower rocker panel. If these goals can't be reached by adjusting the hinge-to-body or hinge-to-door bolts, body alignment shims may have to be purchased and inserted behind the hinges to achieve correct alignment.
11   To adjust the door closed position, scribe a line or mark around the striker plate to provide a reference point, then verify that the door latch is contacting the center of the latch striker. If it isn't, adjust the vertical position of the striker **(see illustration)**.
12   If necessary, adjust the horizontal position of the striker, so that the door panel is flush with the center pillar or rear quarter panel and provides positive engagement with the latch mechanism.

## 20   Trunk lid - removal, installation and adjustment

**Note:** *The trunk lid is heavy and somewhat awkward to remove and install - at least two people should perform this procedure.*

### Removal and installation

*Refer to illustration 20.3*

1    Open the trunk lid and cover the edges of the trunk compartment with pads or cloths to protect the painted surfaces when the lid is removed.
2    Disconnect any cables or wire harness connectors attached to the trunk lid that would interfere with removal.
3    Make alignment marks around the hinge mounting bolts with a marking pen **(see illustration)**.

4    While an assistant supports the trunk lid, remove the lid-to-hinge bolts on both sides and lift it off.
5    Installation is the reverse of removal.
**Note:** *When reinstalling the trunk lid, align the lid-to-hinge bolts with the marks made during removal.*

### Adjustment

6    Fore-and-aft and side-to-side adjustment of the trunk lid is accomplished by moving the lid in relation to the hinge after loosening the bolts or nuts.
7    Scribe a line around the entire hinge plate as described earlier in this Section so you can determine the amount of movement.
8    Loosen the bolts or nuts and move the trunk lid into correct alignment. Move it only a little at a time. Tighten the hinge bolts or nuts and carefully lower the trunk lid to check the alignment.
9    If necessary after installation, the entire trunk lid striker assembly can be adjusted up and down as well as from side to side on the trunk lid so the lid closes securely and is flush with the rear quarter panels. To do this, scribe a line around the trunk lid striker assembly to provide a reference point. Then loosen the bolts and reposition the striker as necessary. Following adjustment, retighten the mounting bolts.
10   The trunk lid latch assembly, as well as the hinges, should be periodically lubricated with white lithium-base grease to prevent sticking and wear.

## 21   Trunk lid latch, release cable and lock cylinder - removal and installation

**Note:** *This procedure applies to sedan models.*

### Latch

*Refer to illustrations 21.2a, 21.2b and 21.5*

1    Open the trunk and remove any trunk lid trim panels around the latch. Scribe or paint a

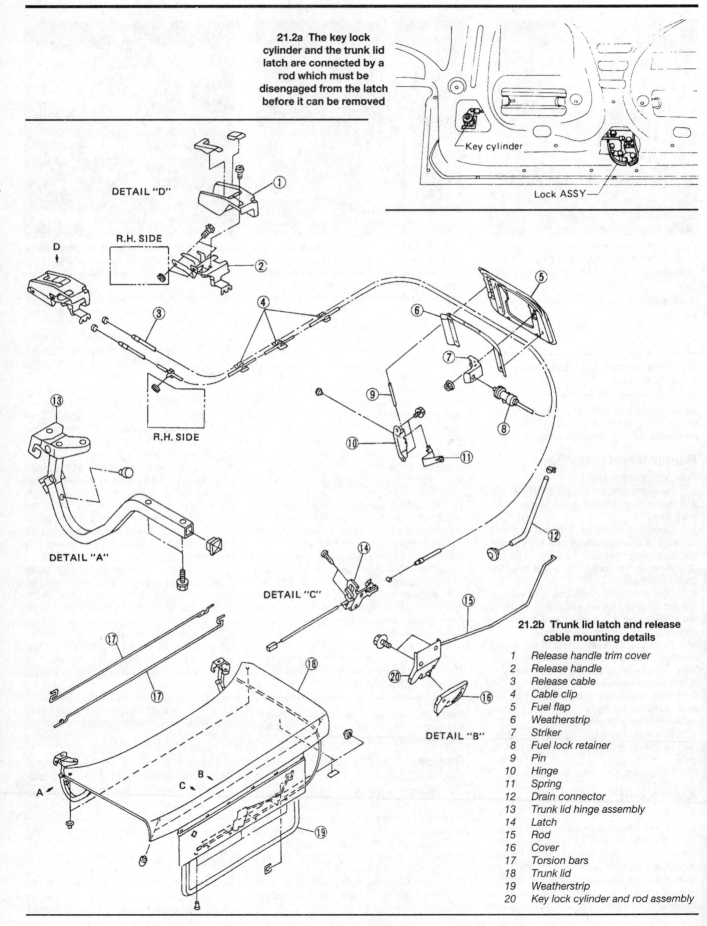

21.2a  The key lock cylinder and the trunk lid latch are connected by a rod which must be disengaged from the latch before it can be removed

—Key cylinder

Lock ASSY—

DETAIL "D"

R.H. SIDE

D

R.H. SIDE

DETAIL "A"

DETAIL "C"

DETAIL "B"

A

B

C

**21.2b  Trunk lid latch and release cable mounting details**

| | |
|---|---|
| 1 | Release handle trim cover |
| 2 | Release handle |
| 3 | Release cable |
| 4 | Cable clip |
| 5 | Fuel flap |
| 6 | Weatherstrip |
| 7 | Striker |
| 8 | Fuel lock retainer |
| 9 | Pin |
| 10 | Hinge |
| 11 | Spring |
| 12 | Drain connector |
| 13 | Trunk lid hinge assembly |
| 14 | Latch |
| 15 | Rod |
| 16 | Cover |
| 17 | Torsion bars |
| 18 | Trunk lid |
| 19 | Weatherstrip |
| 20 | Key lock cylinder and rod assembly |

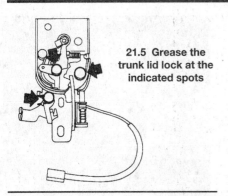

**21.5  Grease the trunk lid lock at the indicated spots**

line around the latch assembly for a reference point to ensure that the latch is correctly aligned when installed again.

2    Disengage the rod connecting the lock cylinder to the latch **(see illustrations)**.

3    Detach any clips securing the release cable to the trunk lid.

4    The trunk lid latch is retained by two bolts. Detach these bolts, then disengage the release cable from the latch assembly and remove the latch.

5    Installation is the reverse of removal. Be sure to grease the latch at the indicated points **(see illustration)**. Make sure the latch

is aligned with the marks you made prior to removal.

### Release cable

*Refer to illustrations 21.9, 21.10 and 21.11*

6    Working in the trunk, remove the latch assembly (see Steps 1 through 4).

7    Remove the driver's seat and the rear seats (see Section 31).

8    Remove the center pillar lower trim panel and the rear quarter trim panel (over the wheel housing hump).

9    Remove the driver's side sill cover **(see illustration)**, the floor mats and the carpeting.

10   Trace the routing of the cable **(see illustration)** and remove all clips securing the cable to the floorpan.

11   Disengage the cable from the release lever assembly **(see illustration)** and the remaining cable retaining clips. Attach a piece of thin wire to the end of the cable to aid in installation.

12   Working in the trunk compartment, pull the cable towards the rear of the vehicle until you can see the wire. Attach the new cable to the wire and pull it back into the passenger compartment.

13   Installation is the reverse of removal.

### Trunk lock cylinder

14   Open the trunk and remove the rear finishing panels (if equipped).

15   Detach the latch to lock cylinder rod and the drain connector from the lock cylinder.

16   Using a pair of pliers remove the lock cylinder retaining clip.

17   Working from the outside of the trunk lid, grasp the lock cylinder and pull it outward to remove it.

18   Installation is the reverse of removal.

## 22  Liftgate support struts - removal and installation

*Refer to illustrations 22.2a and 22.2b*

**Note:** *The liftgate is heavy and somewhat awkward to hold - at least two people should perform this procedure.*

1    Open the rear liftgate and support it securely.

2    Remove the retaining bolts at both ends of the support strut and detach it from the vehicle **(see illustrations)**. **Note:** *The new support struts may not come with the lower mounting stud. If this is the case, you'll have to*

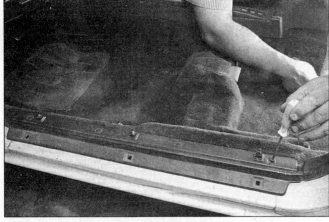

**21.9  Detach the clips and screws securing the driver's side door sill plates**

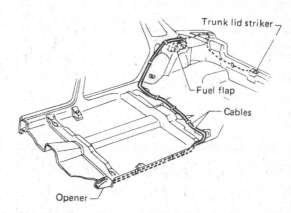

**21.10  Follow the routing of the cable and detach all cable clips and clamps securing the cable to the floorpan**

**21.11  Use a screwdriver to pry the cable out of the lever retaining bracket (arrow), then disengage the cable from the lever assembly**

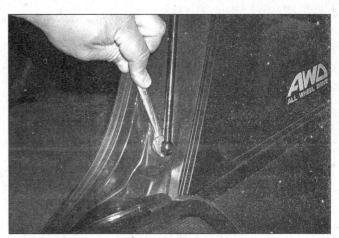

**22.2a  Unscrew the lower end of the liftgate strut from the body as shown . . .**

**22.2b** . . . then detach the upper end of
the strut from the liftgate (don't try to pry
the spherical bearings loose on these
struts - they can't be removed that way)

*grind or cut off the ball socket of the old strut.*
3     Installation is the reverse of removal.

### 23   Liftgate - removal, installation and adjustment

**Note:** *This procedure applies to station
wagon models. The liftgate is heavy and
somewhat awkward to hold - at least two
people should perform this procedure.*

#### Removal and installation

*Refer to illustration 23.4*
1     Open the liftgate and support it securely.
2     Remove the liftgate trim panels and disconnect the rear washer hose and all wiring
harness connectors leading to the liftgate.
3     While an assistant supports the liftgate,
detach the support struts from the liftgate
(see Section 22).
4     Scribe a line around the liftgate hinges
for a reference point to aid the installation
procedure. Then detach the hinge-to-liftgate
bolts **(see illustration)**. and remove the liftgate from the vehicle.
5     Installation is the reverse of removal.

#### Adjustment

*Refer to illustrations 23.7a, 23.7b and 23.7c*
6     Adjustments are made by loosening the
hinge-to liftgate bolts and moving the liftgate.
Proper alignment is achieved when the edges
of the liftgate are parallel with the rear quarter
panel and the top of the tailgate.
7     To provide positive engagement with
the latch mechanism, the latch striker may
need to be adjusted. To get to the striker,
remove the trim piece between the bumper
cover and the carpeting **(see illustrations)**.
Then mark the relationship of the striker to
the body, loose the striker bolts and move
the striker fore-and-aft and/or side-to-side as
necessary to achieve positive engagement.

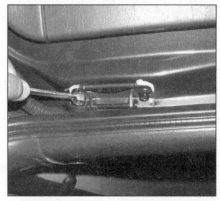

**23.4  Before loosening the liftgate
retaining bolts, draw a line around the
hinge plate for a reinstallation reference**

### 24   Liftgate latch, outside handle and lock cylinder - removal and installation

*Refer to illustration 24.2*
1     Open the liftgate and support it securely.
2     To gain access to most of the following
components, the interior trim panel on the
liftgate must be removed. Using a trim panel
removal tool or a small screwdriver, carefully
pry out the trim panel retaining clips **(see
illustration)** and detach the trim panel from
the liftgate.

#### Latch

*Refer to illustration 24.5*
3     Disengage the latch rod from the lock
cylinder **(see illustration 24.9)**.
4     Remove the bolts from the automatic
door-lock actuator, if equipped.
5     Remove the two latch retaining bolts **(see
illustration)**, unplug the electrical connectors
for the liftgate switch and the automatic door-
lock actuator and remove the latch.
6     Installation is the reverse of removal.

#### Outside handle

*Refer to illustrations 24.7 and 24.8*
7     Disengage the rod from the outside han-

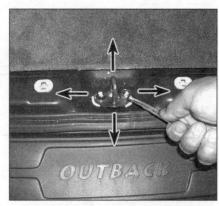

**23.7c  Adjust the liftgate lock striker by
loosening the mounting screws and
gently tapping the striker in the
desired direction (arrows)**

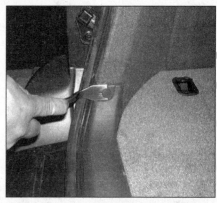

**23.7a  To remove the trim piece between
the carpeting and the bumper cover,
remove these plastic retainers . . .**

**23.7b** . . . then pry off the trim piece

dle **(see illustration)**.
8     Remove the nuts securing the outside
handle **(see illustration)** and detach the handle from the liftgate.

#### Lock cylinder

*Refer to illustrations 24.9 and 24.10*
9     Disengage the rod from the lock cylinder
**(see illustration)**.
10    Remove the lock cylinder retaining nuts
**(see illustration)** and detach the lock cylinder from the liftgate.
11    Installation is the reverse of removal.

**24.2  Pry out the retaining clips securing
the liftgate interior trim panel**

**24.5  To detach the latch from the liftgate, remove the latch retaining bolts**

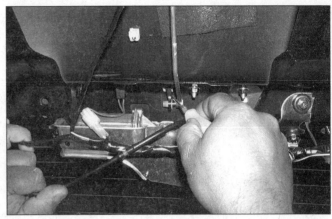

**24.7  Disengage the rod from the outside handle**

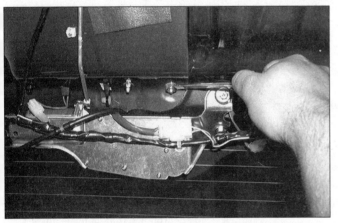

**24.8  Remove the nuts securing the outside handle and detach the handle from the liftgate.**

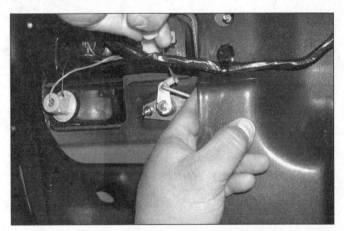

**24.9  Before the lock cylinder (or the liftgate latch) can be removed, this rod must be disengaged from the lock cylinder**

## 25  Steering column cover - removal and installation

*Refer to illustration 25.3 and 25.4*

**Warning:** *Some models covered by this manual are equipped with airbags. Always disconnect the negative battery cable and wait at least one minute before working in the vicinity of the impact sensors, steering column or instrument panel to avoid the possibility of accidental deployment of the airbag, which could cause personal injury (see Chapter 12).*

1    Remove the steering wheel (see Chapter 10).

2    If you need to remove the *upper* half of the steering column cover, remove the instrument cluster trim bezel (see Section 27). (It's not necessary to remove the cluster trim bezel to remove the lower half of the steering column cover.)

3    Remove the steering column cover screws **(see illustration)**.

4    Separate the cover halves and detach them from the steering column **(see illustration)**.

5    Installation is the reverse of removal.

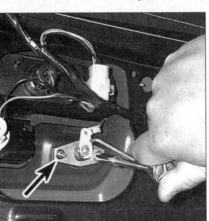

**24.10  To detach the lock cylinder from the liftgate, remove the lock cylinder retaining nuts**

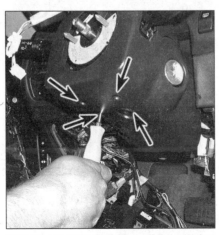

**25.3  To separate the halves of the steering column cover, remove these four screws (arrows) from the bottom cover half**

**25.4  Carefully separate and remove the steering column cover halves**

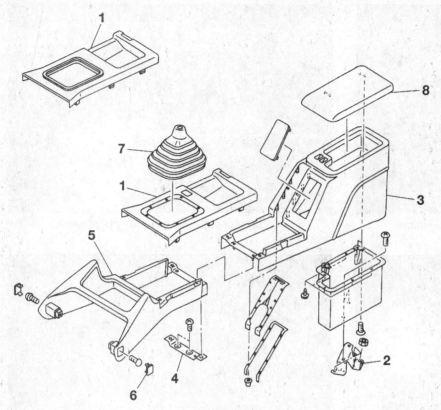

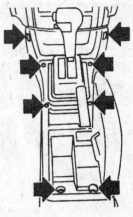

**26.3 Front and rear console retaining screws (1990 through 1994 models)**

**26.6 On automatic models, pry this trim piece from the front console cover (1995 and later models)**

**26.2 Center console assembly mounting details (1990 through 1994 models)**

| | | | | | |
|---|---|---|---|---|---|
| 1 | Center cover | 4 | Bracket | 7 | Boot |
| 2 | Bracket | 5 | Front console box | 8 | Pocket lid |
| 3 | Rear console box | 6 | Cover | | |

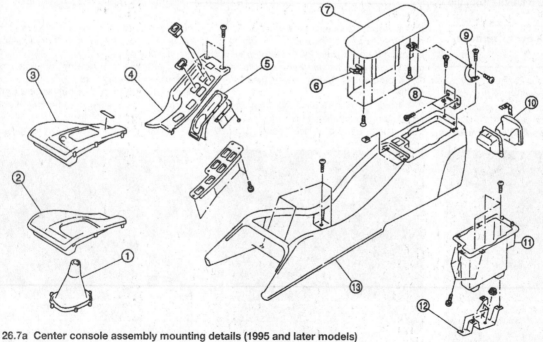

**26.7a Center console assembly mounting details (1995 and later models)**

| | | | | | | | |
|---|---|---|---|---|---|---|---|
| 1 | Shift lever boot (manual transaxle) | 3 | Front cover (automatic transaxle) | 6 | Lock | 10 | Ash tray |
| | | | | 7 | Lid | 11 | Console pocket |
| 2 | Front cover (manual transaxle) | 4 | Console cover | 8 | Hinge | 12 | Console bracket |
| | | 5 | Gasket | 9 | Hinge | 13 | Console box |

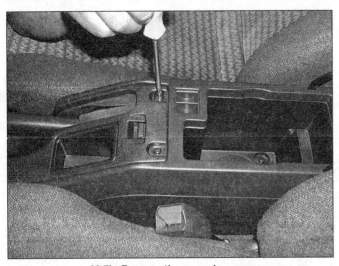

**26.7b Remove the console cover**

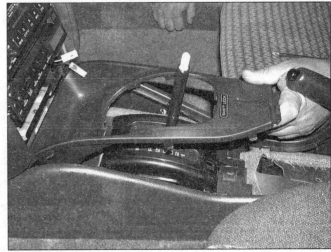

**26.8 Remove the front cover (automatic shown, manual similar)**

## 26 Center console - removal and installation

**Warning:** *Some models covered by this manual are equipped with airbags. Always disconnect the negative battery cable and wait at least one minute before working in the vicinity of the impact sensors, steering column or instrument panel to avoid the possibility of accidental deployment of the airbag, which could cause personal injury (see Chapter 12).*

1    Remove the shift lever knob (see Chapter 7A or 7B).

### 1990 through 1994 models

*Refer to illustrations 26.2 and 26.3*

2    Remove the console cover and, on manual transaxle models, the shift lever boot **(see illustration)**. Detach the parking brake panel cover screws and then remove the cover.

3    Remove the front and rear console retaining screws **(see illustration)**.
4    Unplug any electrical connectors between the front and rear consoles and the vehicle floorpan.
5    Installation is the reverse of removal.

### 1995 and later models

*Refer to illustrations 26.6, 26.7a, 26.7b, 26.8, 26.9a and 26.9b*

6    On manual transaxle models, remove the shift lever boot. On automatic transaxle models, remove the trim piece around the gear position indicator panel **(see illustration)**.
7    Remove the console cover **(see illustrations)**.
8    Remove the front cover **(see illustration)**.
9    Remove the console box **(see illustrations)**.
10   Installation is the reverse of removal.

## 27 Dashboard trim panels - removal and installation

**Warning:** *Some models covered by this manual are equipped with airbags. Always disconnect the negative battery cable and wait at least one minute before working in the vicinity of the impact sensors, steering column or instrument panel to avoid the possibility of accidental deployment of the airbag, which could cause personal injury (see Chapter 12).*

### 1990 through 1994 models

#### Center trim panel

*Refer to illustrations 27.1 and 27.2*

1    Remove the cup holder and the ashtray from the instrument panel **(see illustration on next page)**.
2    Remove the four center trim panel

**26.9a To detach the console box from the floorpan, remove these screws (arrows) . . .**

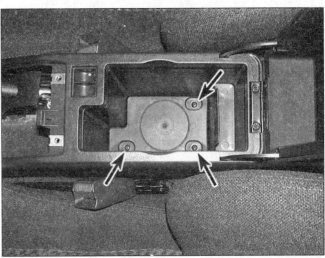

**26.9b . . . and these screws (arrows)**

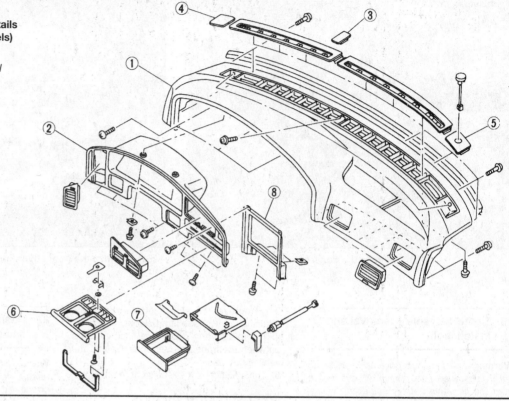

**27.1 Instrument panel details**
**(1990 through 1994 models)**

1   Instrument panel
2   Instrument cluster trim bezel
3   Center upper cover
4   Left upper cover
5   Right upper cover
6   Cup holder
7   Ash tray
8   Center trim panel
9   Left vent grille
10   Center vent grille
11   Right vent grille

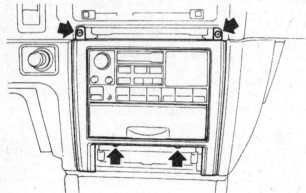

**27.2 The center trim panel is retained by four screws**

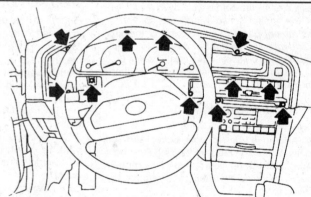

**27.7 Locations of the screws for the instrument cluster bezel**
**(1990 through 1994 models)**

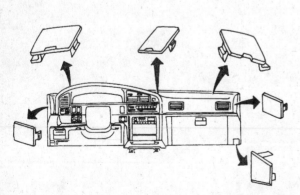

**27.12 Instrument panel screw covers (1990 through 1994 models)**

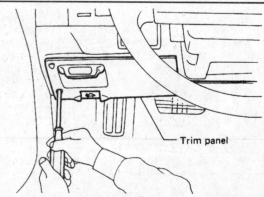

Trim panel

**27.14 To detach the knee bolster trim panels underneath the steering column and the glove box, locate and remove all panel retaining screws; detach the hood release lever from the from the driver's side panel (1990 through 1994 models)**

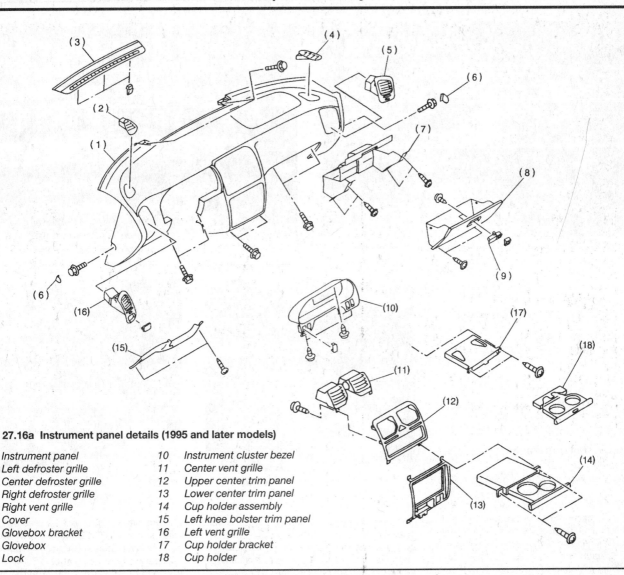

**27.16a Instrument panel details (1995 and later models)**

| | | | |
|---|---|---|---|
| 1 | Instrument panel | 10 | Instrument cluster bezel |
| 2 | Left defroster grille | 11 | Center vent grille |
| 3 | Center defroster grille | 12 | Upper center trim panel |
| 4 | Right defroster grille | 13 | Lower center trim panel |
| 5 | Right vent grille | 14 | Cup holder assembly |
| 6 | Cover | 15 | Left knee bolster trim panel |
| 7 | Glovebox bracket | 16 | Left vent grille |
| 8 | Glovebox | 17 | Cup holder bracket |
| 9 | Lock | 18 | Cup holder |

screws **(see illustration)**. There are two upper screws, (one in each upper corner, and two lower screws, located underneath the trim panel, facing straight down. Remove the center trim panel.

3    Installation is the reverse of removal.

**27.16b To detach the instrument cluster trim bezel from the dash, remove these four screws (arrows) (1995 and later models) . . .**

### Instrument cluster bezel

4    Remove the center trim panel (see Steps 1 and 2).

5    Carefully pry out the left and center vent grilles **(see illustration 27.1)**.

6    Pry out the switch box, the mirror control switch and the height control switch from the instrument cluster bezel, unplug the electrical connectors from these switches and remove them (see Chapter 12).

7    Locate the cluster bezel retaining screws in the lower edge of the holes for each of the components removed in Step 6. Remove these screws **(see illustration)**.

8    Remove the two cluster bezel retaining screws from the upper edge of the heater control panel.

9    Remove the two screws from the upper side of the cluster bezel.

10   Remove the instrument cluster bezel.

11   Installation is the reverse of removal.

### Instrument panel screw covers

*Refer to illustration 27.12*

12   These covers **(see illustration)** provide access to various instrument panel mounting screws. They're easily pried off with a screwdriver. These covers do not use retaining screws. If you're going to remove the instrument panel, remove all of the covers.

13   Installation is the reverse of removal.

### Knee bolster trim panel

*Refer to illustration 27.14*

14   This panel (located underneath the steering column) provides access to the wiring and electrical components located below the instrument cluster. To remove the knee bolster trim panel, remove the trim panel retaining screws **(see illustration)**. Detach the hood release lever and cable (see Section 10).

15   Installation is the reverse of removal.

## 1995 and later models

### Instrument cluster bezel

*Refer to illustration 27.16a, 27.16b and 27.16c*

16   Remove the four instrument cluster bezel retaining screws **(see illustrations)**, tilt the steering wheel down, pull out the cluster

**27.16c ... then pull the trim bezel out and unplug the electrical connectors**

**27.18a  To detach the center trim panels from the dash on 1995 and later models, remove these two screws (arrows) ...**

bezel and unplug the electrical connectors on the backside **(see illustration)**.
17    Installation is the reverse of removal.

### Center trim panels

*Refer to illustrations 27.18a, 27.18b and 27.18c*

18    Pull out the cup holder and remove the two screws between the upper and lower center trim panels, then remove the upper and lower trim panels **(see illustrations)**.
19    Installation is the reverse of removal.

### Knee bolster trim panel

*Refer to illustration 27.20*

20    This panel (located underneath the steering column) provides access to the wiring and electrical components below the instrument cluster. To remove the knee bolster trim panel, remove the trim panel retaining screws and unclip the panel **(see illustration)**. Detach the hood release lever and cable from the panel (see Section 10).
21    Installation is the reverse of removal.

### 28    Instrument panel - removal and installation

**Warning:** *Some models covered by this manual are equipped with airbags. Always*

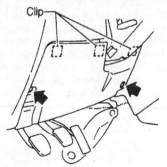

**27.20  To detach the driver's side knee bolster trim panel, remove these two screws and disengage the three clips across the top of the panel**

**27.18b  ... remove the upper center trim panel ...**

*disconnect the negative battery cable and wait at least one minute before working in the vicinity of the impact sensors, steering column or instrument panel to avoid the possibility of accidental deployment of the airbag, which could cause personal injury (see Chapter 12).*

### *1990 through 1994 models*

*Refer to illustration 28.8*

1    Disconnect the negative battery cable.
2    Remove the steering wheel (see Chapter 10).
3    Remove the center console (see Section 26).

**27.18c  ... and remove the lower center trim panel**

4    Pry off the instrument panel screw covers **(see illustration 27.12)** with a screwdriver.
5    Remove the left and right knee bolster trim panels **(see illustration 27.14)**. Detach the hood release lever and cable from the left panel (see Section 10).
6    Remove the instrument cluster trim bezel (see Section 27).
7    Remove the instrument cluster and disconnect the speedometer cable from the cluster (see Chapter 12).
8    Remove the glove box and unplug the electrical connector for the blower motor switch **(see illustration)**.

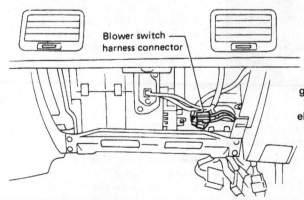

**28.8  After removing the glove box on 1990 through 1994 models, unplug the electrical connector for the blower motor switch**

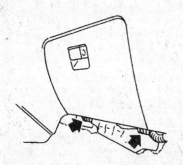

**28.20  To detach the glove box, remove these bolts (arrows)**

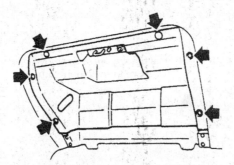

**28.21  To remove the cover back panel, remove these screws (arrows**

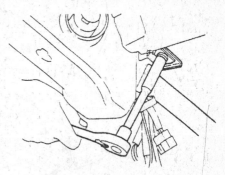

**28.22  To lower the steering column, remove these two bolts (arrows)**

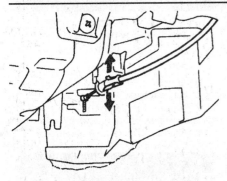

**28.23  Move the temperature control lever to the MAX COLD position, then disengage the temperature control cable from the heater module link**

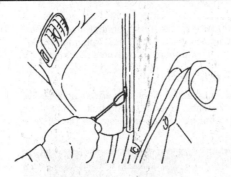

**28.24  Pry off the end covers from the instrument panel and remove the bolts from both ends**

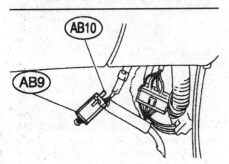

**28.25  On airbag-equipped models, remove the front right sill trim plate and unplug the two yellow electrical connectors**

connectors and vacuum lines interfering with removal.

15    Lift the instrument panel up and out to remove it from the vehicle.

16    Installation is the reverse of removal. Tighten the steering column bolts to 18 ft-lbs.

### 1995 and later models

*Refer to illustrations 28.20 through 28.27*

17    On airbag-equipped models, disable the airbag system (see Chapter 12).

18    Remove the center console (see Section 26).

19    Remove the knee bolster trim panel (see Section 27).

20    Remove the glove box **(see illustration)**.

21    Remove the cover back panel **(see illustration)**.

22    Remove the steering column bolts **(see illustration)** and lower the steering column.

23    Move the temperature control lever to the MAX COLD position, then disengage the temperature control cable from the heater module link **(see illustration)**. Do not move the lever until the cable has been reconnected.

24    Remove the end covers from the instrument panel **(see illustration)** and remove the bolts from both ends.

25    On airbag-equipped models, remove the front right sill trim plate and unplug the yellow electrical connectors **(see illustration)**.

26    Unplug the indicated electrical connectors and remove the instrument panel retaining bolts **(see illustration)**.

9    Remove the four center trim bezel screws (see Section 27) and remove the center trim bezel.

10    Disconnect the ventilation cable and the temperature control cable from the heater unit (see Chapter 3).

11    Remove the radio and disconnect the antenna lead (see Chapter 12).

12    Remove the bolts which secure the steering column to the instrument panel and lower the column.

13    Remove the bolts securing the instrument panel **(see illustration 27.1)** and remove the instrument panel.

14    Pull the instrument panel towards the rear of the vehicle and detach any electrical

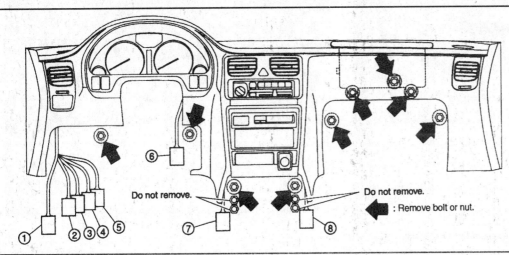

**28.26  To detach the instrument panel from the vehicle, unplug the indicated electrical connectors and remove the indicated retaining bolts (arrows)**

1   *15-pin gray connector*
2   *22-pin brown connector*
3   *22-pin white connector*
4   *20-pin blue connector*
5   *22-pin black connector*
6   *4-pin sky blue connector*
7   *1-pin black connector*
8   *1-pin black connector*

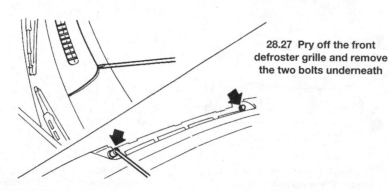

**28.27 Pry off the front defroster grille and remove the two bolts underneath**

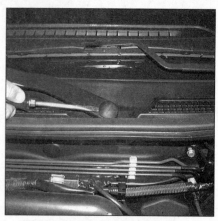

**29.1a Pry off the caps from the windshield wiper arms . . .**

27   Remove the front defroster grille and the two bolts underneath **(see illustration)**.

28   Remove the instrument panel.

29   Installation is the reverse of removal. Tighten the steering column bolts to 18 ft-lbs.

## 29   Cowl vent grille - removal and installation

*Refer to illustrations 29.1a, 29.1b and 29.2*

1   Mark the relationship of the windshield wiper arms to the windshield, then remove the windshield wiper arms **(see illustrations)**.

2   Carefully pry off the cowl and disengage the plastic clips securing it **(see illustration)**.

3   Installation is the reverse of removal.

## 30   Seats - removal and installation

### *Front seat*

*Refer to illustrations 30.2a and 30.2b*

1   Position the seat all the way forward or all the way to the rear to access the retaining bolts.

2   Detach any bolt trim covers and remove the retaining bolts **(see illustrations)**.

3   Tilt the seat upward to access the underneath, then disconnect any electrical connectors and lift the seat from the vehicle.

4   Installation is the reverse of removal.

### *Rear seat*

5   Detach the bolt trim covers and remove the seat cushion retaining bolts. Then lift up on the front edge and remove the cushion from the vehicle.

**29.1b . . . remove the wiper arm retaining nuts and remove the wiper arms**

6   Detach the retaining bolts at the lower edge of the seat back.

7   Lift up on the lower edge of the seat back and remove it from the vehicle.

8   Installation is the reverse of removal.

**29.2 To detach the cowl, carefully pry it loose (its perimeter is secured by a series of push-type clips)**

**30.2a To detach a front seat from the floorpan, remove these two bolts (arrows) from the front end of the seat rails . . .**

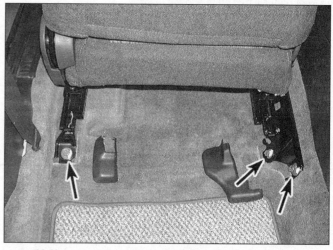

**30.2b . . . and these three bolts (arrows) from the rear**

# Chapter 12
# Chassis electrical system

## Contents

## 1 General information

The electrical system is a 12-volt, negative ground type. Power for the lights and all electrical accessories is supplied by a lead/acid-type battery which is charged by the alternator.

This Chapter covers repair and service procedures for the various electrical components not associated with the engine. Information on the battery, alternator, distributor and starter motor can be found in Chapter 5.

It should be noted that when portions of the electrical system are serviced, the cable should be disconnected from the negative battery terminal to prevent electrical shorts and/or fires.

## 2 Electrical troubleshooting - general information

A typical electrical circuit consists of an electrical component, any switches, relays, motors, fuses, fusible links or circuit breakers related to that component and the wiring and electrical connectors that link the component to both the battery and the chassis. To help you pinpoint an electrical circuit problem, wiring diagrams are included at the end of this Chapter.

Before tackling any troublesome electrical circuit, first study the appropriate wiring diagrams to get a complete understanding of what makes up that individual circuit. Trouble spots, for instance, can often be narrowed down by noting if other components related to the circuit are operating properly. If several components or circuits fail at one time, chances are the problem is in a fuse or ground connection, because several circuits are often routed through the same fuse and ground connections.

Electrical problems usually stem from simple causes, such as loose or corroded connections, a blown fuse, a melted fusible link or a bad relay. Visually inspect the condition of all fuses, wires and connections in a problem circuit before troubleshooting it.

If testing instruments are going to be utilized, use the diagrams to plan ahead of time where you will make the necessary connections in order to accurately pinpoint the trouble spot.

The basic tools needed for electrical troubleshooting include a circuit tester or voltmeter (a 12-volt bulb with a set of test leads can also be used), a continuity tester, which includes a bulb, battery and set of test leads, and a jumper wire, preferably with a circuit breaker incorporated, which can be used to bypass electrical components. Before attempting to locate a problem with test instruments, use the wiring diagram(s) to decide where to make the connections.

## Voltage checks

Voltage checks should be performed if a circuit is not functioning properly. Connect one lead of a circuit tester to either the negative battery terminal or a known good ground. Connect the other lead to a electrical connector in the circuit being tested, preferably nearest to the battery or fuse. If the bulb of the tester lights, voltage is present, which means that the part of the circuit between the electrical connector and the battery is problem free. Continue checking the rest of the circuit in the same fashion. When you reach a point at which no voltage is present, the problem lies between that point and the last test point with voltage. Most of the time the problem can be traced to a loose connection.

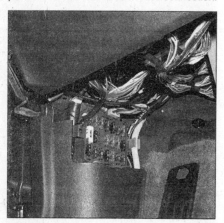

**3.1a One fuse box is located in the upper part of the left (driver's side) kick panel, under the left end of the instrument panel**

**Note:** *Keep in mind that some circuits receive voltage only when the ignition key is in the Accessory or Run position.*

## Finding a short

One method of finding shorts in a circuit is to remove the fuse and connect a test light or voltmeter in its place. There should be no voltage present in the circuit. Move the wiring harness from side to side while watching the test light. If the bulb goes on, there is a short to ground somewhere in that area, probably where the insulation has rubbed through. The same test can be performed on each component in the circuit, even a switch.

## Ground check

Perform a ground test to check whether a component is properly grounded. Disconnect the battery and connect one lead of a self-powered test light, known as a continuity tester, to a known good ground. Connect the other lead to the wire or ground connection being tested. If the bulb goes on, the ground is good. If the bulb does not go on, the ground is not good.

## Continuity check

A continuity check is done to determine if there are any breaks in a circuit - if it is passing electricity properly. With the circuit off (no power in the circuit), a self-powered continuity tester can be used to check the circuit. Connect the test leads to both ends of the circuit (or to the "power" end and a good ground), and if the test light comes on the circuit is passing current properly. If the light doesn't come on, there is a break somewhere in the circuit. The same procedure can be used to test a switch, by connecting the continuity tester to the power in and power out sides of the switch. With the switch turned On, the test light should come on.

## Finding an open circuit

When diagnosing for possible open circuits, it is often difficult to locate them by sight because oxidation or terminal misalign-

ment are hidden by the electrical connectors. Merely wiggling an electrical connector on a sensor or in the wiring harness may correct the open circuit condition. Remember this when an open circuit is indicated when troubleshooting a circuit. Intermittent problems may also be caused by oxidized or loose connections.

Electrical troubleshooting is simple if you keep in mind that all electrical circuits are basically electricity running from the battery, through the wires, switches, relays, fuses and fusible links to each electrical component (light bulb, motor, etc.) and to ground, from which it is passed back to the battery. Any electrical problem is an interruption in the flow of electricity to and from the battery.

## 3   Fuses - general information

*Refer to illustrations 3.1a, 3.1b and 3.3*

The electrical circuits of the vehicle are protected by a combination of fuses, circuit breakers and fusible links. The fuse block is located under the instrument panel on the driver's side of the dashboard and in the engine compartment **(see illustrations)**. Access is gained by simply unsnapping the plastic cover.

Each of the fuses is designed to protect a specific circuit, as identified on the fuse cover. Spare fuses and a special removal tool are included in the fuse box cover.

Miniaturized fuses are employed in the fuse blocks. These compact fuses, with blade terminal design, allow fingertip removal and replacement. If an electrical component fails, always check the fuse first. The best way to check the fuses is with a test light. Check for power at the exposed terminal tips of each fuse. If power is present at one side of the fuse but not the other, the fuse is blown. A blown fuse can also be identified by visually inspecting it **(see illustration)**.

Fuses are replaced by simply pulling out the old one and pushing in the new one.

Be sure to replace blown fuses with the correct type. Fuses of different ratings are

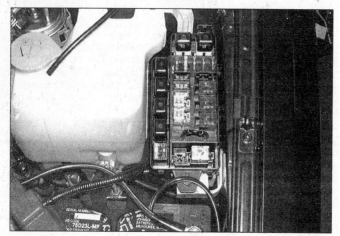

**3.1b  The main fuse box is located in the engine compartment, behind the battery**

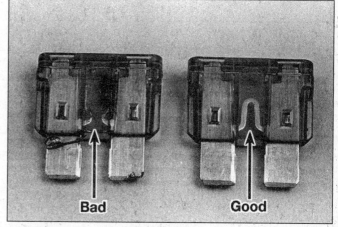

**3.3  The fuses can be checked visually to see if they're blown**

**4.2 One fusible link (arrow) is a short section of wire; the others look like large fuses. They're located in the main fuse box in the engine compartment**

physically interchangeable, but only fuses of the proper rating should be used. Replacing a fuse with one of a higher or lower value than specified is not recommended. Each electrical circuit needs a specific amount of protection. The amperage value of each fuse is molded into the fuse body.

If the replacement fuse immediately fails, don't replace it again until the cause of the problem is isolated and corrected. In most cases, this will be a short circuit in the wiring caused by a broken or deteriorated wire.

**5.2 Perform a continuity test with an ohmmeter to check a circuit breaker - infinite resistance indicates a bad circuit breaker**

**4  Fusible links - general information**

*Refer to illustration 4.2*

Some circuits are protected by fusible links. The links are used in circuits which are not ordinarily fused, such as the ignition circuit.

The fusible links are located in the engine compartment fuse block **(see illustration)**. To replace a fusible link, first discon-

nect the negative cable from the battery. Unplug the burned-out link from the fuse block and replace it with a new one. Always determine the cause for the overload which melted the fusible link before installing a new one.

**5  Circuit breakers - general information**

*Refer to illustration 5.2*

Circuit breakers protect components such as, power windows, power door locks and headlights.

On some models the circuit breaker resets itself automatically, so an electrical overload in a circuit breaker protected system will cause the circuit to fail momentarily, then come back on. If the circuit doesn't come back on, check it immediately **(see illustration)**. Once the condition is corrected, the circuit breaker will resume its normal function. Some circuit breakers must be reset manually.

**6  Relays - general information and testing**

## General information

*Refer to illustrations 6.1a, 6.1b, 6.1c, 6.1d and 6.1e*

1  Several electrical accessories in the vehicle, such as the fuel injection system, horns, starter, and fog lamps use relays to transmit the electrical signal to the component. Relays use a low-current circuit (the control circuit) to open and close a high-current circuit (the power circuit). If the relay is defective, that component will not operate properly. The various relays are mounted in the instrument panel **(see illustrations)** and several locations throughout the vehicle. If a faulty relay is suspected, it can be removed and tested using the procedure below. Defective relays must be replaced as a unit.

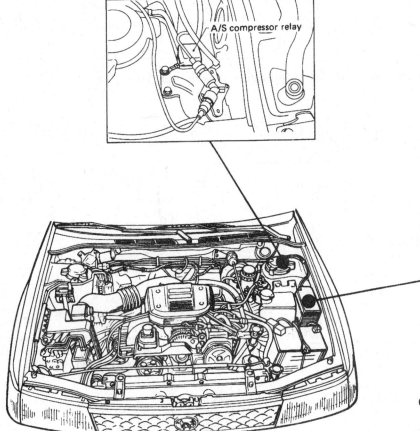

A/S compressor relay

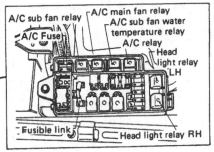

**6.1a  Engine compartment relay locations (1990 through 1994 models)**

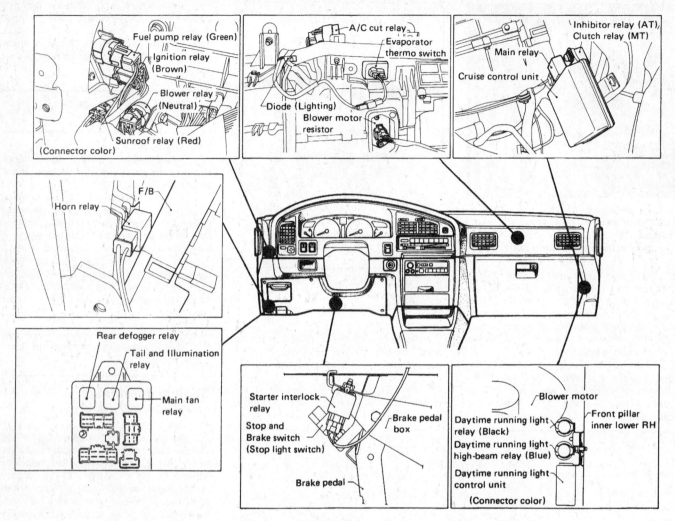

**6.1b  Instrument panel relay and other electrical component locations (1990 through 1994 models)**

## Testing

*Refer to illustration 6.4*

2    It's best to refer to the wiring diagram for the circuit to determine the proper hook-ups for the relay you're testing. However, if you're not able to determine the correct hook-up from the wiring diagrams, you may be able to determine the test hook-ups from the information that follows.

3    On most relays, two of the terminals are the relay's control circuit (they connect to the relay coil which, when energized, closes the large contacts to complete the circuit). The other terminals are the power circuit (they are connected together within the relay when the control-circuit coil is energized).

4    Some relays are marked as an aid to help you determine which terminals are the control circuit and which are the power circuit **(see illustration)**. If the relay isn't marked, check for continuity between the terminals of the relay; the terminals with continuity between them are the ones for the control circuit (this assumes that the control circuit coil is operational). The other terminals are the power circuit.

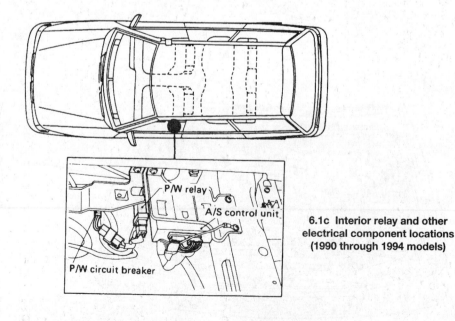

**6.1c  Interior relay and other electrical component locations (1990 through 1994 models)**

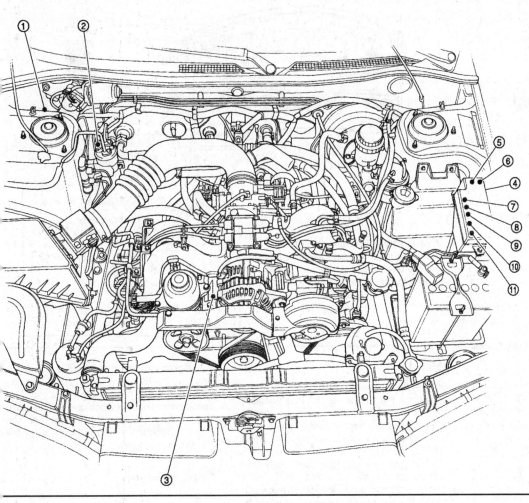

**6.1d Engine compartment relay and other electrical component locations (1995 and later models)**

1  2WD switch (automatics)
2  Air conditioning pressure switch
3  Oil pressure switch
4  Main fuse box
5  Left headlight relay
6  Right headlight relay
7  Air conditioning compressor relay
8  Air conditioning fan relay 2
9  Air conditioning sub-fan relay 2
10  Air conditioning main fan relay 1
11  Air conditioning fuse

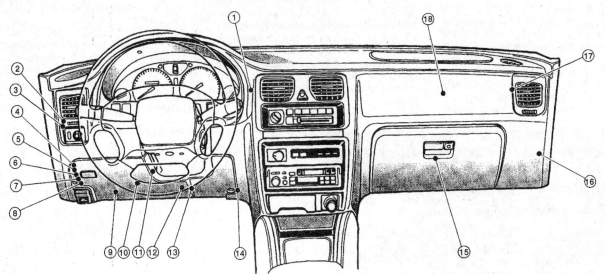

**6.1e Instrument panel relay and other electrical component locations (1995 and later models)**

| | | |
|---|---|---|
| 1  Mode actuator | 7  Main fan relay | 13  Power window and sunroof relay |
| 2  Blower relay | 8  Turn and hazard module | 14  Check connector |
| 3  Horn relay | 9  Seat belt timer | 15  Blower motor resistor |
| 4  Interior fuse box | 10  Illumination control module | 16  Door lock timer |
| 5  Rear defogger relay | 11  Shift lock control module | 17  FRESH/RECIRC actuator |
| 6  Taillight and illumination relay | 12  Power window circuit breaker | 18  Evaporator thermoswitch |

**6.4 Some relays are marked on the outside to easily identify the power circuit and control circuits**

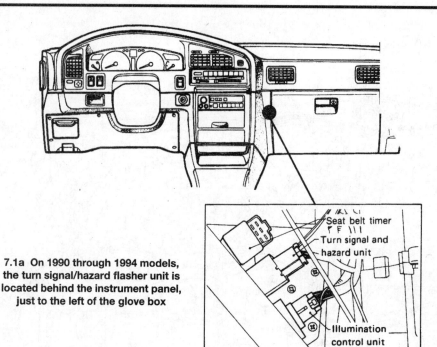

**7.1a On 1990 through 1994 models, the turn signal/hazard flasher unit is located behind the instrument panel, just to the left of the glove box**

5    Connect a fused jumper wire between one of the two control circuit terminals and the positive battery terminal. Connect another jumper wire between the other control circuit terminal and ground. When the connections are made, the relay should click. On some relays, polarity may be critical, so, if the relay doesn't click, try swapping the jumper wires on the control circuit terminals.

6    With the jumper wires connected, check for continuity between the power circuit terminals as indicated by the markings on the relay.

7    If the relay fails any of the above tests, replace it.

## 7   Turn signal/hazard flasher - check and replacement

**Warning:** *Some models covered by this manual are equipped with airbags. Always disconnect the negative battery cable and wait at least one minute before working in the vicinity of the impact sensors, steering column or instrument panel to avoid the possibility of accidental deployment of the airbag, which could cause personal injury (see Section 26).*

### Check

*Refer to illustrations 7.1a and 7.1b*

1    When the turn signal switch is actuated, the flasher unit flashes the turn signal lights; when the hazard flasher switch is actuated, the flasher unit flashes all four turn signal lights simultaneously. On 1990 through 1994 models, the turn signal/hazard flasher is located behind the instrument panel, just to the left of the glove box **(see illustration)**. On 1995 and later models, it's located behind the left end of the instrument panel, right above the hood release lever **(see illustration)**.

2    When the flasher unit is functioning properly, an audible click can be heard during its operation. If the turn signals fail on one side or the other and the flasher unit does not make its characteristic clicking sound, or if it flashes much more rapidly than normal, a faulty turn signal bulb is indicated.

3    If both turn signals fail to blink, the problem may be due to a blown fuse, a faulty flasher unit, a broken switch or a loose or open connection. If a quick check of the fuse box indicates that the turn signal fuse has blown, check the wiring for a short before installing a new fuse.

### Replacement

*Refer to illustrations 7.4a, 7.4b and 7.5*

4    To remove the flasher on 1990 through 1994 models, remove the glove box (see Chapter 11, then remove the screws which secure the glove box frame **(see illustration)**. Unplug the electrical connector from the flasher, remove the flasher bracket screws **(see illustration)** and remove the flasher and bracket. Separate the flasher from the bracket.

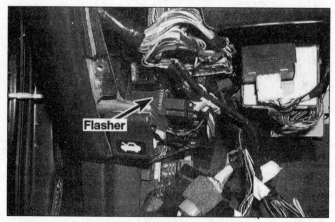

**7.1b On 1995 and later models, the turn signal/hazard flasher unit (arrow) is located behind the left end of the instrument panel (knee bolster removed)**

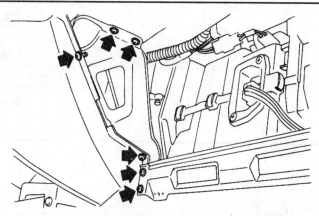

**7.4a To gain access to the turn signal/hazard flasher unit on 1990 through 1994 models, remove these screws and remove the left side of the glove box frame**

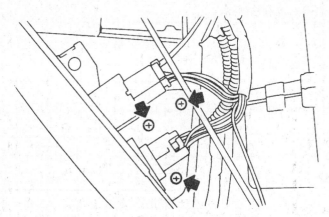

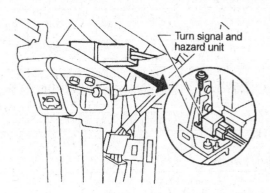

**7.4b To remove the turn signal/hazard flasher unit on 1990 through 1994 models, unplug the electrical connector from the flasher, remove these three bracket screws (arrows), remove the flasher and bracket, then separate the flasher from the bracket**

**7.5 To remove the turn signal/hazard flasher unit on 1995 and later models, remove the knee bolster and the hood release lever, unplug the electrical connector and remove the flasher retaining screw**

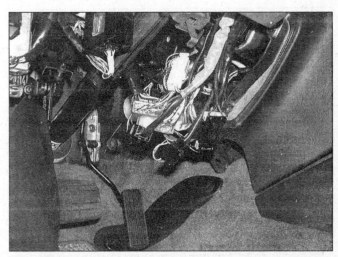

**8.2 After removing the lower half of the steering column cover, remove this steel reinforcement plate to access the steering column switch connectors**

**8.3 The electrical connectors for the steering column switches are located at the base of the steering column; trace the wires down from each switch to make sure you have the right connector before unplugging it**

5    To remove the flasher on 1995 and later models, remove the knee bolster and the hood release lever bracket (see Chapter 11), unplug the electrical connector from the old unit, remove the flasher retaining screw **(see illustration)** and remove the old flasher.
6    Make sure that the replacement unit is identical to the original. Compare the old one to the new one before installing it.
7    Installation is the reverse of removal.

## 8    Steering column switches - check and replacement

**Warning:** *Some models covered by this manual are equipped with airbags. Always disconnect the negative battery cable and wait at least one minute before working in the vicinity of the impact sensors, steering column or instrument panel to avoid the possibility of accidental deployment of the airbag,*

*which could cause personal injury (see Section 26). DO NOT use any electrical test equipment on the airbag system wiring, which can be identified by its bright yellow insulation and connectors.*

### Check

*Refer to illustrations 8.2, 8.3, 8.4a, 8.4b, 8.4c and 8.4d*
1    Remove the lower half of the steering column cover (see Chapter 11).
2    Remove the knee protection plate from the underside of the steering column **(see illustration)**.
3    Trace the wires from the switch assembly, down the steering column, to the connectors at the lower end of the column **(see illustration)** and unplug them.
4    Using an ohmmeter or a self-powered test light, check for continuity between the indicated switch terminals with the switch in each of the indicated positions **(see illustra-**

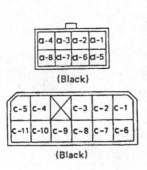

(Black)

(Black)

**8.4a Terminal guide for the turn signal/headlight/dimmer switch**

**tions). Warning:** *DO NOT use electrical test equipment on the yellow airbag connector. If the continuity isn't as specified, replace the switch.*

## Turn signal switch

| Switch position | Terminal | a-5 | a-7 | a-6 |
|---|---|---|---|---|
| Turn | L·L' | ○——|——○ | |
| | ↕ | ×——|———|——× |
| | N | | | |
| | ↕ | ×——|———|——× |
| | R·R' | | ○——|——○ |

## Lighting switch

| Switch position | Terminal | c-1 | c-2 | c-3 |
|---|---|---|---|---|
| OFF | | | | |
| Tail | | ○——|——○ | |
| ↕ | | ○——|——○ | |
| Head | | ○——|——○——|——○ |

## Parking switch

| Switch position | Terminal | c-10 | c-11 | c-9 |
|---|---|---|---|---|
| OFF | | ○——|——○ | |
| ↕ | | ×——|———|——× |
| ON | | | ○——|——○ |

## Dimmer and passing switch

| Switch position | Terminal | a-3 | a-2 | a-1 | a-4 |
|---|---|---|---|---|---|
| Flash | | ○——|———|——○ | ○ |
| ↕ | | ○——|——○ | ○ | |
| Low beam | | ○——|——○ | | |
| ↕ | | ○ | | ○ | |
| HI-beam | | ○——|———|——○ | |

**8.4b   Continuity table for the turn signal/headlight/dimmer switch**

## Front wiper switch

| Switch position | | d-9 (Y) | d-8 (L) | d-6 (LY) | d-7 (LW) | INT1 | INT2 |
|---|---|---|---|---|---|---|---|
| OFF | OFF | ○——|——○ | | | | |
| | | ×——|———|——× | | | |
| | MIST | | | ○——|——○ | | |
| INT | OFF | ○——|——○ | | | ○——|——○ |
| | | ×——|———|——× | | | |
| | MIST | | | ○——|——○ | | ○——|——○ |
| | | ×——|———|——× | | | |
| LO | OFF | | | ○——|——○ | | |
| | MIST | | | ○——|——○ | | |
| HI | OFF | | | | ○——|——○ | |
| | MIST | | | | ○——|——○ | |

## Front Washer switch

| Switch position | Terminal (Wire color) | d-5 (B) | d-2 (W) |
|---|---|---|---|
| OFF | | | |
| ON | | ○——|——○ |

## Rear wiper/washer switch

| Switch position | Terminal (Wire color) | d-2 | d-1 | d-3 |
|---|---|---|---|---|
| WASH | | ○——|——○——|——○ |
| OFF | | | | |
| ON | | ○——|———|——○ |
| WASH | | ○——|——○——|——○ |

**8.4d   Continuity table for the wiper/washer switch**

| d-4 | d-3 | ✕ | d-2 | d-1 |
|---|---|---|---|---|
| d-9 | d-8 | d-7 | d-6 | d-5 |

(Black)

**8.4c   Terminal guide for the wiper/washer switch**

**8.9   To detach the steering column switch assembly from the steering column, remove these two screws**

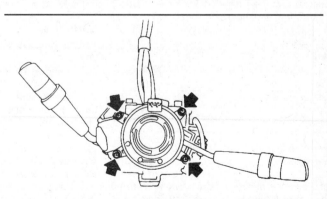

**8.10   To detach the slip ring from the steering column switch assembly, remove these four screws**

## Replacement

*Refer to illustrations 8.9, 8.10 and 8.11*

5    Disconnect the cable from the negative terminal of the battery.
6    Remove the steering wheel (see Chapter 10).
7    Remove the upper and lower halves of the steering column cover (see Chapter 11).
8    Remove the knee protection plate from the underside of the steering column **(see illustration 8.2)**, then trace the wires from the switch assembly, down the steering column, to the connectors at the lower end of the column **(see illustration 8.3)** and unplug them.
9    Remove the two switch retaining screws **(see illustration)** and pull the switch off the steering shaft.
10    Remove the four slip ring retaining screws **(see illustration)** and remove the slip ring.
11    Remove the turn signal/headlight/dimmer switch retaining screws or the windshield wiper/washer switch screws **(see illustration)**.
12    Installation is the reverse the removal. On models equipped with airbags, center the roll connector before installing the steering wheel (see Section 26).

**8.11  To detach the turn signal/headlight/dimmer switch or the windshield wiper/washer switch, remove the indicated switch retaining screws (arrows)**

**9.3  Trace the wires from the ignition switch down to the electrical connector and unplug it**

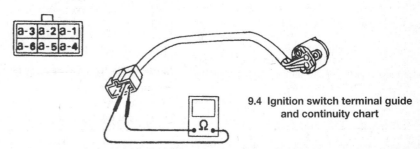

**9.4  Ignition switch terminal guide and continuity chart**

| Position | Terminal | a-1 | a-2 | a-5 | a-4 |
|---|---|---|---|---|---|
| LOCK | | | | | |
| ACC | | ◯—————◯ | | | |
| ON | | ◯————◯ | | ◯ | |
| START | | ◯ | | ◯————◯ | |

## 9    Ignition switch and key lock cylinder - check and replacement

**Warning:** *Some models covered by this manual are equipped with airbags. Always disconnect the negative battery cable and wait at least one minute before working in the vicinity of the impact sensors, steering column or instrument panel to avoid the possibility of accidental deployment of the airbag, which could cause personal injury (see Section 26). DO NOT use any electrical test equipment on the airbag system wiring, which can be identified by its bright yellow insulation and connectors.*

## Check

*Refer to illustrations 9.3 and 9.4*

1    Remove the lower half of the steering column cover (see Chapter 11).
2    Remove the knee protection plate from the underside of the steering column **(see illustration 8.2)**.
3    Trace the wires from the ignition switch, down the steering column, to the connector at the lower end of the column **(see illustration)** and unplug them.
4    Using an ohmmeter or self-powered test light, check for continuity between the indicated switch terminals with the switch in each of the indicated positions **(see illustration)**. **Warning:** *DO NOT use electrical test equipment on the yellow airbag connector.* If the continuity isn't as specified, replace the switch.

## Replacement

### Ignition switch

*Refer to illustration 9.9*

5    Disconnect the cable from the negative

terminal of the battery.
6    Remove the steering column lower cover (see Chapter 11).
7    Remove the knee protection plate from the underside of the steering column **(see illustration 8.2)**.
8    Trace the wires from the ignition switch, down the steering column, to the connectors at the lower end of the column and unplug them.
9    Remove the screw retaining the switch to the lock cylinder housing **(see illustration)**.
10    Pull the switch out of the housing.
11    Installation is the reverse of removal. Be sure to align the slot in the switch with the blade on the lock cylinder.

### Key lock cylinder

*Refer to illustration 9.16*

12    Disconnect the cable from the negative terminal of the battery.
13    Remove the steering column covers (see Chapter 11).

**9.9  The ignition switch is secured to the lock cylinder housing with one screw (arrow)**

14    Remove the steering wheel (see Chapter 10).
15    Remove the ignition switch from the lock cylinder housing (see Steps 9 and 10).
16    Remove the shear-head retaining bolts

**9.16 To remove the key lock cylinder assembly, remove these two shear-head retaining bolts (arrows)**

from the lock cylinder housing **(see illustration)**. You may be able to unscrew them using a hammer and a sharp punch, knocking them in a counterclockwise direction. If they are too tight and won't loosen by using that method, carefully drill into the center of each bolt and remove them with a screw extractor. Separate the bracket halves from the steering column and remove the old lock cyl-

inder/housing assembly.

17   Place the new lock cylinder/housing in position, install the new shear-head bolts and tighten them until the heads snap off.

18   Install the ignition switch (see Step 11).

19   The remainder of the installation is the reverse of removal. On models equipped with airbags, center the roll connector before installing the steering wheel (see Section 26).

---

## 10   Instrument panel switches - check and replacement

---

**Warning:** *Some models covered by this manual are equipped with airbags. Always disconnect the negative battery cable and wait at least one minute before working in the vicinity of the impact sensors, steering column or instrument panel to avoid the possibility of accidental deployment of the airbag, which could cause personal injury (see Section 26).*

**Note:** *For information on heater and air conditioning control switches refer to Chapter 3.*

### 1990 through 1994 models
#### Power mirror switch
*Refer to illustrations 10.1 and 10.3*

1   Using a small slotted screwdriver, pry out the power mirror switch **(see illustration)**.

2   Unplug the electrical connector from the backside the switch.

3   Using an ohmmeter or self-powered test light, check for continuity between the indicated switch terminals with the switch in each of the indicated positions **(see illustration)**. If the continuity isn't as specified, replace the switch.

4   To install the switch, plug in the electrical connector, place the switch in position and pop it into place.

### Hazard warning switch
*Refer to illustration 10.7*

5   Remove the instrument cluster bezel (see Chapter 11).

6   Remove the hazard warning switch retaining screws and remove the switch from the instrument cluster bezel.

7   Using an ohmmeter or self-powered test light, check for continuity between the indicated switch terminals with the switch in each of the indicated positions **(see illustration)**. If the continuity isn't as specified, replace the switch.

8   Place the switch in position, install the switch retaining screws, plug in the electrical connector and install the instrument cluster bezel (see Chapter 11).

---

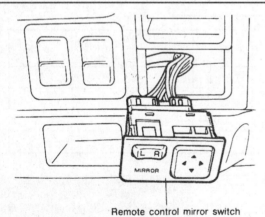

Remote control mirror switch

**10.1 To check and/or replace the power mirror switch, pry it out of the instrument panel and unplug the electrical connector (1990 through 1994 models)**

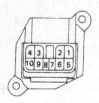

**10.7 Hazard warning switch terminal guide and continuity table (1990 through 1994 models)**

| | 7 | 3 | 9 | 10 | 5 | 6 | 1 | | 2 |
|---|---|---|---|---|---|---|---|---|---|
| ON | O—|—O | O—|—O—|—O | O—|—Ø | | Ø |
| OFF | O—|—O | | | | | O—|—Ø | | Ø |

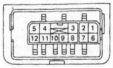

**10.3 Power mirror switch terminal guide and continuity table (1990 through 1994 models)**

| | Mirror switch | | | | | Left/Right changing switch | | |
|---|---|---|---|---|---|---|---|---|
| | OFF | Right | Left | Upper | Down | Left | N | Right |
| 4 | | O | O | O | O | | | |
| | | | | O | O | O | | O |
| 10 | | O | O | O | O | | | |
| 11 | | O | O | O | O | | | O |
| 1 | | | | | | | | O |
| 6 | | | | | | | | O |
| 2 | | | | | | O | | |
| 7 | | | | | | O | | |
| 8 | | | | | | | | |
| 9 | | | | | | | | |
| 5 | | | | | | O | | |
| | | | | | | O | | |
| 12 | | | | | | O | | |

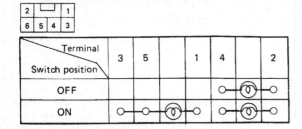

| Switch position \ Terminal | 3 | 5 | 1 | 4 | 2 |
|---|---|---|---|---|---|
| OFF | | | | o—Ⓥ—o | |
| ON | o—o—Ⓥ—o | | | o—Ⓥ—o | |

10.11  Rear window defogger switch terminal guide and continuity table (1990 through 1994 models)

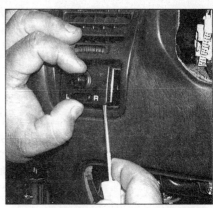

10.13  To remove the power mirror switch from the instrument panel on 1995 and later models, carefully pry it out with a small screwdriver, then unplug the electrical connector

10.15  Power mirror switch terminal guide and continuity table (1995 and later models)

| Switch position Terminal | Mirror switch | | | | | Left/Right changing switch | | |
|---|---|---|---|---|---|---|---|---|
| | OFF | Right | Left | Up | Down | Left | N | Right |
| 7 | | | | | | o | | |
| 9 | | | | | | o | | |
| 6 | | | | | | | | o |
| 8 | | | | | | | | o |
| 2 | | o | | o | | | | |
| | | o | | o | | o | | o |
| 1 | | o | o | o | | | | |
| | | | o | | o | o | | |
| 4 | | o | o | o | o | | | |
| 3 | | | | | | | | |

## Rear window defogger switch

*Refer to illustration 10.11*

9  Using a small slotted screwdriver, pry out the rear widow defogger switch.
10  Unplug the electrical connector from the backside the switch.
11  Using an ohmmeter or self-powered test light, check for continuity between the indicated switch terminals with the switch in each of the indicated positions **(see illustration)**. If the continuity isn't as specified, replace the switch.

10.18  To remove the hazard warning switch on 1995 and later models, remove the upper center trim panel, unplug the electrical connector from the switch and remove the switch retaining screws

replace the switch.
12  To install the switch, plug in the electrical connector, place the switch in position and snap it into place.

## 1995 and later models

### Power mirror switch

*Refer to illustrations 10.13 and 10.15*

13  Using a small slotted screwdriver, carefully pry out the power mirror switch from the instrument panel **(see illustration)**.
14  Unplug the electrical connector from the backside the switch.
15  Using an ohmmeter or self-powered test light, check for continuity between the indicated switch terminals with the switch in each of the indicated positions **(see illustration)**. If the continuity isn't as specified, replace the switch.

16  To install the switch, plug in the electrical connector, place the switch in position and snap it into place.

### Hazard warning switch

*Refer to illustrations 10.18 and 10.19*

17  Remove the upper center trim panel (see Section 27 in Chapter 11).
18  Unplug the electrical connector from the hazard warning switch **(see illustration)**, remove the switch retaining screws and detach the switch from the upper center trim panel.
19  Using an ohmmeter or self-powered test light, check for continuity between the indicated switch terminals with the switch in each of the indicated positions **(see illustration)**. If the continuity isn't as specified, replace the switch.
20  To install the switch, place the switch in position and install the screws, plug in the electrical connector and install the upper center trim panel (see Chapter 11).

### Rear window defogger, cruise control and fog light switches

*Refer to illustrations 10.23a, 10.23b and 10.23c*

21  Remove the instrument cluster bezel (see Chapter 11).
22  Pry the switch you wish to test out of the instrument cluster bezel.
23  Using an ohmmeter or self-powered test light, check for continuity between the indicated switch terminals with the switch in

10.19  Hazard warning switch terminal guide and continuity table (1995 and later models)

| | 7 | 3 | 9 | 10 | 5 | 6 | 1 | | 2 |
|---|---|---|---|---|---|---|---|---|---|
| ON | o—o | | o—o | | o—o | | o—Ⓥ | | —o |
| OFF | o—o | | | | | | o—Ⓥ | | —o |

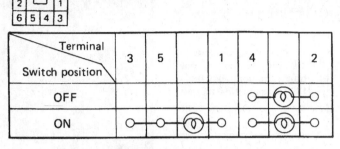

| Terminal / Switch position | 3 | 5 | 1 | 4 | 2 |
|---|---|---|---|---|---|
| OFF | | | | ⊙——⊙ | |
| ON | ⊙——⊙——⊙⊙——⊙ | | | ⊙——⊙⊙——⊙ | |

**10.23a  Rear window defogger switch terminal guide and continuity table (1995 and later models)**

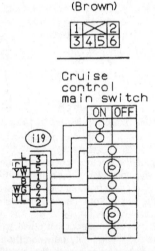

**10.23b  Cruise control main switch terminal guide and continuity table (1995 and later models)**

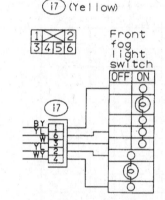

**10.23c  Fog light switch terminal guide and continuity table (1995 and later models)**

each of the indicated positions **(see illustrations)**. If the continuity isn't as specified, replace the switch.

24    Place the switch in position and snap it into place, plug in the electrical connector and install the instrument cluster bezel (see Chapter 11).

### 11    Instrument panel gauges - check

**Warning:** *Some models covered by this manual are equipped with airbags. Always disconnect the negative battery cable and wait at least one minute before working in the vicinity of the impact sensors, steering column or instrument panel to avoid the possibility of accidental deployment of the airbag, which could cause personal injury (see Section 26).*
**Note:** *The procedures described below are for use on analog type gauges only (non-digital).*

### Fuel, oil and temperature gauges

1    All tests below require the ignition switch to be turned to ON position when testing.
2    If the gauge pointer does not move from the empty, low or cold positions, check the fuse. If the fuse is OK, locate the particular sending unit for the circuit you're working on (see Chapter 4 for fuel sending unit location, Chapter 2B for the oil pressure sending unit location or Chapter 3 for the coolant temperature sending unit location). Connect the sending unit connector to ground. If the pointer goes to the full, high or hot position replace the sending unit. If the pointer stays in same position, use a jumper wire to ground the sending unit terminal on the back of the gauge, if necessary, refer to the wiring diagrams at the end of this Chapter. If the pointer moves, the problem lies in the wire between the gauge and the sending unit. If the pointer does not move with the sending unit terminal on the back of the gauge grounded, check for voltage at the other terminal of the gauge. If voltage is present, replace the gauge.

### 12    Instrument cluster - removal and installation

*Refer to illustrations 12.4a and 12.4b*
**Warning:** *Some models covered by this manual are equipped with airbags. Always disconnect the negative battery cable and wait at least one minute before working in the vicinity of the impact sensors, steering column or instrument panel to avoid the possibility of accidental deployment of the airbag, which could cause personal injury (see Section 26).*
1    Disconnect the negative battery cable.
2    Remove the instrument cluster bezel (see Chapter 11).
3    Cover the steering column with a cloth to protect the trim covers.
4    Remove the cluster mounting screws **(see illustrations)** and pull the instrument cluster towards the steering wheel.

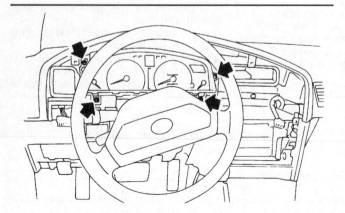

**12.4a  Instrument cluster retaining screws (arrows) (1990 through 1994 models)**

**12.4b  Instrument cluster retaining screws (arrows) (1995 and later models)**

**13.3  Radio and CD player retaining screws (arrows) (late model shown, earlier models similar)**

**13.4  Pull the radio out and disconnect the electrical connectors and the antenna lead**

5   Unplug all electrical connectors and disconnect the speedometer cable (if equipped) from the backside of the instrument cluster. Carefully remove the cluster.
6   Installation is the reverse of removal.

## 13  Radio and speakers - removal and installation

**Warning:** *Some models covered by this manual are equipped with airbags. Always disconnect the negative battery cable and wait at least one minute before working in the vicinity of the impact sensors, steering column or instrument panel to avoid the possibility of accidental deployment of the airbag, which could cause personal injury (see Section 26).*
1   Disconnect the negative battery cable.

### Radio

*Refer to illustration 13.3 and 13.4*
2   Remove the ashtray, cup holder and center trim panel (see Chapter 11).
3   Remove the radio retaining screws **(see illustration)**.
4   Pull out the radio far enough to disconnect the antenna lead and electrical connec-

tors from the backside of the radio **(see illustration)**.
5   Installation is the reverse of removal.

### Speakers

#### Door-mounted speakers

*Refer to illustrations 13.6 and 13.7*
6   On some models, small "tweeters" are mounted behind the mirror trim panels in the front doors. Remove the mirror trim panel (see Chapter 11), pry off the speaker **(see illustration)**, unplug the electrical connector and remove the speaker.
7   To access the main door-mounted speakers in the front or rear doors, remove the door trim panel (see Chapter 11), remove the speaker mounting screws, withdraw the speaker, unplug the electrical connector **(see illustration)** and remove the speaker.
8   Installation is the reverse of removal.

#### Package-shelf mounted speakers (sedan models only)

9   Remove the rear seat cushion and backrest.
10   Remove the rear quarter trim panel.
11   Remove the rear shelf trim panel.
12   Remove the speaker retaining screws,

withdraw the speaker, unplug the electrical connector and remove the speaker from the vehicle.
13   Installation is the reverse of removal.

## 14  Antenna - removal and installation

**Warning:** *Some models covered by this manual are equipped with airbags. Always disconnect the negative battery cable and wait at least one minute before working in the vicinity of the impact sensors, steering column or instrument panel to avoid the possibility of accidental deployment of the airbag, which could cause personal injury (see Section 26).*

### Manual antenna

*Refer to illustration 14.2*
1   Detach the radio and disconnect the antenna lead from the backside of the radio (see Section 13). Attach a piece of stiff wire to the end of the antenna lead, then remove any retaining clips under the instrument panel securing the antenna lead.
2   Remove the antenna retaining screws **(see illustration)**.

**13.6  To remove a door-mounted tweeter, simply pry it out (it's attached by three ball-and-socket type push-in style clips) and unplug the electrical connector**

**13.7  To remove a speaker from a front or rear door, remove the three retaining screws (arrows), pull the speaker out and disconnect the electrical connector**

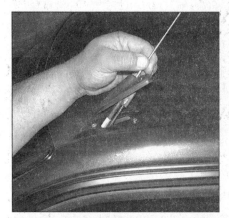

**14.2  Remove the retaining screws, lift the antenna base upward and pull out the antenna lead**

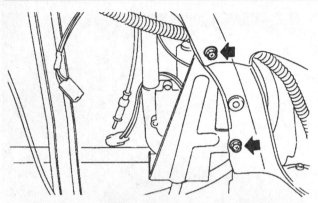

**14.8a  On 1990 through 1994 models, remove these power antenna retaining bolts (arrows)**

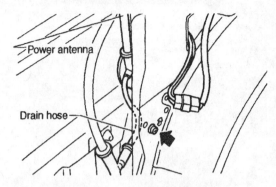

**14.8b  On 1995 and later models, remove this power antenna retaining nut (arrow)**

3    Pull up the antenna base and antenna and pull out the antenna lead.
4    Attach the wire to the new antenna lead and pull the lead back down through the A-pillar. Once the lead has been correctly routed back to the radio, detach the wire.
5    Installation is the reverse of removal.

## Power antenna

*Refer to illustrations 14.8a and 14.8b*
6    Remove the left trunk trim panel (sedan models) or the left rear lower quarter trim panel (wagon models).
7    On 1990 through 1994 wagon models, remove the insulator from the antenna lead.
8    Remove the power antenna retaining bolt(s) or nut **(see illustrations)**.
9    Unplug the electrical connector and the antenna lead, detach the drain tube and remove the power antenna assembly.
10   Installation is the reverse of removal.

## 15  Headlight bulb - replacement

*Refer to illustrations 15.2, 15.3 and 15.5*
**Warning:** *Halogen gas-filled bulbs are under pressure and may shatter if the surface is scratched or the bulb is dropped. Wear eye protection and handle the bulbs carefully, grasping only the base whenever possible.*

**15.2  Unplug the electrical connector from the bulb holder**

*Do not touch the surface of the bulb with your fingers because the oil from your skin could cause it to overheat and fail prematurely. If you do touch the bulb surface, clean it with rubbing alcohol.*
1    Disconnect the negative cable from the battery.
2    Disengage the locking tab and unplug the electrical connector from the bulb holder **(see illustration)**.
3    Remove the rubber cap (if equipped), pull up on the top of the wire retainer to release it and remove the bulb assembly from

**15.3  To detach the bulb holder from the headlight housing, release the wire retainer, then pull out the holder**

the headlight housing **(see illustration)**.
4    Without touching the glass with your bare fingers, insert the new bulb assembly into the headlight housing and lock it into place with the wire retainer.
5    If equipped, install the rubber cap with the word TOP facing up **(see illustration)**, so that the drain hole is facing down. To ensure that the cap is watertight, make sure that the grooved portion of the cap is correctly seated.
6    Plug in the electrical connector and lock

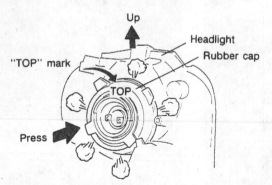

**15.6  Make sure that the rubber cap (if equipped) is installed with the word TOP facing up; press it firmly into place so that the groove seats properly all the way around**

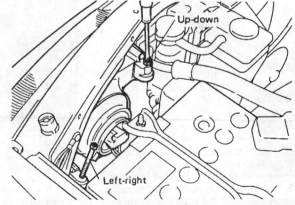

**16.1a  Headlight adjusting screws (1990 through 1994 models)**

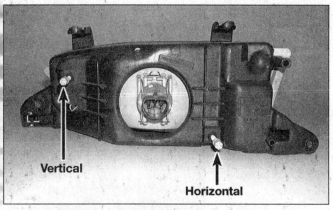

**16.1b  Headlight adjusting screws (1995 and later models)**

Vertical

Horizontal

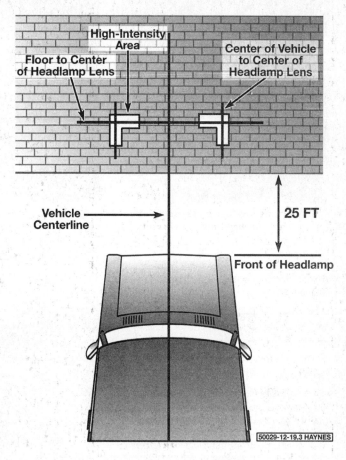

**16.3  Headlight aiming details**

**17.4a  To detach the headlight housing from the body, remove these two bolts from the top . . .**

it into place.
7    Verify that the headlights operate correctly.

## 16   Headlights - adjustment

*Refer to illustrations 16.1a, 16.1b and 16.3*
**Note:** *The headlights must be aimed correctly. If adjusted incorrectly they could blind the driver of an oncoming vehicle and cause a serious accident or seriously reduce your ability to see the road. The headlights should be checked for proper aim every 12 months and any time a new headlight is installed or front end body work is performed. It should be emphasized that the following procedure is only an interim step which will provide temporary adjustment until the headlights can be adjusted by a properly equipped shop.*
1    Headlights have two adjusting screws, one for adjusting up-and-down movement and one for adjusting left-and-right movement **(see illustrations)**.
2    There are several methods for adjusting the headlights. The simplest method requires a blank wall 25 feet in front of the vehicle and a level floor.

3    Position masking tape vertically on the wall in reference to the vehicle centerline and the centerlines of both headlights **(see illustration)**.
4    Position a horizontal tape line in reference to the centerline of all the headlights. **Note:** *It may be easier to position the tape on the wall with the vehicle parked only a few inches away.*
5    Adjustment should be made with the vehicle sitting level, the gas tank half-full and no unusually heavy load in the vehicle.
6    Starting with the low beam adjustment, position the high intensity zone so it is two inches below the horizontal line and two inches to the right of the headlight vertical line. Adjustment is made by turning the top or bottom adjusting screw to raise or lower the beam. The adjusting screw on the side should be used in the same manner to move the beam left or right.
7    With the high beams on, the high intensity zone should be vertically centered with the exact center just below the horizontal line. **Note:** *It may not be possible to position the headlight aim exactly for both high and low beams. If a compromise must be made, keep in mind that the low beams are the most used and have the greatest effect on driver safety.*

8    Have the headlights adjusted by a dealer service department or service station at the earliest opportunity.

## 17   Headlight housing - removal and installation

*Refer to illustration 17.4a, 17.4b and 17.4c*
**Warning:** *These vehicles are equipped with halogen gas-filled headlight bulbs which are under pressure and may shatter if the surface is damaged or the bulb is dropped. Wear eye protection and handle the bulbs carefully, grasping only the base whenever possible. Do not touch the surface of the bulb with your fingers because the oil from your skin could cause it to overheat and fail prematurely. If you do touch the bulb surface, clean it with rubbing alcohol.*
1    Remove the headlight bulb (see Section 15).
2    Remove the radiator grille (see Chapter 11).
3    Remove the side marker light (see Section 18).
4    Remove the headlight housing retaining bolts **(see illustrations)** and remove the

**17.4b** ... remove this bolt (arrow) from the inner end ...

**17.4c** ... and remove this bolt (arrow) from the outer end (1998 Outback model shown, other models similar)

**18.1a** To detach the side marker light housing from the body, remove this screw and maneuver the housing out from the fender (1998 Outback model shown, other models similar)

headlight housing.

5    Installation is the reverse of removal. Adjust the headlight when you're done (see Section 16).

## 18    Bulb replacement

### *Front side marker/turn signal lights*

*Refer to illustrations 18.1a, 18.1b and 18.1c*

1    Remove the screw that secures the side marker light housing **(see illustration)**. Pull off the side marker housing (towards the front of the vehicle), rotate the bulb holder counterclockwise, pull it out and pull the bulb out of the holder **(see illustrations)**.

2    Installation is the reverse of removal. Be sure the small "bayonet" on the rear of the housing engages with its grommet, and the tang on the inner side of the housing engages with its slot on the headlight housing.

### *Rear side marker/brake/turn signal lights*

*Refer to illustrations 18.3a, 18.3b and 18.4*

3    Pry open the access panel **(see illustrations)**.

**18.1b** Rotate the bulb holder counterclockwise to release it from the side marker housing

**18.1c** Rotate the bulb counterclockwise to release it from the bulb holder

4    Rotate the bulb holder counterclockwise to remove it from the housing **(see illustration)**.

5    Push in and rotate the bulb counterclockwise to remove it from the bulb holder.

6    Insert the new bulb in the holder and rotate it clockwise to lock it into the bulb holder. Insert the bulb holder into the housing and rotate it clockwise to lock it into the housing.

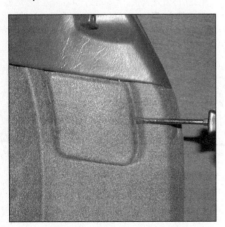

**18.3a** To access the rear side marker/brake/turn signal light bulbs, pry off this panel

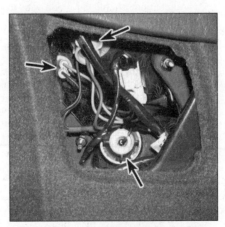

**18.3b** The rear side marker/brake/turn signal light bulbs (arrows) (Outback model shown, other models similar)

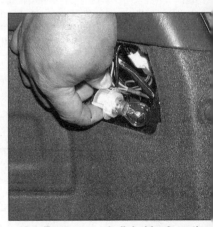

**18.4** To remove a bulb holder from the housing, rotate it counterclockwise and pull it out of the housing

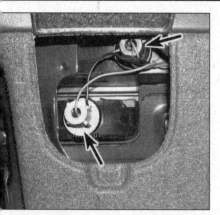

**18.7  On wagon models, you'll find another brake light bulb (upper arrow) and the back-up light bulb (lower arrow) behind two more access panels in the liftgate**

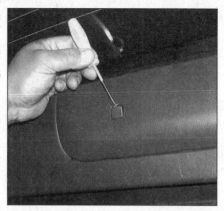

**18.12a  To replace a high-mount brake light bulb on a wagon model, pry off these two screw covers, remove the screws . . .**

**18.12b  . . . flip the access panel down and remove it . . .**

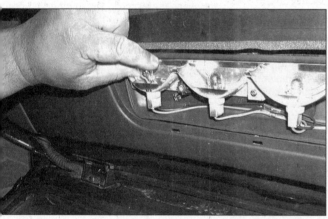

**18.13  . . . and remove the bulb by pulling it straight up**

**18.15  To replace a license plate light bulb, remove the lens/housing retaining screws (arrows)**

### Brake/back-up lights (in trunk lid or liftgate)

*Refer to illustration 18.7*

7    Pry open the access panel **(see illustration)**. The procedure for replacing the bulb is identical to the procedure described in Steps 4 through 6.

**18.16  Separate the lens from the housing**

### High-mount brake lights
#### Sedan models

8    Unplug the electrical connector from the high-mount brake light.
9    Remove the high-mount brake light retaining screws.

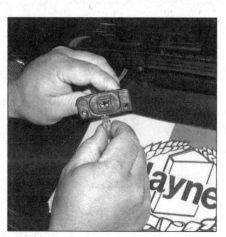

**18.17  Pull the license plate light bulb straight out of the housing**

10    Remove the high-mount brake light.
11    Installation is the reverse of removal.

#### Wagon models

*Refer to illustrations 18.12a, 18.12b and 18.13*

12    Remove the access panel **(see illustrations)**.
13    To remove a bulb, pull it straight up out of the housing **(see illustration)**.
14    Installation is the reverse of removal.

### License plate light

*Refer to illustrations 18.15, 18.16 and 18.17*

15    Remove the license plate light retaining screws **(see illustration)**.
16    Detach the lens and housing as a single assembly and separate the lens from the housing **(see illustration)**.
17    Remove the bulb from its socket by pulling it straight out **(see illustration)**.
18    Installation is the reverse of removal.

### Instrument cluster lights

*Refer to illustration 18.20*

19    Remove the instrument cluster (see Section 12).
20    Rotate the bulb holder counterclockwise

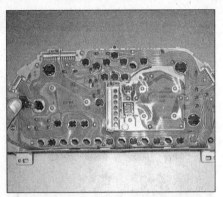

**18.20  Remove the instrument cluster bulbs by rotating them 1/4-turn counterclockwise and pulling straight out**

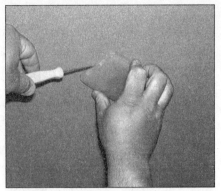

**18.22  Pry off the dome light lens with a small screwdriver**

**18.23  Remove the dome light from the holder (if you have to pry it out, pry against the metal - not the glass - part of the bulb**

to remove it **(see illustration)**.
21    Installation is the reverse of removal.

### Interior light

*Refer to illustrations 18.22 and 18.23*
22    Pry the interior lens off the interior light housing **(see illustration)**.
23    Detach the bulb from the terminals **(see illustration)**. It may be necessary to pry the bulb out - if this is the case, pry only on the ends of the bulb (otherwise the glass may shatter).
24    Installation is the reverse of removal.

---

## 19   Wiper motor - removal and installation

### *Wiper motor circuit check*

*Refer to illustration 19.2*
**Note:** *Refer to the wiring diagrams for wire colors and locations in the following checks.*
1    If the wipers work slowly, make sure the battery is in good condition and has a strong charge (see Chapter 1). If the battery is in good condition, remove the wiper motor (see below) and operate the wiper arms by hand. Check for binding linkage and pivots. Lubricate or repair the linkage or pivots as neces-

sary. Reinstall the wiper motor. If the wipers still operate slowly, check for loose or corroded connections, especially the ground connection. If all connections look OK, replace the motor.
2    If the wipers fail to operate when activated, check the fuse. If the fuse is OK, connect a jumper wire between the wiper motor and ground, then retest. If the motor works now, repair the ground connection. If the motor still doesn't work, turn on the wipers and check for voltage at the motor **(see illustration)**. If there's no voltage at the motor, remove the motor and check it off the vehicle with fused jumper wires from the battery. If the motor now works, check for binding linkage (see Step 1 above). If the motor still doesn't work, replace it. If there's no voltage at the motor, check for voltage at the switch. If there's no voltage at the switch, check the wiring between the switch and fuse panel for continuity. If the wiring is OK, the switch is probably bad.
3    If the wipers only work on one speed, check the continuity of the wires between the switch and motor. If the wires are OK, replace the switch.
4    If the interval (delay) function is inoperative, check the continuity of all the wiring between the switch and motor. If the wiring is OK, replace the interval module.

5    If the wipers stop at the position they're in when the switch is turned off (fail to park) check for voltage at the wiper motor when the wiper switch is OFF but the ignition is ON. If voltage is present, the limit switch in the motor is malfunctioning. Replace the wiper motor. If no voltage is present, trace and repair the limit switch wiring between the fuse panel and wiper motor.
6    If the wipers won't shut off unless the ignition is OFF, disconnect the wiring from the wiper control switch. If the wipers stop replace the switch. If the wipers keep running, there's a defective limit switch in the motor; replace the motor.
7    If the wipers won't retract below the hoodline, check for mechanical obstruction in the wiper linkage or on the vehicle's body which would prevent the wipers from parking If there are no obstructions, check the wiring between the switch and motor for continuity If the wiring is OK, replace the wiper motor.

### *Wiper motor replacement*

#### Front motor and linkage
*Refer to illustrations 19.10a, 19.10b, 19.11a, 19.11b, 19.12a and 19.12b*
8    Remove the windshield wiper arms and the cowl vent grille (see Chapter 11).

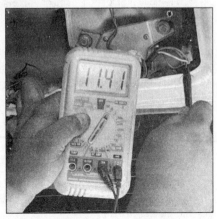

**19.2  Use a voltmeter or test light to check for battery power at the wiper motor (rear wiper motor shown)**

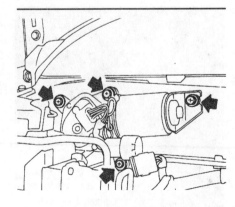

**19.10a  Front wiper motor retaining bolt locations (arrows) (1990 through 1994 models)**

**19.10b  Front wiper motor retaining bolt locations (arrows) (1995 and later models**

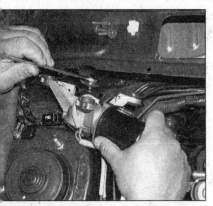

**19.11a  If you're replacing the motor, pull the front wiper motor outward, unscrew the spindle nut (arrow), detach the link arm and install the arm on the new motor . . .**

**19.11b  . . . or, if you're going to install the same motor, disconnect the other end of the link arm from the wiper arm linkage**

**19.12a  To remove the wiper arm linkage, remove all six mounting nuts (other three nuts, not visible here, are in left rear corner of engine compartment) . . .**

**19.12b  . . . then pull it out the far-left access hole**

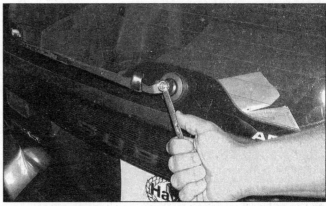

**19.14  Pull off the rear wiper arm cover, then remove the nut and pull the arm straight off its splined shaft**

Disconnect the electrical connector from the wiper motor.

10  Remove the wiper motor retaining bolts (see illustrations).

11  Pull out the wiper motor slightly and disconnect it from the linkage. If you're *replacing* the motor, remove the nut securing the link arm to the motor (see illustration). If you're planning to reuse the same motor, leave the link arm attached to the motor and simply pry the other end of the link arm loose from the wiper arm linkage (see illustration). Remove

the motor from the vehicle.

12  To remove the wiper arm linkage from cowl, remove all six retaining nuts (see illustration) and remove the linkage from the left access hole (see illustration).

13  Installation is the reverse of removal.

### Rear motor

*Refer to illustrations 19.14, 19.15, 19.17a and 19.17b*

14  Remove the wiper arm cover and remove the wiper arm retaining nut (see illus-

tration). Detach the nut and pull the wiper arm straight off the shaft to remove it.

15  Remove the protective cap (see illustration) and remove the drive spindle retaining nut.

16  Remove the liftgate trim panel and the watershield (see Chapter 11).

17  Disconnect the electrical connector from wiper motor and remove the wiper motor retaining bolts (see illustrations), then remove the motor from the vehicle.

18  Installation is the reverse of removal.

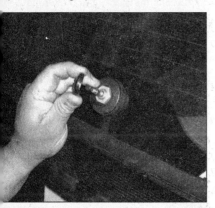

**19.15  Remove the protective cap, then remove the drive spindle retaining nut from the outside of the liftgate**

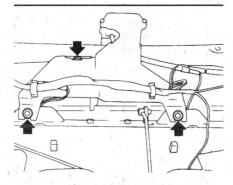

**19.17a  Rear wiper motor retaining bolt locations (arrows) (1990 through 1994 models)**

**19.17b  Rear wiper motor retaining bolt locations (arrows) (1995 and later models)**

20.1  The left horn is located between the battery and the left headlight

20.3  Check for power at the horn terminal with the horn button depressed (right horn shown)

20.8  To detach a horn, remove the mounting bolt (arrow) and unplug the electrical connector

## 20   Horn - check and replacement

### Check

*Refer to illustrations 20.1 and 20.3*
**Note:** *Check the fuses before beginning electrical diagnosis.*
1    The horns are located right behind the headlights **(see illustration).**
2    To test a horn, unplug the electrical connector from the horn, then connect battery voltage to the terminals with a pair of jumper wires. If the horn doesn't sound, replace it.
3    If the horn does sound, check for voltage at the terminal when the horn button is depressed **(see illustration).** If there's voltage at the terminal, check for a bad ground at the horn.
4    If there's no voltage at the horn, check the relay (see Section 6).
5    If the relay is OK, check for voltage to the relay power and control circuits. If either of the circuits is not receiving voltage, inspect the wiring between the relay and the fuse panel.
6    If both relay circuits are receiving voltage, depress the horn button and check the circuit from the relay to the horn button for continuity to ground. If there's no continuity, check the circuit for an open. If there's no open circuit, replace the horn button.
7    If there's continuity to ground through the horn button, check for an open or short in the circuit from the relay to the horn.

### Replacement

*Refer to illustration 20.8*
8    To replace either horn, disconnect the electrical connector and remove the bracket bolt **(see illustration).**
9    Installation is the reverse of removal.

## 21   Rear window defogger - check and repair

1    The rear window defogger consists of a number of horizontal elements baked onto

21.4  When measuring the voltage at the rear window defogger grid, wrap a piece of aluminum foil around the positive probe of the voltmeter and press the foil against the wire with your finger

the glass surface.
2    Small breaks in the element can be repaired without removing the rear window.

### Check

*Refer to illustrations 21.4, 21.5 and 21.7*
3    Turn the ignition switch and defogger system switches to the ON position. Using a voltmeter, place the positive probe against the defogger grid positive terminal and the negative probe against the ground terminal. If battery voltage is not indicated, check the fuse, defogger switch and related wiring. If voltage is indicated, but all or part of the defogger doesn't heat, proceed with the following tests.
4    When measuring voltage during the next two tests, wrap a piece of aluminum foil around the tip of the voltmeter positive probe and press the foil against the heating element with your finger **(see illustration).** Place the negative probe on the defogger grid ground terminal.
5    Check the voltage at the center of each heating element **(see illustration).** If the voltage is 5 to 6-volts, the element is okay (there

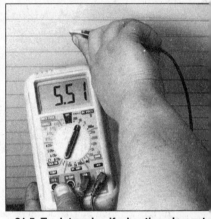

21.5  To determine if a heating element has broken, check the voltage at the center of each element - if the voltage is to 6-volts, the element is unbroken - if the voltage is 10 to 12-volts, the element is broken between the center and the ground side - if there is no voltage, the element is broken between the center an the positive side

is no break). If the voltage is 0-volts, the element is broken between the center of the element and the positive end. If the voltage is 1 to 12-volts the element is broken between the center of the element and ground.
6    If none of the elements are broken, connect the negative lead to a good body ground. The reading should stay the same. it doesn't, the ground connection is bad.
7    To find the break, place the voltmeter negative probe against the defogger negative terminal. Place the voltmeter positive probe with the foil strip against the heating element at the positive terminal end and slide toward the negative terminal end. The point at which the voltmeter deflects from several volts to zero is the point at which the heating element is broken **(see illustration).**

### Repair

*Refer to illustration 21.13*
8    Repair the break in the element using

**21.7  To find the break, place the voltmeter negative lead against the defogger ground terminal, place the voltmeter positive lead with the foil strip against the heating element at the positive terminal end and slide it toward the negative terminal end - the point at which the voltmeter deflects from several volts to zero volts is the point at which the element is broken**

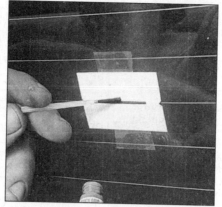

**21.13  To use a defogger repair kit, apply masking tape to the inside of the window at the damaged area, then brush on the special conductive coating**

repair kit specifically recommended for this purpose, available at most auto parts stores. Included in this kit is plastic conductive epoxy.

9    Prior to repairing a break, turn off the system and allow it to cool off for a few minutes.

10    Lightly buff the element area with fine steel wool, then clean it thoroughly with rubbing alcohol.

11    Use masking tape to mask off the area being repaired.

12    Thoroughly mix the epoxy, following the instructions provided with the repair kit.

13    Apply the epoxy material to the slit in the masking tape, overlapping the undamaged area about 3/4-inch on either end **(see illustration)**.

14    Allow the repair to cure for 24 hours before removing the tape and using the system.

## 22  Cruise control system - description and check

1    The cruise control system maintains vehicle speed with a vacuum actuated servo located in the engine compartment, which is connected to the accelerator pedal by a cable. The system consists of the cruise control unit, brake switch, control switches, vacuum hose and vehicle speed sensor. Some features of the system require special testers and diagnostic procedures which are beyond the scope of this manual. Listed below are some general procedures that may be used to locate common problems.

2    Locate and check the fuse (see Section 3).

3    Check the brake light switch (see Chapter 9).

4    Visually inspect the control cable between actuator assembly and accelerator pedal for free movement, replace if necessary.

5    Check the vehicle speed sensor (see Chapter 6).

6    Test drive the vehicle to determine if the cruise control is now working. If it isn't, take it to a an automotive electrical specialist for further diagnosis.

## 23  Power window system - description and check

*Refer to illustrations 23.10a, 23.10b, 23.10c and 23.10d*

1    The power window system operates electric motors, mounted in the doors, which lower and raise the windows. The system consists of the control switches, relays, the motors, regulators and associated wiring.

2    The power windows can be lowered and raised from the master control switch by the driver or by remote switches located at the individual windows. Each window has a separate motor which is reversible. The position of the control switch determines the polarity and therefore the direction of operation.

3    The circuit is protected by a fuse and a circuit breaker. Each motor is also equipped with an internal circuit breaker, this prevents one stuck window from disabling the whole system.

4    The power window system will only operate when the ignition switch is ON. In addition, many models have a window lockout switch at the master control switch which, when activated, disables the switches at the rear windows and, sometimes, the switch at the passenger's window also. Always check these items before troubleshooting a window problem.

5    These procedures are general in nature, so if you can't find the problem using them, take the vehicle to a dealer service department or other properly equipped repair facility.

6    If the power windows won't operate, always check the fuse and circuit breaker first.

7    If only the rear windows are inoperative, or if the windows only operate from the master control switch, check the rear window lockout switch for continuity in the unlocked position. Replace it if it doesn't have continuity.

8    Check the wiring between the switches and fuse panel for continuity. Repair the wiring, if necessary.

9    If only one window is inoperative from the master control switch, try the other control switch at the window. **Note:** *This doesn't apply to the driver's door window.*

10    If the same window works from one

**23.10a  Power window master control switch terminal guide and continuity table (1990 through 1994 models)**

| Lock switch | Switch Position | Front LH | | | | Front RH | | | | Rear RH | | | | Rear LH | | | |
|---|---|---|---|---|---|---|---|---|---|---|---|---|---|---|---|---|---|
| | | 12 | 6 | 5 | 7 | 12 | 9 | 8 | 7 | 12 | 13 | 14 | 7 | 12 | 11 | 10 | 7 |
| NORMAL | UP | | | | | | | | | | | | | | | | |
| | OFF | | | | | | | | | | | | | | | | |
| | DOWN | | | | | | | | | | | | | | | | |
| LOCK | UP | | | | | | | | | | | | | | | | |
| | OFF | | | | | | | | | | | | | | | | |
| | DOWN | | | | | | | | | | | | | | | | |

switch, but not the other, check the switch for continuity (see illustrations). If the continuity is not as specified, replace the switch.

11 If the switch tests OK, check for a short or open in the circuit between the affected switch and the window motor.

12 If one window is inoperative from both switches, remove the trim panel from the affected door and check for voltage at the switch and at the motor while the switch is operated.

13 If voltage is reaching the motor, disconnect the glass from the regulator (see Chapter 11). Move the window up and down by hand while checking for binding and damage. Also check for binding and damage to the regulator. If the regulator is not damaged and the window moves up and down smoothly, replace the motor. If there's binding or damage, lubricate, repair or replace parts, as necessary.

14 If voltage isn't reaching the motor, check the wiring in the circuit for continuity between the switches and motors. You'll need to consult the wiring diagram for the vehicle. If the circuit is equipped with a relay, check that the relay is grounded properly and receiving voltage.

15 Test the windows after you are done to confirm proper repairs.

## 24 Power door lock system - description and check

The power door lock system operates the door lock actuators mounted in each door. The system consists of the switches, actuators, a control unit and associated wiring. Diagnosis can usually be limited to simple checks of the wiring connections and actuators for minor faults which can be easily repaired. On 1995 and later models, the system uses an electronic control unit; in-depth diagnosis should be left to a dealership service department. The door lock control unit is located behind the instrument panel, to the right of the fuse box.

Power door lock systems are operated by bi-directional solenoids located in the doors. The lock switches have two operating positions: Lock and Unlock. When activated, the switch sends a ground signal to the door lock control unit to lock or unlock the doors. Depending on which way the switch is activated, the control unit reverses polarity to the solenoids, allowing the two sides of the circuit to be used alternately as the feed (positive) and ground side.

Some vehicles may have an anti-theft systems incorporated into the power locks. If you are unable to locate the trouble using the following general Steps, consult your a dealer service department.

1 Always check the circuit protection first. Some vehicles use a combination of circuit breakers and fuses.

2 Operate the door lock switches in both directions (Lock and Unlock) with the engine off. Listen for the click of the solenoids operating.

3 Test the switches for continuity. Replace the switch if there's not continuity in both switch positions.

4 Check the wiring between the switches, control unit and solenoids for continuity. Repair the wiring if there's no continuity.

5 Check for a bad ground at the switches or the control unit.

6 If all but one lock solenoids operate, remove the trim panel from the affected door (see Chapter 11) and check for voltage at the solenoid while the lock switch is operated One of the wires should have voltage in the Lock position; the other should have voltage in the Unlock position.

7 If the inoperative solenoid is receiving voltage, replace the solenoid.

8 If the inoperative solenoid isn't receiving voltage, check the relay or for an open or short in the wire between the lock solenoid and the control unit. **Note:** *It's common for wires to break in the portion of the harness between the body and door (opening and closing the door fatigues and eventually breaks the wires).*

## 25 Electric side view mirrors - description and check

*Refer to illustration 25.7*

1 Most electric rear view mirrors use two motors to move the glass; one for up and down adjustments and one for left-right adjustments.

2 The control switch has a selector portion which sends voltage to the left or right side mirror. With the ignition ON but the engine OFF, roll down the windows and operate the mirror control switch through all functions (left-right and up-down) for both the left and right side mirrors.

3 Listen carefully for the sound of the electric motors running in the mirrors.

4 If the motors can be heard but the mirror glass doesn't move, there's probably a problem with the drive mechanism inside the mir-

**23.10b Power window front right door and rear door switch terminal guide and continuity table (1990 through 1994 models)**

| Terminal / Switch position | 3 | 4 | 2 | 5 | 1 |
|---|---|---|---|---|---|
| UP | O | | | O | |
| UP | | O | | | O |
| OFF | x | x | | | |
| OFF | | O | | O | |
| OFF | | | O | | O |
| DOWN | x | | x | | |
| DOWN | | O | | O | |
| DOWN | O | | | | O |

**23.10c Power window master control switch terminal guide and continuity table (1995 and later models)**

Connector terminal guide:
```
 1   2  [X]  3   4
 5   6   7   8   9
10  11  12  13  14
```

| Window lock switch | Switch Position | Front RH 7 | 14 | 9 | 12 | Front LH 7 | 13 | 8 | 12 | Rear RH 7 | 6 | 11 | 12 | Rear LH 7 | 10 | 5 | 12 |
|---|---|---|---|---|---|---|---|---|---|---|---|---|---|---|---|---|---|
| NORMAL | UP | O | O | O | O | O | O | O | O | O | O | O | O | O | O | O | O |
| NORMAL | OFF | | O | O | | | O | O | | | O | O | | | O | O | |
| NORMAL | DOWN | O | O | O | O | O | O | O | O | O | O | O | O | O | O | O | O |
| LOCK | UP | O | O | | | O | O | O | O | O | O | | | | O | O | |
| LOCK | OFF | | O | O | | | O | O | | | O | O | | | O | O | |
| LOCK | DOWN | O | O | | | O | O | O | O | O | O | | | | O | O | |

| Terminal<br>Switch position | 5 | 1 | 3 | 4 | 2 |
|---|---|---|---|---|---|
| UP | o——|——————|———|———o | |
| | | | o———o | | |
| ↕ | | | | | |
| OFF | | o———|———————|———o | |
| | | | o———o | | |
| ↕ | | | | | |
| DOWN | o——|———————|——o | | |
| | | o——|———————|———o | |

**23.10d  Power window front right door and rear door switch terminal guide and continuity table (1995 and later models)**

ror. Remove and disassemble the mirror to locate the problem.

5    If the mirrors don't operate and no sound comes from the mirrors, check the fuse (see Chapter 1).

6    If the fuse is OK, remove the mirror control switch from its mounting without disconnecting the wires attached to it. Turn the ignition ON and check for voltage at the switch. There should be voltage at one terminal. If there's no voltage at the switch, check for an open or short in the circuit between the fuse panel and the switch.

7    If there's voltage at the switch, disconnect it. Check the switch for continuity in all its operating positions **(see illustration)**. If the switch does not have continuity, replace it.

8    Re-connect the switch. Locate the wire going from the switch to ground. Leaving the switch connected, connect a jumper wire between this wire and ground. If the mirror works normally with this wire in place, repair the faulty ground connection.

9    If the mirror still doesn't work, remove the mirror and check the wires at the mirror for voltage. Check with ignition ON and the mirror selector switch on the appropriate side. Operate the mirror switch in all its positions. There should be voltage at one of the switch-to-mirror wires in each switch position (except the neutral "off" position).

10   If there's not voltage in each switch position, check the circuit between the mirror and control switch for opens and shorts.

11   If there's voltage, remove the mirror and test it off the vehicle with jumper wires. Replace the mirror if it fails this test.

## 26  Airbags - general information

*Refer to illustrations 26.1a, 26.1b and 26.1c*

1    Some models are equipped with a Supplemental Restraint System (SRS), more commonly known as an airbag. This system

**26.1a  The airbag control module (arrow) is mounted on the floor pan tunnel, below the center of the instrument panel, just in front of the console**

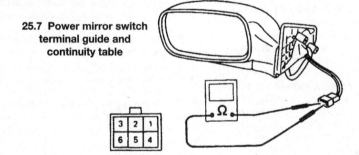

**25.7  Power mirror switch terminal guide and continuity table**

| Operation | Terminal connection | |
|---|---|---|
| | (+) | (−) |
| UP | 1 | 3 |
| DOWN | 3 | 1 |
| RIGHT | 3 | 2 |
| LEFT | 2 | 3 |

**1990 through 1994 models**

| Operation | Terminal connection | |
|---|---|---|
| | (+) | (−) |
| UP | 3 | 1 |
| DOWN | 1 | 3 |
| RIGHT | 1 | 2 |
| LEFT | 2 | 1 |

**1995 and later models**

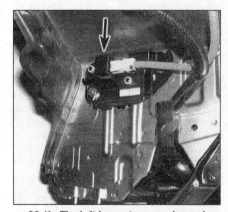

**26.1b  The left impact sensor (arrow)**

**26.1c  The right impact sensor (arrow)**

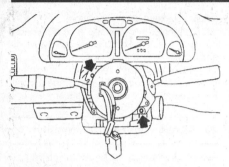

**26.12 To remove the roll connector, remove these two screws (arrows)**

is designed to protect the driver and, on some later models, the front seat passenger as well, from serious injury in the event of a head-on or frontal collision. It consists of an airbag module in the center of the steering wheel and, if equipped, another airbag inside the instrument panel, right above the glove compartment. A control module **(see illustration)** is mounted below the dash, on top of the tunnel, in front of the console. A pair of impact sensors are located at the front of the vehicle, behind the inner fender panels **(see illustrations)**.

## Airbag module

### Driver's side

2   The airbag inflator module contains a housing incorporating the cushion (airbag) and inflator unit, mounted in the center of the steering wheel. The inflator assembly is mounted on the back of the housing over a hole through which gas is expelled, inflating the bag almost instantaneously when an electrical signal is sent from the system. The roll connector on the steering column under the module carries this signal to the module.

The roll connector can transmit an electrical signal regardless of steering wheel position. The igniter in the airbag converts the electrical signal to heat and ignites the sodium azide/copper oxide powder, producing nitrogen gas, which inflates the bag.

### Passenger's side

3   The passenger side airbag is mounted above the glove compartment and designated by the letters SRS (Supplemental Restraint System). It consists of an inflator containing an igniter, a bag assembly, a housing and a trim cover.

4   The passenger airbag is considerably larger than the steering wheel-mounted unit. The trim cover is textured and painted to match the instrument panel and has a molded seam which splits when the bag inflates. As with the steering wheel-mounted airbag, the igniter electrical signal converts to heat, converting sodium azide/iron oxide powder to nitrogen gas, inflating the bag.

## Airbag control module

5   The airbag control module supplies the current to the airbag system in the event of the collision, even if battery power is cut off.

It checks this system every time the vehicle is started, causing the airbag warning light on the instrument cluster to go on then off, if the system is operating properly. If there is a fault in the system, the light will go on and stay on, flash, or the dash will make a beeping sound. If this happens, the vehicle should be taken to your dealer immediately for service.

## Precautions

### Disabling the SRS system

**Warning:** *Failure to follow these precautions could result in accidental deployment of the airbag and personal injury.*

6   Whenever working in the vicinity of the steering wheel, steering column or any of the other SRS system components, the system must be disarmed. To disarm the system:

a)   *Point the wheels straight ahead and turn the ignition key to the LOCK position.*

b)   *Disconnect the cable from the negative battery terminal.*

c)   *Wait at least one minute for the back-up power supply capacitor to be depleted.*

7   Whenever handling an airbag module, always keep the airbag opening (the trim side) pointed away from your body. Never place the airbag module on a bench of other surface with the airbag opening facing the surface. Always place the airbag module on a flat surface in a safe location with the airbag opening facing up (don't set it in a corner or next to a wall). Never dispose of a live airbag module. Return it to your dealer service department for safe deployment, using special equipment, and disposal.

8   Never measure the resistance of any SRS component. An ohmmeter has a built-in battery supply that could accidentally deploy the airbag. When working around the instrument panel and console, you will see several large yellow connectors; they're the harness connectors for the airbag system. Generally speaking, it's a good idea to avoid unplugging these yellow connectors unless absolutely necessary.

9   Always disable the airbag system when working in the vicinity of the front grille or bumper. Use extreme caution when working around the front impact sensors. Do not remove or unplug them unless absolutely necessary.

10   Never use electrical welding equipment on a vehicle equipped with an airbag without first disconnecting the yellow airbag connector, located under the steering column near the steering column switch connectors (driver's airbag) and behind the glove box (passenger's airbag).

### Removing, installing and centering the roll connector

*Refer to illustrations 26.12 and 26.16*

**Warning:** *Once the steering wheel has been removed on an airbag-equipped vehicle, make sure that the steering shaft is not turned. If it is, the roll connector must be re-centered before installing the steering wheel, or the airbag system may be damaged and be*

**26.16 To center the roll connector, wind it up in a clockwise direction until it stops, then unwind it about 2.65 turns and align the two small triangular marks**

rendered inoperative.

11   Unless you're replacing a steering column switch, there should be no need to remove the roll connector. However, should it be necessary, it's easily replaced once the steering wheel (see Chapter 10) and steering column covers (see Chapter 11) are removed.

12   Simply unplug the airbag connector from the roll connector and remove the two retaining screws **(see illustration)**. Follow the wiring harness down the steering column and unplug the electrical connector.

13   The roll connector MUST be centered anytime it is removed and installed (or replaced), or anytime the steering shaft is accidentally turned while the steering wheel is removed, or the steering shaft is disconnected from the steering gear, or if both tie-rod ends are disconnected from the steering knuckle and the steering column has turned.

14   To center the roll connector, verify that the front wheels are pointing straight ahead.

15   Turn the hub of the roll connector clockwise by hand until it stops.

16   Rotate the hub counterclockwise approximately 2.65 turns until the two small triangular marks on the moving and non-moving parts of the roll connector are aligned **(see illustration)**.

## 27   Wiring diagrams - general information

Since it isn't possible to include all wiring diagrams for every year covered by this manual, the following diagrams are those that are typical and most commonly needed.

Prior to troubleshooting any circuits, check the fuse and circuit breakers (if equipped) to make sure they're in good condition. Make sure the battery is properly charged and check the cable connections (see Chapter 1).

When checking a circuit, make sure that all connectors are clean, with no broken or loose terminals. When unplugging a connector, do not pull on the wires. Pull only on the connector housings themselves.

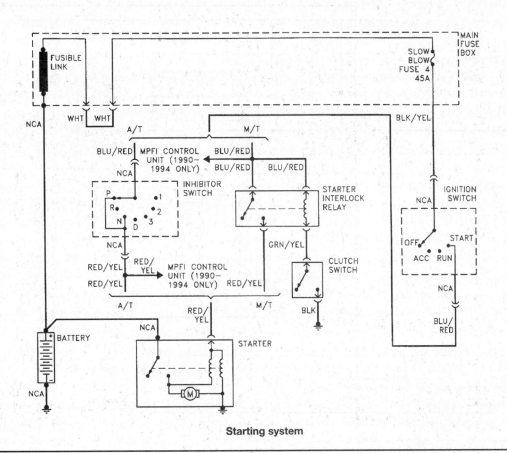

**Starting system**

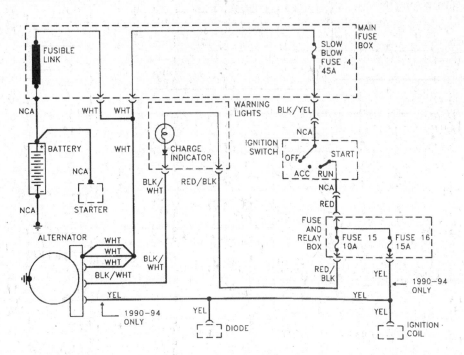

**Charging system**

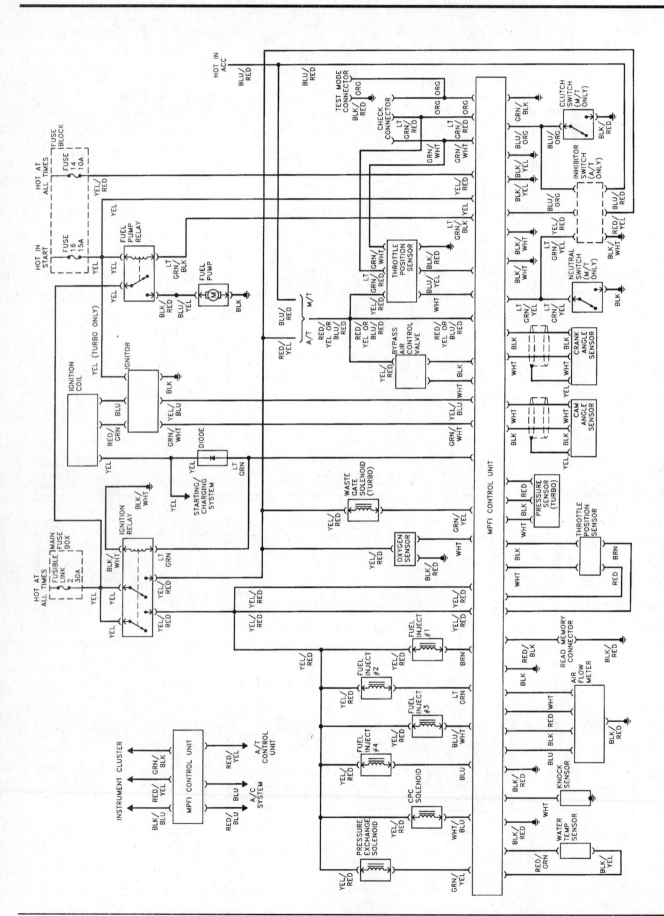

**Engine control system (1990 through 1994 models)**

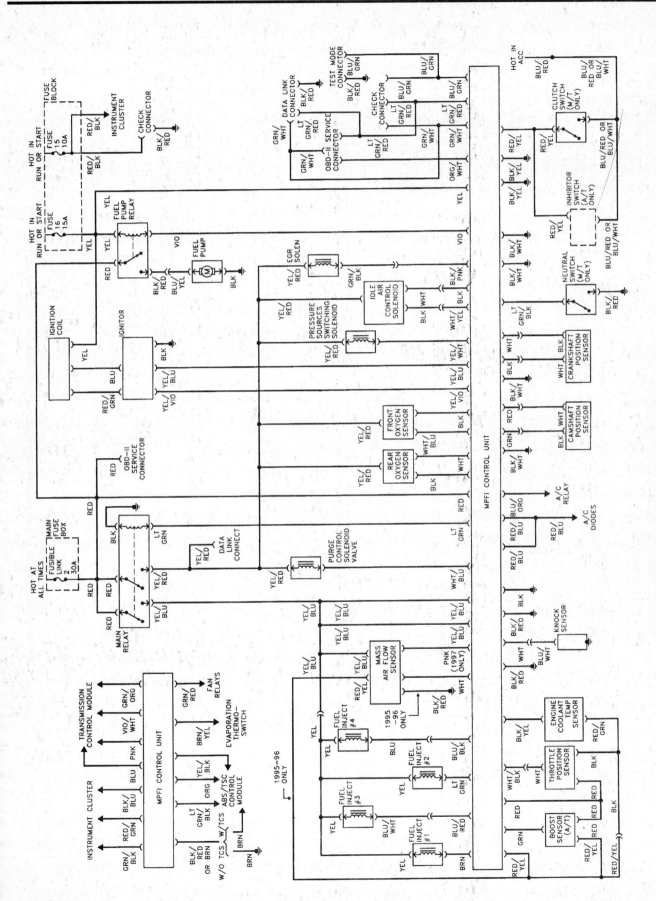

**Engine control system (1995 and later models)**

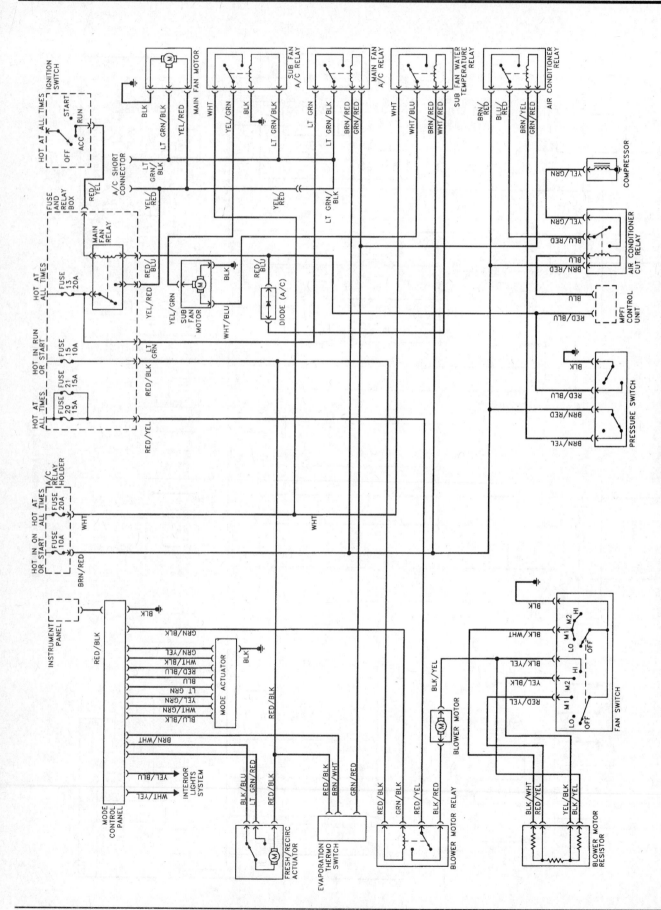

**Engine cooling, heating and air conditioning systems (1990 through 1994 models)**

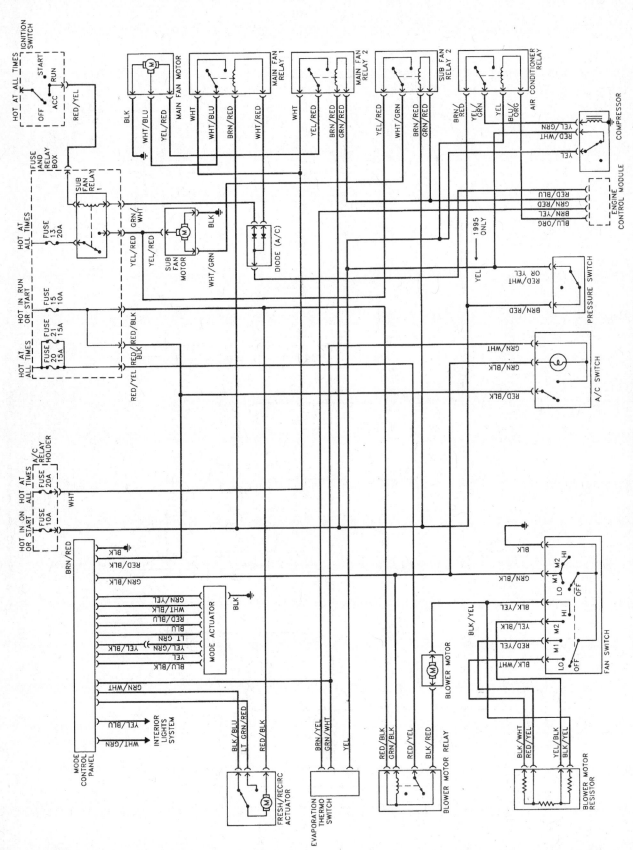

**Engine cooling, heating and air conditioning systems (1995 and later models)**

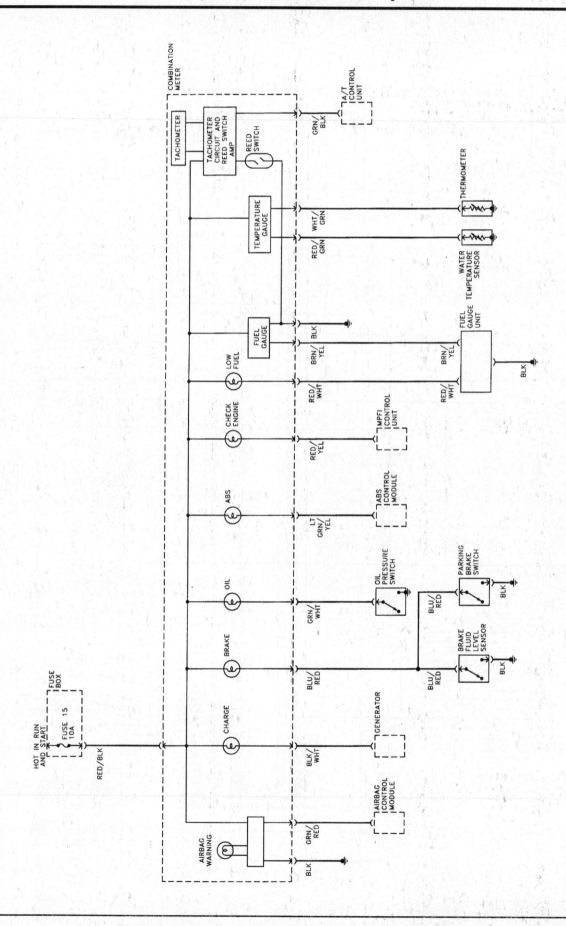

**Instrument panel warning system (1990 through 1994 models)**

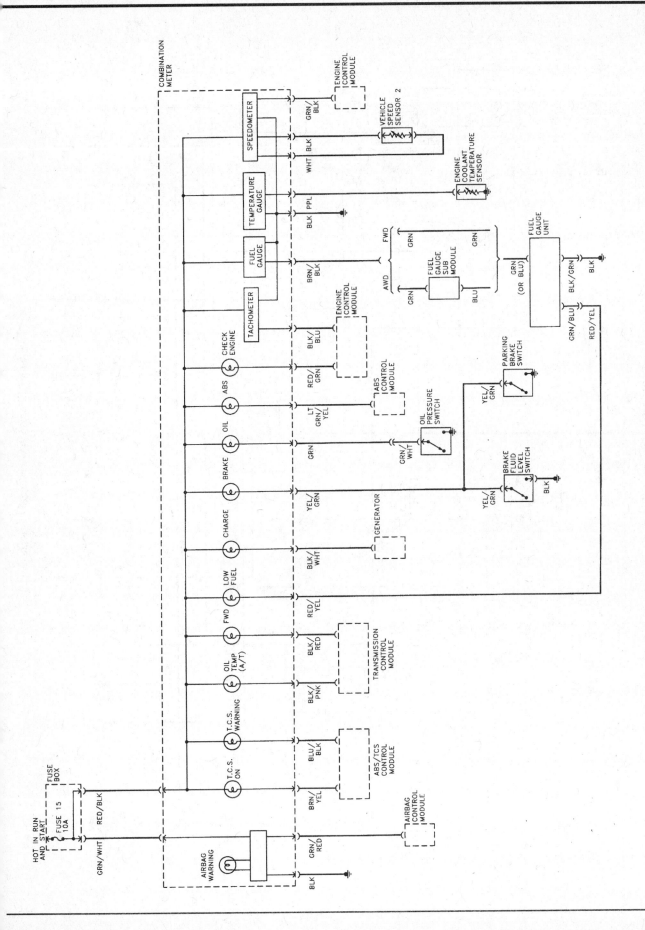

**Instrument panel warning system (1995 and later models)**

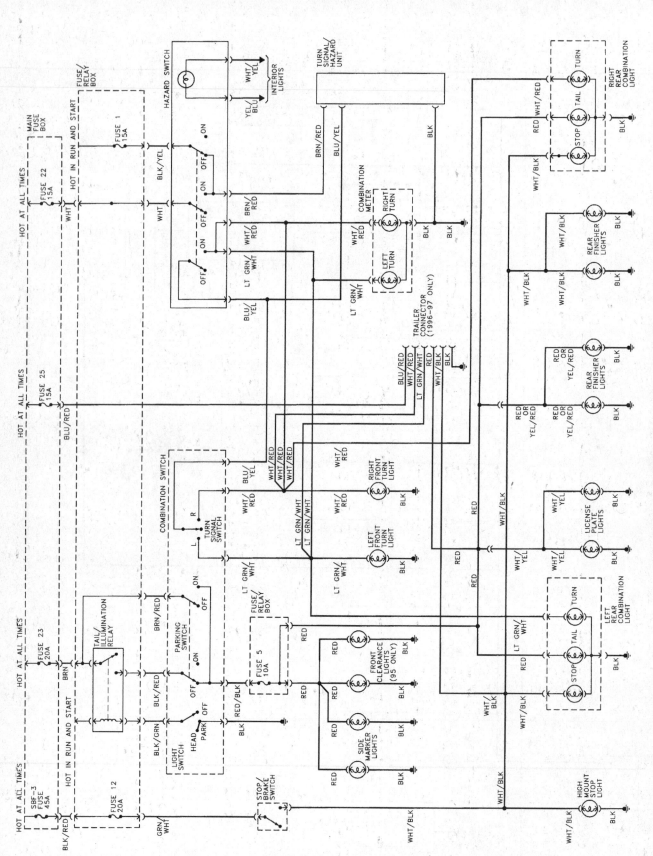

**Typical exterior lighting system (except headlights)**

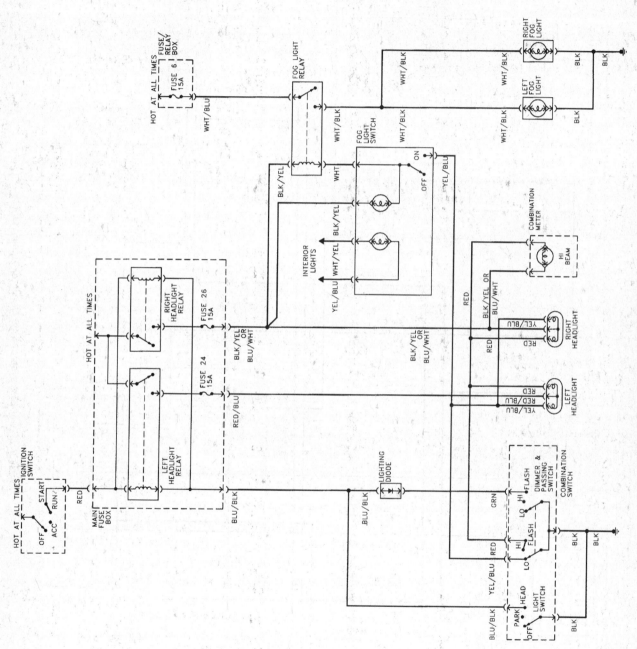

**Typical headlight system (without Daytime Running Lights)**

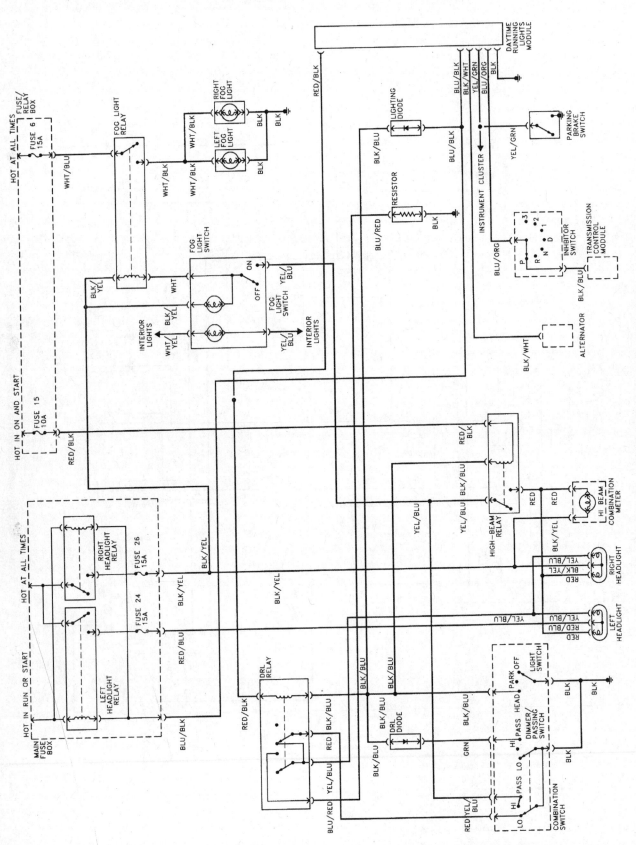

**Typical headlight system (with Daytime Running Lights)**

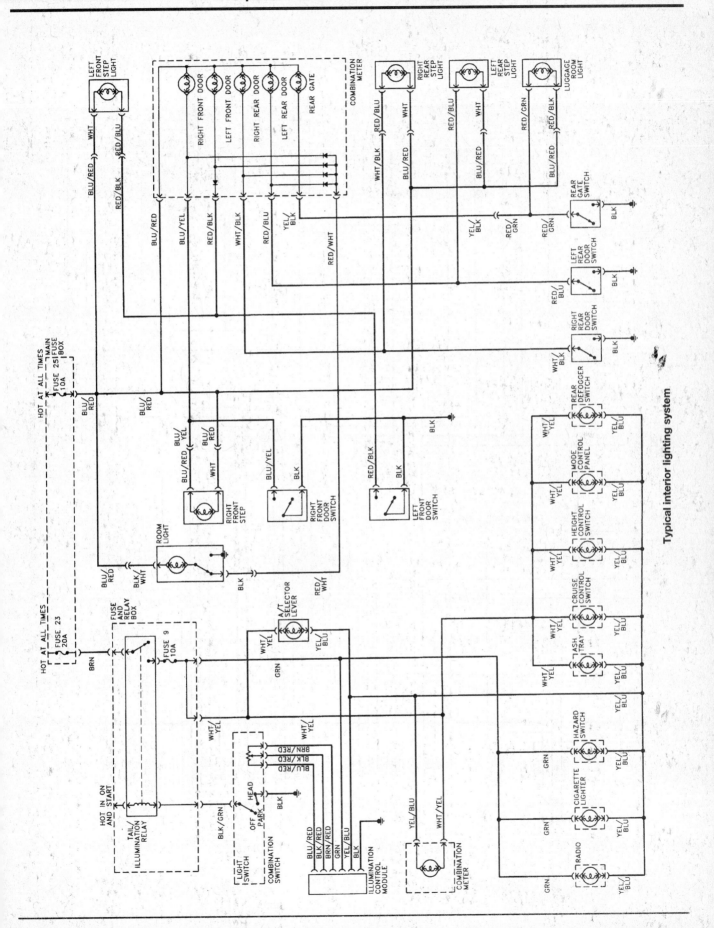

**Typical interior lighting system**

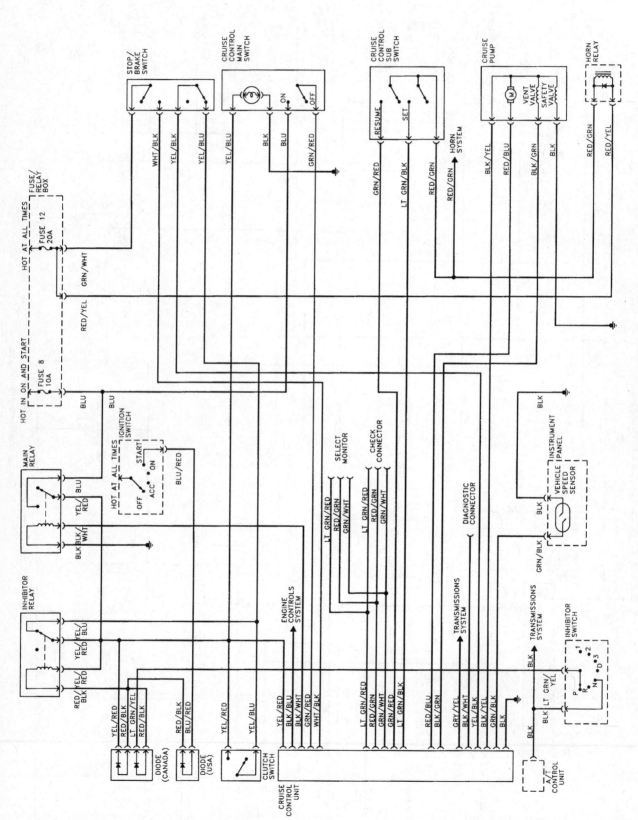

**Cruise control system (1990 through 1994 models)**

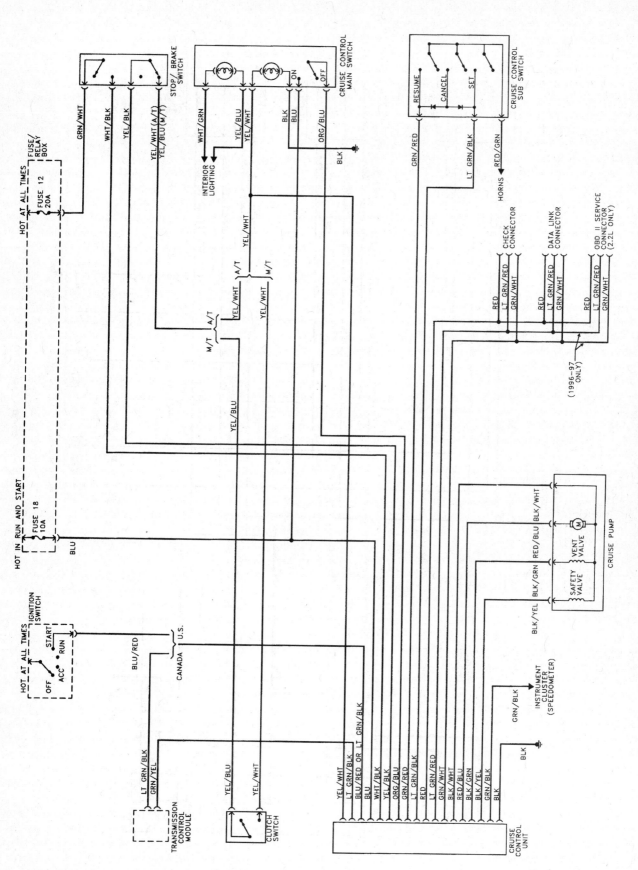

**Cruise control system (1995 and later models)**

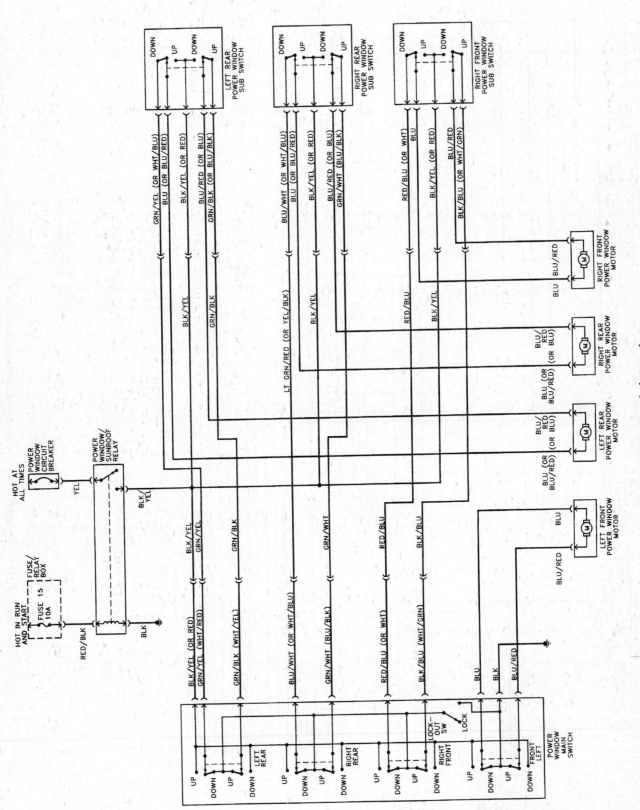

**Typical power window system**

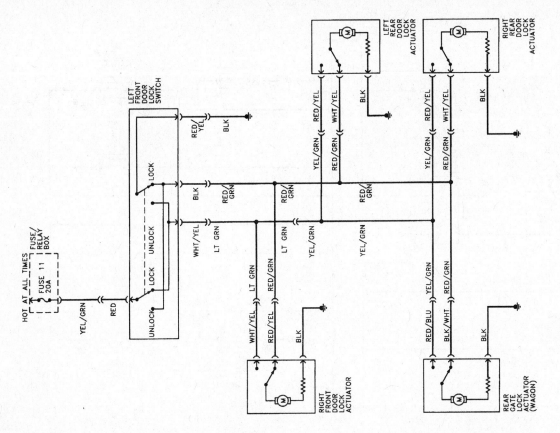

**Power door lock system - (1990 through 1994 Canada models)**

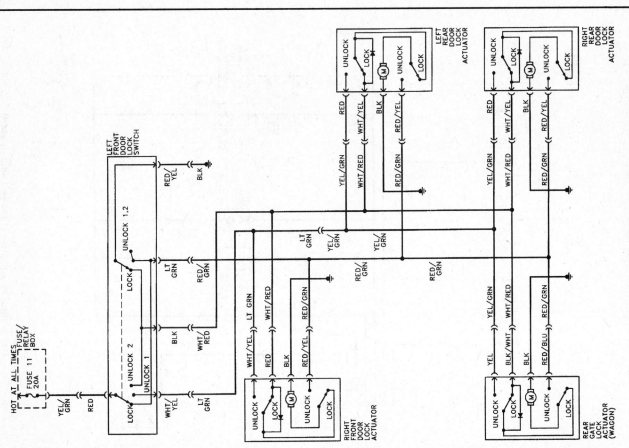

**Power door lock system - (1990 through 1994 USA models)**

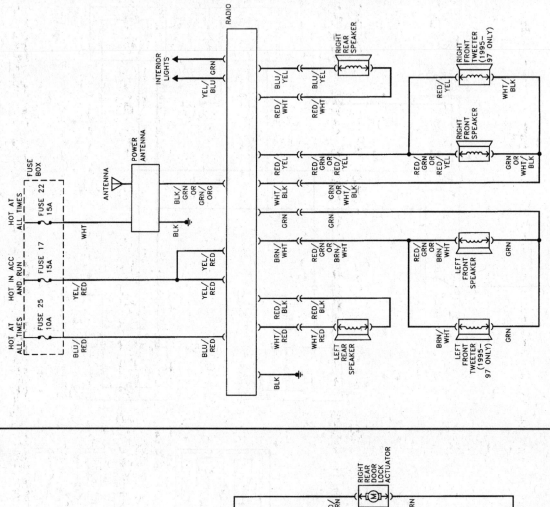

**Typical audio system**

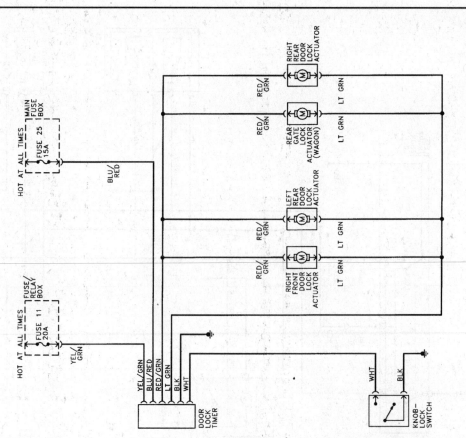

**Power door lock system (1995 and later models)**

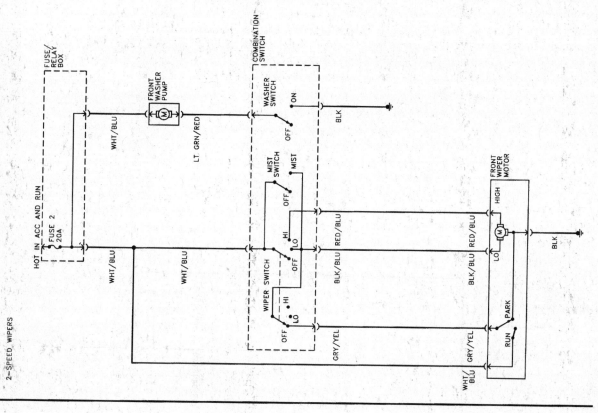

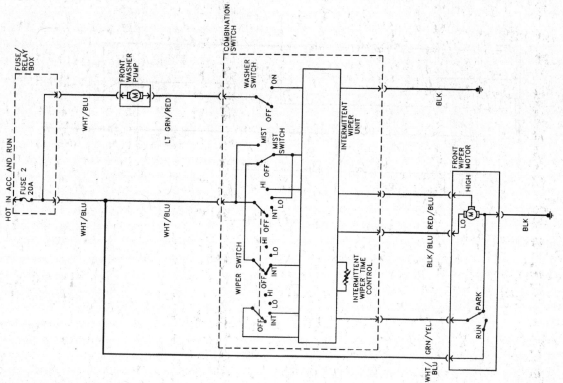

**Windshield wiper and washer system**

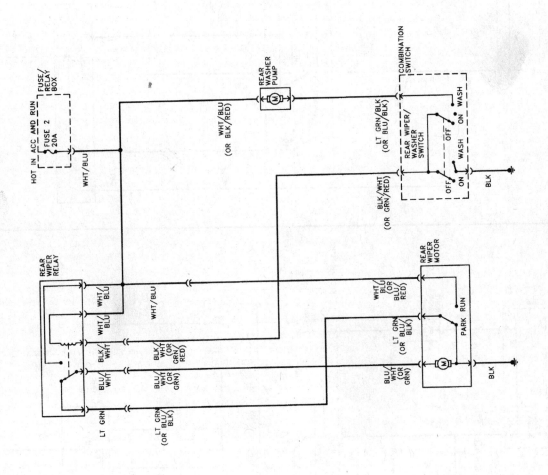

**Rear wiper and washer system**

# Index

# Haynes Automotive Manuals

*NOTE: If you do not see a listing for your vehicle, consult your local Haynes dealer for the latest product information.*

**ACURA**
12020 Integra '86 thru '89 & Legend '86 thru '90
12021 Integra '90 thru '93 & Legend '91 thru '95
Integra '94 thru '00 - see HONDA Civic (42025)
MDX '01 thru '07 - see HONDA Pilot (42037)
12050 Acura TL all models '99 thru '08

**AMC**
Jeep CJ - see JEEP (50020)
14020 Concord/Hornet/Gremlin/Spirit '70 thru '83
14025 (Renault) Alliance & Encore '83 thru '87

**AUDI**
15020 4000 all models '80 thru '87
15025 5000 all models '77 thru '83
15026 5000 all models '84 thru '88
Audi A4 '96 thru '01 - see VW Passat (96023)
15030 Audi A4 '02 thru '08

**AUSTIN**
Healey Sprite - see MG Midget (66015)

**BMW**
18020 3/5 Series '82 thru '92
18021 3-Series including Z3 models '92 thru '98
18022 3-Series incl. Z4 models '99 thru '05
18023 3-Series '06 thru '10
18025 320i all 4 cyl models '75 thru '83
18050 1500 thru 2002 except Turbo '59 thru '77

**BUICK**
19010 Buick Century '97 thru '05
Century (front-wheel drive) - see GM (38005)
19020 Buick, Oldsmobile & Pontiac Full-size (Front wheel drive) '85 thru '05
19025 Buick, Oldsmobile & Pontiac Full-size (Rear wheel drive) '70 thru '90
19030 Mid-size Regal & Century '74 thru '87
Regal - see GENERAL MOTORS (38010)
Skyhawk - see GM (38030)
Skylark - see GM (38020, 38025)
Somerset - see GENERAL MOTORS (38025)

**CADILLAC**
21015 CTS & CTS-V '03 thru '12
21030 Cadillac Rear Wheel Drive '70 thru '93
Cimarron, Eldorado & Seville - see GM (38015, 38030, 38031)

**CHEVROLET**
10305 Chevrolet Engine Overhaul Manual
24010 Astro & GMC Safari Mini-vans '85 thru '05
24015 Camaro V8 all models '70 thru '81
24016 Camaro all models '82 thru '92
Cavalier - see GM (38005)
Celebrity - see GM (38005)
24017 Camaro & Firebird '93 thru '02
24020 Chevelle, Malibu, El Camino '69 thru '87
24024 Chevette & Pontiac T1000 '76 thru '87
Citation - see GENERAL MOTORS (38020)
24027 Colorado & GMC Canyon '04 thru '10
24032 Corsica/Beretta all models '87 thru '96
24040 Corvette all V8 models '68 thru '82
24041 Corvette all models '84 thru '96
24045 Full-size Sedans Caprice, Impala, Biscayne, Bel Air & Wagons '69 thru '90
24046 Impala SS & Caprice and Buick Roadmaster '91 thru '96
Impala '00 thru '05 - see LUMINA (24048)
24047 Impala & Monte Carlo all models '06 thru '11
Lumina '90 thru '94 - see GM (38010)
24048 Lumina & Monte Carlo '95 thru '05
Lumina APV - see GM (38035)
24050 Luv Pick-up all 2WD & 4WD '72 thru '82
Malibu - see GM (38026)
24055 Monte Carlo all models '70 thru '88
Monte Carlo '95 thru '01 - see LUMINA
24059 Nova all V8 models '69 thru '79
24060 Nova/Geo Prizm '85 thru '92
24064 Pick-ups '67 thru '87 - Chevrolet & GMC
24065 Pick-ups '88 thru '98 - Chevrolet & GMC
24066 Pick-ups '99 thru '06 - Chevrolet & GMC
24067 Chevy Silverado & GMC Sierra '07 thru '12
24070 S-10 & GMC S-15 Pick-ups '82 thru '93
24071 S-10, Sonoma & Jimmy '94 thru '04
24072 Chevrolet TrailBlazer, GMC Envoy & Oldsmobile Bravada '02 thru '09
24075 Sprint '85 thru '88, Geo Metro '89 thru '01
24080 Vans - Chevrolet & GMC '68 thru '96
24081 Full-size Vans '96 thru '10

**CHRYSLER**
10310 Chrysler Engine Overhaul Manual
25015 Chrysler Cirrus, Dodge Stratus, Plymouth Breeze, '95 thru '00
25020 Full-size Front-Wheel Drive '88 thru '93
K-Cars - see DODGE Aries (30008)
Laser - see DODGE Daytona (30030)
25025 Chrysler LHS, Concorde & New Yorker, Dodge Intrepid, Eagle Vision, '93 thru '97
25026 Chrysler LHS, Concorde, 300M, Dodge Intrepid '98 thru '04
25027 Chrysler 300, Dodge Charger & Magnum '05 thru '09
25030 Chrysler/Plym. Mid-size '82 thru '95
Rear-wheel Drive - see DODGE (30050)
25035 PT Cruiser all models '01 thru '10
25040 Chrysler Sebring '95 thru '06, Dodge Stratus '01 thru '06, Dodge Avenger '95 thru '00

**DATSUN**
28005 200SX all models '80 thru '83
28007 B-210 all models '73 thru '78
28009 210 all models '78 thru '82
28012 240Z, 260Z & 280Z Coupe '70 thru '78
28014 280ZX Coupe & 2+2 '79 thru '83
300ZX - see NISSAN (72010)
28018 510 & PL521 Pick-up '68 thru '73
28020 510 all models '78 thru '81
28022 620 Series Pick-up all models '73 thru '79
720 Series Pick-up - see NISSAN (72030)
28025 810/Maxima all gas models '77 thru '84

**DODGE**
400 & 600 - see CHRYSLER (25030)
30008 Aries & Plymouth Reliant '81 thru '89
30010 Caravan & Ply. Voyager '84 thru '95
30011 Caravan & Ply. Voyager '96 thru '02
30012 Challenger/Plymouth Sapporo '78 thru '83
Challenger '67-'76 - see DART (30025)
30013 Caravan, Chrysler Voyager, Town & Country '03 thru '07
30016 Colt/Plymouth Champ '78 thru '87
30020 Dakota Pick-ups all models '87 thru '96
30021 Durango '98 & '99, Dakota '97 thru '99
30022 Durango '00 thru '03, Dakota '00 thru '04

30023 Durango '04 thru '09, Dakota '05 thru '11
30025 Dart, Challenger/Plymouth Barracuda & Valiant 6 cyl models '67 thru '76
30030 Daytona & Chrysler Laser '84 thru '89
Intrepid - see Chrysler (25025, 25026)
30034 Dodge & Plymouth Neon '95 thru '99
30035 Omni & Plymouth Horizon '78 thru '90
30036 Dodge and Plymouth Neon '00 thru '05
30040 Pick-ups all full-size models '74 thru '93
30041 Pick-ups all full-size models '94 thru '01
30042 Pick-ups full-size models '02 thru '08
30045 Ram 50/D50 Pick-ups & Raider and Plymouth Arrow Pick-ups '79 thru '93
30050 Dodge/Ply./Chrysler RWD '71 thru '89
30055 Shadow/Plymouth Sundance '87 thru '94
30060 Spirit & Plymouth Acclaim '89 thru '95
30065 Vans - Dodge & Plymouth '71 thru '03

**EAGLE**
Talon - see MITSUBISHI (68030, 68031)
Vision - see CHRYSLER (25025)

**FIAT**
34010 124 Sport Coupe & Spider '68 thru '78
34025 X1/9 all models '74 thru '80

**FORD**
10320 Ford Engine Overhaul Manual
10355 Ford Automatic Transmission Overhaul
11500 Mustang '64-1/2 thru '70 Restoration Guide
36004 Aerostar Mini-vans '86 thru '97
Aspire - see FORD Festiva (36030)
36006 Contour/Mercury Mystique '95 thru '00
36008 Courier Pick-up all models '72 thru '82
36012 Crown Victoria & Mercury Grand Marquis '88 thru '10
36016 Escort/Mercury Lynx '81 thru '90
36020 Escort/Mercury Tracer '91 thru '02
Expedition - see FORD Pick-up (36059)
36022 Escape & Mazda Tribute '01 thru '11
36024 Explorer & Mazda Navajo '91 thru '01
36025 Explorer/Mercury Mountaineer '02 thru '10
36028 Fairmont & Mercury Zephyr '78 thru '83
36030 Festiva & Aspire '88 thru '97
36032 Fiesta all models '77 thru '80
36034 Focus all models '00 thru '11
36036 Ford & Mercury Full-size '75 thru '87
36044 Ford & Mercury Mid-size '75 thru '86
36045 Ford Fusion & Mercury Milan '06 thru '10
36048 Mustang V8 all models '64-1/2 thru '73
36049 Mustang II 4 cyl, V6 & V8 '74 thru '78
36050 Mustang & Mercury Capri '79 thru '93
36051 Mustang all models '94 thru '04
36052 Mustang '05 thru '10
36054 Pick-ups and Bronco '73 thru '79
36058 Pick-ups and Bronco '80 thru '96
36059 Pick-ups & Expedition '97 thru '09
36060 Super Duty Pick-up, Excursion '99 thru '10
36061 F-150 full-size '04 thru '10
36062 Pinto & Mercury Bobcat '75 thru '80
36066 Probe all models '89 thru '92
Probe '93 thru '97 - see MAZDA 626 (61042)
36070 Ranger/Bronco II gas models '83 thru '92
36071 Ford Ranger '93 thru '10 & Mazda Pick-ups '94 thru '09
36074 Taurus & Mercury Sable '86 thru '95
36075 Taurus & Mercury Sable '96 thru '01
36078 Tempo & Mercury Topaz '84 thru '94
36082 Thunderbird/Mercury Cougar '83 thru '88
36086 Thunderbird/Mercury Cougar '89 thru '97
36090 Vans all V8 Econoline models '69 thru '91
36094 Vans full size '92 thru '10
36097 Windstar Mini-van '95 thru '07

**GENERAL MOTORS**
10360 GM Automatic Transmission Overhaul
38005 Buick Century, Chevrolet Celebrity, Olds Cutlass Ciera & Pontiac 6000 '82 thru '96
38010 Buick Regal, Chevrolet Lumina, Oldsmobile Cutlass Supreme & Pontiac Grand Prix front wheel drive '88 thru '07
38015 Buick Skyhawk, Cadillac Cimarron, Chevrolet Cavalier, Oldsmobile Firenza Pontiac J-2000 & Sunbird '82 thru '94
38016 Chevrolet Cavalier/Pontiac Sunfire '95 thru '05
38017 Chevrolet Cobalt & Pontiac G5 '05 thru '11
38020 Buick Skylark, Chevrolet Citation, Olds Omega, Pontiac Phoenix '80 thru '85
38025 Buick Skylark & Somerset, Olds Achieva, Calais & Pontiac Grand Am '85 thru '98
38026 Chevrolet Malibu, Olds Alero & Cutlass, Pontiac Grand Am '97 thru '03
38027 Chevrolet Malibu '04 thru '10
38030 Cadillac Eldorado & Oldsmobile Toronado '71 thru '85, Seville '80 thru '85, Buick Riviera '79 thru '85
38031 Cadillac Eldorado & Seville '86 thru '91, DeVille & Buick Riviera '86 thru '93, Fleetwood & Olds Toronado '86 thru '92
38032 DeVille '94 thru '05, Seville '92 thru '04
Cadillac DTS '06 thru '10
38035 Chevrolet Lumina APV, Olds Silhouette & Pontiac Trans Sport '90 thru '96
38036 Chevrolet Venture, Olds Silhouette, Pontiac Trans Sport & Montana '97 thru '05
GM Full-size RWD - see BUICK (19025)
38040 Chevrolet Equinox '05 thru '09
Pontiac Torrent '06 thru '09
38070 Chevrolet HHR '06 thru '11

**GEO**
Metro - see CHEVROLET Sprint (24075)
Prizm - see CHEVROLET (24060) or TOYOTA (92036)
40030 Storm all models '90 thru '93
Tracker - see SUZUKI Samurai (90010)

**GMC**
Vans & Pick-ups - see CHEVROLET

**HONDA**
42010 Accord CVCC all models '76 thru '83
42011 Accord all models '84 thru '89
42012 Accord all models '90 thru '93
42013 Accord all models '94 thru '97
42014 Accord all models '98 thru '02
42015 Accord '03 thru '07
42020 Civic 1200 all models '73 thru '79
42021 Civic 1300 & 1500 CVCC '80 thru '83
42022 Civic 1500 CVCC all models '75 thru '79
42023 Civic all models '84 thru '91
42024 Civic & del Sol '92 thru '95
42025 Civic '96 thru '00, CR-V '97 thru '01, Acura Integra '94 thru '00
42026 Civic '01 thru '10, CR-V '02 thru '09
42035 Odyssey all models '99 thru '10
Passport - see ISUZU Rodeo (47017)

42037 Honda Pilot '03 thru '07, Acura MDX '01 thru '07
42040 Prelude CVCC all models '79 thru '89

**HYUNDAI**
43010 Elantra all models '96 thru '10
43015 Excel & Accent all models '86 thru '09
43050 Santa Fe all models '01 thru '06
43055 Sonata all models '99 thru '08

**INFINITI**
G35 '03 thru '08 - see NISSAN 350Z (72011)

**ISUZU**
Hombre - see CHEVROLET S-10 (24071)
47017 Rodeo, Amigo & Honda Passport '89 thru '02
47020 Trooper '84 thru '91, Pick-up '81 thru '93

**JAGUAR**
49010 XJ6 all 6 cyl models '68 thru '86
49011 XJ6 all models '88 thru '94
49015 XJ12 & XJS all 12 cyl models '72 thru '85

**JEEP**
50010 Cherokee, Comanche & Wagoneer Limited all models '84 thru '01
50020 CJ all models '49 thru '86
50025 Grand Cherokee all models '93 thru '04
50026 Grand Cherokee '05 thru '09
50029 Grand Wagoneer & Pick-up '72 thru '91
50030 Wrangler all models '87 thru '11
50035 Liberty '02 thru '07

**KIA**
54050 Optima '01 thru '10
54070 Sephia '94 thru '01, Spectra '00 thru '09, Sportage '05 thru '10

**LEXUS**
ES 300/330 - see TOYOTA Camry (92007) (92008)
RX 330 - see TOYOTA Highlander (92095)

**LINCOLN**
Navigator - see FORD Pick-up (36059)
59010 Rear Wheel Drive all models '70 thru '10

**MAZDA**
61010 GLC (rear wheel drive) '77 thru '83
61011 GLC (front wheel drive) '81 thru '85
61012 Mazda3 '04 thru '11
61015 323 & Protegé '90 thru '03
61016 MX-5 Miata '90 thru '09
61020 MPV all models '89 thru '98
Navajo - see FORD Explorer (36024)
61030 Pick-ups '72 thru '93
Pick-ups '94 on - see Ford (36071)
61035 RX-7 all models '79 thru '85
61036 RX-7 all models '86 thru '91
61040 626 (rear wheel drive) '79 thru '82
61041 626 & MX-6 (front wheel drive) '83 thru '92
61042 626 '93 thru '01, & MX-6/Ford Probe '93 thru '02
61043 Mazda6 '03 thru '11

**MERCEDES-BENZ**
63012 123 Series Diesel '76 thru '85
63015 190 Series 4-cyl gas models '84 thru '88
63020 230, 250 & 280 6 cyl sohc '68 thru '72
63025 280 123 Series gas models '77 thru '81
63030 350 & 450 all models '71 thru '80
63040 C-Class: C230/C240/C280/C320/C350 '01 thru '07

**MERCURY**
64200 Villager & Nissan Quest '93 thru '01
All other titles, see FORD listing.

**MG**
66010 MGB Roadster & GT Coupe '62 thru '80
66015 MG Midget & Austin Healey Sprite Roadster '58 thru '80

**MINI**
67020 Mini '02 thru '11

**MITSUBISHI**
68020 Cordia, Tredia, Galant, Precis & Mirage '83 thru '93
68030 Eclipse, Eagle Talon & Plymouth Laser '90 thru '94
68031 Eclipse '95 thru '05, Eagle Talon '95 thru '98
68035 Galant '94 thru '10
68040 Pick-up '83 thru '96, Montero '83 thru '93

**NISSAN**
72010 300ZX all models incl. Turbo '84 thru '89
72011 350Z & Infiniti G35 all models '03 thru '08
72015 Altima all models '93 thru '06
72016 Altima '07 thru '10
72020 Maxima all models '85 thru '92
72021 Maxima all models '93 thru '01
72025 Murano '03 thru '10
72030 Pick-ups '80 thru '97, Pathfinder '87 thru '95
72031 Frontier Pick-up, Xterra, Pathfinder '96 thru '04
72032 Frontier & Xterra '05 thru '11
72040 Pulsar all models '83 thru '86
72050 Sentra all models '82 thru '94
72051 Sentra & 200SX all models '95 thru '06
72060 Stanza all models '82 thru '90
72070 Titan pick-ups '04 thru '10, Armada '05 thru '10

**OLDSMOBILE**
73015 Cutlass '74 thru '88
For other OLDSMOBILE titles, see BUICK, CHEVROLET or GM listings.

**PLYMOUTH**
For PLYMOUTH titles, see DODGE.

**PONTIAC**
79008 Fiero all models '84 thru '88
79018 Firebird V8 models except Turbo '70 thru '81
79019 Firebird all models '82 thru '92
79025 G6 all models '05 thru '09
79040 Mid-size Rear-wheel Drive '70 thru '87
Vibe '03 thru '11 - see TOYOTA Matrix (92060)
For other PONTIAC titles, see BUICK, CHEVROLET or GM listings.

**PORSCHE**
80020 911 Coupe & Targa models '65 thru '89
80025 914 all 4 cyl models '69 thru '76
80030 924 all models incl. Turbo '76 thru '82
80035 944 all models incl. Turbo '83 thru '89

**RENAULT**
Alliance, Encore - see AMC (14020)

**SAAB**
84010 900 including Turbo '79 thru '88

**SATURN**
87010 Saturn all S-series models '91 thru '02
87011 Saturn Ion '03 thru '07

87020 Saturn all L-series models '00 thru '04
87040 Saturn VUE '02 thru '07

**SUBARU**
89002 1100, 1300, 1400 & 1600 '71 thru '79
89003 1600 & 1800 2WD & 4WD '80 thru '94
89100 Legacy all models '90 thru '99
89101 Legacy & Forester '00 thru '06

**SUZUKI**
90010 Samurai/Sidekick/Geo Tracker '86 thru '01

**TOYOTA**
92005 Camry all models '83 thru '91
92006 Camry all models '92 thru '96
92007 Camry/Avalon/Solara/Lexus ES 300 '97 thru '01
92008 Toyota Camry, Avalon and Solara & Lexus ES 300/330 all models '02 thru '06
92009 Camry '07 thru '11
92015 Celica Rear Wheel Drive '71 thru '85
92020 Celica Front Wheel Drive '86 thru '99
92025 Celica Supra all models '79 thru '92
92030 Corolla all models '75 thru '79
92032 Corolla rear wheel drive models '80 thru '87
92035 Corolla front wheel drive models '84 thru '92
92036 Corolla & Geo Prizm '93 thru '02
92037 Corolla models '03 thru '11
92040 Corolla Tercel all models '80 thru '82
92045 Corona all models '74 thru '82
92055 Cressida all models '78 thru '82
92056 Land Cruiser FJ40/43/45/55 '68 thru '82
92056 Land Cruiser FJ60/62/80/FZJ80 '80 thru '96
92060 Matrix & Pontiac Vibe '03 thru '11
92065 MR2 all models '85 thru '87
92070 Pick-up all models '69 thru '78
92075 Pick-up all models '79 thru '95
92076 Tacoma, 4Runner & T100 '93 thru '04
92077 Tacoma all models '05 thru '09
92078 Tundra '00 thru '06, Sequoia '01 thru '07
92079 4Runner all models '03 thru '09
92080 Previa all models '91 thru '95
92081 Prius '01 thru '08
92082 RAV4 all models '96 thru '10
92085 Tercel all models '87 thru '94
92090 Sienna all models '98 thru '09
92095 Highlander & Lexus RX-330 '99 thru '07

**TRIUMPH**
94007 Spitfire all models '62 thru '81
94010 TR7 all models '75 thru '81

**VW**
96008 Beetle & Karmann Ghia '54 thru '79
96009 New Beetle '98 thru '11
96016 Rabbit, Jetta, Scirocco, & Pick-up gas models '75 thru '92 & Convertible '80 thru '92
96017 Golf, GTI & Jetta '93 thru '98, Cabrio '95 thru '02
96018 Golf, GTI & Jetta '98 thru '05
96019 Jetta, Rabbit, GTI & Golf '05 thru '11
96020 Rabbit, Jetta, Pick-up diesel '77 thru '84
96023 Passat '98 thru '05, Audi A4 '96 thru '01
96030 Transporter 1600 all models '68 thru '79
96035 Transporter 1700, 1800, 2000 '72 thru '79
96040 Type 3 1500 & 1600 '63 thru '73
96045 Vanagon air-cooled models '80 thru '83

**VOLVO**
97010 120, 130 Series & 1800 Sports '61 thru '73
97015 140 Series all models '66 thru '74
97020 240 Series all models '76 thru '93
97040 740 & 760 Series all models '82 thru '88

**TECHBOOK MANUALS**
10205 Automotive Computer Codes
10206 OBD-II & Electronic Engine Management
10210 Automotive Emissions Control Manual
10215 Fuel Injection Manual, '78 thru '85
10220 Fuel Injection Manual, '86 thru '99
10225 Holley Carburetor Manual
10230 Rochester Carburetor Manual
10240 Weber/Zenith/Stromberg/SU Carburetor
10305 Chevrolet Engine Overhaul Manual
10310 Chrysler Engine Overhaul Manual
10320 Ford Engine Overhaul Manual
10330 GM and Ford Diesel Engine Repair
10333 Engine Performance Manual
10340 Small Engine Repair Manual
10345 Suspension, Steering & Driveline
10355 Ford Automatic Transmission Overhaul
10360 GM Automatic Transmission Overhaul
10405 Automotive Body Repair & Painting
10410 Automotive Brake Manual
10415 Automotive Detailing Manual
10420 Automotive Electrical Manual
10425 Automotive Heating & Air Conditioning
10430 Automotive Reference Dictionary
10435 Automotive Tools Manual
10440 Used Car Buying Guide
10445 Welding Manual
10450 ATV Basics
10452 Scooters 50cc to 250cc

**SPANISH MANUALS**
98903 Reparación de Carrocería & Pintura
98904 Manual de Carburador Modelos Holley & Rochester
98905 Códigos Automotrices de la Computadora
98906 OBD-II & Sistemas de Control Electrónico del Motor
98910 Frenos Automotriz
98913 Electricidad Automotriz
98915 Inyección de Combustible '86 al '99
99040 Chevrolet & GMC Camionetas '67 al '87
99041 Chevrolet & GMC Camionetas '88 al '98
99042 Chevrolet Camionetas Cerradas '68 al '95
99043 Chevrolet/GMC Camionetas '94 al '04
99048 Chevrolet/GMC Camionetas '99 al '06
99055 Dodge Caravan/Ply. Voyager '84 al '95
99075 Ford Camionetas y Bronco '80 al '94
99076 Ford F-150 '97 al '09
99077 Ford Camionetas Cerradas '69 al '91
99088 Ford Modelos de Tamaño Mediano '75 al '86
99089 Ford Camionetas Ranger '93 al '10
99091 Ford Taurus & Mercury Sable '86 al '95
99095 GM Modelos de Tamaño Grande '70 al '90
99100 GM Modelos de Tamaño Mediano '70 al '88
99106 Jeep Cherokee, Wagoneer & Comanche '84 al '00
99110 Nissan Camionetas & Pathfinder '80 al '96
99118 Nissan Sentra '82 al '94
99125 Toyota Camionetas y 4-Runner '79 al '95

Over 100 Haynes motorcycle manuals also available

7-12